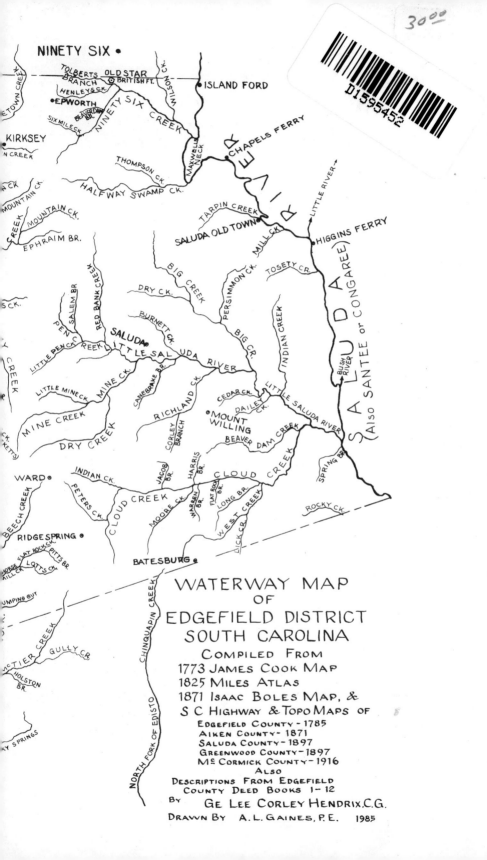

WATERWAY MAP
OF
EDGEFIELD DISTRICT
SOUTH CAROLINA
COMPILED FROM
1773 JAMES COOK MAP
1825 MILES ATLAS
1871 ISAAC BOLES MAP, &
S C HIGHWAY & TOPO MAPS OF
EDGEFIELD COUNTY - 1785
AIKEN COUNTY - 1871
SALUDA COUNTY - 1897
GREENWOOD COUNTY - 1897
MᶜCORMICK COUNTY - 1916
ALSO
DESCRIPTIONS FROM EDGEFIELD
COUNTY DEED BOOKS 1 - 12
BY GE LEE CORLEY HENDRIX, C.G.
DRAWN BY A.L. GAINES, P.E. 1985

EDGEFIELD COUNTY
SOUTH CAROLINA
ABSTRACTS OF DEED BOOKS 1-12
1786-1796
Volume One

From the Collection of
Sara Ann Hale Wales

Abstracted
By
GE LEE CORLEY HENDRIX, C. G.

SOUTHERN HISTORICAL PRESS, INC.
% The Rev. Silas Emmett Lucas, Jr.
P.O. Box 738
Easley, South Carolina 29641-0738

ISBN 0-89308-545-6

To my legacy
CHRISTOPHER RONALD SMOAK
and
BRITTANY GELEE FELTON
the children of my children
and to
the ones who are to be. . .

ACKNOWLEDGMENTS

My everlasting thanks and gratitude to my best friend and companion of the past forty years, my non-genealogist, but supportive husband Chick who allows me the freedom of our home to place and scatter microfilm readers, books and files in whatever area suits my mood at the time. Also, for his wonderful sense of humor when he brags to our friends about my books being "the best list of names he has ever read".

However, this book would not have been possible except for my children Lee, Lynn, Leslie and Lance. They reached their majority and chose to leave the nurturing nest to become "Heads of Households" in their own right, relieving me of many motherly and household tasks and replacing them with their continued love and friendship.

My appreciation and continued love to my mentor, Morn McKoy Lindsay who shares, critiques and listens to the good and bad and has remained my steadfast friend throughout the years.

A special thank you to my publisher, Emmett Lucas for his confidence in me throughout the years. His positive attitude and consultations have continued my interest and appreciation of the ever-expanding availability of records and the publishing of same.

And to my friend, Wilma Copeland Kirkland, who agrees with me that the answers to our genealogical problems do exist, but we have not found them. She has assured me of her continued support in indexing the abstracts I publish—only if I begin at the beginning of a record and continue . . . Thank you Wilma.

All of the above supportive ingredients are necessary for a good book, but cannot come together without the patient, proven proofer. There is none better than Katherine Hester. She has a wonderful way of telling you "your book is full of errors" and I love and appreciate her talent for excellence. Thank you Katherine.

Al Gaines, thank you for sharing your time and talent to draw and letter the maps and titles of this book.

Ge Lee Corley Hendrix, C. G.

MAPS

TABLE OF CONTENTS

Appendixes

The Statutes at Large of South Carolina

DEED BOOK 1: 1786-1790 EDGEFIELD COUNTY S.C.

Pp. 1-6. 12 Jan 1786: JOHN HIX & MARY, his wife, to LUD WILLIAMS, both of Ninety Six Dist. SC for 25 pounds, sold 200 acres in New Windsor Township, adj. LUD WILLIAMS: JOSEPH HIX: JOHN MEYERS & CASPER NAIL. S/ JOHN HIX, MARY (+) HIX. Wit: JOSIAH WILLIAMS, DANIEL (+) HIX, JONATHAN MEYERS, who swore by oath 1 Jan 1790 before JOHN STURZENEGGER, J.P. Rcd. 16 Mar 1790.

Pp. 6-10. 23 Dec 1774: GEORGE ROBINSON of Colleton Co., Orangeburg Dist. SC, Planter, to LUD WILLIAMS of Granville Co., Ninety Six Dist. SC for 200 pounds, sold 100 acres in New Windsor Township, originally granted 21 Apr 1774. S/ GEORGE ROBINSON. Wit: ABRAHAM SPEAR, BRITTAIN DAWSON, who swore by oath 2 Jan 1790 before JOHN STURZENEGGER, J.P. Rcd. 17 Mar 1790.

Pp. 10-16. 16 Mar 1768: ISAAC RAMSEY & SARAH, his wife, of Colleton Co. SC to WILLIAM MARTIN for 200 pounds, sold 100 acres in Berkley Co. SC on Ninety Six branch of the Saluda River. Said land originally granted 17 Jun 1763 to JAMES JOHNSON & sold by JAMES JOHNSON & SARAH, his wife, to ISAAC RAMSEY by L&R 9 & 10 Dec 1763. S/ ISAAC RAMSEY, SARAH (R) RAMSEY. Wit: ELISHA (X) BROOKS, NEOME (N) WOOD, WILLIAM CHRISTIE, who swore by oath 17 Mar 1768 before JOHN SAVAGE, J.P. Rcd. 17 Mar 1790.

Pp. 16-22. 5 Nov 1769: ELISHA BROOKS & FRANCES, his wife, of SC to WILLIAM MARTIN for 300 pounds, sold 300 acres, being part of 400 acres, originally granted 13 Feb 1768 said BROOKS on Ninety Six Mile Creek in Colleton Co. SC, adj. ELISHA FOWLER, ROBERT McCUTCHAN and part by 100 acres of the original survey, now owned by JOHN HARVEY?, & GEORGE BURNS. S/ ELISHA (X) BROOKS, FRANCES BROOKS. Wit: SAMUEL SAVAGE, RICHARD (R) BROOKS, DAVID CUNNINGHAM, who swore by oath 8 Nov 1769 before JOHN SAVAGE, J.P. Rcd. 17 Mar 1790.

Pp. 23-29. 15 Feb 1769: ELISHA BROOKS of SC to WILLIAM MARTIN, Planter, of SC for 250 pounds, sold 105 1/2 acres on Ninety Six Mile Creek in Berkley Co. SC, being part of 450 acres, originally granted 1 Feb 1768 to ELISHA FOWLER, who sold to JAMES JOHNSON 15 & 16 Nov 1768, who sold 400 acres to said BROOKS 26 & 27 Dec 1768...Land adj. JAMES JOHNSON, SAMUEL RAMSEY & ELISHA BROOKS. S/ ELISHA (X) BROOKS. Wit: JOHN CALDWELL, JOSEPH FREEMAN, SAMUEL GOODE, who swore by oath 4 Jul 1771 before JOHN CALDWELL, J.P. for Craven Co SC. Rcd. 18 Mar 1790.

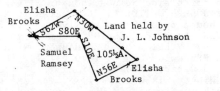

Elisha Brooks

Land held by J. L. Johnson

Samuel Ramsey   105½A.

Elisha Brooks

Plat Certified 14th (sic) 1769 by JOHN CALDWELL.

Pp. 30-36. 9 May 1770: JOHN TOBLER, Sr., Blacksmith, & CHRISTIAN, his wife, to CASPER NAIL, Planter, all of Granville Co. SC for 150 pounds, sold 75 acres, being part of 150 acres originally granted 23 Aug 1765 in Beech Island on Savannah River near New Windsor, adj. TOBLER; DANIEL NAIL; MICHAEL MEYERS...the remainder of 150 acre grant was purchased by ?HAM NAIL. S/ JOHN TOBLER, CHRISTIAN TOBLER. Wit: JOHN STURZENEGGER, DAVID ZUBLY, who swore by oath 22 Jan 1772 before JOHN DICK. Rcd. 19 Mar 1790.

1

DEED BOOK 1: 1786-1790 EDGEFIELD COUNTY, S.C.

Pp. 36-41. 1789: DAVID CUNNINGHAM & JANE his wife, of Aberville Co. SC to JAMES CAMPBELL of Edgefield Co. SC for 24 pounds... sold 100 acres, originally granted 23 Jun 1774 to JOSEPH DREW, who sold by L&R 10 & 11 Jul and four (sic) to said CUNNINGHAM, near waters of Handlies Creek, adj. ROGER McKENNEY, Sr. now deceased; PERSONS, RUTHLEDGE, JOHN SAVAGE now deceased, & DERBY PENDERGRASS. S/ D. CUNNINGHAM, JAIN (X) CUNNINGHAM. Wit: JOHN HIGGINS, ISAAC RAMSEY, who swore by oath 12 Oct 1789 before JOHN MOORE, J.P. Rcd. 25 Mar 1790.

Pp. 42-48. 30 Dec 1773: DANIEL SULIVAN & ANN, his wife, to JOHN ADAMS, both of SC, for 500 pounds, sold 200 acres on waters of Stephens Creek, granted to said SULIVAN 5 Oct 1763. S/ DANIEL (D) SULIVAN, ANN (+) SULIVAN. Wit: THOMAS CAMPBELL, JOHN HUNTER, who swore by oath 31 Dec 1773 before BENJAMIN TUTT, J.P. Rcd. 26 Mar 1790.

Pp. 48-51. 21 Aug 1787: BENJAMIN HARRIS & SOPHIA, his wife, of Augusta GA to CASPER NAIL, Jr. of Edgefield Co. SC, for 125 pounds, sold 200 acres, adj. CASPER NEAL, Sr. & DAVID ZUBLY, granted said BENJAMIN HARRIS 21 Jan 1785. S/ BENJAMIN HARRIS, SOPHIA HARRIS. Wit: GEORGE BENDER, JOHN SAVAGE, who swore by oath before JOHN STURZENEGGAR.

Pp. 52-53. 23 Jan 1786: Bill of Sale: JOHN BARELEY of Washington Co. GA to BENJAMIN TUTT of Edgefield Co. SC, for 1500 pounds, held & bound unto WILLIAM McLEOD & Co. Merchant in Charleston, the receipt whereof I do hereby have bargained & sold 3 negroes Viz: a negro boy, WILL; a negro girl, SULVIAIN my possession, & a negro girl named WINA in possession of Mrs. MILLY LATCHER. S/ JOHN BARELY. Wit: SAMUEL STALNAKER, who swore by oath 12 Apr 1790 before HUGH MIDDLETON, J.P. Condition:...that JOHN BARELY pay debt due WM McLEOD, which BENJAMIN TUTT stands bound for...

Pp. 53-57. 27 Oct 1789: Deed of Trust: The Honorable NICHOLAS EVELEIGH & MARY, his wife, hereunto moving, to Rev. ROBERT SMITH, EDWARD RUTLEDGE & JOHN BEE HOLMES for 5 shillings, transfer tracts of land: (1) 50 acres in Ninety Six on north side of Saluda River granted to JAMES MASON 5 Aug 1785 & conveyed 17 & 18 Nov (sic) to said EVELEIGH. (2) 440 acres in Ninety Six Dist., adj. lands bought of Captain WILLIAM ANDERSON Surv. 12 Apr 1785; granted 1 Aug 1785 to JOHN CAMPFIELD 17 & 18 Nov 1785 to said EVELEIGH. (3) 279 acres on north side Saluda, bought 27 & 28 Mar 1786 by said EVELEIGH of JOSEPH WHITE. (4) 640 acres in Ninety Six Dist., above ancient boundary on Savannah River, called the Cove, sold by JOHN PURVES to said EVELEIGH & certified 3 Jul 1784. (5) 640 acres bought by EVELEIGH of JOHN HAHLESTON on west side of Cape Fair River in Brunswick County 13 Oct 1779. (6) 700 acres in Ninety Six Dist., 350 acres bought 15 Aug 1775 of JAMES & JOHN MARTIN, being on Ninety Six Creek. (7) 379 acres on Dry Creek, branch of Horns Creek in Ninety Six Dist., granted 21 Jul 1775 to JOHN RUTLEDGE & sold by JOHN PURVES to said EVELEIGH about Dec 1779. (8) 200 acres on Crooked Run, branch of Turkey Creek granted about 6 Feb 1773 to DONALD SIMPSON, & sold about Dec 1779 by JOHN PURVES to said EVELEIGH. (9) 100 acres on Black Rocky Creek & bought of RICHARD ANDREW RAPLEY by said EVELEIGH. (10) 350 acres, called Horseshoe, on north side Saludy River bought of ANDREW ROGERS by EVELEIGH. (11) 450 acres on Reedy River bought 9 Mar 1784 of DANIEL WILLIAMS & his son, NIMROD WILLIAMS. (12) 450 acres bought of WILLIAM FALON? being of several tracts; Viz: 200 acres; 100 acres; 50 acres; & 100 acres,

2

in Berkley Co. on north side of Saludy River. (13) 600 acres bought, 4 Jan 1780 of ALEXANDER FRASOR, originally granted to EDWARD EDWARDS, being on west side of Edisto River. (14) 350 acres bought of ALEXANDER FRASER, being 3 miles of former tract in Colleton Co., originally granted to JAMES WALKER. (15) 515 acres bought 18 Mar 1780 from RICHARD ANDREW RAPLEY, as Atty. to JOSEPH SALVADOR, being on Black Rocky Creek, above Ninety Six & is part of a tract granted to WILLIAM LIVINGSTON, Esq. (16) 5689 acres bought 18 Mar 1780 of RICHARD ANDREW RAPLEY, granted to WILLIAM LIVINGSTON, on Saludy River in Ninety Six Dist. (17) 3900 acres bought by L&R 29 & 13 (sic) Apr 1778 of RICHARD ANDREW RAPLEY, granted to WILLIAM LIVINGSTON. (18) 1450 acres on Black Rocky Creek, Ninety Six Dist., being part of land granted to WILLIAM LIVINGSTON, and sold 29 & 13 (sic) Apr 1778 by RICHARD ANDREW RAPLEY to said EVELIEGH. (19) 3022 acres, granted WILLIAM LIVINGSTON, & sold 10 Dec 1777 by RICHARD ANDREW RAPLEY. (20) 1048 acres, part of land granted to WILLIAM LIVINGSTON, & sold 20 (sic) & 13 Apr 1778 by RICHARD ANDREW RAPLEY to said EVELIEGH. (21) All - Plantation in Craven Co. on or near the High Hills of Santee of 1107 acres adj. BENJAMIN WARING & GEORGE JOOR. (22) One undivided moiety of 1000 acres in the North Britain tract on High Hills of Santee. (23) 213 ½ acres on south side of Santee in St. John Parish, adj. RALPH IZARD & SAMUEL IRVING. (24) 274 acres on south side of Santee in St. James Parish, adj. ANTHONY SIMONS & CHARLES PICKNEY, Esq. (25) Undivided moiety of 1375 acres in Craven Co., adj. Berkely Co. line & HENRY MOUSON. (26) 1000 acres on Pedee River, adj. JOHN STONE & ELIZABETH RAVEN. (27) 500 acres in Ninety Six Dist. on br. of Stephens Creek. (28) 500 acres on Turkey Creek betw. Saludy & Savannah Rivers. (29) 1000 acres on cover bridge Creek, a branch of Holmes Creek (30) 640 acres in Ninety Six Dist. on branch of 26 Mile Creek, which several ten? tracts last listed was mortgaged to NICHOLAS EVELEIGH by THOMAS EVELEIGH... Conditions: All tracts sold & money be divided in equal portions to persons named in following schedule... Wit: THOMAS BEE HOLMES, THOMAS EVELEIGH. S/ NICHOLAS EVELEIGH, MARY EVELEIGH...List of Persons Creditors of NICHOLAS EVELEIGH: STATE LONE OFFICE, HANNAH HAYWOOD, REBECCA EVANCE, JOSEPH ALSTON, BENJ. HUGER, R.A. RAPLEY, JANE SIMMONS, Coln. DRY, ANTHONY L???BB, THOS. COCKRAN, ROLLINSON LOWNDS, ALEXAND FARUS?, ANDREW McAN, LIBRARY SOCIETY, ISAAC DACOSTA, Estate of THOS. ?UBROCK, JACOB VANBEBBER, JOHN TIME?, THOS. LAWRENCE, DANIEL HUGER, Estate of HENERY CROUCH, Revd. ROBERT COOPER, JOSEPH BROWN, LEWIS LEDERGITT, Estate of MARY STEPHENS, ANDREW ROGORS, COURTOLD & OGIER, JAS. & EDWARD PONMAN, ROBT. HAZLEHURST & CO., T. EVELEIGH & CO., BENJ. GUERARD, LOCKEY & BRADFORD, COLCOCK & GRAHAM, KEATING & SIMMONS, RD. BOHUN BAKER, THOS. PHIPOC, THOS PHILPOC, McILLS, ADAMUS BURK, WM. BRADSFORD, MICHL. WALSON (sic), JOHN S. GERVAIS, HOOPER & ALXR., GEORGE HOOPER, Dr. FAGPOUX two bonds as Security for T EVELEIGH, JAS. LAURENCE, ROGER SMITH, F. C. MEY, Dr. WITHURAL. Sworn by oath of THOMAS EVELEIGH 19 Mar 1790 before D. L. MAZYCK, J. P.

P. 57. 13 Nov 1786: Bill of Sale. MORRIS CALLEHAM, DUDLEY CARTER & SARAH CARTER to RICHARD McCARY, sold a negro boy, SAMP, for one negro wench, HANNAH. S/ MORRIS (+) CALLAHAM, DUDLEY CARTER, SARAH (+) CARTER. Wit: JOHN G. COOKE, THOMAS WOOD, JOSEPH TUCKER, who swore by oath 17 Jan 1789 before JOHN PURVES, J.P.

Pp. 58-62. 4 Mar 1776: LW&T of HENRY KEY. To 3 sons, HENRY, WILLIAM & TANDY CLERK KEY...all SC lands be divided amongst them as follows: my oldest son, HENRY KEY, lands I bought of ROBERT YOUNG, 200 acres of which was granted to THOMAS RICHARDSON & 75

acres, adj. branch of Turkey Creek of Savannah River; ROBERT KILCREAS, when surveyed 15 Jan 1757...To son, WILLIAM KEY, 200 acres bought of WILLIAM HOLMS, was granted to JOHN GOFF in Granville Co. on Turkey Creek, branch of Stephens Creek when surveyed 20 Jul 1754; also 300 acres in Granville Co. on both sides Turkey & Wine Creek, adj. WILLIAM MINTER; JOHN GOFF's grant; & JOHN ALLEN, dated 7 Apr 1772...To son, TANDY CLERK KEY, 200 acres bought of NIMROD KILCREASE, granted 2 Feb 1762 to ROBERT KILCREASE in Granville Co. on Turkey Creek a branch of Stephens Creek, also 25 acres joins water branch, being part of 100 acre survey I bought of ROBERT YOUNG (& the other part to my son HENRY) & To youngest son, the remainder of 950 acres (after I give my oldest daughter in Granville Co. on Coun Creek & Beard Creek, adj. CALLAHAM YARDRO & WARING; said KEY; WILLIAM ANDERSON, dated 1 Jan 1773...To two sons, HENRY & WILLIAM KEYS, 400 acres in Granville Co. on branch of Turkey Creek, adj. WILLIAM M. (torn), granted 5 Feb 1772; To son, HENRY KEY, negro, SQUIRE; To son, WILLIAM KEY, negro boy, MOSES; To son, TANDY CLERK KEY, negro boy, CATO; To daughter, MARTHA KEY, negro girl, BIDDY; To daughter, MAOMI KEY, negro girl, DEFFENEY; when my 3 daughters become of age...; my lands in Amherst be sold; To daughter, MILLINDA LITCHER; To my beloved wife, MARY KEY, negroes: PHEBE, NAN, PONPY, also 200 acres I bought of NIMROD KILCREASE on Turkey Creek...In event of my wifes death all negroes be kept together until my youngest son comes of age.
Ex's: Captain BENJAMIN TUTT, ROBERT MELVILL, & Son, HENRY KEY. S/ HENRY KEY. Wit: ROBERT MELVILL, JAMES LITCHER, WILLIAM (H) HOLMES & JAMES (X) MURRAY who swore by oath 18 Mar 1777 before JOHN PURVES, J.P.

1 Dec 1778. WILLIAM BURROWS, Esq., Ord. gives JOHN PURVES authority to examine several witnesses to LW&T of HENRY KEY, late of this state, deceased. S/ WM BURROWS.
25 Apr 1779. Secretary's Office certified by WM NESBITT D Regm., MARY KEY, ROBERT MELVILL & HENRY KEY swore to LW&T of HENRY KEY of Ninety Six Dist., Planter, deceased. S/ JOHN PURVES, J.P.

Pp. 63-67. 24 Sep 1789: WILLIAM BUTLER & BETHETHLAND, his wife, to ROBERT ALLEN, Jr., both of Edgefield Co., SC, for 15 pounds, sold 60 acres, granted 3 Mar 1786, on Richland Creek, branch of Little Saluda River, adj. said BUTLER & JACOB SMITH. S/ WM BUTLER, BETHETHLAND BUTLER. Wit: ENOCH GRIGSBY, THOS DOZIER, who swore by oath 24 Sep 1789 before RUSSELL WILSON, J.P. Rcd. 7 May 1790.

Pp. 67-71. 7 Apr 1788: MICHAEL DELOACH to THOMAS WILLIAMS for 30 pounds, sold 200 acres at time of survey in Collenton Co. & now called Edgefield Co., granted 26 Feb 1772, adj. RUSSELL WILSON, JACOB SMITH. S/ MICHAEL DELOACH, DORCUS (X) DELOACH, his wife. Wit: YOUNG ALLEN. SAML. DELOACH & ALEXANDER WILSON swore by oath 19 Apr 1788 before RUSSELL WILSON, J.P. Rcd. 7 May 1790.

Pp. 72-75. 28 Sep 1789: MATTHEW GAYLE & MARY, his wife, of Edgefield Co. SC, to WILLIAM DOZIER for 1000 pounds, sold 250 acres, being part of 300 acres granted 15 May 1772 to ROBERT DAVIS, who sold 250 acres to WILLIAM JONES, who sold 26 Jun 1783 to MATHEW GAYLE. Said land on south side of Little Saluda River. S/ MATTHEW GAYLE, MARY GAYLE. Wit: JOHN BRADSHAW, EDWARD LUTEN. (The release reads differently, same instrument, but conflicting data, gch).

DEED BOOK 1: 1786-1790 EDGEFIELD COUNTY, S.C.

28 Sep 1789: MATTHEW GAYLE & MARY, his wife, to WILLIAM DOZER, both of Edgefield Co. SC, for 1000 pounds, sold 200 (sic) acres, granted 18 May 1775 (sic) to WILLIAM JONES & sold 26 Jun 1773 (sic) said GAYLE, being on a branch of Little Saluda, waters of Santee (sic) River. S/ MATTHEW GAYLE, MARY GALE. Wit: EDWARD LUTEN, JOHN BRADSHAW who swore by oath 13 Oct 1789 before RUSSELL WILSON, J.P.

Pp. 76-81. 1789: JOHN GARRETT & JONES RIVERS, acting Executors to Estate of the late ROBERT GARRETT, deceased, of Edgefield Co. SC to JOHN CANADY of same place, for 100 pounds, sold 100 acres, being part of 1450 acre grant to ROBERT GARRETT on waters of Stevens Creek. S/ JOHN GARRETT, JONES RIVERS. Wit: JOHN C. GARRETT, WM GARRETT, ELISHA PALMER, who swore by oath 19 Oct 1789 before AQUILA MILES, J.P. Rcd. 8 May 1790.

Pp. 82-88. 17 Nov 1787: ROBERT LANG to ROBERT SAMUEL, both of Ninety Six Dist., Edgefield Co. SC for 200 pounds, sold 410 acres, being part of two tracts on Chavors Creek. Viz: 100 acres, granted 18 Jan 1765 to CHRISTIAN BUCKHALTER, who sold by L&R 17 & 18 May 1765 to said LANG...the other 310 acres, granted 5 Jun 1786. S/ ROBERT LANG, SARY LANG, his wife. Wit: GEORGE G. TANKERSLEY, WILLIAM FLIN, who swore by oath 12 Oct 1789 before JOHN PURVES, J.P. Rcd. 8 May 1790.

Pp. 88-93. 5 Nov 1789: ARTHUR WATSON to ABNER WATSON both of Edgefield Co. SC for 10 pounds, sold 200 acres granted said WATSON on Cloud Creek of Saluda River, adj. JOHN WATSON, said ARTHUR WATSON, & MACKENFOOSE Estate. S/ ARTHUR (A) WATSON. Wit: SAMUEL SATCHER, RICHMOND WATSON, HEZEKIAH WATSON, who swore by oath 9 Jan 1790 before RUSSELL WILSON, J.P. Rcd. 8 May 1790.

Pp. 94-104. 29 Sep 1788: ABRAHAM RUMP & ANN, his wife, Planters of St. George Parish SC to ELISHA PALMER, Planter, of Edgefield Co. SC, for 40 pounds, sold 200 acres, granted 10 Feb 1775 & adj. PHILIP GOODE at time of survey. S/ ABRAHAM RUMP. Wit: ROGER WILLIAMS, BENJAMIN MOCK, who swore by oath 29 Sep 1788 before JOHN PURVES, J.P. Rcd. 8 May 1790.

Pp. 104-106. 25 Aug 1778: JOHN SHINHOLSTER & SARAH, his wife, to WILLIAM SHINHOLSTER, both of New Windsor Township, sold 88 1/2 acres on Savannah River & branch formerly called Second Creek, adj. said JOHN SHINHOLSTER; land granted CONRAD EUGSTER, but now DAVID ZUBLY, Esq.; LEONARD ULRICK; MICHAEL MEYER; JOHN TOBLER. S/ JOHN SHINHOLSTER, SARAH (X) SHINHOLSTER. Wit: JOHN STARE, JOHN (X) WARD, NICHOLAS SHAFFER, who swore by oath 31 Dec 1789 before JOHN STURZENEGGER, J.P. Rcd. 11 May 1790.

Pp. 107-108. 22 Jan 1790. Bill of Sale. FRANCIS BENTON, Planter, to CHARLES WAY KING, Schoolmaster, both of Edgefield Co. SC for 29 pounds, sold one bay horse, branded F.B.; one black mare, unbranded; 7 cows; 2 heifers with calf; 1 heifer; 2 steers; 4 yearlings; 9 hogs; 9 shotes; 3 beds & all household furniture. S/ FRANCIS BENTON. Wit: SARAH (X) CAILS, ZACHARIAH MARTIN, who swore by oath 23 Jan 1790 before RUSSELL WILSON, J.P.

Pp. 108-110. 8 May 1789: WILLIAM COVINGTON, Sheriff of Edgefield Co. SC to ZECHARIAH LAMAR, Jr...Whereas THOS. LAMAR was seized of 540 acres at Cherokee Pond, Edgefield Co. SC, adj. FRANCIS LITTLE; WILLIAM TERRANCE; SHADRACK ROGAR...Whereas said THOS. LAMAR became indebted to HUNTER & HAMPTON for 50 pounds...& they did obtain a judgement for payment of such...land sold to last and highest bidder, ZECHARIAH LAMAR for 60 pounds. S/ WM.

5

COVINGTON. Wit: J.P. McQUEEN, ANDREW HARKNESS, who swore by oath 29 Oct 1789 before WILLIAM ANDERSON, J.P.

Pp. 111-114. 4 Aug 1788: JEHIEL McDANIEL, heir at law to Estate of ABSOLOM McDANIEL, deceased, & BARSHABA, his wife, (JEHIEL'S) to WILLIAM & HIGHRAIM McDANIEL, all of Edgefield Co. SC for 10 pounds, sold 200 acres on Cuffetown Creek of Savannah River, adj. lands formerly held by ALLEN ADDERSON. S/ JEHIEL McDANIEL, BARSHA (X) McDANIEL. Wit: JOHN (X) McDANIEL, SAMUEL STALNAKER, who swore by oath 14 Oct 1788 before JOHN PURVES, J.P.

Pp. 115-120. 1 Nov 1789: MORRIS CALLAHAM & MARY, his wife, Planter, to JAMES COURSEY, Planter, both of Edgefield Co. SC, for 100 pounds, sold 100 acres, being part of 250 acres granted 5 Sep 1785 to JOHN RUTLEDGE & sold by L&R 13 & 14 Oct 1785 to JOHN PURVES, who sold by L&R 9 & 10 May 1788 to MORRIS CALLEHAM & was recorded in Edgefield Courthouse in Book C, page 39, 23 Sep 1789. Said land on branch of Turkey Creek of Savannah River, which crosses the Charleston Road, adj. JAMES COURSEY & JOHN RIVERS. S/ MORRIS (M) CALLAHAM, MARY (X) CALLAHAM. Wit: CALL COLLINS, JOHN LYON, who swore by oath 2 Apr 1790 before JOHN PURVES, J.P.

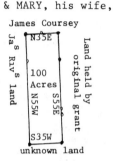

James Coursey

Ja's Riv's land · 100 Acres · Land held by original grant

N35E
N55W S55E
S35W
unknown land

Pp. 120-125. 26 Apr 1789: GEORGE COWAN & ELENDER, his wife, Planter, to JONES RIVERS, both of Edgefield Co. SC for 1000 pounds, sold 450 acres, being part of two tracts; (1) 150 acres originally granted 18 Jan 1765 to NATHAN DAVIS; (2) 300 acres, granted 23 Jun 1774 on Loids Creek, adj. JOSEPH DESUER (or DEPUER); JOHN DAVIS. S/ GEORGE COWAN, ELENDER (X) COWAN. Wit: JOHN C. GARRETT, WILLIAM LONGMIRE, DAVID THOMSON, who swore by oath 19 Jul 1789 before HUGH MIDDLETON, J.P. ELENDER COWAN, wife of GEORGE COWAN, relinquished her dower rights 28 Oct 1789 before R. TUTT, C.E.C., also HUGH MIDDLETON, J.P., & AQUILA MILES, J.P.

Pp. 125-132. 4 Oct 1786: JOSHUA LOCKWOOD, Merchant, of Charleston SC to JOHN STARR of GA, Planter, for 150 pounds, sold 400 acres, granted 8 Dec 1774, being in Granville Co. SC on branch of Savannah River, adj. FORTMAN's Township. S/ JOSHUA LOCKWOOD. Wit: SIMEON CUSHMAN, THOMAS LOCKWOOD, who swore by oath 7 May 1787 in Charleston, SC before PETER HORRY, Esq., J.P.

Pp. 132-136. 10 Mar 1790: CASPER NAIL, Sr., Planter, to WILLIAM SHINHOLSTER, Planter, both of Edgefield County, SC for 20 pounds, sold 26 acres, adj. JOHN TURCLEAR; BENJAMIN HARRIS. S/ CASPER NAIL. Wit: CHARLES RAMSEY, GEORGE BENDER, who swore by oath 11 Mar 1790 before JOHN STURZENEGGER, J.P. Plat: 26 acres surveyed Mar 1789 by WM EVANS D.S.

Casper
N83E
John Turcler · Nail Sr. · Road
S84W
B. Harris

Pp. 137-140. 31 Jul 1789: EDWARD COUCH of Edgefield Co. SC to BIBBY BUSH for 40 pounds, sold 150 acres, granted 5 Feb 1787, on south side Saluda on Rocky Creek of Edisto River. S/ EDWARD COUCH. Wit: WILLIAM BUSH, ISAAC BUSH, FREDERICK(H) HOLMES, who swore by oath 13 Oct 1789 before RUSSELL WILSON, J.P.

DEED BOOK 1: 1786-1790 EDGEFIELD COUNTY S.C.

Pp. 140-146. 5 Nov 1772: SIMEON TUCKER of SC to JAMES HARRISON of Colleton Co. SC for 100 pounds, sold 100 acres on branch of Cuffeetown Creek of Savannah River. S/ SIMEON TUCKER. Wit: JOHN RUGER (sic), PHILIP (sic) WATERS, who swore by oath 19 Apr 1773 before WILLIAM ANDERSON, J.P.

Pp. 146-151. 15 Apr 1789: BENJAMIN TUTT & BARBARY, his wife, to ROBERT CHRISTIE, both of Edgefield Co. SC, for 30 pounds, sold 135 acres, granted 31 Aug 1774, on Indian Creek, a branch of Little Saluda River. S/ BENJ. TUTT, BARBARA (X) TUTT. Wit: GABRIEL TUTT, JAMES TUTT, who swore by oath 10 Oct 1789 before RUSSELL WILSON, J.P.

Pp. 151-155. 28 Dec 1789: JOHN ARLEDGE, Yeoman, to DRURY HEARN, both of Edgefield Co. SC, for 30 pounds, sold 100 acres, granted 10 Jan 1775 to EBENATUS STEPHENS, on Little Stephens Creek of Turkey Creek, adj. JOSEPH STEPHENS. Said land sold by EDWARD MYLS (MILES) to WILLIAM BROWN 6 Oct (sic), who sold by L&R 13 & 14 Jan 1788 to JOHN ARLEDGE. S/ JOHN (X) ARLEDGE. Wit: GEORGE MASON, BARTLETT BLEDSOE, JOHN DRINKARD.

Pp. 156-159. 11 Jul 1789: JOHN GARROTT & JONES RIVERS, Executors of Estate of ROBERT GARROTT, deceased late of Edgefield Co. SC to DANIEL McKEY Sr. same place, for 382 pounds, sold 510 acres, granted & being in 3 different surveys, adj. east side of Stephens Creek; JOHN CUNNINGHAM; JOHN GARRETT; wagon road that leads to JONES RIVERS. Plat surveyed by ROBERT LANG 16 Apr 1789. S/ JOHN GARRETT, JONES RIVERS. Wit: JOHN C. GARRETT, DANIEL BARKSDALE who swore by oath 10 Oct 1789 before HUGH MIDDLETON,J.P.

Pp. 160-163. 31 Jul 1789: EDWARD COUCH to FREDRICK HOMES, both of Edgefield Co. SC, for 40 pounds, sold 150 acres, granted 5 Feb 1787, on Rocky Creek of South Edisto River. S/ EDWARD COUCH. Wit: WILLIAM BUSH, ISAAC BUSH, BIBBY BUSH, who swore by oath 13 Oct 1789 before RUSSELL WILSON, J.P.

Pp. 164-167. 6 Jan 1790: JOHN DURN to MARGARET DURN, both of Edgefield Co. SC, for 30 pounds, sold 100 acres on south side of Saluda River on waters of Sleepy Creek. S/ JOHN (+) DURN. Wit: PETER (P) DURST, TITUS UNDERDUNCK, HENERY(X)ZIMMERMAN, who swore by oath 12 Jan 1790 before BENJ. TUTT, J.P.

Pp. 167-170. 6 Jan 1790: PETER DURN, JOHN DURN & MARGARET DURN to FREDERICK DURN, all of Edgefield Co. SC, for 20 pounds, sold 150 acres on Mountain Creek, a branch of Turkey Creek of Savannah River, adj. said Creek. S/ PETER (N) DURN, JOHN (+) DURN, MARGARET (X) DURN. Wit: PETER (P) DURN, TITUS UNDERDUNCK, HENERY (X) ZIMMERMAN, who swore by oath 12 Jan 1790 before BENJ. TUTT JP

Pp. 170-175. 18 Dec 1788: JONATHAN LIMBACKER to DAVID BOZWELL, both of Edgefield Co. SC, for 200 pounds, sold 100 acres on Chavers Creek, being an equal third part of 300 acres, granted 5 Nov 1755 to MICHAEL BUCKHALTER & sold to GEORGE LIMBAKER, but now said part of 100 acres being invested to JONATHAN LIMBACKER, by LW&T of said GEORGE LIMBACKER, deceased. Land adj. DAVID BOZWELL. S/ JONATHAN (L) LIMBAKER, REBECKA (X) LIMBACKER. Wit: ROBERT MELTON, JOHN (+) CANADY, DRURY MURPHY, who swore by oath 19 Dec 1788 before AQUILA MILES, J.P.

Pp. 175-181. 12 May 1789: RANDOLPH GRIFFIN & DINAH, his wife, of Wilks Co. GA to WILLIAM HOLMES of Edgefield Co. SC, for 100

7

pounds, sold 200 acres, granted 11 Oct 1755 to HENRY OVERSTREET on Turkey Creek. S/ RANDOLPH GRIFFIN, DINAH GRIFFIN. Wit: MORRIS (M) CALEHAM, WILLIAM BROOKS, who swore by oath 23 Jul 1789 before JOHN PURVES, J.P.

P. 181. 15 Jul 1789: ROBERT STARK, Jr. to WILLIAM COVINGTON... Whereas a judgement in Edgefield Court in favor of ROBERT STARK, late Clerk of Court, due him from WILLIAM COVINGTON, Sheriff of said County for fees oblige me as lawful attorney for said STARK... S/ ROBERT STARK, Jr. for ROBERT STARK, Sr. Wit: RICHARD JOHNSON, Captain JOHN MARTIN, who swore by oath 13 Oct 1789 before WILLIAM ANDERSON, J.P.

Pp. 182-183. 27 Feb 1789: SAMUEL MESSER, Blacksmith of Edgefield Co. SC, is bound by Bond...to MARTHA LAREMON & DANIEL LAREMON, concerning 100 acres in Cumberland Co. NC "land which we the said MARTHA & DANIEL LAREMON sold to SAMUEL MESSER.. The obligation... SAMUEL MESSER to stand all law sutes (sic) he shall commence... for the recovery of said land excepting & title made by my husband and my father EDWARD LAREMON, deceased..." S/ SAMUEL MESSER. Wit: WILLIAM MESSER, THOMAS WILLIAMS, who swore by oath 18 Aug 1789 before RUSSELL WILSON, J.P.

Pp. 183-184. 12 Apr 1788: WILLIAM MOSELEY to JOHN AKRIDGE, both of Edgefield Co. SC, for 100 pounds, sold 60 acres, being part of 640 acre survey by ROBERT LANG & granted 5 Jun 1786, adj. JOSEPH DOLITTLE: Wido (sic) HERENDON; THOMAS MOSELEY. S/ WILLIAM (M) MOSELEY. Wit: REZIN DAVIS, CHRISTOPHER (X) EDWARDS, who swore by oath 15 Jan 1790 before AQUILA MILES, J.P.

Pp. 185-186. 12 Apr 1788: WILLIAM MOSELY of Edgefield Co. SC to JOHN AKRIDGE for 100 pounds, sold 130 acres, being part of 640 acre survey by ROBERT LANG & granted 5 Jun 1786, adj. JOHN HERENDON; WILLIAM DOBY; THOMAS MOSELEY & WILLIAM PUSLY on waters of Horns Creek. S/ WILLIAM (M) MOSLEY. Wit: REZIN DAVIS, CHRISTOPHER (X) EDWARDS, who swore by oath 15 Jan 1789 before AQUILA MILES, J.P.

Pp. 186-188. 18 Dec 1787. Deed of Gift: DAVID ZUBLY of Edgefield Co. SC to daughter ANN, wife of WALTER TAYLOR, for love & affection, gives 73 acres as part of her inheritance from her father. S/ DAVID ZUBLY. Wit: CASPER NAIL, JOHN CLARKE, who swore by oath 14 Oct 1788 before JOHN STURZENEGGER, J.P. Plat laid out 4 Dec 1787 by OFFECHTON?

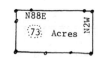

Pp. 188-189. 13 Jul 1789: Bill of Sale: RUSSELL WILSON of Richland Creek, Edgefield Co. SC to MARY LARRANCE for 15 pounds, sold 17 head of Nute Black Cattle, now in possession of JAMES BARRENTINE of same county. S/ RUSSELL WILSON. Wit: LEPARD NOBLES & JAMES HARRISON, who swore by oath 14 Jul 1789 before JOHN MOORE, J.P.

Pp. 189-192. 1 Aug 1789: WILLIAM COVINGTON, Sheriff of Edgefield Co. SC to JAMES VESSELLS... Whereas WILLIAM DAVIS, deceased of said county, was in his lifetime seized in his demesne of 72 acres on waters of Sweetwater Creek, adj. JOHN DAY. And Whereas said WILLIAM DAVIS, deceased, was indebted unto JAMES VESSELLS for 24 pounds... And Whereas said JAMES VESSELS in July term of

Court of Common Pleas of said county... to recover said debt obtained a Judgement in 1788, which was issued 13 Jan 1788 against the Admrs. of the Estate of said WILLIAM DAVIS. Land was publically sold to JAMES VESSELLS for 7 pounds, being the last and highest bidder. Now this indenture witness that said land was paid for by said JAMES CHRISTOPHER...(sic) S/ WM. COVINGTON. Wit: ABRAHAM RICHARDSON, CHARLES BANKS, who swore by oath 1 Aug 1789 before LEROY HAMMOND, J.P.

Pp. 192-194. 17 Mar 1789: CLEMENT CARGILL to GEORGE STROP, both of Edgefield Co. SC, for 50 pounds, sold 150 acres, being part of grant 2 Oct 1786 to ELIZABETH REYNOLDS on Chavores Creek, adj. LUCY ST JONES. S/ CLEMENT CARGILL. Wit: RACHEL CARGILL, KEZIAH MILLER, GEORGE MILLER, who swore by oath 14 Oct 1789 before JOHN STURZENEGGER, J.P.

Pp. 194-195. 22 Oct 1789. Deed of Gift: JOHN SPANN, the Elder, Planter, there unto moving, to JAMES SPANN, both of Edgefield Co. SC, for love I bear my own son, said JAMES SPANN, give 2 negroes to Wit: a boy, BOBB, about 5 yrs. old; a girl, DORCUS, about 3 yrs. old, both in possession of said JAMES SPANN. S/ JOHN (+) SPANN. Wit: WILLIAM BUTLER, RICHARD DOZER, THOMAS DOZER, who swore by oath 22 Oct 1789 before RUSSELL WILSON.

Pp. 195-196. 19 Feb 1787: ENOCK GRIGSBY, Planter, & RUSSELL WILSON, Esq. of Edgefield Co. SC are bound to THOMAS BERRY, Planter, of same place for 10,000 pounds... The condition of obligation is if the above said ENOCK GRIGSBY, do hereafter Indemonify (sic) the above THOMAS BERRY from former leases given to the heirs of said ENOCK GRIGSBY for 3 different tracts of land containing 100 acres each, on Richland Creek of Little Saludy River and said leases shall never come against said THOMAS BERRY... then obligation be void, otherwise to stand in full force. S/ ENOCK GRIGSBY, RUSSELL WILSON. Wit: HENERY KING, DANNETT ABNEY, THOMAS DOZER, who swore by oath 9 Oct 1789 before RUSSELL WILSON, J.P.

Pp. 196-197. 5 Mar 1790. Deed of Gift: MICAJAH PHILLIPS of Edgefield Co. SC, hereunto moving, for love for my son, THOMAS PHILLIPS, give 150 acres on Stallion branch of Horns Creek of Savannah River; 1 negro man, SANDY; 1 woman, PEGGE, 1 boy, SAM, 8 head of cattle; 1 sorrell & 1 bay mare branded 33; 1 horse branded TW; 20 head of hogs; 3 feather beds & furniture; 3 chest; 1 hair trunk; 1 dozen pewter plates; 3 dishes, 1 bason; 1/2 dozen knives & forks; 4 pots; 1 cast oven; 1 spice mortar; 1 frying pan; 2 smothing irons; 1 pr. fire tongs & shovel; 1 looking glass. S/ MICAJAH PHILLIPS. Wit: BETTY TUTT, NATHAN WHITE, who swore by oath 6 Mar 1790 before ARTHUR SIMKINS, J.P.

Pp. 197-201. 20 Nov 1789: ELIZABETH CALLYHAM, widow, to JOHN PURVES, Planter, all of Edgefield Co. SC, for 10 shillings, sold 240 acres, granted 5 Sep 1785, near Savannah River, adj. JOHN PURVES. S/ ELIZABETH (+) CALLYHAM. Wit: JAMES MURRAH, GEORGE COWAN, who swore by oath 15 May 1790 before AQUILA MILES, J.P.

Pp. 201-205. 23 Nov 1789: JOHN PURVES, Planter, of Edgefield Co. SC to JOHN LEWIS GERVAIS, Esq. of Charleston SC, for 10 shillings, sold 640 acres, granted 15 Oct 1784, on Savannah River; also 240 acres, adj. above land, granted 5 Sep 1785 to ELIZABETH CALLYHAM. S / JOHN PURVES. Wit: JAMES COURSEY, WILLIAM PRICHARD.

DEED BOOK 1: 1786-1790 EDGEFIELD COUNTY, S.C.

24 Nov 1789: JOHN PURVES of Ninety Six Dist. to JOHN LEWIS
GERVAIS of Charleston SC... Whereas JOHN PURVES by his Bond of 26
Aug 1774 was bound for 3490 pounds with condition for payment of
1745 pounds... And Whereas Said JOHN PURVES did by another Bond
dated 23 Oct 1784 was bound for 332 pounds with condition of
payment of 153 English Guineas with interest due on the first
Bond to the said GERVAIS 23 Oct 1784 transferred land for said
obligation... And this indenture further grants to JOHN LEWIS
GERVAIS the following negro slaves: POLYDORE; BRAM; BILLY;
PRINCE, fellows; TOBY & FRANK, boys; NELL; CHARLOTTE & PEGG
wenches; SYLVA; HANNAH; PHILLIS; CHLOE; & LUCY, girls; NANCY, a
child of CHARLOTTE's. S/ JOHN PURVES. Wit: JAMES COURSEY, WILLIAM
PRICHARD. Received of JOHN LEWIS GERVAIS 1745 pounds and also 153
Guineas, being the full consideratin within mentioned. S/ JOHN
PURVES. Sworn by oath of WILLIAM PRICHARD 17 May 1790 before
AQUILA MILES, J.P.

Pp. 206-207. 10 Jul 1783: ELIZABETH ALLEN, widow, to JAMES ALLEN,
Batchelor, both of Edgefield Co. SC, for 30 guineas, sold 1/3
part of 150 acres, where JAMES ALLEN now lives, granted 23 May
1763 to MOSES POWEL; also 1/3 part of 100 acres, granted 22 Nov
1770 to JOSIAH ALLEN, deceased, being in Collenton Co. SC,•adj.
said ALLEN; JACOB SMITH...said 1/3 part would be 83 acres. S/
ELIZABETH ALLEN. Wit: HARDWOOD JONES D.S., RUSSELL WILSON, Jr.,
GEORGE MASON, who swore by oath 9 Sep 1789 before RUSSELL WILSON,
J.P.

Pp. 208-212. 16 Jan 1778: NEWBY MANN to RICHARD TUTT, both of
Ninety Six Dist. for 300 pounds, sold 100 acres, granted 28 Oct
1774, on north side Cuffeetown Creek, Granville Co., adj. WILLIAM
ROWAN; THOS. WALLACE. S/ NUBY MANN. Wit: JOHN HAGWOOD, JOHN (X)
MILLS, ALEXANDER (A) MILLS. 14 Oct 1789 BENJAMIN TUTT & JOHN
PURVES being duly sworn by oath that they believe the
subscription to this Release & also the Receipt was endorsed to
be the Handwriting of NUBY MANN & that they were well acquainted
with the writing of NUBY MANN, before LEROY HAMMOND, J.P., AQUILA
MILES, J.P. & JOHN STURGENEGGER, J.P.

Pp. 212-215. 29 Sep 1789: JOHN FREDRICK & RACHEL, his wife, of
Ninety Six Dist. to WILLIAM HOLSTON of Orangeburg Dist. SC for 5
pounds, sold 162 acres, granted said FREDRICK, including
plantation where said FREDRICK now lives. S/ JOHN FREDRICK,
RACHAEL (X) FREDRICK, his wife. Wit: ROLAN WILLIAMS, WILLIS
FREDRICK, JACOB ODOM, who swore by oath 29 Sep 1789 before
RUSSELL WILSON, J.P.

Pp. 215-216. 6 Apr 1787: JOHN STURZENEGGER, Esq. & ELIZABETH, his
wife, to DAVID BOWERS, both of Ninety Six Dist. SC for 10 pounds,
sold 200 acres, granted 3 Apr 1786, all sides vacant at time of
survey. S/ JOHN STURZENEGGER, ELIZABETH (E) STURZENEGGER. Wit:
WILL McCARRA, JOHN CLARK, who swore by oath 14 Apr (blank) before
WILLIAM ANDERSON, J.P.

Pp. 217-218. 3 Mar 1783: JAMES BUTLER & SARAH, his wife, late of
Beach Island Township of New Windsor SC to ADAM HOILS, of same
place, Planter, for 118 pounds, sold all rights, title interest &
claim of dower to lands of JOHN SHINHOLSTER, her former husband,
deceased, being in Beach Island, New Windsor SC. S/ JAMES BUTLER,
SARAH (X) BUTLER. Wit: SIMEON CUSHMAN, WILLIAM EVANS, who swore
by oath 12 Feb 1790 before JOHN STURZENEGGER, J.P.

DEED BOOK 1: 1786-1790 EDGEFIELD COUNTY, S,C,

Pp. 218-222. 5 Mar 1790: JOSEPH COLLIER & AMY, his wife, to WILLIAM HOWLE, Junr. all of Edgefield Co. SC, for 10 pounds, sold 70 acres, adj. WILLIAM HOWLE, Junr.; CHRISTIAN BUCKHALTER; JOHN MARTIN; being land granted JOHN MOORE, but now property of JOSEPH COLLIER & AMY, his wife. S/ JOSEPH COLLIER, AMEY COLLIER. Wit: THOS. H. HOWLE, JUDITHA (X) WINFREY, JAMES LIVINGSTON, who swore by oath 6 Mar 1790 before AQUILA MILES, J.P.

Pp. 222-224. 25 Feb 1790: WILLIAM HERRIN to HENERY CHAMPION both of Edgefield Co. SC, for 10 pounds, sold 94 acres, on branch of Dry Creek, waters of Little Saludy River & part of 184 acres adj. land granted in 1788 to WILLIAM HERRIN; JAMES GILLON; by part of small survey purchased by JAMES SALTER & divided by a branch called LUCES branch. S/ WILL HERRIN. Wit: JOHN (X) RABUN, WM. SISSON, JAMES(X)GILLON, who swore by oath 6 Mar 1790 before RUSSELL WILSON, J.P.

Pp. 224-226. 20 Feb 1790: ROBERT WALTON & BLANCHE, his wife, of Richmond Co. GA to JOHN ANDERSON of Granville Co. SC for 325 pounds, sold 300 acres, granted to JAMES NOLOBOY & PHILIP GOODE, being on Stephens Creek in Granville Co. SC. S/ ROBERT WALTON, BLANCHE WALTON. Wit: JAMES VAUGHAN, ROGER WILLIAMS, who swore by oath 13 Apr 1790 before AQUILA MILES, J.P.

Pp. 226-228. 3 Mar 1790: JAMES TOMLIN to ROBERT CATES, both of Edgefield Co. SC for 1 pound, 2 sh., 2 p, sold 73 acres on Cloud Creek, waters of Little Saluda River, being part of 248 acres on south end of tract, granted 1789 to JAMES TOMLIN & adj. JAMES HARRIS. S/ JAMES TOMLIN. Wit: ENOCH GRIGSBY, WILL WRIGHT, JAS. GRISGBY, who swore by oath 3 Mar 1790 before RUSSELL WILSON, J.P.

Pp. 228-231. 23 Dec 1789: WILLIAM MOSELEY & SARAH, his wife, to ROBERT GLOVER, all of Edgefield Co. SC, for 50 pounds, sold 250 acres, adj. MICHAEL BUCKHALTER; said WILLIAM MOSELEY; REASON DAVIS; JOHN ACRIDGE; ROBERT MELTON; WILLIAM GLOVER; being granted said WILLIAM MOSELEY 5 Jun 1768. S/ WILLIAM (X) MOSELEY, SARAH (X) MOSELEY. Wit: WILLIAM GLOVER, ROBERT MELTON, DAVID GLOVER, who swore by oath 13 Apr 1790 before AQUILA MILES, J.P.

Pp. 232-235. 27 Nov 1789: CILAS GREEN to ROBERT GLOVER, both of Edgefield Co. SC, for 150 pounds, sold 150 acres on Hornes Creek of Savannah River, being granted to JOSEPH BELL 12 Jul 1772 & conveyed 14 Apr 1774 by said BELL to EDWD GREEN, Dec'd. S/ SILAS (sic) (X) GREEN, ANN (X) GREEN. Wit: JOAB WOOTON, DAVID GLOVER, who swore by oath 5 Apr 1790 before AQUILA MILES, J.P.

Pp. 235-240. 7 May 1784: OWEN FORT to WILLIAM HUMPRISS, both of Ninety Six Dist. SC, for 48 pounds, 11 sh., 5 p., sold 150 acres being part of 300 acres on Dry Creek of Little Saludy River, adj. CHARLES PARTIN; GAVEN POU; being originally granted 2 May 1770 to ARTHUR FORT, now dec'd, & conveyed to said OWEN FORT by LW&T of said ARTHUR FORT, his father. S/ OWEN FORT. Wit: JAMES SPULLOCK, JOHN ROGERS, JOSEPH NUNN, J.P., who swore by oath 21 Apr 1785 before SOLOMON POPE, J.P.

Pp. 240-244. 26 Sep 1788: WILLIAM HUMPHREYS to MOSES FELPS, both of Edgefield Co. SC, for 30 pounds, sold 28 acres on Dry & Mine Creek, a branch of Little Saludy River, being part of 300 acres, granted 2 May 1770 to ARTHUR FORT, adj. CHARLES PARTIN; GAVIN PUGH. Said land conveyed by LW&T of ARTHUR FORT to OWEN

11

FORT, who conveyed to said WILLIAM HUMPHREYS. S/ WM HUMPHREYS, ANN HUMPHREYS, his wife. Wit: THOS SMEDLY, SARAH (X) HUMPHREYS, HENERY KING, who swore by oath 24 Mar 1789 before AQUILA MILES J.P.

Pp. 244-248. 18 Jul 1788: BARTHOLOMEW (BARTLETT) CORLEY & DELILAH, his wife, Yeoman, to HEZEKIAH JENTRY, Yeoman, all of Edgefield Co. SC for 20 pounds, sold 73 acres on Indian Creek of Little Saluda River, granted 3 Apr 1786. S/ BARTHOLOMEW CORLEY, DELILAH CORLEY. Wit: SANDERS (X) CORLEY, RUNNELS (X) GENTRY, who swore by oath 20 Apr 1789 before RUSSELL WILSON, J.P.

Pp. 248-250. 29 Jan 1790: WILLIAM HERRIN to JAMES SALTER both of Edgefield Co. SC for 25 pounds, sold 138 acres granted in 1786 on branch of Dry Creek of Little Saludy River to said HERRIN, & adj. JAMES GILLON & (torn) COX land at time of survey by the name of the Mill Place. S/ WILLIAM HERRIN. Wit: WILLIAM SISSON, PHILL IKNOR, who swore by oath 5 Mar 1790 before RUSSELL WILSON, J.P.

Pp. 250-252. 2 Feb 1790: WILLIAM HERRIN to JAMES SALTER, both of Edgefield Co. SC, for 10 pounds, sold 90 acres, being part of 184 acres & taken from the west end, on Little Saludy River, granted in 1788 to said WILLIAM HERRIN, adj. said WILLIAM HERRIN; ARTHUR WATSON at time of survey. S/ WILLIAM HERRIN. Wit: WILLIAM SISSON, WILLIAM (X) RABUN, who swore by oath 25 Mar 1790 before RUSSELL WILSON, J.P.

Pp. 252-255. 20 Jul 1789: CHARLES BANKS, Sr. of Edgefield Co. SC to ELISHA BANKS for 100 pounds, sold 150 acres on Cloud Creek of Little Saluday River, adj. WILLIAM WEST. S/ CHARLES BANKS. Wit: WILLIAM (X) ETHERIDGE, LEWIS ETHERIDGE, FRANCIS DAVIS, who swore by oath 26 Apr 1790 before RUSSELL WILSON.

Pp. 255-259. 16 Feb 1790: SAMUEL WALKER, Planter, of Edgefield Co. SC, qualified & only surviving Executor of BENJAMIN BELL, dec'd, of said county, to WILLIAM DANIEL, Planter, of Fairfield Co. SC for 200 pounds, sold 1000 acres, being of several tracts: (1) 300 acres in Colleton Co., St. Pauls Par. on Little Mine Creek of Little Saludy, granted 2 Jun 1769 to said BELL; (2) 200 acres on Mine Creek of Little Saludy River in Colleton Co., granted 27 Sep 1769 to WOOD TUCKER & conveyed 28 Sep 1771 to said BENJAMIN BELL; (3) 100 acres on Mine Creek, branch of Little Saludy River, granted 5 Oct 1773 to JOHN BELL; (4) 200 acres on Mine Creek, a branch of Little Saludy River, granted 21 May 1772 to BENJAMIN Bell; (5) 200 acres in St. Pauls Par., Berkley Co. SC near Little Mine Creek, a branch of Little Saludy River, granted 23 Jun 1774 to ROBERT STARK, who conveyed to BENJAMIN BELL, dec'd. S/ SAMUEL WALKER. Wit: THOMAS ADAMS, BENJAMIN RHODES, who swore by oath 6 Mar 1790 before ARTHUR SIMKINS, J.P.

Pp. 259-262. 26 Apr 1790: JESSE COPELAND to PETER HILL, both of Edgefield Co. SC, for 15 pounds, sold 102 acres on Wescotes Creek of Savannah River, adj. CELEY WILLIAMS; MAJ. TUTT; JOHN McCOY; THOMAS BUCKHAM. S/ JESSE COPELAND, SALLY (X) COPELAND, his wife. Wit: JEREMIAH MILES, JAMES NEWBY, JOHN MILES, who swore by oath 3 May 1790 before AQUILA MILES, J.P.

Pp. 262-265. 6 Feb 1790: RICHARD FREEMAN to JOHN MILES, both of Edgefield Co. SC, for 25 pounds, sold 120 acres on Wescot Creek of Savannah River, adj. THOMAS BECKHAM. S/ RICHARD (X) FREEMAN.

Wit: JAMES NEWBY, THOMAS (TE) FREEMAN, JEREMIAH MILES, who swore by oath 3 May 1790 before AQUILA MILES, J.P.

Pp. 265-266. 1 Jan 1790: Bill of Sale: RICHARD JOHNSON to HALEY JOHNSON, both of Edgefield Co. SC, for 1000 pounds, sold thirteen negroes. To Wit: BEN; ISAAC: JACK; HARRY; DRUMMER; NANCY; SALLY; MOLL; BECK; BETTY; LUCY; RACHEL; & DINAH. S/ RICHARD JOHNSON. Wit: R.W. CAMPBELL. Certified sale of RICHARD JOHNSON, Jr. (sic) 3 Apr 1790 by JOHN STURZENEGGER, J.P.

Pp. 266-267. 15 Mar 1790: MACK GOODE of Charlotte Co. VA to JOHN THURMOND of Edgefield Co. SC for 36 pounds, sold 250 acres on Camp branch of Beaverdam of Turkey Creek, adj. said THURMOND; JOHN ELAM; & land supposed to belong to DAVID GEORGE; Estate of THOMAS GOODE, dec'd. S/ MACK GOODE. Wit: ELIZABETH D. MARTIN, LANGSTON BACON, JOHN MARTIN, who swore by oath 17 Apr 1790, that he did see MACK GOODE in VA sign instrument of writing, before AQUILA MILES, J.P.

Pp. 267-271. 22 Jul 1787: COL. PHILEMON WATERS to PLEASANT BURNETT, both of Ninety Six Dist. SC, for 10 pounds, sold 120 acres, on Indian Creek of Little Saludy, granted 5 Mar 1787, & adj. JACOB POPE; PETER WHITTEN. S/ PHILEMON WATERS. Wit: HEZEKIAH GENTRY, JACOB POPE, who swore by oath 23 Apr 1789 before RUSSELL WILSON, J.P.

Pp. 271-274. 6 Nov 1777: DAVID THREATT to MATHEW STOKER, both of Ninety Six Dist. SC, for 1000 pounds, sold 200 acres on Stephens Creek in Granville Co. SC, originally granted to JOHN PERKINS, who conveyed to JOHN LAMAR, who conveyed to GEORGE ROGERS, who conveyed to WILLIAM JACKSON, who conveyed to said DAVID THREATT. Said land adj. NOLLOBOY when surveyed. S/ DAVID THREATT. Wit: MAJOR WEATHERFORD, THOS SPRAGINS, JOHN DAVISON, who swore by oath 8 Nov 1777 before LEROY HAMMOND.

Pp. 275-279. 26 Feb 1790: PETER CARNES & ELIZABETH, his wife, to THOMAS MARBURY, all of Edgefield Co. SC, for 10 pounds, sold 100 acres, being part of 300 acres lately belonging to THOMAS EVELIEGH of Charleston SC and was originally granted 7 Jun 1774 to EDWARD COUCH, and was conveyed 7 Mar 1780 by NICHOLAS EVELIEGH to LEONARD MARBURY, late of GA, who conveyed to PETER CARNES. Said land on Buckhalters Creek of Savannah River, adj. THOMAS EVELIEGH. (also reads the 100 acres on Dry Creek, adj. THOMAS PEARIES in Lease, but LEWIS NOBLE in release). S/ PETER CARNES, ELIZABETH CARNES. Wit: DAN RITCHEY, JONATHAN WIGHTT, who swore by oath 12 Apr 1790 before AQUILA MILES, J.P.

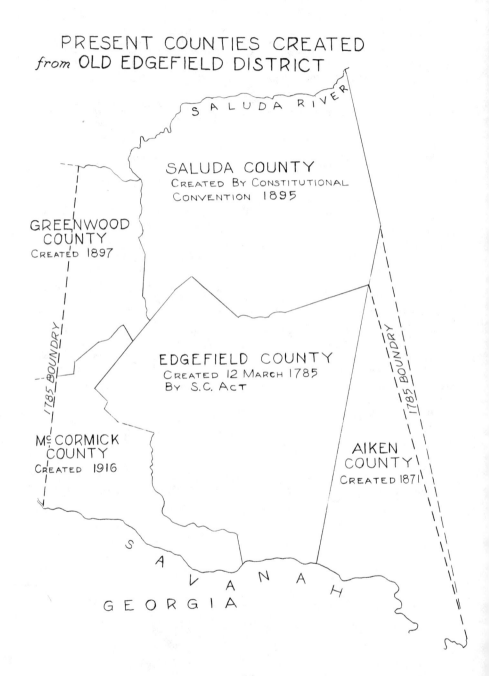

PRESENT COUNTIES CREATED
from OLD EDGEFIELD DISTRICT

SALUDA RIVER

SALUDA COUNTY
CREATED BY CONSTITUTIONAL
CONVENTION 1895

GREENWOOD
COUNTY
CREATED 1897

1785 BOUNDRY

EDGEFIELD COUNTY
CREATED 12 MARCH 1785
BY S.C. ACT

1785 BOUNDRY

Mc CORMICK
COUNTY
CREATED 1916

AIKEN
COUNTY
CREATED 1871

SAVANAH

GEORGIA

DEED BOOK 2: 1787-1788 EDGEFIELD COUNTY, S.C.

Pp. 1-2. 14 Jan 1788: JOSEPH HIGHTOWER, Gentleman, to JOHN HAMMOND, both of Ninety Six Dist. SC, for 5 pounds, sold 306 acres on Savannah River, granted 2 May 1785. S/ JOSEPH HIGHTOWER. Wit: JOHN HAMMOND, SYLVESTER HAMMOND, ROBERT BIRTUN.

Pp. 3-4. 4 Feb 1787: ROBERT BARTLETT to JOHN ROBERTS, both of Edgefield Co. SC, for 35 pounds, sold 150 acres on branch of Turkey Creek of Stevens Creek. S/ ROBERT BARTLETT. Wit: JOHN WILLIAMS, REUBEN ROBERTS, THOMAS LARGN.

Pp. 4-6. ?9 Oct 1787: DANIEL BULLOCK & HANNAH, his wife, to JACOB SMITH & ENOCH GRIGSBY, Executors of LW&T of BURDITT ESKRIDGE, dec'd, all of Edgefield Co. SC, for 10 pounds & benefit of the heirs of said ESKRIDGE, sold their portion, being 1/3rd of said Estate, which falls to HANNAH BULLOCK, wife of DANIEL BULLOCK, as being the widow of the late BURDITT ESKRIDGE. To Wit: 1/3rd of 350 acres on Richland Creek & 1/3rd of 150 acres on Red Bank Creek. S/ DANIEL BULLOCK, HANNAH BULLOCK. Wit: RUSSELL WILSON, ALEXANDER MCDOUGAL, LODOWICK HILL.

Pp. 6-8. 21 Sep 1787: HENRY FOSTER to DANIEL ROGERS, Sr., both of Edgefield Co. SC, for 100 pounds, sold 200 acres on Big Saluda River, adj. DAVID KELLY, dec'd; THOMAS CHAPPEL; when surveyed 3 Feb 1769 & granted 25 Aug 1769. A Memorial was entered in Surveyor Generals office. S/ HENRY FOSTER. Wit: ISAAC KIRKLAND, JOHN FOSTER, ANDREW LOGAN.

Pp. 8-10. 3 Oct 1785: WILLIAM DAVIS, Schoolmaster, & SARAH, his wife, late SARAH MCQUEEN, widow, to THOMAS SPRAGGIN, Planter of Ninety Six Dist. SC, for 75 guineas, sold 153 acres granted 1 Aug 1785 to SARAH MCQUEEN, being on Tossety's Creek. S/ WILLIAM DAVIS, SARAH (X) DAVIS. Wit: ENOCH GRIGSBY, JAMES GRIGSBY, LODOWICK HILL.

Pp. 10-12. 11 Jan 1788: RICHARD WITHERTON of Edgefield Co. SC to THOMAS WITHERTON for 50 pounds, sold 55 acres on branch of Chaver's Creek of Big Stevens Creek, granted 1 May 1786 said WITHERTON & adj. JONATHAN LIMBACKER; JOHN DOOLY. S/ RICHARD (+) WITHERTON. Wit: WILLIAM WATSON, Sr., WILLIAM WATSON, Jr.

Pp. 12-13. 12 Jan 1788: RICHARD JOHNSTON, Sadler, of Edgefield Co. SC to LEROY HAMMOND for 70 pounds, sold 100 acres on branch of Stevens Creek called Chavers Creek, originally granted to said RICHARD JOHNSON. S/ RICHARD (R) JOHNSTON. Wit: JOSHUA HAMMOND, ROLAND SPEER.

Pp. 14-15. 21 Nov 1787: BENAJAH RAMBO & RACHEL, his wife & MARY RAMBO, widow, to EDWARD MITCHELL, all of Edgefield Co. SC, for 10 pounds, sold 152 1/2 acres on Horns Creek & described by Plat dated 7 Mar 1787 by WM COURSEY, Mathamatician. S/ BENJAH RAMBO, RACHEL (X) RAMBO, MARY (O) RAMBO. Wit: JAMES KIND, JOHN HUFFMAN Whereas: by a grant 8 Mar 1755 to JOSEPH NOBLES for 200 acres on branch of Stevens Creek called Toblers now Horns Creek & whereas said JOSEPH NOBLES died & left son & heir, called JOSEPH NOBLES, who conveyed 30 Oct 1765 said 200 acres to LAWRENCE RAMBO, father to said BENAJAH RAMBO & husband to said MARY RAMBO, & said LAWRENCE RAMBO is since dead & willed land to MARY, his widow, during her life & her deceased to said BENAJAH RAMBO. The above 152 1/2 acres being part of said 200 acres...

DEED BOOK 2: 1787-1788 EDGEFIELD COUNTY, S.C.

Pp. 16-17. 12 Jan 1788: EDMOND MARTAIN, Esq. Sheriff of Ninety Six Dist. SC to JAMES HARRISON of same place...Whereas a Judgment in Court of Comman Pleas April Term 1785 for recovery of 40 pounds & a debt of 18 pounds as well, was obtained against CHALMERS & DAVID BLAKENEY, late of said dist. & state, and 100 acres on Mountain Creek originally surveyed & certified 15 Oct 1772 for CATHARINE WHITE, was seized & sold too last & highest bidder, JAMES HARRISON, for 10 pounds. S/ EDMOND MARTIN.

Pp. 17-19. 2 Dec 1786: EDMOND MARTIN, Sheriff of Ninety Six Dist. SC to WILLIAM HAGWOOD...Whereas WILLIAM TERRY in April Term 1786 impleaded THOMAS MURPHEY in Court of Common pleas in an action

Vacant — to Porter's line
Vacant — S50W
Vacant — N40E — 350 Acres — Road to 96 — N30W — Vacant
N60E
Vacant — Land laid out to Alexander McIntosh

for recovery of 32 pounds, as well as 16 pounds 4 sh., 4 p. and obtained a Judgement...and Whereas THOMAS MURPHY late of said Dist. was seized of 350 acres in Edgefield Co. SC on Ninety Six Creek, a branch of Saluda River, adj. ALEXANDER MCINTOSH & FOSTER...Whereas said land was sold at public auction 2 Dec 1786 to last & highest bidder, WILLIAM HAGWOOD for 96 pounds. S/ EDMOND MARTIN. Wit: WILLIAM MOORE,WILLIAM HUGGINS, FRANCIS WILSON.

Pp. 20-24. 26 Oct 1787: BENJAMIN COOKE & MARY, his wife, to CHARLES GOODWIN, Atty. at law, all of Edgefield Co. SC, for 700 pounds, sold four tracts of land: (1) 12 1/2 acres, granted 4 May 1775 & included in survey of 15 acres to JOHN NICHOLAS BOMFOY, who sold to FRANCIS SINQUEFIELD, who conveyed to JACOB FUDGE, who conveyed to BENJAMIN COOKE. Said land adj. lands late of MORRIS CALAHAM; FRANCIS SINQUEFIELD; ROBERT LANG; (2) 150 acres granted to FRANCIS SINQUEFIELD & conveyed to JACOB FUDGE, who conveyed to BENJAMIN COOKE & adj. first described tract; MORRIS CALAHAM; tract conveyed called MILLARS tract; (3) 300 acres granted 24 Dec 1772 to HENRY MILLER, who conveyed to RICHARD KIRKLAND, who conveyed to JOHN ROEBUCK, who conveyed to BENJAMIN COOKE, & adj. MORRIS CALAHAM; THOMAS CARTER; SINQUEFIELD; BENJAMIN COOK; JACOB FUDGE; ROBERT LANG; (4) 1184 acres, granted said BENJAMIN COOKE, adj. MILLAR; THOMAS CARTER; JACOB FUDGE, Sr. S/ BENJAMIN COOKE. Wit: GEORGE WINTER, ROB. G. HARPER.

Pp. 24-26. 14 Jan 1788: CHARLES GOODWIN of SC to EDWARD CHURCH of Edgefield Co. SC, for 120 pounds, sold 1/4th acre called a Town Lot in Campbelton, Edgefield Co. SC., known by No. 6 in original Plat of said town. S/ CHARLES GOODWIN. Wit: R.G. HARPER, JOHN HAMMOND.

Pp. 26-28. 10 Oct 1786: JABASH HENDRICKS, late of Edgefield Co. SC to EDWARD PRINCE, Planter, for 5 pounds, sold 50 acres, granted 5 Sep 1785, being on branch of Savannah River, adj. JOHN SULLIVAN. S/ JABASH HENDRICKS. Wit: HUGH MIDDLETON, JOSEPH PRINCE, LILLEY (W) WILLIAMS.

Pp. 28-31. 12 Nov 1787: JOHN RANDOL of Winton Co., Orangeburg Dist. SC to WILLIAM DAY of Edgefield Co. SC for 20 pounds, sold 50 acres, granted 5 Jun 1786, on Shaws Creek of South Edisto. S/ JOHN (J) RANDOL. Wit: DANIEL (X) DAY, ISHAM (X) MATHEWS, PETER (X) DAY.

Pp. 31-33. 15 Aug 1787: JOHN RANDOL & MARY, his wife, to JOAB WOOTAN, all of Ninety Six Dist. SC for 100 pounds, sold 112 acres on Horse Creek called Kions Fork, adj. ROBIN ROBUCK; JOHN HERNDON. S/ JOHN (J) RANDOL, MARY (M) RANDOL. Wit: THOMAS BECHUM, REUBEN BECHUM.

Pp. 34-38. 1 Aug 1787: DRURY MIMS & LYDIA, his wife, of Edgefield Co. SC, Planters, to JENKINS HARRIS for 50 pounds, sold 1/2 acre, being part of 44 acres in which the Court House of Edgefield County is appointed to be set, granted to DAVID BURKS 5 Sep 1785 & sold 29 Jun 1787 to DRURY MIMS. S/ DRURY MIMS, LYDIA (X) MIMS. Wit: WILLIAM COURSEY, MOSES HARRIS, DAVID MIMS.

original
130 feet N10E
by the
grant
N8OW
Land held
Wm Coursey Math^m

Pp. 38-41. 23 Nov 1787: WILLIAM DOBEY & ANN, his wife, to JOHN OLIPHANT, all of Edgefield Co. SC for 200 pounds, sold 100 acres on Beaver Dam Creek, of Stevens Creek, waters of Savannah River, adj. JOHN SUMMERS. Said land was granted Sep 1768 to VANCE MAGILTON & being invested by LW&T of said VANCE MAGILTON, deceased, unto JAMES MAGILTON. Now said land is invested to PATRICK TARVIS of Augusta GA, being sole Executor at Law to the Estate of said JAMES MAGILTON, deceased, & said PATRICK TARVIS, conveyed to WILLIAM DOBY 13 Mar 1787. S/ WILLIAM DOBEY, ANN (X) DOBEY. Wit: THOMAS HAGINS, RICHARDSON (X) BARTLETT.

Pp. 41-43. 9 Dec 1784: THOMAS BECHUM & NANCY, his wife, to JOSEPH COLLIER all of Ninety Six Dist. SC for $500, sold 120 acres surveyed 12 Mar 1756 for THOMAS LAMAR & granted to THOMAS BECHUM, adj. THOMAS BEAL. S/ THOMAS BECHUM, NANCY (X) BECHUM. Wit: MATT MARTIN, RUSEL (X) BECHUM, ELIZABETH (X) BECHUM.

Pp. 43-46. 13 Aug 1785: PETER GREEN of Abbeville Co. SC to ISHAM GREEN of Edgefield Co. SC for 20 pounds, sold 344 acres on Ninety Six Creek, adj. WILLIAM MARTIN's heirs; JAMES MOORE's heirs; JAMES JONES' land now the property of JOEL LIPSCOMB; JAMES BURTON; ISAAC CROWTHERS & JACOB SMITH. S/ PETER (X) GREEN. Wit: JOHN MOORE, JAMES CHILES, JAMES BEAL.

Pp. 46-48. 8 Jul 1787: FIELDING RENNOLDS & ELIZABETH, his wife, of Dry Creek to JOHN HERNDON, both of Edgefield Co. SC for 50 pounds, sold 100 acres originally granted 3 Apr 1786, being on the main Road from Augusta to the Ridge, known by the name of the wells. S/ FIELDING RENNOLDS, ELIZABETH (X) RENNOLDS. Wit: WILLIAM MURPHEY, DRURY MURPHEY.

Pp. 48-51. 19 Oct 1787: WILLIAM DOBEY & NANCY, his wife, to ABSALOM SHEARLY, both of Ninety Six Dist. SC for 50 pounds, sold 250 acres originally granted 7 Aug 1786, being on the head of Couches Branch of Edisto. S/ WILLIAM DOBEY, NANCY (X) DOBEY. Wit: WM. MURPHEY, DANL. RITCHY, RICHARDSON (X) BARTLETT.

DEED BOOK 2: 1787-1788 EDGEFIELD COUNTY, S.C.

Pp. 51-54. 17 Jul 1787: HENRY SUMMERALL of Wilks Co. Ga, Planter, & FRANCES, his wife, & ANN SUMMERALL, his mother and the widow of JACOB SUMMERALL, dec'd., Adm'trix of JACOB SUMMERALL's Estate, to JOHN RAINFORD of Horns Creek of Edgefield Co. SC, Planter, for 40 pounds, sold 100 acres originally granted 14 Aug 1772 to said JACOB SUMMERALL. S/ HENRY SUMMERALL, ANN SUMMERALL. Wit: PHILIP THOMSON, DANIEL HUFF, ROBERT (R) WILSON.

Pp. 54-56. 9 Nov 1787: ISAAC KIRKLAND to JOHN RYAN, both of Edgefield Co. SC for 20 pounds, sold 300 acres, being part of 643 acres originally granted 7 May 1787 of Chavers Creek & Horns Creek, adj. JACOB FUDGE. S/ ISAAC KIRKLAND. Wit: LEWIS NOBLES, JOHN LUCUS, MARTHA GIBSON.

Pp. 56-59. 25 Aug 1787: ABNER MAYS of Edgefield Co. SC to DAVID LILES, Planter, for 50 pounds, sold 90 acres, being part of 373 acres originally granted 5 Jun 1786 on Halfway Swamp of Saluda River, adj. WILLIAM HILL; PHILEMON BOZMAN; REUBEN HOLLOWAY & vacant land. S/ ABNER MAYS. Wit: REUBEN HOLOWAY, JOSEPH OLDHAM, WILLIAM (X) WARD.

Pp. 59-62. 6 Aug 1788: RICHARD JOHNSTON, Sr. to JOHN OLDRIDGE, Planter, both of Edgefield Co. SC for 15 pounds, sold 464 acres granted 1 May 1786 on Turkey Creek including the mouth of little Turkey Creek or Pucket's Creek, being on both sides of Turkey Creek, adj. JAMES SCOTT & ROBERT BURTON. S/ RICHARD (R) JOHNSTON. Wit: ARTHUR SIMKINS, JOHN SIMKINS, NANCY SIMKINS.

Pp. 62-64. 9 Nov 1787: ISAAC KIRKLAND to WILLIS ODOM, both of Edgefield Co. SC for 25 pounds, sold 343 acres, being part of 643 acres granted 7 May 1787 on waters of Chavers Creek & Horns Creek, adj. JACOB FUDGE. S/ ISAAC KIRKLAND. Wit: JOHN RYAN, MARTHA RYAN, MARTHA GIBSON.

Pp. 64-67. Jan 1788: WILLIAM COVINGTON to JOHN HARDY, all of Edgefield Co. SC for 100 pounds, sold 45 acres, being part of 50 acres granted 7 Nov 1785 on Stevens Creek, adj. JOHN HARDY & JOSEPH COVINGTON. S/ WM. COVINGTON. Wit: RICHARD TUTT, JOHN HERNDON, SHURLEY WHATLEY.

Pp. 67-69. 18 Oct 1787: SYLVANUS STEVENS to JAMES YOUNGBLOOD, both of Edgefield Co. SC for 80 pounds, sold 200 acres on Turkey Creek, originally granted 13 Apr 1769 to WILLIAM BLACKLEY, who conveyed to PETER MEHL, who conveyed to said SYLVANUS STEVENS. S/ SYLVANUS (S) STEVENS. Wit: DAVIS WILLIAMS, JOHN HARKENS, WILLIAM HARKENS.

Pp. 69-72. 28 Dec 1787: DRURY MIMS & LYDIA, his wife, Planters, to MOSES HARRIS, all of Edgefield Co. SC for 50 pounds, sold 1/2 acres, being part of 44 acres granted 5 Sep 1785 to DAVID BURKE & conveyed by L&R 29th & 13th (sic) days of Jun 1787 to DRURY MIMMS, adj. JOHN HARRIS, a lot of 2 acres allotted for the Public Goal & Court House of

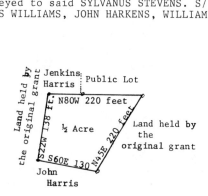

18

DEED BOOK 2: 1787-1788 EDGEFIELD COUNTY S.C.

Edgefield Co., JENKINS HARRIS. S/ DRURY MIMS. Wit: WM. COURSEY, JOHN (X) COTTON, DANIEL HUFF.

Pp. 73-75. 13 Jan 1788: WILLIAM BROWN, Planter, to JOHN ARLEDGE, both of Edgefield Co. SC for 20 pounds, sold 100 acres on Turkey Creek, originally granted 10 Jan 1775 to EBENATUS STEVENS, and was conveyed from EDWARD MILES 6 Oct (sic) to WILLIAM BROWN. Said land adj. JOSEPH STEVENS. S/ WILLIAM BROWN. Wit: JAMES BROWN, WILLIAM DOBEY, LEVI JESTER.

Pp. 75-78. 14 Jan 1788: STEPHEN TILLMAN to FREDERICK TILLMAN, Jr., both of Edgefield Co. SC for 100 pounds, sold 100 acres on both sides of Nobles Creek, now called Horns Creek, being part of 3 tracts, (1) was surveyed by JOSEPH NOBLES, who conveyed to LAWRENCE RAMBO, dec'd. (2 & 3) were surveyed by LAWRENCE RAMBO, dec'd, who conveyed to his son, LAWRENCE RAMBO by LW&T & said LAWRENCE RAMBO conveyed to STEPHEN TILLMAN by L&R described as adj. WALTER JACKSON on RAMBO's Spring, Nobles Creek, now called Horns Creek, mouth of Rogers Creek, Old Mill on north side of Horns Creek, EDWARD MITCHELL, FREDRICK TILLMAN, Jr., & JOSEPH RAMBO. S/ STEPHEN TILLMAN. Wit: ROBERT STARK, Jr., LEWIS NOBLES.

Pp. 78-81. 21 Nov 1787: HENRY BOLTON & MARY, his wife, Planter, to WILLIAM HUMPHREYS, all of Edgefield Co. SC for 50 pounds, sold 135 acres on Mine Creek of Saluda River, adj. BARRETT TRAVIS; DRURY FORT; WILLIAM HUMPHREY & vacant land. S/ HENRY BOALTON, MARY (X) BOALTON. Wit: NATHANIEL BOALTON, WILLIAM FORT, MARY BOALTON.

Pp. 81-84. 14 Jan 1788: JOSHUA HAMMOND to WILLIAM SPENCER, both of Edgefield Co. SC for 200 pounds, sold 164 acres on Sweet Water Creek, being part of 500 acres granted 19 Nov 1772 to JOHN HAMMOND, dec'd, & said 100 acres was invested by LW&T of JOHN HAMMOND, dec'd, to JOSHUA HAMMOND. Said land adj. JOSEPH DAY; WILLIAM COVINGTON; ALLY HINTON; & the main waggon road. S/ JOSHUA HAMMOND. Wit: JOHN HATCHER, WILLIAM COVINGTON.
Plat: p. 84.

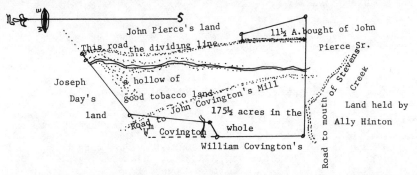

Pp. 84-85. State of South Carolina: Agreeable to request of WILLIAM COVINGTON, I have ameasured & laid out unto WILLIAM SPENCER 175 1/2 acres, being part of 500 acres granted 19 Nov 1772 to JOHN HAMMOND, dec'd, on main Road to Augusta & part of land being invested by LW&T of JOHN HAMMOND, dec'd, unto JOSHUA HAMMOND by virture of his being an Administrator in Will of Estate of JOHN HAMMOND...S/ ROBERT LANG D.S. 3 September.

19

Pp. 85-88. 14 Jan 1788: JOSHUA HAMMOND to WILLIAM COVINGTON, both of Edgefield Co. SC for 100 pounds, sold 14 1/2 acres on waters of Sweet Water Creek, being part of 500 acres granted 19 Nov 1772 to JOHN HAMMOND, dec'd. Said 14 1/2 acres invested by LW&T of JOHN HAMMOND, dec'd, to said JOSHUA HAMMOND...S/ JOSHUA HAMMOND. Wit: JOHN GANETT, WILLIAM WILLIAMS, JOHN HATCHER.

Pp. 88-91. 10 Apr 1787: JOHN ROEBUCK & MARY, his wife, to BENJAMIN COOK, all of Edgefield Co. SC for 500 pounds, sold 300 acres granted 24 Dec 1772 to HENRY MILLER, who conveyed 6 Aug 1773 to RICHARD KIRKLAND, who conveyed 10 Jan 1778 to JOHN ROEBUCK. Said 300 acres, being on Chavers Creek of Stevens Creek, adj. CHRISTIAN BUCKHALTER; FRANCIS SINQUEFIELD; MORRIS CALAHAM; JACOB FUDGE; & ROBERT LANG. S/ JOHN (X) ROEBUCK, MARY (M) ROEBUCK. Wit: ROBERT LANG, Ld. NOBLES, THOMAS DOZER.

Pp. 91-94. 1788: ROBERT SPEERS & ELIZABETH, his wife, Mill right & seamstress, to ASAEL ROBERTS, Planter, all of Edgefield Co. SC for 60 pounds, sold 100 acres granted 14 Sep 1771 to LEVI HARRIS, who conveyed 6 Aug 1779 to DANIEL JONES, who conveyed 29 Nov 1781 to FREDERICK TILLMAN, who conveyed 7 Jul 1786 in the Clerk Office of Edgefield Co. SC in Book A page 65, to said ROBERT SPEER. S/ ROBERT SPEER, ELIZABETH (X) SPEER. Wit: JOHN RAINSFORD, BURGESS WHITE.

Pp. 95-97. 1 Jan 1788: JOHN ARLEDGE & ANN, his wife of Edgefield Co. SC to SAMUEL JENKINS for 30 pounds, sold 100 acres on Turkey Creek a branch of Stevens Creek waters of Savannah River... the lower side on Turkey Creek & running S.E. so as to include the spot whereon the Old Houses stood which JOHN DUKES once lived...on little or Pucket Creek adj. ROBERT BURTON; land called MILLERS old place, said to run by JOHN DOOLY. S/ JOHN (+) ARLEDGE. Wit: ARTHUR SIMKINS, JOHN SIMKINS, NANCY SIMKINS.

Pp. 97-98. 15 Jan 1787: SION FIELDS, son of RICHARD FIELDS, dec'd, of Edgefield Co. SC puts himself Apprentice to JOHN MALLET, blacksmith of same place for 4 years... S/ SION (X) FIELDS, JOHN MALLETT.

P. 98. 16 Jan 1788: Bill of Sale: GEORGE RAGLAND of Edgefield Co. SC for 30 pounds, sold to SHADRACK ROGAR one negroe boy named JEFF & one bay horse. S/ GEORGE RAGLAND. Wit: WM COVINGTON, JOHN (X) COCKBURN.

Pp. 98-101. 13 Feb 1788: JOSEPH WILLIAMS of Orangeburg Dist. of Lexington Co. SC to WILLIAM HOWARD of Edgefield Co. SC for 30 pounds, sold 100 acres, originally granted 31 Aug 1774 to RICHARD WILLIAMS, now dec'd and said JOSEPH WILLIAMS, being son of said RICHARD WILLIAMS. Said land on the road from the Ridge to the Congaree & Cloud Creek. S/ JOSEPH WILLIAMS. Wit: JOHN THOS. FAIRCHILD, NATHAN NORRIS, JESSE JOHNSTON, who swore by oath 12 Apr 1788 before JOHN THOMAS FAIRCHILD, J.P., Lexington Co. SC.

Pp. 101-104. 9 Mar 1788: THOMAS LAMAR, Planter, to SHADRACK ROGAR, both of Edgefield Co. SC for 57 pounds, sold 100 acres, being in Edgefield Co., formerly known by name of Granville Co. SC at Cherokee Ponds. S/ THOMAS LAMAR. Wit: ZACHARIAH LAMAR, Jr., JOHN (X) ROGAR, NANCY ROGAR.
State of SC: At the request of THOMAS LAMAR, Sr., I have ameasured 100 acres at Clouds Cherokee Pond in Edgefield Co. SC. 23 Jun 1788 by H. JONES D.S.

DEED BOOK 2:   1787-1788 EDGEFIELD COUNTY S.C.

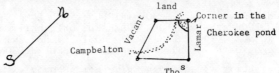

Pp. 105-109. 25 Sep 1787: ALEXANDER MCIVER of Sunbury Ga,
Merchant, to WILLIAM MCWHANN of Charleston SC for 50 pounds...
sold 417 acres called ALEXANDRIA & formerly WILLIAMSON's camp,
being opposite to the Town of Augusta in SC & now in tenure &
occupation of Mr. SAMUEL WILLISSON... Whereas the said ALEXANDER
MCIVER by his Bond stands bound to said WILLIAM MCWHANN the penal
sum 450 pounds... with condition for payment of 225 pounds... with
interest by installments at several periods by an Act of SC
Legislature to Recover & payments of Debts & passed 26 March
last... And Whereas ALEXANDER MCIVER stands indebted in & by the
ballance of an account with ALLANS WILSON & Co. of Glascow,
Merchant of whome the said WILLIAM MCWHANN his Attorney unto them
in the sum of 381 pounds... with interest 12 July 1786... S/ ALEX.
MCIVER. Wit: FRANCIS CODDINGTON, THOMAS HOLMES, who swore by oath
7 Dec 1787 before P. HORRY, J.P.

Pp. 109-110. 28 May 1788: Bill of Sale: EDWARD COUCH, Planter, to
GEORGE MEE for 300 pounds, sold 4 negroes, ISAAC; PHILLIS; TOM; &
JAMES... said EDWARD COUCH appear before the Justices of Court of
Common Pleas in Charleston the first Tuesday in July next then
stand to & abide by the Judication of SC Court in the suit brought
against the said EDWARD COUCH by ROBERT STARK, Esq., then this
Bill of Sale be void otherwise remain in full force. S/ EDWARD
COUCH. Wit: PETER CHASTAIN, THOMAS (X) ADAMS, who swore by oath 30
Aug 1788 before RUSSELL WILSON, J.P.

P. 110. 9 Jun 1788: Bill of Sale: SANDERS NOBLES to JOHN RYAN,
both of Edgefield Co. SC for 50 pounds, sold a young negroe girl
HANNAH. S/ SANDERS NOBLES. Wit: BURGES WHITE, EZEKIAL MCCLENDON,
VAN SWEARINGTON, Jr., JNO. SWEARINGIN, who swore by oath 15 Jul
1788 before BENJ. TUTT, J.P.

P. 111. 20 Oct 1787: LEWIS WATSON, Planter, appoint my loving
Brother SAMUEL WATSON, both of Edgefield Co. SC, my lawful
attorney in my name to collect from ROBERT STARKE & ARTHUR WATSON,
Executors of Captain MICHAEL WATSON's Estate, dec'd.. the sum of 84
pounds. S/ LEWIS WATSON. Sworn by oath of EDWARD COUCH 14 Oct 1788
before JOHN PURVIS, J.P.

Pp. 112-115. 22 Mar 1788: GEORGE MASON, Joiner, to RHYDON GRIGSBY,
both of Edgefield Co. SC for 40 pounds, sold 100 acres on the
bounty, granted 2 Oct 1786 on middle & Palmetto Fork of Pen Creek
of Little Saluda River. S/ GEORGE MASON. Wit: RUSSELL WILSON,
HENRY KING & THOMAS BUTLER, who swore by oath 30 May 1788 before
RUSSELL WILSON, J.P.

Pp. 115-118. 22 Mar 1788: GEORGE MASON, Joiner, to RHYDON GRIGSBY,
both of Edgefield Co. SC for 50 pounds, sold 150 acres in fork of
Pen Creek of Little Saluda River, granted 6 Mar 1786. S/ GEORGE
MASON. Wit: RUSSELL WILSON, Sr., HENRY KING, THOS BUTLER, who
swore by oath 13 Mar 1788 before RUSSELL WILSON, J.P.

Pp. 119-122. 26 Jun 1788: JOSHUA DEEN to SAMUEL MAYS, both of
Edgefield Co. SC for 50 pounds, sold 130 acres on Big Creek of

21

Saluda River, adj. JOHN HIGDON; SAMUEL MAYS; land surveyed for GAVIN PUGH otherwise JOHN GARRARD. Originally granted 3 Oct 1785. S/ JOSHUA (+) DEEN. Wit: JOSIAH ALLEN, WILLIAM (X) DEEN, who swore by oath 14 Jul 1788 before RUSSELL WILSON, J.P.

Pp. 122-125. 2 Apr 1788: BARTLETT BLEDSOE to ENOCH GRIGSBY, both of Edgefield Co. SC for 80 pounds, sold 200 acres on Pen Creek of Little Saluda River, granted 7 Nov 1785 & adj. WRIGHT NICHOLSON. S/ BARTLETT BLEDSOE. Wit: PRESLEY BLAND, JOHN DRINKARD, HENRY KING, who swore by oath 27 Jun 1788 before RUSSELL WILSON, J.P.

Pp. 125-129. 26 Mar 1788: SAMUEL MAYS, D.S. to GEORGE MASON, both of Edgefield Co. SC for 20 pounds, sold 180 acres on Pen Creek of Little Saluda River, adj. SAMUEL LEWIS when granted 4 Dec 1786. S/ SAMUEL MAYS. Wit: AVERILLA (A) KING, HENRY KING, who swore by oath 22 Jun 1788 before RUSSELL WILSON, J.P.

Pp. 129-133. 7 Mar 1788: WILLIAM BROWN to ANNA BLAND, widow and Executrix of Estate of ROBERT BLAND, late of said county, dec'd, both of Edgefield Co. SC for 2 pounds, sold 350 acres on Little Mine Creek of Little Saluda River, adj. WILLIAM DANIELS & HART when granted 1 Jan 1787. S/ WILLIAM (X) BROWN. Wit: HENRY KING, AVERILLA (A) KING, who swore by oath 27 Jun 1788 before RUSSELL WILSON, J.P.

Pp. 133-134. 28 Nov 1787: Power of Attorney: AMBROSE GAINS, Planter of West Florida Chicasaw Nation... thereunto moving, appoint my trusty friend, JESSE GAINS of Edgefield Co. SC, my lawful atty. for & in my name to sell 100 acres on Iscot's Creek of Little Saluda River, well known by the name of AMBROSE's clearing... S/ AMBROSE GAINS. Wit: HENRY KING, JOHN SMEDLEY, who swore by oath 7 Jan 1788 before RUSSELL WILSON, J.P.

Pp. 134-136. 15 Apr 1788: WILLIAM HOLSTON of Lexington Co. SC to MATHEW BURDEN of Edgefield Co. SC for 21 pounds, sold 100 acres on Cloud Creek of Saluda River. S/ WILLIAM HOALSTUN (sic) Wit: JOSHUA BUNTER, JAMES HARRISON, WILLIAM RABORN, who swore by oath 1 Aug 1788 before RUSSELL WILSON, J.P.

Pp. 136-137. 28 Apr 1787: Bill of Sale. JOHN MARSHALL of Abbeville Co. SC to RICHARD MOORE of Edgefield Co. SC for 160 pounds, sold negroe slaves... To Wit: TOE CAK & 3 children named FED, PHIB & CHARITY. S/ JOHN MARSHALL. Wit: JOHN WHITE, HENRY WHITE, who swore by oath 13 Oct 1788 before LEROY HAMMOND, J.P.

Pp. 137- 138. 11 May 1787: Bill of Sale: JOHN MARSHALL of Abbeville Co. SC to WILLIAM WHITE for 150 pounds, sold negroe slaves named TOM, MARINDA, PATIENCE & child BEN. S/ JOHN MARSHALL. Wit: JOHN WHITE, HENRY WHITE, who swore by oath 13 Oct (blank) before LEROY HAMMOND.

Pp. 138-140. 1 Feb 1788: GEORGE MEE to JAMES TOMLIN, both of Edgefield Co. SC for 5 pounds, sold 100 acres on Moores Creek of Little Saluda River, adj. DENNIS MCCARTNEY & JACOB READ. S/ GEORGE MEE. Wit: THOMAS (T) ADAMS, SOLOMAN (S) STRICKLIN, ELENOR (X) BECK, who swore by oath 1 Jun 1788 before RUSSELL WILSON.

Pp. 140-143. 3 Jan 1789: GEORGE SAWYER to AGNESS NORRIS, both of Edgefield Co. SC for 50 pounds, sold 100 acres, originally granted 23 Feb 1768 unto LEWIS POWELL, who sold 8 Feb 1771 to JOHN SAWYER & by LW&T of JOHN SAWYER dated 2 Oct 1784, was bequeathed to said GEORGE SAWYER, being 100 acres taken of east part of 150 acres. S/ GEORGE (+) SAWYER, ELIZABETH (+) SAWYER, his wife. Wit: HOWEL (+) JOHNSTON, NATHAN NORRIS, who swore by oath 12 Apr 1788 before JOHN THOMAS FAIRCHILD.

Pp. 143-145. 22 Mar 1788: DRURY FORT to EDWARD HOMES, both of Edgefield Co. SC for 100 pounds, sold 200 acres on Mine Creek of Little Saluda River, originally granted 23 Aug 1774, adj. said FORT; HENRY BOLTON & BENJAMIN BELL. S/ DRURY FORT. Wit: WILLIAM HOMES, WILLIAM FORT, who swore by oath 21 Aug 1788 before RUSSELL WILSON, J.P.

Pp. 145-147. 26 Jul 1787: WILLIAM ANDERSON to JOSEPH OLDHAM, both of Edgefield Co. SC for 15 pounds, sold 100 acres on Halfway Swamp, originally granted 2 Feb 1773 to EDWARD BUCK, who conveyed 17 Aug 1773 to said WILLIAM ANDERSON & adj. JOHN EDWARDS. S/ WILLIAM ANDERSON. Wit: REUBEN HOLLOWAY, ABNEY MAYS, WILLIAM TAYLOR.

Pp. 147-150. 12 Jul 1788: MATHEW DEVORE, Sr. to ANTHONY BUTLER, both of Edgefield Co. SC, for 38 pounds, sold 100 acres on drains of Stevens Creek, originally granted 4 Dec 1771. S/ MATHEW (M) DEVORE. Wit: ROBERT (T) WHITE, WILLIAM WATSON, Sr., who swore by oath 14 Jul 1788 before JOHN PURVIS, J.P.

Pp. 150-153. 28 Nov 1787: ELISHA BROOKS & NANCY, his wife, of Newberry Co. SC to WILLIAM THOMAS of Lawrence Co. SC for 60 pounds, sold 350 acres on Cuffee Town & hard Labor Creeks, adj. JOHN ANDERSON. S/ ELISHA BROOKS, NANCY BROOKS. Wit: NIMROD WILLIAMS, JOHN SILLS, RICHARD (+) HOGIN, who swore by oath 14 Apr 1788 before RUSSELL WILSON, J.P.

Pp. 153-156. 4 Jan 1788: BENJAMIN MOBLEY & MARY, his wife, to BENJAMIN SUTTON, all of Edgefield Co. SC, for 30 pounds, sold 265 acres originally granted 7 Aug 1786, being on South side Edisto River at head of Bridge Creek, where said MOBLEY now lives. S/ BENJAMIN (X) MOBLEY, MARY (X) MOBLEY. Wit: JNO.SWEARINGIN, MATHEW BETTIS, STEPHEN BETTIS, who swore by oath 3 May 1788 before ARTHUR SIMKINS, J.P.

Pp. 156-158. 16 Jan 1788: CHARLES GOODWIN, Esq. of Edgefield Co. SC to JOHN COOK for 30 pounds, sold a 1/4 acre lot known as No. 26 in the Village of Campbelton. S/ CHARLES GOODWIN. Wit: LEROY HAMMOND, GEORGE WALKER.

Pp. 158-161. 1787: LEVEY MANNING, Planter, to CHARLES BANKS, both of Ninety Six Dist. SC, for 10 pounds, sold 30 acres adj. said LEVY MANNING & said CHARLES BANKS on north side of Saluda River. (Note, gch: This deed poorly written without dates & signatures of Grantor & Witnesses.)

Pp. 161-164. 3 Jan 1788: WILLIAM ANDERSON & RACHEL, his wife of Ninety Six Dist. SC to JOHN POOL for 14 pounds, sold 90 acres on Halfway Swamp Creek, adj. GEORGE BLAKE, THOMAS ?PIKE & JOSH THOMAS. S/ WM. ANDERSON, RACHEL ANDERSON. Wit: TIMOTHY COOPER, JOHN (+) GORMAN.

DEED BOOK 2: 1787-1788 EDGEFIELD COUNTY S.C.

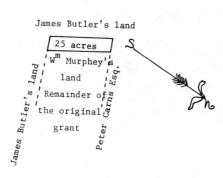

James Butler's land

25 acres

Wᵐ Murphey's land

Remainder of the original grant

James Butler's land

Peter Carns Esq.

Pp. 165-169. 31 Jan 1788: WILLIAM MURPHEY & MARY, his wife, to JOHN MORRIS, all of Edgefield Co. SC, for 50 pounds sold 25 acres, being part of 200 acres originally granted 11 Feb 1773 to WILLIAM ANDERSON, who conveyed 12 Aug 1773 to said MURPHEY being on Buckhalter's Mill Creek of Stevens Creek of Savannah River & adj. JAMES BUTLER & PETER CARNS, Esq. S/ WILLIAM MURPHEY, MARY (X) MURPHEY Wit: ROBERT LAND, WM. WATSON, who swore by oath 15 Apr 1788 before BENJAMIN TUTT, J.P.

Plat: Surveyed 25 Mar 1787 by ROBERT LANG D.S. by request of WILLIAM MURPHEY.

Pp. 169-171. 1 Nov 1787: Mortgage: ISAAC CROTHERS by my bond unto WILLIAM ROBINSON, Merchant, both of Edgefield Co. SC in the penal sum of 226 pounds... with the condition for payment of 113 pounds... & said ISAAC CROUTHERS for the better securing of the sum of 113 pounds... sold WILLIAM ROBINSON 4 slaves: TOM, a field fellow; JENNY a field wench; DOLLY a house wench & field slave; & JAMES a BOY...S/ ISAAC CROUTHER. Wit: CHAS. GOODWIN, TURNER HARRIS.

Pp. 171-175. 29 Nov 1773: PETER YOUNGBLOOD, Sr. to ARTHUR SIMKINS, both of Granville Co., Ninety Six Dist. SC, for 100 pounds sold 300 acres, excepting 100 acres on the south corner, which I have for sometime past conveyed to JOHN FRAZER, which he is now in possession of. Said 300 acres, being on Beaver Dam Creek of Savannah River, originally granted 1 Aug 1758 unto JOHN LAMAR & conveyed 1 Aug 1764 unto PETER YOUNGBLOOD, Sr., adj. NICHOLAS DILLARD; JOHN VARNER; EDWARD VANN; & JENKINS HARRIS. S/ PETER (+) YOUNGBLOOD. Wit: JOHN NIBLETT, ROBURD BIRTIN, who swore by oath 15 Jan 1774 before MOSES KIRKLAND, J.P.

Pp. 175-179. 10 May 1775: FRANCIS BRAZINA, Planter of Camden Dist. SC to ARTHUR SIMKINS, Esq. of Ninety Six Dist. SC for 25 pounds, sold 250 acres on Puckets Creek a branch of Stevens Creek & Savannah River, originally granted 31 Aug 1774, & adj. EPHRAIM PUCKET; land surveyed on Dutch bounty; WILLIAM CARR & ARTHUR SIMKINS. S/ FRANCIS BREZINA. Wit: JESSE DANIEL, WILLIAM DANIEL, who swore by oath 15 Feb 1776 in Orangeburg Dist. SC before JOHN FAIRCHILD, J.P.

Pp. 179-181. 4 Sep 1788: JOHN THOMAS SPENCER & MARY, his wife of Burke Co. GA to LEROY HAMMOND of SC for 150 pounds, sold 250 acres, being part of two tracts of land inherited by JOHN THOMAS SPENCER by the death of his brother, WILLIAM SPENCER, late of SC. Tract #1 of 150 acres on Horns Creek called Cedar Creek, originally granted to DAVID ROBERTSON & transferred to said WILLIAM SPENCER. Tract #2 of 100 acres originally granted to said WILLIAM SPENCER. S/ JOHN T. SPENCER, MARY (X) SPENCER. Wit: THOMAS HANCOCK, WILLIAM MATHEWS, who swore by oath 15 oct 1788 before RUSSEL WILSON, J.P.

Pp. 181-185. 15 May 1776: BENJAMIN ALLEN, Millwright, to LEROY HAMMOND, Merchant, both of Ninety Six Dist. SC, for 100 pounds, sold 250 acres, originally granted 1770, being on Foxes Creek of Savannah River, adj. EPHRIAM SIZEMORE; WARING; & LEROY HAMMON. S/ BENJAMIN ALLEN. Wit: THOMAS HARVEY, JOHN DAVISON, who swore by oath 15 Oct 1788 before RUSSELL WILSON, J.P.

Pp. 185-191. 13 Jun 1788: DAVID ZUBLY of New Windsor Township, Edgefield Co. SC to LEROY HAMMOND of Edgefield Co. SC for 5 shillings, sold 239 acres in Township of New Windsor, adj. Savannah River; CONRAD LUTZ; ULRICK EGGER; LEONARD ULRICK & MICHAEL MYERS, being the plantation whereon said DAVID ZUBLY now lives. Also the following slaves: MINGO; SCIPPO; TELLERY; CORK PRIMUS; HERCULES; ADAM; BETTY; HANNAH; & SUE with the future increase of the females... Whereas 1 Jul 1788 DAVID ZUBLY by his Bond stands bound in penal sum of 500 pounds with condition for payment of 250 pounds with interest in the proportions mentioned of 83 pounds... Now for better securing of payment with interest DAVID ZUBLY sells to LEROY HAMMOND above tract of land and slaves... S/ DAVID ZUBLY. Wit: WILLIAM MATHEWS, LEROY HAMMOND, Jr.

Pp. 191-194. 1 Oct 1787: THOMAS LAMAR of Edgefield Co. SC to Brig. Genl. ANDREW PICKENS of Abbeville Co. SC for 25 pounds, sold 7 acres near mouth of Horse Creek in Edgefield Co. SC. S/ THOMAS LAMAR. Wit: JOSEPH DICK, MELINESE CONCKLING LEAVENCEWORTH, who swore by oath 20 Jun 1788 before LEROY HAMMOND, J.P. The plat represents a small tract of high land in Edgefield Co. SC near the mouth of Horse Creek on the West side next the Ford. The road on the East side of the land being the line bounded as per plat being divided off from a tract of Mr. LAMAR of Horse Creek to Genl. ANDREW PICKENS containing 7 acres by me 1 Oct 1787. S/ WM. EVANS.

Pp. 194-197. 16 Sep 1787: EZEKIEL & OBURN BUFFINGTON of Winton Co. SC to RICHARD JOHNSON for 200 pounds, sold 200 acres on Turkey Creek adj. JOHN RUTLEDGE, Esq. & said RICHARD JOHNSON. S/ OBURN (OB) BUFFINGTON. Wit: CHRISTIAN (X) GOMILLION, RICHARD (X) JOHNSON, JAMES CLEVELAND.

Pp. 197-201. 5 Jul 1773: WILLIAM ANDERSON of Ninety Six Dist. SC to THOMAS ROSS for 100 pounds, sold 69 acres, being part of 100 acres originally granted 12 Dec 1768 on Ninety Six Creek of Saluda River, adj. north by said 100 acres. S/ WM. ANDERSON. Wit: THOS. ANDERSON, STEPHEN ANDERSON. Plat: 69 acres being part of 100 acres granted unto WM. ANDERSON 12 Dec 1768 bounded north by part of 100 acres surveyed 1 Apr 1773.WM.ANDERSON DS.

Pp. 201-204. 27 Aug 1788: ROBERT LANG & SARY, his wife, to ISAAC WOOD, all of Edgefield Co. SC for 50 pounds, sold 340 acres on a road that leads from Fort Moore to Silver Bluff, adj. JAMES PARSON's Estate; GEORGE GALPHIN & GEORGE MILLER. S/ ROBERT LANG, SARY LANG. Wit: LEWIS NOBLES, GEORGE MILLER, who swore by oath 14 Oct 1788 before JOHN STURZENEGGER, J.P.

Pp. 205-208. 26 Nov 1787: JAMES BUCKELEW to JOHN STILL, both of

Ninety Six Dist. SC for 50 pounds, sold 182 acres on branch of Little Stevens Creek, being part of 500 acres originally granted 14 Aug 1772 to RICHARD BUCKELEW & by his decease fell to his son & heir, GEORGE BUCKELEW, who conveyed to said JAMES BUCKELEW, adj. CHRISTOPHER WARD. S/ JAMES BUCKELEW, RACHEL (R) BUCKELEW. Wit: CHRISTOPHER WARD, OGDEN COCKCROFT, who swore by oath 14 Apr 1788 before ARTHUR SIMKINS, J.P.

Pp. 208-211. 22 Feb 1788: BENJAMIN WARING of Claremont Co. SC to MATHEW WILLS of Ninety Six Dist. SC for 60 pounds, sold 200 acres originally granted 26 Sep 1772 in Colleton Co. SC on branch called Mill Creek, adj. land formerly called a Dutch Survey. S/ B. WARING. Wit: WILLIAM BUTLER, WILLIAM ANDERSON, who swore by oath 1 May 1788 before LEROY HAMMOND, J.P.

Pp. 211-215. 21 Jul 1787: LEONARD MARBURRY of Georgia to JOHN JOLSON LOW for 75 pounds, sold 100 acres in Granville Co. SC, formerly but now Edgefield Co. SC, on a branch of Stevens Creek, adj. lands lately JOHN BUCKHALTER & WILLIAM BUCKHALTER. Said land was formerly sold by ROBERT STARK, Sheriff of Ninety Six Dist. SC 5 Jan 1774 unto THOMAS EVELEIGH. S/ LEOD. MARBURRY, JOHN JOLSON LOW. Wit: PETER CARNS, GEO OGG, EDWARD TELFIAR.
Mrs. ANN MARBURY, wife of LEONARD MARBURY, relinquishes her dower 9 Jul 1788 before LEROY HAMMOND, J.P.

Pp. 215-219. 21 Jul 1788: LEONARD MARBURRY & ANN, his wife, of Georgia to PETER CARNS for 400 pounds, sold two tracts of land of 1300 acres between Saluda & Savannah Rivers, being (1) 1000 acres, originally granted 13 Mar 1772 unto WILLIAM ELLIOTT, dec'd, on Buckhalters Creek adj. JOHN HARRITON; LAWRENCE RAMBO; JOHN WARD; RICHARD JONES; EDWARD COUCH; & JOHN BUCKHALTER. (2) 300 acres adj. lands late belonging to THOMAS EVELEIGH, originally granted 7 Jun 1774 to one EDWARD COUCH. S/ LEOD. MARBURY, PETER CARNS. Wit: JOHN LOW, GEO OGG, EDWD. TELFAIR, THOMAS MARBURY, THOMAS PEARCE, who swore by oath 14 Oct 1788 before JOHN STURZENEGGER, J.P.

Pp. 219-223. 23 Feb 1773: JOHN TANNER, Planter of NC to MOSES KIRKLAND of Ninety Six Dist. SC for 1000 pounds, sold 750 acres being part of two tracts; (1) 500 acres in Colleton Co. SC on Little Saluda Creek, adj. SAMUEL MARSH, FRANCIS SINQUEFIELD, PATRICK THOMAS & one HOLLAN. (2) 300 acres granted to PATRICK THOMAS in Colleton Co. SC on Little Saluda Creek & conveyed 19 Sep 1770 to said JOHN TANNER, adj. said TANNER; ELIZABETH MEATZO & FRANCIS SINQUEFIELD, excepting 50 acres surveyed & granted 22 Nov 1771 unto said JOHN TANNER. S/ JOHN TANNER. Wit: WILLIAM CHENEY, DRURY FORT, JOSIAH ALLEN, who swore by oath 27 Feb 1773 before JOHN CALDWELL, J.P.

Pp. 223-227. 31 Aug 1773: WILLIAM ANDERSON to THOMAS ROSS, both of Ninety Six Dist. SC for 50 pounds, sold 50 acres on Wilson Creek, adj. ANDERSON; land not yet divided & remainder part of 200 acres granted 2 Feb 1773 to EDWARD BUCK & by him & SARA, his wife, sold to said ANDERSON 17 Aug 1773. S/ WILLIAM ANDERSON. Wit: STEPHEN ANDERSON, AZARIAH LEWIS, BENJAMIN LEWIS.

Land not yet divided

50 acres

Land granted to   old mark
William Anderson

Plat: Pursuant to a sale to THOMAS ROSS...50 acres adj. land he now lives on being part of 200 acre grant EDWARD BUCK & has such marks as plat represents. 25 Aug 1773. S/ WM ANDERSON.

Pp. 228-229. 26 Sep 1788: LEONARD MARBURY to PETER CARNS for $500.00, sold 1000 acres granted in 1772 to JAMES PARSONS & purchased by said MARBURY of NICHOLAS EVELEIGH, on Cedar Creek in Edgefield Co. SC, adj. WILLIAM MOSES; LAWRENCE RAMBO; DILLARD; JAMES THOMAS; ALLEN ANDERSON; GEORGE STRAWDERS & JOHN BARIN. S/ LEOD. MARBURY, PETER CARNS. Wit: THOMAS MARBURY, THOMAS PEARCE, who swore by oath 14 Oct 1788 before JOHN STURZENEGGER, J.P.

Pp. 229-233. 19 Sep 1770: PATRICK THOMAS & ANN, his wife, to JOHN TANNER, all of Ninety Six Dist. SC for 10 shillings, sold 300 acres on Little Saluda River, adj. ELIZABETH MANTZ. Said tract surveyed 18 Dec 1754 & granted May 1757. S/ PATRICK (P) THOMAS, ANN (O) THOMAS. Wit: MICHEL (MB) BUCKHALTER, WM. BUCKHALTER, FRANCIS SINQUEFIELD, who swore by oath 21 Dec 1771 in Granville Co. SC before LEROY HAMMOND, J.P.

Pp. 233-236. 13 May 1775: JAMES ROBERTSON & GRIZEL, his wife, to DANIEL ROGERS, all of Ninety Six Dist. SC for 200 pounds, sold 200 acres surveyed 8 Jul 1770, certified 15 Oct 1772 & granted 9 Sep 1774 in Granville Co. SC on both sides Beaver Dam, adj. YOUNGBLOOD. S/ JAMES ROBERTSON. Wit: JOSEPH NOBLES, JAMES SCOT, JOHN VERNON, who swore by oath 4 Nov 1775 before ARTHUR SIMKINS, J.P.

Pp. 236-238. 1 May 1788: NATHAN JOHNSON & SHABEY, his wife of Edgefield Co. SC, for love & affection for his sons & daughters, NATHAN JOHNSON, Jr.; ESTHER JOHNSON; MARY JOHNSON; RACHEAL JOHNSON; JAMES JOHNSON; JOHN JOHNSON & AARON JOHNSON for 5 shillings each, gives to each of his children 200 acres on both sides of Beaver Dam Creek purchased of JOHN MASON's heirs, granted to said JOHN MASON, dec'd. Also unto ESTHER JOHNSON, my dau., the negro that JOHN ELAM owes me, she paying half her value to her sister MARY JOHNSON. Also unto JAMES JOHNSON, my son, 200 & 70 odd acres on both sides Little Beaver Dam Creek, being part of 300 & 70 odd acre grant in my own name, whereof I have sold 100 acres to JOHN KELLY. Also unto JOHN JOHNSON, my son, 125 acres on both sides of waggon road that leads from the Long Cain to Charleston below Beaver Dam Creek, granted in my own name. Also unto AARON JOHNSON, my son, one Negroe girl named VENUS. All cattle, household goods, lands etc... to above named children provided said NATHAN JOHNSON, Sr. & SHABEY, his wife, have use of as long as they may live... S/ NATHAN JOHNSON. Wit: ELLEN MASON, W. COURSEY, who swore by oath 8 Oct 1788 before AQUILLA MILES, J.P.

Pp. 238-241. 20 Jul 1787: WILLIAM ANDERSON to JAMES ANDERSON, both of Edgefield Co. SC for 200 pounds, sold 750 acres, being part of two tracts: (1) 500 acres originally granted 4 Nov 1772 unto JAMES SIMPSON on Turkey Creek, (2) 250 acres granted 21 Jan 1785 said ANDERSON on Bird Creek of Savannah River, adj. HENRY CALDWELL. S/ WM. ANDERSON. Wit: JOHN WALDROP, RACHEL SINQUEFIELD.

Pp. 241-244. 13 Dec 1784: JAMES RISHTAN of Ninety Six Dist. SC to CHRISTOPHER WARD for 14 pounds, sold 100 acres originally granted 13 Apr 1769 said JAMES RISHTAN, being on Manchestor Branch & Waggon Road from Charleston to Ninety Six. S/ JAMES RISHTAN. Wit: JAMES HART, JOHN SILLS, WILLIAM SALMON, who swore by oath 14 Dec. 1784 before WILLIAM MOORE, J.P.

DEED BOOK 2: 1787-1788 EDGEFIELD COUNTY S.C.

Pp. 244-248. 22 Feb 1788: JOHN GORMAN & HANNAH, his wife, to THOMAS BERRY, Sr., all of Edgefield Co. SC for 60 pounds, sold 177 acres, being part of 2 surveys on Mill Creek of Saluda River: (1) 163 acres granted 5 Dec 1785 said JOHN GORMAN, & (2) 14 acres, being part of 200 acres originally granted Oct 1772 unto MICHAEL ABNEY & is now property of JOHN GORMAN. S/ JOHN (+) GORMAN, HANNAH GORMAN. Wit: NATHAN ABNEY, MARTHA GORMAN, JOSEPH (X) GORMAN.

Pp. 248-251. 8 Sep 1774: ROBERT STARK, Sheriff, to JAMES MARTIN & JOHN MARTIN for 500 pounds, sold 500 acres in Granville Co. SC on branch of Cuffy Town and Birds Creek, adj. said MARTINS & ROBERT WALLACE...Whereas CHARLES PINCKNEY, Atty. at law, obtained a Judgement in July Term 1773 against WILLIAM MARTIN for a debt of 8090 pounds... & Whereas ROBERT STARK, Sheriff, did seize 500 acres originally granted said WILLIAM MARTIN...S/ ROBERT STARK, Sheriff. Wit: GEORGE MARTIN, JOSIAH TURPIN, EDMOND MARTIN, who swore by oath before HUGH MIDDLETON, J.P.

Pp. 251-252. 2 Jul 1788: MARTIN CLOUD of Edgefield Co. SC to ANNA CLOUD, my dau., for love & affection & 5 shilllings, sold all household furniture, stock, Bonds, Notes, Bills & c & all the crop now growing in the property of said MARTIN CLOUD. S/ MARTIN CLOUD. Wit: JOHN BALLARD, ROBERT MOSELEY, who swore by oath 15 Jul 1788 before LEROY HAMMOND, J.P.

Pp. 252-255. 23 Jan 1788: DANIEL DAY to JOHN MAYS, both of Edgefield Co. SC for 25 pounds, sold 100 acres, originally granted 13 Apr 1769 unto EZEKEIL TOWNSEND & was conveyed 3 May 1769 unto JESSE DRAKE, being on Benfield Creek of Savannah River, adj. HENRY BENFIELD when granted. S/ DANIEL DAY. Wit: THOMAS CARTER, JAS. TUTT, who swore by oath 14 Jul 1788 before BENJAMIN TUTT, J.P.

Pp. 255-257. 29 Apr 1788: JOSEPH MILLER of Winton Co. SC to GEORGE MILLER for 50 pounds, sold 200 acres originally granted 7 May 1771 unto LAURENCE RAMBO, being on Chavus Creek. S/ JOSEPH MILLER. Wit: JAMES BOOTH, Sr., JAMES BOOTH, Jr., who swore by oath 25 Oct 1788 before AQUILA MILES, J.P.

Pp. 257-259. 5 Sep 1788: DRURY FORT, Planter, to HENRY BOALTON, both of Edgefield Co. SC for 40 pounds, sold 50 acres, being part of 100 acres grant 31 Oct 1765 on Mine Creek of Little Saluda River, adj. when surveyed FREDERICK SISSON, BARROT TRAVIS, HENRY BOALTON, WILLIAM HUMPHRIES . S/ DRURY FORT. Wit: NATHANIEL BOALTON, LYDIA (X) FORT, WILLIAM HUMPHRIES, who swore by oath 19 Sep 1788 before RUSSELL WILSON, J.P.

Pp. 260-261. 15 Oct 1788: NANCY REYNOLDS of Edgefield Co. SC to CLEMENT CARGILL for 40 pounds, sold one negroe girl named EASTER. S/ NANCY (X) REYNOLDS. Wit: CORNELIUS CARGILL, MARTHY CARGILL, JESSE SKINNER, who swore by oath 16 Oct 1788 before ROBERT STARK.

P. 261. 10 Jul 1788: ABRAHAM ODOM, Sr. to ABRAHAM ODOM, Jr., both of Edgefield Co. SC, sold horse branded with IB; bay mare branded IB with a young colt; 1 feather bed including all household furniture; heifer; white stear; red stear; 9 sheep. S/ ABRAHAM (X) ODOM. Wit: HENRY SWEARINGEN who swore by oath 14 Oct 1788 before AQUILA MILES, J.P.

Pp. 1-5. 23 Oct 1787: BENJAMIN HUGHS & ANNA, his wife, ESTHER MASON & ELLENDER MASON of Ninety Six Dist. SC, Planter & Spinster, to NATHAN JOHNSON, Planter of Edgefield Co. SC, for 100 pounds, sold 200 acres surveyed 21 Jul 1772 & granted 24 Dec 1772 unto JOHN MASON & by his decease, descended unto said ANNA MASON, now HUGHS; ESTHER MASON, widow of JOHN MASON; ELLENDER MASON, dau. of him; & BENJAMIN HUGHS, husband of said ANNA. Said 200 acres being on Beaverdam Creek of Turkey Creek, a fork of Stephens Creek of Savannah River, adj. THOMAS BOON, NATHAN JOHNSON, WARD TAYLOR & JAMES BOON. S/ BENJAMIN (B) HUGHS, ANNA (+) HUGHS, EASTER (X) MASON, ELLEN MASON. Wit: W. COURSEY, LEVI JESTER, CHARITY (her X) MOCK.

Pp. 5-6. 15 Jun 1788: SAUNDERS NOBLES of Edgefield Co. SC to the children of NANCY JONES for 10 pounds, sold at the death of LEONARD NOBLES two negroe boys: PRINCE & STEPHEN. S/ SANDERS NOBLES. Wit: ARTHUR BENNET, JOHN RYAN, who swore by oath 1 Aug 1789 before LEROY HAMMOND, J.P.

Pp. 6-7. 22 Apr 1772: JAMES MCCORD of Marklinburg Co. NC is bound unto JOHN WILLIAMS, Merchant of Craven Co. SC for 2000 pounds. The obligation is such that lawful titles to 650 acres secured by a warrant 7 Apr 1772 as soon as a grant can be got in name of said JAMES MCCORD be made unto said JOHN WILLIAMS... the obligation be void... S/ JAMES MCCORD. Wit: THOMAS NORTH, DANIEL CLARK, who swore by oath 2 May 1789 in Abbeville Co. SC before WILLIAM MOORE, J.P.

Pp. 8-12. 23 Jun 1789: LW&T of GEORGE STROOP. Bequeaths all household furniture, stock & all debts due me to MARY MURPHEY, WILLIAM MURPHEY & NANCY STROOP... to be equally divided them when NANCY STROOP marries or becomes of age. Bequeaths to my three sons, JACOB, GEORGE, & HENRY STROOP all my lands of 524 acres to be equally divided among them when HENRY comes of age... Ordain MARY MURPHEY my Executrix & my well & trusted friend, CLEMENT CARGILL, my sole Executor. S/ GEORGE (+) STROOP. Wit: G. MILLER, KEZIH MILLER, MARY (X) SAINGOHN (sic). Proven in open Court by oath of GEORGE MILLER.

Pp. 8-12. 13 Oct 1785: JOHN RUTLEDGE to JOHN PURVES for 5 shillings, sold 550 acres, being on three tracts granted 5 Sep last: (1) 150 acres in Ninety Six Dist. on Stevens Creek of Savannah River; (2) 250 acres on Crooked Run a branch of Turkey Creek; (3) 150 acres on branch of Stevens Creek. S/ JOHN RUTLEDGE. Wit: JOHN RUTLEDGE, Jr., E. RUTLEDGE, Jr.

Pp. 12-17. 18 Jul 1785: SARAH BRYANT & ROBERT BRYANT, widow & son of ROBERT BRYANT, dec'd, to BENJAMIN TUTT, all of Ninety Six Dist. SC for 80 pounds, sold 150 acres originally surveyed 1 Apr 1757 for HUMPHRY PARROT, but granted 18 Jan 1765 unto ROBERT BRYANT (dec'd), being on Hawtree Creek of Stephens Creek of Savannah River. S/ SARAH (+) BRYANT, ROBERT BRYANT. Wit: MARSHALL LEWIS, JAMES TUTT, RICHARD TUTT, who swore by oath 10 Aug 1789 before JOHN PURVES, J.P. (Note, gch: Lease dated 18 Jul 1785, Release dated 19 Jul 1784).

Pp. 18-19. 13 Mar 1775: ROBERT WALLACE to DAVID MAXWELL, both of Ninety Six Dist. SC for 10 shillings, sold 132 acres on Cuffee Town Creek of Savannah River, adj. BENJAMIN TUTT; THOMAS WALLACE;

& said ROBERT WALLACE. S/ ROBERT WALLACE. Wit: ROBERT BRYANT, JOHN STUART.

Pp. 20-24. 31 Mar 1775: ROBERT WALLACE & ISABELL, his wife, to DAVID MAXWELL, all of Ninety Six Dist. SC for 800 pounds, sold 250 acres granted 24 Jan 1770 said WALLACE in Granville Co. SC on Cuffey Town Creek of Savannah River, adj. SARAH BLACKNEY; THOMAS WALLACE; & ROBERT WALLACE. Also in addition to above mentioned land, did convey part of another tract of 132 acres. S/ ROBERT WALLACE, ISABELL (+) WALLACE. Wit: ROBERT WALLACE, JOHN STEWART, who swore by oath 1 Apr 1775 before BENJAMIN TUTT, J.P

P. 24. PLAT: By request of ROBERT WALLACE, I have ameasured 132 acres, part of 2 surveys on Cuffey Town Creek of Savannah River in Ninety Six Dist. SC. One granted said ROBERT WALLACE & the other laid out for him on a warrant of JOHN ULRICK, adj. SE, NE, NW, & SW on BENJAMIN TUTT; S by THOMAS WALLACE; NE said ROBERT WALLACE. 28 Mar 1775. M. GOODE, D.S.

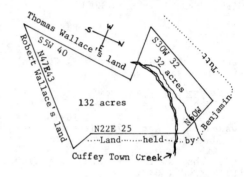

Pp. 25-28. 14 Dec 1788: DAVID MAXWELL to BENJAMIN TUTT, both of Edgefield Co. SC for 100 pounds, sold 132 acres on Cuffee Town Creek of Savannah River, being part of two surveys, one granted to ROBERT WALLACE & the other laid out on a Warrant of JOHN ULRICK, adj. BENJAMIN TUTT; THOMAS WALLACE & ROBERT WALLACE. Said 132 acres conveyed by L&R 30 & 31 Mar 1775 by ROBERT WALLACE & ISABELL, his wife to DAVID MAXWELL. S/ DAVID MAXWELL. Wit: HUGH MIDDLETON, GABRIEL TUTT.

P. 29. 8 Jun 1789: LW&T of JOHN TOBLER: I, JOHN TOBLER of Edgefield Co. SC bequeaths to wife, CHRISTIAN, all of my estate for the maintaining of her & her children during her life, then after her death... to my son JOHN's daughter, CHRISTIAN, five shillings... to my two daughters, CHRISTIAN & ANN, 5 shillings and also the following negroes named: CATE; NANCY; ISAAC; MOLY; QUA; & SILVIA, together with a bed and furniture to each of them. The remainder of my estate both real & personal to my three sons, FREDERICK, ULRICK; & JOHN JOAKIM, provided they pay to my daughter, ELIZABETH, the sum of 60 pounds, being the full amount of her portion left me by my father... Appoint wife, CHRISTIAN, Executrix & son, JOHN JOAKIM Executor. S/ JOHN TOBLER. Wit: JOHN MEYER, CHAS. WILLIAMS, GOODRICK HOWELL. Proved by the oath of JOHN MEYER.

Pp. 30-36. 3 Mar 1789: EBENEZER HILL to NIMROD SHINALT, both Planters of Edgefield Co. SC for 37 pounds, sold 50 acres, being part of 100 acres granted to JACOB RAUGH, but now in possessin of EBENEZER HILL & is on north side of Stevens Creek. S/ EBENEZER (H) HILL & MARY (X) HARRISON (sic). Wit: JOHN (+) SHINALT, EDMOND FRANKLIN, JOHN GLANTON, who swore by oath 24 Jul 1789 before BENJAMIN TUTT, J.P.

DEED BOOK 3: 1787-1789 EDGEFIELD COUNTY S.C.

Pp. 37-42. 19 Aug 1787: MARTIN CLOUD to NATHANIEL FORD, both Planters of Edgefield Co. SC, for 125 pounds, sold 75 acres, being part of 220 acres originally granted 6 Feb 1786 to said CLOUD on Beaver Dam Creek of Turkey Creek and adj. LEVY JESTER; JOHN OLIPHANT; & MARTIN CLOUD. S/ MARTIN CLOUD. Wit: JOHN CHENEY, ELIZABETH CHENEY; DRURY MIMS, who swore by oath 2 Jul 1788 before ARTHUR SIMKINS, J.P.

Pp. 42-46. 3 Sep 1788: WARD TAYLOR of Georgia to MOSES TAYLOR of Edgefield Co. SC for 5 pounds, sold 100 acres, being half of 200 acres granted 9 Sep 1775 said WARD TAYLOR on branch of Turkey Creek of Savannah River. The other 100 acres now in possession of CALL COLLINS. S/ WARD (W) TAYLOR. Wit: J. MORRIS, CALL COLLINS, who swore by oath 4 Sep 1788 before JOHN PURVES, J.P.
PLAT: This is a true Plat of the land conveyed by me to MOSES TAYLOR 4 Jul 1788. S/ WARD (W) TAYLOR. JOHN PURVES, J.P.

Coll Collin's land
100 acres — Crooked Run

Pp. 46-49. 16 Feb 1789: JOHN ALLEN, Planter, of Turkey Creek, Ninety Six Dist. SC to JOHN LEWIS GERVAIS, the younger son of the Honorable JOHN LEWIS GERVAIS of Charleston SC for 5 shillings, sold 1169 acres, being part of several tracts viz: (1) 100 acres originally granted about 3 Nov 1762 to said JOHN ALLEN & being the land where he now lives on Turkey Creek; (2) 200 acres originally granted about 3 Jul 1772 said JOHN ALLEN on Turkey Creek & adj. above said land; (3) 100 acres adj. above said lands on both sides of Turkey Creek where said JOHN ALLEN formerly was building a Mill; MICHL. WATSON; & said JOHN ALLEN; (4) 200 acres originally granted 22 Aug 1771 to said JOHN ALLEN on Beaver Dam Creek about 2 miles from last mentioned tract where said JOHN ALLEN resides; (5) 100 acres called Springfield, being part of 500 acres originally granted about May 1772 unto WILLIAM COURSEY, who with his wife, conveyed about 16 Apr 1774 to said JOHN ALLEN; (6) 469 acres including Pole Cat Pond granted said JOHN ALLEN.

Pp. 49-53. WHEREAS:... in the year 1774 JOHN ALLEN of Turkey Creek, Ninety Six Dist. SC was indebted to JOHN LEWIS GERVAIS, Esq., the father by Bond for several negroes & other articles to the amount of 1320 pounds, & said JOHN ALLEN about the last of the year 1778 made a considerable payment of above sum & did by several after payments in 1779 wholly discharge the balance of the Bond aforesaid. And WHEREAS from the depreaciation of the paper currency which was then in circulation and a legal tender, the said JOHN LEWIS GERVAIS, Esq. sustained almost a total loss of his just debt aforesaid by the payment being (left blank) per the circumstances above mention (blank) order that a just and reasonable satisfaction of the natural love and affection which said JOHN ALLEN has for the said JOHN LEWIS GERVAIS, the younger, and the sum of 5 shillings, conveys all the above several tracts of land. S/ JOHN ALLEN. Wit: ABRAM. MARKLEY, JOHN EWING CALHOUN, Esq., who swore by oath 18 Mar 1789 before PETER FRENEAU, J.P. in Charleston Dist. SC. Registors Office: 18 Mar 1789. Rcd. in Bk. 6, p. 239. PETER HORRY, Regr.

Pp. 53-55. 17 Feb 1789: JOHN ALLEN of Turkey Creek, Edgefield Co. SC to JOHN LEWIS GERVAIS, the younger, for & in consideration of loss sustained by JOHN LEWIS GERVAIS, Esq. from my paying off in the year 1779 as depreciated money his Bond dated Jan 1774 for

31

payment of 1320 pounds & also for sum of 10 shillings, sold a negroe fellow called SIMITY; a negro wench called BELLANEY & her two children, a boy JACK & a girl DINAH; a young wench called BETT... horses, mares colts, cattle & hogs with the household furniture. S/ JOHN ALLEN. Wit: JOHN E. COLHOUN, ABRAM MARKLEY, who swore by oath 13 Mar 1789 before D. MAZYCK, J.P. SC, Secretary Office. Rcd. in Bill of Sale Bk. 20, pp. 626-627, 21 Nov 1789. S/ D. MAZYCK.

Pp. 55-59. 13 Nov 1788: JAMES WEST to WILLIAM JETER, Sr., both of Edgefield Co. SC for 15 pounds, sold 19 acres, being part of 75 acres originally granted 17 Aug 1786 said JAMES WEST on North side of Horns Creek, adj. widow FERNEDO & said JETER. S/ JAMES (+) WEST. Wit: THOMAS CHILDERS, MOSES ASHFORD, W. JETER, Jr.

Pp. 59-62. 28 Jun 1789: LEROY HAMMOND & MARY ANN, his wife, to JOHN HAMMOND, Sr. all of Edgefield Co. SC for 5 pounds, sold 15 1/2 acres granted 6 Jun 1785 said LEROY HAMMOND on Savannah River, adj. heirs of GEORGE GOLPHIN & MCCARTIN CAMPBELL. S/ LEROY HAMMOND, MARY ANN HAMMOND. Wit: HENRY SMERDON, JOSHUA HAMMOND.

Pp. 62-65. 29 Jun 1789: JOHN HAMMOND & ELIZABETH, his wife, Merchant, to LEROY HAMMOND, all of Edgefield Co. SC for 5 shillings, sold 6 acres, being near a Villiage commonly called Campbelton, adj. Savannah River & down a row in the center of a Street to be called Union Street in a town intended to be laid out. S/ JOHN HAMMOND, ELIZABETH HAMMOND. Wit: JOSHUA HAMMOND, HENRY SMERDON, who swore by oath with JUNE ROUNTREE 8 Jul 1789 before JOHN HAMMOND.

Pp. 65-68. 17 Jul 1789: JOHN HAMMOND & ELIZABETH, his wife, to LEROY HAMMOND, Merchant, all of Edgefield Co. SC, for 5 pounds, sold 104 feet square on Union Street & Broad Street of a town intended to be laid out by said JOHN HAMMOND & LEROY HAMMOND on their lands joining a Villiage known as Campbeleton. S/ JOHN HAMMOND, ELIZABETH HAMMOND. Wit: HENERY SMERDON, EPHRIAM HENDREN.

Pp. 69-73. 27 Mar 1789: THOMAS BUTLER to JAMES TOMLIN all of Edgefield Co. SC for 25 pounds, sold 163 acres, excepting such part that may run into a survey held by DENNIS MCCARTA, on Mores Creek of Cloud Creek of Saludy River, adj. GEO. MEE & SOLOMAN EDWARDS. S/ THOMAS BUTLER. Wit: WILLIAM CORLEY, WILLIAM (+) MCCARTY, DANIEL BULLOCK, who swore by oath 28 Mar 1789 before RUSSELL WILSON, J.P.

Pp. 73-74. 12 Jan 1789: ROBERT MOSELEY & PENNY, his wife, to JOHN RAINSFORD, both Planters of Horns Creek, Edgefield Co. SC, for 100 pounds make sure & perfect title by Bond, obligation to be met by March next, to 8 1/2 acres that has been in dispute for sometime. Said 8 1/2 acres granted or laid out to JACOB SUMMERALL, Jr. & adj. GEORGE EILAND; said SUMMERALL... now belongs said JOHN RAINSFORD's possession. S/ ROBERT (+) MOSELEY, PENNY (+) MOSELY. Wit: JACOB ODOM, JAMES (+) WEST, who swore by oath 8 Jun 1789 before AQUILA MILES, J.P.

Pp. 74-75. 8 Dec 1786: ANN SUMMERALL, widow of JACOB SUMMERALL, of Horns Creek, Edgefield Co. SC to JOHN RAINSFORD for 50 pounds, make sure & perfect title by Bond, obligation to be met by 10 Jan next, to a tract of land containing 1/3rd of 100 acres being her dower of her late husband & was originally granted 14 Aug 1772 to JACOB SUMMERALL. S/ ANN (+) SUMMERALL. Wit: JOSHUA (+) MARQUES, DANL. MARQUES, who swore by oath 19 Jun 1789 before AQUILA MILES, J.P.

Pp. 76-77. 24 Oct 1788: PHILIP JOHNSON & MARGARET, his wife, to JOHN RAINSFORD, all of Horns Creek, Edgefield Co. SC, for 100 pounds, make sure & perfect title by Bond, obligation to be met by 25 Dec next, to a tract of 4 1/4 acres, being part of survey originally granted to JOHN SHAW & by said SHAW to WILLIAM JEETER, adj. PHILIP JOHNSON. S/ PHILIP JOHNSON, MARGARET (X) JOHNSON. Wit: ROBERT (A) WILSON, JAMES COBB, Jr., who swore by oath 8 Jun 1789 before AQUILA MILES, J.P.

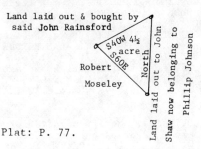

Land laid out & bought by said John Rainsford

S40W 4½ acre S60E

Robert Moseley

North Land laid out to John Shaw now belonging to Phillip Johnson

Plat: P. 77.

P. 77. 19 Nov 1788: SUSANNAH BILLINS (BILLINGS) to SALLY BILLINS for 10 pounds, sold all household furniture, 1 mare & sadle. S/ SUSANNAH (X) BILLINS. Wit: LEORNARD NOBLES, who swore by oath 28 Feb (blank) before LEROY HAMMOND, J.P.

Pp. 78-79. 14 Jul 1789: RICHARD HAMPTON to my beloved children, to wit: GALE HAMPTON, CHARLOTTE HAMPTON, JONNAH HAMPTON, LUCY HAMPTON, MARY HAMPTON, EDWARD HAMPTON & RICHARD HAMPTON for love & affection & me hereunto moving... give & grant the following goods & chattels to them to wit: Negroes, DICK, HANNAH, JUDY, NANCY, SIMON, CRESEY, also beds, household furniture, wagon, horses with gear & all stock of cattle & hoggs. Property to be divided equally with conditions & this condition annexed that the eldest to wit: GALE, CHARLOTTE, JOANNAH, LUCY & MARY be obliged to support me out of above estate, together with my two younger children EDWARD & RICHARD as long as I live & till said EDWARD & RICHARD become of age. S/ RICHARD HAMPTON. Wit: THOMAS PETER CARNES, WILLIAM COVINGTON, who swore by oath 14 Jul 1789 before JOHN PURVES, J.P.

Pp. 79-80. 10 Apr 1789: WHEDEN PINES of Edgefield Co. SC & ther unto moving to WILLIAM HERN for 43 pounds, sold a certain negroe boy named PRINCE, nine or ten years old. S/ WHEDEN (M) PINES. Wit: ROLAN WILLIAMS, GEORGE MEE, who swore by oath 9 Apr 1789 (sic) before RUSSELL WILSON, J.P.

Pp. 80-81. 16 Apr 1789: MARTHA LAREMON to my loving daughter, SARAH LAREMON for love & affection give and grant my cattle, hogs, horses & household stuff, all my property which was left to me by LW&T of my husband, EDWARD LAREMON, dec'd, 24 Mar 1785, except those articles as bequeathed by said will to my son, DANIEL LAREMON. S/ MARTHA LAREMON. Wit: ISREAL MARTIN, DANIEL LAREMON, who swore by oath 30 May 1789 before RUSSELL WILSON, J.P.

Pp. 81-84. 13 Apr 1789: WILLIAM COVINGTON, Sheriff of Edgefield Co. SC to JOSEPH RAMBO for 39 pounds, sold 100 acres on Stevens Creek, adj. ISAAC EVANS & SAMUEL CRAFTON. WHEREAS... WILLIAM

HERNDON, dec'd, was in his lifetime became indebted to BENJAMIN
JOINER for 39 pounds & BENJAMIN JOINER in the Court of Common
Pleas obtained a Judgement for recovery in Nov 1787 & the tract
was sold to the last and highest bidder JOSEPH RAMBO. S/ WILLIAM
COVINGTON. Wit: DAVID ZUBLY, W. ANDERSON. Ordered to be rcd. in
Open Court Jul Term 1789.

Pp. 84-87. 18 Apr 1789: WILLIAM COVINGTON, Sheriff of Edgefield
Co. SC to JAMES COODY for 15 pounds, sold 90 acres on Horns
Creek, adj. DRURY MIMS; EDITH COODY's thirds of said tract; JOHN
POUNDS; & BURRELL JOHNSON. WHEREAS... LEWIS COODY, dec'd, became
indebted to ADAM PERDUE for 34 pounds... & WHEREAS... ADAM PERDUE
obtained a Judgement against Estate of LEWIS COODY 10 Oct 1788...
the said WILLIAM COVINGTON, Sheriff, sold to the last & highest
bidder JAMES COODY. S/ WILLIAM COVINGTON. Wit: JAMES CARSON,
ZEPHENIAH CLEMENT, who swore by oath 15 Jul 1789 before AQUILA
MILES, J.P.

Pp. 87-90. 18 Apr 1789: WILLIAM COVINGTON, Sheriff of Edgefield
Co. SC to JAMES COODY for 5 pounds, sold 12 acres on Horns Creek,
adj. EDITH COODY's of said tract; WILLEBY TILLERY; HENRY PARKMAN
& land least unto MORRIS PARDUE. WHEREAS...ADAM PARDUE having
impleaded the Administrators of the said LEWIS COODY, Dec'd, in
Court of Common Pleas for the recovery of 34 pounds... in 1788...
S/ WILLIAM COVINGTON. Wit: JOSHUA HAMMOND, ZEPHANIAH CLEMENT, who
swore by oath 15 Jul 1789 before AQUILA MILES, J.P.

Pp. 91-94. 18 Apr 1789: WILLIAM COVINGTON, Sheriff of Edgefield
Co. SC to JAMES COODY for 10 pounds, sold 100 acres on Horns
Creek, adj. DRURY MIMS, BURELL JOHNSON, WM. PARDUE, EDMAN BOYD,
WILLERBY TILLERY. WHEREAS... LEWIS COODY, deceased in his life
became indebted unto ADAM PARDUE for 34 pounds... & WHEREAS...
ADAM PARDUE obtained a Judgement for recovery against the Admrs.
of Estate of LEWIS COODY, dec'd. S/ WM. COVINGTON. Wit: JOSHUA
HAMMOND, WEST COOK, who swore by oath 15 Jul 1789 before AQUILA
MILES, J.P.

Pp. 94-98. 31 Aug 1784: JOHN SHAW of Hollow Creek to WILLIAM
JETER of Horns Creek, both of Edgefield Co. SC for 60 pounds,
sold 100 acres, originally granted 29 Apr 1768 unto JOHN SHAW on
Nobles Creek S/ JOHN (+) SHAW. Wit: ABSOLOM JACKSON, JAS. LAMAR,
Jr.
"I do certify that I give JOHN SHAW 20 feet square of land, part
of the 100 acres, the spot where his brother, DANIEL, lies in his
grave on said land"...
Sworn by oath of ABSOLUM JACKSON 1 Sep 1784 before JOHN HERNDON,
J.P.

Pp. 98-102. 31 Aug 1784: JOHN SHAW of Hollow Creek to WILLIAM
JETER OF Horns Creek, both of Edgefield Co. SC, for 120 pounds,
sold 100 acres, originally granted 27 Aug 1764 unto said SHAW on
Nobles Creek. S/ JOHN SHAW. Wit: JAMES LAMAR, Jr., ABSOLOM
JACKSON, who swore by oath 1 Sep 1784 before JOHN HERNDON, J.P.

Pp. 102-105. 15 May 1789: JAMES KING & SALLY, his wife, to
COALLER & STUART, all of Edgefield Co. SC for 170 pounds, sold
200 acres, being part of 400 acres originally granted 3 Nov 1770
unto JOHN BROUGHTON in Granville Co. SC, but now Edgefield Co.
SC., being the 200 acres not sold to DANIEL HUFF and is that part
where the plantation now is... S/ JAMES KING, SALLY (X) KING.
Wit: WILLIAM PARDUE, ULYSSES ROGERS, who swore by oath 14 Jun
1789 before JOHN PURVES, J.P.

Pp. 105-109. 13 Jul 1789: JAMES TUTT, Trader, to JOSEPH MORRIS, Planter, both of Edgefield Co. SC, for 100 pounds, sold 120 acres near Logg Creek & adj. an Old line formerly made for 5 acres & sold from the original grant for a Mill seat; TIMOTHY RAIRDEN & THOMAS BOON as shown by a plat on the Release hereof Indorsed & certified by WILLIAM COURSEY, mathemationer. Said land being part of 250 acres granted Bounty 6 Feb 1773 unto ANNA MILLER & memorialized 16 Jul 1773. Said 120 acres transferred by ANNE MILLER to JAMES MUREHEAD, who conveyed to NEWBY MANN, who conveyed to said JAMES TUTT. S/ JAS. TUTT. Wit: WILLIAM PARDUE, DANIEL BIRD, who swore by oath 14 Jul 1789 before JOHN PURVES, J.P.
PLAT: p. 109.

Vacant at time of Original Survey

Thomas Boon's land / N10W 70 ——— N80E — Log Creek

Land sold from original survey / S17W / S10E 50

Timothy Readon

Pp. 110-114. 23 May 1789: NATHAN JOHNSTON & SHABA, his wife, Planter & Spinster, to JOHN ELAM, all of Edgefield Co. SC for 100 pounds, sold 200 acres originally granted unto said JOHNSTON 8 Jul 1774 & rcd. 23 Dec 1774, as can be seen by a plat certified 27 Jun 1774, being on Beaver Dam Creek of Savannah River, adj. THOMAS BOON & WILLIAM GOODE. S/ NATHAN JOHNSTON, SHABA (X) JOHNSTON, JOHN ELAM. Wit: W. COURSEY, CHARLES BRODWATER, WILLIAM TERRY, who swore by oath 27 Jun 1789 before JOHN PURVES, J.P.

Pp. 114-118. 4 Feb 1789: CHESLY DANIEL & JUDITH, his wife, of Granville Co. NC to WILLIAM GLOVER of Edgefield Co. SC for 200 pounds, sold 400 acres originally granted 14 Sep 1771 unto CHAMPNESS TERRY & conveyed by deed 8 Mar 1774 to CHESLY DANIEL, adj. MICHAEL BUCKHALTER & GEORGE LIMBECKER. S/ CHESLY DANIEL, JUDITH W (J) DANIEL. Wit: WM. COCKE, Jr., HENRY KEY, DAVID GLOVER, ROBERT GLOVER, who swore by oath 10 Jul 1789 before AQUILA MILES, J.P.

Pp. 118-121. 7 Apr 1789: RICHARD JOHNSON, Jr. & MARY, his wife, to ROBERT BURT, all of Edgefield Co. SC for 100 pounds, sold 275 acres, being part of Gen. S. Plat by No. 1 confiscated lands on Turkey Creek of Savannah River, adj. RUTLEDGE. S/ RICHARD JOHNSON, MARY JOHNSON. Wit: HARWOOD BURT, MOODY BURT, who swore by oath 13 Apr 1789 before HUGH MIDDLETON, J.P.

Pp. 122-125. 31 Jan 1785: MICHAEL BECKMAN to JOHN JACOB MESSER SMITH, all of Ninety Six Dist. SC, for 50 pounds, sold 350 acres originally granted 13 Aug 1765 unto ALDBRIGHT BECHMAN, dec'd, father of MICHAEL BECHMAN, being on Sleepy Creek otherwise called Rocky Creek of Savannah River, adj. FREDERICK TIMBERMAN. S/ MICHAEL BECKMAN. Wit: JAMES PRICHARD, JOSEPH MORRIS, who swore by oath 1 Feb 1785 before JOHN PURVES, J.P.
29 Nov 1785: "I do certify I have measured & resurveyed a tract of land granted to ALBRIGHT BECHMAN 30 Aug 1765 on Turkey Creek near the mouth of Sleepy Creek." S/ DAVID BURKS D.S.

Pp. 126-130. 15 Feb 1785: JACOB HUITT & CHRISTINA BARBARA, his wife, to JOHN JACOB MESSER SMITH, Planters of Ninety Six Dist. SC for 30 pounds, sold 150 acres originally granted 30 Aug 1765 unto JOHN GEORGE SHOEMAKER, father of CHRISTINA BARBARA & came by Heirship by his "will" to CHRISTINA BARBARA, wife of said JACOB

DEED BOOK 3: 1787 - 1789 EDGEFIELD COUNTY S.C.

HUITT, being on Little Stevens Creek of Savannah River, adj.
JOHANNES KEEK & VALENTINE KUNE. S/ JACOB (X) HUITT, CHRISTINA
BARBARA HUITT. Wit: GEORGE (C) TILDMAN, JOHN MICHL. KUBLER, who
swore by oath 16 Feb 1785 before WM. HOUSEAL, J.P.

Pp. 130-134. 19 Jan 1789: BLASSENGAME HARVEY of Burke Co. GA
to WILLIAM HOWLE, Jr. of Edgefield Co. SC for 50 pounds, sold 81
acres, originally granted HANNAH FLEEK (now the lawful wife of
ABRAM TAYLOR) & conveyed by them 20 Dec 1779 unto BLASSENGAME
HARVEY, adj. CHRISTIAN BUCKHALTER & JOHN MOORE. S/ BLAS. HARVEY.
Wit: PETER CHASTAIN, JAS. COALTER, JOHN MARTIN, who swore by oath
14 Jul 1789 before AQUILA MILES, J.P.

Pp. 134-138. 13 Jun 1789: ROLAND WILLIAMS to JOHN FORTNER,
Planter, both of Edgefield Co. SC, for 15 pounds, sold 75 acres,
being part of 762 acres granted 1 Jan 1787 unto ROLAND WILLIAMS,
being on a branch of Mine Creek called Dry Creek of Little Saludy
River. S/ ROLAN WILLIAMS. Wit: GEORGE MEE, THOMAS (X) FORTNER,
EDWARD COUCH, who swore by oath 15 Jul 1789 before BENJAMIN TUTT,
J.P.

Pp. 139-146. 7 Jan 1788: SIMEON CUSHMAN & JUDITH, his wife,
Planter, to JOSEPH FULLER, Docter, all of Edgefield Co. SC, for
60 pounds, sold two tracts of land: (1) 140 acres originally
granted 2 Oct 1786 unto THOMAS ROGERS, being on head branch of
Savannah River, adj. ADAM HOIL; (2) 72 acres, being 30 or 40
acres of the old survey granted 2 Oct 1786 unto THOMAS ROGERS &
transferred 22 Jan 1787 by conveyance unto said SIMEON CUSHMAN.
S/ SIMEON CUSHMAN, JUDITH CUSHMAN. Wit: JOSEPH HIX, WILLIAM
STEWART, who swore by oath 15 Mar 1788 before JOHN STURZENEGGER,
J.P.

Pp. 147-153. 10 Jan 1789: BRYANT GREEN, Planter, to DUDLY CARTER,
both of Edgefield Co. SC for 300 pounds, sold 100 acres, being
part of 400 acres originally granted 5 May 1773 unto JOHN DAY &
was conveyed 26 Oct 1783 to BRYANT GREEN, being on Chavers Creek,
adj. LEROY HAMMOND; JOHN CLEKLER; JAMES BUTLER; JOHN LOW; & JOHN
SCOTT. S/ BRYAN (B) GREEN, PHEBY (X) GREEN. Wit: ANTHONEY BUTLER,
JOHN G. COOKE, who swore by oath 10 Jan 1789 before AQUILA MILES,
J.P.

P. 153. 13 Nov 1786: RICHARD MCCAREY sold to MORRIS CALLEHAM his
life then DUDLEY CARTER & SARAH CARTER a negroe wench named
HANNAH for consideration of one negroe boy named SAMP which said
negroe wench HANNAH, I, the said RICHARD MCCAREY defend with her
increase unto the said MORRIS CALLEHAM his lifetime then to DUDLY
CARTER & SARAH CARTER. S/ RICHARD MCCARY. Wit: JOSEPH TUCKER,
THOMAS WOOD, JOHN G. COOKE, who swore by oath 13 Jan (blank)
before AQUILA MILES, J.P.

Pp. 154-161. 16 Jan 1788: ARTHUR WATSON to JOHN WATSON, Sr. for
10 shillings, ‘sold 35 acres, originally granted 5 Feb 1787 unto
said ARTHUR WATSON, being in Ninety Six Dist. now cald (sic)
Cambridge on Cloud Creek in Edgefield Co. SC. S/ ARTHUR (A)
WATSON. Wit: ABNER WTASON, HEZEKIAH WATSON.

Pp. 161-166. 14 Mar 1789: JAMES CARSON & SARAH, his wife, to
WILLIAM MOORE, all of Edgefield Co. SC for 15 pounds, sold 12
acres granted 1785 unto said JAMES CARSON, being on Saludy River
near Mill Creek of Saludy River, adj. a Dutch Survey; VACIH
CLARY; WATSON, dec'd; & MATTHEW WILLS. S/ JAMES CARSON, SARAH

DEED BOOK 3: EDGEFIELD COUNTY S.C.

CARSON. Wit: GILSON YARBROUGH, THOMAS BUTLER, who swore by oath 5 Aug 1789 before WILLIAM ANDERSON, J.P.

Pp. 167-172. 10 Oct 1788: THOMAS MCGINNES to THOMAS SELLERS, Planters of Edgefield Co. SC, for 42 pounds... sold 100 acres granted 13 Feb 1768 to him, being on Log Creek of Savannah River, adj. EBENEZER WESTCOAT. S/ THOMAS MCGINNES. Wit: HOWEL SELLERS, SILAS SELLERS, who swore by oath 13 Oct 1786 before RUSSELL WILSON, J.P.

Pp. 172-177. 5 Oct 1787: GEORGE DEEN, Eldest son & heir at law of ANN DEEN, to SAMUEL MAYS, all of Edgefield Co. SC for 75 pounds, sold 200 acres, being part of 300 acres originally granted 8 Jul 1774 unto ANN DEEN, being on Bigg Creek of Saluda River, adj. DANNITH ABNEY; JOHN BROOKS; GAVIN POU otherwise JOHN GURRARD; & ISAAC DECOSTA. S/ GEORGE DEEN. Wit: WILLIAM ANDERSON, WILLIAM CARSON, JOHN LOVE, who swore by oath 6 Jul 1786 before WILLIAM ANDERSON, J.P.

Pp. 177-186. 22 Jan 1787: THOMAS ROGERS, Shoemaker, to SIMEON CUSHMAN, Planter, both of Edgefield Co. SC, for 75 pounds, sold 212 acres, being part of two tracts: (1) 142 acres granted 21 Jan 1785 unto THOMAS ROGERS, being on the head branch of Savannah River below the Ancient Boundary, adj. ADAM HOIL; & (2) 72 acres granted 2 Oct 1786 unto THOMAS ROGERS, adj. said THOMAS ROGERS. S/ THOMAS ROGERS. Wit: ISAAC (IP) PARKER, WILLIAM STEWART, who swore by oath 15 Mar 1788 before JOHN STURZENEGGER, J.P.

Pp. 186-191. 9 May 1788: JOHN PURVES to MORRIS CALLYHAM for 10 pounds, sold 250 acres, originally granted by State 5 Sep 1785 in Fee simple unto JOHN RUTLEDGE, who conveyed 14 Oct same year unto JOHN PURVES, being in Ninety Six Dist. on Crooked Run of Turkey Creek of Savannah River. S/ JOHN PURVES. Wit: BURGES WHITE, JOHN BLOCKER, who swore by oath 10 May 1788 before AQUILA MILES, J.P.

Pp. 191-197. 6 Sep 1784: BENJAMIN SMITH to JOHN GORMAN, both of Ninety Six Dist. SC for 142 pounds... sold 200 acres, being of two tracts of land: (1) 100 acres originally granted 15 Mar 1771 unto said BENJAMIN SMITH, being on south side of Saludy River, adj. JOHN FOSTER & Saludy River; (2) 100 acres, being part of 250 acres originally granted 21 Feb 1772 unto JOSEPH JOHNSON & conveyed 22 Aug 1772 to THOMAS EASTLAND, who conveyed 14 Dec 1778 to BENJAMIN COOK, who conveyed 26 Feb 1779 to BENJAMIN SMITH, adj. above said land on east and west. S/ BENJA. SMITH. Wit: WILLIAM ANDERSON, MORRIS (M) GWIN, RACHEL ANDERSON, who swore by oath 9 Jul 1788 before WILLIAM ANDERSON, J.P. Rcd. 23 Jun 1789.

Pp. 197-203. 14 Oct 1788: JOHN RANDALL & MARY, his wife, to JOSHUA HAMMOND, all of Edgefield Co. SC for 75 pounds, sold 200 acres on waters of Savannah River (survey is in the name of RICHARD POND & executed by P. CUNNINGHAM). S/ JOHN (J) RANDALL, MARY (X) RANDAL. Wit: WM. WATSON, WILLIAM BROWN, JESSE ROUNDTREE, who swore by oath 15 Oct 1788 before JOHN PURVES, J.P.

Pp. 204-210. 13 Jan 1787: WILLIAM CALDWELL & ELIZABETH ANN, his wife, of Newberry Co. SC to DANIEL BULLOCK of Edgefield Co. SC for 100 pounds, sold 250 acres originally granted 5 May 1773 unto JOHN BURK, who conveyed 1 Jan 1787 to said WILLIAM CALDWELL, being in Edgefield Co. SC on Cainbrack Branch of Little Saludy River, adj. JOHN DUGLAS. S/ WILLIAM CALDWELL, ELIZABETH ANN CALDWELL. Wit: USLEY GOODMAN, NATHANIEL TATE, who swore by oath 26 May 1788 before WILLIAM ANDERSON, J.P.

DEED BOOK 3: 1787-1789 EDGEFIELD COUNTY S.C.

Pp. 210-218. 25 Jun 1788: NICHOLAS EVELEIGH, Esq. of Edgefield Co. SC to JOHN GORDON of Northampton Co. VA for 200 pounds, sold 500 acres, originally granted 1769 unto JACOB FUDGE & known as FUDGE's tract, being on waters of Stephens Creek. S/ NICHOLAS EVELEIGH. Wit: STEPHEN WAYNE, ROBERT GOODLOE HARPER, who swore by oath 4 Jul 1786 before WILLIAM MOORE, J.P.

Pp. 218-223. 16 May 1788: ROBERT STARK, Esq., to JOHN DAY, both of Edgefield Co. SC for 30 pounds, sold 200 acres on Shaws Creek of South Edisto River. S/ ROBERT STARK. Wit: GEO. MEE, WILLIAM (O) DEASE.

Pp. 223-226. 11 Jan 1789: CHARLES BANKS & SUSANNAH, his wife, of Edgefield Co. SC to ABRAHAM RICHARDSON for 5 pounds, sold 200 acres, originally granted 5 Feb 1787 unto said CHARLES BANKS, being near the Cherokee ponds, adj. RICHARDSON. S/ CHARLES BANKS, SUSANNA (+) BANKS. Wit: JOSHUA HAMMOND, FRANCES SETTLE, JOHN HAMMOND.

Pp. 227-231. 29 Mar 1788: CHARLES BANKS & SUSANNA, his wife, to ABRAHAM RICHARDSON, all of Edgefield Co. SC for 100 pounds, sold 275 acres on Stephens Creek on a small creek called Sweetwater adj. by ROGERS corner, being part of 350 acres granted 6 Feb 1773 unto FREDERICK GLAZIER (which said tract was conveyed 177[blank] to WILLIAM BANKS & afterwards part from said BANKS to said ROGERS, being the N.E. corner of a tract of 75 acres, the remainder part of said tract was left to said CHARLES BANKS by above named WILLIAM BANKS as his only Heir). S/ CHARLES BANKS, SUSANNA (+) BANKS. Wit: ISAAC DAVIS, MARRY (X) ROGERS, RICHARD POND.

Pp. 231-234. 14 Nov 1788: CHARLES BANKS & SUSANNA BANKS, his wife, to ROBERT SPEER, all of Edgefield Co. SC for 5 pounds, sold 200 acres granted 5 Feb 1787 unto CHARLES BANKS, being on Horse Creek, adj. BENJAMIN FRANKLIN. S/ CHARLES BANKS. Wit: GEO. WINTER, MATT (M) DORTON.

Pp. 235-241. 25 Feb 1779: BENJAMIN COOK to BENJAMIN SMITH, both of Ninety Six Dist. SC for 200 pounds, sold 100 acres, being part of 250 acres originally granted 21 Feb 1772 unto JOSEPH JOHNSTON, who conveyed 22 Aug 1772 unto THOMAS EASTLAND, who conveyed 14 Dec 1778 unto BENJAMIN COOK, being on south side of Saluday River, adj. BENJAMIN SMITH. S/ BENJ. COOK. Wit: BENJAMIN MOORE, ROBERT LANG, who swore by oath 15 Jul 1780 before BENJAMIN TUTT, J.P.

Pp. 241-245. 16 Feb 1787: JAMES MUREHEAD to DANIEL BIRD, both of Edgefield Co. SC for 50 pounds, sold 125 acres, being part of 250 acres granted 6 Feb 1773 unto ANNE MILLAR in Granville Co. on Logg Creek, adj. TIMOTHEY RAIRDEN; & a Dutch Bounty Warrant. S/ JAS. MUREHEAD. Wit: ABRAHAM (X) RIGS, JOHN BLOCKER, who swore by oath 14 Jul 1788 before JOHN PURVES, J.P.

Pp. 245-250. 3 Jan 1788: DAVID BURKS & JEAN, his wife, to ROBERT MOSELEY, both of Edgefield Co. SC for 50 pounds, sold 54 acres granted 6 Nov 1786 on Horns Creek of Stephens Creek of Savannah River. S/ DAVID BURKS, JEAN (X) BURKS. Wit: CONSTANT (his mark) OGLESBEY ALLEN COURSEY. Sworn by oath 14 Jul 1788 of DAVID BURKS (sic) before BENJ. TUTT, J.P.

Pp. 250-255. 19 Oct 1785: GEORGE SWILLING to JAMES TUTT of Ninety Six Dist. SC for 50 pounds, sold 100 acres, granted 23 Jan 1773 unto JOHN SWILLING, being in Colleton Co. SC on Cuffe Town Creek, adj. ROBERT MICHAEL. S/ GEORGE (+) SWILLING. Wit: GEORGE PERRIN, SAMUEL STALNAKER, who swore by oath.

Pp. 255-260. 10 Jan 1788: EDWARD COEE to ELLEXANDER BURNET, both of SC, for 50 pounds, sold 100 acres, being part of 300 acres granted 18 Oct 1774 unto EDWARD COEE, adj. Beaver Dam Creek of Little Saludy in Ninety Six Dist. SC; the original tract; & DANIEL TOLLOWSON. S/ EDWARD (m) COEE, LUCY COE. Wit: JOSEPH RABOURN, CATLET CORLEY, who swore by oath 9 Jul 1788 before RUSSELL WILSON, J.P.

Pp. 260-265. 14 Oct 1788: JAMES MARTIN & MILLY, his wife, to JAMES VESSELS, Jr., all of Edgefield Co. SC for 20 pounds, sold 100 acres, being part of 346 acres originally granted 7 Nov 1785 unto JAMES MARTIN, adj. MORGAN; Col. LEROY HAMMOND & WARING & JAS. MARTIN. S/ JAMES MARTIN. Wit: DRURY PACE, JOHN DAY, CHARLES HAMMOND, who swore by oath 13 (sic) Oct 1788 before RUSSELL WILSON, J.P.

Pp. 265-269. 15 Jul 1788: TOBIAS MYRES of Charlestown Dist. SC to JOHN GIBSON, Blacksmith, of Ninety Six Dist. for 100 pounds, sold 150 acres, granted 27 Nov 1770 unto TOBIAS MYRES, being on Big Creek of Little Salude River. S/ TOBIAS MYERS. Wit: JOHN DAVIS, CHURCHILL GIBSON, ABNOR (X) CORLEY, who swore by oath 10 Jan 1789 before RUSSELL WILSON, J.P.

Pp. 270-275. 4 Jun 1787: JOSEPH REED & JANE, his wife, of Rocky Creek of Reedy River, Greenville Co. SC to JAMES FRAZIER of Edgefield Co. SC for 100 pounds, sold 215 acres, being part of 330 acres granted 15 Jun 1786 unto JOSEPH REED, on Rocky Creek of Reedy River which crosses Parrises Wagon Road. S/ JOSEPH REED, JANE (+) REED. Wit: WILLIAM FRAZIER, DANIEL ROGERS, Jr., who swore by oath 8 Mar 1788 before ARTHUR SIMKINS, J.P.

Pp. 275-279. 1 Sep 1789: WILLIAM EVANS, D.S. of Ninety Six Dist. to JOHN DICK of Orangeburg Dist. SC for 200 pounds, sold 346 acres originally granted unto JAMES PARSONS, being in Beech Island, adj. JAMES PARSONS, Esq., dec'd; PARSON ZUBLEY & land granted to LAMAR, late property of ISAAC WOOD, dec'd; EDWARD ROWELL; JOHN CLERKE; ALBERT FREDERICK; GASPER STRUBLE; & GEORGE BENDER. S/ WM. EVANS. Wit: DAVID MEYER, ALEXANDER GRAHAM, who swore by oath 9 Oct 1789 before JOHN STURZENEGGER, J.P.

Pp. 279-283. 25 Feb 1788: REBECCA HOGAINS, Alias GAINS, Widow, to ROBERT STARK, the Elder, both of Edgefield Co. SC for 30 pounds, sold 200 acres originally granted 11 Aug 1774 unto said REBECCA HOGAINS, Widow of WILLIAM GAINES, dec'd, on Shaws Creek, a branch of the South fork of Edisto River. S/ REBECCA (+) HOGAINS. Wit: HENRY KING, RUSSELL WILSON, Jr., who swore by oath 13 Oct 1788 before JOHN MOORE, J.P.

Pp. 284-288. 24 Mar 1789: WILLIAM RUNNALDS to TALLIAFERO COX, both of Edgefield Co. SC, for 57 pounds, sold 130 acres, being part of 200 acres originally granted 6 Aug 1774 unto JAMES HARRIS, who conveyed to said WILLIAM RUNNALDS on West side of Stephens Creek of Savannah River, adj. ROSS; TALIAFERO COX; lands surveyed for the Irish; DAVID CALLAHAM; & JNO. HERINGTON. S/ WILLIAM RENALDS. Wit: JOSEPH TUCKER, JOEL (X) COX, JOHN SEARLS, who swore by oath 12 Aug 1789 before BENJ. TUTT, J.P.

Pp. 288-293. 24 Jul 1787: THOMAS ROBERSON to ALSOLUM FARRIS, both of Ninety Six District SC for 20 pounds, sold 104 acres originally granted 3 Apr 1786 on Catfish Creek of Savannah River, adj. CALAHAM; THOMAS ROBERSON; & SCOTTE. S/ THOMAS (T) ROBERSON. Wit: CHARLES ASHLEY, JOEL (X) COX, who swore by oath 12 Aug 1789 before BENJ. TUTT, J.P.

Pp. 293-298. 20 Apr 1789: ROBERT KILLCREASE, Planter, to BENJAMIN COCKRAM, Planter, both of Edgefield Co. SC for 80 pounds, sold 100 acres, being part of 305 acres shown by plat surveyed 24 Sep 1775 by WILLIAM GOODE & by plat of the original granted 1 Dec 1772 unto SANDIFORD KEZIAH, being in the fork of Stephens Creek & Turkey Creek, adj. BENJAMIN KILLCREASE; WILLIAM THOMAS; & MARY HILL. S/ ROBERT (R) KILLCREASE. Wit: JOHN GLANTON, CHRISTOPHER GLANTON, who swore by oath 10 Aug 1789 before BENJ. TUTT, J.P.

Pp. 298-302. 13 Oct 1788: DANIEL ROGERS to SAMUEL STALNAKER, both of Edgefield Co. SC for 140 pounds, sold 200 acres, being part of two surveys: (1) 100 acres originally granted 7 May 1762 unto ALLEN ADDISON; & (2) 100 acres originally granted 4 Jul 1789 unto DANIEL ROGERS, being on Haw Creek of Stephens Creek of Savannah River, adj. ALLEN ADDISON & BENJAMIN BELLS. S/ DANIEL (+) ROGERS. Wit: GABRIEL TUTT, JAMES TUTT, who swore by oath 10 Apr 1789 before BENJ. TUTT, J.P.

Pp. 302-306. 8 Apr 1789: EZEKIEL HARLIN to JAMES TUTT, both of Edgefield Co. SC for 75 pounds, sold 75 acres, being part of 150 acres originally granted 4 Dec 1771 unto EZEKIEL HARLIN, Sr., the father of said HARLIN... the other 75 acres was conveyed unto RICHARD FREEMAN. Said land is on Savannah River & adj. RICHARD FREEMAN. S/ EZEKIEL (X) HARLIN. Wit: RICHARD (X) FREEMAN, GABRIEL TUTT, who swore by oath 11 Apr 1789 before BENJ. TUTT, J.P.

Pp. 307-311. 1 Jul 1789: JOHN PURVES, Planter, to ABRAHAM RICHARDSON, Trader, both of Ninety Six Dist. SC for 130 pounds, sold 500 acres originally survey granted 17 Feb 1773 unto SARAH BAKER & was conveyed by BENJAMIN BAKER, her son, 13 Oct 1785 unto said JOHN PURVIS, being on Foxes Creek & adj. SIZEMORE. S/ JOHN PURVES. Wit: SAML. CRAFTON, JOSEPH HIGHTOWER, who swore by oath 12 Oct 1789 before BENJ. TUTT, J.P.

Pp. 311-314. 17 Sep 1787: MICHAEL BUCKHALTER to JAMES LOW for 50 pounds, sold 101 1/2 acres, being part of 200 acres surveyed 2 May 1758 on Horns Creek, adj. EDWARD MARTIN; JOHN BUCKHALTER; & REUBEN BECKUM. S/ MICHAEL (MB) BUCKHALTER. Wit: THOMAS MILES, DAVID BUCKHALTER, who swore by oath 12 Sep 1788 before AQUILA MILES, J.P.

Pp. 315-316. 28 Sep 1789: MATHEW GAYLE & MARY, his wife, to WILLIAM DOZER, all of Edgefield Co. SC for 10 Shillings, sold 200 acres originally granted 18 May 1771 unto WILLIAM JONES, who conveyed 24 Jun 1783 unto MATHEW GAYLE, being on a branch of Little Saluda of Santee River, adj. WM. JONES at time of survey. S/ MATHEW GALE, MARY GALE. Wit: JOHN BRADSHAW, EDWARD LUTEN. RUSSELL WILSON, J.P.

DEED BOOK 3: 1787-1789 EDGEFIELD COUNTY S.C.

Pp. 316-318. 28 Sep 1789: MATHEW GAYLE & MARY, his wife, to WILLIAM DOZER, all of Edgefield Co. SC for 10 Shillings, sold 250 acres, being part of 300 acres originally granted 15 May 1772 unto ROBERT DAVIS, who conveyed 12 Jun 1773 unto WILLIAM JONES, who conveyed 25 Jun 1783 unto MATHEW GAYLE, being on South side of Little Saluda River, adj. MOSES ?RIRKS at time of survey. S/ MATHEW GAYLE, MARY GAYLE. Wit: EDWARD LUTIN, JOHN BRADSHAW, who swore by oath 13 Oct 1789 before RUSSELL WILSON.

Pp. 319-325. 9 Feb 1789: THOMAS BECKUM, Sr. & MARY, his wife, to AQUILA MILES, Esq., all of Ninety Six Dist. SC for 300 pounds, sold 300 acres originally granted 6 Feb 1786 unto THOMAS BECKUM, being on Horns Creek, adj. lands formerly THOMAS; AQUILA MILES; & MARTIN. S/ THOMAS (T) BECKUM, Sr., MARY (+) BECKUM. Wit: HUGH MIDDLETON, JAMES TALBERT, who swore by oath 12 Oct 1789 before JOHN STURZENEGGER, J.P.

Pp. 325-331. 25 Jul 1789: ARTHUR WATSON to CHRISTIAN CURRY (her), both of Edgefield Co. SC for 10 pounds, sold 100 acres, being part of 420 acres originally granted 3 Sep 1787 unto ARTHUR WATSON, being on branch of Dry Creek of Mine Creek, adj. WILLIS MURPHY WATSON (?one or two surnames?, gch); JACOB WATSON & ARTHUR WATSON. S/ ARTHUR (A) WATSON. Wit: GEO. MEE, ROLAN WILLIAMS, JAMES HARRISON, who swore by oath 25 Jul 1789 before RUSSELL WILSON, J.P.

Pp. 331-338. 19 Aug 1789: JOHN MARTIN & ELIZABETH, his wife, to CHARLES MARTIN, all of Edgefield Co. SC for 300 pounds, sold 300 acres, being of two tracts: (1) 150 acres originally granted 9 Jan 1756 unto HENRY SUMMERALL, who conveyed 30 Nov 1783 unto JOHN MARTIN & was Recorded in Registers Office in Book A, No 5, pages 1-3, 29 Mar 1784?, being on both sides of Nobles Creek of Stephens Creek, adj. JOSEPH SUMMERALL & HENRY SUMMERALL at time of survey; (2) 150 acres originally granted 12 Jul 1772 unto JACOB SUMMERALL, Dec'd, who died intestate and his heir, HENRY SUMMERALL, did convey unto said JOHN MARTIN and was Recorded in Clerks Office in Book A, page 79 in 1786. S/ JNO. MARTIN, ELIZABETH D. MARTIN. Wit: JOHN C. GARRET, WM. MORGAN, MATT MARTIN, who swore by oath 5 Sep 1789 before AQUILA MILES, J.P.

Pp. 338-339. 2 Sep 1789: JOSEPH RAMBO, Yeoman, to MARY RAMBO, both of Edgefield Co. SC, for 3 Guineas, sold 1 Mare, 2 colts & 7 hogs. S/ JOSEPH RAMBO. Wit: PETER CARNES, THOMAS ADAMS, who swore by oath 5 Oct 1789 before AQUILA MILES, J.P.

Pp. 339-341. 29 Aug 1789: JOSEPH RAMBO to MARY RAMBO, both of Edgefield Co. SC, for 5 Guineas sold 400 acres on Horns Creek, where MARY now lives, being that Plantation devised to said JOSEPH RAMBO by LAURENCE RAMBO, his dec'd Father after the Death of said MARY RAMBO and the said MARY, being now in possession of said land as tenant for life under said Devise. S/ JOSEPH RAMBO. Wit: PETER CARNES, THOMAS ADAMS, who swore by oath 5 Oct 1789 before AQUILA MILES, J.P.

Pp. 341-345. 16 Feb 1785: HARMON GALMAN to EDWARD MITCHEL, both of Horns Creek, Ninety Six Dist. SC for 50 pounds, sold 50 acres, being part of 400 acres originally granted 14 Sep 1775 unto said HARMON GALMAN on North side of Marshels Creek, adj. JENKINS HARRIS land that he sold to GEORGE TILLMAN; & JOHN GRAY, being

41

the land he bought of said HARMAN GALMAN. S/ HARMAN GALLMAN. Wit: WILLIAM BROWN, GASPER GALLMAN, who swore by oath 6 Jul 1785 before JOHN HERNDON, J.P.

Pp. 346-351. 12 Sep 1782: LEWIS TILLMAN to EDWARD MITCHEL, both of Ninety Six Dist. SC for 1000 pounds, sold 125 acres, being part of 250 acres originally granted 25 Oct 1764 unto DANIEL ROGERS, who conveyed unto JENKINS HARRIS, who conveyed 14 Feb 1774 unto GEORGE TILLMAN and fell to LEWIS TILLMAN, being his oldest son & Heir at Law. Said land adj. Mrs. TILLMAN's Spring Branch. S/ LEWIS TILLMAN, FRANCES (+) TILLMAN. Wit: LITTLEBERRY TILLMAN, STEPHEN TILLMAN, LITTLESTON PARDUE, who swore by oath 12 Aug 1784 before JOHN HERNDON, J.P.

Pp. 351-357. 11 May 1772: EPHRAIM JONES & RACHEL, his wife, to LEWIS TILLMAN, Planter, all of Granville Co. SC for 150 pounds, sold 500 acres originally granted 23 Dec 1771 unto EPHRAIM JONES on Cedar Creek of Stephens Creek of Savannah River. Wit: XMAS RAY, JAMES (+) VANN, JAMES MARTIN, who swore by oath 5 Oct 1772 in Granville Co. SC before LEROY HAMMOND, J.P.

Pp. 357-364. 10 Apr 1789: JAMES WEST & CELEY, his wife, to JOHN WALLS, all of Edgefield Co. SC, for 50 pounds, sold 150 acres, being part of 380 acres originally granted 6 Feb 1786 unto JAMES WEST on Ceder Creek of Horns Creek, adj. WM. MURPHEY & SPENCER. S/ JAMES (+) WEST, CELEY (X) WEST. Wit: JOHN (+) WILSON, JOHN LYON, who swore by oath 13 Oct 1789 before RUSSELL WILSON, J.P. PLAT: p. 364.

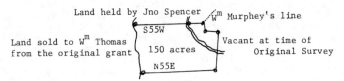

Land held by Jno Spencer / Wm Murphey's line

Land sold to Wm Thomas from the original grant

S55W

150 acres

Vacant at time of Original Survey

N55E

Land held by the Original Grant

Pp. 364. JOSEPH LEWIS, late of Liberty Co. GA, to DEMSEY LEWIS of Edgefield Co. SC for 700 pounds...(The rest of the original deed is gone. The following information was taken from the WPA Abstract, gch) sold the following Negroes To Wit: Two Negro men named HENRY & CHARLES, 3 women named SILVIA, CLACY & JANE, also 7 Negroe boys named CUTOR, TOM, HENRY, DICK, JOHN, JACOB & ABRAM & also 2 negro girls named CAT & LUCY remaining & being in the County of Edgefield, this 10 Nov 1789. S/ JOSEPH LEWIS. Wit: ROBERT TATE, ISAAC LEWIS, JOHN TUNE, who swore by oath 12 Nov 1789 before WM. ANDERSON, J.P.

Pp. 1-4. 8 Jan 1790: RICHARD TATE, Jr., Heir at law of RICHARD TATE, Sr. to JONES WILLS, both of Edgefield Co. SC for 25 pounds, sold 17 acres, being part of 100 acres originally granted 27 Aug 1764 unto RICHARD TATE, Sr. on South side of the Saluda River. S/ RICHARD (O) TATE. Wit: WM. SPRAGINS, THOS. BERRY, who swore by oath 24 Feb 1790 before W. ANDERSON, J.P.

Pp. 4-8. 18 Jan 1790: THOMAS BOONE of Georgia to ARVIN MOORE of Edgefield Co. Sc for 50 pounds, sold 287 acres, being part of two tracts of land: (1) 150 acres originally granted 26 Jun 1774 unto said BOONE on the drains of Turkey Creek; & (2) 137 acres originally granted 1 Jan 1787 unto said BOONE near Log Creek where said BOONE lately resided. S/ THOMAS BOONE. Wit: JOHN STIDHAM, JOHN BLOCKER, who swore by oath 12 Apr 1790 before RUSSELL WILSON, J.P.

Pp. 8-13. 2 Apr 1790: BENJAMIN TUTT, Esq. & BARBARA, his wife, of Edgefield Co. SC to THOMAS BACON for 1700 pounds, sold 5509 acres, being of two tracts: (1) 2871 acres on Cuffeetown Creek of Stephens Creek of Savannah River, adj. Heirs of ANDREW WILLIAMSON; HUGH MIDDLETON; JOHN WALLACE & BENJAMIN TUTT; & (2) 2638 acres on Hardlabour Creek of Stephens Creek of Savannah River, adj. ABNER PERRIN; Maj. TUTT; BENJ. BLAKE; LOGANS; & Mrs. YELDON. S/ BENJ. TUTT, BARBARY (X) TUTT. Wit: JAS SANDERS, RICHARD TUTT, Jr., JAS TUTT, who swore by oath 13 Apr 1790 before JOHN STURZENEGGER, J.P.

Pp. 13-17. 2 Dec 1789: JOHN SPENCER & MARY, his wife, of Burke Co. GA to PHILLIP MAY, Jr. of Edgefield Co. SC for 100 pounds, sold 87 acres, being part of 100 acres originally granted 19 Jun 1772 unto JOHN SPENCER on the East of Chavers Creek, adj. land formerly held by JINKINS HARRIS; RUBIN RAMBO; & part of original grant. S/ JOHN SPENCER, MARY SPENCER. Wit: JOHN (+) MURPHY, JNO McCOLLA, ZACHARIAH (+) JAMES, who swore by oath 13 Apr 1790 before RUSSELL WILSON, J.P.

Pp. 18-21. 16 Nov 1789: JAMES HARRIS & ELIZABETH, his wife, to PHILLIP MAY, Jr., all of Edgefield Co. SC, for 60 pounds, sold 88 acres, being part of 100 acres originally granted 15 May 1771 unto said HARRIS on Chavers Creek. S/ JAMES (H) HARRIS, ELIZABETH HARRIS. Wit: WILLIAM HARRIS, PHILLIP MAY, Sr., who swore by oath 13 Apr 1790 before RUSSELL WILSON, J.P.

Pp. 22-26. 25 Dec 1789: JOHN CARTER to WILLIAM TARRANCE, Planter, both of Edgefield Co. SC for 260 pounds, sold 260 acres originally granted 6 Feb 1786 unto JOHN CARTER on a branch near the Cherokee Pond in Ninety Six District. S/ JOHN CARTER. Wit: JOHN HARDY, JOHN TARRANCE, ISAAC DAVIS, who swore by oath 27 May 1790 before JOHN PURVES, J.P.

Pp. 26-29. 29 Jan 1790: MACARTAN CAMPBLE, Esq. of Charleston SC to WEST COOK of Edgefield Co. SC for 20 pounds, sold 1/4 acre known as Lot No. 4 in the Village of Campbeleton of Edgefield Co. SC. S/ MACARTAN CAMPBLE. Wit: JAMES STUART, JOHN COOK, who swore by oath 10 April 1790 before LEROY HAMMOND, J.P.

Pp. 29-31. 13 Apr 1790: WEST COOK to PETER CARNES both of Edgefield Co. SC for 20 pounds, sold 1/4 acre known as Lot No. 4 in the Village of Campbeleton of Edgefield Co. SC. S/ WEST

DEED BOOK 4: 1790 EDGEFIELD COUNTY S.C.

COOK. Wit: DAVIS MOORE, E. HOLLEMAN, R. TUTT. Ack. in Open Court 14 Apr 1790.

Pp. 32-36. 12 Mar 1790: Mortgage: ISAAC CROTHERS to WILLIAM SHAW, Atty at Law, both of Edgefield Co. SC for 40 pounds, sold Lot No. Seven in the old town of Ninety Six, containing 82 feet in front & on the west side 214 feet in depth & on the south side 294 feet adj. North by Lot No. Eight, South by Lot No. Six, East by the late JAMES PARSONS, & West by a back street. Also 4 cows & calves; 2 yearlings; 2 horses; 20 hogs; 4 bedsteads; 3 feather beds; 3 bolsters; 4 pillows; 6 pillow cases; 5 pair of sheets; 4 quilts; 2 rugs; 4 pair of blankets; 1 silk gause pavillion; 6 towels; 2 walnut tables; 1 mahogony stand; 3 pine tables; 14 chairs; 2 large trunks; 1 large chest; 1 corner culbord; 1 clothes skren; 3 china boals; 4 tea pots; 2 milk pots; 2 sugar dishes; 2 quart mugs; 3 cups & saucers; 2 glasses; 1 glass pint decanter; 3 glass mugs; 3 glass tumblers; 2 wine glasses; 3 Queensware dishes; 1 small dish; 6 plates; 6 pewter soup plates; 6 pewter shallow plates; 7 stone jares; 5 candlesticks; 1 tin candle box; Japan tea board; 1 smaller waiter; 2 large looking glasses; 1 small looking glass; 1 copper tea kittle; 1 coffee pot; 1 iron tea kettle; 5 iron pots; 2 dutch ovens; 2 frying pans; 1 copper skillet; 2 pair smothing irons; 4 pott hooks; 2 pair fire dogs; 1 pair tongs; 2 shovels; 4 pewter basons; 1 corn mill; 1 coffee mill; 1 pepper mill; 2 large stone jars with the appurtenances. IF THE SAID 40 pounds with Interest is paid...this Indenture becomes Void... S/ ISAAC CROWTHER. Wit: JAS GOUEDY, HENRY WILSON, who swore by oath 10 Apr 1790 before WILLIAM MOORE, J.P.

Pp. 36-39. 28 Jul 1789: WILLIAM BROOKS & SUSANNAH, his wife, to JAMES McDONAL, all of SC, for 100 pounds, sold 210 acres originally granted 3 Apr 1786 unto AMON ROBERTS, who conveyed to said WILLIAM BROOKS on Stephens Creek of Savannah River, adj. JNO DAVIS; JNO SWILLIVANT; & HILLERY PHILLIPS. S/ WILLIAM BROOKS, SUSANNAH BROOKS. Wit: ROGER TRIPLETT, GEORGE FARRAR, who swore by oath 10 Apr 1790 before HUGH MIDDLETON, J.P.

Pp. 40-42. 29 Jul 1789: WILLIAM BROOKS & SUSANNAH, his wife, to JAMES McDONAL of SC for 100 pounds, sold 100 acres originally granted 5 Sep 1785 unto JOHN DAVIS on waters of the Savannah River, adj. AMON ROBERTS; & HILLERY PHILLIPS. S/ WM BROOKS, SUSANNAH BROOKS. Wit: ROGER TRIPLETT, GEORGE FARRAR, who swore by oath 10 Apr 1790 before HUGH MIDDLETON, J.P.

Pp. 42-43. 16 Feb 1783: Deed of Gift: AGNESS UMPHRESS, widow, of Ninety Six Dist. SC to my daughter, AGNESS HUNTER, for love and affection my Goods & Chattles, except two cows, one to my Grandson, THOMAS HILL, & the other cow to my Granddaughter, NANCY HILL, now being in my present Dwelling House in the District. S/ AGNESS (+) UMPRESS. Wit: THOMAS CLARK, JONATHAN DAWSON, who swore by oath 13 Apr 1790 before RUSSELL WILSON, J.P.

Pp. 43-45. 28 Nov 1789: WILLIAM COURSEY, Schoolmaster, of Edgefield Co. SC to CONSTANT OGLESBY & ANNY, his wife, my Son-in-law & daughter, for love & affection...convey 50 acres, (now in possession of CONSTANT OGLESBY & ANNA, his wife), being part of 946 acres originally granted 7 Aug 1786 unto WILLIAM COURSEY on Beaver Dam Creek of Turkey Creek of Savannah River.

S/ W. COURSEY. Wit: ALLEN COURSEY, ISAAC BRUNSON, Jr., who swore by oath 28 Nov 1789 before JOHN PURVES, J.P.

Pp. 45-46. 5 Oct 1782: Deed of Gift: MARK LOTT of Colleton Co. SC to my loving daughters, JEANN LOTT & ELIZABETH LOTT for love & affection... two young negroes, DICK & HANNAH. I deliver DICK to my dau., JEANN LOTT & likewise HANNAH to my dau., ELIZABETH LOTT, said negroes being in my present possession on my plantation on Edisto River. S/ MARK LOTT, Sr. Wit: JAS COCKS, Sr., NICHOLAS BAKER, APSELIA COUCH, EDWARD COUCH, who swore by oath 9 Apr 1789 before RUSSELL WILSON, J.P.

Pp. 46-51. 4 Apr 1790: DAVID BURKS & JANE, his wife, to RICHARD JOHNSON, Jr., all of Edgefield Co. SC for 50 pounds, sold 334 acres originally granted 7 Aug 1786 unto said BURKS on Turkey Creek & Rockey Creek by the Richland Pond. S/ DAVID BURKS. Wit: JOHN THURMOND, MARSHALL MARTIN, who swore by oath 5 Jun 1790 before JOHN PURVES, J.P.
PLAT: p. 50.

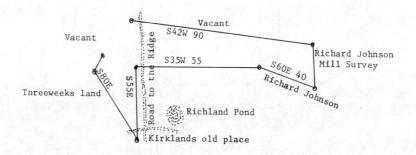

Surveyed by: DAVID BURKS, Deputy Surveyor.
Certified: 17 Feb 1786/ BREMAR, Surv. Genl.

Pp. 51-53. 1 Sep 1788: ROBERT STARK of Edgefield Co. SC to JOHN WIN, RICHARD WIN, JOSEPH KIRKLAND & THOMAS TAYLOR, being his securities to WILSON BLUNT, for $4,000.00 for goods purchased of said BLUNT in Charleston SC, sold 750 acres on the head of Cloud Creek, near the ridges, where said ROBERT STARK now lives & being the former property of MOSES KIRKLAND; DAVID HARTLY; & DAVID ANDREWS. Said Condition be null & void upon payment of $4,000.00... Wit: JAMES (X) BARRENTINE, EDWARD COUCH, who swore by oath 16 Feb 1789 before WILLIAM ANDERSON, J.P.

Pp. 53-56. 9 Jul 1790: JOHN HAMMOND & ELIZABETH, his wife, of Edgefield Co. SC to CHARLES COTESWORTH PINCKNEY, Esq. of Charleston SC for 5 pounds, sold Lot No. 39, being 75 feet in front & 155 feet in length fronting on Pinckney St. in the Town called Fallmouth, laid out by JOHN HAMMOND & LEROY HAMMOND on their lands, adj. a Town called Camplbelltown. S/ JOHN HAMMOND, ELIZABEH HAMMOND. Wit: JNO PERRY, DAVID SANDIDGE, CATHARINE D. HAMMOND. Ack. in Open Court July Term 1790. R. TUTT, C.E.C.

Pp. 58-62. 9 Jul 1790: JOHN HAMMOND & ELIZABETH, his wife, of Edgefield Co. SC to EDWARD RUTLEDGE of Charleston SC for 5 pounds, sold Lot No. 40, being 70 feet in front & 155 feet in length fronting on Pinckney St. of a Town called Falmouth, laid out by JOHN HAMMOND & LEROY HAMMOND on their lands, adj. a small Village of Campbell Town. S/ JOHN HAMMOND, ELIZ. HAMMOND. Wit: JNᵒ PERRY, DAVID SANDEDGE. Ack. in Open Court July Term 1790. R. Tutt, C.E.C.

Pp. 62-64. 5 Jul 1790: DAVID SHOCKLEY, Planter, of Edgefield Co. SC to DAVID MOCK, Grandson of MARTHA SHOCKLEY, wife of DAVID SHOCKLEY, for good will & affection, sold 100 acres on both sides of Beaver Dam Creek & the wagon road from the Long Canes to Charleston... provided DAVID SHOCKLEY & MARTHA, his wife, shall be permitted to live & occupy the said tract. S/ DAVID (D) SHOCKLEY. Wit: W. COURSEY, MARY (+) CALLEHAM, MORRIS (W) CALLEHAM, who swore by oath 6 Jul 1790 before JOHN PURVES, J.P.

Pp. 65-67. 5 Jul 1790: DAVID SHOCKLEY of Edgefield Co. SC to his step Granddaughter, PATTY STOTT, granddaughter of MARTHA SHOCKLEY, wife of DAVID SHOCKLEY, for good will & affection, give 2 feather beds & furniture, my stock of horses & cattle & other property that may increase during the life of said DAVID SHOCKLEY & MARTHA, his wife, provided they may have use of above during their said lives. S/ DAVID (X) SHOCKLEY. Wit: W. COURSEY, MARY (X) CALLYHAM, MORRIS (W) CALLYHAM, who swore by oath 9 Jul 1790 before JOHN PURVES, J.P.

Pp. 67-71. 9 Jul 1790: JOHN HAMMOND & ELIZABETH, his wife, of Edgefield Co. SC to ISAAC COURSE of Charleston SC for 5 pounds, sold five lotts of land, known as Lot No. 26,27,28,29, & 30, in the Town of Falmouth near Campbelton, each 70 feet in front & 155 feet in length fronting on Teasdale St. S/ JOHN HAMMOND, ELIZABETH HAMMOND. Wit: CATHARINE D. HAMMOND, JNᵒ PERRY, DAVID SANDRIDGE. Ack. in Open Court July Term 1790. R. Tutt, C.E.C.

Pp. 71-80. 15 Feb 1790: RICHARD JOHNSON, Jr. & MARY, his wife of Edgefield Co. S to MOODY BURT of Augusta GA for 1000 pounds, sold 300 acres, being part of three tracts: (1) 200 acres, of which 50 acres was part of a grant to RICHARD JOHNSON, joining the other land granted 27 Sep 1769 unto MARY BUFFINGTON on Turkey Creek adj. BENJAMIN GARROTT at time of survey; (2) 50 acres, adj. GARROTT; ROBERT BURTS; & BUFFINGTON; (3) 50 acres, being part of a tract of MOSES KIRKLAND & sold by act of Confiscation to RICHARD JOHNSON. S/ RICHD. JOHNSON. Wit: MOODY BURT, Jr., STEPHEN EVANS. Ack. in Open Court July Term 1790. Mrs. MARY JOHNSON, relinq. Dower before HUGH MIDDLETON, Esq. & was ordered Recorded. R. TUTT, C.E.C.

Pp. 80-82. 21 Apr 1790: JAMES SCOTT to SAMUEL SCOTT for 500 pounds,. Quit Claim to all my right title, interest or claim to 8 tracts of land totaling 1800 acres belonging to my father, JOHN SCOTT, dec'd Estate, being on Savannah River in Ninety Six Dist. SC known by the name of Pleasant Hill or Scotts Ferry. S/ JAMES SCOTT. Wit: JOSEPH WOOD, MARY WOOD, JAMES GRAY, who swore by oath 20 Aug 1790 before HUGH MIDDLETON, J.P.

P. 82. 1770: Deed of Gift: SOLOMON NEWSOM to my son, DAVID NEWSOM, after my decease when he comes of age, fore Negroes, one

wench named AG; a garl named ANNER; a boy named TOM; a boy named
SQUASH. If son should died without Heirs, then said fore Negroes
shall be divided between my son, SOLOMON, & my daughter, ANN. S/
SOLOMON (+) NEWSOM. Wit: JOHN BUCKHALTER, THOMAS PEARCE, who
swore by oath 12 Oct 1790 before HUGH MIDDLETON, J.P. Rcd. 12 Oct
1790.

Pp. 82-87. 2 May 1780: ELENOR McKINNEY to my grandchildren, ROGER
McKINNEY, ROBERT DITTON McKINNEY & TIMOTHEY McKINNEY for love &
affection, I did execute a certain Instrument of writing
purporting to be a Plat & grant of all my goods & chattles then
being in my possessin with three Negroes, JACK; & SARAH; & JACK
their children; also 1 yelding; my stock of hogs; 2 feather beds
with their trimmings; said Instrument was executed by me in
presence of KEATING SMITH, ROBERT HUGGINS & TIMOTHEY McKINNEY...
and as I being an Ignorant Person & not having the opportunity of
advising with council learned in the law & approaching near my
last Breath & to relieve me from all fears that my said provision
for above named grand children be defeated or deprised from any
bounty on account of any informatity in the said deed, I have
requested the present writing should be drawn up to better
express my meaning...
2 May 1785 WHEREAS my said 3 grandchildren being minors since the
execution of said Deed, I have been informed that Trustees ought
to have been appointed the better to preserve the said property
for the use of said Grandchildren & to prevent the provision I
made from being defeated which Trustees from my Ignorance of the
law was neglected in my said Deed of Gift and WHEREAS I have
acquired other goods & chattles not mentioned in said Instrument
of writing, I do for 10 Shillings paid by TOM KEELING SMITH &
JOHN CAREW sell all my goods & property as Trustees for 1 negro
wench named CATE & her issue; 2 horses; 1 mare; 1 red cow &
yearling; 1 heffer; 1 bridle cow & yearling; bull; 2 sets of plow
irons; 2 hoes; 3 axes; 1 bed & bed cloaths; 1 flax wheel; 2 iron
pots; 1 dutch oven; 6 pewter plates; 6 earthen plates; 1 tea
kettle; 2 tables; 1 set of tea cups & sausers; 4 bowles; 2 bed
steads & 1 trunk. Said Trustees for my said grandchildren in &
over the property given and granted to them by my deed of 2 May
1785 to be divided when my youngest grandson living becomes of
age of 18, hereby requesting that when the division is made that
my grandson, WILLIAM JOHNSON McKINNEY has a share equal to the
rest & if his said brothers refuse, then the deficiency be made
up out of sale of property.
THIS LAST DEED OF INSTRUMENT WAS WRITTEN & SIGNED 19 Jan 1789. S/
ELEONOR (E) McKINNY, Sr. Wit: SAMPSON (C) WALL, SUSANNAH CAREW,
JOHN LEWIS POAGE, who swore by oath 20 Jan 1789 before JOHN
MOORE, J.P.

Pp. 88-90. 8 May 1790: DAVID JOHNSON to SAMUEL RAMSEY, both of
Edgefield Co. SC... WHEREAS being indebted for 21,200 weight of
Tobacco to be delivered at Augusta as follows: 1200 pounds to be
delivered Nov 1790; also 6000 pounds in Nov 1792; & also 8000
pounds in the year 1793; for 5 Shillings, sell 150 acres
originally granted 25 Apr 1765 unto MATHEW RAMSY on the South
side of The Saludy River in Edgefield Co. SC... S/ DAVID JOHNSON.
Wit: WM. MOORE, JAMES McMILLAN at Abbeville Co. SC, who swore by
oath 23 Oct 1790 before Wm MOORE, J.P.

Pp. 90-96. 22 Sep 1790: LOTT WARREN of GA to ISAAC FOREMAN of

DEED BOOK 4: 1790 EDGEFIELD COUNTY S.C.

Edgefield Co. SC for 50 pounds, sold 100 acres originally granted 5 Jun 1786 unto said WARREN on Horns Creek of Stephens Creek, adj. DANIEL MARSHEL; NATHAN WHITE & JNº CONRAD COLEMAN at the time of survey. S/ LOTT WARREN, REBECCA (X) WARREN, his wife. Wit: JNº GRAVES, TRAVIS HILL, who swore by oath 11 Oct 1790 before ARTHUR SIMKINS, J.P.

Pp. 96-100. 11 Jul 1789: BRYANT GREEN to THOMAS KEY, both Planters of Edgefield Co. SC for 10 pounds, sold 50 acres on branch of Bedingfields Creek, adj. Estate of JOHN DOOLY, dec'd; MATHEW STOKER; & THOMAS KEY. S/ BRYANT (B) GREEN. Wit: JACOB ZINN, DAVID BURKS, who swore by oath 13 Jul 1790 before JOHN PURVIS, J.P. Relinq. of Dower Ack. July Term 1790 (no name).

Pp. 100-105. 28 Apr 1790: JOHN CARTER & ELIZABETH, his wife to JOHN HARDY, all of Edgefield Co. SC for 50 pounds, sold 1000 acres, being part of 7893 acres originally granted unto said JOHN CARTER, adj. said HARDY's Coal Kiln; THOMAS CARTER; Five Notch Road; JOHN CARTER; HALL; JOSEPH HIGHTOWER; CHARLES HAMMOND; JAMES VESSEL; JOHN DAY; & JOHN HANDCOCK. S/ JOHN CARTER, ELIZABETH CARTER. Wit: ISAAC DAVIS, JOHN TERRANCE, WILLIAM TERRANCE, who swore by oath 13 Jul 1790 before ARTHUR SIMKINS.

Pp. 106-110. 29 Jan 1790: WILLIAM BROOKS, Planter, to THOMAS DALTON, both of Edgefield Co. SC for 5 pounds, sold 100 acres originally granted 3 Jul 1786 said BROOKS on Savannah River in Ninety Six Dist. SC, adj. KENNEDY. S/ WILLIAM BROOKS. Wit: JOHN THURMOND, MICHAEL BLOCKER, who swore by oath 13 Jul 1790 before JOHN PURVIS, J.P.

Pp. 110-115. 16 Jul 1790: ELLIS PALMORE & ANN, his wife, to RUSSELL PALMORE, Planter, for 50 pounds, sold 89 acres originally granted 1 Oct 1787 unto said PALMORE, on Horns Creek, adj. JOHN GARRETT; GEORGE MOCK; PHILIP GOOD; & ABRAHAM RUMP. S/ ELLIS PALMER, ANN (X) PALMER. Wit: JESSE (X) PUCKET, ELIJAH PALMOR, who swore by oath 12 Oct 1790 before HUGH MIDDLETON, J.P.

Pp. 116-120. 17 Jul 1789: MAYSON IZARD to JOHN GARRETT, both of Edgefield Co. SC for 130 pounds, sold 200 acres originally granted 22 Aug 1771 unto MARY HINDS, the present wife of said MAYSON IZARD. S/ MAYSON (M) IZARD, MARY (W) IZARD. Wit: FRANCES DAVIS, JOHN IZARD, JOHN WEST, who swore by oath 28 Aug 1789 before RUSSELL WILSON, J.P.

Pp. 121-127. 7 Apr 1789: RICHARD JOHNSON, Jr. & MARY, his wife, to ROBERT BURT, all of Edgefield Co. SC for 100 pounds, sold 275 acres known as Plat No. 1 of confiscated lands on Turkey Creek of Savannah River, adj. RUTLEDGE. S/ RICHd JOHNSON, MARY JOHNSON. Wit: HARWOOD BURT, MOODY BURT, who swore by oath 13 Apr 1789 before HUGH MIDDLETON, J.P. Edgefield Co. SC: July Court 1790, MARY JOHNSON, relinqishes her Dower... R. TUTT, C.E.C.

Pp. 127-129. 13 Apr 1790: JOSEPH COVINGTON & DARKES, his wife, to JOHN HARDY, all of Edgefield Co. SC for 10 pounds, sold 30 acres on Stephens Creek of Savannah River, adj. the mouth of Sweetwater Creek; COOK; & JOHN HARDY. S/ JOs COVINGTON. Wit: LEONARD NOBLES, SAMUEL WRIGHT, who swore by oath 13 Jul 1790 before ARTHUR SIMKINS, J.P.

DEED BOOK 4: 1790 EDGEFIELD COUNTY S.C.

Pp. - 130-135. 16 Mar 1790: EZEKIEL HARLEN to JOHN McCOY, both of Edgefield Co. SC for 200 pounds, sold 200 acres on Savannah River, adj. said River. S/ EZEKIEL (X) HARLEN. Wit: JEREMIAH MILES, SIMS (X) MIDDLEBROOKS, JOHN MILES, who swore by oath 13 Jul 1790 before JOHN PURVES, J.P.

Pp. 135-144. 24 Feb 1790: WILLIAM LONGMIRE & ANNE, his wife, Planter & Spinstress, to ISAAC BRUNSON, Sr., Planter, all of Edgefield Co. SC for 70 pounds, sold 150 acres being part of 500 acres originally granted 21 May 1772 unto WILLIAM COURSEY, who sold 24 Sep 1786 & is Rcd. in Clerk's Office in Book A, page 105, 1786. Said 150 acres on branch called Springfield of Beaver Dam Creek of Turkey Creek a fork of Stevens Creek of Savannah River, adj. WILLIAM GOODE; ROBERT MELVEL, dec'd; JOHN ALLEN; ABRAM MARTIN & WILLIAM COURSEY. S/ WILLIAM LONGMIRE, ISAAC BRUNSON. Wit: W. COURSEY, JOSEPH BRUNSON, who swore by oath 8 Jul 1790 before JOHN PURVIS, J.P.

PLAT: p. 144.
7 Jan 1790 - True Plat of 150 acres sold by WILLIAM LONGMIRE to ISAAC BRUNSON. S/ Wm COURSEY, Mathemat (torn).

Pp. 145-151. 23 Apr 1790: LEROY HAMMOND & MARY ANN, his wife, to JOHN HAMMOND, all of Edgefield Co. SC for 5 pounds, sold a Lot containing 104 square feet, adj. Union St. & Broad St. of a Town laid out by said LEROY HAMMOND & JOHN HAMMOND on their lands adj. a Little Village named Cambelton. S/ LEROY HAMMOND. Wit: SUSANNAH WINTERS, GEORGE WINTER, SHADRACK ROZAR, who swore by oath 13 Jul 1790 before WILLIAM ANDERSON, J.P.

Pp. 151-157. 26 Apr 1790: JOHN HAMMOND & ELIZABETH, his wife, to SHADRACK ROZAR, all of Edgefield Co. SC for 5 pounds, sold Town Lot No. 5, being 83 feet wide in front and 132 feet in length, adj. Union St. & Broad St. in a town called Fallmouth, which was laid out by said JOHN HAMMOND & LEROY HAMMOND on their land adj. a Little Village called Campbelton. S/ JOHN HAMMOND, ELIZ. HAMMOND. Wit: JN. PERRY, DAVID SANDIDGE. Ack. in open Court Oct Term 1790.

Pp. 157-159. 19 Nov 1790: JAMES TUTT to GABRIEL TUTT, both of Edgefield Co. SC, for 40 pounds, sold six negroes To Wit: BOB; JACK; CHARLES; CHARITY; SAM; & PATT. S/ JAMES TUTT. Wit: LARKIN SULLIVANT, BENJ. PIBURN, RICHARD TUTT, Jr., WILLIAM P. TIBBS, who swore by oath 20 Nov 1790 before AQUILLA MILES, J.P.

Pp. 159-166. 23 May 1787: ROBERT DAVIS, Sr. & PATTY, his wife, Yeoman, to WILLIAM ENGLISH, Planter, all of Edgefield Co. SC for 30 pounds, sold 100 acres, being part of 200 acres originally granted 15 May 1772 unto said DAVIS, adj. MOSES KIRKLAND at time of survey. S/ ROBERT (R) DAVIS, PATTY (X) DAVIS. Wit: THOS PULLEY, JAMES (+) SMEDLY, who proved in Jan. Court. Dower relinquished. Capt. MOORE (sic) & proved by THOMAS PULLEY in Jul Term Court 1790. R. TUTT, C.E.C.

Pp. 167-174. 3 May 1789: RICHARD JOHNSON, Planter, & MARY, his wife, to RICHARD BURTON, all of Edgefield Co. SC for 50 pounds, sold 500 acres originally granted 1 May 1786 unto said JOHNSON (except about 15 acres where said RICHARD JOHNSON now lives, which he purchased of OBURN BUFFINGTON) on both sides of Turkey Creek of Stephens Creek adj. land formerly held by OBURN BUFFINGTON, now in possession of said RICHARD JOHNSON. S/ RICHd JOHNSON. Wit: EDWARD (X) CUDY (also COUDY), JOHN SIMKINS, who swore by oath 5 May 1789 before ARTHUR SIMKINS, J.P. Relinquished Dower by Mrs. MARY JOHNSON in Open Court July Term 1790 before HUGH MIDDLETON, Esq., J.P. Rcd. by R. TUTT, C.E.C.

Pp. 175-180. 17 Jun 1790: WILLIAM ROBINSON to VAN SWEARINGEN, Jr., both of Edgefield Co. SC for indebtiness of 93 pounds... & better & effectual securing of payment... sold 364 acres, being part of two tracts: (1) 50 acres granted unto LAWRENCE HALL with a Griss Mill thereon; & (2) 314 acres, being part of 492 acres granted unto JOHN RYAN on Shaws Creek, adj. said 50 acres. If said debt with Interest is paid by 17 Jun 1795... said Indenture be null & void. S/ WILL ROBINSON. Wit: ELIZABETH (X) WILLIAMS, EZEKIEL McCLENDON, who swore by oath 27 Sep 1790 before ARTHUR SIMKINS, J.P.
Memorandum:... that Mill & land was delivered by said WILLIAM ROBERTSON unto said VAN SWEARINGAM in the name of all the goods & chattles within mentioned.

Pp. 180-184. 18 Feb 1790: JOHN HAMMOND & ELIZABETH, his wife, to DRURY MIMS, all of Edgefield Co. SC for 5 pounds, sold two Lots No. 6 & 7, each containing 65 2/3rd feet on front on Union St. & 155 feet deep in the town of Fallmouth, laid out on land of said JOHN HAMMOND near a little village called Campbelton. S/ JOHN HAMMOND, ELIZTH. HAMMOND. Wit: JN. PERRY, BEN RHODES. Received in Office 14 Jul 1790.

Pp. 185-191. 3 Jan 1776: AARON WEAVER, Planter, to JOHN DUGLAS, Planter, both of Colleton Co. SC for 100 pounds, sold 50 acres, being part of 200 acres granted unto said WEAVER in Colleton Co. SC on waters of Saludy River. S/ AARON WEAVER. Wit: SHAROD DUGLAS, JOHN DUGLAS, SAMUEL EATHERAGE, who swore by oath 21 Oct 1784 before SOLOMAN POPE, Justice Person.

Pp. 192-193. 30 Aug 1790: Bill of Sale: BARKLEY MARTIN, High Sheriff of Edgefield Co. SC to JOHN HAMMOND for 10 pounds... sold 1 negroe boy named JOHNNY, having been taken by me as directed by Clerk of County Court to satisfy a debt of ISAAC TASDALE & COMPANY against LEONARD MARBURY late of the state, of the state of Georgia (sic) & sold to the last & highest bider at a Public Auction... S/ BARKLEY MARTIN, S.E.C. Wit: JOHN SIMKINS, ELLIS PALMER, who swore by oath 10 Jan 1791 before RUSSELL WILSON, Esq., J.P. Rcd. Jan Term 1791.

Pp. 193-207. 11 Dec 1789: (Deed titled WILLIAM MATTHEWS & DRURY MATTHEWS, but DRURY MATTHEWS is not mentioned in the content of the deed, gch). WILLIAM MATHEWS, Planter of SC to LEROY HAMMOND, Esq. of Edgefield Co. SC for 2100 pounds, sold 3 tracts of land in Ninety Six Dist.: (1) 200 acres granted to PATRICK DOOLY & conveyed by GEORGE DOOLY to said WILLIAM MATTHEWS being on branch of Ninety Six Creek, adj. JOHN ANDERSON, Ninety Six Creek, JOHN ANDERSON, JAMES ANDERSON & COLBERT ANDERSON... (2) 100 acres granted to JOHN ANDERSON & conveyed by THOMAS ANDERSON to said WILLIAM MATTHEWS, adj. JAMES ANDERSON... (3) 150 acres granted JOHN HOLLOWAY & conveyed to said MATTHEWS, being on Machones Creek adj. MACHONES GOODE & JAMES ANDERSON. S/ WILLIAM (+) MATTHEWS. Wit: WM. GARRETT, CHAS. GOODWIN, Atty. at Law, who swore by oath 12 Jul 1790 before ARTHUR SIMKINS, J.P.

Pp. 207-214. 17 Jan 1780: JOSEPH DAVENPORT to JOHN ELAM, both of Ninety Six Dist. SC for 1500 pounds, sold 400 acres originally granted 21 Feb 1772 unto said DAVENPORT, adj. all sides vacant at time of survey. S/ JOSEPH DAVENPORT. Wit: BARTLETT SATTERWHITE, SAMUEL GOODE, who swore by oath 20 Jan 1780 before Wᵐ ANDERSON, J.P.

Pp. 214-220. 1 May 1790: DANIEL MARSHALL & ABRAHAM MARSHALL, Planters of Richmond Co. GA to JOHN GREY, Planter of Edgefield Co. SC for 140 pounds, sold 400 acres where said JOHN GREY now lives, being part of 500 acres originally granted 12 Jul 1771 unto REVEREND DANIEL MARSHALL & a Memorial of 1 Aug 1771, on Marshalls Creek a branch of Hornes Creek of Stevens Creek in St. Paul Parrish of Colleton Co. SC then called, but now Edgefield, adj. THOMAS HUGHS; JOHN CONN; DAVID LOCKER; JOHN VARNER; SAMUEL WALKER & ALLEN ADERSON at time of survey. S/ DANIEL MARSHALL, A. MARSHALL. Wit: THOMAS HANCOCK, JAMES WHITLOCK, who swore by oath 5 May 1790 before HUGH MIDDLETON, J.P. Rcd. 12 Oct 1790.

Pp. 220-222. 6 May 1788: Articles of an Agreement: DAVID ZUBLY, Planter, to JOHN PRIOR, Millwright, of Edgefield Co. SC for one pair of Grist Mill stones & hand Mill stones reserved & following considerations sell 1000 acres with a Grist Mill on Town Creek & laid out by ROBERT LANG, Surveyor, for said JOHN PRYOR to build the said DAVID ZUBY on the upper Mill Seat, one Saw Mill 23 feet by 15 feet compleat for one Saw in six months, after said ZUBLY brings the timber & materials to the directions of said PRYOR. Said ZUBLY will hew the timber & furnish three hands or more that is capable of takingdirections, and five or more white pileing & put down the ground works & sufficient help to raise the Mill as given by the directions of PRYOR. Said PRYOR is to give ZUBLY 50,000 merchantable Inch boards delivered at his mill, and is to have 9 months to build his own mills & then after said ZUBLY is to have his lumber as fast as it can be sawed & after said PRYOR builds & pays him the lumber, ZUBLY is to make Titles to the land & Mills and moreover PRYOR agrees that if the Mill blows up for a space of 3 years after the mill is delivered, except the water runs over the dam then said PRYOR is to put her in place again at his own expense & said PRYOR promises to furnish his own board, washing & lodging while he is doing DAVID ZUBLY's work. Said PRYOR promises to give ZUBLY as much two inch plank sufficient to pile said ZUBLY's Mill. S/ DAVID ZUBLEY, JOHN (P) PRYER. Wit: JONATHAN MYER, JOHN CLARK, who swore by oath 27 Sep 1790 before JOHN STURGENNEGGER, J.P.

Pp. 222-223. 6 Jan 1791: JOHN WATSON, Sr., Planter, to my son, JOHN WATSON, Jr., both of Edgefield Co SC for love & affection, gives one negroe man called JOE. S/ JOHN (+) WATSON. Wit: EDWARD COUCH, WILLIAM WATSON, who swore by oath 1 Feb 1791 before RUSSELL WILSON, J.P. Rcd. 2 Feb 1792.

P. 224. 5 Jan 1791: JOHN WATSON, Sr., Planter, to my daughter, MARY ODUM, Widow, both of Edgefield Co. SC for love & affection, gives 100 acres on Moores Creek of Little Saludy, adj. THOMAS WARREN, Moores Creek & a road. S/ JOHN (+) WATSON. Wit: EDWARD COUCH, WILLIAM ANDERSON, THOMAS WILLIAM BENSON, who swore by oath 29 Jan 1791 before RUSSEL WILSON, J.P.

Pp. 225-228. 26 Jul 1788: DRURY FORT, Yeoman, to WILLIAM

HUMPHREY, both of Edgefield Co. SC for 42 pounds, sold 50 acres being part of 100 acres originally granted 31 Oct 1765 unto said FORT on Mine Creek of Little Saludy River and is equally divided between said WILLIAM HUMPHREYS & BARROT TRAVIS. Said HUMPHRYS is to have the NE part of the 100 acres. S/ DRURY FORT. Wit: NATHANIEL BOALTON, LODOWICK HILL, HENRY BOALTON, who swore by oath 19 Sep 1788 before RUSSELL WILSON, J.P.

P. 229. 19 Jan 1790: JOHN POUND to DAVID WALKER of Richmond Co. GA for 55 pounds, sold one negroe woman named PHILIS with her increase. S/ JOHN POUND. Wit: LEROY HAMMOND, DAVID WALKER, Jr., who swore by oath 12 Jul 1790 before JOHN MOORE, J.P.

P. 230. 7 Jul 1790: JOHN POUND to DAVID WALKER, Sr. of Richmond Co. GA for 32 pounds, sold 7 head of cattle; 2 fether beds & furniture; & 2 pair of bedsteads; 2 tables & 1 chest; 1 case of bottles; 1 pewter dish; 5 basons & 5 plates; 1 case of nives & forks; 2 iron pot ; 1 dutch oven. S/ JOHN POUND. Wit: FREDERICK TILLMAN, DAVID WALKER, Jr., who swore by oath 12 Jul 1791 before JOHN MOORE, J.P.

Pp. 231-240. 24 Apr 1770: JAMES GREER & MARY his wife, Planter, to EZEKIEL BUFFINGTON & OBURN BUFFINGTON, all of Granville Co. SC for 240 pounds, sold 200 acres originally granted 27 Sep 1769 unto said MARY GREER on Turkey Creek of Granville Co. SC. S/ JAMES GREER, MARY GREER. Wit: JAs SCOTT, NATHAN HARLEN. 24 Apr 1770: Received of EZEKIEL & OBURN BUFFINGTON 250 pounds, it being the full consideration & their full part or share of their Father, the late THOMAS BUFFINGTON's Estate. We say received by us JAMES GREER, MARY GREER. Wit: JAs SCOTT, NATHAN HARLEN, who swore by oath Nov 1770 before JOHN PICKENS, Jr., Esq., J.P.

Pp. 240-241. 7 Aug 1790: JAMES VESSELS, Sr. of Edgefield Co. SC to JOHN FLINT for 20 pounds, sold one negroe man named JAMES BLACK, Corker by Trade. S/ JAMES VESSELS, Sr. Wit: ISAAC WINGATE, FRANCES OGILVES.
Richmond Co. GA: ISAAC WINGATE of Augusta swore by oath 5 Jan 1791 before DATZIRL HUNTER, J.P.

Pp. 241-242. 7 Oct 1790: Bond: JOHN CHENEY, Planter, bound to JOHN COGBOURN, Planter, both of Ninety Six Dist. SC for 1000 pounds, the conditions... to make lawfull right of 200 acres, whereon JOHN CHENEY now lives on branch of Cedar Creek of Savannah River when Heirs of JOSEPH REE's come to the age of twenty one years... then this obligation to be void or otherwise remain in full force... S/ JOHN CHENEY. Wit: THOs HAGENS, RICH. TUTT, Jr., who swore by oath 7 Oct 1790 before ARTHUR SIMKINS, J.P.

P. 243. 5 Jan 1790: Sworn Statement: ARTHUR WATSON of Edgefield Co. SC gave oath that in 1779 he, with MICHAEL WATSON & JOSEPH HOWEL subscribed their names as witnesses to a set of conveyances of land made from WILLIAM WATSON to JESSE PARTIN. Said tract of 100 acres originally granted 26 Aug 1774 unto WILLIAM WATSON on Indian Creek of Cloud Creek. S/ ARTHUR (A) WATSON. Sworn before RUSSELL WILSON, J.P.

P. 243. 28 Nov 1789: Sworn Statement: Received of Mr. JOHN PRYOR 50,000 feet of Merchantable boards as measured by SAMUEL

DEED BOOK 4: 1790 EDGEFIELD COUNTY S.C.

BURGES in part pay of Mill Seat on Town Creek. S/ DAVID ZUBLY. SAMUEL BURGES & WILLIAM STUART swore by oath 27 Sep 1790 before JOHN STURZENEGGER, J.P.

Pp. 244-248. 5 Jan 1790: JOHN PURVES, Planter, to WILLIAM TERRY, Planter, both of Edgefield Co. SC for 40 pounds, sold 240 acres originally granted 5 Sep 1785 unto JOHN RUTLEDGE, who conveyed to said JOHN PURVES on Turkey Creek of Savannah River. S/ JOHN PURVES. Wit: DAVID BURKS, MARSHALL MARTIN, who swore by oath 5 Jun 1790 before AQUILA MILES, J.P.

Pp. 248-253. 29 May 1789: ANDERSON CRAWFORD & RACHEL, his wife, of GA to MAURICE GUIN for 25 pounds, sold 50 acres originally granted 10 Apr 1771 unto WILLIAM ANDERSON, who conveyed to MAURICE GUIN, who conveyed to FRANCES SINQUEFIELD, now dec'd, & said tract amongst other lands was given in LW&T of FRANCIS SINGUEFIELD to RACHEL SINQUEFIELD, now wife of ANDERSON CRAWFORD & JANE SINQUEFIELD, now the Widow MAXWELL. Land being on Saludy River, adj. WILLIAM LOWE & MAURICE GUIN. S/ A. CRAWFORD, RACHEL CRAWFORD. Wit: JOSEPH TOWLES, JOHN CLARK, JOHN LOWE, who swore by oath 31 Mar 1789 before W. ANDERSON, J.P.

Pp. 253-257. 11 Feb 1789: JAMES BELVEN of Edgefield Co. SC to ZACHARIAH MARTIN for 30 pounds, sold 100 acres, being part of 200 acres originally granted 5 Mar 1787 unto PHILEMON WATERS, who conveyed 6 Sep 1787 unto said BELVEN on Cloud Creek of Saludy River, adj. JOSEPH WRIGHT. S/ JAMES BELVEN, FRANKEY (X) BELVEN, his wife. Wit: JOHN MITCHEL, DANIEL LANGSDON, who swore by oath 11 Feb 1789 before RUSSEL WILSON, J.P.

Pp. 257-263. 14 Aug 1790: GEORGE FORREST of Newberry Co. SC, Planter to the Reverend JOHN SPRINGER of Wilks Co. GA for 170 pounds, sold 200 acres, being part of 350 acres originally granted 13 Jul 1762 unto ROBERT McCUTCHEN, who conveyed unto THOMAS HERD in two seperate tracts: (1) 100 acres conveyed 26 Apr 1768; & (2) conveyed 24 Dec 1768. Said THOMAS HERD conveyed to JAMES PETEGREW by two deeds of conveyance of 100 acres each 11 May 1770, and said PETEGREW conveyed to said GEORGE FORREST. Land being on Beaver Dam, a branch of Ninety Six Creek, adj. WILLIAM ROBERSON; THOMAS HERD; & MARY SMITH. S/ GEORGE FORREST. Wit: THOS W. FAKES, R. WATTS, JAMES CRESWELL, who swore by oath 5 Oct 1790 before JOHN MOORE, J.P.

Pp. 263-269. 16 Jan 1787: SIMON MARTIN & CELIA, his wife, to ALLEN HINTON, all of Edgefield Co. SC for 12 pounds, sold 100 acres originally granted 5 Sep 1785 unto said MARTIN on each side of the road from Augusta to Ninety Six by Sweetwater Creek, adj. COVINGTON PIERCE & WILLIAM MORGAN. S/ SIMON MARTIN. Wit: ABRAHAM PIERCE, JAMES MARTIN, JOSHUA THORN, who swore by oath 14 Oct 1790 before AQUILA MILES, J.P.

Pp. 269-274. 5 Mar 1790: ALLEN HINTON to SAMUEL WRIGHT, both of Edgefield Co. SC for 10 pounds, sold 100 acres, adj. WILLIAM COVINGTON; DANIEL GILL; MORGAN; JOHN PEARCE, Sr.; & JOHN HAMMOND, dec'd. S/ ALLEN HINTON. Wit: JOHN (+) PIERCE, REUBIN FRAZIER, who swore by oath 6 Mar 1790 before LEROY HAMMOND, J.P.

P. 274. 23 Dec 1790: Bill of Sale: NICHOLAS DILLARD to CASPER GALLMON sold one negroe man named JEFFRE. S/ NICHOLAS DILLARD. Wit: PHILLIP DILLARD, CONRAD GALMAN, who swore by oath 9 Jul 1791 before ARTHUR SIMKINS, J.E.C.   Rec. (torn).

Pp. 1-6. 3 Jul 1789: JOHN ROEBUCK to GEORGE RANDAL, both of Edgefield Co. SC for 50 pounds, sold 103 acres originally granted 3 Dec 1787 unto said ROEBUCK on branch of Horse Creek of Ninety Six Dist. SC. S/ JOHN (+) ROEBUCK. Wit: DANIEL RILELY, JOAB WOOTEN, who swore by oath 4 Jul 1789 before LEROY HAMMOND, J.P. Rcd. 12 Apr 1791.

Pp. 7-12. 1 Oct 1790: DAVID SIGLAR, Sr. to GEORGE SIGLER, both of Edgefield Co. SC for 25 pounds, sold 126 acres, being part of a grant unto said SIGLAR, Sr., adj. JOHN HANDCOCK; DAVID SIGLAR; JOHN HILLY; JAMES BREWER, formerly, but now held by JOHN HARDY; & JOHN CURRY. S/ DAVID SEGLAR, Sr. Wit: WM. WATSON, Sr., JOHN (+) GENTRY, who swore by oath 4 Dec 1791 before HUGH MIDDLETON, J.P. Rcd. 6 Jun 1791.

Pp. 12-18. 17 May 1784: THOMAS CLARK & PATIENCE CLARK of Granville Co. SC, Planter, to ROBERT WARE of Caroline Co. VA Planter, for 200 pounds, sold 300 acres originally granted 23 Jan 1773 unto JOHN CLARK in Granville Co. SC, adj. Stephens Creek & HENRY WARE. S/ THOS. CLARK & PATIENCE CLARK. Wit: GEORGE CAMMOCK, NICHOLAS WARE, HENRY WARE, who swore by oath 6 Jun 1791 before HUGH MIDDLETON, J.P. Rcd. 6 Jun 1791.

P. 19. 7 Jun 1790: Bill of Sale: ALLEN HINTON of Edgefield Co. SC to CHARNAL HIGHTOWER THORN, sold four negroes named SILVEY; WINNEY; PETER; & POLL. S/ ALLEN HINTON. Wit: STERLING HIGHTOWER, JOHN HAMMOND, Jr., who swore by oath 27 Jul 1790 before HUGH MIDDLETON, J.P. Rcd. 6 Jun 1791.

Pp. 20-22. 1 Dec 1790: LEONARD NOBLES, Planter, to LEROY HAMMOND, Merchant, both of Edgefield Co. SC for 100 pounds, the Receipt whereby I am fully content & satisfied, have sold & delivered ten Negroe Slaves to Wit: CESAR; STEPHEN; SILVA; BINAH; PRINCE; TIM; LUCY; STEPNEY; FANCY; & LETTIE; also, 30 head of cattle; 30 hoggs; 6 head of horses & mares; 4 feather beds & furniture to his own use (LEONARD NOBLES) provided he pay the full sum of 100 pounds with Interest of his bond dated 1 Dec 1791. Also a note to the Estate of LEROY HAMMOND dated 26 Apr 1790 on or before 1 Jan 1792. Should LEONARD NOBLES default payment of two bond & note... LEROY HAMMOND shall take as his goods & chattles... S/ LRD NOBLES. Wit: ABRAHAM RICHARDSON, WM. MORGAN, who swore by oath 2 May 1791 before ARTHUR SIMKINS, J.C.C. Rcd. 6 Jun 1791.

Pp. 23-28. 15 Jun 1791: ELISHA ROBERSON to THOMAS ROBERSON & SAMUEL GARNER, Planters of Edgefield Co. SC for 5 pounds, sold 250 acres originally granted 23 Jun 1774 unto ELISHA ROBERSON on waters of Savannah River in Ninety Six Dist. SC. S/ ELISHA (E) ROBERSON. Wit: R. TUTT, RICH^d TUTT, Jr., who swore by oath 15 Jun 1791 before THOS. BACON, J.P. Rcd. 15 Jun 1791.

Pp. 28-34. 15 Jun 1791: ELISHA ROBERSON to ALLEN ROBERSON, both of Edgefield Co. SC for 5 pounds, sold several tracts of land: (1) 150 acres originally granted 28 Nov 1771 unto ELISHA ROBERSON on south side of Stephens Creek of Savannah River; (2) part of 200 acres originally granted 2 Apr 1773 unto said ROBERSON on both sides of Stephens Creek, adj. above tract; & (3) 100 acres surveyed 4 May 1756 for JAMES MUSE & granted 27 Aug 1765 unto BENJ. HORN. S/ ELISHA (E) ROBERSON. Wit: RICHARD TUTT, Sr., RICHARD TUTT, Jr., who swore by oath 15 Jun 1791 before THOMAS BACON, J.P.

DEED BOOK 5: 1791 EDGEFIELD COUNTY S.C.

Pp. 34-41. 16 Jun 1791: ELISHA ROBERSON to WILLIAM ROBERSON, Planters of Edgefield Co. SC for 5 pounds, sold unmeasured acres in his actual possession on North side of Stephens Creek of Savannah River containing in the whole 100 acres originally surveyed 4 May 1756 for JAMES MUSE & granted 27 Aug 1765 unto BENJAMIN HORN, who conveyed by L&R 13 (blank) 17 (blank). Also, part of 250 acres originally granted 3 Apr 1773 unto ELISHA ROBERSON on both sides of Stephens Creek. S/ ELISHA (E) ROBERSON. Wit: R. TUTT, Sr., RICHARD TUTT, Jr., who swore by oath 15 Jun 1791 before THOMAS BACON, J.P.

Pp. 41-47. 1 Dec 1790: ABRAHAM RICHARDSON & WINFORD, his wife, to JOSEPH HIGHTOWER, all of Edgefield Co. SC for 100 pounds, sold 50 acres originally granted 19 Nov 1772 unto EPHRIAM FRANKLIN at the Cherokee Ponds, adj. JAMES JOHNSON; JOSEPH HIGHTOWER; & CHARLES BANKS. S/ ABRAM RICHARDSON, WINFORD (X) RICHARDSON. Wit: ROBERT SPEER, JOHN (X) CHERRY, CHRISTOPHER HALL, who swore by oath 4 Dec 1790 before HUGH MIDDLETON, J.P. Rcd. 2 Jul 1791.

Pp. 47-52. 1 Dec 1790: ABRAHAM RICHARDSON & WINFORD, his wife, of Edgefield Co. SC to JOSEPH HIGHTOWER for 150 pounds, sold 100 acres originally granted 1 Feb 1768 unto JAMES JOHNSON, Sr., on the Cherokee pond. S/ ABRAHAM RICHARDSON, WINEFORD (X) RICHARDSON. Wit: ROBERT SPEER, JOHN (X) CHERRY, CHRISTOPHER HALL, who swore by oath 4 Dec 1790 before HUGH MIDDLETON, J.P. Rcd. 2 Jul 1791.

Pp. 52-58. 1 Dec 1790: ABRAHAM RICHARDSON & WINEFORD, his wife, to JOSEPH HIGHTOWER, all of Edgefield Co. SC for 50 pounds, sold 200 acres originally granted 1 Feb 1787 unto CHARLES BANKS near the Cherokee pond. S/ ABRAM RICHARDSON, WINEFORD (X) RICHARDSON. Wit: ROBERT SPEER, JNᵒ (X) CHERRY, CHRISTOPHER HALL, who swore by oath 4 Dec 1790 before HUGH MIDDLETON, J.P. Rcd. 2 Jul 1791.

Pp. 58-68. 5 Dec 1788: BENJAMIN DRUMMON & ANN, his wife, of Laurence Co. SC to JOHN OLIPHANT of Edgefield Co. SC for 25 pounds, sold 50 acres, being part of 400 acres granted 1 Sep 1768 unto JOHN SUMMERS, dec'd, then fell by heirship to his eldest son, GEORGE SUMMERS, who conveyed 19 & 20 Jan 1778 & was witnessed by NICHOLAS DILLARD & JAMES CARMICAL. Said land being on Pinckney branch, Beaverdam Creek, mouth of a little branch called Jesters branch & joins OLIPHANT's land. S/ BENJAMIN (B) DRUMMON, ANN (X) DRUMMON. Wit: ABRAHAM (X) RIGGS, THOMAS HAGINS, who swore by oath 26 Dec 1789 before ARTHUR SIMKINS,J.P. Rcd. 9 Jul 1791.

Pp. 68-81. 8 Jul 1791: JOHN RYAN to BENJAMIN RYAN, both of Edgefield Co. SC for the consideration of the sum of 4560 acres in GA, within 20 miles of the Rock Landing on Ocone River have sold 4560 acres, being of twelve tracts: (1) 100 acres granted 1 Feb 1786 unto MARTHA RYAN; (2) 150 acres granted 23 Jun 1774 unto JAMES BARRENTINE, adj. DANIEL ELLIS; JAMES HARRIS; JOHN RYAN; MOSES KIRKLAND; JOHN WHITE; & HARMON GALMAN at time of survey; (3) 352 acres, late the property of MOSES KIRKLAND known by Plat No. 3, adj. lands lately the property of MOSES KIRKLAND; RICHARD KIRKLAND; ROLLEY ROBUCK; JOSEPH & GEORGE MILLER; (4) 384 acres late the property of MOSES KIRKLAND known by Plat No. 4, adj. JOHN RYAN; JOHN RUTLEDGE; lands late the property of

MOSES KIRKLAND; & JOHN LUCAS; (5) 100 acres, adj. JOHN RYAN; WILLIS ODUM; & EDWARD RUTLEDGE; (6) 300 acres, being part of 643 acres granted 7 May 1787 unto ISAAC KIRKLAND, adj. JOHN RYAN; WILLIS ODUM; EDWARD RUTLEDGE, Esq.; FRANCIS SINQUEFIELD; WILLIAM HARGROVE; & JACOB FUDGE at time of survey. The above tracts all join each other and are on Chavers & Horns Creek of Savannah River. (7) 200 acres granted Jul 1768 unto JOHN HARVEY, adj. BENJAMIN RYAN & JOSEPH WALKER on Nobles Creek at time of survey, but now called Horns Creek; (8) 84 acres granted 5 Jun 1786 unto JOHN RYAN, adj. aforesaid lands & EDWARD RUTLEDGE at time of survey; (9) 660 acres granted 1 Oct 1787 unto JOHN RYAN, adj. BOLEN STARK; REUBIN ROBERTS; ROBERT LANG, CHRISTIAN GOMILLIAN; DAVID BURKS; & WILLIAM ROTTEN; (10) 637 acres granted 3 Mar 1788 unto JOHN RYAN near the head of Turkey Creek, adj. above lands; CHRISTIAN GOMILLIAN & REUBIN ROBERTS; (11) 593 acres granted 7 May 1787 unto JOHN RYAN on Paces branch of Shaws Creek, adj. THOMAS SWEARENGHAM & ABRAHAM ODEN; (12) 1000 acres granted 3 Mar 1788 unto JOHN RYAN on Horns Creek, adj. REBECCA STARK; VAN SWEARENGHAM; BENJAMIN RYAN; EDWARD RUTLEDGE & Capt RYAN. S/ JOHN RYAN. Wit: BENJAMIN HIGHTOWER, ABRAHAM HERNDON, ISAAC KIRKLAND, who swore by oath 9 Jul 1791 before JOSEPH HIGHTOWER, J.P. Rcd. 11 Jul 1791.

Pp. 81-88. 13 Jan 1791: JAMES THOMAS of Washington Co. GA to JONATHAN WIGHTT of Edgefield Co. SC for 200 pounds, sold 307 acres, being part of two tracts on Horns Creek: (1) 250 acres granted 21 Jul 1769 unto said THOMAS; & (2) 57 acres granted 26 Jul 1774 unto LANCLOT WARREN, who conveyed 27 May 1775 unto said THOMAS & adj. TILMAN, COLEMAN, & ADERSON at time of survey. S/ JAMES THOMAS. Wit: FREMON WIGHTT, BENJAMIN TENELLE, JAMES (+) WEST, who swore by oath 18 Jul 1791 before JOSEPH HIGHTOWER, J.P. Rcd. 20 Jul 1791.

Pp. 89-96. 16 Jan 1789: THOMAS HAGINS to PHILLIP DILLARD, both of Edgefield Co. SC for 5 pounds, sold 33 acres, being part of 66 acres granted in 1789 on waters of Cedar Creek of Savannah River. S/ THOS. HAGINS. Wit: SAMUEL MARSH, Jr., WILLIAM HAGINS, who swore by oath 12 Jan 1789 before AQUILA MILES, J.P. Rcd. 25 Jul 1791.

Pp. 96-103. 16 Jan 1789: NICHOLAS DILLARD to PHILIP DILLARD, both of Edgefield Co. SC for 10 pounds, sold 50 acres, being part of 200 acres originally granted in 1775 unto said NICHOLAS DILLARD (reads 1775 in Lease & 1770 in Release, gch), being on Cedar Creek of Savannah River. S/ NICHL.DILLARD. Wit: SAML.MARSH, Jr., WILLIAM HAGINS, who swore by oath 20 Jan 1789 before A. MILES, J.P. Rcd. 25 Jul 1791.

Pp. 104-107. 13 Jun 1785: OMY MONS to WILLIAM TERRY, both of Ninety Six Dist. SC for 5 pounds, sold 100 acres originally granted 16 Jan 1765 unto RICHARD MONS on Turkey Creek of Stephens Creek of Savannah River & vacant on all sides at time of survey, but now adj. WILLIAM DAWSON; CHARLES WILLIAMS; JAMES ROWEN; & JOHN PURVES. S/ OMY (her mark) MONS. Wit: ELIZABETH (+) LINEAR (also LORIN), EZABELL RHODES, ARTHUR RHODES, who swore by oath 18 Jan 1785 before LEROY HAMMOND, J.P. Rcd. 25 Jul 1791.

Pp. 108-111. 13 Jan 1791: JAMES THOMAS of Washington Co. GA to JONATHAN WIGHTT of Edgefield Co. SC for 200 pounds, sold two tracts in Edgefield Co. SC on Horns Creek. Viz: (1) 250 acres granted 21 Jul 1769 unto JAMES THOMAS; & (2) 57 acres granted 26 Jul 1774 unto LANCELOT WARREN, adj. TILMAN COLEMAN & ADDERSON & was conveyed 27 May 1775 unto said JAMES THOMAS. S/ JAMES THOMAS. Wit: JAMES (X) WEST, BENJAMIN TENNILLE, FREEMAN WIGHTT. Rcd. 20 Jul 1791.

Pp. 112-116. 17 Mar 1773: JAMES ROBERSON to JOHN OLIPHANT, both of Granville Co. SC for 100 pounds, sold 100 acres originally granted 28 Aug 1772 & a Memorial entered 30 Oct 1772, being on head of Seder Creek, adj. NICHOLAS DILLARD. S/ JAMES ROBERSON. Wit: JOHN VERNON, WILLIAM VANN, THOS. HAGEN, who swore by oath 30 Jul 1774 before MOSES KIRKLAND, J.P. Rcd. 28 Jul 1791.

Pp. 116-121. 26 Nov 1778: JAMES HARRIS to JOHN OLIPHANT, both of Ninety Six Dist. SC for 1000 pounds, sold 50 acres, being part of 100 acres originally granted 8 Jun 1768 unto MARGARET DOUGALL, who conveyed by L&R 15 & 16 Jan 1771 unto TULLY BOWLING, who conveyed to EDWARD VANN, who conveyed 14 & 15 Nov 1776 unto said JAMES HARRIS. The remaining 50 acres was sold to SAMUEL MARSH, being on South side of branch called Lasies Creek of Stephens Creek, adj. NICHOLAS DILLARD, said OLIPHANT; & SAMUEL MARSH. S/ JAMES (X) HARRIS, ELIZABETH HARRIS. Wit: SAML. MARSH, NICHOLAS DILLARD, THOMAS HAGENS, who swore by oath 27 Dec 1778 before ARTHUR SIMKINS, J.P. Rcd. 28 Jul 1791.

Pp. 121-127. 14 Jul 1788: THOMAS RAY of Abbeville Co. SC to LEVI JESTER of Edgefield Co. SC for 50 pounds, sold 100 acres originally granted 14 Aug 1772 unto JAMES RAY & was invested to THOMAS RAY by being the elder Brother in the Law as JAMES RAY died without heirs or will. Said land on Beaver Dam Creek of Stephens Creek of Savannah River. S/ THOMAS (T) RAY. Wit: THOS. HAGENS, JOHN FRAZIER, WILLIAM HAGENS, who swore by oath 26 Jul 1788 before ARTHUR SIMKINS, J.P. Rcd. 28 Jul 1791.

Pp. 127-133. 22 Jun 1772: CHAMPNESS TERRY & SARAH, his wife, Planter, to JAMES HARRISON, Carpenter, all of Coleton Co. SC for 100 pounds, sold 600 acres granted 3 Apr 1772 unto said TERRY on branch of Coffetown Creek of Stephens Creek. S/ CHAMP. TERRY, SARAH TERRY. Wit: TIMOTHY McKINNEY, ROGER (R) McKINNEY, JAMES MARTIN, who swore by oath 18 Nov 1772 before JAMES MASON, Esq., J.P. Rcd. 1 Aug 1791.

Pp. 133-134. 1 Dec 1790: Bill of Sale: ROBERT LEVERET, Sr., of Edgefield Co. SC to HEZEKIAH GENTRY, Sr. for 150 pounds, sold two negro boys named JACK & SAM. Likewise one Negro woman named JUDE... the boys forever to him & the woman during the said LEVERET's natural life with all stock & household furniture & C. with all moneys due to me. S/ ROBERT (X) LEVERET. Wit: DAVID MARTIN, NATHAN MELTON, who swore by oath 23 Aug 1791 before RUSSELL WILSON, J.P. Rcd. 23 Aug 1791.

P. 135. 17 Jun 1791: MORIS CALLAHAM, EDWARD WHING, & WM. BURGES, Planters, all of Orangeburg District SC, to THOMAS WARREN of Edgefield Co. SC for 33 pounds, sold one negro boy named BEN. S/ MORRIS (N) CALLAHAM, EDWARD WHING (also WING), WM. BURGES. Wit: RACHAL (+) FOX, MARY (+) HOWEL, ELIJAH (+) FOX, who swore by oath in Orangeburg Distict 17 Jun 1791 before JOHN THOMAS FAIRCHILD, J. P. Rcd. 1 Sep 1791.

P. 136. 29 Jul 1791: Bill of Sale: CHARNEL HIGHTOWER THORN certifies that ALLEN HINTON payed in full a certain Bill of Sale left in your Office to be Recorded and please deliver the Bill of Sale to BARKLEY MARTIN, Esq. & his Receipt shall be discharge against me & my heirs. S/ CHARNEL HIGHTOWER THORN. Wit: RICHARD TUTT, Esq. Clerk Edgefield Co., GEORGE COWAN, JOHN HALL, who swore by oath 30 Jul 1791 before JOSEPH HIGHTOWER, J.P. Rcd. 29 Aug 1791.

Pp. 136-139. 27 Sep 1788: JOHN PIERCE, Sr. to JOHN PIERCE, Jr., both of Edgefield Co. SC for 10 Shillings, sold 148 acres being part of a tract granted JOHN HAMMOND 1772, bounded by WILLIAM PIERCE, Ninety Six Road, WILLIAM SPENCER. S/ JOHN PIERCE. Wit: THOMAS MATHEWS, WILLIAM MATHEWS, ISAAC MATHEWS, who swore by oath 3 May 1791 before JOSEPH HIGHTOWER, J.P. Rcd. 1 Sep 1791.

Pp. 140-147. 22 Apr 1791: JOSEPH TUCKER, Planter, of Edgefield Co., SC to TANDY CLARK KEY of Burk Co. GA, Planter, for 25 pounds, sold 100 acres, being part of 280 acres surveyed by WILLIAM GOODE 20 Mar 1775 & granted said JOSEPH TUCKER 5 Nov 1787, on a branch of Cuffey Town Creek in Edgefield Co. SC and is bounded by lands held by SAMUEL ANDERSON & the Widow BELCHER. S/ JOSEPH TUCKER. Wit: WILLIAM LEWIS, THOMAS JENNINGS, WILLIAM BALEY, who swore by oath 13 Aug 1791 before THOMAS BACON, Esq., J.P. Rcd. 23 Aug 1791.

Pp. 147-151. 19 Sep 1791: WILLIAM BROOKS of Pendleton Co. SC to WILLIAM MOORE of Edgefield Co. SC for 40 pounds, sold 100 acres near Saluda Old Town bounded to NW by land surveyed for DANIEL BURNET, now claimed by Mr. WAGGONER of Charleston, SC, SE by land surveyed for JAMES CARSON, now claimed by WM. MOORE, E by land surveyed for PETER WERTS now claimed by WM. MOORE, bounded SE on lands claimed by MOSES MARTIN (also read MOSES WALTON in release). S/ WILLIAM BROOKS. Wit: WILLIAM YARBOROUGH, GIBSON YARBOROUGH, who swore by oath 20 Oct 1791 before RUSSELL WILSON, J.P. Rcd. 21 Oct 1791.

P. 151. 3 May 1791: Bill of Sale: JINKIN HARRIS to JOHN HILL, sold one negro fellow named SAM, about twenty five years old. S/ JINKIN (H) HARRIS. Wit: BURGES WHITE, who swore by oath 1 Sep 1791 before AQUILA MILES, J.P. Rcd. 1 Sep 1791.

Pp. 152-155. 3 Jan 1791: JOHN THOMAS & ELIZABETH, his wife, of Edgefield Co. SC to JAMES ELBERT DAWSON, son of WILLIAM DAWSON of same place for 100 pounds, sold 300 acres granted to said JOHN THOMAS 5 Jun 1786 being near Turkey Creek in Edgefield Co. SC. S/ JOHN THOMAS, ELIZABETH (X) THOMAS. Wit: CALL COLLINS, JANE STEDAM, JAMES COURSEY, who swore by oath 20 Jan 1791 before JOHN PURVES, J.P. Rcd. 1 Sep 1791.

Pp. 155-159. 3 Jan 1791: JOHN THOMAS & ELIZABETH, his wife of Edgefield Co. SC to JONATHAN DAWSON of same place for 100 pounds, sold unto WILLIAM WADE DAWSON, son of WILLIAM DAWSON of same place for 100 pounds, (sic); 200 acres granted unto JOHN THOMAS 21 Jan 1785 being on Turkey Creek, a branch of Stephens Creek. S/ JOHN THOMAS, ELIZABETH (X) THOMAS. Wit: CALL COLLINS, JANE (+) STEDAM, JAMES COURSEY, who swore by oath 20 Jan 1791 before JOHN PURVES, Esq., J.P. Rcd. 1 Sep 1791.

Pp. 159-162. 26 Sep 1788: JOHN PIERCE to ABRAHAM PIERCE both of Edgefield Co. SC for 10 Shillings, sold 148 acres being parts of tracts granted to JOHN HAMMOND and remainder granted to JOHN CURRY and bounded by lands of JAMES VESSELS, JOHN PIERCE, N by WILLIAM PIERCE & CHARLES BANKS. S/ JOHN PIERCE. Wit: THOMAS MATTHEWS, WILLIAM MATTHEWS, ISAAC MATTHEWS, who swore by oath 3 May 1791, that he did see JOHN PIERCE Senr sign above, before JOSEPH HGIHTOWER, J.P. Rcd. 1 Sep 1791.

Pp. 163-166. 26 Sep 1788: JOHN PIERCE Senr. to WILLIAM PIERCE both of Edgefield Co. SC for 10 Shillings, sold 148 acres being part of a tract granted to JOHN HAMMOND 1772 and part of a tract granted to JOHN CURRY 1785, on a waggon road that leads from Augusta to Ninety Six, bounded by said JOHN PIERCE, SPENCER, NE by A. PIERCE, N by BANKS, & SW by PETER DAY. S/ JOHN PIERCE. Wit: THOMAS MATTHEWS, WILLIAM MATTHEWS, ISAAC MATTHEWS, who swore by oath 3 May 1791 before JOSEPH HIGHTOWER, J.P. Rcd. 1 Sep 1791.

Pp. 166-170. 16 Aug 1791: EZEKIEL HARLING of Abaville Co. SC to THOMAS FREEMAN of Edgefield Co. SC for 50 pounds, sold 75 acres in Edgefield Co. on the Savannah River bounded by JOHN McCOY, SW Savannah River & W by vacant land. Said land was granted unto EZEKIEL HARLING's father (to wit) EZEKIEL HARLING Senr. 4 Dec 1771. S/ EZEKIEL (X) HARLING. Wit: EZEPHANIAH (X) NOBLES, JOHN McCOY, who swore by oath 1 Sep 1791 before AQUILA MILES, J.P.

Pp. 170-175. 3 Oct 1788: SAMUEL LEWIS of Ninety Six Dist SC to WILLIAM DEAN of same place for 35 pounds, sold 200 acres granted 5 Jun 1786 on a branch of Little Stevens Creek bounded on the S by lands of ANSIL BEARDEN, formerly GARRET BUCKELEW's land. S/ SAMUEL LEWIS. Wit: FREDERICK (F) BUCKLEW, CHRISTOPHER (R) WARD, who swore by oath 30 Aug 1791 before JAMES SPANN, J.P. Rcd. 1 Sep 1791.

Pp. 175-179. 4 Mar 1791: JESSE PITTS of Edgefield Co. SC to JOSIAH PADGET of same place for 20 pounds, sold 156 acres originally granted Esquire BROWN 2 Mar 1789, being in Edgefield Co. on a branch of Clouds Creek on the South side of Saluda River bounded SW by ROBERT CATES. S/ JESSE PITTS, SARY PITTS, his wife. Wit: JOSIAH THOMAS, PUDY PITTS (+) BROWN, SAMUEL ESKRIDGE, who swore by oath 31 Aug 1791 before RUSSEL WILSON, J.P. Rcd. 1 Sep 1791.

Pp. 179-180. 6 Aug 1791: JOHN SPANN Senr. of Edgefield Co. SC to JAMES SPANN, Esq. of Edgefield Co. SC and FRANCIS SPANN of Washington Co. GA for 150 pounds, sold four country born negroes, one negroe man named DICK about forty years of age, one negroe woman named HANNAH about thirty years of age, One negroe girl named RACHEL about seven years of age, and another negro girl ELEY about one and one half years old. S/ JOHN SPANN. Wit: ELIZABETH (+) RAILY (also RILY), SUSANNAH (+) STANDLEY (also STANLEY), who swore by oath 30 Aug 1791 before JOHN MOORE, J.P. Rcd. 1 Sep 1791.

Pp. 180-185. 15 Aug 1786: MICHAEL LEIGH & DRUSILLA, his wife, of Edgefield Co. SC (Release states they are of Orangeburg Dist. SC, Planter), to SAMUEL CRAFTON of Edgefield Co. SC for 150 pounds, sold 150 acres originally granted 20 Apr 1774 to WILLIAM WARREN & was conveyed in 1780 to MICHAEL LEIGH, lying in Granville Co. on Stephens Creek bounded SE & NE by WILLIAM BOIDE's land & SW & SE by WM USSERY. S/ MICHAEL LEIGH, DRUSILLA LEIGH. Wit: WILLIAM (+) KEY, CHARLES BANKS, who swore by oath 9 Jul 1791 before JOSEPH HIGHTOWER, J.P. Rcd. 2 Sep 1791.

Pp. 186-191. 20 Jul 1791: ROBERT MOSELY & PENELLOPE, his wife of Edgefield Co. SC to WILLIAM MORGAN of same place for 45 pounds, sold 45 1/2 acres, being part of a tract granted said MOSELY 27 Sep 1784 on Horse Creek, bounded NE by CHARLES MARTIN, N by JOHN RENSFORD, & SW & SE by JOHN MARTIN. S/ ROBERT (R) MOSELY, PENELOPE (X) MOSELY. Wit: CHAS. MARTIN, DANL. MARCUS, JAMES COBB, Junr., who swore by oath 2 Sep 1791 before JOSEPH HIGHTOWER, J.P. Rcd. 2 Sep 1791.

Pp. 191-197. 30 Aug 1791: WILLIAM SPENCER of Richmond Co. GA to WILLIAM COVINGTON of Edgefield Co. SC for 200 pounds, sold 164 acres on Sweet Water Creek being part of 500 acres granted to JOHN HAMMOND, dec'd, 19 Nov 1772, but now said part of land containing 164 acres being invested to JOSHUA HAMMOND by LW&T of said JOHN HAMMOND, dec'd. Said land bounded SW by JOSEPH DAY, SE & S by WILLIAM COVINGTON, NE by ALLY HINTON & NW by the main Waggon Road. S/ WILLIAM SPENCER. Wit: HENRY KEY, HENRY SMERDON, who swore by oath 2 Sep 1791 before JOHN STURZENEGGER, J.P. Rcd. 2 Sep 1791.

Pp. 197-201. 8 Mar 1791: JAMES McBRIDE, Planter of Abbeville Co. SC to GEORGE SWILLING, Hunter, of Edgefield Co. SC for 10 Shillings, sold 300 acres of land on Rockey Creek of the Savannah River bounded NE by WILLIAM McBRIDE. S/ JAMES McBRIDE. Wit: THOMAS McBRIDE, ABNER PERRIN, who swore by oath 15 Aug 1791 before THOMAS BACON, Esq., J.P. Rcd. 3 Sep 1791.

Pp. 201-206. 15 Jan 1791: PHILIP ZIMMERMAN of Edgefield Co. SC to PETER ZIMMERMAN of same place for 5 Shillings, sold 200 acres where the said PETER ZIMMERMAN now lives, being on Hardlabour Creek a branch of Savannah River, bounded on the N by JAMES STEPHEL, E by MARKS, S. by PHILLIP ZIMMERMAN & W by Hard Labor Cr. S/ PHILLIP ZIMMERMAN. (Clerk made a note "the signature was wrote in dutch"). Wit: HENRY (+) ZIMMERMAN, ABNER PERRIN, who swore by oath 3 Sep 1791 before JOHN PURVES, Judge of Edgefield Co. Rcd. 3 Sep 1791.

Pp. 206-210. 6 Jun 1791: JAMES TUTT of Edgefield Co. SC to THOMAS FREEMAN of same place for 75 pounds, sold 75 acres on Savannah River, being part of an original grant of 150 acres to EZEKIEL HARLIN Senr., dec'd, 4 Dec 1771 and was conveyed to JAMES TUTT by EZEKIEL HARLIN Junr., son of EZEKIEL HARLIN Senr. 8 & 9 Apr 1789 and was Recorded in Clerk's Office in Book C, page 62, 16 Nov 1789. S/ JAMES TUTT. Wit: ISAM MITCHELL, EDMOND MARTIN, RICHARD TUTT Junr., who swore by oath 3 Sep 1791 before JOHN PURVES, J.C.C.E. Rcd. 3 Sep 1791.

Pp. 210-214. 3 Sep 1791: BARKLEY MARTIN, Sheriff of Edgefield Co. SC to EDWARD PRINCE of same place for 35 pounds, sold 127 acres of land sold at Public Auction...WHEREAS...ROBERT STARK, the absent debtor, was seized of said 127 acres... and Whereas WILSON BLUNT of Lexeton Co. SC, the plaintiff in the County Court SC of June Term 1789 did obtain & Recover a Judgement for 1414 pounds... S/ BARKLEY MARTIN, S.E.C. Wit: PETER CHASTAIN, RICHARD TUTT, Junr., who swore by oath 6 Sep 1791 before JOSEPH HIGHTOWER, J.P. Rcd. 6 Sep 1791.

DEED BOOK 5: 1791 EDGEFIELD COUNTY S.C.

Pp. 214-218. 3 Sep 1791: BARKLEY MARTIN, Sheriff of Edgefield Co. SC, Esquire, to EDWARD PRINCE of same place for 37 Pounds, sold 122 acres of land sold at Public Auction..WHEREAS ROBERT STARK, the absent debtor of Edgefield Co. SC was seized of said 122 acres and Whereas WILSON BLUNT, the Plaintiff in the County Court of Lexeton at June Term 1789 obtained & Recovered a Judgement of said court for 1414 pounds, and whereas said MARTIN then & now Sherriff of County did seize and give Legal notice to impose Sale of all that tract. S/ BARKLEY MARTIN. Wit: PETER CHASTAIN, RICHARD TUTT, Junr., who swore by oath 6 Sep 1791 before JOSEPH HIGHTOWER, J.P. Rcd. 6 Sep 1791.

Pp. 218-222. 3 Sep 1790 (sic): BARKLEY MARTIN, Esquire, Sheriff of Edgefield Co. SC to JOHN WALKER, Junr. for 4 pounds, sold at Public Auction 100 acres on Cuffee Town Creek bounded SE by PHILLIP PETER KNOBB and SW by MARIE ELIZABETH KNOBB. Said land granted to MARGARET KNOBB 24 Dec 1764 & conveyed by MARGARET KNOBB & NICHOLAS RAMSEY, her husband, to DAVID HUNTER 4 & 5 May 1779. and WHEREAS...DAVID HUNTER, the absent debtor was Seized of said 100 acres and WHEREAS.. MARY ROBERTS, widow & Executrix of goods & rights, & credits, which were of THOMAS ROBERTS, dec'd, The Plaintiff in Edgefield County Court Jan Term 1790 did obtain & Recover a Judgement in the sum of twenty nine four & five pence Sterling to be Levied against DAVID HUNTER and WHEREAS the said BARKLEY MARTIN then & now Sheriff did seize and give Legal notice, expose to Sale said tract. S/ BARKLEY MARTIN, S.E.C. Wit: PETER CHASTAIN, RICHARD TUTT, Junr., who swore by oath 6 Sep 1791 before JOSEPH HIGHTOWER, J.P. Rcd. 6 Sep 1791.

Pp. 222-226. 3 Sep 1791: BARKLEY MARTIN, Sherriff of Edgefield Co. SC to JOHN WALKER, Junr. of same place for 5 pounds, sold at Public Auction 100 acres on Reedy Creek of Cuffy Town Creek, granted to MARIA ELIZABETH KNOBB. and WHEREAS DAVID HUNTER, the absent debtor was seized of said property and Whereas MARY ROBERTS, widow & Executrix of THOMAS ROBERTS, dec'd, the Plaintiff in the Edgefield County Court Jan Term 1790 did obtain & recover a Judgement for 29 pounds...and Whereas said BARKLEY MARTIN, Sherriff, did seize and give Legal notice to expose to sale of land. S/ BARKLEY MARTIN, S.E.C. Wit: PETER CHASTAIN, RICHARD TUTT, Junr., who swore by oath 6 Sep 1791 before JOSEPH HIGHTOWER, J.P. Rcd. 6 Sep 1791.

Pp. 226-230. 3 Sep 1791: BARKLEY MARTIN, Esq., Sherriff of Edgefield Co. SC to DAVID TILLMAN of same place for 10 pounds, sold at Public Auction 120 acres on Cedar Creek a branch of Horns Creek...WHEREAS FREDERICK TILLMAN, the absent Debtor of Edgefield Co. SC was seized of 120 acres and Whereas JOHN JACOB MESSER SMITH, the Plaintiff in the county court of Edgefield Jan Term 1790 did obtain & Recover a Judgement for 90 pounds...and Whereas BARKLEY MARTIN did seize and give Legal notice to expose to sale of land. S/ BARKLEY MARTIN, S.E.C. Wit: PETER CHASTAIN, RICHARD TUTT, JUNR., who swore by oath 6 Sep 1791 before JOSEPH HIGHTOWER, J.P. Rcd. 6 Sep 1791.

Pp. 230-232. 23 Aug 1791: WILLIAM MARTIN & GEORGE D. MOORE of Edgefield Co. SC to CHARLES MARTIN for 100 pounds, Release and Forever Quit Claim 100 acres on Horns Creek, waters of Stephens Creek of Savannah River surveyed by PATRICK CUNNINGHAM 5 Feb 1771 or Certified 12 Feb 1771 and granted to JOSEPH SUMMERALL 10 Apr

1771, bounded NE by GEORGE EILAND and all other sides vacant at time of survey. The above said land was conveyed by JOSEPH SUMMERALL to WILLIAM MARTIN 28 Jan 1791 and he said WILLIAM MARTIN & GEORGE D. MOORE do convey to CHARLES MARTIN. S/ WILLIAM MARTIN, GEORGE D. MOORE. 24 Aug 1791 AQUILA MILES, J.P. witnessed above signing of Instrument. Rcd. 6 Sep 1791.

Pp. 232-235. 28 Jan 1791: JOSEPH SUMMERALL & SARAH, his wife, on Mileses Swamp the draught of Nassaw, the province of East Florida, Late from Ninety Six Dist., Edgefield Co. SC to WILLIAM MARTIN of SC for 80 pounds, Released and forever Quit Claim, 100 acres on Horns Creek of Stephens Creek of Savannah River, surveyed by PATRICK CUNNINGHAM by a Warrant dated 5 Feb 1771 bounded NE by GEORGE EILAND at time of survey & granted to JOSEPH SUMMERALL 10 Apr 1771. S/ JOSEPH SUMMERALL, SARAH (X) SUMMERALL. Wit: MILLS DRURY, GEORGE DRADON MOORE, who swore by oath 24 Aug 1791 before AQUILA MILES, J.P. Rcd. 6 Sep 1791.

Pp. 235-240. 5 May 1791: JAMES BROOKS of Edgefield Co. SC to STEPHEN TOMKINS of same plce for 50 pounds, sold 120 acres, being part of 2 tracts granted JAMES BROOK 22 Feb 1773 lying on the south side of Persimon Creek, bounded NE & SW on tracts belonging to said JAMES BROOKS & GEORGE ABNEY & NW by JAMES DAVIS. S/ JAMES (X) BROOKS. Wit: CHURCHILL GIBSON, AARON (X) BROOKS, who swore by oath 2 Jul 1791 before RUSSELL WILSON, J.P. Rcd. 6 Sep 1791.

Persimon Creek

At Request of JAMES BROOKS, I have ameasured out 120 acres unto STEPHEN TOMPKINS on south side of Persimmon Creek of Saluda River. 11 Mar 1791. Signed: SAML. MAYS, D.S.

Pp. 240-242. 11 May 1791: Bond: WILLIAM WILLIAMS of Montgomery Co. VA is bound unto DAVIS BOSWELL of Edgefield Co. SC for 1000 pounds, the condition of above obligation is that WILLIAM WILLIAMS & DAVID BOSWELL exchanged a small parcel of land on Chavers Creek and established the lines in the presence of REUBEN COOPER, ELIJAH HUTSON & ASIA WADE. Should the agreement of said line not be peaceably and quietly from this day forward, in that case the above obligation should be void & of none effect or else remain in full force & Virtue in Law. S/ WILLIAM WILLIAMS. Sworn by oath of JOSEPH HIGHTOWER, J.P. 7 Sep 1791 before AQUILLA MILES, J.P. Rcd. 7 Sep 1791.

Pp. 242-243. 17 Jun 1782: PHILIP JONES of the Commonwealth of Virginia to DANIEL EVANS of SC for 50 pounds, sold 200 acres in Beech Island on Savannah River, bounded NW by said river, SW by SARAH LAMAR and other sides vacant at time of survey. Said land was conveyed to MORDICAE JONES by THOMAS LAMAR and by the decease of said MORDICAI JONES, it fell to said PHILIP JONES his brother, being heir at law. S/ PHILIP JONES. Wit: THEODORICK GOODWYN, EDWARD BUGG, Junr. Rcd. 7 Sep 1791.

Pp. 244-245. 1 Dec 1791: DANIEL EVANS & POLLY, his wife, Planter of Burke Co. GA to ROBERT LAMAR of Edgefield Co. SC for 90

pounds, sold 100 acres being one-half (the other half being sold
to EDWARD ROWELL by the said DANIEL EVANS & POLLY, his wife) of
200 acres granted 8 Sep 1756 to THOMAS LAMAR, being on Savannah
River in Beech Island and bounded by SARAH LAMAR at the time of
the survey. S/ DANIEL EVANS, MARY EVANS. Wit: VINSON ROWELL,
JEMIMA JONES. Rcd. 7 Sep 1791.

Pp. 245-250. 1 Dec 1791: DANIEL EVANS & POLLY, his wife, Planter,
of Burke Co. GA to EDWARD ROWELL, Planter of Richmond Co. GA for
90 pounds, sold 100 acres being one-half (the other half being
sold to ROBERT LAMAR by said DANIEL EVANS & POLLY, his wife) of
200 acres granted 8 Sep 1756 to THOMAS LAMAR, being on Savannah
River in Beech Island and bounded by SARAH LAMAR at the time of
the survey. S/ DANIEL EVANS, MARY EVANS. Wit: JEMIMA JONES,
VINSON ROWELL, who swore by oath 14 May 1791 before JOHN
STURZENEGGER, J.P. Rcd. 7 Sep 1791.

Pp. 254-258. 1 Jun 1791: SAMUEL EDWARDS & MARY, his wife, of
Edgefield Co. SC to ABRAHAM RICHARDSON of same place for 30
pounds, sold 100 acres on the deer Savannah in Winton County,
being part of 200 acres granted to ELIJAH MERRY BAITIE 19 Aug
1774. Said tract was divided and the 100 acres above being on the
SE side of said tract or the opposite side from the Deer
Savannah. S/ SAMUEL (X) EDWARDS, MARY (X) EDWARDS. Wit: WILLIAM
JORDAN, DANIEL HEARN, CHARLES BANKS, who swore by oath 29 Aug
1791 before JOSEPH HIGHTOWER, J.P. Rcd. 12 Sep 1791.

Pp. 258-260. 26 Jul 1791: SARAH HOWARD, Spinster of Edgefield Co.
SC to THOMAS HOWARD, son of said SARAH HOWARD, for love and
affection and 21 Shillings paid to her by JNO. WALLACE, conveys
to THOMAS HOWARD all of Real and personal property before the
time said THOMAS HOWARD doth Marry may be Improved or Increased,
under the condition that said SARAH HOWARD may use, occupy &
enjoy said estate so long as said THOMAS HOWARD shall remain
unmarried. SARAH HOWARD for herself, her executors and
administrators, doth Covenant, grant & agree & with the said
THOMAS HOWARD his executors & administrators under the conditions
aforesaid shall peaceably & quietly hold. S/ SARAH (+) HOWARD.
Wit: HENRY (H) GUESS, JOHN LYON, who swore by oath 27 Jul 1791
before THOMAS BACON, J.P. Rcd. 20 Sep 1791.

Pp. 260-265. 14 Sep 1791 (sic): JAMES ROBINSON, Planter of Winton
Co. SC to ARTHUR SIMKINS, Esq. of Edgefield Co. SC for 10 pounds,
sold 100 acres, granted said ROBINSON 21 Apr 1774, being in
Edgefield Co. SC on the N, S, & W by ARTHUR SIMKINS & the
South side a line on Log Creek, a branch of Stephens Creek. S/
JAMES ROBERSON, SARAH (X) ROBERSON. Wit: BENJN. CLARK, WILLIAM
McCLENDON, JOHN RYAN, who swore by oath 8 Sep 1791 before WM.
ANDERSON, J.E.C. Rcd. 24 Sep 1791. (The second Indenture read
"this Indenture made & concluded this eightt day of Sept 1791.")

Pp. 1-10. 23 Jun 1791: JINKIN HARRIS, Planter of Edgefield Co. SC to JOHN SIMKINS, Planter of same place for 50 pounds, sold one-half acre, being part of 44 acres on which the Courthouse of Edgefield now stands, granted to DAVID BURKS 4 Sep 1785 & conveyed by him 29 & 30 Jun 1787 to DRURY MIMS and was conveyed by said MIMS to said JENKIN HARRIS 1 & 2 Aug 1787. S/ JINKIN (H) HARRIS. Wit: GEORGE YOUNGBLOOD, PEGGY (+) SIMKINS, NANCY DALBY, who swore by oath 26 Sep 1791 before ARTHUR SIMKINS, J.E.C. Rcd. 26 Sep 1791.

P. 10. 23 Sep 1791: Bill of Sale: RICHARD HAMPTON of Edgefield Co. SC to HERON & FRAZER for 12 pounds, sold a certain Yellow Sorrel horse, branded on shoulder with YU. S/ RICH. HAMPTON. Wit: WM. HERON, NATHANILE BACON, who swore by oath 23 Sep 1791 before JOHN PURVES, J.E.C. Rcd. 11 Oct 1791.

Pp. 11-17. 8 Aug 1791: JINKIN HARRIS & SARAH HARRIS of Edgefield Co. SC to RICHARD TUTT, Senr. of same place for 140 pounds, sold 140 acres, being a part of two tracts (1) 100 acres being on a branch of Turkey Creek & Stephens Creek called Beaver Dam and being a part of 300 acres granted 2 Mar 1768 to JAMES ROBERSON and transferred by Deed of Gift to his son, THOMAS ROBERSON & transferred 30 & 31 Jan 1778 by said THOMAS ROBERSON to JENKIN HARRIS, Senr., dec'd & by LW&T to SARAH & JENKIN HARRIS. (2) 40 acres, being part of above 300 acres which descended to JOHN HARRIS to JENKIN HARRIS by Lease 20 & 21 Dec 1787 & joins above 100 acres & is bounded by YOUNGBLOOD FURNACE & part of the original survey held by MOSES HARRIS & RACHEL OLIVER. S/ SARAH (S) HARRIS, JENKIN (H) HARRIS. Wit: MOSES HARRIS, ELIJAH YARD, RICHARD TUTT, Junr., who swore by oath 14 Oct 1791 before AQUILLA MILES, J.P. Rcd. 14 Oct 1791.

Pp. 17-18. 17 Sep 1791: Bill of Sale: GABRIEL TUTT of Edgefield Co. SC to BARKLEY MARTIN of same place for 80 pounds, sold a Negroe man named JACK of a Black Complexion about 23 years old. S/ GABRIEL TUTT. Wit: RICHARD TUTT, Junr., who swore by oath 7 Nov 1791 before RUSSELL WILSON, J.P. Rcd. 7 Nov 1791.

Pp. 18-26. 6 Sep 1790: Capt. VANN SWEARENGEN, Junr. of Edgefield Co. SC to EZEKIEL McCLENDON of same place for 100 pounds, sold 270 acres, being part of many surveys in particular part of a 200 acre tract granted to RICHARD PACE 19 Sep 1758 & is known by the name of the Pine Woods House lying West of same. Said land is bounded on the North by ISAAC KIRKLAND, W by JOHN RYAN - which part of said tract with the parts of the other tracts is now sold to said EZEKIEL McCLENDON. S/ VAN SWEARINGEN. Wit: THOMAS SWEARINGEN, ISAAC KIRKLAND, who swore by oath 7 Nov 1791 before RUSSELL WILSON. J.P. Rcd 7 Nov 1791.

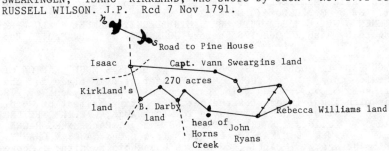

Road to Pine House

Isaac   Capt. Vann Sweargins land

Kirkland's   270 acres

land   B. Darby land   Rebecca Williams land

head of John Horns Ryans Creek

Pp. 26-30. 13 Apr 1791: ROBERT WARING of Claremont Co. SC Camden Dist. to WILLIAM BUTLER of Edgefield Co. SC for 50 pounds, sold 200 acres on Red Bank Creek, bounded E by JOHN SPANN & AMOS RICHARDSON & W by HENRY BRATCHEY. S/ ROBERT WARING. Wit: WM. COVINGTON, FREEMAN WIGHTT, RICHARD TUTT, Junr., who swore by oath 7 Nov 1791 before RUSSELL WILSON, J.P. Rcd. 7 Nov 1791.

Pp. 30-36. 8 Jan 1790: JOHN CHESNUT of Camden SC, Planter, to ISAAC MATHIS of Ninety Six Dist. SC for 100 pounds, sold 250 acres originally granted to WILLIAM WHITAKER 4 Oct 1768 & conveyed by said WHITAKER to JOHN CHESNUTT 27 & 28 Sep 1769. Said land bounded E by WILLIAM WEST at time of survey. S/ JOHN CHESTNUT. Wit: Camden Dist. SC JOHN KERSHAW, ZACHARIAH CANTEY, who swore by oath 9 Jan 1790 before J. ALEXANDER, J.P. Rcd. 7 Nov 1791.

Pp. 36-44. 24 Nov 1785: WILLIAM BOYD & ANN, his wife, of Chester Co. SC to ISAAC EVANS of Chester Co. SC for 100 pounds, sold 100 acres granted said BOYD 31 Oct 1769, being on Stephens Creek of Savannah River in Granville Co. S/ WILL BOYD, ANN BOYD. Wit: BENJAMIN CARTER, GEORGE BLESSET, who swore by oath 1 Feb 1791 before JOHN BELL, J.P. in Camden Dist. SC. Rcd. 26 Nov 1791.

Pp. 44-49. 3 Nov 1791: JOHN LOGAN, Esq. of Charleston SC to JOHN KILLCREASE, Planter, of Edgefield Co. SC for 50 pounds, sold 200 acres on Gunnels Creek a branch of Stephens Creek, bounded by RAILEY's line & STRAWDER's line. Said land granted to CHAMPNESS TERRY, dec'd, 9 Nov 1774 and was surveyed by WM. GOODE, D.S. 27 Sep 1774 and a Memorial entered 18 May 1775. Said land with other certain reasons & LW&T of JOHN LOGAN, Senr. was desired sold by his Executors and JOHN LOGAN, Junr., being an Executor does sell above property. S/ JOHN LOGAN. Wit: ISAAC PERRY, DEMSEY BUSSEY, who swore by oath 10 Nov 1791 before HUGH MIDDLETON, J.P. Rcd. 28 Nov 1791.

Pp. 50-54. 8 Jan 1790: ABSALOM GRIFFIN & SUSANNA, his wife, Planters of Edgefield Co. SC to CARY COX, Planter of same place for 50 pounds, sold 350 acres on branches of Turkey Creek of Savannah River, granted to THOMAS GRIFFIN 23 Jun 1774 and by him conveyed by deed of Gift to his son, ABSALOM GRIFFIN. S/ ABSALOM GRIFFIN, SUSANNAH (X) GRIFFIN. Wit: WILLIAM COX, CHARLES ASHLEY, TOLIVER COX, who swore by oath 10 Jan 1790 before JOHN PURVES, J.P. Rcd. 3 Dec 1791.

Pp. 54-60. 23 Jan 1785: PATRICK McCUTCHEN of Ninety Six Dist. to BENJAMIN TUTT of same place for 500 pounds, sold 640 acres granted said McCUTCHEN 15 Oct 1784, being South on Savannah River, SW by Mr. CROOK's, NW & NE by vacant land. S/ PATRICK (P) McCUTCHEN. Wit: JAS. TUTT, BENJAMIN BLACKEY, SAMUEL STALNAKER, who swore by oath 23 Dec 1785 before JOHN PURVES, J.P. Rcd. 3 Dec 1791.

Pp. 60-63. 11 Oct 1791: Mortgage & Bond: SAMUEL CRAFTON of Edgefield Co. SC to THOMAS KEY, Planter of same place for the penal sum of 566 pounds principal & condition of payment of 278 pounds with legal interest & the better securing payment of such, sold the following Negroes Slaves To Wit: JAMES, WILLIAM, PETER, & JACK - fellows, HARRY & STERLING - boys, CALLIENER, HAGER, SIMMERIA, TAMER & MIMA - women, two girls named NANCY & CHANEY. Also 8 horses, 17 cattle, 80 hogs & household furniture. Above obligation be paid then this bond be utterly void and of none effect. S/ SAML.CRAFTON. Wit: F. PARDUE, JOHN PURVES, who swore by oath 24 Oct 1791. Received this 11 Oct 1791, 278 pounds from THOMAS KEY by SAML. CRAFTON. Rcd 3 Dec 1791.

Pp. 64-65. 1 Dec 1791: Article of Agreement: JINKINS HARRIS of Edgefield Co. SC bargains with RACHEL OLIVER, alias CHENEY, concerning 60 acres of land joining ULYSES RODGERS, RICHARD TUTT, MOSES HARRIS & ARTHUR SIMKINS. Know ye that I RACHEL OLIVER for Love & affection I bear my two sons, EVIN CHAINY HARRIS & AUSTIN CHAINEY HARRIS, do give above land and that EVIN CHAINEY HARRIS will pay his sister TEMP 25 pounds when she married & 25 pounds to ELIZABETH CHENEY HARRIS when she marries. And that said RACHEL OLIVER may rent said land for their maintenance during her lifetime. S/ JINKINS (H) HARRIS, RACHEL OLIVER. Wit: ELIJAH YARD, ROBERT HATCHER, who swore by oath 12 Dec 1791 before AQUILA MILES, J.P. Rcd. 12 Dec 1791.

Pp. 65-71. 18 Oct 1791: LEONARD NOBLES & ANN, his wife, Planter of Edgefield Co. SC to LEROY HAMMOND of same place for 100 pounds, sold 213 acres on Walnutt Creek of Hornes Creek bounded NE by HENRY PARKMAN & WILLIAM ROADES, NW by BURREL JOHNSON, & SE by LEWIS COODY. Said land originally granted LEONARD NOBLES. S/ LEONARD NOBLES. Wit: A. WILLIAMSON, WILLIAM GARRETT, who swore by oath 21 Oct 1791 before JOHN PURVES, J.E.C. Rcd. 16 Dec 1791.

Pp. 72-77. 18 Nov 1791: JOHN HILL & JANE, his wife of Edgefield Co. SC to THOMAS PALMER of same place for 60 pounds, sold 150 acres on Mountain Creek, a branch of Stephens Creek, granted said JOHN HILL 23 Jan 1774 all sides vacant at time of survey. S/ JOHN HILL, JANE (X) HILL. Wit: JOHN WHITE, ALEXR.EDMONDS, THOMAS MILES, who swore by oath 21 Nov 1790 (sic) before AQUILA MILES, J.P. Rcd. 21 Dec 1791.

Pp. 77-82. 6 Jan 1791: JEREMIAH ROBERTS & ANN, his wife of Horns Creek, Ninety Six Dist. to THOMAS PALMER of same place for 5 shillings & 30 guineas sold 50 acres being part of 200 acres granted BENJAMIN HORN 4 Feb 1755 on Horns creek and joins a branch called ADAMS to a dividing line agreed on between said ROBERTS & PALMER, N by DRURY ADAMS, SE by THOMAS PALMER & Horns Creek. S/ JEREMIAH ROBERTS, NANCY (X) ROBERTS. Wit: DEMPSY BECKHAM, SHURROD (X) WHATLEY, DRURY ADAMS, who swore by oath 5 Feb 1791 before AQUILA MILES. Rcd. 21 Dec 1791.

Pp. 82-87. 26 Jan 1791: GEORGE HUNT, Merchant of Richman Co. GA to JOHN FREDERICK, Planter of Edgefield Co. SC for 20 pounds, sold 100 acres on each side of Clear Water & Horse Creek, branches of South fork of Eddisto River, which was once the property of MOSES KIRKLAND. S/ GEORGE HUNT. Wit: HUGH CRAMER, WILLIS FREDERICK.
Orangeburg Dist, Lexenton Co. SC: Sworn by oath of WILLIS FREDRICK 24 Dec 1791 before JOHN THOMAS FAIRCHILD, J.P. Rcd. 28 Dec 1791.

Pp. 87-88. 7 Mar 1792: ELIZABETH JONES of Columbia GA do appoint ABENIGO WRIGHT of same place my lawful attorney to sue for recovery from JAMES THOMPSON & WILLIAM SLEE of Charleston SC, Executors of LW&T of JESSE JONES, late husband of said ELIZABETH JONES now dec'd, a Legacy of 40 Pounds, with lawful interest 18

Dec 1789 and also interest of 54 pounds from the last mentioned date by LW&T of said JESSE JONES, dec'd from the maintainance of his Infant son, JOSHUA JONES. S/ ELIZABETH JONES. March Term 1792: Acknowledged in open court before R. TUTT, C.E.C. Wit: 7 Mar 1792 before RUSSELL WILSON, J.P. Rcd. 12 Mar 1792.

Pp. 88-93. 8 Jul 1783: JOHN EWING CALHOUN & THOMAS WARING, Senr., Commissioners of Forfited Estates of SC to THOMAS LAMAR, Senior of Ninety Six Dist., Planter for 34 pounds, sold 115 acres known as No. 9 being part of the land late the property of MOSES KIRKLAND bounded SW by RICHARD KIRKLAND as per Plat. S/ JOHN EWING CALHOUN, ROBT. WARING, Senr. (sic). Wit: JOHN ABNEY, WILLIAM ANDERSON, who swore by oath 5 Mar 1792 before JOSEPH HIGHTOWER, J.P. Rcd. 14 Apr 1792.

Pp. 93-94. 14 Feb 1791: Bill of Sale: JOSEPH COOK to OBEDIAH HENDERSON for 50 pounds, sold a quanity of Cattle, horses, marked with the brand IK and A. S/ JOS. COOK. Wit: ELIJAH LYON, WILLIAM COOK, both of whom swore by oath 25 Feb 1792 before AQUILA MILES, J.P. Rcd. 7 Mar 1792.

Pp. 94-96. 28 Mar 1792: Mortgage: JOSEPH HUSTON, Taylor, to WHITE & MOORE, Merchants, all of Edgefield Co. SC for 15 pounds, sold Smoaker - a bay horse, a mare & colt, 1 feather bed & furniture, 2 bedsteds, 1 brinded cow & calf, 1 heifer, 1 woman's saddle, 1 man's saddle, 2 bridles, 1 Silver Watch, 6 chairs, 1 hair trunk, 1 pot, 1 Dutch oven, 1 sett knives & forks, & 1 case bottles. If payment of above obligation be made this deed null & void. S/ JOSEPH HUSTON. Wit: RICHARD WALER THOMAS (sic) & RICHARD MOORE, both of whom swore by oath 20 Apr 1792 before ARTHUR SIMKINS. Rcd. 2 May 1792.

Pp. 96-104. 15 Mar 1792: TOLAVER DAVIS, Senr., Planter to DAVIS MOORE, Merchant, both of Edgefield Co. SC for 100 pounds, sold 150 acres surveyed for JOSEPH NOBLE 11 Sep 1767 and was conveyed by said JOSEPH NOBLE & RACHEL, his wife to JOHN MOCK, & was conveyed by said JOHN MOCK & MARY his wife to JOHN CHANEY & was conveyed by said JOHN CHANEY & MARTHA, his wife to said TOLAVER DAVIS. S/ TOLAVER DAVIS, Senr. Wit: JOHN WHITE, FREEMAN WIGHTT, who swore by oath 2 May 1792 before RICHARD TUTT, Esq., J.P. Rcd. 2 May 1792.

Pp. 105-106. 15 Mar 1792: Bill of Sale: TOLAVER DAVIS, Senr. of Edgefield Co. SC to DAVIS MOORE for 65 pounds, sold 1 negroe man slave named MAT, 1 negroe woman slave named GRACE, 1 mare 9 yrs old, 1 mare 4 yrs old, 4 beds, seven blankets, 9 sheets, 4 bolsters, 4 bedsteads, 6 chairs, 2 plows, 6 hoes, 4 axes, 1 loom, 8 head of cattle & 27 hogs. S/ TOLAVER DAVIS, Sr. Wit: JOHN WHITE, FREEMAN WIGHTT, who swore by oath 2 May 1792 before RICHARD TUTT, Esqr., J.P. Rcd. 2 May 1792.

Pp. 107-108. 14 Oct 1790: Letters of Attorney: JOSEPH DREW of Kingston in Kings County & province of New Brunswick, to WILLIAM ANDERSON, Esq. of Ninety Six Dist. SC Letters of Attorney to sell 150 acres on North prong of Halfway Swamp bounded NE by PAUL TRAPEN, SE by JOHN EDWARDS & SW by JOSEPH THOMAS. S/ JOSEPH DREW. Wit: CORNELIUS NICE, MARY HAMILTON.
Providence of New Brunswick, Kings Co: Signed before JOHN HAMILTON, J.P.

DEED BOOK 6: 1791-1792 EDGEFIELD COUNTY S.C.

Abbeville Co. SC: Sworn by oath of JOHN HAMILTON 29 Aug 1791 before JULIUS NICHOLS, Esq., J.P. Rcd. 12 Mar 1792.

Pp. 108-109. 25 Nov 1790: RICHARD KIRKLAND of Effingham Co. GA to ROLLY ROEBUCK for 25 pounds, sold 1 negroe girl named PEGG who is about 5 years old. S/ RICHARD KIRKLAND. Wit: STEPHEN MILLS, ROBERT (R) ROBUCK, who swore by oath 2 Jan 1792 before JOSEPH HIGHTOWER, J.P. Rcd 6 Jun 1792 by R. TUTT, C.E.C.

Pp. 110-112. 1 Jun 1792: Mortgage: HENRY FLEMING to BENJAMIN GLOVER for 29 pounds, mortgages for period not less than 8 months, which will be 1 Feb 1793, horses, cattle & household furniture to wit: 3 mares, 1 cow & calf, 2 feather beds, 1 chest, 1 trunk, 1 looking glass, 1 barrel & bushel salt, 1 table, 5 chairs, 2 smoothing irons, 2 Bibles, 40 milk pans, 10 crocks, 27 bowles, 2 pewter dishes, 8 plates, 6 basons, 1 tea & coffee pot, 1 dutch oven, 1 pott, 1 kettle, 1 gag, 1 saddle & 600 pounds of bacon, also 1 spinning wheel. S/ HENRY FLEMING. Wit: JOHN SMITHERS, JOHN E.GLOVER, who swore by oath in Abbeville Co. SC 1 Jun 1792 before JULIUS NICHOLS, Junr. 12 o'clock. Satisfaction entered R. TUTT, C.E.C. Rcd. 4 Jun 1792.

Pp. 112-115. 24 Apr 1792: Mortgage: SAMUEL CRAFTON to ROBERT ANDERSON, Esq. in penal sum of 172 pounds and payment of 81 pounds, not to be demanded before 24 Oct 1793 have sold negroe slaves, to Wit: JOHN CALUNER & HAGER. S/ SAML. CRAFTON. Signed, Sealed & Delivered in the Presence of open Knife WM. LESLEY, GABRIEL SMITHERS.
Abbeville Co. SC: Sworn by oath of GABRIEL SMITHERS 22 May 1792 before JULIUS NICHOLS, Junr. R. TUTT, C.E.C. Rcd. 4 Jun 1792.

Pp. 115-116. 25 Mar 1792: Bill of Sale: EDWARD BABER, Planter of Edgefield Co. SC to CHRISTOPHER BROOKS, Junr. of same place for 20 pounds, sold one negroe boy named HAMPTON, about 6 years old. S/ EDWD. BABER. Wit: CHRISTOPHER (Z) BROOKS, Senr., JAMES (+) VAUNN, Senr., who swore by oath 25 Mar 1792 before HENRY KING, J.P., R. TUTT, C.E.C. Rcd. 3 Sep 1792.

Pp. 116-117: 25 Mar 1792: Bill of Sale: EDWARD BABER, Planter, to JAMES VAUNN, Planter, both of Edgefield Co. SC for 20 pounds, sold one negroe boy named SAMBO, about 4 years old. S/ EDWARD BABER. Wit: LUCEY (X) DRINKARD, JOHN DRINKARD, who swore by oath 25 Mar 1792 before HENRY KING, J.P., RD. TUTT, C.E.C. Rcd. 3 Sep 1792.

Pp. 117-118. 5 Mar 1792: JOHN TURNER of Edgefield Co. SC to GABRIEL TUTT of same place for 50 pounds, sold 1 mare, 3 cows & calves & 35 head of hogs & all my household furniture. S/ JOHN TURNER. Wit: PATRICK GIBSON, RICHD. TUTT, Junr., who swore by oath 13 Mar 1792 before AQUILA MILES, J.P.

Pp. 118-119: 28 Sep 1792: We, the Heirs & Legatees of the Estate of WILLIAM BAKER of Jacksonburg SC, dec'd, empower BENJAMIN POSTELL, Executor to dispose of 1500 acres, sold to RICHARD JOHNSON at Jacksonburg 5 Apr 1787 & released BENJAMIN POSTELL, Executor from any damages of such sale & authorize to Cancel the first Sale to the said RICHARD JOHNSON. S/ RACHEL (X) MALLETT. Wit: RICHARD TUTT, J.P., JAMES MALLETT, who swore by oath 28 Sep 1792 before RICHARD TUTT, J.P.

69

Pp. 119-120. 21 Sep 1792: RACHEL MALLETT of Randolph Co. NC, widow, authorises my son, JAMES MALLETTE to go to BENJAMIN POSTELL of Charleston Dist. SC, Executor of WILLIAM BAKER Estate and apply for my proportion of said WILLIAM BAKER's Estate as willed to me, his sister, RACHEL MALLETT & said JAMES MALLETT is at Liberty to Settle with said Executor in my behalf. S/ RACHEL (+) MALLETT. Wit: SEALY (X his mark) HAYES, RICHARD JOHNSON, who swore by oath 28 Sep 1792 before RICHARD TUTT, J.P. Rcd. 28 Sep 1792.

Pp. 120-126. 12 Nov 1792: Bond: JOHN HAMMOND of Mount Airy of Edgefield Co. SC to ISAAC TEASDALE of Charleston SC for 3000 pounds on condition of payment of 1500 pounds with Interest at the rate of 7 pounds for 100 pounds for the year on 1st April next, sold two tracts of land, (1) 306 acres called Mount Airy now occupied by said JOHN HAMMOND and was granted JOSEPH HIGHTOWER 2 May 1785 and (2) 640 acres granted ROBERT COCKRAN in 1786 and is bounded partly on old Chickesaw land in Edgefield Co. SC. Also forty negroes: RACHAEL, BIG SAM, PATT, ALECK, BETTY, HANNAH, LITTLE RACHAEL, SILVA, BIG FORTUNE, PHILLIS, BIG AMY, MANSFIELD, JACK, LITTLE FORTUNE, BRAM, SILLER, LITTLE AMY, LITTLE MARY, PEG, SOLSBURY, PETER, JENNY, BILLY, ISABELLE, TOM, GRACE, BEN, MINGOE & TALLEY, APRIL, CASAR, SUE, BIG LEWIS, SINAH, LITTLE LEWIS, LANCE, BIG MARY, MARY ANN, LITTLE SAM & BRISTON. Also the horses cattle and sheep. S/ JOHN HAMMOND. Wit: W. DREW, GEO. TAYLOR.
14 Nov 1792: Whereas JOHN HAMMOND purchased of said ISAAC TEASDALE, Merchant of Charleston SC a large amount of goods, wares & merchandise entered in Book of Accounts of ISAAC TEASDALE & signed by JOHN HAMMOND subject to the Proviso within contained. S/ JOHN HAMMOND. Wit: ROBERT TROY, GEO. TAYLOR, who, with WILLIAM DREW, all of Charleston SC, swore by oath 8 Dec 1792 before J. BENTHAM. Rcd. 20 Dec 1792. R. TUTT, C.E.C.

Pp. 127-129. 6 Jan 1792: PHINIAS SUTTON of Edgefield Co. SC to BENJAMIN SUTTON of same place for 50 pounds, sold 299 acres being in fork between Edisto & Shaws Creek and was originally surveyed 7 Aug 1786. S/ PHINIAS SUTTON. Wit: CHARLES (his mark) SUTTON, MARY (X) FAIRCHILD.
Oringburg Dist. SC: Sworn by oath of CHARLES SUTTON 7 Jan 1792 before THOMAS FAIRCHILD, J.P.

Pp. 130-134. 27 Jan 1774: PETER YOUNGBLOOD of Granville Co. SC to JOHN FRAZIER, Planter, of same place for 100 pounds, sold 100 acres, being part of 300 acres granted to JOHN LAMAR, Senr. 1 Aug 1758 & conveyed unto said PETER YOUNGBLOOD. Said 100 acres is on the south & lower side of Beaverdam Creek of Savannah River in Granville Co. SC. S/ PETER (his mark) YOUNGBLOOD, MARY (M) YOUNG - BLOOD.

Wit: XMAS (THOM also) RAY, JENKIN (IH) HARRIS, MOSES HARRIS, who swore by oath 9 Jul 1774 before MOSES KIRKLAND, J.P.

Pp. 134-137. 16 Jan 1792: DANIEL DAY of Edgefield Co. SC to LEROY HAMMOND of same place for 200 pounds, sold 400 acres on Savannah

River commony called New Richmond. S/ DANIEL(O) DAY. Wit: GEO. HENNESSEY, THOMAS VOILETT, JOSHUA HAMMOND, who swore by oath 17 Jan 1792 before JOHN PURVES, J.P.

Pp. 137-141. 2 Aug 1790: WILLIAM ABNEY of Edgefield Co. SC to JOHN CLARK of same place for 100 pounds, sold 200 acres on the Middle Tarupen Creek of Saluda River bounded N by ABRAHAM LITTLE, W by STOUKLEY TOWLES & WILLIAM ABNEY at time of survey when granted to said WILLIAM ABNEY 21 Jan 1785. S/ WM ABNEY. Wit: EDWARD THURATT, JACOB NORRELL, ROBERT McKEE (also McKIE), who swore by oath 5 Aug 1790 before W. ANDERSON, J.P. Rcd. 26 Jan 1792.

Pp. 141-143. 21 Dec 1790: NATHANIEL FOOSHE of Winton Co. SC to JOHN CLARK of Edgefield Co. SC for 50 pounds, sold 100 acres on the Taripan Creek granted to STOCKLY TOWLES & conveyed by him to NATHANIEL FOOSHE. S/ NATHANIEL (X) FOOSHE. Wit: BENJAMIN TAYLOR, JOHN (X) TOWLES. Rcd. 26 Jan 1792. W. ANDERSON, J.C.E.

Pp. 144-146. 28 Feb 1791: JOSIAH STEVENS of Little Stevens Creek, Edgefield Co. SC to ELISHA STEVENS of the creek, Edgefield Co. SC for Love & Affection of said ELISHA STEVENS and for the better maintainence & livelyhood of him, do grant 200 acres where said JOSIAH STEVENS now lives and also all cattle, horses, hoggs, house furniture, plantation tools & every article moveable & immoveable that said JOSIAH STEVENS possesses. S/ ISIAH STEVENS (written JOSIAH in content of deed & signed ISIAH) Wit: FREDERICK WILLIAMS, JOSIAH (X) THOMAS, ALEXANDER BEAN, who swore by oath 17 Dec 1791 before RUSSELL WILSON, J.P.

Pp. 146-149. 1 Dec 1790: CHARLES JOHNSTON of Charleston SC to ABNER PERRIN of Edgefield Co. SC for 100 pounds, sold a certain 100 acre tract of land near Hard Labour Creek of Stevens Creek, a branch of Savannah River, originally granted JOHN MURRAY, Esq. for 1000 acres, but dimished in Quantity by Smaller Grants. S/ CHAS. JOHNSTON. Wit: ROBERT M. JOHNSTON, JOHN PURVIS, Esq., who swore by oath 11 Jan 1791 before W. ANDERSON, J.P. Rcd. 11 Feb 1792.

Pp. 149-151. 15 Aug 1791: SARAH BARNS, Widow of Edgefield Co. SC hath put her son, JAMES BARNS, age 13 years & 6 months, to be apprentice to RICHARD WITHINGTON, Farmer of Edgefield Co. SC until JAMES BARNS reaches the age of 21 years. Said JAMES BARNS is to serve his Master and said Master is to furnish food, clothing and lodging and 1 year of schooling. S/ SARAH (ᴓ) BURNS, RICHARD (W) WITHINGTON. Wit: MENOAH (+) WITHINGTON (also WEATHINGTON), SUSANER WATSON, WILLIAM WATSON, Senr., who swore by oath 11 Feb 1792 before JOSEPH HIGHTOWER, J.P. Rcd. 13 Feb 1792.

Pp. 151-154. 14 Feb 1792: Whereas BENJAMIN BLACKEY of Edgefield Co. SC, Farmer, hereunto moving and being justly indebted unto JOHN & MARY CLIMM of same place for the sum of 50 pounds (25 pounds to each) payment of such by 2 Jan 1799 and their better securing payment, sells 12 head of meat cattle, 1 waggon, household furniture, plantation tools & stock of hogs. Should payment be made then agreement be null & void. S/ BENJAMIN BLACKEY. Wit: BETTY TUTT, LEWIS BRYANT, who swore by oath 14 Feb 1792 before R. TUTT, J.P. Rcd. 14 Feb 1792.

Pp. 154-160. 25 Feb 1792: BARKLEY MARTIN, Esq., Sheriff of

DEED BOOK 6: 1791-1792 EDGEFIELD COUNTY S.C.

Edgefield Co. SC to CHRISTOPHER SHAW of same place for 21 pounds, sold 400 acres...WHEREAS...JAMES VESSELS, Senr. the absent Debtor was seized of a tract of 400 acres, being part of 638 acres granted JAMES VESSELS 13 Nov 1784 being on the South fork of Foxes Creek waters of Savannah River, bounded SE by LOGGINGS, BENJ. WARRING, NE by land surveyed for WILL: DAVIS, NW by JOSHUA HAMMOND & DAVISON line, and WHEREAS... JOHN HIGHTOWER, the plaintiff did obtain a Judgement of the Court to be levied of the goods & Chattles of JAMES VESSELS, Senr. S/ BARKLEY MARTIN. Wit: JUDAH CHASTAIN, RICHARD TUTT, Junr., who swore by oath 27 Feb 1792 before R. TUTT, J.P.

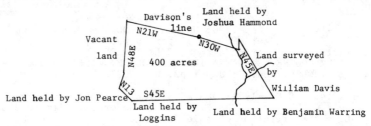

Plat of 400 acres surveyed for JAMES VESSELS 13 Nov 1784 on a warrant dated 12 Sep 1784, being part of 638 acres on South fork of Foxes Creek of Savannah River. Surveyed 7 Jan 1792 by CHARLES BANKS, D.S.

Pp. 160-161. 2 Apr 1791: CHARLES DUPONT of Lyncoln Co. SC to JOHN CHENEY of SC for 80 pounds, sold one negro man named TOM. S/ CHARLES DUPONT. Wit: MARY M. MILAR.
19 May 1791: JOHN CHENEY to BARKLEY MARTIN, Esq. of Edgefield Co. SC for 80 pounds, sold one negro man named TOM. S/ JOHN CHENEY. Wit: JOHN C. GARRETT, JAMES LIVINGSTON, who swore by oath 2 Mar 1792 the Bill of Sale of JOHN CHANEY before AQUILA MILES, J.P. Rcd. 8 Mar 1792.

Pp. 161-167. 5 Mar 1792: JOHN RYAN & MARTHA, his wife, of Horns Creek of Edgefield Co. SC to ABRAHAM HERNDON of Edgefield Co. SC for 100 pounds, sold 147 acres that was granted JOHN RYAN 1 Jan 1787 being on the waggon road that leads from the Pine woods House to Augusta. S/ JOHN RYAN, MARTHA RYAN. Wit: JOHN LUCAS, Junr., JAMES WALKER, who swore by oath 8 Mar 1792 before JOSEPH HIGHTOWER, J.P. Rcd. 9 Mar 1792.

Pp. 167-173. 5 Mar 1792: GEORGE RANDOL & PHEBE, his wife, of Edgefield Co. SC to ABRAHAM HERNDON of same place for 25 pounds, sold 100 acres that was granted said RANDOL 7 Jun 1790, being on the new road from Congree to Augusta on West side of Shaws Creek. S/ GEORGE (X) RANDOL, PHEBE RANDOL. Wit: EZEKIEL ROEBUCK, DANIEL RITCHY, who swore by oath 8 Mar 1792 before JOSEPH HIGHTOWER, J.P. Rcd. 9 Mar 1792.

Pp. 174-180. 7 Feb 1792: BRIENT GREEN & PHEBE, his wife of Edgefield Co. SC to ABRAHAM HERNDON of same place for 200 pounds, sold 350 acres, originally granted to SOLOMON WOOD 28 Jul 1775, and bounded South by WM. PINES at the time of the survey. S/ BRIENT (B) GREEN, PHEBE GREEN. Wit: WM. FUDGE, DANIEL RITCHY, who swore by oath 8 Mar 1792 before JOSEPH HIGHTOWER, J.P. Rcd. 9 Mar 1792.

72

DEED BOOK 6: 1791-1792 EDGEFIELD COUNTY S.C.

Pp. 180-181. 7 Feb 1792: JOHN HERNDON of Edgefield Co. SC to ABRAHAM HERNDON of same place for 317 pounds, sold All my house hold furniture, 1 stud horse named Sweet Larry, 1- 10 yr old mare named Driver with her colt, 1 - 7 or 8 yr old yelding, 1 grey yelding named Tuckery Grey, 1 grey yelding, 1 bay yelding named Punch (6 yrs old), 10 head of cattle, 30 head of hogs, 200 bushels of corn, & plantation tools of all kins. (for descriptions of brands & marks get original deed). S/ JOHN HERNDON. Wit: BENJAMIN REYNOLDS, DANIEL RITCHY, who swore by oath (no date) before JOSEPH HIGHTOWER, J.P. Rcd. 9 Mar 1792.

Pp. 182-183. 17 Feb 1792: JOHN HERNDON of Edgefield Co. SC to ABRAHAM HERNDON of same place for 350 pounds, sold the following negroes Namely: a 21 yr old negroe fillow named QUACH of brown complexion: WILL a negroe fellow about 22 yrs old of dark complected; HAGAR a negro wench 18 yrs old also her son HARRY, both dark complected & a negro wench named HAGAR 38 yrs old of a dark complexion. S/ JOHN HERNDON. Wit: BENJ. REYNOLDS, DANIEL RITCHY, who swore by oath 8 Mar 1792 before JOSEPH HIGHTOWER. Rcd. 9 Mar 1792.

Pp. 183-189. 1792: JOHN HERNDON of Edgefield Co. SC to ABRAHAM HERNDON of same place for 150 pounds, sold 100 acres on the main Road from Augusta to the Ridge known by the name of the old Well Granted to FIELDING REYNOLDS 3 Apr 1786. S/ JOHN HERNDON. Wit: BENJ. REYNOLDS, DANIEL RITCHY, who swore by oath 8 Mar 1792 before JOSEPH HIGHTOWER, J.P.

Pp. 189-192. 28 Feb 1792: Bond & Mortgage: ALEXANDER NEWMAN, Planter of SC is firmly bound to WALTER TAYLOR, Planter of Edgefield Co. SC for the penal sum of 400 pounds for payment of 200 pounds on or before 10 Jun 1792 and for the better securing of payment do sell fore negroes: BILLY, FRED, SAM, & WILL. S/ ALEXR NEWMAN.
Signed, Sealed & Delivered a knife in Lue of the whole in the presents of J. McELHENNY, SAML.DUNBAR, who swore by oath 7 Mar 1792 before JOHN STURZENEGGER, J.P. Rcd. 12 Mar 1792.

Pp. 192-193. 17 Jun 1791: Bill of Sale: MOSES HARRIS of Wilks Co. GA to REUBEN KIRKLAND of Edgefield Co. SC for 60 pounds, sold a negroe boy about 9 years old named DANIEL. S/ MOSES HARRISS. Wit: JOHN (B) MILLER, JONATHAN WEVER, who swore by oath 3 Feb 1792 before HENRY KING, J.P. Rcd. 12 Mar 1792.

Pp. 193-200. 10 Nov 1788: ROBERDS THOMAS of Green Co. GA, Planter, to WILLIAM LITTLE of Edgefield Co. SC for 15 pounds, sold 55 acres on Burnetts Creek of Little Saludy River, bounded NE by JOHN SIMKINS when surveyed and granted 5 Jun 1786. S/ ROBERDS THOMAS. Wit: SOLOMON POPE, SAML. ESKRIDGE, JOSIAH (O) THOMAS, who swore by oath 23 Apr 1791 before RUSSELL WILSON, J.P. Rcd. 12 Mar 1792.

Pp. 200-205, 9 Apr 1791: AMBROSE GORDON & ELIZABETH, his wife of Richmond Co. GA, Esquire, to GEORGE BENDER of Beech Island, Edgefield Co. SC for 400 pounds, sold 200 acres in Beech Island bounded S by GEORGE BENDER, E by LUD WILLIAMS, N by heirs of JOHN NEALE & W by Savannah River. Said 200 acres was originally granted to LEONARD SWITZER, now dec'd & was conveyed by LEONARD SWITZER, his heir at law to said AMBROSE GORDON. S/ AMBROSE

73

DEED BOOK 6: 1791-1792 EDGEFIELD COUNTY S.C.

GORDON, ELIZABETH GORDON. Wit: HENRY ARINTON, JONA MEYER, who swore by oath 2 Sep 1791 before JOHN STURZENEGGER, J.P. Rcd. 12 Mar 1792.

Pp. 206-214. 19 Jan 1785: LEONARD SWITZER to AMBROSE GORDON of Richmond Co. GA for 500 pounds, sold a certain tract of land on Beach Island in Granville Co. SC bounded S by GEORGE BENDER, E by LUD WILLIAMS, N by heirs of JOHN NEALE & W by Savannah River, being originally granted LEONARD SWITZER, dec'd. S/ LEONARD SWITZER. Wit: JOSEPH MILLER, THEO WYATT, JOHN MEALS, who swore by oath 9 Sep 1791 before DALZIEL HUNTER, Esq. of Richmond Co. GA. Received from within named AMBROSE GORDON 5 negroe fellows, his obligation being equal to 500 pounds being the full consideration S/ LEONARD SWITZER.

Pp. 215-216. 10 Feb 1792: Bill of Sale: JOSIAH THOMAS, Yeoman, of Edgefield Co. SC to BARROTT TRAVIS, Planter, of same place for 50 pounds, sold one negroe girl named BETT, about 9 yrs old. S/ JOSIAH THOMAS. Wit: RAYDON GRIGSBY, ALEXANDER WILSON, who swore by oath 10 Feb 1792 before HENRY KING, J.P. Rcd. 12 Mar 1792.

Pp. 216-217. 19 Nov 1789: Bill of Sale: BARTLETT BLEDSOE of Edgefield Co. SC to DUDLEY PREWIT of same place for 50 pounds, sold one negro boy named JUBE about 12 years old. S/ BARTLET (B) BLEDSOE. Wit: JOHN BLEDSOE, JEREMIAH MOBLEY, who swore by oath 23 Jan 1792 before HENRY KING, J.P.
27 Nov 1790: I, DUDLEY PUET to BARRET TRAVIS for 45 pounds, sell one negroe boy named JUBE. S/ DUDLEY (X) PUET. Wit: CHARLES (X) PARTAIN, ALEXANDER WILSON, who swore by oath 23 Jan 1792 before HENRY KING, J.P.

Pp. 217-222. 26 Apr 1788: ROBERDS THOMAS of GA to WILLIAM LITTLE of Edgefield Co. SC for 19 pounds, sold 100 acres on Burnetts Creek of Little Saluday River. S/ ROBERDS THOMAS. Wit: HIGDON BORROUM, JOHN THOMAS, Junr., JON THORN (or THOM), JOHN POPE, who swore by oath 28 May 1791 before JAMES SPANN, J.P. Rcd. 12 Mar 1792.

Pp. 222-230. 13 Aug 1790: FRANCIS HIGGINS & SARAH, his wife of Newberry Co. SC to THOMAS WILLOUGHBY WATERS, Esqr. of same place for 160 pounds, sold 400 acres granted HENRY MEDCALF 16 Dec 1766 on South side of Saluda River with all sides vacant, but now surveyed by NATHANIEL ABNEY and bounded on upper side by NATHANIEL ABNEY & the Widow ABNEY the lower side on said river & by JNO. ABNEY. Said land was conveyed by LW&T of HENRY MEDCALF to his son, HENRY MEDCALF & conveyed by Lease by said HENRY MEDCALF to FRANCIS HIGGINS. S/ FRANCIS HIGGINS, SARAH (her mark) HIGGINS. Wit: JOHN GIGLETILER, JAMES COX, who swore by oath 23 Feb 1792 before NATHANIEL ABNEY, J.P. Rcd. 12 Mar 1792.

Pp. 230-238. 6 Jan 1791: THOMAS WILLOUGHBY WATERS & FRANCES, his wife, of Newberry Co. SC to NATHANIEL ABNEY of Edgefield Co. SC for 180 pounds, sold 400 acres (Same description as above deed). S/ THOMAS W. WATERS, FANNEY WATERS. Wit: MATTHEW WILLS, JOEL ABNEY, WILLIAM SPRAGINS, who swore by oath 19 Jan 1791 before JOHN MOORE, J.P.

Pp. 239-246. 4 Jan 1792: WILLIAM ODOM of Ninety Six Dist. SC to JOHN MURFEY of Fairfield Co. SC, Planter, for 50 pounds, sold 100 acres on the Ridge of Clouds Creek of Saluday River, bounded NW by PEARSON's land and other 3 sides vacant at time granted 21 Jan 1785. S/ WILLIAM ODOM, MARY (~) ODOM. Wit: JOHN VARDELL, MOSES HARRISON, JESSE (+) HOUSE (also HOUS), who swore by oath 3 Mar 1792 before RUSSELL WILSON, J.P. Rcd. 12 Mar 1792.

Pp. 247-248. 10 Nov 1792: DANIEL BRUNER, Trader of the Creek Naition appoint my lawful attorney, Mr. JOHN MURRAY Planter, of SC to recover all dues & impower him to sell any or all my said tracts of land & make ample titles. S/ DANIEL (DB) BRUNER. Wit: ALEXANDER McGILLURAY of CN, ISAAC PERRY, who swore by oath 14 Feb 1793 (sic) before JOSEPH HIGHTOWER, J.P. Rcd. 23 Feb 1793 (sic).

Pp. 248-249. 10 Feb 1792: Bill of Sale: ALLEN HINTON of Edgefield Co. SC to BARKLEY MARTIN for 40 pounds, sold one negroe girl named WINNEY. S/ ALLEN HINTON. Wit: EDMOND MARTIN, JOHN MARTIN, who swore by oath 13 Mar 1792 before RICHARD TUTT, J.P. Rcd. 13 Mar 1792.

Pp. 249-250. 20 Feb 1793: ANDREW HARKNESS swore before JOSEPH HIGHTOWER, J.P. of Edgefield Co. SC that sometime in the beginning of the month of January last, this deponant left a Bond given by JAMES KING & JOHN ANDERSON security for 500 pounds to make him & JOHN PUSSELL rights to Lot #23 in Campbelton with THOMAS HERRON to take care of for him & he this deponant never traded said Bond nor Indorsed it to any person & that he has since demanded it of said HERRON & could not get it. S/ ANDREW HARKNESS. Rcd. 26 Feb 1793.

Pp. 250-257. 20 Feb 1792: JOHN HERNDON of Edgefield Co. SC to THOMAS WITHINGTON of same place for 27 pounds, sold 77 1/3 acres granted 5 Jun 1786 and is bounded by lands of THOMAS WITHINGTON, Heirs of JOHN DOOLY, CLACKLER, LEROY HAMMOND, JOHN HERNDON. S/ JOHN HERNDON. Wit: BENJAMIN HIGHTOWER, ABSALOM (A) ROBERTS, THOS. (T) MOSLEY, who swore by oath 21 Feb 1792 before JOSEPH HIGHTOWER, J.P.
Mrs. RUTH HERNDON released her dower & thirds before ARTHUR SIMKINS, Esq. Rcd. March Term 1792.

Pp. 258-260. 18 Feb 1791: WILLIAM THOMAS of Saint Mathews Parish & Orangeburg Dist. SC to JOHN POOL of Edgefield Co. SC for 30 pounds, sold 150 acres on the Half Way Swamp of Saluday River joining lands of the said JOHN POOL. S/ WM. THOMAS. Wit: WILLIAM HOLLOWAY, JAMES ADAMS, JOHN (I) HOLLOWAY, Sen., who swore by oath 10 Mar 1792 before JOHN MOORE, J.P. Rcd. 12 Mar 1792.

Pp. 260-267. 13 Mar 1792: PETER CARNS, Attorney at Law, of Augusta, Richmond Co. GA to JAMES JONES of Edgefield Co. SC for 100 pounds, sold 120 acres on Buckhalters Creek being part of a tract where said PETER CARNES formerly resided being on Carnes Spring Branch, Lows Creek, formerly known as Buckhalters Creek and joins JOHN LOW's line. S/ PETER CARNS. Wit: LEWIS NOBLES, JOHN RYAN, who swore by oath 14 Mar 1792 before JOSEPH HIGHTOWER, J.P. Rcd. 14 Mar 1792.

Pp. 267-269. 5 Sep 1791: JOHN HARRIS of Edgefield Co. SC to WILLEY GLOVER for 100 pounds, sold one negroe wench about 16 yrs old named SUCK & a negro boy about 12 yrs old named GEORGE. 1 mare about 8 yrs old named Sweep Stackes. S/ JOHN HARRIS. Wit:

DEED BOOK 6: 1791-1792 EDGEFIELD COUNTY S.C.

JOHN NORWOOD, ELIJAH MOORE, who swore by oath in open court 14 Mar 1792.

Pp. 269-278. 23 Feb 1792: JOSEPH THOMAS & JOICE, his wife, of GA to PETER CHASTAIN of Edgefield Co. SC for 100 pounds, sold 150 acres on both sides of Lloyds Creek with all sides vacant when surveyed & granted said JOSEPH THOMAS 14 Aug 1775. S/ JOSEPH THOMAS, JOYCE THOMAS. Wit: WILLIAM KEY, WILLIAM (H) HOWLE, Senr., JAMES CHASTAIN, who swore by oath 19 Mar 1792 before R. TUTT, J.P. Rcd. 19 Mar 1792.

Pp. 278-285. 9 Mar 1792: ANN ZUBLY, Executrix of LW&T of the late DAVID ZUBLY, Esq., dec'd, & by power invested by said Will to CHARLES RANSAY, both of Edgefield Co. SC, for 12 pounds, sold 100 acres being in the fork of Town & Hollow Creeks, at the time of Survey in Granville Co. now Winton Dist. of Orangeburgh. Said tract originally granted to CRONOMUS ZINN 1 Mar 1775 and was conveyed by Lease 15 Sep 1787 by JACOB ZINN, Junr. unto DAVID ZUBLY. S/ ANN ZUBLY, Executrix. Wit: JONA MEYER, CASPER NAIL, Junr., who swore by oath 15_ 1792 before JOHN STURZENEGGER, J.P. Rcd. 16 Mar 1792.

Pp. 285-294. 15 Mar 1792: ANN ZUBLY, Executrix of LW&T of the late DAVID ZUBLY, Esq., dec'd, & by power invested by said will to JOHN PRYOR, Mill Wright, both of Edgefield Co. SC for 147 pounds, sold 1480 acres, being taken out of 3 tracts of lands; (1) part of 640 acres called the Old Mill Seat, originally granted to DAVID ZUBLY 21 Jan 1785 bounded NE by BURGESS & SE by JOHN HIX, (2) being part of 640 acres originally granted JOHN HIX 1 Jan 1785 bounded on NW by DAVID ZUBLY and was conveyed 10 Sep 1787 by said JOHN HIX to DAVID ZUBLY, (3) being part of 1200 acres granted DAVID ZUBLY 4 Dec 1786 bounded NW by DAVID ZUBLY & one PARKER & the remaining 1000 acres was sold to JOHN PRYOR by said DAVID ZUBLY. S/ ANN ZUBLY, Executrix. Wit: WILLIAM STEWART, JONA MEYER, SAMUEL BURGESS, who swore by oath 15 Mar 1792 before JOHN STURZENEGGER, J.P. Rcd. 16 Mar 1792.

Pp. 295-306. 25 Jan 1792: DRURY MIMS & LIDIA, his wife, Planter of Edgefield Co. SC to ARTHUR SIMKINS, Esq. of same place for 300 pounds, sold 43 acres on Beaverdam Creek of Stephens Creek of Savannah River, bounded South on land formerly belonging to JOHN HARRISS, but now held by RACHEL OLIVER. Said 43 acres being part of 44 acre Grant to DAVID BURKS 5 Sep 1785 & was conveyed by him & his wife, JANE unto DRURY MIMS 29 Jun 1787, except two half acre lots which was conveyed to MOSES HARRIS & JENKINS HARRIS. S/ DRURY MIMS, LYDIA (X) MIMS. Wit: MARY (M) BARRONTINE, DANIEL PARKER, JOHN SIMKINS, who swore by oath 19 Mar 1792 before W. ANDERSON, J.E.C. Rcd. 19 Mar 1792.
LYDIA MIMS relinquished Dower 12 Mar 1792.

Pp. 306-311. 14 Dec 1791: JOHN WALLACE & JOSEPH WALLACE of Edgefield Co. SC to JOSEPH MORTON of same place for 300 pounds, sold 445 acres of land, being of 3 tracts of land; (1) a tract of 155 acres; (2) a tract of 100 acres; & (3) a tract of 190 acres. Said land runs near Mr. JAMES' store. Two of the tracts was granted to ROBERT WALLACE, dec'd, and the other tract was granted to JOHN WALLACE now on record in the Clerk's Office. S/ JOHN WALLACE, JOSEPH WALLACE. Wit: WILLIAM EVANS, JOHN BACON, JAMES SANDERS, who swore by oath 3 Apr 1792 before RICHARD TUTT, J.P.

76

DEED BOOK 6: 1791-1792 EDGEFIELD COUNTY S.C.

27 Feb 1792: ISBELL WALLACE, Relict of ROBERT WALLACE, received a valuable consideration from JOSEPH MORTON & do hereby release Quit Claim to all my rights title dower & claim to described property by annexed conveyance made said MORTON by my sons, JOHN & JOSEPH WALLACE. S/ ISBEL (X) WALLACE. Rcd. 3 Apr 1792.

Pp. 311-312. Title of Deed - THOMAS BELL to THOMAS YATES: Know all men that I the Subscriber sold to THOS. YATES of North Carolina a tract of land, the property of Colonal BELL of Hard Labour Creek for 200 pounds to be paid the said Colonal THOS. BELL at or before 3 Dec 1768, & I do give YATES possession by Colonal BELL's orders to me this 14 Nov 1767. S/ JAMES MAYSON.

Glasgow - 23 Sep 1768: I approve of the Sale made by JAMES MAYSON, Esq. of 200 acres lying on Wilsons Creek & make titles unto THOMAS YEATS. S/ THOS. BELL.
Ninety Six Dist. SC: Lessee of ANDERSON for Yates agt. JAMES MAYSON accor.

PATRICK CALHOUN & LEROY HAMMOND, Esq. made oath they are well acquainted with the hand writing of Colonel THOMAS BELL and that the paper now produced was of the writing of the named THOS. BELL. S/ PAT CALHOUN. Sworn by oath 3 Dec 1789 before WILLIAM MOORE, J.P. Rcd. 6 Apr 1792.

Pp. 312-322. 7 Mar 1792: BARTLETT BLEDSOE, Yeoman, of Edgefield Co. SC to LODOWICK HILL of same place for 25 pounds, sold 180 acres, being part of 793 acres granted said BLEDSOE 1 Oct 1787 on Penn Creek of Little Saludy River and is bounded by LODOWICK, WRIGHT NICHOLSON, ROBERT STARK & GEORGE MASON's lands. S/ BARTLET BLEDSOE. Wit: WRIGHT NICHOLSON, GEORGE MASON, who swore by oath 26 Mar 1792 before HENRY KING, J.P. Rcd. 6 Apr 1792.

Pp. 323-329. 20 Mar 1792: Bond & Mortgage: SAMUEL WRIGHT of Edgefield Co. SC to JOSEPH DAY by bond bound the penal sum of 50 pounds or 8000 weight of crop Tobacco, that the condition of payment of 25 pounds or 4000 weight Tobacco be paid by 1 Nov next. Also for better securityship do sell one sorril horse with 111 1/2 acres, being the plantation I now live on generally know by the name of Poverty Hill. S/ SAML. WRIGHT. Wit: JOHN GRISSAM, ANDREW HARKNESS, who swore by oath 9 Apr 1792 before WM. ANDERSON, J.E.C. Rcd. 11 Apr 1792.

Pp. 330-332. 4 Apr 1792: ISAAC HOPKINS of Edgefield Co. SC to JOHN RYAN for 25 pounds, sold a certain parcel of property Viz: 2 feather beds, 4 plates, 1 bason & 9 head of hogs. S/ ISAAC HOPKINS. Wit: GEORGE MILLER, CLEMENT CARGILL, who swore by oath 5 Apr 1792 before JOSEPH HIGHTOWER, J.P. Rcd. 16 Apr 1792.

Pp. 332-335. 2 Apr 1792: WILLIAM EVANS, Dept. Surv. of Edgefield Co. SC to WILLIAM SHINHOLSER, Planter of same place for 100 pounds, sold 240 acres in New Windsor, Edgefield Co. SC that joins BENJAMIN HARRIS' corner, DAVID ZUBLY's line, dec'd, then with several lines of JOHN RICHARDSON's plat of which it is a part of. S/ WM. EVANS. Wit: JOHN SAVAGE, CASPER NAIL, Junr., who swore by oath 17 Apr 1792 before JOHN STURZENEGGER, J.P. Rcd. 18 Apr 1792.

Pp. 335-343. 8 Jan 1792: EPHRIAM PUCKITT of Winton Co. SC, Planter, to ARTHUR SIMKINS, Esq. of Edgefield Co. SC for 60 pounds, sold 250 acres between Saluda & Savannah Rivers, now Edgefield Co. on Little Turkey Creek of Stephens Creek of Savannah River bounded NW by ARTHUR SIMKINS, SE & NW by bounty land and all other sides vacant when surveyed & granted EPHRIAM PUCKITT 7 May 1774. S/ EPHRIAM PUCKITT. Wit: ELIZABETH PUCKITT, THOMAS PUCKITT, CHARLES BANKS, who swore by oath 2 Apr 1792 before JOSEPH HIGHTOWER, J.P. Rcd. 18 Apr 1792.

Pp. 343-353. 12 Apr 1792: Reverant JOHN 'SPRINGER of Wilks Co. GA to WILLIAM ROBINSON of Edgefield Co. SC for 170 pounds, sold 200 acres on branch of Ninety Six Creek called Beaverdam branch, bounded at the time of survey SW by WILLIAM ROBERTSON & THOMAS HEARDS, NW by MARY SMITH. The said 200 acres was a part of 350 acres granted to ROBERT McCUTCHEN 13 Jul 1762 and was conveyed to THOMAS HEARD in 2 seperate tracts of 100 acres each by Deed 24 & 26 Dec 1768 & conveyed by THOMAS HEARD to JAMES PETIGREW by 2 Deeds of 100 acres dated 11 May 1770 & conveyed from JAMES PETIGREW to GEORGE FORREST & from GEORGE FORREST a transfer of said 100 acres 14 Aug 1790 and now said SPRINGER to WILLIAM ROBINSON. S/ JOHN SPRINGER. Wit: JOHN BULLOCK, JAMES McMILLAN, DAVID CUNNINGHAM, who swore by oath 23 Apr 1792 before JOHN MOORE, J.P. Rcd. 24 Apr 1792.

P. 353. 28 May 1792: Bill of Sale: THOMAS LAMAR of Horse Creek to EPHRAIM FERRELL of Edgefield Co. SC for 48 pounds, sold four Negroes, known by the names of GEORGE CRESE, SELA & DAVY. S/ THOMAS LAMAR. Wit: HALEY JOHNSON, who swore by oath 8 Jan 1793 before JOSEPH HIGHTOWER, J.P. Rcd. 4 Feb 1793.

Pp. 1-5. 22 Aug 1785: JAMES WALLACE, Planter, Ninety Six Dist. SC to JOHANAS HOOSE, Planter of same place for 21 pounds, sold 100 acres lying on Stephensons Creek, originally granted 4 May 1775 unto WILLIAM THOMSON & said THOMSON granted unto said JAMES WALLACE by L&R 14 & 15 Nov 1784. S/ JAMES (X) WALLACE. Wit: MARY PERRIN, ABNER PERRIN, who swore by oath 25 Apr 1792 before RICHARD TUTT, J.P. Rcd. 25 Apr 1792.

Pp. 5-9. 9 Jan 1786: JOHANNES HOOSE, Planter of Edgefield Co. SC to PETER RAMBEY, Planter of same place for 5 shillings, sold 100 acres on Stephenses (sic) Creek originally granted 4 May 1775 to WM. THOMSON & said THOMSON sold to JAMES WALLACE BY L&R 16 & 17 Aug 1785. S/ JOHANNES HOOSE. Wit: GEORGE PERRIN, ABNER PERRIN, who swore by oath 25 Apr 1792 before RICHARD TUTT, J.P. Rcd. 25 Apr 1792.

Pp. 9-14. 6 Feb 1792: EDWARD PENMAN, Merchant of Charleston SC to PATRICK CUNNINGHAM, Planter, for 100 pounds, sold 200 acres being part of 500 acres granted 28 Aug 1772 to JAMES SIMPSON on Dry Creek, a branch of Buckhalters Creek of Savannah River adj. NE to SE by LAWRENCE RAMBO & SW & SE by remainder of tract. Said tract being land whereon WILLIAM JEETER now lives. S/ ED PENMAN. Wit: Abbeville C.H. SC: JAMES GAIRDNER, CHARLES COLCOCK, who swore by oath 18 Apr 1792 before JULIUS NICHOLS Junr, J.P. Rcd. 1 May 1792

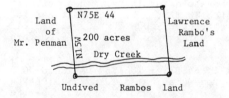

Land of Mr. Penman — N75E 44 — N15W — 200 acres — Dry Creek — Lawrence Rambo's Land — Undived Rambos land

SC: Pursuant to request of EDWARD PENMAN, Esq. of Charleston, SC, I have measured off 200 acres of a 500 acre tract, granted 28 Aur 1772 unto JAMES SIMPSON on Dry Creek. S/ W. ANDERSON, D. S.

Pp. 15-20. 17 Apr 1792: PATRICK CUNNINGHAM, Planter & ANN, his wife, of Ninety Six Dist. SC to SAMUEL DOOLITTLE, Planter of same place for 60 pounds, sold 200 acres being part of 500 acres originally granted 28 Aug 1772 to JAMES SIMPSON, Esqr., being land whereon WILLIAM JEETER now lives on Dry Creek, a branch of Buckhalters Creek of Savannah River adj. NE & SE by LAWRENCE RAMBO; SW & SE by remainder of said tract & was sold by said JAMES SIMPSON, Esq. unto EDWARD PENMAN, Esq. & was sold by said PENMON to PATRICK CUNNINGHAM by L&R 6 & 7 Feb 1792. Said tract being same 200 acres conveyed by CUNNINGHAM originally sold to said SAMUEL DOOLITTLE by L&R 1 & 2 Jun 1780 which land was originally granted WILLIAM CLARK 20 Nov 1772 & happened to be of a later date than the JAMES SIMPSON Esqr. grant. S/ P. CUNNINGHAM, ANN CUNNINGHAM. Wit: LEWIS SAXON, SAMUEL STEDMAN, who swore by oath 20 Apr 1792 before ARTHUR SIMKINS Esq., J.E.F.C.C. Rcd. 1 May 1792.

P. 21. 14 Dec 1791: Bill of Sale: JOSEPH MORTON, Planter of Edgefield Co. SC to JOHN WALLACE for 300 pounds, sold 4 negroes Viz: DOMINY; SINAH; DARKISS & SILVY. S/ JOSEPH MORTON. Wit: WILLIAM EVANS, JAMES SANDERS, JOHN BACON, who swore by oath 2 May 1792 before THOS. BACON, J.P. Rcd. 4 May 1792.

Pp. 21-22. 2 May 1792: Bill of Sale: PETER MORGAN to JOHN RYAN, for 50 pounds, sold 1 negroe woman named LETTICE. S/ PETER (X) MORGAN. Wit: JN. PERRY, ISAAC FOREMAN, LEWIS TILMAN, who swore by oath 4 May 1792 before RICHARD TUTT, J.P. Rcd. 4 May 1792.

P. 22. 14 Apr 1792: Bill of Sale: JOHN WALLACE of Cuffee Town, Planter, Edgefield Co. SC to RUTH WALLACE, Spinster of same place for 65 pounds, sold a negro woman slave named DARKEES dark colour aged 17 yrs, 5 ft. 6 in. S/ JOHN WALLACE. Wit: ALEXR HAMMONTREE, EVANS STOKES, JOHN CHANNING, who swore by oath 16 Apr 1792 before THOS. BACON, J.P. Rcd. 4 May 1792.

Pp. 22-23. 14 Dec 1791: Bill of Sale: JOSEPH MORTON, Planter, of Edgefield Co. SC to JOHN WALLACE for 65 pounds, sold one negro boy named HARRY. S/ JOSEPH MORTON. Wit: WILLIAM EVANS, JAMES SANDERS, JOHN BACON, who swore by oath 2 May 1792 before THOS. BACON, J.P. Rcd. 4 May 1792.

Pp. 23-24. 16 Apr 1792: Bill of Sale: CONRAD GALLMAN of Edgefield Co. SC to JOHN OLLIPHANT for 50 pounds, sold one negroe man named TONEY. S/ CONRAD GALLMAN. Wit: JOHN FRAZIER, who swore by oath 5 May 1792 before RICHARD TUTT, J.P. Rcd. 5 May 1792.

Pp. 24-25. 13 Apr 1792: Deed of Gift: JOHN THOMAS, Planter of Edgefield Co. SC to his children, MATTEE THOMAS, daughter, SILAS THOMAS & HOWEL THOMAS, sons, for love & affection & 35 shillings, to MATTEE THOMAS, all my household furniture, 5 head of neat cattle, branded J.T.; To son SILAS THOMAS, 5 head of neat cattle; To HOWEL THOMAS, 5 head neat cattle. S/ JOHN THOMAS. Wit: SILAS SELLERS, CONRAD GALLMAN, who swore by oath 5 May 1792 before RICHARD TUTT, J.P. Rcd. 5 May 1792.

Pp. 25-26. 11 Dec 1790: Bill of Sale: TOLAVER DAVIS to JOHN OLLIPHANT for 50 pounds, a negroe woman named QUEEN. S/ TOLAVER DAVIS. Wit: BETTY TUTT, who swore by oath 10 May 1792 before RICHARD TUTT, J.P. Rcd. 10 May 1792.

Pp. 26-28. 1 Jun 1792: Mortgage: LEVY STARNES, Planter of Edgefield Co. SC, hereunto moving, to WILLIAM TERRY of same place for 9 pounds, sold 100 acres being part of 500 acres originally granted WILLIAM COURSEY who conveyed by L&R to said STARNES, being on a branch called Springfield.
If said 9 pounds interest is paid before next 25 Dec. Instrument becomes null & void. S/ LEVY (X) STARNES. Wit: W. COURSEY, ALLEN COURSEY, CHARLES COURSEY, who swore by oath 12 July 1792 before AQUILLA MILES, J.P. Rcd. 3 Jul 1792.

Pp. 28-34. 1778: L&R: STEPHEN RUSSELL & KEZIAH, his wife, Planters of Edgefield Co. SC to ZEBEDEE TAYLOR, Planter of same place for 500 pounds, sold 100 acres...In the third year of this our United States in America, granted 21 Dec 1769 on Bennefields (also Benfield) Creek of Savannah River as shown by plat surveyed 6 Nov 1767 by JNO NELSON D.S. & certified 6 Dec 1769 by JOHN BRENNAR, D Sur G^l. S/ STEPHEN RUSSELL, KISIAH (+) RUSSELL. Wit: JOHN (↦) BENEFIELD, CHARLES WILLIAMS, THOMAS (TF) FREEMAN, who swore by oath 13 Feb 1792 before THOS. BACON, J.P. Rcd. 15 May 1792.

Pp. 34-37. 13 July 1790: JOHN CHENEY of Edgefield Co. SC to

SAMUEL MAYS of same place for 100 pounds, sold 200 acres being part of 400 acres originally granted 29 Apr 1768 to said CHENEY, on Bigg Creek of Saluda adj. E by part of tract conveyed to THOMAS BERRY. S/ JOHN CHENEY. Wit: JAMES SPANN, THOMAS BUTLER,' who swore by oath 14 July 1790 before RICHARD TUTT, J.P. Rcd. 17 May 1792.

Pp. 37-39. 21 May 1792: Deed of Gift: WILLIAM EVANS Planter of Edgefield Co. SC to my loving son & daughter WILLIAM & ANN EVANS, for love & affection all my goods & chattles as follows - To son WILLIAM - horse, bridle, mare, bull, cow & calf, 3 volumes of Mr. Wesley's works, 1 testament, 1 spelling book, with some other books, 1 plow & 2 axes. To daughter ANN, 1 feather bed, bedding, 1 pot & hook, 1 dutch oven, 1 hocket, Bible, 1 testament & spelling book, 2 cows & calfs, 1 pewter bason, 7 pewter plates, 6 pewter spoons, 1 silver watch, 1 rifle gun, (the silver watch & gun to be disposed of for a young mare for the said ANN), 25 bushels of corn. The condition is the use of above until the children come of age. S/ WILLM. EVANS. Wit: WILLIAM GLEN, MARK (+) NOBLES, who swore by oath 25 May 1792 before RICHARD TUTT, J.P. Rcd. 25 May 1792.

Pp. 39-41. 14 Nov 1792: Mortgage: ROBERT LANGFORD, to BENJAMIN GLOVER, note of hand unto BENJAMIN GLOVER for 12 pounds, payable 1 Jan 1794 & for better securing of payment sell one negro man slave about 20 yrs old named JEM, one horse, trots & paces & formerly the property of JOHN LANE; 1 bay mare, 4 cows; 3 yearlings; 25 hogs, 4 feather beds & furniture with my household & kitchen furniture, my plantation tools, carpenter & cooper tools, & 50 bushels of corn. Should above note be paid with interest this instrument becomes null & void. S/ ROBERT LANGFORD. Wit: JOHN LANE, JOHN SMITHERS, who swore by oath 25 May 1793 (sic). Rcd. 28 May 1793. (sic)

Pp. 41-45. 3 Jan 1785: GEORGE BUCKLUE, Planter of Ninety Six Dist. SC, to OGDEN COCKCROFT, Planter of same place for 10 pounds, sold 50 acres, being part of original grant 14 Jun 1772, surveyed 2 Jun 1772 by WM ANDERSON, certified 17 Jun 1772 in Colleton Co. SC, unto RICHARD BUCKLUE on little Stevens Creek of Savannah River adj. lands of ALEXANDER BEEN & WILLIAM GREEN. Said RICHARD BUCKLUE being dead & said GEORGE BUCKLUE, his son, being his heir in law. S/ GEORGE BUCKELEW, MARY (X) BUCKELEW. Wit: AZARIAH LEWIS, ELIZABETH (+) GREEN, WILLIAM (I) GREEN, who swore by oath 31 Mar 1789 before ARTHUR SIMKINS, J.P.

Pp. 45-48. 1 Oct 1791: L&R: WILLIAM BUTLER, Esq. of Edgefield Co. SC to RICHARD DOZER of same place for 50 pounds, sold 200 acres, originally granted 16 Sep 1774 to ROBERT WARING on Red Bank Creek adj. E by JOHN SPAN & AMOS RICHARDSON & W by HENRY BRATCHEY & was conveyed by said WARING by L&R 13 Apr 1791 to said BUTLER. S/ WM. BUTLER. Wit: SAMUEL MAYS, EDWARD BLAND, SAMUEL LEWIS, who swore by oath 22 Oct 1791 before RUSSELL WILSON, J.P. Rcd. 4 Jun 1792.

Pp. 48-50. 3 Nov 1788: WILLIAM RHENY & SARAH, his wife, of Burke Co. GA. to ROBERT BOYD of Richmon Co. GA for 40 pounds, sold 100 acres originally granted 20 Jan 1773 in Granville Co. SC to SILAS PACE who conveyed to KNOWLES PACE who conveyed to WILLIAM RHENY by L&R 21 Feb 1779. S/ WILLIAM RHENY. Wit: JAMES BOYD, JOHN GRAY, Junr., SAMUEL (SP) PAYNE, Senr. of Edgefield Co. SC, who swore by oath 2 Jun 1792 before HUGH MIDDLETON, J.P.

Burk Co. GA: 11 Nov 1788 SARAH RHENY relinquished dower before JOHN MORRISON, J.P. Rcd. 4 Jun 1792.

Pp. 50-51. 3 Nov 1788: WILLIAM RHENY & SARAH, his wife of Burke Co. GA to ROBERT BOYD of Richmond Co. GA for 10 pounds, sold 10 acres being in Wilkes Co. GA surrounded on all sides by Savannah River originally granted in Georgia 10 Apr 1784 to said RHENY. S/ WILLIAM RHENY. Wit: JAMES BOYD, JOHN GRAY, SAMUEL (SP) PAYNE, Senr., who swore by oath 2 Jun 1792 before HUGH MIDDLETON, J.P. Burke Co. Ga: 11 Nov 1788 SARAH RHENY relinquished dower before JOHN MORRISON, J.P. Rcd. 4 Jun 1792.

Pp. 51-52. 3 Jan 1792: JOHN LEWIS, late of SC but now of Burke Co. GA to ROBERT & JOHN BOYD in complying with a bargain made 17 Mar 1791, release 500 acres on Savannah River & adj. SE RICHARD MEDORS. S/ JNO. LEWIS. Wit: RICHARD WHITE, NICHOLAS MERIWETHER, BENJAMIN SAMUELL, JAMES BOYD, who swore by oath 2 Jun 1792 before HUGH MIDDLETON, J.P. Rcd. 4 Jun 1792.

Pp. 52-53. 23 Apr 1792: Deed of Gift: JOHN WOOTAN of Edgefield Co. SC to ANN STREET, dau. of JOSIAH STREET & MARY, his wife, 2 cows & a calf. S/ JOHN WOOTAN. Wit: REDICK (+) GANEY, DANIEL (D) WOOTAN, who swore by oath 4 Jun 1792 before RICHARD TUTT, J.P. Rcd. 4 Jun 1792.

Pp. 53-58. 10 Dec 1791. JOHN PURSELL of Edgefield Co. SC to JOHN SWILLIVAN of same place for 40 pounds, 25 acres being part of 95 acres granted to JOHN MORICE 3 Nov 1772 on East side of Stevens Creek; land N by MARY SULLIVAN, W by SAMUEL GARDNER, SAMUEL GOODE & TOBLER, TEETs old line land held by CHARLES LEE; SW by ARON HERREN. S/ JOHN (ʧ) PURSELL, BARBARY (+) PURSELL. Wit: WILLIAM PURSELL, JAS WM ROBERTS, JONATHAN SWILLIVAN, who swore by oath 24 Feb 1792 before AQUILLA MILES, J.P. Rcd. 4 Jun 1792.

Pp. 58-61. 24 May 1786. MARY KISES & CATHRON WEAVER of Chesterfield Co. SC to DAVIS WILLIAMS of Edgefield Co. SC for 28 pounds, Release 250 acres originally granted NICKLESS CISES Aug 1765 & was left by LW&T of NICKLES CISES to said MARY KISES & CATHRON WEAVER. Said land being on North side of Cuffey Town Creek adj. lands of DRURY GLOVER & said NICKLES heir. S/ MARY (X) KISES, CATHRON (W) WEAVER. Wit: HORATIO JETER, MARY GLOVER, DRURY GLOVER, who swore by oath 4 Jun 1792 before RICHARD TUTT, J.P. Rcd. 4 Jun 1792.

Pp. 61-63. 13 Dec 1790. JOHN DAY of Edgefield Co. SC to JOHN HARDY of same place for 30 pounds, sold 163 acres originally granted 21 Jan 1785 to said DAY, being on Sweet Water Creek & adj. lands W by JAMES BENNETT & JOHN HANCOCK. S/ JOHN (D) DAY. Wit: J. PULLIAM, ANN HARDY, JOSEPH CUNNINGHAM, who swore by oath 7 May 1791 before JOSEPH HIGHTOWER, J.P. Rcd. 5 Jun 1792.

Pp. 63-65. 13 Dec 1790. JOHN DAY of Edgefield Co. SC to JOHN HARDY for 20 pounds, sold 70 acres originally granted 21 Jan 1785 unto JOHN HANCOCK being on Sweet Water Creek adj. lands by JAMES ROGERS, JOHN DAY & JAMES VESSELLS, Senr. S/ JOHN (D) DAY. Wit: J. PULLIAM, ANN HARDY, JOSEPH CUNINGHAM, who swore by oath 7 May 1791 before JOSEPH HIGHTOWER, J.P. Rcd. 5 Jun 1792.

Pp. 66-72. 20 Feb 1788: JAMES MALONE & ELIZABETH, his wife, of

Edgefield Co. SC to HENRY ZINN, Planter of same place for 5 shillings, 156 acres originally granted 5 Jun 1786 said MALONE being in Edgefield Co. SC adj. lands of HENRY ZINN; LEMAR; & the Red House land. S/ JAMES (9) MALONE, ELIZABETH (X) MALONE. Wit: JACOB ZINN, ISAAC ARDIS, who swore by oath 5 Dec 1788 before JOHN STURZENEGGER, Esq., J.P. Rcd. 6 Jun 1792.

Pp. 72-76. 24 Jul 1790: HENRY ZINN, Planter of Edgefield Co. SC to HARMON BOZEMAN, Boatwright of same place for 25 pounds, sold 156 acres originally granted 5 Jun 1786 unto JAMES MELONE being on the head of a branch of Savannah River and was conveyed by said JAMES MALONE & ELIZABETH, his wife, to said HENRY ZINN by L&R 17 Feb 1788 adj. lands of HENRY ZINN, Red House Tract. S/ HENRY ZINN. Wit: AX HAWKINS, WILLIAM STEWART, who swore by oath 6 Nov 1790 before JOHN STURZENEGGER, J.P. Rcd. 6 Jun 1792.
Memo: Agreement between HENRY ZINN & HARMON BOZEMAN that if an older Right take place of within mentioned land - then HENRY ZINN will pay HARMON BOZEMAN 25 pounds purchase money & likewise pay him for improvements. S/ HENRY ZINN, HARMON BOZEMAN.

Pp. 77-79. 8 Oct 1788: JOSEPH JENKINS of Abervill Co. SC to WILLIAM BAILEY of same place for 90 pounds, sold 437 acres originally granted 1786 to said JENKINS on a branch of Turkey Creek of Savannah River adj. ROWAN & SIMSON. S/ JOSEPH JENKINS. Wit: ROBERT MAXWELL, GEORGE LIDDELL, THOMAS (+) HOMES, GEORGE WILSON, who swore by oath 11 Jun 1792 before THOS. BACON, J.P. Rcd. 14 Jun 1792.

Pp. 80-85. 14 Jun 1792: JOHN ARLEDGE & ANN, his wife, of Turkey Creek, Edgefield Co. SC to DAVID BAKER CHENDLER, a miner & son of JOEL CHANDLER of same place for 150, sold 519 acres being a part of two tracts (1) 364 acres part of a 464 acre tract granted RICHARD JOHNSON Sr., 1 May 1786 & was conveyed to said ARLEDGE by L&R 6 & 7 Aug 1788 and was recorded in Edgefield Deed Book B p. 25, 1788 being on Turkey Creek and the mouth of Little Turkey Creek or Puckett Creek on both sides of said creek adj. S by ARTHUR SIMKINS Esq, & JAMES SCOTT & JENKINS line which takes off 100 acres of the 464 acre tract & (2) a tract of 155 acres which joins the 364 acres, granted said ARLEDGE 3 Oct 1791 adj. NE & SE by THOMAS McGINNIS's land; NE JOHN ARLEDGE; NW by WILLIAM FRAZER & SW by MOTT's land. S/ JOHN (I) ARLEDGE, ANN (I) ARLEDGE. Wit: JAMES SCOTT, PATIENCE (P) ARLEDGE, JOEL CHANDLER, who swore by oath 20 Jun 1792 before RICHARD TUTT, J.P.
Nov. Term 1792: Dower Relinquished. Rcd. Nov term 1792.

Pp. 85-88. 17 Feb 1792: WILLIAM PRICHARD, surveyor of Edgefield Co. SC to ROBERT GARDNER of same place for 50 pounds, sold 150 acres originally granted 15 Oct 1784 said PRICHARD being on Savannah River & Stevens Creek adj. said creek & land formerly JERMYN WRIGHT's & SE by HENRY DEA. S/ WILLIAM PRICHARD. Wit: JOHN PURVES, JAMES PRICHARD, who swore by oath 15 Jun 1792 before JOSEPH HIGHTOWER, J.P. Rcd. 23 Jun 1792.

P. 88. 21 Dec 1792: Bill of Sale: JOHN RIVERS to PHILIP DILLARD for 50 pounds sold one negro woman named VICE. S/ JOHN RIVERS. Wit: SALEY (+) RIVERS, CHARLES RIVERS, who swore by oath 21 Dec 1792 before AQUILLA MILES, J.P. Rcd. 21 Dec 1792.

Pp. 89-90. 26 May 1792: Bill of Sale: JOHN MOCK, GEORGE MOCK & BENJAMIN MOCK of Edgefield Co. SC to MICAJAH PHILLIPS of same place for 100 pounds, sold the after named property viz: one negro man named WILL; one negro woman named HAGAR; one bay mare named PRIMROSE, one mare named SNIP, colt, 11 head of cattle, 1 feather bed & bedsted, 2 plows, & gear, 1 flax wheel, 1 cotton wheel, 1 table & 4 chairs, 2 large pots, 1 small pot, 1 pad lock, 2 hoes, 1 ax, a parcel of pewter, 1 iron pot rack, 3 pales, 1 hogshead, 1 beer tub, 1 tub, 1 chest, 1 bottle, 1 churn, Box Iron, 2 sides good of Leather, 1 wash tub, 1 pr. fire tongs & pot hooks also a parcel of hogs 15 head. S/ JOHN MOCK, GEORGE MOCK, BENJAMIN MOCK. Wit: THOMAS PHILLIPS, THOMAS HOWLE, who swore by oath 4 Jun 1792 before AQUILA MILES, J.P. Rcd. 2 Jul 1792.

P. 90. 15 May 1792: Bond: GEORGE MOCK to MICAJAH & ELIZABETH PHILLIPS Rent for two shillings per year paid annually 70 acres adj. JOHN MOCK's lines. S/ GEORGE MOCK. Wit: BENJAMIN MOCK, THOMAS H. HOWLE, who swore by oath 4 Jun 1792 before AQUILA MILES, J.P. Rcd. 2 Jul 1792.

Pp. 90-91. 17 Jan 1792: MARY ITSON of Edgefield Co. SC to JAMES MURFEY of same place for Consideration of having a good plantation made suteable buildings & a good peach & apple orchard made by said JAMES MURPHEY assign 50 acres for a term of thirteen years, being on Cedar Creek adj. COLERD's line & WILLIAM MURFEY. S/ MARY (X) ITSON. Wit: WILLIAM WALLS, JOHN WALLS, who swore by oath 3 Jul 1792 before AQUILA MILES, J.P. Rcd. 3 Jul 1792.

Pp. 91-96. 24 Apr 1790: RICHARD JOHNSON, Junr. of Edgefield Co. SC to RICHARD JOHNSON Senr. of same place for 20 pounds, sold 200 acres being the remaining part of that plantation whereon Coll. MOSES KIRKLAND formerly lived & whereon the said RICHARD JOHNSON, Senr. now lives excepting 100 acres laid off to MOODY BURTS, Junr. Said tract was confiscated & sold to RICHARD JOHNSON, Junr. & is near the head of Turkey Creek adj. JOHN RUTLEDGE & RICHARD WILLIAMS. S/ RICHD. JOHNSON. Wit: JOEL CHANDLER, MOOR JOHNSON, ROBERT WILLIS, who swore by oath 6 Jul 1792 before RD. TUTT, J.P. Rcd. 6 Jul 1792.

Pp. 96-97. 30 Mar 1792: Mortgage: THOMAS GOLPHIN of SC to JOHN ROLSTON & HUGH NESBIT, Merchants of Augusta GA for 100 pounds, sell one boat called the "Good Intent" together with 7 negros, boat hands, to wit: Negros BENTER, ZADOCK, NARY, ABEY, STEPHEN, PUMPKIN, and ABRAHAM. Should said obligation be paid before 1 Jul 1793 the said Bill of Sale be null & void & property reverts back to me. S/ THOS. GOLPHIN. Wit: MATTHIAS MAKER.
GA: 30 Mar 1792 sworn by oath of MATTHIAS MAKER, Merchant of Augusta GA before JNO. MILTON, Mayor of town of Augusta.
Edgefield Co. SC: 21 Jul 1792 sworn by oath of MATTHIAS MAKER before HUGH MIDDLETON, J.P. Rcd. 21 Jul 1792.

Pp. 98-99. 27 Mar 1792: Bond: THOMAS GOLPHIN of Edgefield Co. SC to MATTHIAS MAKER, QUINTON HAMILTON & ARTHUR HARPER, Merchants for imperial sum of 800 pounds, sold 1 Flatt called the "Bold Hornet" and eight negros named SANDY, CATO, CYRUS, TOM, GOODGAME, ANDREW, BEN & JUNE. Should 400 pounds be paid on or before 1 Jan next said condition becomes null & void. S/ THOS GOLPHIN. Wit: GA: HUGH NESBITT swore by oath 30 Mar 1792 before JNO. MILTON, Mayor of the town of Augusta.
Edgefield SC: HUGH NESBITT swore by oath 21 Jul 1792 before HUGH MIDDLETON, J.P. Rcd. 21 Jul 1792.

Pp. 100-101. 16 Apr 1792: WILLIAM COURSEY, Mathematition of Edgefield Co. SC to JOHN THURMOND for 20 pounds sold 200 acres being part of 946 acres granted 7 Aug 1786 said COURSEY on a branch called Horsepen, a branch of Beaverdam which is a branch of Turkey Creek, a branch of Stephens Creek of Savannah River adj. lines of said THURMOND & TALLEY. S/ W. COURSEY. Wit: ALLEN COURSEY, CHARLES THURMOND, who swore by oath 28 Jul 1792 before RICHARD TUTT, J.P. Rcd. 28 Jul 1792.

land sold from original to
Scarbourgh
Broadwater

land held by Jno Thurmond

200 acres

S85W

Horsepen branch

N5W

land sold from original to Ben Griffin

land sold to Jourdan Brooks from the original

N80E

land held by Nathan Talley

Pp. 101-104. 19 Feb 1793: Mortgage: ISAAC CROWTHER, Planter of Ninety Six Dist. SC to PATRICK McDOWALL, Merchant of same place ...Whereon said ISAAC CROWTHERS has taken & purchased of said McDOWALL good wares & merchandise in amount of 25 pounds & for better securing of payment in the penal sum of 51 pounds condition for payment of said 25 pounds & whereas said ISAAC CROWTHERS by his note dated 17 Aug 1791 stands bound to said PATRICK McDOWEL, as Assinee of WADSWORTH & TURPIN in the further sum of 11 pounds with interest from 17 Oct 1791. Said CROWTHERS does sell one negroe wench named RACHEL & her child named NANCY. Should sum be paid with interest by 14 Feb next this sale be null & void. S/ ISAAC CROWTHERS. Wit: GABRIEL SMITHERS, THOMAS ROBERTSON, who swore by oath in Abberville 13 Mar 1793 before JULIUS NICHOLS, Junr.
Memo: If payment not made said negro wench RACHEL & child NANCY to be sold at public auction & the overplus be returned to ISAAC CROWTHERS after interest & other expenses are paid. S/ P. McDOWALL. Rcd. 13 Mar 1793.

Pp. 104-105. 6 Jan 1791: JOSEPH WALKER of Edgefield Co. SC to LEWIS CLARK of same place for 50 pounds sold 150 acres being part of 598 acres surveyed 16 Dec 1786 & granted 1 Oct 1787 to said JOSEPH WALKER, being on the North side of south Edisto River adj. said CLARK's land. S/ JOSEPH WALKER. Wit: BENJAMIN CLARK, JOSIAH (X) THOMAS, SHILES MARSH, who swore by oath 1 Aug 1792 before RICHARD TUTT, J.P. Rcd. 1 Aug 1792.

Pp. 106-109. 16 Aug 1791: JOHN HOMES & ELIZABETH, his wife of Edgefield Co. SC to JOHN COTTON of same place for 10 pounds, sold 40 acres being part of 260 acres surveyed by WILLIAM FRAZIER 31 Oct 1786 & granted 1 Feb 1790 unto JOHN WALLER & conveyed to said JOHN HOMES by L&R. Said land being on the Beaverdam Creek a branch of Turkey Creek of Savannah River adj. NE by JOHN FRAZIER, NW by JOHN CARTER, SE by JOHN COTTEN, and by BURNE's land to STERKs old road. S/ JOHN HOMES. Wit: SAMUEL MARSH, BRYANT

HOMES, SHILES MARSH, who swore by oath 1 Aug 1792 before RICHARD TUTT, J.P. Rcd. 1 Aug 1792.

Pp. 109-112. 14 May 1785: DANIEL ROGERS, Senr & SARAH, his wife of Edgefield Co. SC to JOHN COTTON for 50 pounds, 88 acres being part of 200 acres granted 9 Sep 1774 unto JAMES ROBERTSON & conveyed by L&R 12 & 13 May 1775 unto DANIEL ROGERS being on South side of the Beaverdam Creek adj. JOHN FRAZIER's land that he bought out of said tract. S/ DANIEL (D) ROGERS, SARAH ROGERS. Wit: THOS. COTTEN, WILLIAM MARSH, SHILES MARSH, who swore by oath 1 Aug 1792 before RICHARD TUTT, J.P. Rcd. 1 Aug 1792.

Pp. 112-117. 10 Mar 1792: ANN ZUBLY, (Executrix of LW&T of the late DAVID ZUBLY Esqr., dec'd.), to WALTER TAYLOR for 50 pounds, sold 248 acres being two tracts of land (1) 100 acres granted HANS & JOHN ZURCHER & transferred by L & R by NICHOLAS SHUBDREIN (in right of his wife, who being heir to said HANS & JOHN ZURCHER) unto DAVID ZUBLY & adj. lands E by HANS ZURCHER & N by ULRICK EGGER (2) 148 acres originally granted ULRICK EGGER & transferred by WILLIAM EGGER (son & heir to ULRICH EGGER) to CHRISTOPHER SMITHERS who transferred by L & R 27 Feb 1779 unto DAVID ZUBLY. Said land when surveyed being in Township of New Windsor now Edgefield Co., adj. W on ZURCHER's land, S CONRAD LUTZ & ANN & ELIZABETH MEYER. S/ ANN ZUBLY, Executrix. Wit: WILLIAM STEWART, GEO. WALKER, GEORGE SAVAGE, who swore by oath 10 Mar 1792 before JOHN STURZENEGGER, Esq., J.P. Rcd. 2 Aug 1792.

Pp. 118-122. 15 Apr 1790: WRIGHT NICHOLSON, Planter, & MARY, his wife of Edgefield Co. SC to JEREMIAH MOBLEY of same place for 20 pounds, 400 acres granted 2 Feb 1789 being on branch of Pen Creek of Little Saluda River adj. SAMUEL MAYS, YOUNG ALLEN, WILLIAM HART, JOHN MOBLEY, ROBERT STARK, Junr. S/ WRIGHT NICHOLSON, MARY NICHOLSON. Wit: HANNAH BULLOCK, ASAEL ROBERTS, who swore by oath 31 Jul 1792 before HENRY KING, J.P. Rcd. 4 Aug 1792.

Pp. 122-125. 3 Aug 1792: VANN SWEARRENGEN, Senr. of Edgefield Co. SC to JULIUS NICHOLS (son of WILLIAM NICHOLS, Junr.) of same place for 5 pounds, sold 340 acres granted 5 Sep 1791 said SWEARENGEN being on head of Turkey Creek adj. NW, NE & SE by SWEARENGEN's old survey, NW JOHN RYAN, SW JAMES BARRINGTON & DAVID BURK, NE DRURY MIMS & Widow CARPENTER. S/ VAN SWEARINGEN. Wit: MARY (X) SWEARINGEN, EZEKIAL ROEBUCK, who swore by oath 17 Aug 1792 before RICHARD TUTT, J.P.

Pp. 125-129. 16 Aug 1792: VAN SWEARINGEN, Senr. of Edgefield Co. SC to WILLIAM NICHOLS, the younger (son to WILLIAM NICHOLS, Junr.), for 60 pounds, sold 150 acres originally granted 26 Jul 1774 to LACON RYAN being on the ridge between Turkey & Shaw Creeks. S/ VANN SWEARINGEN. Wit: MARY (X) SWEARINGEN, EZEKIEL ROEBUCK, who swore by oath 17 Aug 1792 before RICHARD TUTT, J.P. Rcd. 17 Aug 1792.

Pp. 129-133. 9 Sep 1770: JOSEPH WALKER, Planter of St. Paul's Parish SC to SAMUEL WALKER of same place for 100 pounds, sold 250 acres originally granted 27 Aug ?1765? in Granville Co. St. Paul's Parish SC. S/ JOSEPH (‡W) WALKER. Wit: JESSE DANIELL, RICHARD KIRKLAND, who swore by oath 15 Nov 1771 before MOSES KIRKLAND, J.P. Rcd. 23 Aug 1792.

P. 133. 10 Jun 1784. LEWIS CLARK, Planter of Ninety Six Dist. SC to SAMUEL WALKER of same place for (blank) sold 100 acres being on Rogers Creek a branch of Horns Creek adj. SE by LACON RYAN's land. (This deed clearly written but stops mid page, p. 134 is blank as if clerk did not finish his recording. See DBK 7, p. 144 for complete deed, gch).

Pp. 135-137. Apr 1793: Deed of Gift: RICHARD MOORE of Edgefield Co. SC to CRESWELL MOORE, for natural love & affection I bear my son for the better support & maintance of him & his family after my decease, gives 150 acres originally granted unto JOHN WALKER who conveyed to said RICHARD MOORE being on branch of Cuffetown Creek of Savannah River adj. NW JOHN SAVAGE, Esqr., & SE & NE WILLIAM DAVIS. S/ RICHARD MOORE. Wit: DAVID LILLY, WILLIAM WHITE, THOMAS JOHNSON, who swore by oath 1 Apr 1793 before JOHN MOORE, J.P. Rcd. 20 May 1793.

Pp. 137-138. 1 Apr 1793: RICHARD MOORE of Edgefield Co. SC hereunto moving, to CRISWELL MOORE, my son, for love & affection & better maintance of him & his family after my decease, grant the following negroes to wit: HARRY, SYLVY & HANNAH also 2 feather beds & furniture & 2 horses, 1 waggon & geers. S/ RICHARD MOORE. Wit: DAVID LILLY, WILLIAM WHITE, THOMAS JOHNSON, who swore by oath 1 Apr 1793 before JOHN MOORE, J.P. Rcd. 20 May 1793.

Pp. 138-139. 1793: RICHARD MOORE of Edgefield Co. SC hereunto moving to JOHN M. MOORE, my son for love & affection and for better support & maintenance of him & his family after my decease grant & give three negroes to wit: JOE, CLARY, & SAMPSON: also 2 feather beds & furniture & 2 horses & other goods & chattels. S/ RICHARD MOORE. Wit: DAVID LILLY, WILLIAM WHITE, THOMAS JOHNSON, who swore by oath 1 Apr 1793 before JOHN MOORE, J.P. Rcd. 20 May 1793.

Pp. 140-141. 1 Apr 1793: Deed of Gift: RICHARD MOORE of Edgefield Co. SC hereunto moving, to TABITHA MOORE, my daughter, for love & affection & better support of her & her family after my decease, give four negroes to wit: FRANK, LUCY, JIMMY & BOB; also 2 feather beds & furniture, 1 riding chair, 2 horses. S/ RICHARD MOORE. Wit: DAVID LILLY, WILLIAM WHITE, THOMAS JOHNSON, who swore by oath Apr 1793 before JOHN MOORE, J.P. Rcd. 20 May 1793.

Pp. 141-143. 1793: Deed of Gift: RICHARD MOORE of Edgefield Co. SC hereunto moving, to WILLIAM MOORE, my son of same place for love & affection... give six negroes to wit: BASON, BIG BETTY, GEORGE, FANNY, JIM, & little BETTY; also 2 feather beds & furniture, 3 horses, 24 head of cattle, 14 sheep, 40 hogs. S/ RICHARD MOORE. Wit: DAVID LILLY, WILLIAM WHITE, THOMAS JOHNSON, who swore by oath 1 Apr 1793 before JOHN MOORE, J.P. Rcd. 20 May 1793.

Pp. 143-144. 21 Jan 1793: Bill of Sale: ROBERT ROBERTSON, Planter of GA to RANDAL ROBERSON, Planter of Edgefield Co. SC for 124 pounds, sell 4 negroes viz: SARAH, a negro woman about 31 yrs.; NELL about 13 yrs.; WILL about 11 yrs.; & PAT about 9 yrs. old. S/ ROBERT ROBINSON. Wit: THOMAS KEY, SAMUEL (X) GARDNER, who swore by oath 12 Mar 1793 before JOSEPH HIGHTOWER, J.P. Rcd. 12 Mar 1793.

Pp. 144-148. 10 Jun 1784: LEWIS CLARK, planter of Ninety Six Dist. SC to SAMUEL WALKER of same place for 50 Guineas, sold 100

acres being part of 500 acres originally granted 12 Jul 1771 unto
DANIEL MARSHALL being on Rogers Creek branch of Horns Creek adj.
SW & SW LACON RYAN, NW & SW by SAMUEL WALKER & NW & NE by DANIEL
MARSHALL. S/ LEWIS CLARK. Wit: JOHN WALKER, JAS McPHERSON, who
swore by oath 10 Jun 1784 before JOHN RYAN, J.P. Rcd. 23 Aug
1792.

Pp. 148-152. 29 Aug 1779: DANIEL MARSHALL of ?Kickey Creek GA to
LEWIS CLARK of Ninety Six Dist. SC for 1600 pounds, sold 100
acres being part of 500 acres granted 12 Jul 1771 to said
MARSHALL being on Rogers Creek of Stephen Creek adj. SE & SW by
LACON RYAN, NW & SW by SAMUEL WALKER & NW & NE by DANIEL
MARSHALL. S/ DANIEL MARSHALL. Wit: ATHA THOMAS, ISAAC FOREMAN,
who swore by oath 24 May 1780 before ARTHUR SIMKINS, J.P. Rcd. 23
Aug 1792.

Pp. 153-157. 2 Oct 1791: JOHN ADAMS Planter of Red Bank of
Edgefield Co. SC to WILLIAM PRICE CLARK, Planter of Rockey Creek
of Edgefield Co. SC for 67 pounds, sold 150 acres originally
granted 4 Dec 1786 unto JOSEPH NUNN being on Red Bank on South
side of the Saluda River & was conveyed by said NUNN by L&R 9 &
10 Mar 1787 unto said JOHN ADAMS. S/ JOHN ADAMS. Wit: AARON
CLARK, ALEXR. PATERSON, JOHN BRATCHER, who swore by oath 13 Apr
1792 before HENRY KING, J.P. Rcd. 1 Sep 1792.

Pp. 158-161. 9 Jun 1789: THOMAS FARGUHAR to JAMES FARGUHAR for 30
pounds, sold 200 acres originally granted 13 May 1768 to said
FARGUHAR being on Ninety Six Creek in Edgefield Co. SC. S/ THOMAS
FARGUHAR. Wit: JOHN LOWE, THOMAS ROSS, JOHN ANDERSON, who swore
by oath 30 Aug 1792 before WILLIAM ANDERSON, Esq., J.E.C. Rcd. 1
Sep 1792.

Pp. 161-165. ROBERT THOMPSON & BARBARA, his wife of Burke Co. GA
to FEDRICK WARD of Edgefield Co. SC for 128 pounds, sold 300
acres originally granted 16 Jun 1768 to said THOMPSON. S/ ROBERT
(R) THOMPSON. Wit: WILLIAM MOORE, DAVIS MOORE, THOMAS ROSS, who
swore by oath 22 Aug 1792 before W. ANDERSON, J.E.C. Rcd. 1 Sep
1792.

Pp. 165-167. 15 Dec 1789: EDWARD HOMES of Edgefield Co. SC to
FREDERICK SISSON of same place for 50 pounds, sold 100 acres
being part of 200 acres originally granted 23 Aug 1774 unto DRURY
FORT being on Mine Creek of little Saluda River adj. E & NW DRURY
FORT & HENRY BOLTON; W by said BOLTON & BENJAMIN BELL. S/ EDWARD
HOMES. Wit: WILLIAM SISSON, WILLIAM HERIN, who swore by oath 1
Jan 1791 before RUSSELL WILSON, J.P. Rcd. 1 Sep 1792.

Pp. 167-171. 1792: ABDELL STOTT, Yeoman of Edgefield Co. SC to
WILLIAM HALL of same place for (blank) sold 100 acres being part
of 200 acres originally granted 3 Apr 1786 said STOTT being on
Mine Creek of Little Saluda River adj. WILLIAM NICHOLSON's part
of said tract; JANE WEAVER; HAYES line. S/ ABDELL (X) STOTT. Wit:
VANN SWEARINGEN, MUMFORD PERRYMAN, who swore by oath 7 May 1792
before HENRY KING, J.P. Rcd. 3 Sep 1792.

Pp. 171-173. 20 Jan 1791: JAMES MUNDAY of Ninety Six Dist. SC to
GEORGE HOGWOOD of same place for 20 pounds, sold 100 acres
Bennefield Creek. S/ JAMES MUNDAY. Wit: EZEKIEL HUDNALL, JAMES
HAGOOD, who swore by oath before THOMAS BACON, Esq., J.P. Rcd. 4
Feb 1792.

Pp. 173-176. 21 Jan 1791: JAMES MUNDAY of Ninety Six Dist. SC to GEORGE HOGWOOD of same place for 20 pounds, sold 100 acres being part of 800 originally granted 31 Aug 1774 unto HENRY WARE on Rocky Creek, Stephens Creek & Martins of the Savannah River adj. SW MURPHEYS NE by GEBARES NW by JAMES MUNDAY & JAMES HOGWOOD. S/ JAMES MUNDAY. Wit: EZEKIEL HUDNALL, JAMES HAGOOD, who swore by oath 4 Feb 1792 before THOMAS BACON, J.P. Rcd. 3 (sic) Sep 1792.

Pp. 176-178. 12 Sep 1793: JOHN TODD, LUCY (LUCINDA), his wife, & JENNET (JEANNY), mother to the said JOHN, to DAVID BURN for 50 pounds, sold 250 acres on the head of Ninety Six Creek adj. MACERNESS GOOD, JANE BROWNLEE, ROBERT DICKE. S/ JOHN TODD, LYCINDY (O) TODD, JEANNY (also JENNET) (O) TODD. Wit: THOMAS CLEMENT WADE, JOSEPH McSHOUN, WILLIAM TODD, who swore by oath 18 Nov 1793 before JOHN MOORE, J.P. Rcd. 29 Jan 1794.

Pp. 178-182. 21 Nov 1793: Mortgage: DAVID BURN of Edgefield Co. SC to THOMAS WADSWORTH & WILLIAM TURPIN, Merchants by a bond of 10 May 1793 in penal sum of 52 pounds, with a condition of payment of 26 pounds & for better securing payment, conveys 250 acres on which said DAVID BURNS now lives being on the head of Ninety Six Creek adj. MERCNESS GOOD, JANE BROWNLEE, ROBERT DICKE & was conveyed to said BURNS by JOHN TODD, LISY TODD & JEANNY TODD 12 Sep 1793. Should payment be made with interest said deed becomes null & void. S/ DAVID (D) BURN. Wit: THO (X) MILLS, JOHN TROTTER, who swore by oath 20 Jan 1794 before JULIUS NICHOLS, J.P. Rcd. 29 Jan 1794.

Pp. 182-183. 9 Aug 1790: Deed of Gift: EDWARD FLETCHER of Edgefield Co. SC hereunto moving, to my wife, HANNAH, and my children JOHN FLETCHER, JAMES FLETCHER & MARY JONES for love of wife & children, my property viz: to wife HANNAH: all the cattle & house furniture she bought of her & 1/3 of the land I now live, & the land I have in Georgey & land on Long Cain be sold & a 1/3 of money to son JOHN FLETCHER also a mar. To daughter MARY JONES, 2/3 of money from sale of Long Cain Land & a hunting saddle. To son JAMES FLETCHER all the rest of my property. S/ EDWARD FLETCHER. Wit: CHARLES BUSSEY, MOSES FRAZER, JOHN (Y) WIDMAN, who swore by oath 20 Sep 1790 before HUGH MIDDLETON, J.P. Rcd. 3 Sep 1792.

Pp. 183-185. 4 May 1792: JAMES HOLT, Carpenter of Edgefield Co. SC to RICHARD LEWIS for 60 pounds, 107 acres granted 5 Dec 1791 unto JAMES HOLT being on Penn Creek of Little Saluda River & on the Circut Road leading from Cambridge to Charleston. S/ JAMES HOLT. Wit: ALEXR. WILSON, JOHN SMEDLY, who swore by oath 4 May 1792 before HENRY KING, J.P. Rcd. 3 Sep 1792.

Pp. 186-188. 28 Mar 1792: WRIGHT NICHOLSON of Edgefield Co. SC to RICHARD LEWIS for 80 pounds, 190 acres granted 6 Mar 1786 unto said NICHOLSON on Penn Creek of Little Saluda River. S/ WRIGHT NICHOLSON. Wit: JOHN McMANUS, JOHN LEWIS, who swore by oath 16 Jun 1792 before HENRY KING, J.P. Rcd. 3 Sep 1792.

Pp. 188-189. 25 Mar 1792: Bill of Sale: EDWARD BABER of Edgefield Co. SC to JOHN DRINKARD of same place for 20 pounds, one negro boy named JIMMY. S/ EDWARD BABER. Wit: CHRISR. BROOKS, Senr., JAMES (+) VAUNN, who swore by oath 25 Mar 1792 before HENRY KING, J.P. Rcd. 3 Sep 1792.

Pp. 189-193. 7 Aug 1792: WILLIAM THOMAS CALDWELL, eldest brother & heir at law of JOHN CALDWELL dec'd of Newberry Co. SC to NATHANIEL ABNEY of Edgefield Co. SC for 50 pounds, sold 100 acres originally granted 2 Apr 1773 to JOHN CALDWELL now dec'd being (when surveyed), in Colleton Co., (now Edgefield), on Saluda River adj. E by NATHANIEL ABNEY,& N by FRANCES BROWN. S/ WILLIAM CALDWELL. Wit: PHILLEMON WATERS, JOHN ABNEY, JOEL ABNEY, who swore by oath 3 Sep 1792 before AQUILA MILES, J.P. Rcd. 4 Sep 1792.

Pp. 193-196. 7 Jan 1794: Mortgage: FANNY BURT, widow of the late MOODY BURT, Senior, dec'd. of Edgefield Co. SC to FRANCIS BURT of same place, by her Bond for the penal sum 153 pounds with condition of payment of 76 pounds on or before 7 Jan1795 & for better securing of payment convey one negro wench named GRACE & her child named JACOB, 1 mare, 1 riding chair & harness, 1 sow, 1 lot plantation tools, 1 lot of kitchen furniture, 1 trunk, 1 morble slab, 1 pine table, 1 Bible, 1 bed & furniture, 7 chairs, 1 shot gun, 1 hand saw & 3 pad locks. S/ FANNY (X) BURT. Wit: LUCY W. EVANS, E. BRENAN, who swore by oath 7 Feb 1794 before RICHARD TUTT, J.P. Rcd. 7 Feb 1794.

Pp. 196-198. 5 Feb 1794: Mortgage: DAVID JOHNSON of Edgefield Co. SC to SAMUEL RAMSEY Indebted for 95 pounds by a note dated 21 Dec 1793 to be paid in 12 months & for better securing of payment convey 150 acres originally granted 25 Apr 1765 unto MATHEW RAMSEY bounded to the North by Saluda River. S/ DAVID JOHNSON. Wit: JOHN MOORE, GREEN MOORE, who swore by oath 3 Feb 1794 before JOHN MOORE, J.P. Rcd. 11 Feb 1794.

Pp. 198-202. 3 Mar 1792: ABNER PERIN, Planter to CATHARINE FRITZ for 5 shillings, 180 acres on Hard Labour Creek of Savannah River adj. E by said PERRIN; N by PRICE; W by GIBSON & CON & S by McBRIDE. S/ ABNER PERRIN. Wit: PHILIP ZIMMERMAN, PETER RAMBEY, JOHN JAMES STIEFEL, who swore by oath 14 Jul 1792 before THOS. BACON, J.P. Rcd. 4 Sep 1792.

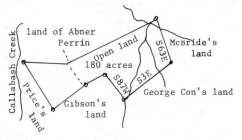

Plat laid out & surveyed 26 Jan 1792 by ABNER PERRIN, D.S.

Pp. 202-206. 18 Jul 1792: GEORGE MILLER & KEZIAH, his wife, Planter of Edgefield Co. SC to WILLIAM TOBLER, Planter of same place for 26 pounds, 112 acres being part of 1110 acres originally granted said MILLER 6 Mar 1786 opposite Beach Island adj. NE on remainder part of original grant; N by WILLIAM EVANS; SW by JOHN CLARK; SE by JOHN STURZENEGGER, Esq. & SW by JAMES PARSONS. S/ GEO. MILLER, KEZIAH MILLER. Wit: GEORGE BENDER, WILLIAM EVANS, who swore by oath 25 Aug 1792 before JOSEPH HIGHTOWER, J.P. Rcd. 4 Sep 1792.

Pp. 206-210. 15 Oct 1791: JOHN STURZENEGGER, Esq & ELIZABETH his wife to GEORGE BENDER, Planter for 50 pounds, sold 139 acres being part of 166 acres originally granted said STURZZENEGGER 21 Jan 1785, the remaining 27 acres being exchanged with JOHN CLARK; adj. N by JOHN RICHARDSON, S by JOHN TOBLER Senr & SAMUEL BURGESS, & W by JOHN TOBLER, Senr. S/ JOHN STURZENEGGER, ELIZABETH STURZENEGGER. Wit: CASPER NAIL, Senr., CASPER NAIL, Junr., who swore by oath 4 Sep 1792 before RICHARD TUTT, Esq., J.P. Rcd. 4 Sep 1792.

Pp. 210-212. 7 Aug 1792: WILLIAM EVANS, Surveyor to CASPER NAIL, Junr., Planter for 100 pounds, sold 50 acres being part of 640 acres originally granted 15 Oct 1784 unto JOHN RICHARDSON and was conveyed to said WILLIAM EVANS by L&R 18 Sep 1790 adj. N & E by CASPER NAIL, Senr; W by BENJAMIN HARRIS & all other sides by JOHN RICHARDSON. S/ WM. EVANS. Wit: JOHN SAVAGE, GEO. BENDER, who swore by oath 4 Sep 1792 before RICHARD TUTT, J.P. Rcd. 4 Sep 1792.

Pp. 212-214. 29 Aug 1792: Mrs. ANN ZUBLY, Gentlewoman, to GEORGE BENDER, Gentleman for 20 Guineas sold 12 acres being part of land granted to said Mrs ANN ZUBLY & Mrs ELIZABETH STURZZENEGGER his sisters, whereon the said Mrs ANN ZUBLY now lives in New Windsor near the upper end of Beach Island adj. WALTER TAYLOR; ULRICK EGGER & W on said tract of land to the said sisters granted in 1762; Mr MICHAEL MAYERS. S/ ANN ZUBLY. Wit: WM. SHINHOLSER, CASPER NAIL, Junr., who swore by oath 4 Sep 1792 before RICHARD TUTT, J.P. Rcd. 4 Sep 1792. Plat pg. 214.

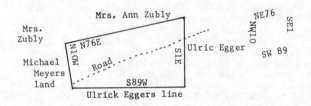

Pp. 214-218. 16 Apr 1786: MICHAEL BURKHALTER to DAVID BURKHALTER for 50 pounds, sold 100 acres being part of 200 acres originally granted 21 Jan 1761 unto JNO. FEDRICK DUBBER & was conveyed to MICHAEL BURKHALTER by L&R 17 & 18 Oct 1773 being on the South side of Horns Creek of Stephens Creek. S/ MICHAEL (MB) BURKHALTER. Wit: WILLIAM STRINGER, JOHN (‡B) BURKHALTER, who swore by oath 17 Mar 1792 before AQUILA MILES, J.P. Rcd. 5 Sep 1792.

Pp. 218-220. 1791: THOMAS KEY & ELIZABETH his wife of Edgefield Co. SC to ELISHA PALMER of same place for 200 pounds, sold 450 acres on waters of Savannah River. S/ THOMAS KEY, BETSY KEY. Wit: GEORGE GOODWIN, JESSE LANIER, who swore by oath 31 Oct 1791 before AQUILA MILES, J.P. Rcd. 5 Sep 1792.

Pp. 221-223. 10 Jan 1792: Mortgage: SAMUEL BURGESS, Planter of Edgefield Co. SC to JOHN CLARK, Planter of same place by my bond in the penal sum of 312 pounds, with condition of payment of 156 pounds on or before June next do for better securing of payments sell 640 acres where I live in Winton & Edgefield also five negroes namely JACK; TENAH; DINAH; JOE; & LONDON. Should payment be made with interest this deed becomes null & void. S/ SAMUEL BURGESS. Wit: JESSE FOUNTAIN, WALTER TAYLOR, who swore by oath 5 Sep 1792 before JOSEPH HIGHTOWER, J.P. Rcd. 5 Sep 1792.

Pp. 223-227. 30 May 1791: EDMUND WHATLEY & PHILLIS, his wife of Edgefield Co. SC to CHARLES MARTIN for 70 pounds, sold 60 acres being part of an original grant to HENRY SUMMERALL, lying on Horns Creek adj. N by JOHN MARTIN; E by CHARLES MARTIN & W by ANN SUMMERALL. S/ EDMUND WHATLEY, PHILLIS (+) WHATLEY. Wit: ALEXR. EDMONDS, TRUMAN WIGHTT, JAMES CHASTAIN. (See DBK 7, p. 234). Rcd. (no date).

P. 227. 29 Sep 1794: Power of Attorney: JOHN HANCOCK, the Elder of Edgefield Co. to my Brother, WILLIAM HANCOCK of Kentucky, for the purpose of collecting a certain debt from JOHN GRANT, who formerly lived in Surry Co. NC but now Kentucky, grant power of attorney to collect in my name in Kentucky. S/ JOHN HANCOCK, Senr. Wit: JOSHUA HAMMOND, who swore by oath 29 Sep 1794 before JOSEPH HIGHTOWER, J.P. Rcd. 30 Sep 1794.

Pp. 228-233. 20 Dec 1790: ROBERT MOSELY & PENELLEPE, his wife of Edgefield Co. SC to CHARLES MARTIN of same place for 80 pounds, sold 47 1/2 acres being part of an original grant 27 Sep 1784 to said MOSELY being on Horns Creek of Stephens Creek adj. CHARLES MARTIN; JOHN RANSFORD; & JOSEPH SUMERLIN. S/ ROBERT (+) MOSELY, PENELLEPEI (X) MOSELY. Wit: WILLIAM MORGAN, DANIEL MARQUIS (also MARCUS), JAMES COBB, Junr., who swore by oath 2 Sep 1794 before JOSEPH HIGHTOWER, J.P. Rcd. 6 Sep 1792.

Pp. 233-238. 30 May 1791: EDMUND WHATLEY & PHILLIS, his wife of Edgefield Co. SC to CHARLES MARTIN of same place for 75 pounds, sold 60 acres being part of an original grant to HENRY SUMMERALL being on Horns Creek adj. N by JOHN MARTIN; E & S by CHARLES MARTIN & W by ANN SUMMARALL. S/ EDMUND WHATLEY, PHILLIS (+) WHATLEY. Wit: ALEXANDER EDMONDS, JAMES CHASTAIN, TRUMAN WIGHTT, who swore by oath 5 Sep 1792 before RICHARD TUTT, J.P. Rcd. 6 Sep 1792. [This is the completed deed started on page 223-227 which has no oath or recording date, gch.]

Pp. 238-241. 3 Apr 1792: FRANCIS SETTLE (?LITTLE?) of Edgefield Co. SC to JOSHUA HAMMOND of same place for 100 pounds, sold 200 acres originally granted HENRY SIZEMORE 26 Sep 1772 being at Cherokee ponds. S/ FRS. LITTLE. Wit: JOSEY PARKER, JOHN HATCHER, who swore by oath 3 Sep 1792 before JOSEPH HIGHTOWER, J.P. Rcd. 12 Sep 1792.

Pp. 241-245. 7 Nov 1791: ALEXANDER ROBERTSON & JANE, his wife alias BROWNLEE, of Charleston SC to WILLIAM FARGUHAR of Edgefield Co. SC for 20 pounds, sold 100 acres originally surveyed 13 Feb 1768 for JANE BROWNLEE being in Granville Co. (when surveyed) on Wilson Creek adj. E by JAMES ANDERSON; NW by ARCHIBALD BEARD; & S by Wilson Creek. S/ ALEXDR. ROBERTSON, JANE (+) ROBERTSON. Wit: JOHN BROWNLEE, JOHN GAMBLE, THOMAS ROSS, who swore by oath 10 Aug 1792 before WILLIAM ANDERSON, J.P. Rcd. 1 Jan 1792.

Pp. 245-247. 11 Jul 1792: Mortgage: SIMON GENTRY to my step-sons JEREMIAH COBB & SANDERS COBB property made use of belonging to said step-sons; am bound for 50 pounds provided said 50 pounds is not demanded in less time than 4 yrs & for better securing of payment have sold 147 acres on head of little Creek adj. N by WILLIAM THOMAS & the land where said GENTRY now lives; also horses, cattle & household furniture. S/ SIMON GENTRY. Wit: GREEN MOORE, MARTIN MORGAN, who swore by oath 11 Jul 1792 before JOHN MOORE, J.P. Rcd. 15 Jul 1792.

Pp. 247-252. 29 Dec 1789: THOMAS LAMAR of Edgefield Co. SC to JOHN PARKER of same place for 20 pounds, sold 125 acres being part of an original grant to said LAMAR on Town Creek adj. CRANNAMOS ZINN & said LAMAR's land. S/ THOMS. LAMAR. Wit: JOHN BUTLER, WILLIAM STEWART, who swore by oath 2 Jan 1792 before JOHN STURZENEGGER, Esq., J.P. Rcd. 3 Sep 1792.

Pp. 252-256. 21 Mar 1792: JACOB YOUNGBLOOD, Planter of Edgefield Co. SC to JOHN ALDRIDGE, Planter of same place for 15 pounds, sold 185 acres being part of 370 acres granted said YOUNGBLOOD 5 Jun 1786 on South side of Turkey Creek of Stephens Creek of Savannah River. S/ JACOB YOUNGBLOOD. Wit: PATIENCE (P) ALDRIDGE, JAS. SCOTT, ISAAC (I) ALDRIDGE, who swore by oath 19 Sep 1792 before RICHARD TUTT, J.P. Rcd. 19 Sep 1792.

P. 256. SC Orangeburgh Dist: 10 Sep 1792; MARIA JACOBO HOFFMAN made oath that she was lawfully married to PETER KEABLOR in St. Andrews Church in London in Oct 1763 & that she had four children by said KEABLER which are all dead. S/ MARIA JACOBO (+) HOFFMAN before WM. HEATLY, J.Q.
CHRISTOPHER WITTS made oath that he knew PETER KEABLER and MARIA JACOBO HOFFMAN & they lived as man & wife in Charleston & they had several children about 25 years ago. WM. HEATLY, J.Q. Rcd. 26 Sep 1792.

Pp. 257-260. 10 May 1787: MELCHIOR HOFFMAN of SC & his wife, MARIA JACOBO, (Relick of PETER KIBBER), to JOHN STEDHAM of Edgefield Co. SC for 37 pounds, sold 200 acres originally granted PETER KIBBER 13 Aug 1765 being on Turkey Creek adj. SW by NICHOLAS GLASSER. S/ (German script) MELCHOIR HOFFMAN, MARIA ZACOBNI (+) HOFFMAN. Wit: JOHN HOFMAN, ZACHARIAH STEDHAM, who swore by oath 26 Sep 1792 before RICHARD TUTT, J.P. Rcd. 26 Sep 1792.

P. 260. 31 Dec 1792: Bill of Sale: JAMES LYON, Planter of Wilkes Co. GA to JOHN LYON for 45 pounds, sold 1 negro boy named GEORGE. Wit: WILLIAM LYON, ROBERT JENNINGS, who swore by oath 8 Oct 1792 (sic) before THOS. BACON, J.P. Rcd. 8 Oct (sic) 1792.

Pp. 261-265. 13 May 1792: JOHN KIRKLAND, Planter of Edgefield Co. SC to ARTHUR SIMKINS, Esq. of same place for 10 pounds, 100 acres originally granted 7 Mar 1791 said KIRKLAND being in Orangeburgh Dist. in Winton Co. on a branch of South fork called Shaws Creek of Edisto River adj. branches of Shaws Creek called Joices branch. S/ JOHN (J) KIRKLAND. Wit: JONATHAN WEVER, CHARLES (X) SUTTON, CHRISTIAN (X) GOMILION, who swore by oath 8 Oct 1792 before RICHARD TUTT, J.P. Rcd. 8 Oct 1792.

Pp. 265-267. 17 Jan 1791: JOHN LEYSATH, (also JOHN WILLIAM

LIZARD), Planter of Orangeburgh Dist. SC to LUD WILLIAMS of Edgefield Co. SC for 30 pounds, 50 acres originally granted 2 Jan 1754. S/ JOHN LEYSATH. Wit: JOHN STURZENEGGER, J.P., JONATHAN MEYER, who swore by oath 9 Oct 1792 before RICHARD TUTT, J.P. Rcd. 9 Oct 1792.

Pp. 267-269. 18 Jul 1792: GEORGE MILLER & KEZIAH, his wife of Edgefield Co. SC to JOSEPH HIX, Planter of same place for 15 pounds, sold 108 acres being part of a tract originally granted said MILLER & divided off from it by WILLIAM EVANS, D.S. being near the Musterfield Branch. S/ GO. MILLER, KEZIAH MILLER. Wit: WILLIAM EVANS, GEO. BENDER, who swore by oath 9 Oct 1792 before RICHARD TUTT, J.P. Rcd. 9 Oct 1792.

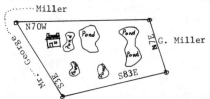

This tract of 108 acres in Edgefield Co. SC within half a mile of Beech Island swamp divided from a large tract granted GEORGE MILLER - certified 10 Jul 1792 by WILLIAM EVANS, Dept Surv.

Pp. 269-270. 2 Aug 1792: Bill of Sale: THOMAS FREEMAN of Edgefield Co. SC to RICHARD FREEMAN of same place for 124 pounds, sold one small negro man named JACK & one negro wench named PHILLIS & one negro boy child named MACK. S/ THOMAS (TF) FREEMAN. Wit: DAVID BURK, JESSE COPELAND, who swore by oath 20 Oct 1792 before RICHARD TUTT, J.P. Rcd. 20 Oct 1792.

Pp. 270-274. 11 Oct 1792: THOMAS FREEMAN of Edgefield Co. SC to RICHARD FREEMAN of same place for 100 pounds, sold 404 acres originally granted 6 Mar 1786 said THOMAS FREEMAN being on Bedingfield Creek of Savannah River adj. SW by land formerly of THOMAS FREEMAN which was sold at Columbia; & by PETER GEBARR. S/ THOMAS (TF) FREEMAN. Wit: DAVID BURK, JESSE (X) TAYLOR, JESSE COPELAND, who swore by oath 20 Oct 1792 before RICHARD TUTT, J.P. Rcd. 20 Oct 1792.

Pp. 274-276. 20 Apr 1790: JOHN COOK of Edgefield Co. SC to WEST COOK for 10 pounds, sold Lot #25 in Village of Campbelton containing 1/4 acre. S/ JOHN COOK. Wit: HENRY ALLEN, ROBERT B. WASHINGTON, who swore by oath 16 Oct 1790 before AQUILA MILES, J.P. Rcd. 5 Oct 1793.

Pp. 277-279. 20 Apr 1790: WEST COOK of Edgefield Co. SC to JNO. PURSELL & ANDW.HARKNESS for 10 pounds, sold Lot No 25 in Village of Campbelton containing 1/4 acre. S/ WEST COOK. Wit: JAMES TALBERT, EDMOND MARTIN, who swore by oath 2 Mar 1792 before AQUILA MILES, J.P. Rcd. 5 Oct 1793.

Pp. 279-282. 7 May 1793: ANDW. HARKNESS of Edgefield Co. SC to JNO. PURSELL of same place for 10 pounds, sold 1/2 of Lot #25 in Village of Campbelton being 1/2 or 1/4 acre. S/ ANDREW HARKNESS. Wit: MARY PURSELL, ZACHEUS PURSELL, SAML (X) LYON, who swore by oath 5 Oct 1793 before AQUILA MILES, J.P. Rcd. 5 Oct 1793.

Pp. 282-287. 18 Oct 1792: THOMAS PALMER & REBECCA, his wife of Edgefield Co. SC to JOHN HILL of same place for 60 pounds, sold

150 acres originally granted 23 Jun 1774 & recorded in Audrs. Office 22 Nov 1774 & was transferred to said THOMAS PALMER by L&R 18 & 19 Nov 1791 & recorded at Edgefield Book H pp 72-77 being on branch of Mountain Creek of Stevens Creek of Savana River. S/ THOMAS PALMER, REBECA (+) PALMER. Wit: JAMES GOLMAN, JOHN (0) HILL, WILLIAM GLEN, who swore by oath 22 Oct 1792 before AQUILA MILES, J.P. Rcd. 22 Oct 1792.

Pp. 287-288. 12 Mar 1792: Bill of Sale: THOMAS BELLEW of Edgefield Co. SC to CHARLES LAVENDER for 10 pounds, sold a horse, & working tools. S/ THOMAS (+) BELLEW. Wit: WILLIAM JETER, Junr., who swore by oath 24 Oct 1792 before AQUILA MILES, J.P. Rcd. 30 Oct 1792.

Pp. 288-291. 14 Sep 1792: SAMUEL WRIGHT of Edgefield Co. SC to WILLIAM COVINGTON for 10 pounds, sold 100 acres originally granted SIMON MARTIN 5 Sep 1785 on the main road leading from Campbellton to Ninety Six. Said land was conveyed from said MARTIN to ALLEN HINTON & from HINTON to SAMUEL WRIGHT adj. NW by WILLIAM COVINGTON; W by DANL. GILL; E by WM MORGAN; NE by JNO PIERCE & N by JNO. HAMMOND, dec'd. S/ SAML. WRIGHT. Wit: JOHN McMULLAN, THOMAS HERON, who swore by oath 20 Oct 1792 before JOSEPH HIGHTOWER, J.P. Rcd. 2 Nov 1792.

Pp. 291-297. 6 Nov 1791: RICHARD JOHNSON Junr., Joyner, & MARY, his wife of Edgefield Co. SC to JOHN WILLIAMS for 46 pounds, sold 334 acres originally granted 7 Aug 1786 unto DAVID BURKS & was conveyed by L&R 2 & 3 Apr 1790 unto said JOHNSON being on a branch of Turkey Creek of Stephens Creek. Said 334 acres excepting such part of an older grant to MOSES KIRKLAND now in possession of ROBERT BURTS on SW & except such part as an older survey may be taken on E part of tract which is said to be the property of JOHN THREEWITT which said two surveys is suppose to run within said lines of tract. S/ RICHD. JOHNSON. Wit: WILLIAM SIMKINS, JOHN (‡) GORMAN, JOHN SIMKINS, who swore by oath 25 Nov 1791 before ARTHUR SIMKINS, J.C.C. Rcd. 1 Nov 1792.
NB Aforesaid parties have agreed that a straight line should be run by RUTLEDGE's tract to BUFFINGTON's old tract, ROBERT BERT & said JOHN WILLIAMS.

Pp. 297-302. 1 Nov 1792: ANNE BLAND of Edgefield Co. SC to WORMLY BLAND of same place for 20 pounds, sold 120 acres being part of 2 surveys (1) part of a tract conveyed by GEORGE MASON to said ANNE BLAND being on the main road leading from Ninety Six to Charleston & (2) part of a tract originally granted 1 Jan 1787 to WILLIAM LITTLE & conveyed to ANNE BLAND 8 Jun 1787. S/ ANNE (X) BLAND. Wit: SAMUEL HUMPHREYS, SAMUEL LEWIS, WILLIAM HUMPHREYS, who swore by oath 5 Nov 1792 before JOSEPH HIGHTOWER, J.P. Rcd. 5 Nov 1792.

P. 303. 7 Jul 1792: CHARLES PINCKNEY, Governor & Commander in Chief of SC Appoint THOMAS BACON, Esq. be a Judge of Edgefield County Court in SC in the room of JOHN PURVIS, Esq. dec'd. S/ CHARLES PINCKNEY. PETER FRENEAU, Secretary. Rcd. Nov Term 1792.

Pp. 303-309. 25 Apr 1792: RICHARD JOHNSON, Junr., Planter & MARY his wife & JOEL CHANDLER, Planter of Edgefield Co. SC to JAMES HALL, Planter of same place for 233 pounds, sold 500 acres being land formerly held by MOSES KIRKLAND & confiscated & sold by the

DEED BOOK 7:   1792-1794   EDGEFIELD COUNTY S.C.

Commissioners known as ground plat No. 2 to said JOHNSON by L&R 8
& 9 Jul 1783 being on Turkey Creek of Stephens Creek of Savannah
River adj. N by land formerly held by RICHARD WILLIAMS, now by
JOHN JONES; E by RICHARD JOHNSON, Senr. & MOODY BURT formerly
held by JOHN RUTLEDGE, Esq.; S by RICHARD JOHNSON & JAMES SCOTT;
W by said SCOTT & land surveyed by FRAZER as having recourse to a
plat made by ROBERT LANG, D.S. 26 Sep 1788. S/ RICHARD JOHNSON,
MARY JOHNSON, JOEL CHANDLER. Wit: WILLIAM HALL, BENJAMIN
HIGHTOWER, who swore by oath 25 Apr 1792 before JOSEPH HIGHTOWER,
J.P.
Edgefield Co. Court Nov Term 1792: Mrs MARY JOHNSON, wife of
RICHARD, relinquishes dower & 1/3 before RICHARD TUTT, C.E.C.
Rcd. (no date).

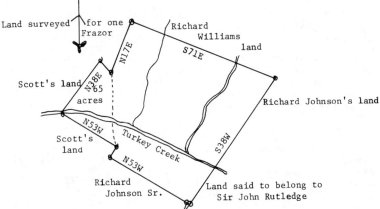

Capt. RICHARD JOHNSON requested a resurvey of a piece of land
where JOEL CHANDLER now lives & found to contain 570 acres as
seen by plat. 26 Sep 1788. S/ ROBERT LONG, D.S.

Pp. 310-311. 20 Sep 1791: RUBEN FARLEY of Edgefield Co. SC to
JACOB GUYTON of same place for 25 pounds, sold 139 acres being
part of an original grant to PHILIP LAMAR on Horse Creek adj. S &
SW by original lines; N by WILLIAM GIBSON; E & NE by RICHARD
JOHNSON; SE by JAMES JONES. S/ RUBEN FARLEY. Wit: PHILIP
LAMAR, JAMES JONES, who
swore by oath 5 Nov 1792
before RICHARD TUTT J.P.

PHILIP LAMAR requested
that 139 acres be divided
off to RUBEN FARLEY. Plat
certified 19 Dec 1788.
S/ WM. EVANS, D.S.

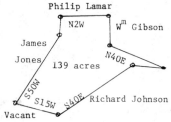

Pp. 311-314. 9 Nov 1792: THOMAS FREEMAN & MARTHA his wife of
Edgefield Co. SC to JOSEPH TOLBERT of same place for 58 pounds
sold 150 acres originally granted 4 Dec 1771 to EZEKIEL HARLEN on
Savannah River near the mouth of Long Cain Creek adj. E by HARLAN
& SW by Savannah River. S/ THOMAS (TF) FREEMAN, MARTHA (M)
FREEMAN. Wit: THOMAS MILES, JEREMIAH TOLBORT, JOHN TOLBORT, who
swore by oath 13 Nov 1793 before RICHARD TUTT, J.P. Rcd. 13 Nov
1793.

96

DEED BOOK 7: 1792-1794 EDGEFIELD COUNTY S.C.

Pp. 315-320. 20 Sep 1786: JAMES WILSON, Planter Ninety Six Dist
SC to SAMUEL HALL of same place for 70 pounds, sold 150 acres
being part of 350 originally granted 2 Mar 1768 unto said WILSON
on Stephens Creek and east branch of Savannah River adj. W by
JAMES HARRISON; E by original survey & plantation where BRYAN
COCRUM, dec'd., "did live when he died" son in law to said JAMES
WILSON. S/ JAMES (𝓋𝓸) WILSON. Wit: WILLIAM (+) HALL, ALEXANDER
HALL, who swore by oath 6 Nov 1792 before RICHARD TUTT, J.P. Rcd.
6 Nov 1792.

Pp. 320-326. 17 May 1792: SAMUEL DOOLITTLE & ANN, his wife of
Edgefield Co. SC to STEPHEN TILLMAN of same place for 200 pounds,
sold 72 acres being part of 200 acres originally granted 8 Mar
1755 unto JOSEPH NOBLES & conveyed to LAURENCE RAMBO, dec'd., by
L&R 29 & 30 Oct 1765 & by LW&T of said RAMBO was given to his son
BENJAH RAMBO who conveyed to said DOOLITTLE by L&R 8 & 9 Sep 1786
being on North side of Horns Creek. Said land adj. N by PETER
CARNES; NE by said STEPHEN TILLMAN & EDWARD MITCHELL; Marshels
Creek. S/ SAMUEL (X) DOOLITTLE, ANN (X) DOOLITTLE. Wit: JOSEPH
DOOLITTLE, WILLIAM (X) FLINN, FREDRICK TILLMAN, Junr., who swore
by oath 3 Nov 1792 before RICHARD TUTT, J.P.
E.F.C. Nov Term 1792: Mrs ANN DOOLITTLE, wife of SAMUEL,
relinquished dower & 1/3 before RICHARD TUTT, C.E.C. Rcd. 3 Nov
1792.

Pp. 326-329. 24 Mar 1792: Article of Agreement: JAMES COURSEY,
WILLIAM KEY, & E. COX all of Edgefield, agree on a copartnership
to keep a tavern on 6 acres Lot now let for use by said COURSEY
of his said adj. property. All to share equally in expense &
profits of such for period of 10 years. S/ JAMES COURSEY, WILLIAM
KEY, E. WWWWWCox(sic) Wit: COLL COLLINS, WILLIAM DAVIS, who swore
by oath 1 Nov 1792 before THOMAS BACON, J.P. Rcd. 17 Dec 1792.
[Note ; gch: Terms for buildings & obligations very descriptive.]

P. 329. Letter to RICHARD TUTT, Esq.: PHILEMON BOZEMAN to WILLIAM
BLAKE : 14 Dec 1792: Sir: Deliver to WILLIAM BLAKE a Deed of Gift
(Alias conveyance) 2 negroes viz: LETT & NIMROD & 1 horse given
to me by BLAKE & recorded in your office. Said BLAKE having fully
satisfied me for the same & I relinquish any claim to said
property under said Deed of Gift or Conveyance. S/ PHILEMON
BOZEMAN. WILLIAM NEWTON swore by oath 22 Dec 1792 before JOHN
MOORE, J.P. Rcd. 23 Dec 1792.

Pp. 329-332. 1 Jun 1792: NATHAN EVANS, Planter, & LUCY his wife
of SC to JOHN WRIGHT, Teacher, for (blank) sold 70 acres granted
5 Jul 1790 on Horn Creek of Stephens Creek of Savannah River adj.
NW an old survey; SW by WILLIAM HOWLS & NE by JOHN GARRETT. S/
NATHAN (ᴄᴐ) EVENS, LUCY (W) EVANS. Wit: THOS. HOWEL, HOPKINS
(𝒴) HOWELL, who swore by oath 26 Nov 1792 before AQUILA MILES,
J.P. Rcd. 23 Dec 1792.

Pp. 333-334. 10 Sep 1788: ELISABETH RENOLDS of Edgefield Co. SC
to CLEMENT CARGILL of same place for 30 pounds, sold 299 acres
granted 2 Oct 1786 to said RENOLDS on Chavis Creek adj. LUCY
SAINJONS; FRANCIS MENS & ROBERT LANG. S/ ELISABETH (X) RENOLDS.
Wit: GEORGE RICHARDS, MATT POLLOCK, JOHN ELLIOT, JOHN HERNDON,
who swore by oath 13 Jan 1789 before WILLIAM ANDERSON, J.P. Rcd.
15 Jan 1793.

DEED BOOK 7: 1792-1794 EDGEFIELD COUNTY S.C.

Pp. 334-340. JOHN ROBERTS & SALLY, his wife of Edgefield Co. SC
to ABSOLOM ROBERTS of same place for 50 pounds, sold 37 acres
being part of 200 acres originally granted 6 Dec 1755 unto THOMAS
ROBERTS, dec'd. & conveyed to JOHN ROBERTS L&R 7 & 8 Jul 1786
being on waters of Dry Creek of Chaveses Creek. S/ JOHN (Ɨ)
ROBERTS, SALEY ROBERTS. Wit: RICHARD WITHENTON, WILLIAM ROBERTS,
JNO. SWILLIVAN, who swore by oath 1 Jan 1793 before AQUILA MILES,
J.P. Rcd. 2 Jan 1793.

Pp. 340-341. 10 Apr 1790: MARY RODGERS of Edgefield Co. SC
hereunto moving appoint my Trusty friend ABRAHAM RICHARDSON of
said County my attorney to recover & receive in my name from the
Estate of JOHN DOOLY, dec'd. of Wilkes Co. GA 552 pounds with
Interest from 1792 (sic). S/ MARY (X) RODGERS. Wit: ROBERT SPEAR,
JOHN COLLINS, CHARLES BANKS, who swore by oath 1 Jul 1790 before
HUGH MIDDLETON, J.P. Rcd. 28 Jan 1793.

Pp. 341-346. 4 Feb 1793: RICHARD JOHNSON, Junr, Planter & MARY,
his wife & RICHARD JOHNSON, Senr. of Edgefield Co. SC to JAMES
HALL of same place for 30 pounds, sold 185 acres being part of
202 acres originally granted 1 Aug 1790 to said RICHARD JOHNSON,
Junr. being on Turkey Creek of Savanna River adj. when surveyed
NE by JOHN RUTLEDGE, Esq., & now held by MATTHEW BURT; N by
RICHARD JOHNSTON; on the Great Road leading from Augusta to the
Ridge & by ROBERT BURTON's line. S/ RICHARD JOHNSTON, MAREY
JOHNSTON, RICHARD (R) JOHNSTON, Senr. Wit: THOMAS HALL, ISAAC
FOREMAN, who swore by oath 4 Feb 1793 before JOSEPH HIGHTOWER,
J.P. Rcd. 4 Feb 1793.

Pp. 346-350. 18 Dec 1792: STEPHEN LEE, Gentleman, & DORTHEA, his
wife of Charleston SC, said DORATHEA being surviving Executrix of
LW&T of HUGH ALISON, dec'd., to JOHN BLOCKER of Edgefield Co. SC
for 151 pounds, sold a tract of land originally granted 3 Jul
1772 unto HUGH ALISON & by LW&T to be sold by his Executrix for
benefit of his Devisees Said land on both sides of Log Creek adj.
when surveyed SE by TIMOTHY REARDON & land granted on Dutch
Survey; E by MOSES KIRKLAND. S/ STEPHEN LEE, DORTHEA LEE. Wit:
JACOB H. ALISON, ALEXR. McDOWALL, who swore by oath 4 Feb 1793
before RICHARD TUTT, J.P. Rcd. 4 Feb 1793.

Pp. 350-354. 4 Mar 1793: WM. COVINGTON & PHEBE, his wife of
Edgefield Co. SC to THOS. JEDG of same place for 40 pounds, sold
188 acres originally granted 1 Jan 1787 unto CHARLES RHODES lying
on Jones branch of Savanna River & since conveyed by L&R Jan 1791
unto said COVINGTON adj. NE by DANIEL GILL & SIMON MARTIN; SE by
Colo. JNO. PURVIS; SW by JAMES MARTIN; NW & SW by Colo LEROY
HAMMOND. S/ WM. COVINGTON, PHEBE COVINGTON. Wit: JOHN COVINGTON,
WILLIAM WILLIAMS, who swore by oath March Term Edgefield Court
before RICHARD TUTT, C.E.C. Rcd. (no date).

Pp. 354-356. 28 Jan 1793: PATRICK SULLIVANT of Edgefield Co. SC
to SAMUEL CARTER of same place for 10 pounds, sold 102 acres
originally granted to said SULLIVANT being on Cuffy Town Creek a
branch of Stephens Creek of Savannah River. S/ PATRICK SULLIVANT.
Wit: ALEXANDER HALL, WILLIAM BIBB, JOHN GLANTON, who swore by
oath 28 Jan 1793 before JAMES HARRISON. Rcd. 1 Mar 1793.

Pp. 356-357. 28 Jan 1793: JOHN GLANTON of Edgefield Co. SC to
SAMUEL CARTER of same place for 80 pounds, sold 63 acres being

part of 200 acres originally granted RICHARD WALLACE being on waters of Cuffy Town Creek a branch of Stephens Creek of Savannah River. S/ JOHN GLANTON, PEGGY (X) GLANTON. Wit: JOSEPH WALLACE, ALEXANDER HALL, JACOB HIBBLER, who swore by oath 28 Jan 1793 before JAMES HARRISON, J.P. Rcd. 1 Mar 1793.

Pp. 357-358. 3 Jan 1793: DANIEL WEITMAN of Edgefield Co. SC to SAMUEL CARTER of same place for 40 pounds, sold 150 acres originally granted to CHARLES WEITMAN being on Cuffy Town Creek a branch of Stephens Creek of Savannah River. S/ DANIEL WEITMAN. Wit: GARRETT LONGMIRE, WILLIAM BIBB, JACOB HIBBLER, who swore by oath 8 Jan 1793 before JAMES HARRISON, J.P. Rcd. 1 Mar 1793.

Pp. 359-363. 16 Dec 1790: JOHN HARRIS, Planter & MARY his wife of Edgefield Co. to DAVID SHOCKLEY, Planter of same place for 50 pounds, sold 100 acres being part of 295 acres granted 1 Jan 1787 to JAMES HARRIS & 100 acres conveyed by L&R 28 Aug 1787 unto JOHN HARRIS being on Beaver dam creek on the waggon road from Long Cain to Charleston. S/ JOHN (X) HARRIS, MARY (X) HARRIS. Wit: JOHN FRAZIER, FREDERICK HOLMES, THOS. HAGERS, who swore by oath 2 Mar 1793 before RICHARD TUTT, J.P. Rcd. 2 Mar 1793.

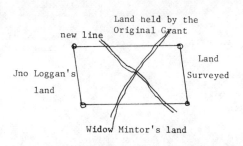

Land held by the Original Grant

new line

Jno Loggan's land

Land Surveyed

Widow Mintor's land

Surveyed by WM. COURSY, M.M.

Pp. 364-366. 3 Apr 1792: FRANCIS SETTLE of Edgefield Co. SC to JOSHUA HAMMOND of same place for 100 pounds 352 acres originally granted 5 Feb 1787 to said SETTLES adj. the Cherokee Ponds. S/ FRS. SETTLE. Wit: JOSEY PARKER, JOHN HATCHER, who swore by oath 10 Sep 1792 before JOSEPH HIGHTOWER, J.P. Rcd. 12 Sep 1792.

Pp. 366-371. 6 Dec 1792: MACKNESS GOOD of Edgefield Co. SC to CHRISTIAN LIMBACKER of same place for 150 pounds, 50 acres being part of 200 acres granted 10 Feb 1775 ABRAHAM RUMPH & was conveyed to ELIJAH PALMER who conveyed said land unto MACKNESS GOOD; adj. ELLIS PALMER; JOHN CANADY & by CUNNINGHAM's 10 acres, said land between Horns Creek & Stephens Creek. S/ MACK GOODE. Wit: THOMAS PHILLIPS, ELLIS PALMER, who swore by oath 7 Dec 1792 before AQUILA MILES, J.P. Rcd. 11 Mar 1793.

Pp. 371-375. 25 Dec 1789: JOHN GIBSON, Blacksmith of Edgefield Co. SC to JESSE GRIFFIN of same place for (blank), sold 150 acres originally granted 27 Nov 1770 unto TOBIAS MIRES being on Big Creek a branch of Little Saluda River of Saluda River. S/ JOHN GIBSON. Wit: WILLIAM SPANN, ABNER (X) CORLEY, CHURCHILL GIBSON, who swore by oath 20 Mar 1790 before RUSSELL WILSON. Rcd. 12 Mar 1793.

Pp. 375-379. 17 Sep 1792: BENJAMIN RYAN, Senr. to BENJAMIN RYAN the second, both of Edgefield Co. SC for 100 pounds, sold 250 acres originally granted 25 Oct 1764 being on Nobles Creek, now called Horns Creek of Stephens Creek. S/ BENJAMIN RYAN. Wit: RICHD. NEWMAN, ISAAC KIRKLAND, who swore by oath 12 Mar 1793

DEED BOOK 7: 1792-1794 EDGEFIELD COUNTY S.C

before JOSEPH HIGHTOWER, J.P. Rcd. 12 Mar 1793.

Pp. 379-382. 20 Dec 1792: MACKERNESS & SAMUEL GOODE to EDMOND
PURSELL for 50 pounds, sold 70 acres being a tract of land willed
to said MACKERNESS & SAMUEL GOODE by their father adj. lands of
WILLIAM & JAMES CLARK. S/ MACK GOODE, SAMUEL GOODE. Wit: W.H.
HOWARD, AARON (A) HERRING, who swore by oath 26 Jan 1793 before
HUGH MIDDLETON, J.P. Rcd. 12 Mar 1793.

DEED BOOK 8: 1793-1794 EDGEFIELD COUNTY S.C.

Pp. 1-5. 13 Feb 1793: JESSE ROUNTREE to JOSHUA HAMMOND, both of Edgefield Co. SC for 25 pounds, sold 100 acres originally granted 26 July 1774 unto JETHRO ROUNTREE adj. the Cherokee pond; JOSHUA HAMMOND; WILLIAM TARRENCE; JOSEPH HIGHTOWER & ZACHARIAH LAMAR. S/ JESSE ROUNTREE. Wit: ANDREW GLOVER, JOHN GLOVER, who swore by oath 15 Feb 1793 before JOSEPH HIGHTOWER, J.P. Rcd. 12 Mar 1793.

Pp. 5-10. 26 Dec 1792: GEORGE SEGLAR to JOHN HARDY, both of Edgefield Co. SC for 50 pounds, sold 128 acres where said SEGLAR now lives adj. NW by JOHN HANCOCK; N by DAVID SEGLAR; W by JOHN HETTY; S by JOHN HARDY; & E by JOHN CURRY. S/ GEORGE (X) SEGLAR. Wit: JAMES BAKER, CHEARLS BUSSEY, JOHN (X) GENTRY, who swore by oath 2 Mar 1793 before JOSEPH HIGHTOWER, J.P. Rcd. 12 Mar 1793.

Pp. 10-16. 11 Feb 1793: CHRISTOPHER BROOKS Senr., Planter & HONOUR his wife of Edgefield Co. SC to ALEXANDER WILSON of same place for 75 pounds, sold 170 acres originally granted 14 Dec 1786 to said BROOKS, on Deloaches branch of Little Saluda River adj. NW by MICHAL DELOACH. S/ CHRISTOPHER BROOKS, Senr., HONOR (S) BROOKS. Wit: MUMFORD PERRYMAN, MATHEW BOLTON, who swore by oath 13 Feb 1793 before HENRY KING, J.P. Rcd. 12 Mar 1793.

Pp. 16-22. 7 Dec 1792: MATTHEW STOKER, Planter of Edgefield Co. SC to RANDOL ROBINSON for 10 pounds, sold 25 acres being part of a survey granted to JOHN PERKINS who conveyed to JOHN LAMAR who conveyed to GEORGE RODGERS who conveyed to WILLIAM JACKSON who conveyed to DAVID THREATT who conveyed to said STOKER, said land being on Stephens Creek adj. lands of said STOKER. S/ MATTHEW STOKER, ELIZABETH (X) STOKER. Wit: JOHN GARDNER, LEVI SLATER, WILLIAM QUARLS, who swore by oath 9 Mar 1793 before JOSEPH HIGHTOWER, J.P. Rcd. 12 Mar 1793.

Pp. 22-27. 7 Dec 1792: MATTHEW STOKER to RANDOL ROBINSON, both of Edgefield Co. SC for 50 pounds, 102 acres originally granted 5 Feb 1787 to said STOKER adj. SE by said STOKER & JOHN DOOLEY. S/ MATTHEW STOKER, ELIZABETH (X) STOKER. Wit: JOHN GARDNER, LEVI SLATER, WILLIAM QUARLES, who swore by oath 9 Mar 1793 before JOSEPH HIGHTOWER, J.P. Rcd. 12 Mar 1793.

Pp. 27-33. 4 Feb 1793: JOSHUA HAMMOND & SARAH, his wife of Edgefield Co. SC to WILLIAM MORGAN of same place for 75 pounds, sold 200 acres on the Savannah River. S/ JOSHUA HAMMOND, SARAH HAMMOND.
Recd. 150 pounds full consideration from WM. MORGAN S/ JOSHUA HAMMOND. Wit: JOHN HAMMOND, BENJAMIN HIGHTOWER, who swore by oath 13 Feb 1793 before JOSEPH HIGHTOWER, J.P. Rcd. 12 Mar 1793.

Pp. 33-38. 12 Feb 1793: JOHN MOBLEY, Senr., Cooper, & ELIZABETH his wife to ALEXANDER WILSON, both of Edgefield Co. SC for 30 pounds, sold 123 acres originally granted 5 Nov 1792 unto said MOBLEY being on Pen Creek of Little Saludy River adj. NW by WRIGHT NICHOLSON; W by WM. HART; & SE by ROBT. STARK, Junr. S/ JOHN (X) MOBLEY, ELIZABETH (X) MOBLEY. Wit: JOHN (‡) DUGLAS, (also DOUGLESS), MATHEW BOLTON, who swore by oath 13 Feb 1793 before HENRY KING, J.P. Rcd. 12 Mar 1793.

P. 39. 2 May 1792: EZL. BELL to ANNE BELL, both of Edgefield Co. SC for 20 pounds, sold 100 acres on Reedy Creek (?Rudy?); 12 hogs; 1 mare & cold; 1 horse; 1 cow & calf; 1 bed & furniture;

pewter dishes; bason; 8 plates; 1 pot; Dutch oven; Iron Kettle; skillet; loome; womans saddle; 1/2 doz. chairs; 1 eap; 2 pr. cotton cords; 1 pr toe; spinning wheel; 2 bed & slead; check reel; & 1 hacle. S/ EZL. (X) BELL. Wit: MARY (X) BELL, WILLIAM POWL. KENNETT, who swore by oath 23 Jun 1792 before JOHN MOORE, J.P. Rcd. 14 Mar 1793.

P. 40. 4 Feb 1793: Bill of Sale: RICHARD & JOHN MOORE, Executors of JAMES MOORE, dec'd., to JOHN WHITE for 70 pounds, sold a negro slave named CHARLES. S/ RICHARD MOORE, JOHN MOORE. Wit: WILLIAM MOORE, R. ROBT. McCOMB. Rcd. (no date).

Pp. 41-45. 17 Sep 1792: WILLIAM ANDERSON, Esq. to THOMAS JOHNSON, Planter both of Edgefield Co. SC for 12 pounds, sold 25 acres originally granted 2 Oct 1786 said ANDERSON's being land where the said THOMAS JOHNSON now lives. S/ W. ANDERSON. Wit: THOMAS FARGUHAR, JOHN ANDERSON, who swore by oath 3 Nov 1792 before JOHN MOORE, J.P. Rcd. 14 Mar 1793.

Pp. 45-47. No date: Deed of Gift: JOHN CHERRY, Blacksmith of Edgefield Co. SC, for love & affection for my children give to loving son EDWARD GASKINS a horse, cow, 10 hogs; to two daughters (to wit) BETSEY CHERRY & NANCY CHERRY, all my household furniture to be divided between them; to my loving son JOSEPH CHERRY, all my blacksmith tools. S/ JOHN CHERRY, B'smith. Wit: GEORGE (X) HORN, WILLIAM WATSON, Senr., who swore by oath 15 Mar 1793 before HUGH MIDDLETON, J.P. Rcd. 15 Mar 1793.

Pp. 47-49. 7 Jun 1793: JOHN McDANIEL & MARY, his wife, of Wilks Co. GA to JAMES THOMAS of Edgefield Co. SC for 50 pounds, sold 50 acres originally granted 3 Sep 1754 unto JOSEPH CHATWIN on Stephens Creek of Savannah River. S/ JOHN (1) McDANIEL, MARY (X) McDANIEL. Wit: JOSEPH McMATH, JOHN SALLIS, who swore by oath 10 Jan 1793 before HUGH MIDDLETON, J.P. Rcd. 15 Mar 1793.

Pp. 49-51. 29 Jan 1793: ROGER SMITH of Charleston SC to JAMES THOMAS of Edgefield Co. SC for 100 pounds, sold 500 acres originally granted 12 Jul 1771 unto JAMES SIMPSON & conveyed by L&R 7 Jul 1774 unto JOHN LOGAN who conveyed by L&R 28 Jan 1784 to ROGER SMITH. Said land on Stephens Creek of Savannah River; adj. NE JOHN MAINER & said creek. S/ ROGER SMITH. Wit: CHARLES McDANIEL, SAMUEL SCOTT, who swore by oath 14 Mar 1793 before HUGH MIDDLETON, J.P. Rcd. 15 Mar 1793.

Pp. 51-56. 10 Jan 1790: BARKLEY MARTIN, Esq. Sheriff of Edgefield Co. SC to ROBERT STARK the younger, & ALEXANDER BOLIN STARK late of said county, Esqs., for 100 pds, sold 1570 acres..Whereas ROBERT STARK was seized in his demesne as of fee of 1570 acres commonly known as the Level or Stark's Old place being on head of branch of Cloud Creek of Saluda river & also branch of South Edisto...Whereas by his bond of 1 Feb 1783 did himself with THOMAS TAYLOR, JOHN WINN, RICHARD WINN, JOSEPH KIRKLAND & WILLIAM RIEVES as his securities therefore unto WILSON BLOUNT, Merchant of Charleston SC in penal sum of 87 silver Spanish milled dollars conditioned for payment of 4363 silver spanish milled dollars before Nov next...& Whereas WILSON BLOUNT for recovery of said

DEED BOOK 8: 1793-1794 EDGEFIELD COUNTY S.C.

land begun action in Lexington Court in 1789 & obtained a
Judgement by JOHN BYNUM, Esq. Clerk of said court 10 Dec 1789 &
directed the Sheriff of Edgefield Co. SC to the goods & Chattles
of ROBERT STARK be levied for 1481 pounds & cost of suit...
Whereas BARKLEY, Esq. Sheriff of Edgefield Co. SC did seize &
sell to the highest & last bidder.
Disc. of land: NE persons unknown & Irish tract the Hartly tract
& Colo. JACOB REID; NW Colo. REID & Estate of MICHAEL WATSON; SE
JOHN FREDRICK. S/ BARK MARTIN. Wit: PENIX (P) HOWLET, SAML.
WILLSON, who swore by oath 15 Mar 1793 before JOSEPH HIGHTOWER,
J.P. Rcd. 15 Mar 1793.

Pp. 56-57. 13 Dec 1788: JAMES KING & JOHN ANDERSON to JOHN
PURSELL & ANDREW HARKNESS for 500 pounds; Condition a clear title
be made to Lot No 23 in Town in Campbelton should payment not be
made by next 1 Jul. S/ JAMES KING, JOHN ANDERSON. Wit: PETER
McKINNEY.
18 Mar 1793: WEST COOK swore by oath that he saw ANDREW HARKNESS
endorse the within bond & deliver it to THOMAS HERON & that
WILLIAM COVINGTON witnessed the endorsement also before JOSEPH
HIGHTOWER, J.P. Rcd. 18 Mar 1793.

Pp. 57-61. 25 Feb 1793: FIELDS PARDUE, Planter & LUCY his wife to
THOMAS HERON, both of Edgefield Co. SC for 20 pounds, 1 lott No
23 containing 1/4 acre in village Campbelton. S/ F. PARDUE, LUCY
PARDUE. Wit: GIDN. PARDUE, DAVID NEAL, who swore by oath 26 Feb
1793 before JOSEPH HIGHTOWER, J.P. Rcd. 18 Mar 1793.

Pp. 61-62. 8 Sep 1792: WILLIAM WILLIAMS & RACHEL, Administrators
of the Estate of JACOB FOREMAN, dec'd, did give all right to all
indent that was drawn by Mr. JOHN HERNDON from office in
Charleston & delivered to JOHN WILLIAMS of the Estate of JACOB
FOREMAN, dec'd., to ISAAC FOREMAN as guardian for the children of
the said deceased which is the Principle of 34 pounds & the
Interest 14 pounds which said Indents I never sold to the said
JOHN WILLIAMS; only gave him an order to draw the said Indents
for me & we do hereby give all our rights to indents unto said
FOREMAN as guardian for the children. S/ W. WILLIAMS, RACHEL (R)
WILLIAMS. Wit: OLIFE (+) DARBY, BENJAMIN DARBY, who swore by oath
19 Mar 1793 before RICHARD TUTT, J.P. Rcd. 19 Mar 1793.

P. 63. 14 Oct 1793: B. Sale: GEORGE COWAN of Edgefield Co.
SC is bound unto THOS. LAMAR of Horse Creek of same place for 160
pounds. The condition of above is that GEORGE COWAN make over a
negro fellow named DICK & a negro boy named LESAR & said THOS.
LAMAR being security for said COWAN agreeable to the Installment
Act in sum of 83 pounds due EDWARD KEATING & JNO. DAVISON. S/
GEORGE COWAN. Wit: THOMAS BECKHAM.
19 Mar 1794: JAMES McQUEEN swore by oath to the best of his
knowledge he believes the signature to be GEORGE COWAN before
AQUILA MILES, J.P. Rcd. 19 Mar 1794.

Pp. 64-70. 6 Feb 1789: BARTLETT BLEDSOE, Yeoman, and LYDIA his
wife of Ninety Six Dist. SC, to JESSE SAMFORD of same place for
100 pounds, sold 235 acres being part of 470 acres originally
granted 1 Oct 1787, being on Indian Creek of Little Saluda River
adj. NW by ELIJAH MARTIN & JOHN ABNEY, SW by APPLETON, SE & NE by
ZACHEUS CORLEY, NW & SE by SAMFORD's land. Said 470 grant being
divided by a conditional line through the tract where ZACHEUS
CORLEY now lives & the said JESSE SAMFORD now lives. S/ BARTLETT

DEED BOOK 8: 1793-1794 EDGEFIELD COUNTY S.C.

BLEDSOE. Wit: VALENTINE CORLEY, ASA SAMFORD, ZACHEUS (+) CORLEY, who swore by oath 9 Feb 1793 before HENRY KING, J.P. Rcd. 9 Feb 1793.

Pp. 70-77. 7 May 1784: WILLIAM HUGGINS, Joint Executor with MARY HUGGINS his wife, real Executrix of BENJAMIN DURBORON, dec'd, Estate of Ninety Six Dist. SC, to JOHN HARRIS, on Ninety Six Store Keeper for 100 pounds, sold 88 acres originally granted 15 Feb 1769 unto MICHAEL THOMSON, who conveyed by L&R 7 & 8 Jul 1769 unto BENJAMIN DURBORON, being on Ninety Six creek adj. N by Heirs of THO. BROWN; W by DANIEL MICKLAR; & S by EMANUEL MILLAR at the time of survey. S/ WILLIAM HUGGINS, MARY HUGGINS. Wit: THOMAS (T) RAY, D. CUNNINGHAM, DRURY GLOVER, who swore by oath 12 Nov 1787 before WILLIAM ANDERSON, J.P. Rcd. 19 Mar 1793.

Pp. 77-82. 27 Aug 1792: JOHN HARRIS & WILLEY, his wife to JOSEPH BURTON, Tavern Keeper of Ninety Six for 100 pounds, sold 88 acres originally granted 15 Feb 1769 on waters of Ninety Six Creek unto MICHAEL THOMSON who conveyed by L&R 7 & 8 Jul 1769 to BENJAMIN DURBORON, now dec'd; adj. N by heirs of THOMAS BROWN; W by DANIEL MICKEL; S by EMANUEL MILLAR at time of survey. S/ JOHN HARRIS, WILLEY (+) HARRIS. Wit: ALLEN GLOVER, WILLIAM PERRY, LUKE McAHAN, DRURY GLOVER, who swore by oath 16 Dec 1793 before JOHN MOORE, J.P. Rcd. 19 Mar 1793.

Pp. 83-87. 19 Dec 1792: TOLIVER DAVIS, Senior, to DAVIS MOORE, both of Edgefield Co. SC for 50 pounds, sold 150 acres originally surveyed unto JOSEPH NOBLE 11 Sep 1767 & was conveyed by NOBLE & his wife, RACHEL by L&R 17 & 18 Dec 1768 to JOHN MOCH who with his wife MARY conveyed by Deed of 15 & 16 Apr 1783 to JOHN CHENEY who conveyed by L&R 9 & 10 Apr 1789 to said TOLIVER DAVIS. Said land is at the head of a branch of Horns Creek of Stephens Creek. S/ TOLAVER DAVIS, Senr. Wit: PETER CHASTAIN, ARGE GARNER, JOHN CHASTAIN, who swore by oath 28 Mar 1793 before RICHARD TUTT, J.P. Rcd. 27 Mar 1793.

Pp. 87-89. 20 Apr 1791: ·Bond: JAMES WEST, Planter & CELIA, his wife of Horns Creek, Edgefield Co. SC, bound to JOHN RAINSFORD, Planter of same place for the sum of 100 pounds to be paid on the 20th July next; for better securing of payment sell 25 acres being part of a grant to said JAMES WEST 7 Aug 1786 being on South part of Horns Creek, the Northern part of survey having been sold unto WILLIAM JEETER, the said 25 acres adj. land by Widow ADAM, Widow FUNNED, WILLIAM JEETER & Widow MOSELEY. S/ JAMES (⊢⊣) WEST, CELIA (X) WEST. Wit: JOHN WALLS, CHARLES WALLS, who swore by oath 13 Mar 1793 before RICHARD TUTT, J.P. Rcd. 13 Mar 1793.

Pp. 89-90. 12 Jan 1793: Bill of Sale: FIELDS PARDUE, Planter of Edgefield Co. SC to KEVAN TAYLOR & MURREN, Merchants of Campbellton for 60 pounds, to deliver a negro man named CEASER about 23 yrs. old. S/ FIELD PARDUE. Wit: JESSE CLARK, who swore by oath 8 Apr 1793 before RICHARD TUTT, J.P. Rcd. 8 Apr 1793.

Pp. 90-94. 1 Nov 1770: WILLIAM DOOLY to EDWARD COUCH, both of SC for 250 pounds, sold 150 acres originally granted 24 Jan 1770 being near Cloud creek a branch of little Saluda River adj. E by HENRY HARTLEY & N by MOSES POWEL. S/ WILLIAM DOOLY. Wit: PATRICK McDOUGAL, MICHAEL WALTON, WILLIAM CLARK, who swore by oath 29 Apr 1793 before HENRY KING, J.P. Rcd. 30 Apr 1793.

Pp. 94-95. 21 Apr 1788: ANN HAMMOND to JAMES MARTIN sold 1 horse, 2 beds & furniture, 4 hogs, 1 side saddle, 2 dishes, 1 dozen plates, 2 pots, 1 oven, 1 cow & calf. S/ ANN (↦) HAMMOND. Wit: CHARLES HAMMOND, SIMON MARTIN, who swore by oath 17 Nov 1792 before JOSEPH HIGHTOWER, J. P. Rcd. 1 May 1793.

Pp. 95-97. 5 Apr 1793: FRANCIS BREMAR of Charleston SC to ELIJAH BIRD of Edgefield Co. SC for 40 pounds, sold 150 acres originally surveyed 17 May 1771 for JOSEPH GUNNELLS & granted unto ROBERT McCRACKAN 8 Dec 1774 & was conveyed by L&R 10 & 11 Feb 1775 to said BREMAR. Said tract is on Long & Turkey Creek adj. NE by ROBERT OSBORN at time of survey. S/ F. BREMAR. Wit: LEWIS NEWHOUSE, ALEX. McDOWAL, DANIEL JAMES RAVENEL, who swore by oath 6 Apr 1793 before STEPHEN RAVENEL, J.P. Rcd. 4 May 1793.

Pp. 97-98. 9 May 1793: JOSIAH THOMAS of Edgefield Co. SC to Capt. JOHN THOMAS of Green Co. GA for 50 pounds, sold 1 negro woman named JENNY said to be 47 yrs. old. S/ JOSIAH THOMAS. Wit: SAML. ESKRIDGE, LODOWICK HILL, who swore by oath 9 May 1793 before HENRY KING, J.P. Rcd. 10 May 1793.

Pp. 98-99. 7 Sep 1771: GEORGE STROTHERS of Craven Co. SC to MICHAEL WATSON of Coleton Co. SC bound for 500 pounds & for better securing of payment sell 100 acres laid out originally unto BENJAMIN SIMS on Cloud Creek and also 50 acres surveyed for THOMAS TAYLOR. S/ GEORGE STROTHERS. Wit: BENJ. TUTT, who swore by oath 14 Jul 1788 before HUGH MIDDLETON, J.P. Rcd. 10 May 1793.

Pp. 100-102. 11 May 1793: MICHAEL BUCKHALTER & AGNESS, his wife to CHRISTIAN BUCKHALTER, both of Edgefield Co. SC for 5 pounds, sold 6 acres being part of 300 acres originally granted MICHAEL BUCKHALTER adj. S by JOHN MARTIN; W by WILLIAM HOWLS, N by said CHRISTIAN BUCKHALTER. S/ MICHAEL (MB) BURCKHALTER. Wit: HENRY BURCKHALTER, JOHN GRIFFIS, who swore by oath 13 May 1793 before RICHARD TUTT, J.P. Rcd. 13 May 1793.

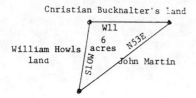

Cnristian Bucknalter's land

W11
6 acres
N53E
William Howls land
S1OW
John Martin

Pursuent to a request of CHRISTIAN BUCKHALTER I have laid out 6 acres of land, being part of the original grant to MICHAEL BUCKHALTER. Certified 1 Dec 1792. By JOHN BOYD, D. S.

Pp. 102-104. 14 Feb 1791: MOSES POWELL of Wilks Co. GA to THOMAS HOLSEL, Planter of Edgefield Co. SC for 40 pounds, sold 100 acres originally granted 1 Jun 1762 near Cloud Creek a branch of Saluda adj. NE by WM. WATSON, SE by ANDREW SHIPES when surveyed. S/ MOSES POWELL. Wit: LEWIS POWELL, SOLOMON MINGHAM, JACOB GIBSON, Senr., who swore by oath 26 Oct 1792 before ARTHUR SIMKINS, J.P. Rcd. 18 May 1793.

Pp. 104-109. 2 May 1793: EDWARD COUCH to THOMAS HOLSEL, both of Edgefield Co. SC for 100 pounds, sold 150 acres originally granted 24 Jan 1770 near Clouds Creek of little Saludy river adj. SE by HENRY HARTLEY, NE by MOSES POWELL at time of survey. S/

EDWARD COUCH, APSELA COUCH. Wit: ABRAHAM (A) SMITH, REASEIGN HOLSEL, who swore by oath 18 May 1793 before RICHARD TUTT, J.P. Rcd. 18 May 1793.

Pp. 109-111. 25 Apr 1788: JOHN GREEN to WILLIAM ADAMS for 50 pounds, sold 74 acres originally granted 6 Nov 1786 on Red Bank a branch of little Saludy River adj. said ADAMS & WM. CASH. S/ JOHN GREEN, ESTHER (g) GREEN. Wit: JAMES (X) HOLLANDSWORTH, JOHN (X) ADAMS, THOMAS SCOTT, who swore by oath 13 May 1793 before HENRY KING, J.P. Rcd. 20 May 1793.

Pp. 111-119. 1 May 1793: THOMAS ANDERSON, Planter to SAMUEL GOODE, Planter both of Edgefield Co. SC for 21 pounds, sold 100 acres originally granted 3 Jun 1766 unto JOHN ANDERSON, Dec'd., adj. NW by JAMES ANDERSON at time of survey. Now said THOMAS ANDERSON being in possession by being heir at law of said JOHN ANDERSON. S/ THOS. ANDERSON. Wit: MATTHEW WILLS, GEORGE WHITEFIELD, who swore by oath 3 May 1793 before JULIUS NICHOLS, Junr., J.P. Rcd. 20 May 179?.

Pp. 119-123. 11 Dec 1767: PATRICK DOOLY & ANN, his wife of Ninety Six SC to MAKNERNESS GOOD, Planter of same place but late Virginia, for 5 pounds, sold 300 acres originally granted 20 Aug 1767 unto PATRICK DOULY on Ninety Six Creek in Barkley Co. SC adj. lands by MOSES THOMPSON & COLBERT ANDERSON & JAS. ANDERSON. S/ PATRICK DOOLY, ANN (X) DOOLY. Wit: RICHARD ALLISON, WILLIAM CHRISTIE.
I was also present & witnessed above signatures. S/ JOHN SAVAGE, J.P. Rcd. 20 May 1793.

Pp. 123-127. 29 Dec 1792: JOHN HOLLOWAY, Planter to SAMUEL GOODE, Planter both of Edgefield Co. SC for 43 pounds, sold 150 acres originally granted 2 May 1770 in Edgefield Co. SC (formerly Colleton Co. SC), adj. SW & SE by MACKONESS GOODE, NW & NE by JAMES ANDERSON when surveyed. S/ JOHN (Ɨ) HOLLOWAY, Senr. Wit: RICHARD LANIER, JAMES LANIER, GARLAND GOODE, who swore by oath 17 May 1793 before JOHN MOORE, J.P. Rcd. 20 May 1793.

Pp. 127-130. 19? Sep 1771: JOHN DOOLY of Saluda of Berkley Co. SC to SAMUEL GOODE of Ninety Six in Colleton Co. SC for 100 pounds, sold 100 acres originally granted 29 Apr 1767 unto JOHN DOOLY on a small branch of Ninety Six Creek in Colleton Co. SC adj. NE MACKERNESS GOODE, NW & SW by ROBERT MITCHEL. S/ JNO DOOLY. Wit: ROBT. MITCHELL, MOSES YARBOROUGH, who swore by oath 29 Nov 1771 before JAMES MAYSON. Rcd. 20 May 1793.

Pp. 130-133. 6 Nov 1789: MACKERNESS GOODE, Eldest son & heir at law of PHILLIP GOODE, dec'd., to SAMUEL GOODE, both of Edgefield Co. SC for 50 pounds, sold 50 acres originally granted PHILLIP GOODE now deceased being in Colleton County (formerly) but now Edgefield on waters of Ninety-Six Creek adj. NW by THOMSON; SE by PATRICK DOOLY & COLBERT ANDERSON & NW by SAMUEL RAMSEY at time of survey. S/ MACKERNESS GOODE. Wit: GEORGE MOCK, Senior, GEORGE MOCK, Junior, who swore by oath 20 May 1793 before AQUILA MILES, J.P. Rcd. 20 May 1793.

Pp. 133-136. 4 Dec 1792: JOHN KENNEDY & ANN his wife, of Edgefield Co. SC to JOHN & JOSEPH WALLACE of same place for 100 pounds, sold 193 acres being part of 300 acres granted unto DAVID

KENNEDY on Cuffee Town & Hard Labour Creek, branches of Stephens Creek of Savannah River, adj. W by JOHN CLEM, S & E by heirs of CHARLES WILLIAMS & all other sides by JOHN LONGMIRE. S/ JOHN KENNEDY, ANN (Ⓠ) KENNEDY. Wit: BATTE EVANS, JAMES BROWN, WILLIAM EVANS, who swore by oath 14 Jan 1793 before JAMES HARRISON, J.P. Rcd. 27 May 1793.

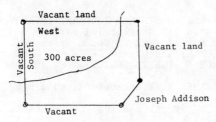

Pursuant to a precept of 22 Jun 1767 I have ameasured out unto DAVID KENNEDY 300 acres on the fork of Stephens Creek known by the name of Chevees & Hard Labor Creek bounded at SE corner by JOSEPH ADDISON. Certified 25 Aug 1767, JNO. NELSON, D.S. The above is true copy taken from original & examined by me. S/ PETER BREMAR pro Survr Genl: SC Survr Genl Office 17 Sep 1785.

Pp. 136-138. 4 Dec 1792: JOHN KENNEDY & ANN, his wife of Edgefield Co. SC to JOHN LONGMIRE, for 50 pounds, sold 107 acres on east side Cuffetown Creek adj. land of THORN FREEMAN, SW by SAMUEL STALNAKER & all other sides by JAMES & JOSEPH WALLACE, who has in their possession a copy of a 300 acre plat. S/ JOHN KENADY ANN (O) KENADY. Wit: BATTE EVANS, JAMES BROWN, WILLIAM EVANS, who swore by oath before JAMES HARRISON, J.P. Rcd. 27 May 1793.

Pp. 138-141. 1 Jun 1793: Power of Attorney: JAMES WEATHERFORD of Edgefield Co. SC appoints Maj. PARSONS of SC my attorney to sue & recover two negroes & their increase in possession of JOHN WILKERSON of the frontiers of Virginia in Caintucket settlement as follows viz: 1 girl about 21 yrs. old named SAL of Yellowish complexion, & a boy, her brother, of a black complexion named BURTON, about 19 yrs old, but I have been informed their names have been changed. Said negroes were plundered from my father, MARTIN WEATHERFORD in Augusta about 1780 or 1781 & sold said WILKERSON by a party of men going over the mountain & likewise to take my papers out of the hands of TURNER WILLIAMS given him some time ago unless said WILLIAMS pays said PARSON 406 pounds for negroes recovered in Cumberland which I empower said PARSONS to receive. S/ JAMES WEATHERFORD. Wit: JOHN HALL, THOMAS ROLLAN, who swore by oath before JOSEPH HIGHTOWER, J.P. Rcd. 1 Jun 1793.

Pp. 141-144. 23 May 1793: WILLIAM HUMPHREYS to JOHN RUSHTON, both of Edgefield Co. SC for 5 pounds, sold 250 acres being part of 922 acres granted 1792 to said HUMPHREYS on Dry Creek of Little Saludah. Said tract on East end of tract adj. JOHN GILLON, COXES land, & JAMES GILLON. S/ WILLIAM HUMPHREYS. Wit: WM. SISSON, JOHN DRINKARD, JAMES (J) GILLON, who swore by oath 29 May 1793 before RUSSELL WILSON, J.P. Rcd. 1 Jun 1793.

Pp. 144-148. 14 Feb 1792: PETER HILLARD to THOMAS SWEARINGIN, both of Edgefield Co. SC for 10 pounds, sold 200 acres originally granted 3 Apr 1786 unto PETER HILLARD on Shaws Creek of Edisto River. S/ PETER (8) HILLARD. Wit: JOSIAH McDANIEL, HENRY SWEARINGIN, who swore by oath 12 Mar 1793 before JOSEPH HIGHTOWER, J.P. Rcd. 3 Jun 1793.

DEED BOOK 8: 1793-1794 EDGEFIELD COUNTY S.C.

Pp. 148-153. 27 Apr 1792: THOMAS SWEARINGEN to ISAAC KIRKLAND, both of Edgefield Co. SC for 60 pounds, sold 200 acres originally granted 3 Apr 1786 to PETER HILLARD & was conveyed 14 Feb 1792 unto said SWEARINGEN being on Shaws creek of Edisto River. S/ THOS. SWEARINGEN. Wit: SILAS DOLIHIDE, FREDRICK SWEARINGEN, who swore by oath 12 Mar 1793 before JOSEPH HIGHTOWER, J.P. Rcd. 3 Jun 1793.

Pp. 154-159. 3 Mar 1793: JAMES WEST to STEPHEN TILLMAN, both of Edgefield Co. SC for 100 pounds, sold 210 acres being part of 380 originally granted 6 Feb 1786 unto said WEST on Cedar Creek adj. said WEST; JOHN WALLS; WILLIAM THOMAS; & BENJAMIN HARRY. S/ JAMES (↔) WEST, CELAH (+) WEST. Wit: TRUMAN WIGHTT, DANIEL HUFF, JOSEPH T. BELL.
E.F. Co. Ct. Jun Term 1793: JAMES WEST acknowledge said Deed before RICHARD TUTT, C.E.C.
Mrs CELAH WEST, wife of said JAMES WEST relinquished dower before RICHARD TUTT, J.P. Rcd. 3 Jun 1793.

Pp. 159-168. 30 May 1793: BENJAMIN RYAN, the second & MILLA, his wife to JOHN RYAN, both of Edgefield Co. SC for 1060 pounds, sold 4560 acres being 12 tracts that was conveyed by L&R 8 & 9 Jul 1791 viz:
(1) 100 acres originally granted MARTHA RYAN 1 Feb 1768.

(2) 150 acres originally granted JAMES BARRENTINE 23 Jun 1774 adj. DANIEL ELLIS; JAMES HARRIS; JOHN RYAN; MOSES KIRKLAND; JOHN WHITE; & HARMON GALMON at time of survey.

(3) 352 acres adj. N late property of MOSES KIRKLAND; S by RICHARD KIRKLAND; & W by ROLLEY ROBUCK, JOSEPH & GEORGE MILLAR.

(4) 384 acres adj. NE JOHN RYAN & JOHN RUTLEDGE; S by late property of MOSES KIRKLAND & W by JOHN LUCAS.

(5) 100 acre tract of JOHN RYAN adj. SE & NE by JOHN RYAN; NW by WILLIS ODOM & SW by ISAAC KIRKLAND.

(6) 300 acres being part of 643 acres originally granted 7 May 1787 to ISAAC KIRKLAND, adj. JOHN RYAN; WILLIS ODOM; EDWARD RUTLEDGE, Esq; FRANCIS SINQUEFIELD; WILLIAM HARGROVE & JACOB FUDGE.
The above tracts all join each other & are on waters of Chavers & Horn Creek of Savannah River.

(7) 200 acres originally granted July 1768 to JOHN HARVEY adj. BENJAMIN RYAN & JOSEPH WALKER at time of survey being on Nobles Creek, but now called Horns Creek.

(8) 84 acres granted 5 Jun 1786 to JOHN RYAN adj. aforesaid land & EDWARD RUTLEDGE at time of survey.

(9) 660 acres granted 1 Oct 1787 to JOHN RYAN on head of Turkey Creek adj. BOLIN STARK; RUBIN ROBERTS; ROBERT LANG; CHRISTIAN GOMILLION; DAVID BURKS & WILLIAM ROTTEN.

(10) 637 acres granted 3 Mar 1788 to JOHN RYAN near head of Turkey Creek adj. CHRISTIAN GOMILLION & RUBIN ROBERTS.

DEED BOOK 8: 1793-1794 EDGEFIELD COUNTY S.C.

(11) 593 acres granted 7 May 1787 to JOHN RYAN on Paces branch of Shaws Creek adj. THOS SWEARINGEN & ABRAHAM ODOM.

(12) 1000 acres granted 3 Mar 1788 to JOHN RYANS on Horns Creek adj. REBECCA STARK; VAN SWEARINGEN; BENJN. DARBY; LACON RYAN; BENJN. RYAN; EDWARD RUTLEDGE & Capt. RYAN. S/ BENJAMIN (B) RYAN, MILLA (M) RYAN. Wit: RICHD. NEWMAN, MOSES McWHORTER, ISAAC KIRKLAND, who swore by oath 3 Jun 1793 before JOSEPH HIGHTOWER, J.P.
EF Co. Ct 3 Jun 1793: Mrs. MILLEY RYAN, wife of BENJAMIN RYAN, relinquished dower before RICHARD TUTT, C.E.C. Rcd. 3 Jun 1793.

Pp. 168-173. 13 Jan 1793: JAMES WALKER, Planter of Edgefield Co. SC to JOSEPH RAYBOURN, Planter of Rocky Creek of same place for 70 pounds, sold 200 acres survey certified 1 Mar 1770 unto BENJAMIN BELL who conveyed to FRANCIS SINQUEFIELD who sold to ISAAC KIRKLAND who sold to said JAMES WALKER as will appear by the Deposition of JOSHUA HAMMOND & JOHN FOREACRES, Recorded in Public Registers office in Charlestown Book M No. 5 pg. 550, 4 Oct 1785 & examined by D. MAZUCK, Register.
Said 200 acres being on Rocky Creek of Turkey Creek of Savannah River & is where said JOSEPH RAYBOURN now lives. S/ JAMES WALKER. Wit: JOHN JONES, SANDERS (+) DAY, MOSES CLARK, who swore by oath 9 Mar 1793 before ARTHUR SIMKINS, J.E.C. Rcd. 3 Jun 1793.

Pp. 173-181. 13 Dec 1787: WILLIAM CORLEY, Hatter, of Ninety Six Dist. SC to JESSE SAMFORD of same place for 100 pounds, sold 205 acres being part of 327 acres granted 6 Feb 1786 unto said CORLEY on Indian Creek of little Saluda River adj. VOLENTINE CORLEY when surveyed. Said tract measured off by JOSEPH WRIGHT, D.S. S/ WILLIAM CORLEY, PATSY (X) CORLEY. Wit: HEZEKIAH GENTRY, JOSEPH (X) WHITTLE, JOHN (X) GRIFFIN, who swore by oath 9 Feb 1793 before HENRY KING, J.P. Rcd. 3 Jun 1793.

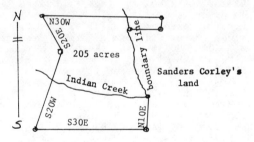

At the request of JESSE SAMFORD & SANDERS CORLEY, I have measured off 205 acres being part of 327 acres granted 6 Feb 1786 unto WILLIAM CORLEY. Surveyed 28 Feb 1787 by JOS. WRIGHT, D.S.

Pp. 181-188. 26 Nov 1792: ANTHONY ARGO & MARY, his wife of Edgefield Co. SC to PLEASANT BURNET of same place for 10 pounds, sold 105 acres being part of 325 acres originally granted 3 Jul 1786 unto ARGO being on the fork of Little Saluda & Big Creek. Said 325 being divided into several parts & sold all except the said 105 acres being the last of the original tract adj. CUZECK's; NE by JAMES BARROT & JOHN WRIGHT; NE & S AARON ETHEREDGE. S/ ANTHONY ARGO, MARY (X) ARGO. Wit: JOHN (X) COLTON, HEZEKIAH (X) BURNET, who swore by oath 14 Jan 1793 before HENRY KING, J.P. Rcd. 3 Jan 1793.

Pp. 188-189. 18 Mar 1793: Affidavit: Oringburg Dist. SC: MORRIS CALLIHAM gave oath before J. THOS. FAIRCHILD that a certain negro boy named BEN which Deponent sold to THOMAS WARNER was born the property of this Deponant 7 May 1787. S/ MORRIS (M) CALLIHAN. Also MARY CALLEHAN & MARTHA SMITH gave same above oath. S/ MARY (X) CALLIHAN, MARTHA (X) SMITH.

Pp. 189-190. 15 Apr 1793: Bill of Sale: ALLEN HINTON of Edgefield Co. SC to JOSHUA THORN for 30 pounds sold a negro boy named PETTER about 8 yrs. old. S/ ALLEN (X) HINTON. Wit: THOMAS HERON, who swore by oath 20 Apr 1793 before JOSEPH HIGHTOWER, J.P. Rcd. 3 Jun 1793.

Pp. 190-191. 8 Apr 1793: JOHN CHENEY, Planter of Edgefield Co. to KEVAN TAYLOR & MURREN, Merchants of Campbelton, SC for 65 pounds, sold a negro woman named SILVIA about 25 yrs. old. S/ JOHN CHENEY. Wit: MORGAN MURRAH, who swore by oath 21 May 1793 before JOSEPH HIGHTOWER, J.P. Rcd. 3 Jun 1793.

Pp. 191-193. Abbeville Co. SC: HENRY FLEMING of Edgefield Co. SC: am indebted to JOSIAH BRADLEY for 200 pounds referring to a bond given by me 31 Mar 1791 & Whereas bond is now on demand & it being at present out of my power to discharge same...but in order to make satisfaction do mortgage viz: Roan mare branded IG, bay horse formerly property of JOHN RAY, 2 cows & calves, 3 feather beds & furniture, 1 chest, trunk, looking glass, table & 5 chairs, 2 smothing irons, 2 Bibles, 1 churn, 20 bowls, 2 pewter dishes, 8 pewter plates, 6 pewter basons, 10 spoons, 1 set knives & forks, 1 set of cups & saucers, 1 tea & coffee pot, 1 dutch oven, 1 pot, 1 kettle, 1 bag, 1 saddle & bridle, 2 spinning wheels. If payment made by 1 Jun 1796 then becomes null & void. S/ HENRY FLEMING. Wit: JOHN CONNER, J. CALHOUN, Abbeville Co. SC, swore by oath 1 Jun 1793 before JULIUS NICHOLS, Junr., J.P. Rcd. 8 Jun 1793.

Pp. 193-199. 29 Jun 1793: GEORGE RANDAL of Edgefield Co. SC to JAMES BROWN of same place for 40 pounds, sold 200 acres being part of 943 acres originally granted 4 Mar 1793 unto GEORGE RANDAL on the NE side of Keninsis fork of big Horse creek adj. JONATHAN RICHARDSON, JOAB WOOTAN & said RANDAL. S/ GEORGE (X) RANDAL. Wit: JOAB WOOTAN, DANIEL RITCHY, who swore by oath 29 Jun 1793 before RICHARD TUTT, J.P. Rcd. 29 Jun 1793.

Pp. 199-206. 7 Jun 1793: GEORGE RANDAL of Edgefield Co. SC to JOAB WOOTAN of same place for 50 pounds, sold 100 acres being part of 943 acres originally granted 4 Mar 1793 said RANDAL being on Kinins fork of big Horse Creek adj. said JOAB WOOTAN, BENJAMIN REYNOLDS, JONATHAN RICHARDSON & said RANDAL. S/ GEORGE (X) RANDAL. Wit: JAMES (‡) BROWN, DANIEL RITCHY, JONATHAN (‡) RICHARDSON, who swore by oath 11 Jun 1793 before RICHARD TUTT, J.P. Rcd. 11 Jun 1793.

Pp. 206-213. 20 Feb 1793: CHARLES BANKS of Edgefield Co. SC to JOAB WOOTAN of same place for 50 pounds, sold 245 acres being part of 361 acres originally granted 3 Dec 1792 unto said BANKS being on Drafts of Kines fork of Horse Creek of Savannah River adj. NE, SE & NW by JOHN HERNDON, NW said JOAB WOOTAN, SW & NW by JONATHAN RICHARDSON. S/ CHARLES BANKS. Wit: EZEKIEL McCLENDON, JOHATHAN (‡) RICHARDSON, who swore by oath 11 Jun 1793 before RICHARD TUTT, J.P. Rcd. 11 Jun 1793.

DEED BOOK 8: 1793-1794 EDGEFIELD COUNTY S.C.

Pp. 213-219. 7 Aug 1789: THOMAS MOSELEY to JONATHAN RICHARDSON, both of Edgefield Co. SC for 75 pounds?, 150 acres being part of 547 acres originally granted 2 Oct 1786 unto JOHN HERNDON & conveyed by L&R unto THOMAS MOSELEY, being on Coins fork of Horse Creek adj. JOHN RANDOL. S/ THOMAS (T) MOSELY, PRISCILLA (ℑ) MOSLY. Wit: NATHANIEL (X) SHEARLY, JOAB WOOTAN, who swore by oath 11 Jun 1793 before RICHARD TUTT, J.P. Rcd. 11 Jun 1793.

Pp. 219-221. 13 Jun 1793: Deed of Gift: CHARLES LANDRUM, Senr., Planter of Edgefield Co. SC to his Children, THOMAS LANDRUM, CHARLES LANDRUM, MARY LANDRUM, PATIENCE LANDRUM, sons & daughters, for love & affection:
Son: THOMAS - horse branded CL; mare branded CL; rifle gun;
Son, CHARLES - mare branded CL;
Dau., MARY - mare & 1/2 part of household furniture;
Dau., PATIENCE - mare branded B, also 1/2 part of household furniture.
My present crop to be equally divided among my children. S/ CHARLES LANDRUM. Wit: THOMAS SELLERS, SILAS SELLERS, who swore by oath 13 Jun 1793 before RICHARD TUTT, J.P. Rcd. 13 Jun 1793.

Pp. 221-223. 15 Jan 1793: Release Quit Claim: JOSEPH WOOD of Beach Island in Edgefield Co. SC to SAMUEL SCOTT against all action of sales bonds, debts, etc... S/ JOSEPH WOOD. Wit: JAMES GRAY, who swore by oath 6 May 1793 before HUGH MIDDLETON, J.P. Rcd. 25 Jun 1793.

Pp. 223-229. 29 Apr 1793: WILLIAM MORGAN & MARGARET, his wife to ROBERT MOSELEY, both of Edgefield Co. SC for 45 pounds, sold 45 1/2 acres being part of grant of 27 Sep 1784 unto said MORGAN being on Horns Creek adj. NE CHARLES MARTIN; N by JOHN RENSFORD; SW & SE by JOHN MARTIN. S/ WM. MORGAN, MARGARET (M) MORGAN. Wit: ROBERT LAMAR, ROBERT FARISH, who swore by oath 18 Jun 1793 before JOSEPH HIGHTOWER, J.P. Rcd. 26 Jun 1793.

Pp. 229-235. 3 Jan 1785: GEORGE BUCKLUE, Planter to WILLIAM GREEN, Planter both of Ninety Six Dist. SC for 10 pounds, sold 50 acres being part of a tract surveyed by WILLIAM ANDERSON, D.S. 2 Jun 1772 & certified 17 Jun 1772 & entered in Auditr. Generals office 9 Oct 1772 & granted 14 --- 1772 unto RICHARD BUCKLUE being now dead & said GEORGE BUCKLUE, his son, became heir at law. Said tract on little Stephens Creek of Savannah River adj. OGDEN COCKEROFF; RICHARD BUCKLUE, dec'd., now belonging to said GEORGE BUCKLUE; JAMES BUCKLUE; GARRET BUCKLUE at time of survey. S/ GEORGE BUCKELEW, MARY (X) BUCKELEW. Wit: AZARIAH LEWIS, EFPHAMA (+ her mark) BUCKELEW, OGDEN COCKEROFF, who swore by oath 31 Mar 1789 before ARTHUR SIMKINS, J.P. Rcd. 26 Jun 1793.

Pp. 235-237. 11 Nov 1789: JOSEPH LEWIS to WILLIAM MORRIS, both of Edgefield Co. SC for 40 pounds, sold 200 acres originally granted 6 Aug 1787 unto said LEWIS on little Stephens Creek of Savanna River. S/ JOSEPH LEWIS. Wit: SAMUEL LEWIS, JOHN STILL, ELISHA STEPHENS, who swore by oath 10 Mar 1790 before JOHN MOORE, J.P. Rcd. 6 Jul 1793.

Pp. 238-243. 19 Dec 1789: (Release dated 20 Dec 1792) PHILIP DILLARD & FANNY, his wife to DRURY MIMS, both of Edgefield Co. SC for 25 pounds, sold 50 acres being part of 200 acres granted 1772 unto NICHOLAS DILLARD being on Cedar Creek of Savanna River adj.

DEED BOOK 8: 1793-1794 EDGEFIELD COUNTY S.C.

THOMAS HAGENS. S/ PHILLIP DILLARD, PHANEY (X) DILLARD. Wit: CHARLES RIVERS, BRITON MIMS, who swore by oath 6 July 1793 before RICHARD TUTT, J.P. Rcd. 6 Jul 1793.

Pp. 243-248. 19 Dec 1792: PHILLIP DILLARD & FANNEY, his wife, to DRURY MIMS, both of Edgefield Co. SC for 25 pounds, sold 33 acres being part of 66 acres granted 1787 unto THOS. HAGENS, being on Cedar Creek of Savannah River \ & adj. OLIPHANT, CHENEY & said DILLARD. S/ PHILIP DILLARD, PHANEY (X her mark) DILLARD. Wit: BRITON MIMS, CHARLES RIVERS, who swore by oath 6 Jul 1793 before RICHARD TUTT, J.P. Rcd. 6 Jul 1793.

Pp. 248-251. 2 Oct 1792: WILLIAM BURDITT & PATIENCE, his wife of Edgefield Co. SC to MUMFORD PERRYMAN of same place for 20 pounds, sold 100 acres being part of two tracts (1) 80 acres originally granted 3 Mar 1787 to said BURDITT & (2) 2 acres being part of 100 acres originally granted 4 Jun 1787 unto JAMES HUNT who conveyed by L&R to said BURDITT, being in the fork of Deloaches Branch & a branch called the Long Branch. S/ WILLIAM (X) BURDITT, PATIENCE (X) BURDITT. Wit: SOLOMON POPE, **ALEXANDER** WILSON, who swore by oath 5 Jan 1793 before HENRY KING, J.P. Rcd. 6 Jul 1793.

Pp. 251-255. 8 Jan (sic) 1793: JAMES TOMLIN to MUMFORD PERRYMAN, both of Edgefield Co. SC for 5 pounds, sold 199 acres originally granted 4 Jun 1792 unto JAMES TOMLIN being between Mine Creek & Red Bank, branches of little Saludy River adj. SW FREDK. SISSON & WILLIAM BURDITT, NE by WM. BROWN & JAMES BAYLEY, & NW & NE by WM. HUMPHREY. S/ JAMES TOMLIN. Wit: DANIEL BULLOCK, WILLIS ANDERSON, ALEXR. WILSON, who swore by oath 5 Jan 1793 before HENRY KING, J.P. Rcd. 6 Jul 1793.

Pp. 255-258. 23 Jul 1791: WILLIAM HUMPHREYS, Planter to MUMFORD PERRYMAN, both of Edgefield Co. SC for 25 pounds, sold 80 acres; (1) 62 acres originally granted 22 May 1772 unto ARTHUR FORT who conveyed to GEORGE MASON who conveyed to ANNA BLAND who conveyed to said HUMPHREY, & (2) 18 acres adj. above tract being part of 312 acres originally granted 4 Dec 1786 unto said HUMPHREYS & adj. E by JOSEPH NUNN. S/ WILLIAM HUMPHREYS. Wit: SAMPSON WILLIAMS, ALEXR. WILSON, who swore by oath 6 Aug 1791 before JAMES SPANN, J.P. Rcd. 6 Jul 1793.

Pp. 258-264. 25 Jun 1793: JOSIAH THOMAS & ELIZABETH his wife, to JACOB SMITH, both of Edgefield Co. SC for 100 pounds, sold 128 acres being part of two tracts that adj. each other; (1) 63 acres originally granted 5 Feb 1787 unto LEWIS CLARK & was conveyed by L&R 14 & 15 Nov 1788 unto said THOMAS & (2) 65 acres originally granted 31 Aug 1774 unto THOMAS DELOACH who conveyed by L&R 12 & 13 May 1789 to said THOMAS. Both tracts being on Red Bank Creek of Little Saluda River. S/ JOSIAH THOMAS, ELIZABETH (X) THOMAS. Wit: WILLIAM BROWN, REBEKAH ESKRIDGE, SAMUEL ESKRIDGE, who swore by oath 26 Jun 1793 before HENRY KING Esq., J.P. Rcd. 6 Jul 1793.

Pp. 265-266. 8 Dec 1792: DAVID DAVIS of Edgefield Co. SC to DRURY MIMS for 100 pounds, sold one negro man named JAMES. S/ DAVID DAVIS. Wit: TOLAVER DAVIS Junr., HENRY WARE Junr., who swore by oath 9 Jul 1793 before RICHARD TUTT, J.P. Rcd. 9 Jul 1793.

Pp. 266-273. 25 Jul 1785: ELIJAH MERRY BAILEY & LEAH his wife, of Camden Dist. SC to HARMON GOLMAN of Edgefield Co. SC for 60

112

pounds, sold 200 acres originally granted 31 Aug 1775 unto JOHN BAILEY being on Rogers Creek a branch of Horns Creek of Savannah River, adj. SW & SE by ALLEN ADDISON, NE by HARMON GOLMAN, NE & SE by JOSEPH WALKER, NE by Bounty land & NW & NE by DANIEL MARSHEL. Said JOHN BAILEY is now dead & ELIJAH MERRY BAILEY as oldest brother & heir at law came in possession of land. S/ ELIJAH MERE BAYLY, LEAH BAYLY. Wit: BAGWELL BAYLY, CALEB BAYLY, JOSEPH ADDISON, who swore by oath 10 Oct 1793 before JOHN PURVIS, J.P. Rcd. 15 Jul 1793.

Pp. 273-274. Plat: MARCANTAN CAMPBELL to THOMAS LAMAR.

Thomas Lamar's land

negroe grave yard

Big Horse Creek

Savannah River

Swamp land

Thomas Lamar's land

750 acres

Road to Phillip Lamars

Thomas Lamar's land

Thomas Lamar's land

Agreeable to request of Mr. MACARTON CAMPBELL of Augusta & Mr. THOMAS LAMAR of Edgefield Co. SC I have made a resurvey of Mr. CAMPBELL's land of 750 acres. Surveyed in Presence of THOMAS LAMAR & WILLIAM JACKSON & Certified 2 May 1792 by ROBERT LANG, D.S. GEORGE RINGLAND, JOSEPH COX, Chain Carriers. ROBERT LANG swore by oath 9 Jul 1793 to above before RICHARD TUTT, J.P. Rcd. 19 Jul 1793.

Pp. 275-277. 10 May 1792: THOMAS BACON to JAMES JAMES, both of Edgefield Co. SC for 5 pounds, sold 5 acres being part of a tract granted ROBERT WALLACE who conveyed to BENJAMIN TUTT who conveyed to said BACON being on waters of Cuffytown Creek a branch of Stephens Creek of Savannah River on the road leading from Senaca to Augusta, adj. JOSEPH MORTON, & said JAMES & his Store house. Wit: ONAN ELLISON, WILLIAM EVANS, JOHN LYON, who swore by oath 8 Feb 1793 before JAMES HARRISON, J.P. Rcd. 22 Jul 1793

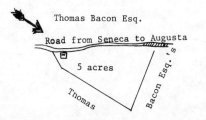

Thomas Bacon Esq.

Road from Seneca to Augusta

5 acres

Thomas Bacon Esq.

Pp. 277-279. 22 Dec 1792: JAMES JAMES of Liberty Co. GA to JACOB HIBBLER of Edgefield Co. SC for 50 pounds, sold 5 acres being part of a tract granted unto ROBERT WALLACE who conveyed to BENJAMIN TUTT who conveyed to THOMAS BACON who conveyed to said

DEED BOOK 8:   1793-1794   EDGEFIELD COUNTY S.C.

JAMES being on Cuffytown Creek of Stephens Creek of Savannah
River. Said tract on the road leading from Seneca to Augusta on
JOSEPH MORTON's line near the Store House of JAMES JAMES.

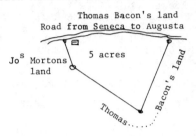

Thomas Bacon's land
Road from Seneca to Augusta

Jo^s Mortons
land

5 acres

S/   JAMES JAMES. Wit:
SAMPSON WOOD, JOHN LYON,
who swore by oath 8 Feb
1793   before   JAMES
HARRISON. Plat: p. 278.
Rcd. 22 July 1793.

Pp. 279-283. 28 Sep 1792: AARON BOOTH of SC to JOSEPH SUMMERS of
Newberry Co.   SC for $166.33 sold 166 acres being 1/3 of a 500
acre tract granted WILLIAM MOULTREE, Esq. being on Big Creek adj.
JESSE GRIFFIN. S/ AARON (X) BOOTH, RUTH (X) BOOTH. Wit: JESSE
GRIFFIN, THOS. W. WATERS, Newberry Co. SC, who swore by oath 12
Oct 1792 before PET. JULIEN, J.P. Rcd. 23 July 1793.

Pp. 283-284. 25 Oct 1789: JOSEPH WALKER, Planter to my beloved
son, HEZEKIAH WALKER, both of Edgefield Co. SC for love &
affection one negro man named BOB. S/ JOSEPH (ŦW) WALKER. Wit:
SOLOMAN (X) LUCAS, JAMES WALKER, who swore by oath 13 Aug 1793
before RICHARD TUTT, J.P. Rcd. 30 Aug 1793.

Pp. 285-290. 9 Nov 1792: JOHN HAZEL & RHODA, his wife of
Edgefield Co. SC to JAMES COX of Newberry Co. SC for 100 pounds,
sold 225 acres originally granted 1 Aug 1785 unto SAMUEL MAYS who
conveyed to said HAZEL 17 July 1789 being on the North side of
the half way swamp a branch of Saluda River; adj. NE by orphans
of OBED HOLLOWAY & NW by Mr. JERVEY. S/ JOHN (X) HAZEL, RHODA (X)
HAZEL. Wit: JAMES ALLEN, WALTER ABNEY, JOHN LOWE, who swore by
oath 5 Mar 1793 before NATHANIEL ABNEY, J.P. Rcd. 30 Jul 1793.

Pp. 290-296. 1 Feb 1793: WILLIAM ANDERSON, Esq. to THOMAS CHAPELL
for 25 pounds, 78 acres being part of 572 originally granted 5
Jan 1787 adj. SW by land granted CATHERINE YOUNGBLOOD; SE by
HENRY FORSTER; & NW by THOMAS CHAPELL. S/ W. ANDERSON. Wit:
THOMAS ANDERSON, JOHN ANDERSON, who swore by oath 9 Feb 1793
before WILLIAM ANDERSON, J.E.C. Rcd. 30 Jul 1793.

Plat: p.295. Plat by THOS.
ANDERSON. 78 acres part of
572   acres   granted   to
WILLIAM   ANDERSON   5   Jan
1787.

Land granted Catharine Youngblood

S11E
78 acres

Thomas
Chappell's land

Henry
Forster's
land

Henry Forster's
land

Pp. 296-299. 24 Apr 1793: SAMUEL SAXON, Sheriff of Ninety Six
Dist. SC to SAMUEL MAYS of Edgefield Co. SC for 62 pounds, sold
600 acres...Whereas JOHN GORDON of lately in Ct. of Common Pleas
of Orangeburg SC obtained a judgement entered up in the Clerk's
office of Common Pleas against Adms. of JOHN CALDWELL of Amelia

114

township for 1005 pounds & Cost did seize said 600 acres & sold said SAMUEL MAYS. S/ S. SAXON, Sheriff. Wit: JAMES CRESWELL, WILLIAM BULTER, who swore by oath 29 Apr 1793 before RUSSELL WILSON, J.P. Rcd. 3 Aug 1793.

Pp. 299-301. 19 Apr 1784: ABIGAL WILLIAMS, Widow of Orangeburg Dist. SC, hereunto moving, to JOSHUA DEEN to be my lawful attorney to recover three negroes viz: 1 fellow named PETER, 1 wench named FLORAH, 1 girl named DORCAS, who were illegally taken from me since the commence of this last war. S/ ABIGAL (X) WILLIAMS. Wit: WILLIAM MAYS, SAMUEL MAYS, who swore by oath 3 Aug 1793 before RICHARD TUTT, J.P. Rcd. 3 Aug 1793.
10 Jul 1784: JOHN WYLD, J.Q., swore by oath to above power of attorney.

Pp. 301-303. 13 Jun 1783: Deed of Gift: ARTHUR KILLCREASE, Planter of Ninety Six Dist. SC to loving grandson JOHN SCOTT of same place for love & affection do give a cow branded AK, a cow branded with O, 3 other heifers, & a sow. S/ ARTHUR (A) KILLCREASE. Wit: CHRISTOPHER GLANTON, THOMAS PENNINGTON, who swore by oath 6 Jun 1793 before HUGH MIDDLETON, J.P. Rcd. 6 Aug 1793.

Pp. 303-305. 5 Aug 1793: JOHN REED of Greenville Co. SC to JAMES FRAZIER of Edgefield Co. SC for 64 pounds, sold 128 acres being part of 300 acres originally granted 8 Jul 1774 unto JOSEPH REED & by his LW&T of said JOSEPH REED was given to said JOHN REED being on both sides of Rocky Creek of Stephens Creek of Savannah River adj. lands of JABER, & ROBERT RUSSELL. S/ JOHN (‡R) REED. Wit: JOSEPH REED, DRURE (M) MORRES JOHN FRAZIER, who swore by oath 9 Aug 1793 before RICHARD TUTT, J.P. Rcd. 9 Aug 1793.

Pp. 306-308. 19 Jul 1793: Deed of Gift: WILLIAM BELL of Edgefield Co. SC to my loving children, MARY BELL, AGNESS BELL, ZACHARIAH BELL, WILLIAM HARRISON BELL, ELIZABETH BELL, LOCREACIA BELL & ARTIMOTIA TABITHA BELL, for love & affection:

Dau. MARY BELL - a bed & furniture, her horse, saddle & briddle, 2 cows & calves, spinning wheel, 2 tables & a trunk;

Dau. AGNESS BELL - Ibid;

Two sons ZACHARIAH & WILLIAM HARRISON BELL - a waggon, 4 horses, harness, 5 plows & all other plantation tools, 4 Bonds on WILLIAM MINOR amounting to 175 pounds;

Dau. ELIZABETH BELL - bed & furniture, mare, 2 cows & calves, a cotton wheel & table;

Dau. LOCRACY BELL - a bed & furniture, mare, 2 cows & calves, spinning wheel & table;

Dau. ARTIMETIA TABETHA BELL - 5 negroes named: 1 man named DUBLIN, 1 man named PRIME, 1 woman named EASTHER, 1 woman named EAMY, 1 girl named JENNY & 2 beds with furniture & all other household furniture, 1 cow, 2 heifers, & all other stock of hogs & geese. S/ WILLIAM BELL. Wit: MARGARET McGOWER, JAMES McGOWER, who swore by oath 1 Aug 1793 before RUSSELL WILSON, J.P. Rcd. 7 Aug 1793.

DEED BOOK 8: 1793-1794 EDGEFIELD COUNTY S.C.

Pp. 308-312. 5 Apr 1793: JAMES LITTLE of Edgefield County SC to WILLIAM MOORE & GILSON YARBOROUGH of same place for 20 pounds, obligated to pay 5 Apr 1795 & for better securing of payment sell a mare branded NB, 2 feather beds & furniture, 2 pots, 1 dutch oven, 1/2 dozen pewter plates, 1 pewter dish, 2 pewter bason, & 2 cows & 2 calves. Should payment with interest be made this be void. S/ JAMES (X) LITTLE. Wit: DAVID CURETON, GEORGE B. MOORE, who swore by oath 8 Aug 1793 before JOSEPH HIGHTOWER, J.P. Rcd. 15 Aug 1793.

Pp. 312-317. 18 Jul 1793: DRURY MIMS & LYDIA, his wife of Edgefield Co. SC for 20 pounds, sold 33 acres being part of 66 acres originally granted 1787 unto THOMAS HAGENS being on Cedar Creek of Savannah River adj. lands of OLIPHANT, PHILLIP DILLARD, JOHN CHENEY. Said land sold by THOMAS HAGENS unto PHILLIP DILLARD 16 & 17 Jan 1789 who sold by L&R to DRURY MIMS 19 & 20 Dec 1792. S/ DRURY MIMS, LYDDA (X) MIMS. Wit: BRITON MIMS, THOMAS HAGENS, who swore by oath 29 Aug 1793 before RICHARD TUTT, J.P. Rcd. 29 Aug 1793.

Pp. 317-323. 12 Aug 1793: BENJAMIN RYAN the 3rd & FRANKEE his wife, to BENJAMIN RYAN the 2nd, both of Edgefield Co. SC for 200 pounds, sold 125 acres being part of 200 acres originally granted 8 Jul 1774 unto LACON RYAN. being on branches of Horns Creek of Savannah River. Said LACON RYAN now dec'd., & land adjs. N by SWAIN RAMBO; SE MOSES KIRKLAND & SW BENJAMIN RYAN & LACON RYAN. S/ BENJ. RYAN 3rd, FRANKEE (₣) RYAN (also FRANCES). Wit: ISAAC KIRKLAND, JOHN RYAN, who swore by oath 2 Sep 1793 before JOSEPH HIGHTOWER, J.P. Rcd. 2 Sep 1793.

Pp. 323-328. 4 Jun 1793: SAMUEL MAYS to THOMAS READ, both of Edgefield Co. SC for 100 pounds, sold 200 acres being part of 300 acres originally granted 8 Jul 1774 unto ANN DEAN being on Bigg Creek of Saluda River adj. NW DANNETT ABNEY, SW by JOHN BROOKS, SE by GAVEN POU, otherwise JOHN GARRARD, NE ISAAC DE COSTA which said tract was conveyed by GEORGE DEEN, son & heir at law to ANN DEEN by L&R 5 & 6 Oct 1787 unto SAMUEL MAYS. S/ SAML. MAYS. Wit: THOMAS CASON (also CARSON), JEREMIAH HATCHER, who swore by oath 5 Jun 1793 before RICHARD TUTT, J.P. Rcd. 2 Sep 1793.

Pp. 328-329. 23 Aug 1791: AARON BOOTH to WILLIAM MOULTRIE of Charleston SC bound for sum of 1000 pounds, said 500 pounds should be paid:
Received 24 Aug 1791 of A. BOOTH 10 pounds in part of Bond;
Received 19 Nov 1791 of A. BOOTH 20 pounds in part of Bond;
Received 23 Apr 1793 37 pounds of JESSE GRIFFIN being the balance of bond & 60 pounds of T.W. WATERS, all which sums I received in horses. S/ WILLM. MOULTRIE. Wit: JACOB DRAYTON.

Pp. 329-337. 23 Aug 1791: Mortgage: AARON BOOTH of SC to WILLIAM MOULTRIE of Charleston for the penal sum of 1000 pounds & upon payment of 500 pounds with interest by a bond made 23 Aug 1791 & for better securing of payment sells 500 acres being on Bigg Creek of Saluda River adj. lands of THOMAS LEPHARD, JOHN PHILLIPS, & THOMAS COTTON. S/ AARON (X) BOOTH. Wit: JACOB DRAYTON, RICHARD SMITH, Charleston SC, who swore by oath 24 Aug 1791 before JOHN SANFORD DART, J.P.Q.U.
23 Apr 1793: I do hereby assign over to JESSE GRIFFIN the rights & title to property within Mortgage S/ WILLIAM MOULTRIE. Wit: JAMES HAMILTON. Rcd. 2 Sep 1793.

116

Pp. 338-344. 28 Aug 1793: JOHN ADDISON to JOHN GRAY, both of Edgefield Co. SC for 50 pounds, sold 100 acres being part of 2 tracts (1) 10 acres being part of 200 acres originally granted 20 Apr 1764 unto ALLEN ADISON being on Horns Creek & land where HERMAN GALLMAN formerly lived; (2) 90 acres on Horns Creek being part of 200 acres originally granted 31 Aug 1774 unto JOHN BAYLY & at his death fell to ELIJAH MERRY BAYLY, his oldest brother & heir at law who with his wife LEAH sold to HARMON GALLMAN 26 Jul 1785 & who with his wife LUCRETIA sold to JOHN ADDISON 5 Nov 1790. Said tract adj. lands of WILLIAM BROWN, SAMUEL MARSH, & said JOHN ADDISON. S/ JOHN ADDISON. Wit: JOSIAH GREY, SAMUEL MARSH, who swore by oath 2 Sep 1793 before AQUILA MILES, J.P. EF Co. Ct. Sep term 1793: AMY ADDISON, wife of JOHN, relinquished dower & thirds before RICHARD TUTT, J.P. Rcd. 2 Sep 1793.

Pp. 344-348. 15 Apr 1793: MATTHEW WILLS to WILLIAM CARTER, both of Edgefield Co. SC for 40 pounds, sold 96 acres being part of 200 acres originally granted 26 Sep 1772 unto BENJAMIN WARING being upon Mills Creek of Saluda river & was conveyed to said WILLS. Said tract adj. THOMAS BERRY. S/ MATTHEW WILLS. Wit: HARRIS SMITH, SAMUEL SPRAGENS, WILLIAM SPRAGINS, who swore by oath 16 Apr 1793 before NATHANIEL ABNEY, J.P. Rcd. 2 Sep 1793.

Pp. 348-353. 8 Jul 1783: JOHN BERWICH, THOMAS WARING & JOHN EWING CALHOUN, Commissioners of Forfeited Estates of SC to RICHARD JOHNSON of Ninety Six Dist. SC for 422 pounds, at a public sale to highest bidder, sold 866 acres being two tracts formerly belonging to MOSES KIRKLAND known as tract No. 1 & 2. Tract No. 1 contains 406 acres. Tract No. 2 contains 460 & adj. lands of RICHARD WILLIAMS & JOHN RUTLEDGE, Esq.; SE by a small creek of Turkey Creek. S/ JOHN BERWICK, THOS. WARING, Senr. Wit: JAMES O'HARA, WILLIAM EVANS, who swore by oath 12 Aug 1793 before JOHN CLARKE, J.P. Rcd. 2 Sep 1793.

Pp. 353-355. 8 Jun 1793: JOHN COURSEY & ELIZABETH his wife, Planter & Spinstress to WILLIAM VANN, both of Edgefield Co. SC for 30 pounds, sold 153 acres originally granted 21 Jan 1785 said COURSEY being on branches of Turkey Creek of Savannah River. S/ JOHN (X) COURSEY, ELISABETH (C) COURSEY. Wit: ELISHA STEVENS, JONATHAN CLEGG, who swore by oath 2 Sep 1793 before RICHARD TUTT, J.P. Rcd. 2 Sep 1793.

Pp. 355-357. 1 May 1789: RICHARD STOKES of Lunenburg Co. VA to his grandchildren, EVAN STOKES, LUDWELL STOKES, BATT STOKES, WILMYRTH STOKES, GREENBERRY STOKES & ROBERT STOKES, for love & affection give a negroe girl named ESTHER with her increase, use of waggon & horses, plantation utensils & household furniture. S/ RICHD. STOKES. Wit: HENRY STOKES, GEORGE BARNES, WOODSON KNIGHT, JAMES BARNES, WILLIAM CAIN, WILLIAM BLACKLEY, who swore by oath 19 Aug 1793 before JAMES HARRISON, J.P. Rcd. 2 Sep 1793.

Pp. 357-359. 15 Aug 1793: Division of LACON RYAN, Dec'd., Estate. BENJAMIN RYAN - his part - 11 negroes named WILL; SALLEY; SUIE; HANNAR; CLEARK; DAVID; JOE; SUE; SILLVEY; LUCK; ROSE, also 2 horses, small stock of cattle & hogs.

SARAH RYAN - her part - 12 negroes named POMP; NAN; SILAS; BEN;

BOB; FIB; WILL; SEAL; FERIBEE; BRISTO; PETER; & BEN also 2 horses & a small stock of cattle & hogs. The above division was made by JOHN RYAN & BENJAMIN RYAN, Extrs. of Estate. S/ JOHN RYAN, BENJM. (B) RYAN, Extrs. Wit: SAMUEL WALKER, ISAAC KIRKLAND, who swore by oath 2 Sep 1793 before JOSEPH HIGHTOWER, J.P.
15 Aug 1793: BENJAMIN RYAN, Junr. received above from his father's Estate, LACON RYAN from his guardian, JOHN RYAN, Ex. & gave his Quit Claim. Wit: RICHARD JOHNSON, SAMUEL MAYS, ISAAC KIRKLAND. Rcd. 2 Sep 1793

Pp. 359-361. 31 Aug 1793: JOHN PARKER to JOHN PRYOR, both of Edgefield Co. SC for 16 pounds, 125 acres being part of a tract originally granted to THOMAS LAMAR & conveyed by L&R 13 Dec 1789 being on Town Creek adj. N by HECRONIMUS ZINN & THOMAS LAMAR. S/ JOHN (X) PARKER. Wit: NICHOLAS (T) THOMAS, WILLIAM STEWART, who swore by oath 31 Aug 1793 before JOHN CLARK, J.P. Rcd. 2 Sep 1793.

Pp. 362-366. 1791 (sic): DANIEL MICKLAR & MARIAH (also ANAMARIAH), his wife to THOMAS HENDERSON, both of Edgefield Co. SC for 100 pounds, sold 250 acres of which 150 acres originally granted 20 Aug 1765 unto ANAMARIAH STRUB & by entering Matromony with said MICKLAR said 150 acres fell to him; the other 150 (sic) being part of 250 acres granted 3 Jul 1773 unto DANIEL MICKLAR being on Cuffytown Creek adj. lands NE MICHEL PETERS & MARY STRUMS; SE PETER STRUM; & SW by GEORGE GREMINGER. S/ DANIEL MICKLER. Wit: SAMUEL ROBERTSON, JOHN HAYNIE, who swore by oath 21 Sep 1790 before JOHN BROWNLEE, J.P.
Release: DANIEL MICKLAR & EVE his wife, sells to THOMAS HENDERSON of Edgefield Co. SC witnesses that the said DANIEL MICKLAR & ANAMARISH, his wife for 100 pounds to them are satisfied & said DANIEL MICKLAR & EVE his wife sells...
Rcd. 8 Oct 1793? (Note, gch: This deed has date 1791 in L&R).

Pp. 367-370. 30 Dec 1790: RUFUS INMAN, Blacksmith to JOSEPH CULBREATH, Planter both of Edgefield Co. SC for 40 pounds, sold 102 acres originally granted 2 Oct 1786 unto INMAN on Saluda River. S/ RUFUS INMAN. Wit: ISAAC NORRELL, JOHN ABNEY, EDWARD CULBREATH, who swore by oath 30 Jul 1793 before WILLIAM ANDERSON, J.P. Rcd. 2 Sep 1793.

Pp. 370-372. 14 Jul 1792: THOMAS LAMAR of Horse Creek & ANN his wife, to JOHN PRYOR, Mill wright of Edgefield Co. SC for 100 pounds, sold 427 acres being part of a large survey granted to THOMAS LAMAR on Town Creek adj. lands of CHROMOUS ZINN; JOHN PARKER; JAMES ASHBERRY; JOHN GRAY; DAVID ZUBLY; ISAAC PARKER & GASPER NAGEL known as the red House; & JOSEPH LAMBETH. S/ THOS. LAMAR, ANN LAMAR. Wit: JOHN HOWARD, HODGEN HOLMES, who swore by oath 22 Jul 1793 before JOHN CLARKE, J.P. Rcd. 2 Sep 1793.

Pp. 373-375. 7 Nov 1792: WILLIAM ANDERSON to HENRY HAZELL for 40 pounds, sold 132 acres being part of 185 acres originally granted 3 Apr 1786 unto BENJAMIN SMITH being on Tarpin Creek of Saludy River & was conveyed by said SMITH to said ANDERSON. Said tract adj. lands N by SAMUEL SAVAGE; W by JOHN SMITH; E by TOWLES; S by NATHANIEL FOSHEE. S/ W. ANDERSON. Wit: JOHN ANDERSON, THOMAS (X) TURK, JOHN GWYN, who swore by oath 10 Nov 1792 before JOHN MOORE, J.P. Rcd. 2 Sep 1793.

Pp. 376-379. 28 Nov 1774: PHILLILP HAZELL to JOSEPH CULBREATH, both of Ninety Six Dist. SC for 350 pounds sold 250 acres originally granted 11 Feb 1773 unto said HAZELL being on Halfway swamp & Tarrapin Creek of Saludy river in Colleton Co. SC adj. WILLIAM ABNEY. S/ PHILIP (P) HAZELL, ELIZABETH (X) HAZELL. Wit: RICHARD GRIFFIN, Senr., RICHARD GRIFFIN, Junr., HENARY (H) HAZELL, who swore by oath 23 Oct 1776 before JOHN SATTERWHITE, J.P. Rcd. 2 Sep 1793.

Pp. 379-382. 2 Aug 1793: Mortgage: ALLEN HINTON of Edgefield Co. SC, hereunto moving to BARKLEY MARTIN Of Village of Campbelltown, being indebted for 30 pounds & for better securing of debt sell a negroe womin named SILVIA & her child named WILL. S/ ALLEN HINTON. Wit: MORGAN MURRAH, JOSIAS H. McPHERSON, who swore by oath 24 Aug 1793 before JOSEPH HIGHTOWER, J.P. Rcd. 3 Sep 1793.

Pp. 382-385. 31 Aug 1793: ANN ZUBLY spinster of Edgefield Co. SC, Executrix of LW&T of DAVID ZUBLY, dec'd., to JOHN CLARKE, Esq., highest bidder at Public Sale 29 Dec 1791 for 5 pounds, sold 200 acres being part of 5858 acres originally granted to DAVID ZUBLY in County of Winton, Orangburg Dist. SC adj. said JOHN CLARKE...Said notice of sale was published in State Gazette. S/ ANN ZUBY, Extx. Wit: JAMES WEATHERFORD, WILLIAM STEWART, who swore by oath 31 Aug 1793 before JOHN CLARKE, J.P. Rcd. 3 Sep 1793.

Pp. 385-388. 31 Aug 1793: ANN ZUBLY, Executrix of LW&T of DAVID ZUBLY, dec'd., to ANN ZUBLY, Spinster, being highest bidder of public sale 29 Dec 1793...Notice of sale published in State Gazette, for 20 pounds sold 200 acres in Township of New Windsor originally granted unto HANS & JOHN ZEUCHER & on their decease, the late wife of NICHOLAS SHUBDREIN became heir at law & said NICHOLAS SHUBDREIN conveyed unto DAVID ZUBLY, dec'd., & ANN ZUBLY became the purshaser. S/ ANN ZUBLY, Extr. Wit: JAMES WEATHERFORD, WILLIAM STEWART, who swore by oath 31 Aug 1793 before JOHN CLARKE, J.P. Rcd. 3 Sep 1793.

Pp. 388-393. 30 Jan 1792: NATHANIEL ABNEY to JOHN ABNEY,Depy. Surveyor, both of Edgefield County SC for 100 pounds, sold 250 acres being part of 400 acres originally granted 16 Dec 1766 unto HENRY MEDSCALFE & by LW&T given to his son HENRY who conveyed by L&R to FRANCIS HIGGINS who with his wife SARAH conveyed to THOMAS WILLOUGHBY WATERS who with his wife FANNY conveyed to said ABNEY. Said tract on South side of Saluda River adj. Saluda River, the Long branch of Tosety's Creek, crosses head of Wolf Trap's Branch, the Widow ABNEY; PAUL ABNEY & ALEXANDER KENIDA. S/ NATHAL. ABNEY. Wit: AZARIAH ABNEY, THOS. PULLEY, JOEL ABNEY, who swore by oath 27 Oct 1792 before HENRY KING, J.P. Rcd. 3 Sep 1793.

Pp. 393-397. 15 Jun 1791: THOMAS SPRAGINS to JOHN ABNEY, Depy. Surveyor, both of Edgefield Co. SC for 20 pounds, 125 acres being part of 250 acres originally granted 1 Aug 1785 on a branch of Indian Creek of Saluda River adj. lands of JOHN COLEMAN. S/ THOS. SPRAGINS. Wit: FRANCIS JONES, PAUL ABNEY, who swore by oath 16 Jun 1792 before NATHAL. ABNEY, J.P. Rcd. 3 Sep 1793.

Pp. 397-401. 23 May 1793: ROLAND COURTNEY of Orangeburg Dist. SC to JOHN ABNEY, Depy. Surveyor of Edgefield Co. SC for 20 pounds, sold 150 acres originally granted 2 Mar 1789 to said COURTNEY on Bigg Creek a branch of Little Saluda river adj. SE by ISAAC CROWTHERS; NE by EMANUEL LEPPERD; NW by CHANEY & WILLIAM WILSON; SE WILLIAM HILL. S/ ROLAND (X) COURTNEY. Wit: JAMES COURTNEY, JAMES (J) MILLS, who swore by oath 27 Aug 1793 before NATHANIEL ABNEY, J.P. Rcd. 3 Sep 1793.

Pp. 401-403. 23 Mar 1793: ANN SUMMERAL to MARY SUMMERAL, both of Edgefield Co. SC for 10 pounds, sold 33 1/3 acres being 1/3 of 100 acres originally granted 3 Nov 1770 unto JACOB SUMMERAL on Horns Creek. S/ ANNE (A) SUMMERAL. Wit: DAVID SIGLAR, DANIEL PARKER, JOHN HALL, who swore by oath 23 Mar 1793 before JOSEPH HIGHTOWER, J.P. Rcd. 3 Sep 1793.

Pp. 403-408. 26 Aug 1791: CHRISTOPHER WARD to YOUNG ALLEN, both of Edgefield Co. SC for 14 pounds, sold 100 acres originally granted 13 Apr 1769 being on Manchester Creek on the old wagon Road leading from Charleston to Cambridge adj. lands of JOHN RUSHTON. S/ CHRISTOPHER (R) WARD. Wit: JOHN (‡) STILL, AMOS RICHARDSON, who swore by oath 19 Aug 1792 before HENRY KING, J.P. Rcd. 3 Sep 1793.

Pp. 408-412. 16 Nov 1789: AYRES GORELY of Laurens Co. SC to REUBEN PYLES of same place for 80 pounds sold 3314 acres being 6 tracts of land originally granted said GORELY 1 Jan 1787:

(1) 1317 acres originally granted 1 Jan 1787 on a long branch of Town Creek adj. GEORGE MILLER; ROBERT LANG; JAMES GRAY; DAVID BOWERS; & DAVID ZUBLY:

(2) 816 acres originally granted 1 Jan 1787 on waters of Savannah River adj. THOMAS LAMAR; & VALENTINE ZINN:

(3) 188 acres originally granted 1 Jan 1787 on Little River the NW fork of Savannah River;

(4) 203 acres originally granted 1 Jan 1787 on Stephens Creek adj. NICHOLS MINOR & YANCY;

(5) 490 acres originally granted 1 Jan 1787 adj. Hatchess ponds on the new road from Long Cane to Charleston;

(6) 300 acres originally granted 1 Jan 1787 being cn Clarks branch of Savannah River. S/ AYRES GORLEY. Wit: ALLEN GLOVER, WILEY GLOVER, Abbeville Co. SC, who swore by oath 11 May 1793 before JULIUS NICHOLS, Junr., J.P. Rcd. 3 Sep 1793.

Pp. 412-415. 31 Aug 1793: ANN ZUBLY, Executrix of LW&T of DAVID ZUBLY, dec'd. to JOHN CLARKE, Planter, both of Edgefield Co. SC for 5 pounds, sold 5206 acres being part of 5858 acres originally granted 2 Oct 1786 unto DAVID ZUBLY being in Winton Co. Orangeburg Dist. SC adj. SE SAMUEL BURGESS, NE JANE GRAY, JOHN HEATH, PATRICK GORDEN, & DAVID ZUBLY. Said tract sold to highest bidder at public sale. S/ ANN ZUBLY, Exx. Wit: JAMES WEATHERFORD, WILLIAM STEWART, who swore by oath 2 Sep 1793 before JOSEPH HIGHTOWER, J.P. Rcd. 3 Sep 1793.

P. 415. Affidavit: DAVID GLOVER gave oath that he had a note dated 1 Nov 1791 given by WILLIAM CALDWELL to AMOS MITCHELL for 5 negroes - namely - NED, LEAH, JODAH, DAPHNEY & MILLEY which said

:ote had credit on it for all above mentioned negroes but NED. Also another note for 10,000 weight of tobacco which was payable to MITCHELL upon settlement by said MITCHELL & said WILLIAM CALDWELL. The note appears to be fully satisfied but there was no credit entered upon said note & said deponant has lost or mislaid & he said that he never traded said notes to no person whatsoever. S/ DAVID GLOVER. 2 Feb 1793 before JOSEPH HIGHTOWER, J.P. Rcd. 4 Sep 1793.

Pp. 416-420. 14 Aug 1793: SAMUEL ABNEY to THOS. SPRAGINS, both of Edgefield Co. SC for 8 pounds, sold 18 acres being part of 150 originally granted 20 May 1769 unto STEPHEN COLLENS & conveyed to SAMUEL ABNEY, dec'd., & being the father of said SAMUEL ABNEY & he being heir at law. Said tract being on Saluda river adj. branches of Tosetys creek & said THOS. SPRAGIN. S/ SAMUEL ABNEY. Wit: WILLIAM KENNEDY, JOHN ABNEY, who swore by oath 4 Sep 1793 before HENRY KING, J.P. Rcd. 4 Sep 1793.

Pp. 420-422. 3 Nov 1792: HARMON GABLE & ROSANAH, his wife to JACOB IDOM for 10 pounds, sold 100 acres originally granted 23 Jan 1793 (sic) unto ROSANAH MARK wife of said HARMON GABLE (being on the bounty) on waters of Hardlabour Creek adj. E by BRYAN COCKRAM; S by LAURENCE MARK. S/ HARMON GABLE. Wit: PETER ZIMMERMAN, JAMES STIFEL, ABNER PERRIN, who swore by oath 4 Sep 1793 before RICHARD TUTT, J.P. Rcd. 4 Sep 1793.

Pp. 424-430. 21 May 1792: AMOS MITCHELL Planter of Edgefield Co SC to WILLIAM CALDWELL of Newberry SC for 500 pounds, sold 700 acres being two tracts of land: (1) 350 acres originally granted 1751 unto JOSEPH CHATWIN on Savannah River NE by PATRICK CARDIFFS & SE by THOMAS BRYAN at time of survey & also (2) 350 acres originally granted 2 Jan 1754 unto PATRICK CARDIFF & by sundry conveyances became the property of DANIEL MITCHELL. First tract of 350 acres was conveyed 2 Jun 1765 by JOSEPH CHATWIN unto JAMES COLLENS who conveyed to DANIEL MITCHELL. The second tract of 350 acres was conveyed by PATRICK CARDIFF to above mentioned JOSEPH CHATWIN who conveyed to JAMES COLLENS who conveyed to DANIEL MITCHELL. S/ AMOS (X) MITCHELL. Wit: JOSIAH GATES, ANN WHITE, ROBERT GILLAM, Junr., who swore by oath 3 Sep 1793 before ROBERT GILLAM, J.P. Rcd. 4 Sep 1793.

Pp. 430-433. 4 Jun 1793: WILLIAM FORT, Adm. of HENRY BOLTON, dec'd., of Washington Co. GA to WILLIAM HUMPHREYS of Edgefield Co. SC for 25 pounds, sold 25 acres being part of 100 acres originally granted DRURY FORT who conveyed to said HENRY BOLTON & which said WILLIAM FORT is now administrator of the 25 acres being on mine Creek of Little Saluda River adj. W by BARROT TRAVIS, & N & NE by said HUMPHREYS & S by Mine Creek. S/ WILLIAM FORT. Wit: ARNOLD BERRY, NATHANIEL BOLTON, who swore by oath 24 Jun 1793 before HENRY KING, J.P. Rcd. 4 Sep 1793.

Pp. 433-436. 9 May 1789: ANNA BLAND, widow of Edgefield Co. SC to WILLIAM HUMPHREYS of same place for 20 pounds, sold 62 acres being part of 200 acres originally granted 22 May 1772 unto ARTHUR FORT being on a branch of Mine Creek of Little Saludy River who conveyed to GEORGE MASON who conveyed to said ANNA BLAND adj. WILLIAM HUMPHREYS & JOSEPH NUNN. S/ ANN (X) BLAND. Wit: HENRY KING, PRESLEY BLAND, who swore by oath 3 Mar 1790 before RUSSELL WILSON, J.P. Rcd. 4 Sep 1793.

Pp. 436-440. Jan 1793: JOHN TEDDERS to GABRIEL TUTT, both of Edgefield Co. SC for 150 pounds, sold 200 acres originally granted 29 Apr 1786 being on SW side of Savannah River at the mouth of Swifts Creek. S/ JOHN TEDDERS. Wit: BARNARD COFFERY, RICHARD TUTT, Junr., JAMES TUTT, who swore by oath 6 Sep 1793 before RICHARD TUTT, J.P. Rcd. 6 Sep 1793.

Pp. 440-442. 29 Oct 1792: Power of Attorney: THOMAS DAVIS, JOHN COLVARD, WILLIAM COLVARD, JONATHAN HARVEY, all of Edgefield Co. SC now the proper heirs of WILLIAM GRIMES agreeable to LW&T of said GRIMES made in Hanover Co. VA; Appoint ARGE GARNER their attorney to ask & receive all property from WILLIAM & JOHN GRIMES, Executors of said dec'd. WILLIAM GRIMES. S/ THOMAS DAVIS, JOHN COLVARD, WILLIAM COLVARD, JONATHAN HARVEY . Wit: JOHN BOSTICK, TOLIVER DAVIS, Junr., who swore by oath 7 Sep 1793 before RICHARD TUTT, J.P. Rcd. 7 Sep 1793.

Pp. 442-446. 21 Jun 1793: ENOCH GRIGSBY to LODOWICK HILL of Edgefield Co. SC for 100 pounds, sold 200 acres originally granted 7 Nov 1785 unto BARTLETT BLEDSOE, being on Pen Creek of Saluda River adj. NE by WRIGHT NICHOLSON. Said BLEDSOE conveyed by L&R 2 & 3 Apr 1788 unto ENOCH GRIGSBY. S/ ENOCH GRIGSBY. Wit: MOSES (X) BROWN, SAML. MAYS, who swore by oath 30 Aug 1793 before HENRY KING, J.P. Rcd. 25 Sep 1793.

Pp. 447-451. 28 Jun 1793: RHYDON GRIGSBY to LODOWICK HILL, both of Edgefield Co. SC for 50 pounds, sold 100 acres originally granted on a bounty 2 Oct 1786 unto GEORGE MASON & who conveyed by L&R 22 & 23 Mar 1788 unto RHYDON GRIGSBY being on Pen Creek of Saluda River. S/ RHYDON GRIGSBY. Wit: JAMES BARNETT, ENOCH GRIGSBY, who swore by oath 30 Aug 1793 before HENRY KING, J.P. Rcd. 25 Sep 1793.

Pp. 451-456. 28 Jun 1793: RHYDON GRIGSBY to LODOWICK HILL, both of Edgefield Co. SC for 60 pounds, sold 150 acres originally granted 6 Mar 1786 unto GEORGE MASON & who conveyed by L&R 22 & 23 Mar 1788 unto RHYDON GRIGSBY being on the fork of Pen Creek of Saluda River. S/ RHYDON GRIGSBY. Wit: JAMES BARNETT, ENOCH GRIGSBY, who swore by oath 30 Aug 1793 before HENRY KING, J.P. Rcd. 25 Sep 1793.

Pp. 456-460. 18 Apr 1793: ANDREW JONES, Planter of Abbeville Co. SC to JOSEPH DAWSON, Planter of Edgefield Co. SC for 50 pounds, sold 100 acres originally granted by bounty 12 Sep 1768 unto ANDREW JONES being on both sides of Turkey Creek of Savannah River originally surveyed by JOHN NELSON Depty. 6 Nov 1767. S/ ANDREW JONES, MARY (M) JONES. Wit: ROBERT CRAWFORD, ANDREW CRAWFORD, JAMES NELSON, who swore by oath 19 Apr 1793 before JAMES HARRISON, J.P. Rcd. 28 Sep 1793. [Note: gch: Clerk made error of grant date in Lease - year 1786 instead of 1768. Was correct in Release by survey & grant date]

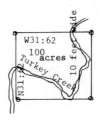

Plat: p. 460. Originally certified 8 Nov 1767 by JOHN NELSON, D. S. being taken from original tract 7 Mar 1793 by WM. COURSEY, D. S.

<u>Pp. 461-465.</u> 16 Aug 1793: THOMAS HAGENS to WILLIAM HAGENS, both of Edgefield Co. SC for 5 pounds, sold 33 acres on Cedar Creek of Savannah River being part of 66 acres originally granted 1787 unto THOMAS HAGENS, adj. JOHN CHANEY's land that he sold JOHN COCKBURN; the remaining 33 acres that said HAGENS sold to PHILLIP DILLARD; said THOMAS HAGANs land where he now lives; JOHN OLIPHANT; LENNARD MARBERY. S/ THOS. HAGENS. Wit: MOSES (M) GUNNELLS, LILLESTUN PARDUE, who swore by oath 10 Oct 1793 before RICHARD TUTT, J. P. Rcd. 10 Oct 1793.

Pp. 1-3. 2 Nov 1793: RICHARD JOEL (also JOWEL), to DANIEL GUNNELS Planter both of Edgefield Co. SC for 20 pounds, sold 40 acres being part of 200 acres originally granted 9 Sep 1774 unto JAMES ROBERSON being on North side of Beaverdam Creek of Turkey Creek of Savannah River & was conveyed by said ROBERSON unto DANIEL ROGERS who conveyed unto BENJAMIN RODES who conveyed unto RICHARD JOEL. S/ RICHARD JOWEL.

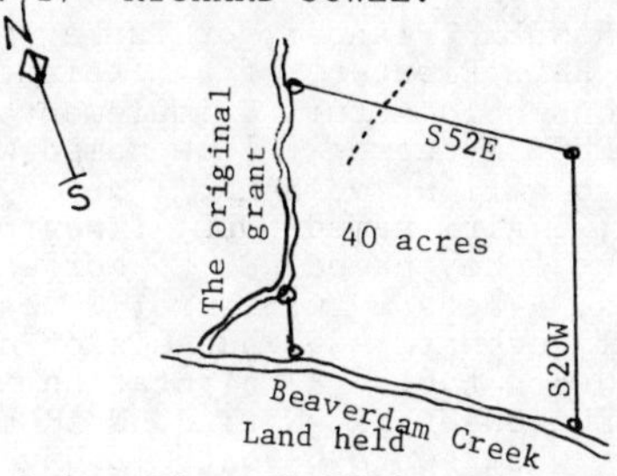

[Plat diagram: N compass, "The original grant", "S52E", "40 acres", "S20W", "Beaverdam Creek", "Land held"]

Wit: HENRY WARE, Junr., BRITON MIMS, who swore by oath 2 Nov 1793 before RICHARD TUTT, J.P.

Mrs (sic) JOWEL ackd. her dower 4 Nov 1793 in open court before RICHARD TUTT, C.E.C. Rcd. 2 Nov 1793.

Pp. 3-4. 26 Jul 1793: Bill of Sale: JOHN RENNALDS to PHILL MAY for 100 pounds, sold one negroe lad named DANIEL, formerly the property of THOMAS RUNNELS, dec'd. S/ JOHN RENNALDS. Wit: WILLIAM GRIFFIN, Saddler, FIELDING RENNALDS, who swore by oath 4 Nov 1793 before RICHARD TUTT, J.P. Rcd. 4 Nov 1793.

Pp. 4-8. 17 Aug 1791: JOSEPH RAMBO & SUSANNA his wife to FIELDING RENNOLDS, both of Edgefield Co. SC for 200 pounds, sold 200 acres adj. lands of WALTER JACKSON; my spring branch; Horns Creek to FARNED; LITTLEBERRY ADAMS; to top of ridge that divides Horns Creek & Dry creek; to JACKSON's but now COBB's line. S/ JOS. RAMBO, SUSANNAH RAMBO. Wit: WM. ROBERTSON, THOMAS ADAMS, who swore by oath 18 Aug 1791 before AQUILA MILES, J.P. Rcd. 4 Nov 1793.

Pp. 9-12. 13 Sep 1793: HEZEKIAH GENTRY to JOHN ABNEY, D.S., both of Edgefield Co. SC for 20 pounds, sold 100 acres originally granted 6 Mar 1786 unto said GENTRY being on head of Indian Creek of Little Saluda River. S/ HEZEKIAH GENTRY. Wit: THOMAS (X) GENTRY, JOHN BOLGER, who swore by oath 14 Sep 1793 before NATHAL. ABNEY, J.P. Rcd. 4 Nov 1793.

Pp. 13-16. 16 Jul 1792: ELISHA PALMORE to GEORGE BUSSEY, Junr both of SC for 100 pounds, sold 208 acres by a survey made 6 Jan 1792 by JOHN BRYDE being on Gunnels creek adj. SE by ELISHA PALMORE & NW by JOHN HOOFMAN. S/ ELISHA (X) PALMOR. Wit: GEORGE BUSSEY, Senr., DEMCY BUSSEY, who swore by oath 24 oct 1793 before HUGH MIDDLETON, J.P. Rcd. 4 Nov 1793.

Pp. 16-18. 20 Jun 1793: Deed of Gift: CATHARINE GLOVER, widow living in Edgefield Co. SC but hereunto moving, to MARY CLARK, my dauter of Edgefield Co. SC, all my household stuff & other substance except a hefer I give to my grandson, ASA CLARK: cow & calf to granddaughter MARY CLARK: a cow & calf to my grandson JESSE GLOVER; LOWRY GLOVER son, a horse; to my grandson THOMAS CLARK... S/ CATREN ( ) GLOVER. Wit: PATRICK SULLIVAN, DANIEL (C) SULLIVAN, who swore by oath 5 Nov 1793 before RICHARD TUTT, J.P. Rcd. 5 Nov 1793.

Pp. 18-21. 8 Nov 1793: Mortgage: RICHARD TUTT, Junr. Planter to GEORGE B. MOORE, Merchant, both of Edgefield Co. SC, The penal sum of 5 pounds, for better securing of payment of 27 pounds with interest do sell 1 negroe girl named ANNICA about 8 or 9 yrs old. Should payment be made this be null & void. S/ RICHARD TUTT, Junr. Wit: GEORGE HOGARTH, ALEXANDER KEVAN, who swore by oath 8 Nov 1793 before JOSEPH HIGHTOWER, J.P. Rcd. 11 Nov 1793.

Pp. 21-23. Bill of Sale: JOEL CHANDLER, Planter, of Turkey Creek of Edgefield Co. SC to WILLIAM HALL, Planter, of same place for 250 pounds, sold all goods household stuff & implements per schedule: 1 negroe man named CHARLES; 1 negroe fellow named WILL; 1 negro wench named JOAN; 1 negro girl named SALL; 1 negro girl named RACHEL; 1 girl named LYDDA; 1 girl named DOLL; 1 negro boy named ABRAM; 1 boy named PETER; 1 boy named NED; 5 horses; 18 horned cattle; 6 sheep; 60 hogs; 4 beds & furniture; 1 desk; 1 chest of drawers; 1 close chest; 1 cupboard; 400 bushels of corn; 1 set blacksmith tools; carpenter tools & plantation tools some chairs & 3 pots. S/ JOEL CHANDLER. Wit: JOHN ARLEDGE, JAMES SCOTT, JEREMIAH HATCHER, who swore by oath 15 Nov 1793 before RICHARD TUTT, J.P. Rcd. 15 Nov 1793.

Pp. 23-28. 14 Nov 1793: SAMUEL BURGES & ELIZABETH his wife to JOHN HAMMOND, Senr. Merchant, both of Edgefield Co. SC for 5 pounds, sold 50 acres originally granted unto JOHN TOBLER, Esq. now dec'd. being in New Windsor Township adj. Savannah River; THOMAS SMITH; & land in possession of DARBY M GOULAND. S/ SAMUEL BURGES, ELIZABETH BURGES. Wit: HELENA CLARKE, WILLIAM STEWART, who swore by oath 15 Nov 1793 before JOHN CLARKE, J.P. Rcd. 19 Nov 1793.
Interlining in deed witnessed by CHARLES RAMSEY & MARY ANN BOWERS.

Pp. 28-31. 16 Jul 1793: PETER CARNS, Attorney at law to JOHN RYAN for 500 pounds, sold 2000 acres being part of 2 tracts (1) 1000 acres being on Buckhalter creek known by the name of Independant Hill being the land where said CARNS now resides. Said tract is the remainder of a tract now already sold to different persons & (2) 1000 acres on Cedar creek that adj. above land; Mrs. WHITE; JAS. WEST; & STEPHEN TILMAN. S/ PETER CARNS. Wit: WINFREY WHITLOCK, MOSES McWHIRTER, who swore by oath 5 Dec 1793 before RICHARD TUTT, J.P. Rcd. 5 Dec 1793.

Pp. 31-32. 14 Oct 1793: Bill of Sale Newberry Co. SC: ALEXANDER BOOCKTER of Newberry Co. SC to WILLIAM NICHOLS, Senr. of Georgia for 40 pounds, sold one mare & colt branded AB. S/ ALEXR. BOOCKTER. Wit: PETER STULEY, SILAS (X) GREEN, Lexington Co. SC, who swore by oath 16 Oct 1793 before JOHN HAMPTON, J.Q. Rcd. 10 Dec 1793.

Pp. 32-37. 1 Oct 1793: SHADRACK ROZER & PRIOR, his wife of Campbelton, SC to BARCLAY MARTIN of same place for 10 Shillings, sold 1/4 acre Lot being 1/2 of original Lot No. 27 fronting a lot sold by MARTIN CAMPBELL to JOHN COOK in the Village of Campbelton of Edgefield Co. SC. S/ SHADRACK ROZER, PRIOR (+) ROZAR. Wit: NANCY ROZER, JAMES GARRETT, who swore by oath 21 Oct 1793 before JOSEPH HIGHTOWER, J.P. Rcd. 13 Dec 1793.

Pp. 37-38. 23 Aug 1793: Bill of Sale: BENJAMIN RYAN the 3rd to BENJAMIN RYAN the 2nd for 100 pounds, sold a negro wench named

HANNAH & her two children one named CLARK & the other named GREENBERRY BOLING. S/ BENJ. RYAN. Wit: JAMES WHITLOCK, who swore by oath 24 Dec 1793 before RICHARD TUTT, J.P. Rcd. 24 Dec 1793.

Pp. 38-43. 25 Mar 1790: ROBERT ANDERSON, Planter, to JOHN ANDERSON, Planter, both of Edgefield Co. SC for 30 pounds, sold 140 acres being part of 200 acres originally granted 21 Jan 1785 unto ROBERT ANDERSON being on Rockey Creek of Turkey Creek of Savannah River adj. NE by JOHN SPRAT; NW by JAMES HARRISON; SW by HENRY PARKMAN & SE by ROBERT ANDERSON. S/ ROBERT ANDERSON. Wit: SAMPSON BUTLER, SAMUEL MAYS, who swore by oath 26 Mar 1793 before JAMES HARRISON, J.P. Rcd. 27 Dec 1793.

Surveyed 12 Jan 1793 by ABNER PERRIN, D.S.

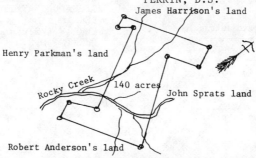

James Harrison's land

Henry Parkman's land

Rocky Creek — 140 acres — John Sprats land

Robert Anderson's land

Pp. 43-44. 10 Aug 1793: Bill of Sale: BENJAMIN RYAN to JOHN RYAN for 200 pounds, sold 4 negroes viz: LUCK, ROSE, GUYE & JOE. S/ BENJ. RYAN. Wit: JONATHAN TAYLOR, LEWIS NOBLE, who swore by oath 27 Dec 1793 before RICHARD TUTT, J.P. Rcd. 27 Dec 1793.

Pp. 44-50. 25 Jun 1793: EDWARD COUCH to JOSEPH HORSEY, both of Ninety Six Dist. SC for 40 pounds, sold 150 acres being part of 206 acres originally granted 5 Sep 1791 unto EDWARD COUCH being on Beach Creek of South Edisto adj. NE by JAMES GUNNELS; SE by EDWARD COUCH. S/ EDWARD COUCH, APSELIA COUCH. Wit: RICHARD BUSH, Junr., CHARITY (X) COUCH, JAMES TOMLIN, who swore by oath 5 Aug 1793 before RUSSELL WILSON, J.P. Rcd. 30 Dec 1793.

Pp. 50-57. 27 Dec 1793: WILLIAM HILL & ANN his wife to AMBRUS RIPLEY, both of Edgefield Co. SC for 60 pounds, sold 206 acres being part of two tracts (1) 100 acres originally granted 31 Aug 1774 unto JAMES ROBINSON & (2) 106 acres originally granted 1 Jan 1787 unto JAMES HARRIS being on Cyder Creek adj. JNO. OLIPHANT; Mrs MARSH; & JNO FRAZIER, Senr. Said land was conveyed to WILLIAM HILL by L&R. S/ WILLIAM HILL. Wit: JOHN (X) COGBOURN, PRESLEY BLAND, who swore by oath 28 Dec 1793 before RICHARD TUTT, J.P. EF Co. SC Court 13 Mar 1794: Mrs ANN HILL, wife of WILLIAM relinqushed dower before ARTHUR SIMKINS & WILLIAM ANDERSON, Judges. Recorded by RICHARD TUTT, C.E.C. Rcd. 28 Dec 1793.

Pp. 57-63. 25 Dec 1793: NATHAN WHITE & REBEKAH, his wife to WILLIAM HILL, both of Edgefield Co. SC for 150 pounds, sold 150 acres surveyed 4 Apr 1769 by JNO DOOLY, D.S., certified 10 Jun 1769 JNO BREMAR, Esq., D.S. Genl., originally granted 31 Oct 1769 unto BENJAMIN RYAN & conveyed 16 Oct 1773 to said WHITE being on Marchels Creek adj. SW by lands formerly held by DANIEL MARCHEL; E by part of original grant unto JOHN COON. S/ NATHAN WHITE,

REBEKAH WHITE. Wit: DAVID LEECH, BETTY TUTT, who swore by oath 4 Jan 1794 before RICHARD TUTT, J.P.
17 Mar 1793 Mrs REBEKAH WHITE, wife of NATHAN relinquished dower & her 1/3 before Judge WILLIAM ANDERSON, RICHARD TUTT, C.E.C.

Pp. 63-68. 22 Oct 1793: ABNER PERRIN & SALLY his wife to GEORGE SULLIVAN, both of Edgefield Co. SC for 80 pounds, sold 170 acres being part in Edgefield County & part in Abbeville Co. SC on Hardlabour Creek. S/ ABNER PERRIN, SALLY PERRIN. Wit: WILLIAM PERRIN, Senr., WILLIAM PEN SULLIVANT, WILLIAM PERRIN, Junr., who swore by oath 4 Jan 1794 before RICHARD TUTT, J.P. Rcd. 4 Jan 1794.

Surveyed 10 Nov 1791 for GEORGE SULLIVAN. East by RICHARD TUTT, NE by WM. PERRIN, N & NW by ABNER PERRIN, S unknown. By ABNER PERRIN, D.S. Plat; p. 67

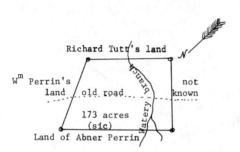

Pp. 68-71. 4 Jun 1793: JOHN HOLMES Planter, to his son FREDERICK HOLMES, Junr both of Edgefield Co. SC for 50 pounds, 300 acres being part of two tracts on the head of Marshals Creek (1) 182 acres originally surveyed 24 Sep 1785 for LOTT WARREN & granted 4 Nov 1786 unto JOHN WALKER by Gov. MOULTRIE at Charleston & sold by L&R 18 & 19 Aug 1790 unto said JOHN HOLMES: & (2) 118 acres on branch of Beaverdam of Turkey Creek of Savannah River being part of 260 acres surveyed by WM. COURSEY, D.S., originally granted 1 Feb 1790 by Gov. CHARLES PINCKNEY at Columbia & unto JOHN WALKER who conveyed by L&R 18 & 19 Aug 1790 unto said JOHN HOLMES. S/ JOHN HOLMES. Wit: WILLIAM DOOLY, JEREMIAH JOHNSON, JAMES (‡) BARRENTINE, who swore by oath 4 Jan 1794 before RICHARD TUTT, J.P. Rcd. 4 Jan 1794. Plat: p. 71.

Pp. 72-75. 25 Nov 1793: FREDERICK HOLMES Junr., son of JOHN HOLMES to KEVAN TAYLOR & MURREN, Merchants for 50 pounds, 300 acres being part of 2 tracts of land (1) 182 acres originally surveyed 24 Sep 1785 for LOTT WARREN & granted to JOHN WALKER by Gov. WILLIAM MOULTRIE at Charleston 4 Nov 1786 being on the head of Marshals branch & was conveyed by L&R 18 & 19 Aug 1790 unto JOHN HOLMES who conveyed to his son FREDERICK HOLMES, Junr. by L&R 4 Jun 1792; also (2) 118 acres originally granted 1 Feb 1790 unto JOHN WALKER by Gov. CHARLES PINCKNEY at Columbia & was conveyed by said WALKER by L&R 18 & 19 Aug 1790 being on Beaverdam a branch of Turkey Creek of Savannah River. S/ FREDERICK HOLMES, Junr. Wit: AMBROUS RIPLY, BURGESS WHITE, who swore by oath 27 Nov 1793 bef. RICHARD TUTT J.P. Rcd. 4 Jan 1794.

Pp. 75-82. 28 Nov 1793: JOHN HOLMES of Edgefield Co. to KEVAN TAYLOR & MURREN, Merchants for 50 pounds, sold 102 acres being part of 260 acres originally surveyed by WILLIAM FRAZIER 31 Oct 1786 & granted 1 Feb 1790 unto JOHN WALKER who conveyed by L&R 18 & 19 Aug 1790 to JOHN HOLMES; 40 acres of which was conveyed by said HOLMES to JOHN COTTON; also 118 acres of the above tract was conveyed by said HOLMES to his son FREDERICK HOLMES 4 Jun 1792 which said two conveyances being deducted out leaves 102 acres of the original survey. Said tract being on Beaverdam, a branch of Turkey Creek of Savannah River adj. NE JOHN FRAZIER, SW & NE JOHN CARTER; SW JOHN MYZICK; NE SAMUEL MARSH & BURNS, SE by DANIEL ROGERS. S/ JOHN HOMES. Wit: GEORGE HOGARTH, MORGAN MURRAH, who swore by oath 9 Dec 1793 before JOSEPH HIGHTOWER, J.P. 13 Mar 1794 ELIZABETH HOMES, wife of JOHN relinquished dower before W. ANDERSON, J.E.C. Rcd. 4 Jan 1794.

Pp. 82-83. 9 Sep 1790: Power of Attorney: ANDREW PICKENS to JOSEPH HIGHTOWER of Edgefield Co. to collect & recieve money due ANDREW PICKENS & Co. for transactions at their later store opposite Augusta. S/ ANDW. PICKENS. Wit: JOHN TAYLOR, GIDEON PURDUE, who swore by oath 13 Nov 1793 before JOHN CLARKE, J.P. Rcd. 16 Jan 1794.

Pp. 83-87. 26 Jun 1792: MACARTON CAMPBELL & SARAH his wife of Augusta GA to ABRAHAM RICHARDSON of Edgefield Co. SC for 275 pounds, sold a lot 163' 8" in front on the street & 180' 6" in depth in the Village of Campbellton, Edgefield Co. SC whereon the Tobacco warehouse commonly called CAMPBELL's Warehouse is errected. S/ MACARTON CAMPBELL, SARAH CAMPBELL. Wit: WM. BUGG, DALZIEL HUNTER, who swore by oath 18 Nov 1793 before JOSEPH HIGHTOWER, J.P.
Richmond Co. GA: 26 Jun 1792: Mrs SARAH CAMPBELL, wife of MACARTON relinquishes dower before DALZIEL HUNTER, J.P. Rcd. 16 Jan 1794. Plat: p. 86.

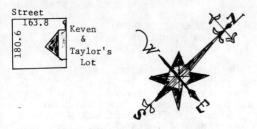

Street
163.8
180.6
Keven & Taylor's Lot

Plat represents a Warehouse Lott in Campbellton that was formerly Mr. MACARTON CAMPBELL's, but now possessed by Mr. SANDRIDGE.
Certified 10 May 1792.
ROBERT LANG, D. S.

Pp. 87-95. 20 Aug 1770: ROBERT GILLAM Planter of Barkley Co. SC to JOHN DOOLY a Dealer of Collenton Co. SC for 30 pounds, sold 250 acres originally granted 7 Apr 1770 being on Turkey Creek of Stephens Creek in Colenton Co. All sides vacant at time of survey. S/ ROBT. GILLAM. Wit: CHARLES CARSON, CHARLES GILLIAM, PATRICK McDOUGAL, who swore by oath 3 Aug 1771 before ROBERT CUNNINGHAM, J.P. Rcd. 19 Feb 1794.

Pp. 95-99. 13 Sep 1793: THOMAS DOOLY of Georgia, son of JOHN DOOLY dec'd., & his heir at law, to DAVID GLOVER of Edgefield Co. SC for 200 pounds, sold 250 acres originally granted 7 Apr 1770 & was conveyed by L&R 20 & 21 Aug 1770 unto JOHN DOOLY, dec'd., being on Turkey Creek a branch of Stephens Creek. S/ THOS. DOOLY

DEED BOOK 9: 1793-1794 EDGEFIELD COUNTY S.C.

Wit: RICHARD WHITHERNTON, JOAB (X) GLOVER, NATHANIEL PARROT, who swore by oath 13 Feb 1794 before JOSEPH HIGHTOWER, J.P. Rcd. 19 Feb 1794.

Pp. 99-101. 25 Jan 1794: Deed of Gift: JOHN GRAY, Senr of Edgefield Co. SC but hereunto moving to DAVID GRAY for 10 pounds, sell the following negroe slaves named ADAM; RACHEL, & SHARLOTT. S/ JOHN GRAY. Wit: JOHN SIMKINS, FRANCIS BURT, who swore by oath 25 Jan 1794 before RICHARD TUTT, J.P. Rcd. 25 Jan 1794.

Pp. 101-102. 25 Jan 1794: Deed of Gift: JOHN GRAY, Senr. of Edgefield Co. but hereunto moving, to my daughter, SUSANNA GRAY for 10 pounds, sells the following negroe slaves named NED, CHARITY & DORCAS. S/ JOHN GRAY. Wit: JOHN SIMKINS, FRANCIS BURT, who swore by oath 25 Jan 1794 before RICHARD TUTT, J.P. Rcd. 25 Jan 1794.

Pp. 103-104. Deed of Gift: JOHN GRAY, Senr. of Edgefield Co. SC but hereunto moving, to my daughter, ELIZABETH GRAY for 10 pounds, sell the following negroes named MOSES, TAMAR & SAVIAY. S/ JOHN GRAY. Wit: JOHN SIMKINS, FRANCIS BURT, who swore by oath 25 Jan 1794 before RICHARD TUTT, J.P. Rcd. 25 Jan 1794.

Pp. 104-106. 29 Sep 1791: Power of Attorney: ROBERT ETHERIDGE, WILLIAM ETHRIDGE, & LEWIS ETHERIDGE of SC & Georgia, Power of Attorney to our brother, AARON ETHERIDGE to collect our portion which our father CALEB ETHERIDGE in Halifax Co. NC has willed. S/ ROBERT ETHRIDGE, WILLIAM (X) ETHERIDGE, LEWIS (1) ETHERIDGE. Wit: JESSE SAMFORD, ABEL ETHRIDGE, who swore by oath 18 Sep 1793 before RUSSELL WILSON, J.P. Rcd. 25 Jan 1794.

Pp. 106-109. 12 Jan 1794: DAVIS WILLIAMS & ABIGAIL his wife & DRURY GLOVER of Edgefield Co. SC, to ANTHONY COOPER for 65 pounds, sold 250 acres originally granted 1 Feb 1765 unto MICHAEL KAISE being on Cuffeytown Creek adj. SW by creek; NW by PETER HEN & ANNA ELIZABETH KEISE, part on Horsepen Creek to NE by ADAM HEN. S/ DAVIS WILLIAMS, ABIGAIL WILLIAMS, DRURY GLOVER. Wit: ISAAC RAMSEY, JOHN COOPER, THOMAS (T) RAMSEY, who swore by oath 12 Jan 1794 before JAMES HARRISON, J.P. Rcd. 27 Jan 1794.

Pp. 109-111. 12 Jan 1794: THOMAS HENDERSON & ELIZABETH his wife to ANTHONY COOPER, both of Edgefield Co. SC for 10 pounds, sold 50 acres being part of 100 acres originally granted Aug 1765 unto ANNA ELIZABETH KAISE on Cuffeytown Creek adj. JACOB WITHROW; E & W by NICHOLAS KAISES & North side of Cuffeytown Creek & STUFELL RUPARD. S/ THOMAS HENDERSON, ELIZABETH (D) HENDERSON. Wit: ISAAC RAMSEY, JAMES McMILLAN, JOHN FEWDERS, THOS. (T) RAMSEY, who swore by oath 12 Jan 1794 before JAMES HARRISON, J.P. Rcd. 27 Jan 1794.

Pp. 111-116. 14 May 1793: JOHN GARRETT to WILLIAM LITTLE, both of Edgefield Co. SC for 30 pounds, sold 200 acres originally granted 22 Aug 1771 MARY HINDS, who afterwards married MASON IZARD , who conveyed to said JOHN GARRET, being on Little Saluda River. S/ JOHN (X) GARRET, ELIZABETH (X) GARRET, his wife. Wit: THOMAS PITTS, JOHN ROBERTS, who swore by oath 29 Oct 1793 before HENRY KING, J.P. Rcd. 30 Jan 1794.

Pp. 116-118. 28 Dec 1792: WILLOUGHBY TILLERY of Edgefield Co. SC to WILLIAM TILLERY for 10 pds. sold 60 ac. being part of 100 ac.

130

originally granted 6 Feb 1786 unto ROBERT MOSELEY on creek adj.
EDMOND BOYD, TALLEY, COODES (also COODY). S/ WILOBY TILLERY.
Wit: BUTLER WILLIAMS, JOHN TILLERY, who swore by oath 1 Feb 1794
before RICHARD TUTT, J.P. Rcd. 1 Feb 1794.

Pp. 119-121. 27 Dec 1792: WILLOUGHBY TILLERY to JOHN TILLERY,
both of Edgefield Co. SC for 10 pounds, sold 60 acres being part
of 200 acres conveyed unto TILLERY by ROBERT MOSLEY, Patent date
15 Oct 1784 & Patent bearing date 1786 adj. EDMOND BOYD, LEWIS
TILLMAN & said WILLOUGHBY TILLERY. S/ WILLOBY TILLERY. BUTLER
WILLIAMS, JESSE MEACHUM, WILLIAM TILLERY, who swore by oath 1 Feb
1794 before RICHARD TUTT, J.P. Rcd. 1 Feb 1794.

Pp. 121-125. 25 Dec 1793: JOHN HARDY to JOSEPH HIGHTOWER, both of
Edgefield Co. SC for 10 pounds, sold 88 acres adj. Cherokee ponds
originally granted JOHN CARTER & conveyed to said HARDY. S/ JOHN
HARDY. Wit: JOSEPH COVINGTON, CHARLES BUSSEY, who swore by oath
10 Feb 1794 before HUGH MIDDLETON, J.P. Rcd. 22 Feb 1794.

Pp. 125-130. 26 Sep 1793: THOMAS DOOLY of Georgia, son of JOHN
DOOLY dec'd. & heir at law & also heir at law to the Estate of
THOMAS DOOLY, dec'd., to DAVID GLOVER of Edgefield Co. SC for 250
pounds, sold 1000 acres originally granted 14 Aug 1772 unto
DANIEL MITCHELL who conveyed by L&R 27 & 28 Nov 1772 unto THOMAS
DOOLY dec'd. on Buckhalters Mill Creek of Stevens Creek adj.
CASTLEMAN; THOMAS ADAMS; MICHAEL BUCKHALTER; & PHILLIP GOODE at
the time of survey. Wit: ABRAHAM HERNDON, BENJAMIN RYAN, JOHN
RYAN, who swore by oath 1 Mar 1794 before RICHARD TUTT, J.P. Rcd.
1 Mar 1794.

Pp. 130-135. 3 Sep 1789: JAMES ALLEN Planter, Eldest son & heir
of JOSIAH ALLEN to ENOCH GRIGSBY, both of Edgefield Co. SC for 50
pounds, sold 100 acres originally granted 21 May 1772 unto JOSIAH
ALLEN, now dec'd. on Richland Creek of Little Saluda River adj.
said ALLEN & JACOB SMITH. S/ JAMES ALLEN. Wit: JAMES GRIGSBY,
HENRY KING, who swore by oath 4 Sep 1789 before RUSSELL WILSON,
J.P. Rcd. 1 Mar 1794.

Pp. 135-140. 1 Mar 1793: JACOB SMITH, Planter, to ENOCH GRIGSBY,
Planter both of Edgefield Co. SC for 4 pds. sold 100 acres being

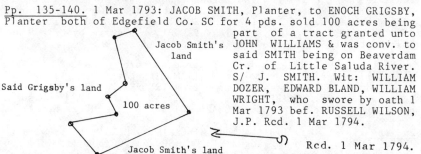

Jacob Smith's land

Said Grigsby's land

100 acres

Jacob Smith's land

part of a tract granted unto
JOHN WILLIAMS & was conv. to
said SMITH being on Beaverdam
Cr. of Little Saluda River.
S/ J. SMITH. Wit: WILLIAM
DOZER, EDWARD BLAND, WILLIAM
WRIGHT, who swore by oath 1
Mar 1793 bef. RUSSELL WILSON,
J.P. Rcd. 1 Mar 1794.

Rcd. 1 Mar 1794.

Pp. 140-145. 3 Sep 1789: JAMES ALLEN, Planter, & Eldest son &
heir of JOSIAH ALLEN, Dec'd., to ENOCH GRIGSBY, both of Edgefield
Co. SC for 80 pounds, sold 150 acres originally granted 18 Aug
1763 unto MOSES POWELL on Richland Creek of Little Saludy River.
Said tract conveyed 13 Jan 1764 by MOSES POWELL & MARY his wife
to JOSIAH ALLEN. S/ JAMES ALLEN. Wit: JAMES GRIGSBY, HENRY
KING, who swore by oath 4 Sep 1789 before RUSSELL WILSON, J. P.
Rcd. 1 Mar 1794.

Pp. 145-152. 4 Feb 1794: GEORGE DEEN, heir at law to ABNER DEEN, JOHN DEEN & ABSOLEM DEEN, his brothers dec'd., to JOHN ABNEY, both of Edgefield Co. SC for 200 pounds, sold 455 acres being of 5 tracts of land (1) 150 acres originally granted 1 Jul 1793 to JOHN DEEN, dec'd., on the Bounty being on the meadow branch of Tosety creek of Saludy River adj. NATHANIEL ABNEY, JOHN GORMAN & WILLIAM YARBROUGH; (2) 50 acres originally granted same time as above 150 acre tract unto JOHN DEEN, dec'd. adj. PAUL ABNEY & JAMES SUMMER; (3) 120 acres originally granted 1 Jul 1793 unto ABNER DEEN, dec'd., on the bounty being on Big Creek of Little Saluda River adj. WILLIAM DEEN & THOMAS BROWN; (4) 80 acres originally granted on the Bounty unto ABNER DEEN, dec'd., being on Persiomon Lick of Big Creek of Little Saluda River adj. DANNETT ABNEY, ZACHERIAH RILEY, GEORGE ABNEY & WILLIAM BOWLERS; (5) 55 acres originally granted 1 Jul 1793 on the Bounty unto ABSOLEM DEEN being on Opossom Branch of Big Creek of Little Saluda River adj. THOMAS DOZER, JOSHUA DEEN & EMANUEL LEPPERD. S/ GEORGE DEEN. Wit: REBEKAH ABNEY, SARAH (M) MILLS, LEWIS WATSON, who swore by oath 7 Feb 1794. Rcd. 11 Mar 1794.

Pp. 152-154. 31 Jul 1793: GEORGE BUSSEY & LIBBA his wife, to beloved son DEMCY BUSSEY, both of Edgefield Co. SC for 5 shillings, sold 150 acres originally granted unto ROBERT RUSSELL. S/ GEORGE BUSSY, Sr., LIBBY (X) BUSSY. Wit: JOSHUA BUSSEY, GEORGE BUSSY, Junr., who swore by oath 24 Oct 1793 before HUGH MIDDLETON, J.P. Rcd. 11 Mar 1794.

Run by John Logan
Now David Thompson's land
Vacant land
150 acres
Vacant land
Path
Vacant
Now Zodack Bussey's land

Pp. 154-157. 27 Jul 1793: WILLIAM HOLSTON to EDWARD EDSON, both of Edgefield Co. SC for 40 pounds, sold 100 acres being part of 200 acres originally granted ELIJAH PADGET 1773 on Cloud Creek of Little Saluda River. Said tract on South side of Cloud Creek adj. MICHAEL WATSON. S/ WILLIAM HOLSTON, SARAH HOLSTON. Wit: MOSES HOLSTON, JOHN GREGORY, JOSIAH PADGET, who swore by oath 9 Nov 1793 before RUSSELL WILSON, J.P. Rcd. 11 Mar 1794.

Pp. 157-158. 21 Sep 1794: Power of Attorney: MARGARET CLARK, widow of Edgefield appoints WILLIAM WILSON my trusty friend of same place to collect in my name from FREDERICK STUMP OF Cumberland 23 pds. S/ MARGARET (Q) CLARK. Wit: DANIEL TILLMAN who swore by oath 22 Sep 1794 bef. RICHARD TUTT, C.E.C. Rcd. 22 Sep 1794.

Pp. 158-164. 17 Apr 1791: ARTHUR GILCHRIST & MARGARET his wife to JAMES SCOTT, both of Edgefield Co. SC for 200 pounds, sold 350 acres being of two tracts; (1) 100 acres being on Stephens Creek; & (2) 250 being on Stephens Creek Adj. W by CHAMPIONS TERRY; one tract granted 15 May 1771 & the other 17 May 1774 unto said GILCHRIST. S/ ARTHUR (A) GILCHRIST, MARGARET (X) GILCHRIST. Wit: JAMES SMITH, CHARITY (+) GILCHRIST, EDMOND FRANKLIN, who swore by oath 11 Mar 1794 before JOSEPH HIGHTOWER, J.P. Rcd. 11 Mar 1794.

Pp. 164-170. 18 Feb 1793: JOHN ROBERTS & SALLY his wife to

JONATHAN LIMBACKERS, both of Edgefield Co. SC for 50 pounds, sold 63 acres being part of 200 acres originally granted 6 Dec 1755 unto THOMAS ROBERTS, dec'd., & was conveyed by L&R 7 & 8 Jul 1786 being on Dry Creek of Chavers Creek adj. SE by JONATHAN SWILLAVANT; NE by JOHN DOOLY. S/ JOHN (Ɨ) ROBERTS, SALLY ROBERTS. Wit: MACK GOODE, JOHN GARDNER, FREDERICK WHATLEY, who swore by oath 24 Dec 1793 before AQUILA MILES, J.P. Rcd. 11 Mar 1794.

Pp. 170-176. 27 Mar 1793: WINFREY WHITLOCK to GASPER GALLMAN, both of Edgefield Co. SC for 5 pounds, sold 48 acres being part of a tract originally granted M. JELTON & conveyed by him to WILLIAM MILLS who conveyed to WINFREY WHITLOCK. Said tract being on Horns Creek adj. DANIEL PARKER & RUTLEDGE at time of survey. S/ WINFREY WHITLOCK, ELIZABETH (X) WHITLOCK. Wit: JOHN BOOTHE, JNO. ADDISON. Rcd. 11 Mar 1794.
11 Mar 1794: ELIZABETH WHITLOCK, wife of WINFREY relinquished dower rights before W. ANDERSON, J.E.C. & RICHARD TUTT, C.E.C.

Pp. 176-182. 13 Apr 1792: JESSE GAINS Planter, to DAVID PITTS & pursuant power of attorney from AMBROSE GAINS for 35 pounds, sold 100 acres originally granted 11 Aug 1774 unto AMBROSE GAINS, being on Red Bank Creek of Saluda River adj. JAMES GRIGSBY & JOSEPH HOGAIN at the time of survey. S/ JESSE GAINS, ELIZABETH GAINS, his wife. Wit: EDWARD BABER, JOHN (X) PARNALT, who swore by oath 14 Apr 1792 before HENRY KING, J.P. Rcd. 11 Mar 1794.

Pp. 182-188. 9 Jun 1791: HILLERY PHILIPS & ANN his wife late of SC to ROBERT WARE for 200 pounds, sold 170 acres being part of 220 acres by a deed of grant 5 Sep 1785 being on Stephens Creek adj. NW by AMON ROBERTS & JOHN DAVIS. S/ HILLERY PHILLIPS. Wit: HENRY GRAYBILL, JOHN HARVEY, HUGH MIDDLETON, J.P., who swore by oath 18 Jan 1794 before AQUILA MILES, J.P. Rcd. 11 Mar 1794.
June Court Edgefield Co: Motion of ROBERT WARE that a Didemus Issue directed to any two Justices of Green Co. GA take acknowledgement of right of dowery from ANN PHILLIPS before RICHARD TUTT, C.E.C.
12 Apr 1791 (sic) Green Co. GA: ANN PHILLIPS, wife of HILLERY, relinquished dower certified 10 Jun 1791 HENRY GRAYBILL, J.P., EDWARD HUNTER, J.P.

Pp. 188-192. 1793: JOHN SMITH to JOB PADGETT, both of Edgefield Co. SC for 100 pounds, sold 250 acres originally granted 18 Oct 1774 being on Cloud Creek of Little Saludy River. S/ JOHN (⊢⊣) SMITH. Wit: ROBERT DIXSON, ROBEN McADAMS, ROBERT CALDWELL, of Newberry Co. SC, who swore by oath 9 Dec 1793 before PROVIDENCE WILLIAMS, J.P. Rcd. 11 Mar 1794.

Pp. 192-199. 31 Nov 1788: THOMAS FARRAR, Sheriff of Ninety Six Dist. SC to JAMES HAYS, Planter for 27 pds, being highest bidder at public auction, sold 300 acres...Whereas 8 Jan 1788 LOVE WARD, Widow Extrx. & WILLIAM SKIRVING & ROGER PARKER SAUNDERS, Execs. of LW&T of JOHN WARD dec'd., whom one PETER LEGER he survived, started a suit & obtained a Judgement in Ct. of Common Pleas in Charleston against JAMES HAYES, Adm. of DENIS HAYS, dec'd., goods & Chatels at the time of his death for recovery of money which said JAMES HAYS detained. Said Sheriff FARRAR did seize 300 acres in Colleton Co. on Mine Creek of Little Saluda River adj. JOSEPH ALLEN at time of survey. S/ THOMAS FARRAR, Shff. Ninety Six Dist. Wit: EDWARD (E) SNELGROVE, GABRIAL FRIDIG, who swore by oath 2 Dec 1788 before WILLIAM MOORE, J.P. Rcd. 11 Mar 1794.

DEED BOOK 9: 1793-1794 EDGEFIELD COUNTY S.C.

Pp. 200-204. 20 Feb 1794: JOHN RUTLEDGE, Esq. of Charleston, by JAMES MASON, agent, to MATTHEW BURT of Edgefield Co. SC for 360 pounds, sold 500 acres originally granted to JOHN GUVARD by HENRY LITTLETON, Governor of then province, now SC, on Turkey Creek. S/ JOHN RUTLEDGE, by his agent, JAS. MAYSON. (JAMES MAYSON, Junr.) Wit: ROBERT MAYSON, JOHN MAYSON, WILLIAM MAYSON, who swore by oath 20 Feb 1794 before W. ANDERSON, J.P. Rcd. 11 Mar 1794.

Pp. 204-207. 16 Jan 1792: JAMES SALTER to WILLIAM BURGES, both of Edgefield Co. SC for 20 pounds, sold 90 acres being part of 184 acres originally granted 1788 unto WILLIAM HEARIN being on Little Saluda River adj. old Lucas Branch; WILLIAM HEARIN, ARTHUR WATSON, at time of survey. S/ JAMES (+)SALTER, ANN (X) SALTER. Wit: WILLIAM (X) RABAN, CHARLES (CP) PARTAIN, who swore by oath 10 Mar 1794 before HENRY KING, J.P. Rcd. 11 Mar 1794.

Pp. 207-209. 12 Jan 1792: JAMES SALTER to WILLIAM BURGES, both of Edgefield Co. SC for 45 pounds, sold 138 acres on branch of Dry Creek of Little Saluda River originally granted 1786 unto WILLIAM HEARRIN, adj. NE by JAMES GILLAND, SW by JAMES. S/ JAMES (+) SALTER, ANN (X) SALTER, his wife. Wit: WILLIAM (+) RABAN, (also RABOURN), CHARLES (CP) PARTAIN, who swore by oath 10 Mar 1794 before HENRY KING, J.P. Rcd. 11 Mar 1794.

Pp. 209-215. 18 May 1793: WINFREY WHITLOCK & ELIZABETH his wife to DANIEL PARKER, both of Edgefield Co. SC for 100 pounds, sold 96 acres being part of a tract of land originally granted ANDREW McGILTON being on South side of Horns Creek, whereon the said PARKER now lives & adj. SAMUEL WALKER's mill, JOHN RYAN, GASPER GALLMON, & TERY FIKE. S/ WINFREY WHITLOCK, ELIZABETH (+) WHITLOCK Wit: ABRAHAM LUCAS, JOHN LUCAS, Junr. ELIZABETH WHITLOCK, wife of WINFREY relinquished dower before W. ANDERSON J.C.E. & was recorded in the minutes by RICHARD TUTT, C.E.C. Rcd. 11 Mar 1794.

Pp. 215-221. 25 Jul 1792: WILLIAM POU, of the fork of Edisto River in Orangeburg Dist & ANN, his wife & JOHN POU & MARGARET, his wife of same place to ROBERT POU of Mine Creek in Edgefield Co. SC for 100 pounds, sold 200 acres originally granted 21 May 1759 unto GAVIN POU being on Little Saluda River. Said GAVIN POU by LW&T 16 Dec 1773 bequeathed said tract & others to WILLIAM POU a joint heir & a part thereof dissolved to JOHN POU, son & heir of JOHN POU, dec'd & grandson to GAVIN POU, dec'd. S/ WILLIAM POU, ANN POU, JOHN POU, MARGARET POU. Wit: HENRY JONES, JOHN FANNIN, who swore by oath 28 Aug 1792 before WITTENHALL WARNER, J. P. in Orangeburg Dist. SC. Rcd. 11 Mar 1794.

Pp. 221-227. 25 Jul 1792: WILLIAM POU & ANN his wife of the fork of Edisto River, Orangeburgh Dist & JOHN POU & MARGARET, his wife of same place to ROBERT POU of Mine Creek in Edgefield Co. SC for 80 pounds, sold 200 acres originally surveyed 19 May 1759, & granted 4 Sep 1759 by Gov. HENRY LITTLETON, unto GAVEN POU on Mine Creek of Little Saluda River. Said tract bequeathed by LW&T of GAVEN POU 16 Dec 1773 to said WILLIAM POU a joint heir & a part thereof dissolved to JOHN POU, son & heir of JOHN POU, dec'd., & grandson of said GAVIN POU, dec'd. S/ WILLIAM POU, ANN POU, JOHN POU, MARGARET POU. Wit: HENRY JONES, JOHN FANNIN, who swore by oath 28 Aug 1792 before WITTENHALL WARNER, J.P., Orangeburgh Dist. Rcd. 11 Mar 1794.

Pp. 227-233. 3 Nov 1793: ROBERT BURTON, House Carpenter, of Turkey Cr. to JAMES HALL, Planter of Turkey Cr. both of Edgefield Co. SC for 20 pds. sold 220 acres on Turkey Cr. leading from Chappel's Bridge on Saludy to Augusta adj. ARTHUR SIMKINS, Esq. & said BURTON. S/ ROBERT BURTON. Wit: BENJAMIN RYAN, Junr., DANIEL ROGERS, WILLIAM HALL, who swore by oath 11 Mar 1794 before JOSEPH HIGHTOWER JP. Rcd. 11 Mar 1794. 11 Mar 1794: SARAH BURTON wife of ROBERT relinq. dower bef. W. ANDERSON J.C.E, RICHARD TUTT, C.E.C.

Pp. 233-237. 13 May 1793: JOHN CALLAHAM & LUCY, his wife to THOMAS CASON, both of Ninety Six Dist. SC for 102 pounds, sold 400 acres originally granted 14 Aug 1772 unto DAVID CALLAHAM whereon said JOHN CALLAHAM now lives, being on Stevenson Creek adj. NATHANIEL HARRIS, DAVID CALLAHAM, at time of survey. Said tract bequeathed by DAVID CALLAHAM by LW&T unto his son JOHN CALLAHAM. S/ JOHN CALLIHAM, LUCY (X) CALLIHAM. Wit: THOMAS CASON, DAVID CALLIHAM, JAMES THOMAS, who swore by oath 11 Mar 1794 before HUGH MIDDLETON, J.P. Rcd. 11 Mar 1794.

Pp. 237-239. Feb 1794: Power of Attorney: SILAS GREEN of Edgefield Co. SC, but hereunto moving, appoint my trusty friend, HENRY ZIMMERMAN of same place my attorney to collect in my name from the Estate of JOHN GREEN, Senr., dec'd. formerly in his lifetime lived on Enoree River now Newberry Co. SC & died Intestate. S/ SILAS GREEN. Wit: WILLIAM LINTON, PHILIP ZIMMERMAN, "wrote in Dutch", sworn by oath 8 Mar 1794 before JAMES HARRISON, J.P. Rcd. 11 Mar 1794.

Pp. 239-241. 5 Mar 1787: A grant for THOMAS LEHRE for 14 pounds, sold 628 acres was recorded in Grant Book by PETER FRENEAU, Secretary of SC, being surveyed for BENJAMIN LOVELESS 27 May 1786 in Ninety Six Dist. on Edisto River & granted to said THOMAS LEHRE. S/ THOMAS PINCKNEY.

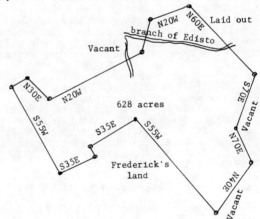

Vacant
branch of Edisto
Laid out
N20W
N60E
N30E
N20W
628 acres
S70E
Vacant
S55W
S35E
S55W
N70E
S35E
Frederick's land
N40E
Vacant

Plat: page 240.

NATHANIEL ABNEY, D.S.
8 Aug 1792: I do assign over the right of me the within grant to BENJAMIN LOVELESS. S/ THOMAS LEHRE.
6 Oct 1792: JOHN LOVELESS swore by oath he was present at above before RUSSELL WILSON, J.P. Rcd. 10 Dec. 1793.

Pp. 242-245. 7 Oct 1793: SAMUEL SAXON, Sheriff of Ninety Six District to DAVID GLOVER for 250 pounds, sold 1000 acres...Whereas MARY RODGERS lately in the Court of Common Pleas in Cambridge obtained a judgement against CHARLES BANKS, Exec. of JOHN DOOLY, dec'd. for the sum of 198 pounds. Said Judgement was issued 29 Apr 1793 directed to said Sheriff to seize said tract which was put up to public auction 5 Aug 1793 to the highest bidder. Said tract was originally granted 2 Jun 1772 unto DANIEL MITCHELL adj. NW by BUCKHALTER, & CASTLEMAN; SE by PHILIP GOODE &

SW by ADAM's land. S. SAXON, Shiff. Ninety Six Dist. Wit: JOHN TROTTER, THOS BUTLER, who swore by oath 12 Mar 1794 before RICHARD TUTT. Rcd. 12 Mar 1794.

Pp. 245-246. 27 Feb 1794: THOMAS WALKER, Planter to THOMAS WARREN, Mill Stone Cutter, both of Edgefield Co. for 58 pounds, sold one negro man named SAMPSON. S/ THOMAS WALKER. Wit: RICHARD (RO) ODOM, DENNY (D) HARBIN, SAMUEL MESSER, who swore by oath 12 Mar 1794 before NATHANIEL ABNEY, J.P. Rcd. 12 Mar 1794.

Pp. 246-252. 27 Feb 1792: ROBERT McCOMBS, & MARY, his wife to LENNARD WALKER for 55 pounds, sold 137 acres which was conveyed to said McCOMB by THOMAS KEELING SMITH & ELLENOR his wife being part of 300 acre tract conveyed to SMITH by TIMOTHY McKINNEY which was part of 450 acres conveyed to said McKINNEY by ROGER McKINNEY, Junr., dec'd. which said 450 acres fell to ROGER McKINNEY Junr., dec'd. by ROGER McKINNEY, Senr. dec'd. Said tract being on Ninety Six Creek adj. SW by GOVERNOR BEE; NW by HECKLOR DICKIE; NE by BEATTEY; SE & NE by PENDERGRASS; SE by ROGER McKINEY, at time of survey. S/ ROBERT McCOMBS, MARY McCOMBS. Wit: THOMAS LIVINGSTON, T.K. SMITH, JAMES GOUEDY, who swore by oath 19 Apr 1792 before WILLIAM ANDERSON, J.P. Rcd. 12 Mar 1794.

Pp. 252-258. 11 Mar 1794: JOSEPH JONES to EDITH COODY, both of Edgefield Co. SC for 20 pounds, sold 100 acres originally granted 16 Mar 1787 unto said JONES being on Turkey Creek of Stephens Cr. S/ JOSEPH JONES. Wit: JOSHA JOWELL, REUBIN ROBERTS, who swore by oath 12 Mar 1794 before HENRY KING, J.P. Rcd. 12 Mar 1794. [Note: gch: The first part of the Release reads ROBERT BARTON to EDITH COODY & the remaining content states JOSEPH JONES to EDITH COODY. It appears to be a clerical error].

Pp. 258-264. 5 Nov 1792: ARTHUR SIMKINS to JUDGES of Edgefield Co. SC for 10 Shillings, sold 2 acres where on the Courthouse & goal now stands of Edgefield Co. SC adj. SW by MOSES HARRIS; W by JOHN SIMKINS & all other sides by ARTHUR SIMKINS. Also 1/4 acre adj. the fourth side of said 2 acres where the Clerk of the County lately built a house for the sole purpose of keeping the Clerk's & Sheriff's Office of said County. S/ ARTHUR SIMKINS. Wit: J. HATCHER, JOHN RYAN, JAMES COBB, Junr. Acknowledged before RICHARD TUTT, C.E.C. 12 Mar 1794: Mrs MARGARET SIMKINS, wife of ARTHUR SIMKINS, relinquished dower before RICHARD TUTT, J.P. Rcd. 12 Mar 1794.

Pp. 264-269. 20 Feb 1794: ANDREW BROWN to NATHAN TOD, both of Edgefield Co. SC for 5 shillings, sold 200 acres in Berkley Co. but now Edgefield, originally granted ELIZABETH VERDITLY, who in her lifetime conveyed said land to GEORGE HAIG now dec'd. & GEORGE HAIG, son of GEORGE HAIG, dec'd., conveyed to ANDREW BROWN being on Santee otherwise called Saludy River. S/ ANDREW BROWN, RUTHY (I) BROWN. Wit: BENJ. BENTON, JOHN ABNEY, who swore by oath 21 Feb 1794 before NATHANIEL ABNEY, J.P. Rcd. 12 Mar 1794.

Pp. 269-272. 7 Oct 1794: MOSES PHELPS to JAMES ITSON, (also IDSON), both of Edgefield Co. SC for 30 pounds, 28 acres being part of 300 acres originally granted 2 May 1770 unto ARTHUR FORT & conveyed to OWEN FORT by will. Said OWEN FORT conveyed by L&R to WILLIAM HUMPHREY who conveyed to said MOSES PHELPS. Said tract being on Mine Creek of Little Saluda adj. POU; & CHARLES

PARTIN. S/ MOSES (X) PHELPS. Wit: WILLIAM SISSON, WILLIAM HUMPHREYS, who swore by oath 5 Nov 1792 before RUSSELL WILSON, J.P. Rcd. 12 Mar 1794.

Pp. 272-273. 20 Mar 1792: Bill of Sale: AMOS MITCHELL to WILLIAM CALDWELL for 39 pounds, sold one negro man named DICK. S/ AMOS (X) MITCHELL. Wit: RICHARD P. WHITE, SAMUEL CRAFTON, who swore by oath 12 Mar 1794 before JOSEPH HIGHTOWER, J.P. Rcd. 12 Mar 1794.

Pp. 274-275. 8 Mar 1794: Bill of Sale: DANIEL BULLOCK to JOHN BULLOCK, for 75 pounds, sold 2 negroes named MOLL & BOBB, 2 feather beds & furniture & more. S/ DAN BULLOCK. Wit: JOSEPH WILLIAMS, JOHN WILLIAMS, SD, who swore by oath 12 Mar 1792 before AQUILA MILES, J.P. Rcd. 12 Mar 1794.

Pp. 275-280. 9 Feb 1790: BARBARA RUFF & GEORGE & BARBARA YOUNG of Charleston SC to WILLIAM MOORE of Edgefield Co. SC for 40 pounds, sold 100 acres near Saludy Old Town adj. NE by THOMAS CURTIS; SW vacant; NW by DANIEL BURNETT, at time of survey. S/ BARBARA (X) RUFF, GEO. YOUNG, BARBARA YOUNG. Wit: JOHN CUNNINGHAM, WILLIAM TURPIN, who swore by oath 18 Jul 1793 before ROBERT GILLIAM, J.P., of Newberry Co. SC. Rcd. 13 Mar 1794.

Pp. 280-285. 28 Jun 1793: WILLIAM ADAMS, Senr. to WILLIAM CLARK, both of Ninety Six Dist. SC for 20 pounds, sold 63 acres being part of 74 acres originally granted 6 Nov 1786 to JOHN GREEN on Red Bank Creek of Little Saluda River adj. WM. CASHE's land & WILLIAM ADAMS. S/ WILLIAM (X) ADAMS, ELISEBETH (E) ADAMS, his wife. Wit: ALEXANDER PATTERSON, WILLIAM BRISON, JOHN BRATCHER, who swore by oath 24 Jan 1794 before HENRY KING, J.P. Rcd. 13 Mar 1794.

Pp. 285-289. 13 Mar 1794: DRURY MIMS & LYDDA, his wife to JOHN HAMMOND, both of Edgefield Co. SC for 5 pounds, sold Lot # 6 & # 7 facing Union Street in Town of Falmouth near a little village called Campbelton being laid out on lands of JOHN HAMMOND, Each Lot contains 65 2/3 feet in Bredth & 155 ft. in length. S/ DRURY MIMS, LYDIA (X) MIMS. Wit: AQUILA MILES, HENRY WARE Junr., who swore by oath 14 Mar 1794 before JOHN CLARKE, J.P. Rcd. 14 Mar 1794.

Pp. 289-294. 19 Nov 1793: SHADRACK ROZER & PRIOR, his wife to JOHN HAMMOND, both of Edgefield Co. SC for 5 pounds, sold Lot bounded by Main & Broad Street in a Town called Falmouth laid out by JOHN & LEROY HAMMOND joining a little village known as Campbelton. S/ SHADRACH ROZER, PRIER (X) ROZAR. Wit: GILES Y. RAINES, WILLIAM COVINGTON, who swore by oath 13 Mar 1794 before JOHN CLARKE, J.P. Rcd. 14 Mar 1794.

Pp. 294-298. 8 Jan 1794: ABRAHAM RICHARDSON to JOSEPH HIGHTOWER, both of Edgefield County for 300 pounds, sold 350 acres at the Cherokee pond, being part of three tracts (1) 100 acres originally granted 1 Feb 1768 unto JAMES JOHNSON who conveyed by L&R 22 & 23 Feb 1769 to THOMAS FRANKLIN who conveyed to said RICHARDSON; (2) 50 acres originally granted 19 Nov 1772 unto EPHRAIM FRANKLIN & conveyed by L&R unto JOHN SKADERS who conveyed to said RICHARDSON: (3) 200 acres originally granted 5 Feb 1787 unto CHARLES BANKS who conveyed to said RICHARDSON. S/ ABRAHAM RICHARDSON. Wit: JOHN HATCHER, JAMES PICKETT, who swore by oath 18 Mar 1794 before HUGH MIDDLETON, J.P. Rcd. 18 Mar 1794.

DEED BOOK 9: 1793-1794 EDGEFIELD COUNTY S.C.

Pp. 299-301. 12 Mar 1794: SAMUEL MAYS, Sheriff of Edgefield Co. SC to JAMES THOMAS, being highest & last bidder for 15 pounds, sold 250 acres...Whereas MICHAEL McKEE, lately obtained in Edgefield County Court a judgment against THOMAS CLERK for 8 pounds & a writ was issued 19 Dec 1793 directing the Sheriff of Edgefield Co. to seize & recover from THOMAS CLERK said land adj. HUGH MIDDLETON, Esq., EDWARD PRINCE on a road leading from Long Cane to Cambleton. S/ SAML. MAYS, Sheriff of Edgefield Co. Wit: DRURY PACE, DAVID MIMS, who swore by oath 12 Mar 1794 before HUGH MIDDLETON, J.P. Rcd. 18 Mar 1794.

Pp. 301-302. 6 Dec 1793: Bill of Sale: COALTER & GLOVER of Abbeville Co. SC to BARNET TRAVIS of Edgefield Co. SC for 85 pounds sell 2 negroe boys POMPEY, about 15 yrs. old & PRINCE, about 7 yrs. old. S/ COALTER & GLOVER. Wit: JESSSE (⊢⊣) JERNAGAN, ALEXANDER WILSON, who swore by oath 30 Jan 1794 before HENRY KING, J.P. Rcd. 19 Mar. 1794.

Pp. 302-309. 1 Jun 1792: LAURENCE RAMBO & MARY his wife of Orangeburg Dist. of Orange SC to JAMES COBBS, Jr. of Edgefield Co., Ninety Six Dist., for 165 pounds, sold 300 acres originally granted 1771 (sic) unto WALTER JACKSON who conveyed to said RAMBO, 11 & 12 Jan 1773 being at the time of survey in Granville Co. but now Edgefield Co. & at time of original plat on Harrises Branch but at present, waters of Dry & Horns Creek. Said Plat was intered in Auditor's office 1 Jul 1772 adj. lands of RICHARD JONES. S/ LAURENCE RAMBO, MARY RAMBO. Wit: WILLIAM WASH, EDWARD VANN, Senr. (in the oath listed as Junr.), LITTLEBERRY ADAMS, who swore by oath 12 Mar 1794 before RICHARD TUTT, J.P. Rcd. 20 Mar 1794.

P. 309. 21 Mar 1794: Agreement: RICHARD JOHNSON to RICHARD BURTON - The two suits brought by me against RICHARD BURTON (one in Cambridge Court & one in Edgefield Court, one hereby dismissed upon each party paying his own cost & all matters in dispute respecting the estate of WILLIAM BAKER & JAMES BAKER are finally settled. S/ RICHD. JOHNSON, RICHARD BURTON. Wit: EPHRAIM RAMSEY, who swore by oath 21 Mar 1794 before RICHARD TUTT. Rcd. 21 Mar 1794.

Pp. 310: 21 Mar 1794: Bill of Sale: RICHARD JOHNSON to RICHARD BURTON for 50 pounds, two negroe children; a girl about 12 called ELSEY & a boy about 8 called JANUARY being negroes late the property of JAMES BAKER's distributive share of WILLIAM BAKERS estate. S/ RICHD. JOHNSON. Wit: EPHRAIM RAMSEY, who swore by oath 21 Mar 1794 before RICHARD TUTT, J.P. Rcd. 21 Mar 1794.

Pp. 310-311. 21 Mar 1794: Receipt: RICHARD BURTON acknowledges receipt from RICHARD JOHNSON, Junr. Admor. of JAMES BAKER dec'd. full satisfaction & payment of any claim to any part of the Estate of JAMES BAKER in right of my wife. S/ RICHARD BURTON. Wit: EPHRAIM RAMSEY, Esq. & Attorney at Law, who swore by oath 25 Mar 1794 before RICHARD TUTT, J.P. Rcd. 21 Mar 1794.

Pp. 311-312. 21 Mar 1794: OBURN BUFFINGTON to RICHARD JOHNSON Junr., releases & forever Quit Claim any claim which I have by Judgement obtained against said JOHNSON in Edgefield County Court which said Judgement being revised in March Term & do authorize Clerk of Court to enter into record of complete satisfaction.

S/ OBURN (+) BUFFINGTON. Wit: EPHRAIM RAMSEY, Esq. Attorney at law, who swore by oath 21 Mar 1794 before RICHARD TUTT, J.P. Rcd. 21 Mar 1794.

Pp. 312-317. 24 Mar 1794: DANIEL GUNNELS & ELIZABETH, his wife to JESSE FRAZIER for 30 pounds, sold 40 acres being part of 250 acres originally granted 9 Sep 1774 unto JAMES ROBINSON who conveyed to DANIEL ROGERS who transferred to BENJM. RHODES who transferred to RICHARD JOWEL who transferred to said GUNNELS being on Beaverdam Creek. S/ DANL. GUNNELS. Wit: DAVIS MOORE, RICHARD JOWELL, BRITON MIMS, who swore by oath 24 Mar 1794 before RICHARD TUTT, J.P. Rcd. 24 Mar 1794.

Pp. 317-321. 13 Jul 1793: Bond: JENKINS HARRIS, bound unto DRURY MIMS, in sum of 75 pounds ...Condition to pay 37 pounds on or before 13 Oct 1794 for better securing of payment, sell one negro man named SAM, 4 feather beds, furniture, 1 dozen pewter plates, a doz knives & forks, 3 doz. earthenware plates, 4 pewter dishes, 4 pewter basons, 2 Iron potts, 1 dutch oven, 10 pewter spoons, 9 chairs, 3 tables, 4 cows & calves, 30 head of hogs. S/ JENKIN (H) HARRIS. Wit: WILLIAM SIMKINS, EUGENE BRENAN, who swore by oath 2 Aug 1793. Rcd. 2 Aug 1793.

Pp. 321-323. 15 Dec 1791: GEORGE BUCKELEW of Edgefield Co. SC to my son, MOSES BUCKELEW for love & affection 50 acres being land where said GEORGE BUCKELEW now lives also a horse branded EU & 1 cow. S/ GEORGE BUCKELEW. Wit: JAMES SCOTT, JOHN (‡) BRIDGES, who swore by oath 21 Jan 1792 before HENRY KING, J.P. Rcd. 29 Mar 1794.

Pp. 323-327. 12 Mar 1794: DAVID GLOVER to JEREMIAH HATCHER, both of Edgefield Co. SC for 60 pounds, sold 250 acres on Turkey Creek a branch of Stevens originally granted 7 Apr 1770 unto ROBERT GILLAM & was conveyed by L&R 20 & 21 Aug 1770 unto JOHN DOOLY, dec'd. & conveyed by THOMAS DOOLY heir at Law to DAVID GLOVER 30 & 31 Oct 1793. S/ DAVID GLOVER. Wit: JAMES McCRACKAN, PHILIP BURT, EUGENE BRENAN, who swore by oath 13 Mar 1794 before RICHARD TUTT, J.P. Rcd. 30 Mar 1794.

Pp. 327-328. 11 Oct 1793: JOHN LAWSON of Edgefield Co. SC to MORDICAI McKENNY for 15 pounds, sold one mare & colt; 5 head of Cattle; 1 feather bed & furniture; 1 iron pot; pewter dish; 2 pewter basons, 6 pewter plates, 6 knives & forks, & 8 pewter spoons with all the rest of my household furniture; working tools; & all my Tabaces in the house. S/ JOHN LAWSON. Wit: JOSEPH TUCKER, who swore by oath 14 Feb 1794 before J. HARRISON, J.P. Rcd. 16 Apr 1794.

Pp. 328-334. 18 Aug 1784: JAMES ALLEN, Eldest son & heir at law of JOSIAH ALLEN, late of SC now deceased, to SOLOMON POPE for 17 pounds, sold 100 acres being on branch of Little Saluda River called Mine Creek. S/ JAMES ALLEN. Wit: WILLIAM BUTLER, THOMAS BUTLER, BARTLET BLEDSOE, who swore by oath 3 Nov 1785 before WM. ANDERSON, J.P. Rcd. 16 Apr 1794. Plat p. 333.

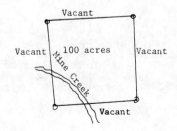

DEED BOOK 9: 1793-1794 EDGEFIELD COUNTY S.C.

Pursuant to a precept dated 5 Sep 1762 I have admeasured out 100 acres of land unto JOSIAH ALLINS this 12 Oct 1762. S/ PATRICK CALHOUN, D.S.
Sur. General's Office 10 Aug 1784 the above plat is a true copy. S/ EPHRAIM MITCHELL, Surv. General.

Pp. 334-337. 22 Jan 1794: Sheriff's Title: SAMUEL SAXON, Sheriff of Ninety Six Dist. to ARTHUR SIMKINS, Esq., being highest & last bidder for 75 pounds ... Whereas JOHN GORDON lately in the Court of Common Pleas at Cambridge obtained a Judgement against the Admrs. of JOHN CALDWELL for 1000 pounds dated 18 Apr 1792 directing goods & chattels of JOHN CALDWELL dec'd. a certain 300 acres of land originally granted 2 May 1758 unto E. WAISTCOAT being on Log Creek & now adj. lands of said ARTHUR SIMKINS. S/ S. SAXON, Sheriff, Ninety Six Dist. Wit: JOHN TROTTER, WHITF. WILSON, ALLEN GLOVER, Abbeville Co. SC who swore by oath 3 Feb 1794 before JULIUS NICHOLS, J.P. Rcd. 22 Apr 1794.

Pp. 337-346. 28 Apr 1794: Bond: WILLIAM HARKINS of Edgefield Co. SC firmly bound unto HENRY WILSON, Merchant for 39 pounds, Condition is that sum of 19 pounds be paid on or before 1 Jan 1795. S/ WILLIAM HARKINS. Wit: RICHARD GANT.
Lease, 28 Apr 1794: WILLIAM HARKINS of Edgefield to HENRY WILSON of Cambridge, Merchant for by bond & obligation for better securing of payment, sold 320 acres being on Sleepy Creek adj. JOHN HARKINS & THOMAS YOUNGBLOOD. S/ WILLIAM HARKINS, HENRY WILSON. Wit: JM. WILSON, RICHARD GANTT, who swore by oath 1 May 1794 before RICHARD TUTT, J.P. Rcd. 1 May 1794.

Pp. 346-348. 21 May 1793: Power of Attorney: CLABOURN RHODES of Edgefield Co. SC appoint WILLIAM MAXWELL my lawful attorney to sue for & recover of JOHN BOSTICK, Jr., a mare he took up as an Estray & wook'd to Charleston & either disposed of or hurt her as not to be able to travel, an acknowledgement of which said BOSTICK made before RICHARD JOWELL who you will call upon as an Evidence. Said mare was branded with S & EVP & I believe was sold & advertized by him. You may get information on that head from the Clerk. S/ CLAIBORNE RHODES. Wit: NATHAN PARKER, JOHN WILLIAMS, Cap., who swore by oath 1 Mar 1794 before RICHARD TUTT, J.P. Rcd. 5 May 1794.

Pp. 348-349. 1 May 1794: Bill of Sale: SHADRACH ROZAR, Constable of Edgefield Co. SC to GEORGE B. MOORE, being highest & last bidder for 51 pounds...at a suit of JOHN GRISHAM to levy goods & Chattels of THOMAS LAMAR both of Edgefield Co. for a debt of 73 pounds...have executed the law & sold 2 negroes, one boy named DICK about 35 yrs. old, the other named FRANK about 12 yrs. old at a public sale. S/ SHADRACK ROZAR. Wit: RICHARD GANTT, who swore by oath 9 May 1794 before RICHARD TUTT, J.P. Rcd. 9 May 1794.

Pp. 349-355. 25 Feb 1790: THOMAS SNELSON to JOHN FINLEY, both of Ninety Six Dist. SC for 15 pounds, sold 50 acres being part of 200 acres originally granted 6 Nov 1786 to THOMAS SNELSON on Hamlines Creek a branch of Savannah River adj. DRURY PACE, & SILAS PACE. S/ THOMAS SNELSON. Wit: DRURY PACE, JOHN (X) FENDLEY, MOSES (X) FINDLEY, who swore by oath 29 Jan 1794 before HUGH MIDDLETON, J.P. Rcd. 16 May 1794.

DEED BOOK 9: 1793-1794 EDGEFIELD COUNTY S.C.

Pp. 355-361. 21 Feb 1790: THOMAS SNELSON to MOSES FENDLEY, both of Ninety Six Dist. SC for 15 pounds, sold 50 acres being part of 200 acres originally granted 6 Nov 1790 (sic) to said SNELSON, being on Hamblin's creek branch of Savannah River adj. DRURY PACE, JOHN FENLEY, & MATHIAS DALTON. S/ THOMAS SNELSON. Wit: DRURY PACE, MOSES FINDLY, JOHN (X) FENDLEY, who swore by oath 29 Jan 1794 before HUGH MIDDLETON, J.P. Rcd. 16 May 1794.

Pp. 361-363. 29 Jan 1794: JOHN FINLEY to MOSES FINLEY, both of Edgefield Co. SC for 20 pounds, sold 50 acres on waters of Savannah River adj. S by DRURY PACE; W by SILAS PACE & N by said FINLY. S/ JOHN (J) FINDLEY. Wit: ELIJAH FINDLEY, JOHN PACE, who swore by oath 29 Jan 1794 before HUGH MIDDLETON, J.P. Rcd. 16 May 1794.

Pp. 363-366. 1 Apr 1793: ABSOLOM GRIFFIN & SUSANNAH his wife of Burke Co. GA to JOSEPH ROBERTSON of Edgefield Co. SC for 30 pounds, sold 247 acres being part of a grant to SAM SCOTT adj. N by ELIJAH FINDLEY, S by said ROBERTSON, & E by JAMES SCOTT. S/ ABSALEM GRIFFIN, SUSANNAH (X) GRIFFIN. Wit: EZEKIEL (+) KEER, ELIJAH (X) FINDLEY, who swore by oath 24 Aug 1793 before HUGH MIDDLETON, J.P. Rcd. 16 May 1794.
Plat: p. 365

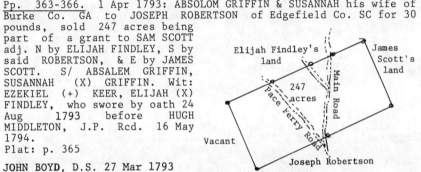

Elijah Findley's land

James Scott's land

247 acres

Main Road

Pace Ferry Road

Vacant

Joseph Robertson

JOHN BOYD, D.S. 27 Mar 1793

Pp. 366-369. 1 May 1794: Mortgage: THOMAS LAMAR of Horns creek Edgefield Co. SC to GEORGE B. MOORE & Co....by a Bond dated 1 May 1794 for 100 pounds on condition of payment of 50 pounds with lawful interest payable on or before 1 Jun next & for better securing of payment, sell 3 female negroes viz: one named NANNEY about 35 yrs. old, one small girl named PHILLES about 4 yrs old & another small girl named BETTY, both the children of above NANNEY. S/ THOS. LAMAR. Wit: PATSY MOORE, MORGAN MURRAH, who swore by oath 19 May 1794 before JOSEPH HIGHTOWER, J.P. Rcd. 21 May 1794.

Pp. 369-372. 7 May 1794: WILLIAM COURSEY, Mathemation of Edgefield Co. SC to WILLIAM TERRY, Planter of same place for 20 pounds, sold 100 acres being part of 500 acres originally granted 20 May 1772 unto said COURSEY being on Beaverdam a branch of Turkey Creek of Savannah River with lines on MARTIN & COURSEY's land at the fork of Springfield branch & then JOHN ALLEN. S/ W. COURSEY. Wit: WILLIAM BROOKS, JOHN TERRY, who swore by oath 22 May 1794 before RICHARD TUTT, J.P. Rcd. 22 May 1794. Plat: p. 371.

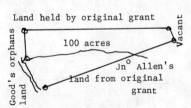

Land held by original grant

Good's orphans land

100 acres

Vacant

Jnᵒ Allen's land from original grant

Pp. 372-377. 25 May 1794: ISAAC KIRKLAND to DERICK HOLSONBAKE, both of Edgefield Co. SC for 100 pounds, sold 400 acres surveyed 24 Oct 1787 & granted 7 Apr 1788 to said KIRKLAND on Mill Creek of Big Horse Creek including the Beaver pond near the head of said creek adj. SE by PETER McCOVENLEY. S/ ISAAC KIRKLAND. Wit: JOHN HOLSONBAKE, JOAB WOOTAN, who swore by oath 26 May 1794 before RICHARD TUTT, J.P. Rcd. 26 May 1794.

Pp. 378-381. 27 Nov 1793: SAMUEL SAXON, Sheriff of Ninety Six to ROBERT COCKRAN, being the highest & last bidder at Public auction for 107 pounds...Whereas WILLIAM FRAZIER, Esq. of Charleston lately in a court of Common Pleas at Cambridge obtained a judgement against JOHN PURVIS & others for 4000 pounds & the Sheriff did seize 385 acres being part of 1500 acres near the Savannah River originally granted 5 May 1775 to FRANCIS BREMAR & was conveyed by him to JOHN PURVIS in Mar 1776. S/ SAMUEL SAXON, Sheriff of Ninety Six Dist. Wit: JOHN TROTTER, who swore by oath 21 Apr 1794 before JULIUS NICHOLS, J.P. Rcd. 26 May 1794. Plat: p. 381. 385 acres surveyed 15 Sep 1791 ROBERT LANG, D.S.

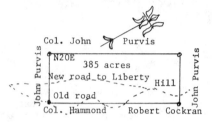

Pp. 382-388. 12 Aug 1773: WILLIAM ANDERSON of Ninety Six Dist. SC to WILLIAM MURPHEY of same place for 100 pounds, sold 200 acres originally granted 11 Feb 1773 unto said WILLIAM ANDERSON being on waters of Savannah River Granville Co. SC adj. NE by SWAN RAMBO & NW by MOSES KIRKLAND. S/ WM. ANDERSON. Wit: JAMES LAMAR, Junr., JOHN DOOLY, EDWARD GREEN, who swore by oath 9 Mar 1774 before LEROY HAMMOND, J.P. Rcd. 28 May 1794.

Pp. 389-396. 2 Mar 1774: SWAN RAMBO to WILLIAM MURPHEY, both of Ninety Six Dist. SC for 100 pounds, sold 50 acres being part of 300 acres originally granted 26 Sep 1772 unto SWAN RAMBO on waters of Savannah River adj. NW & NE by SWAN RAMBO, SW by WILLIAM ANDERSON, & SE by FRANCIS SINKFIELD. S/ SWAN (X) RAMBO. Wit: DANIEL ELLIS, RICHARD (R) BUSSEY, EDWARD GREEN, who swore by oath 9 Mar 1774 before LEROY HAMMOND, J.P.

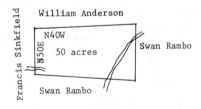

Plat: p. 396. At the request of SWAN RAMBO I have ameasured 50 acres unto WILLIAM MURPHY surveyed 11 Jun 1772 (sic) by WILLIAM ANDERSON, D. S.

Pp. 396-403. 2 Oct 1777: JOHN ANDERSON Planter, of Georgia to LEROY HAMMOND, Merchant of Ninety Six Dist. SC for 200 pounds, sold 250 acres originally granted 4 Apr 1771 on drains of Buckhalter's Mill Creek adj. North by JACOB SUMMERALL. S/ JOHN (I A) ANDERSON. Wit: ABRAHAM SPEAR, DAVID THWEATT, JOHN DAVISON, who swore by oath 4 Feb 1782 before WILLIAM JONES, J.P. Rcd. 2 Jun 1794.

142

Pp. 403-409. 19 Mar 1794: CHRISTIAN LIMBACKER & JANE ANNE, his wife to WILLIS WHATLEY, both of Edgefield Co. SC for 50 pounds, sold 55 acres˙ being part of a survey originally granted 4 Aug 1772 unto ABRAHAM HOLSENBACK who conveyed by L&R 28 Jul 1775 to MATHEW DEVORE, Junr. & said DEVORE conveyed 5 Oct 1787 to said LIMBACKER being on Dry Creek of Stevens Creek beginning on a stake in the road now called the Five Notched Road adj. MOSES KIRKLAND & POLLY DEVORE, & ABRAHAM HOLSENBACK. S/ CHRISTIAN LIMBACKER, JANE ANNE (+) LIMBACKER. Wit: EDMUND PURSSELL, SHURLEY WHATLEY, who swore by oath 23 May 1794 before JOSEPH HIGHTOWER, J.P. Rcd. 2 Jun 1794.

Pp. 409-416. 31 Aug 1789: THOMAS CURTIS to WILLIAM SPRAGINS of Edgefield Co. SC for 100 pounds, sold 250 acres originally granted 24 Apr 1752 unto PETER HUBER lying & being above bever creek now called Mill Creek on South side of Saluda River. Said tract was conveyed 10 Nov 1768 by JOHN HUBER, son & heir at law of PETER HUBER now deceased, unto THOMAS CURTIS. S/ THOMAS CURTIS, FRANCES (O) CURTIS. Wit: JOSHUA WHITMORE, JOHN THOMAS (X) DUGLAS, THOMAS CARSON, who swore by oath 9 Jan 1790 before WILLIAM ANDERSON, J.P. Rcd. 2 Jun 1794.

Pp. 416. 31 May 1794: Bill of Sale: THOMAS DOZER to BARRETT TRAVIS, both of Edgefield Co. SC for 30 pounds, sold a negro girl named AGGEY. S/ THOS. DOZER. Wit: WM. BUTLER, ALEXANDER WILSON, who swore by oath 2 Jun 1794 before NATHANIEL ABNEY, J.P. Rcd. 2 Jun 1794.

Pp. 416-422. 1794: TYREE FYKE to SAMUEL WALKER, both of Edgefield Co. SC for 100 pounds, sold 8 acres being part of 2 tracts; (1) 6 acres being part of original grant MAJILLON being the land where said FYKE now lives being on Horse Creek adj. SAMUEL WALKER's Grist Mill; (2) 2 acres being part also of a tract granted MAJILLON joining the fork of Horns Creek & the main road that leads to Edgefield Courthouse to Augusta. S/ TYRE (X) FYKE. Wit: DANIEL PARKER, GASPER GALLMAN, who swore by oath 2 Jun 1794 before NATHANIEL ABNEY, J.P.
Jun Term 1794: Mrs SARAH FYKE, wife of TYRE, relinquished dower. Rcd. 2 Jun 1794.

Pp. 422-427. 14 Apr 1790: CHARLES BANKS to JOHN CARTER, both of Edgefield Co. SC for 50 pounds, sold 200 acres originally granted 8 Jul 1774 unto JOHN MORRIS being on waters of Nobles Creek adj. BENJAMIN RYAN. Wit: WILLIAM ROBINSON, ADAM STALNAKER, VAN SWEARINGEN, Junr., who swore by oath 14 Apr 1790 before RUSSELL WILSON, J.P. Rcd. 2 Jun 1794.

Pp. 427-429. 16 Jan 1794: ABSOLEM GRIFFEN of Burke Co. NC to ELIJAH FENLEY of Edgefield Co. SC for 20 pounds, sold 50 acres being part of original grant to SAMUEL SCOTT being on Savannah River adj. N DRURY PACE; S JOSEPH ROBERTSON & E JAMES SCOTT including all held by the original grant excluding 250 acres said ABSOLEM GRIFFEN sold to JOSEPH ROBERTSON & also excepted a certain quanity of land in the west corner of above which is taken by an older grant of DRURY PACE. S/ ABSALOM GRIFFEN. Wit: ELIJ. (X) GRIFFIN, JOHN CALLIHAM, RICHARD (X) FINLY, who swore by oath 29 Jan 1794 before HUGH MIDDLETON, J.P. Rcd. 2 Jun 1794.

Pp. 429-435. 10 Nov 1793: BARTLET BLEDSOE to WILLIAM ENGLISH for

50 pounds, sold 100 acres being part of 907 acres surveyed &
granted 3 Oct 1791 unto JOHN MOBLEY in Columbia SC & released to
said BLEDSOE being on Little Saluda River adj. N by JONATHAN
RUTH; NE by WM. DOZER; SE by WM. ENGLISH & ARTHUR SIMKINS;
WILLIAM DEY, old field called Manuels old field; Lick branch. S/
BARTLET BLEDSOE, LIDDIA (X) BLEDSOE. Wit; THEOPHILES GOODWIN,
RICHARD (R) NORWOOD, WILEY KEMP, who swore by oath 31 May 1794
before HENRY KING, J.P. Rcd. 2 Jun 1794.

Pp. 435-438. 4 Mar 1776: HENRY KEY Planter, Granville Co. SC to
my loving daughter MILINDA, wife of JAMES LITCHER, for love &

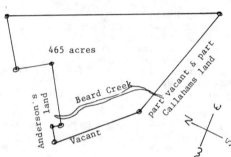

affection 465 acres being
part of 950 acres granted
5 Jan 1773 being in
Granville Co. SC on Coun
Creek & Beard Creek adj.
S by CALLAHAM YARBRO; NE
by said KEY; NW by
WILLIAM ANDERSON. S/
HENRY KEY. Wit: JAMES (+)
MURREY, WILLIAM (H)
HOLMES, ROBERT MELVILLE,
who swore by oath 28 Apr
1777 before JOHN PURVES,
J.P. Rcd. 2 Jun 1794.

Pp. 438-441. 18 Feb 1792: MARY ANN HAMMOND, LEROY HAMMOND &
GEORGE WHITEFIELD, Executrix & Executors of LW&T of LEROY
HAMMOND, late of Edgefield Co. SC, dec'd., to THOMAS BURNETT of
same place for 125 pounds, sold 250 acres originally granted 10
Apr 1771 to JOHN ANDERSON being on drains of Buckhalter's Mill
Creek adj. JACOB SUMMERAL. Said JOHN ANDERSON conveyed said land
2 & 3 Oct 1775 unto LEROY HAMMOND, Esq., dec'd. S/ MARY ANN
HAMMOND, LEROY HAMMOND, GEO. WHITEFIELD. Wit: RICHARD QUARLES,
JOSHUA HAMMOND, who swore by oath 2 Jun 1792 before JOSEPH
HIGHTOWER, J.P. Rcd. 2 Jun 1794.

Pp. 441-443. 17 Apr 1793: JOHN McCOY & SARAH his wife to JOSEPH
TOLBERT, both of Edgefield Co. SC for 140 pounds, sold 200 acres
being on Savannah river. S/ JOHN McCOY, SARAH (J+) McCOY. Wit:
THOMAS MILES, JEREMIAH TOLBERT, who swore by oath 2 Jun 1794
before JAMES HARRISON, J.P. Rcd. 2 Jun 1794.

Pp. 443-449. 9 Nov 1792: ANN DAY of Chatham Co. GA to LEROY
HAMMOND of Edgefield Co. SC for 10 pounds, sold 400 acres being
on Savannah river originally granted 11 Feb 1762 unto WILLIAM
DRAKE who died intestate about 15 Apr 1768 leaving issue his
eldest son JESSE & said JESSE intermarried with MARY JONES & had
issue an only daughter named ANN. Said JESSE DRAKE died intestate
leaving his daughter heir to above land. S/ ANN (+) DAY. Wit:
JAMES (X) BENNETT, CRESSE (+ her mark) BLANTON, SAMUEL HAMMOND,
who swore by oath 10 Dec 1792 before JOSEPH HIGHTOWER, J.P. Rcd.
13 Mar 1794.

Pp. 449-451. 2 Nov 1792: JOSEPH THOMAS, Planter to ZELPHA COBB in
behalf of her son JESSE COBB, all of Edgefield Co. SC for 20
pounds, sold 50 acres between Stephens & Turkey Creek being part
of 100 acres which was part of 305 acres granted 23rd of ----
1775 unto SANDFORD KEZIAH who conveyed 100 acres (blank) unto

WILLIAM THOMAS & said THOMAS
conveyed said 100 acres 13 & 14
Oct 1778. S/ JOSEPH THOMAS. Wit:
ABSALOM GRIFFEN, DAVID THOMAS,
JAMES THOMAS, who swore by oath 6
Jun 1793 before HUGH MIDDLETON,
J.P. Rcd. 3 Jun 1794.
Plat: p. 451.
WM. COURSEY, D.S.

Pp. 451-453. 11 Apr 1794: Bill of Sale: WILLIAM MATHEWS, Planter
to WILLIAM ANDERSON, Esq., both of Edgefield Co. SC for 12
pounds...for my two years Taxes & Cost due the public convey an
old negro wench named JANE, 1 mare & 8 head of cattle, two
feather beds & their furniture & all the furniture that belonged
to his said wife, MARY MATHEWS at the time of his, said WILLIAM
MATHEWS marriage in payment of 12 pounds & after repayment of
said 12 pounds as agreed, the property shall remain the property
of said ANDERSON in trust for his said wife MARY MATHEWS. S/
WILLIAM(I) MATHEWS. Wit: NATHAN WRIGHT, JAMES MOORE, who swore by
oath 12 Apr 1794 in Newberry Co. SC before JAMES MAYSON Esq.,
J.P. Rcd. 3 Jun 1794.

Pp. 453-456. 2 Nov 1792: JOSEPH THOMAS to MARY SUMMERALL in
behalf of her son HARDY SUMMERALL, all of Edgefield Co. SC for 20
pounds, sold 50 acres being on NE side of Stephens Creek being
part of 100 acres which is part of 305 acres granted 3 --- 1774
unto SANDFORD KEZIAH & was conveyed unto WM. THOMAS & above 100
acres conveyed 13 & 14 Oct 1778
by said WM. THOMAS to JOSEPH
THOMAS adj. MITCHEL & STROM.
Said land is to be MARY
SUMMERALL's as long as she
lives & after her death falls
to HARDY SUMMERALL, her son. S/
JOSEPH THOMAS. Wit: ABSOLOM
GRIFFEN, DAVID THOMAS, JAMES
THOMAS, who swore by oath 6 Jun
1793 before HUGH MIDDLETON,
J.P. Rcd. 3 Jun 1794. Plat: p.
455. WM COURSEY, D.S.

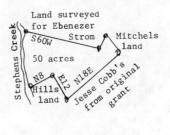

Pp. 456-457. 3 Jun 1793: Deposition: EDWARD COUCH said that he
was present when RACHEL BRAZEL & her son JOHN McKENNEY had a
conversation respecting a negro boy named PRINCE, who was the
property of VALENTINE BRAZEL, husband of said RACHEL BRAZEL. That
said RACHEL told the desponent that she was unwilling VALENTINE
BRAZEL should ever have the boy & since her son had no money she
would lend him a dollar which might be returned to be
imprescences of the deponent as evidence of a contract..that the
deponant is well convinced from the conversation that she
intended to defraud her husband who was absent in Georgia of his
right to said boy as she was provided with other property of less
value which might have been sold in case of distress but to his
knowledge said VALENTINE BRAZEL had furnished her with such
necessities... S/ EDWARD COUCH. Sworn by oath 3 Jun 1793 before
JOSEPH HIGHTOWER, J.P. Rcd. 3 Jun 1794.

Pp. 457-461. 2 Apr 1787: JAMES KETCHERSIDES & SARAH, his wife to MICHAEL CAY, both of Ninety Six District for 100 pounds, sold 100 acres originally granted 5 Jun 1786 said KETCHERSIDES on Persimon Lick Creek of Big Creek of Little Saluda River. S/ JAMES KETCHERSIDE, SARAH (X) KETCHERSIDES. Wit: JOSEPH TOWLES, THOMAS CURB, JOHN WATSON, who swore by oath 23 Aug ---- before NATHANIEL ABNEY, J.P. Rcd. 3 Jun 1794.

Pp. 462-464. 18 Dec 1793: JAMES SCOTT & MARY, his wife, to SAMUEL SCOTT, all of Edgefield for 150 pounds, sold 350 acres being part of 2 tracts; (1) 100 acres originally granted 15 May 1771 to ARTHUR GILCHRIST on Stephens creek adj. CHAMPION TERRY; & (2) 250 acres originally granted 17 May 1774 to ARTHUR GILCHRIST and were conveyed 17 Apr 1791 by GILCHRIST & wife to JAMES SCOTT. S/ JAMES SCOTT, MARY (+) SCOTT. Wit: JOHN FARRAR, JAMES GRAY, ROBERT OLIPHANT, who swore by oath 3 Jun 1794 before HUGH MIDDLETON, J.P. Rcd. 6 Jun 1794.

Pp. 464-468. 25 Feb 1794: MARTHA SAVAGE & THOMAS BEE acting Executrix & Executor of WILLIAM SAVAGE, Merchant of Charleston, dec'd., to SAMUEL MAYS for $100.00, sold 100 acres originally surveyed for RICHARD ALLISON afterwards granted to SARAH STANTENBOUGH, who conveyed to said WILLIAM SAVAGE being on half way Swamp. S/ MARTHA SAVAGE, THOS. BEE, Exrs. of WM. SAVAGE. Wit: WILLIAM ANDERSON, who swore by oath 25 Apr 1794 in Newberry Co. SC before JAMES MAYSON, Esq., J.P. Rcd. 7 Jun 1794.

Pp. 1-19. 2 Nov 1790: JOHN BOWMAN, Esq. of Charleston SC &
SABINA, his wife & RICHARD WELD, Esq. of the Kingdom of Great
Britain who authorized by Letter of Attorney to said BOWMAN to
sell to EDWARD PENMAN Merchant of Charleston SC. The following
tracts were sold: Whereas ROGER PINCKNEY, Esq. late Provost
Marshall of SC the 28 Jun 177- (1) sold to JAMES SIMPSON a tract
of land with property being seized of ISAAC PYTHRHLYN & sold
under execution 20,000 acres, but upon resurvey by PATRICK
CUNNINGHAM, Esq. found to be 17,786 acres & had the deed of
release 20 Apr 1779 by said JAMES SIMPSON by BARBARA SIMPSON his
attorney; 7099 acres for 3668 pounds to EDWARD PENMAN being NW
part of 50,000 acres originally granted WILLIAM LIVINGSTON, Esq.
& his associates bounding SE on another part of 50,000 acres
formerly belonging to JOHN MURRAY, Esq. to the NE on Saludy
river, to SW on lands part of tract & NW on lands late of JOSEPH
SALVADORE, dec'd.; (2) 1000 acres in Craven Co. SC on Fergusen's
creek of Tyger river adj. S lands surveyed on the bounty, E by
JAMES PADEN; (3) 1000 acres in Craven Co. SC on N side of South
fork of Tyger River, E by ISAAC HUGENS - the last two tracts
originally granted 2 Apr 1773 to DANIEL HEYWOOD & sold 28 Feb
1775 to JAMES SIMPSON; (4) 500 acres in Craven Co. SC on small
branch called Abner's creek of Enoree river adj. CHARLES MOORE;
(5) 500 acres in Craven Co. SC on Painters creek of Enoree River;
(6) 300 acres on waters of Middle fork of Tyger River adj. JOHN
WIN & the Indian land; (7) 300 acres in Craven Co. on ?Ben's?
creek of Tyger river; (8) 300 acres on Middle fork of Tyger river
adj. land late of ROBERT PHILLIP & E by ROBERT CARR; (9) 300
acres in Craven Co. on William's creek of Tyger river; (10) 300
acres on Enoree river adj. JOHN FORD & WILLIAM STAUTENBOUGH,
which last seven tracts were originally granted to ROBERT
PHILLIPS 23 Jun 1774 also; (11) 300 acres originally granted 9
Nov 1774 to said ROBERT PHILLIPS & last eight tracts sold 25 Jun
1775: (12) 250 acres originally granted 13 Oct 1769 to JAMES
SIMPSON in Waxsaw settlement adj. at time of grant Dr. CANTZON,
THOMAS McMAN, DAVID ADAMS & JOHN McELHONEY; (13) 500 acres
originally granted 21 Dec 1769 to JAMES SIMPSON being on Four
Hole Swamp adj. land lately of GEORGE SHULER; (14) 950 acres
originally granted 7 Apr 1770 in Craven Co. SC to JAMES SIMPSON
being on North side of Pedee river adj. at time of grant JOHN
GOODWIN, Mr LAROCKE, Mr HUGH CAVANT & SW on Pedee River; (15) 500
acres originally granted 12 Jul 1771 to JAMES SIMPSON on Stephens
creek of Savannah River adj. at time of Grant by WILLIAM MAINER;
(16) 500 acres originally granted 17 Jan 1772 to JAMES SIMPSON on
Bird creek of Stevens Creek; (17) 1000 acres originally granted
15 May 1772 to JAMES SIMPSON on Loyds creek of Stevens Creek adj.
CHRISTIAN BUCKHALTER & JAMES THOMAS; (18) 200 acres originally
granted 28 Aug 1772 to JAMES SIMPSON on Dry branch of Buckhalters
creek of Savannah River adj. LAURENCE RAMBO, SAMUEL & JOSEPH
DOOLITTLE & MOSES KIRKLAND; (19) 1000 acres on Rockey Creek of
Turkey Creek; (20) 200 acres on Bird Creek of Stevens Creek adj.
JAMES SIMPSON & WILLIAM ANDERSON... The last two tracts
originally granted 6 Sep 1772 to JAMES SIMPSON; (21) 500 acres in
Granville Co. SC on Rocky Creek; (22) 500 acres in Colleton Co.
SC on Mountain Creek of Savannah River adj. lands of said JAMES
SIMPSON; (23) 500 acres in Granville Co. SC on Mountain Creek of

Turkey Creek of Savannah River adj. said JAMES SIMPSON's land;
(24) 500 acres in Colleton Co. SC on Turkey Creek of Savannah
river adj. lands of said JAMES SIMPSON...the last 4 tracts
originally granted 4 Nov 1772; (25) 200 acres originally granted
8 Feb 1773 in Craven Co. SC on North side Enoree River; (26) 400
acres originally granted 3 Apr 1775 on Savannah river in Ninety
Six Dist. adj. --CRAWFORD, FRANCES KITTS & --- ABNEY; (27) 800
acres on Stephens Creek near Savanna River in Ninety Six Dist;
(28) 500 acres in Orangeburg Dist. on North side of South fork of
Edisto River on Cedar Creek; (29) 500 acres in Orangeburg Dist on
South fork of Edisto River & Shaws creek adj. THOMAS LYNCH
...last 3 tracts originally granted 1 Jun 1775 to said JAMES
SIMPSON; (30) 500 acres on Horse Creek of Savannah River in
Ninety Six Dist.; (31) 350 acres on Horse Creek adj. THOMAS
FERGUSON...last 2 tracts originally granted 21 Jul 1775 said
JAMES SIMPSON; (32) 1/2 of ten tracts as discribed: 500 acres on
Raybourns creek in Ninety Six Dist. adj. WILLIAM SAVAGE, JAMES
SIMPSON on the indian line land of HENERY POWELL; 500 acres on
Raybourns creek adj. WILLIAM SAVAGE, JAMES SIMPSON, HENRY POWELL,
Indians land line, Mr ADAMSON, MOSES KIRKLAND; 500 acres ibid
adj. THOS. McDONALD & JOHN MAHARTY; 500 acres on Raybourns creek
& Dartons creek adj. SAVAGE, SIMPSON & Cherokee Indian line; 500
acres on Raybourns creek adj. SAVAGE, SIMPSON & Indian land
line...said last six tracts originally granted WILLIAM SAVAGE,
now dec'd., & the said JAMES SIMPSON 5 May 1773; 500 acres in
Ninety Six Dist. on Stevens Creek of Savannah River at a place
called Ridges Old Plantation on land of DRURY MORRIS; 500 acres
in Ninety Six on branch of Saludy river adj. PATRICK WELCH,
ROBERT CUNNINGHAM, WILLIAM SMITH, THOMAS YATES, & JOHN LONG; 500
acres in Ninety Six Dist. on Stevens Creek adj. ROBERT RUSSELL;
500 acres on Turkey creek of Savannah River near LEVI
HARRIS...last four tracts originally granted 9 Nov 1774 to
WILLIAM SAVAGE & said JAMES SIMPSON. A total of 29349 acres.

24 Nov. 1780: Power of Attorney: RICHARD WELD of Parish of St.
Dunston in the west in the county of Middlesex, Esq. appoint JOHN
BOWMAN now of St. Martin Parrish in the Fields in the County of
Middlesex, but intending shortly to sail for the Colony of S.C.
in America, to execute one or more lands unto JAMES SIMPSON of
Charles Town in SC for payment. S/ RICHARD WELD by his atty. JOHN
BOWMAN. JOHN BOWMAN, SABINA BOWMAN. Wit: WM. ROBERTSON, ROBERT
MITCHELL, who swore by oath 8 Nov 1790 before J.P. NICHOLSON,
J.P. Rcd. 11 Jan 1791.

Pp. 20-24. 23 Jul 1790: ARTHUR WATSON to THOMAS FORTNER, both of
Edgefield Co. SC for 10 pounds, sold 157 acres on Peters Creek of
Cloud Creek adj. N JAMES DANIELS; SE ROBERT PRINGLES; due W
ROBERT STARK; ARTHUR MIDDLETON & NE THOMAS WATERS. S/ ARTHUR (A)
WATSON. Wit: ABNER WATSON, ARTHUR RICE WATSON, JOHN FORTNER, who
swore by oath 13 Oct 1790 before ARTHUR SIMKINS, J.P. Rcd. (no
date).

Pp. 24-26. 26 Jul 1790: ISAAC LEAFERER & MILLINDA, his wife of
Wilks Co. GA to JOHN TALBERT of Edgefield Co. SC for 25 pounds &
by virtue of sale made for during MILLINDA LEFERER's natural life
sold 465 acres being part of 950 acres originally granted 5 Jan
1773 on Coun & Bird creek adj. S by CALLEHAM YARBRO; NE by land
held by said KEY (sic); & NW by WILLIAM ANDERSON. S/ ISAAC
LAFERER, MELLINDA LAFERER. Wit: JAMES LYON, JOHN McCOY, who

swore by oath 13 Oct 1790 before AQUILA MILES, J.P. Rcd. (no date).

Pp. 26-33. 2 Nov 1787: JOHN GOODE of Winton Co. SC, Planter to THOMAS DALTON for 100 pounds, sold 150 acres being part of a tract originally granted 1 Dec 1772 to RICHARD CANNADY whole tract & since sold to JOHN GOODE below the mouth of Bedingfield Creek of Savannah River. S/ JOHN (X) GOODE, GOICE (+) GOODE. Wit: WILLIAM GOODE, THOMAS MORRIS, NATHANIEL SANDRES, before me 2 Nov 1787 DANIEL GREEN, J.P..
Winton Co. SC: JESSE WINBORNE, J.P. made oath 15 Oct 1790 before DANIEL GREEN, Esq.

Pp. 33-34. 5 Oct 1790: Bill of Sale: DANIEL BIRD, Planter of Edgefield Co. to JEAN NOBLES, spinstress & housekeeper of same place for 60 pounds, sold a negro woman slave named BETTY & her girl child slave named ALESEY. S/ DANIEL BIRD. Wit: JOHN RYAN, WILLIAM COURSEY, who swore by oath 12 Oct 1790 before JOHN STURZENNEGER, J.P. Rcd. (no date).

Pp. 34-36. 27 Sep 1790: Deed of Gift: TIMOTHEY REARDIN, Farmer of Edgefield to JEAN NOBLES, housekeeper for said REARDIN, of same place for good conduct, behavior as housekeeper & also her great attachment for my benefit, Interest & her better Maintenance, gives 150 acres, land being part of 250 acres granted 1765 to said REARDIN on Logg creek a branch of Turkey Creek of Savannah River. S/ TIMOTHY REARDAN. Wit: WILLIAM COURSEY, DANIEL BIRD, who swore by oath 12 Oct 1790 before JOHN STURZENNEGER, J.P. Rcd. (no date).

Pp. 36-37. 27 Sep 1790: TIMOTHEY REARDIN, Farmer of Edgefield to JEAN NOBLES, housekeeper of said REARDIN of same place, for Esteem & affection & Consideration, me hereunto moving, all my goods chattels, debts, stocks of horses, cattle, hoggs & what kind so ever, Beds, household goods & furniture & all other substance whatsoever moveable & immovable...S/ TIMOTHY REARDIN. Wit: WILLIAM COURSEY, DANIEL BIRD, who swore by oath 12 Oct 1790 before JOHN STURZENEGGER, J.P. Rcd. (no date).

Pp. 37-38. 15 Dec 1789: AMERY DAY of Ninety Six Dist. SC to THOMAS CHAPPEL of same place for 30 pounds, sold one set of Blacksmith tools, a mare, sow & pigs, 2 cows & calves, 2 feather beds & furniture & all other household furniture. S/ AM (+) DAY. Wit: CHARLES (X) CLARK, WILLIAM ROBINSON.
Newberry Co. SC: CHARLES CLARK swore by oath 2 Oct 1790 before JOHN LINDSEY, J.P. Rcd. (no date).

Pp. 39-40. 16 Nov 1790: PRICILLA THOMAS to JOSEPH LEWIS, Jr. both of Edgefield Co. SC for 10 pounds, sold 100 acres part of 300 acres granted 1775 to JAMES THOMAS on Rocky Creek adj. WILLIAM CLARK, JOEL THREEWITS & THOMAS WHITEHEAD. S/ PRICILLA (X) THOMAS. Wit: MARY (X) RAUTIN, ISAAC LEWIS, who swore by oath 12 Nov 1790 before ARTHUR SIMKINS, J.P. Rcd. (no date).

Pp. 41-45. 8 Dec 1789: ANDREW PICKENS, Esq. & REBECCA his wife of Pendleton Co. SC to JAMES MOORE of Edgefield Co. for 935 pounds, sold 407 acres adj. SW by JAMES ARMSTRONG, W by Savannah River, THOMAS LAMAR, Horse Creek. S/ ANDW. PICKENS, REBECCA PICKENS. Wit: ROBERT ANDERSON, HUGH MAXWELL, who swore by oath 31 Dec 1789

DEED BOOK 10:   1791-1794   EDGEFIELD COUNTY S.C.

before ROBERT ANDERSON, J.P. of Pendleton Co. SC. Rcd. (no date).

Pp. 45-53.   3 May 1790: JOHN BOSTICK of Ninety Six Dist.
SC to EDWARD PENMAN, Merchant of Charleston SC for Bond penal sum 454
pounds, condition of payment of 227 pounds at 4 equal payments
beginning 26 Nov 1790, with interest, 350 acres originally
granted 1751 to PATRICK WELCH on South side Saluda river adj. N &
E said River; S by WILLIAM ANDERSON & JOHN WAIT & W by JAMES
ANDERSON. S/ JOHN BOSTICK. Wit: ANDREW WILLIAMSON, EPHRAIM
RAMSEY, who swore by oath 11 Jan 1791 before WILLIAM ANDERSON,
J.P. Rcd. (no date).

Pp. 54-58. 1 Jul 1789: THOMAS FARRAR, Sheriff of Ninety Six Dist.
SC to CHARLES GOODWIN of same place for 18 pounds, sold 300 acres
on Little Stevens Creek... Whereas THOMAS YOUNG the Absent
Debtor, was seized in his demesnes of fee of 300 acres; And Where
as ELIZABETH BEARD, widow & adm. of Chattels which were of DANIEL
BEARD, dec'd., the Plaintiff in 1789 obtained a judgement for 35
pounds... And Whereas THOMAS FARRAR, Sheriff executed by Writ of
Fieri facias & sold at public auction to CHARLES GOODWIN, being
the last and highest bidder. S/ THOMAS FARRAR, Sheriff of Ninety
Six Dist. Wit: WILLIAM MOORE, WILLIAM GARNETT, who swore by oath
27 Nov 1790 before WILLIAM MOORE, J.P. (no date).

Pp. 59-63. 11 Oct 1790: SAMUEL CRAFTON, Planter of Edgefield, to
MELINE CONKLING LEAVENSWORTH of same place for 20 pounds, sold
445 acres on Big & Little Horse Creek & the long branch known in
the General plat of Chikesaw land by the number 24. S/ SAMUEL
CRAFTON. Wit: PHILLIP JOHNSON, RICHARD TUTT, C.E.C., who swore by
oath 11 Jan 1791 before RUSSELL WILSON, J.P. Rcd. (no date).

Pp. 63-66. 19 Nov 1785: CHRISTOPHER HAGER to ALEXANDER HANNA for
15 pounds, sold 150 acres in Granville Co. Adj. SW CATHARINE
BURKMYERS. S/ CHRISTOPHER HAGER. Wit: NATH. BRADWELL, GEORGE
WILKIE, who swore by oath 27 Sep 1783 (sic) before JOHN MURRAY,
J.P. Rcd. (no date).

Pp. 67-71. 16 Sep 1790: EDWARD PRINCE & LUCY, his wife, of
Edgefield... to THOMAS HART for 15 pounds, sold 50 acres granted
5 Sep 1785 JABATH HENDRICKS on a branch of Savannah River. S/
EDWARD PRINCE, LUCY PRINCE. Wit: THOMAS McKIE, JAMES McDANIEL,
who swore by oath 16 Oct 1791 before HUGH MIDDLETON, J.P.

Pp. 72-77. 14 Nov 1788: LEWIS CLARK, Planter, & CATHARINE, his
wife of Edgefield Co. SC to JOSIAH THOMAS of same place for 30
pounds, sold 63 acres granted 5 Feb 1787 on Red Bank Creek of
Little Saluda River adj. SW by ESKRIDGE; S said LEWIS CLARK. S/
LEWIS CLARK, CATHARINE (X) CLARK. Wit: THOMAS SMEDLEY, HENRY
KING, who swore by oath 6 Jan 1791 before JAMES SPANN, J.P. Rcd.
(no date).

Pp. 77-82. 7 Jan 1789: DAVID GEORGE of SC to PHILLIP ZIMMERMAN,
Planter of Edgefield Co. SC for 5 shillings, sold 100 acres
originally granted 7 Jul 1772 to MARY ADOLPH on the bounty in
Londonborough Township waters of Hardlabour Creek adj. W BRIAN
COCKRAM. S/ DAVID (X) GEORGE. Wit: JOHN SMITH, HENRY (X)
ZIMMERMAN, who swore by oath 11 Jan 1791 before RUSSELL WILSON,
J.P. Rcd. (no date).

Pp. 82-90. 14 Nov 1774: JOHN CLARK, Ninety Six Dist. Granville Co. SC, Planter, to WILLIAM MINTOR, Planter of same place for 500 pounds, sold 200 acres surveyed 26 Mar 1772 by WILLIAM GOODE, D.S. certified 2 Mar 1773 by JAMES PURSELL D.S., originally granted 18 May 1773 said JOHN CLARK on branch of Turkey Creek called Beaverdam. S/ JOHN CLARK. Wit: THOMAS GOODE, JOHN GOODE, Jr., PHILLIP GOODE, who swore by oath 16 Nov 1774 before CHAMPNESS TERRY, J.P. Rcd. (no date).

Pp. 90-95. 25 Nov 1790: JOHN POUND & MARY his wife, of Edgefield Co. SC to JOHN CHENEY of same place for 300 pounds, sold 200 + 100 acres, being part of 2 tracts; (1) on Walnut creek of Stevens Creek adj. S. by EDWARD VANN, granted to JOHN SALLEY 3 Dec 1771 & conveyed to said JOHN POUND 27 Feb 1786 &; (2) 100 acres granted 1 Mar 1775 to TULLEY BOWLING on waters of Ceador Creek , Stevens Creek adj. W by ROBERT MOSELY, N&E by EDWARD VAN & conveyed 5 Jun 1778 to said POUND. S/ JOHN POUND, MARY (M) POUND. Wit: GEORGE CHENEY, JOHN RAINSFORD, who swore by oath 24 Jan 1791 before AQUILA MILES, J.P. Rcd. (no date).

Pp. 95-100. 12 May 1789: THOMAS DELOACH, Senr Planter, & PATIENCE his wife to JOSIAH THOMAS, both of Edgefield Co. SC for 60 pounds, sold 65 acres being part of 400 acres originally granted 31 Aug 1774 to said DELOACH on Red Bank Creek & Penn Creek of Little Saluda River, NE by S. WALKER, JACOB SMITH. S/ THOS. DELOACH, Senr., PATIENCE (X) DELOACHE. Wit: WILLIAM BURDITT, SAMUEL DELOACH, HENRY KING, who swore by oath 6 Jan 1791 before JAMES SPANN, J.P. Rcd. (no date).

Pp. 101-104. 2 Jan 1776: CORNELIUS GARDNER & ANNA CARRADESSAN, his wife of Ninety Six Dist. SC to THOMAS NORRELL of same place for 50 pounds, sold 61 acres originally granted ANNA CARRADESSAN EDDMANSIN, wife to the said GARDNER, on a branch of Halfway swamp. S/ CORNELIUS GARDNER, ANNA CARRADESSAN (X) GARDNER. Wit: ELIZABETH (X) MUIRHEAD, JAMES MUIRHEAD, who swore by oath 2 Jan 1776 before WILLIAM ANDERSON, J.P. Rcd. (no date).

Pp. 104-107. 13 Jul 1785: THOMAS NORRELL to RUFUS INMAN, Blacksmith, both of Edgefield Co. SC for 27 pounds, sold 61 acres granted 4 May 1775 to ANNA CARRADESSAN EDALMANSON, being on a branch of Halfway swamp & was conveyed by said EDALMOSON & her husband CORNELIUS GARDNER 2 Jan 1776 to THOMAS NORRELL. S/ THOS. NORRELL. Wit: WILLIAM HUTCHISON, RACHEL SINQUEFIELD, who swore by oath 15 Jul 1785 before WILLIAM ANDERSON, J.P. Rcd. (no date).

Pp. 107-119. 25 Jul ----: JOSEPH TUCKER BELL Planter to DRURY MIMS, Planter, both of Edgefield Co. SC for 150 pounds, sold 550 acres being two tracts of land; (1) 100 acres granted 1 Sep 1768 to JOHN SNEED in Granville Co. SC near lick fork of Cedar Creek of Savannah River who conveyed 25 Jan 1771 to GEORGE STROTHERS & whereas said GEORGE STROTHERS by his LW&T dated 16 Sep 1772 appointed his beloved friend JOHN HOPKINS sole Executor to sell & dispose of said property; (2) 450 acres granted 8 Feb 1773 to SOLOMON PETERS being on Cedar Creek of the Savannah River adj. North by JOHN SNEAD & THOMAS RAY; West by SNEAD, RAY & JOHN SPENCER's, DAVID DUNCAN; S by DUNCAN & Colonel BARNARD. Whereas SOLOMON PETERS conveyed 9 Oct 1773 unto JOHN HOPKINS & Whereas was conveyed 8 Jun 1775 unto BENJAMIN BELL & Whereas said BELL made bonds & obligation to make title unto DRURY MIMS & whereas BENJAMIN BELL died intestate before title could be made & said

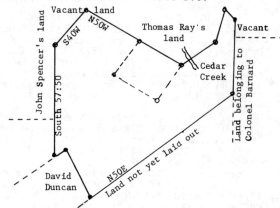

lands descended to
JOSEPH TUCKER BELL
heir at Law of said
lands. Plat
certified by WILLIAM
COURSEY, 19 Jul
1790. S/ JOSEPH T.
BELL. Wit: DAVID
MIMS, HENRY WARE,
Junr., who swore by
oath 11 Dec 1790
before ARTHUR
SIMKINS, J.P. Rcd.
(no date)

Pp. 119-125. 3 Jun 1790: JOHN SPANN & SARAH his wife to JAMES
SPANN, both of Edgefield Co. SC for 100 pounds, sold 200 acres
originally granted 5 Mar 1770 to MARY FERRELL & was conveyed to
said SPANN, being on Red Bank Creek of Little Saluda River. S/
JOHN (I) SPANN, SARAH (S) SPANN. Wit: AVENILLAH (A) KING, HENRY
KING, who swore by oath 27 Jul 1790 before RUSSELL WILSON, J.P.
Rcd. (no date).

Pp. 125-130. 3 Jun 1790: JOHN SPANN, Planter, & SARAH his wife to
JAMES SPANN, both of Edgefield for 100 pounds, sold 350 acres
originally granted 26 Jul 1774 to said JOHN SPANN, being on Red
Bank Creek of Little Saluda River adj. S & SE by AMOS RITCHARDSON,
JOHN SPANN & PETER FOY, & NW owners unknown. S/ JOHN (I) SPANN,
SARAH (A) SPANN. Wit: AVENILLA (A) KING, HENRY KING, who swore by
oath 27 Jul 1790 before RUSSELL WILSON, J.P. Rcd. (no date).

Pp. 130-135. 5 Oct 1785: THOMAS WARING, Senr. & JOHN EWING
CALHOUN, Commissioners of Confiscated Estates, to GEORGE HUNT,
Planter, Ninety Six Dist. SC for 13 pounds, sold 100 acres being
land late the property of MOSES KIRKLAND on Mill & Clear Water
Creeks of Edisto River adj. S & W by Mr. FAIRCHILD. S/ JNO. EWING
CALHOUN, THOS. WARING, Senr. Wit: DANIEL MAZYECK, Esq., C.H.
SIMMONS, THOMAS BRIDE, PHILEMON WATERS, Esq., who swore by oath 12
Jan 1790 before PETER FRENEAU, J.P. Rcd. (no date).

Pp. 136-141. 15 Dec 1788: JOHN ANDERSON, Weaver of Abbeville Co.
SC to ROBERT ANDERSON, Planter of Edgefield Co. SC for 45 pounds,
sold 91 acres being part of 115 acres originally granted 4 Feb
1788 on Cuffee Town Creek of Stephens Creek of Savannah River adj.
lands of SAMUEL ANDERSON. S/ JOHN (X) ANDERSON, ELIZABETH (a)
ANDERSON. Wit: JAMES HARRISON, JOHN ANDERSON, Junr., who swore by
oath 2 Jan 1790 before JOHN PURVES, J.P. Rcd. (no date).

Pp. 142-143. 24 Oct 1785: JOHN EDWARDS of Newberry Co. SC to
WILLIAM HILL, Planter, of Edgefield Co. SC for 120 pounds, sold
200 acres originally granted 4 Jul 1754 to HANS GEORGE DUGHTELL,
who conveyed to RICHARD ALLISON who conveyed to said JOHN EDWARDS
on Halfway swamp creek of Saluda River. S/ JOHN EDWARDS. Mary (M)
EDWARDS, wife of JOHN EDWARDS, resigns all right & title to above
conveyed land. Wit: ROBERT TATE, MICHAEL ABNEY, SAMUEL MAYS, who
swore by oath 5 Sep 1788 before WILLIAM ANDERSON, J.P. Rcd. (no
date).

Pp. 144-146. 4 Mar 1789: MICHAEL ARTERBERY of Orangeburg & District of Winton Co. SC to BENJAMIN CLARK of Edgefield Co., Ninety Six Dist. for 200 pounds, sold 610 acres being part of two tracts; (1) 191 acres surveyed for GEORGE RODAN 12 Jan 1786 on E side of S fork of Edisto River on both sides of Gramping (sic) Gret (sic) adj. W & NW by WILLIAM GOGINS & DAVID RICHARDSON; (2) 419 acres being round the other tract of 191 acres belonging to said ARTERBERY, adj. SE & SW by EZEKIEL WALKER & DANIEL GOGIAN's land, NE & SE on DAVID RICHARDSON, originally granted 5 Nov 1787. S/ MICHAEL (h) ARTERBERY, ELIZABETH (X) ARTERBERY. Wit: THOMAS McCLENDON, HENRY McCLENDON, ROBERT DEWACK, LEWIS CLARK, who swore by oath 10 Jan 1791 before JOHN PERVIS, J.P. Rcd. (no date).

Pp. 147-148. 29 Aug 1787: THOMAS GRIFFIN of Amherst Co. VA to ABSOLUM GRIFFIN of Edgefield Co. SC for 40 pounds, sold 350 acres originally granted 23 Jun 1774 to HENRY KEY being on branches of Turkey Creek. S/ THOS. GRIFFIN. Wit: JOHN TALIAFERRO, THOS. (X) GRIFFIN, Junr., WILLIAM GRIFFIN, JAMES (X) GRIFFIN, JOHN GRIFFIN, ANTHONY (X) GRIFFIN, THOS. WORTHAM, WILLIAM THURMOND, ELY (X) GRIFFIN, who swore by oath 2 Jul 1789 before HUGH MIDDLETON, J.P. Rcd. (no date).

Pp. 149-150. 5 Jan 1791: Deed of Gift: JOHN WATSON, Senior, Planter of Edgefield Co. SC, for love & affection for my wife ANNE WATSON, gives 40 acres on Cloud Creek of Little Saluda River, including houses on plantation, also 10 head of hogs & 1 horse called Jockey, my own riding horse as long as the said ANNE lives. S/ JOHN (X) WATSON. Wit: EDWARD COUCH, WILLIS ANDERSON, THOMAS WILLIAMS BENSON, who swore by oath 29 Jan 1791 before RUSSELL WILSON, J.P. Rcd. (no date).

P. 150. 8 Feb 1772: Marriage Certificate: WILLIAM MARTIN, formerly merchant on the Congaree & GRACEY WARING, was, on the 8 Feb 1772 joined by me in Holy wedlock as witnessed by my hand this 12 Mar 1792. CHRISTIAN THEUS.
Richland Co. S.C.: WILLIAM MORTIMER swore by oath 25 Mar 1791 before JOHN CALVERT, J.P. Rcd. (no date).

Pp. 151-152. 17 Feb 1787: Deed of Gift: JOSEPH WALKER of Edgefield Co. SC for Love & affection for my son JAMES WALKER of same place, all my estate both real & personal except one negro man named BOB, a mare & a cow. All the remainder I give to my son JAMES WALKER. S/ JOSEPH (iW) WALKER. Wit: BARTLETT BROWN, ATHANATHAN THOMAS, WILLIAM BROWN, who swore by oath 15 Apr 1788 before BENJ. TUTT, J.P. Rcd. (no date).

Pp. 152-153. 7 Apr 1790: Agreement: JOHN CLACKLER to JOHN PURSLEY, 50 acres, all that part of his father's Estate which was left to him by LW&T. S/ JOHN (+) CLACKLER, JOHN (X) PURSLEY. Wit: AQUILA MILES, REUBEN BECKUM, who swore by oath 7 Apr 1790 before AQUILA MILES, J.P. Rcd. (no date).

Pp. 153-162. 20 Dec 1789: Mortgage: JAMES MOORE of Edgefield Co. to ANDREW PICKENS for better securing payment for sum of 935 pounds with payments of (1) 200 pounds by 1 Jan 1791; (2) 183 pounds by 1 Jan 1792; (3) 183 pounds by 1 Jan 1793; (4) 183 pounds by 1 Jan 1794; (5) 183 pounds by 1 Jan 1795, sold 407 acres on the Savannah River adj. JAMES ARMSTRONG & THOMAS LAMAR of Horse Creek. S/ JAMES MOORE, ANDW. PICKENS. Wit: NATHANIEL BACON, FIELDS PARDUE, who swore by oath 14 Jan 1790 before JOHN PURVES, J.P. Rcd. (no date).

DEED BOOK 10: 1791-1794 EDGEFIELD COUNTY S.C.

Pp. 163-164. 27 Dec 1790: Deed of Gift: WILLIAM BLACK, for love & affection for my dear friend, PHILEMON BOZMAN, my goods & chatels being two negroe slaves - one named LETT & the other her son NIM, 1 bay with saddle, bags & bridle, wearing clothes. S/ WILLIAM BLACK. Wit: THOMAS SWEARINGHAM, ISAAC KIRKLAND, VAN SWEARINGHAM, Junr., who swore by oath 11 Jan 1791 before RUSSELL WILSON, J.P. Rcd. (no date).

Pp. 164-165. 5 Jan 1791: Bill of Sale: ELISHA WALKER of Edgefield Co. SC to DAVID WALKER, Senr. of Columbia Co. GA for 400 pounds, sold 4 negroes named STEPHEN, JUDAH, CLARY & BETTY; 8 horses; 8 cows, 3 feather beds & furniture, 4 pots, 2 side saddles, 2 silver spoons, 1 cart, 2 spinning wheels, 2 chest, 2 trunks, 1 desk, 1 case of bottles, 1 frying pan & grid Iron, 7 chears, 6 plates, 3 dishes, 2 basons, lot of crocaw(?) ware, 1 loom, 4 slays, 2 pair chane traces & collars, 2 plows, 3 hoes, 1 lot of books, 4 briddles, 1 pr. of smoothing irons, 1 slate & 1 looking glass, 1 table, 2 iron wedges & 2 razors. S/ ELISHA WALKER. Wit: GEORGE CHENEY, JOHN CHENEY, who swore by oath 11 Jan 1791 before JOHN PURVES, J.P. Rcd. (no date).

Pp. 166-167. 23 Apr 1791: SARAH BOWERS of Edgefield Co. SC to ISAAC ARDIS, Planter for 70 pounds, sold 37 1/2 acres on Savannah River adj. by MARTHA McGILBRAY & ROBERT VAUGHN & all other sides by MATHIAS ARDIS. S/ SARAH (X) BOWERS. Wit: HENRY JONES, ALEXD. DOWNER, CHADOCK BURNELL, who swore by oath 23 Apr 1791 before JOHN STURZENEGGER, J.P. Rcd. (no date).

Pp. 167-169. 28 Jan 1778: PHILIP JONES of VA to HENRY JONES of Burk Co. GA for 1000 pounds, sold 188 acres in Beech Island in province of SC on Savannah River adj. lands of JOHN JOACKIM ZUBLY & possessed at present by DAVID BOWERS. The said land was conveyed by said JOHN JOACKIM ZUBLY to DANIEL JONES & by his decease fell to his brother the said PHILIP JONES, his heir at law. S/ PHILIP JONES. Wit: ROBERT JONES, ROBERT WYNNE, DANIEL EVANS, who swore by oath 29 Aug 1783 before JOHN MURRAY, J.P., Ninety Six Dist. SC. Rcd. (no date).

Pp. 169-176. 18 Aug 1773: JOHN JOACKIM ZUBLY, Clerk, of Savannah GA to DANIEL JONES of New Windsor, SC for 200 pounds, sold 188 acres being in Beech Island in Township of New Windsor, fronting the Savannah River being part of land granted said ZUBLY. S/ J.J. ZUBLY, ANNE ZUBLY. Wit: DAVID ZUBLY, JOHN MYERS - 10 Aug 1774: before me DAVID ZUBLY, J.P. at my house in New Windsor.
SC Dept. of Archives, Columbia, SC: This is to certify that page 177 of this volume was misnumbered at the time of microfilming 10 Jan 1975. S/ Steve Gunter, Cameraman.

Pp. 178-179. 5 Nov 1758: PATRICK KELTY (KELLY), of Berkley Co. SC to PATRICK TROY of same place for 10 pounds, sold 200 acres on SW side of Saluda surveyed 9 May 1756 for said KELLEY adj. E the Saluda river, SW by JAMES ANDERSON, W vacant & N by ROBERT SMITH. S/ PATRT. KELTY, MARY (n) KELTY, his wife. Wit: THOS. BICKHAM, CHARLES (CR) ROBISON.
Memo: JAMS. FRANCES of Berkly Co., J.P. was present to witness signatures.

Pp. 180-184. 6 Nov 1758: PATRICK KELTY & MARY his wife, of Berkley Co. SC to PATRICK TROY for 75 pounds, sold 200 acres originally granted 19 Sep 1758 unto PATRICK KELTY, surveyed 9 May

154

1756 for said KELTY on SW side of Saludy river; E on the River; S by JAMES ANDERSON & N by ROBERT SMITH. S/ PATRICK KELTY, MARY(M) KELTY. Wit: THOMAS BECKHAM, CHARLES (CR) ROBINSON. Full consideration received 26 Feb 1759 by PATRICK KELTY. JAMES FRANCIS of Berkley Co., J.P. saw above sign.

Pp. 184-193. 3 May 1790: WILLIAM PANTON of Great Brittain by EDWARD PENMAN, Merchant of Charleston & Lawful Attorney of said PANTON, to WILLIAM ANDERSON of Ninety Six Dist. SC for 120 pounds, sold 200 acres on SW side of Saluda River adj. E said River; S by lands surveyed JAMES ANDERSON; N by JAMES SMITH. S/ WM. PANTON. Wit: CHARLES J. COLCOCK, HENRY WM. DE SAUSSURE. Extract of a letter from WILLIAM PANTON, Esq., to EDWARD PENMAN, Esq.
Dear Sir - Mr. McGILLICRAY is now on his way to meet the Commissioners of Congress. I expect (and with some degree of confidence), that peace will take place betwixt his Nation and the Georgians in which case I shall have frequent opportunities to write you by that rout and as soon as I can lay my hands on a proper form I shall forward to you a power of attorney for the sale of my lands in Carolina. In the meantime you may be looking out for purchases and any bargain you make in my Behalf I will readily confirm. believe to be your much Obliged & Obedient Servt. S/ WM. PANTON, Pensacola, 24 August 1789.
1 Apr 1791: D. MAZYICK Asst Sec. certifies the Extract is a true copy of original letter recorded in Book Y, p. 16-161 for Miscellanious Deeds.
Abbeville Co. SC, 5 May 1790: sworn by oath of HENRY WM. DE SAUSSURE before WM. MOORE, J.P. Rcd. (no date).

Pp. 193-198. 19 Aug 1790: ISHAM LANGLEY Planter of Orangeburg Dist. SC to MICHAEL SEE for 2 pounds, sold 150 acres being part of two grants of land to said LANGLEY; (1) granted 5 May 1773 &; (2) granted 1 Oct 1789 being on Cloud creek of Little Saluda River. S/ ISAM (X) LANGLEY, ELIZTH. (X) (also ⌐⌐ᵢ) LANGLEY, his wife. Wit: WILLIAM WRIGHT, ANNE HILL, GEORGE (I) HILL, who swore by oath in Lexington Co. SC 23 Oct 1790 before THOMAS FAIRCHILD, J.P. Rcd. (no date).

Pp. 199-203. 6 May 1791: Mortgage: JOHN PURVES to JOHN EWING CALHOUN (date blank) - JOHN PURVES gave his bond to ANDREW LORD & GEORGE LORD of Charleston 1100 pounds...Whereas JOHN PURVES is bound to MARTIN CAMPBELL & McCARTON CAMPBELL then Executors & by his bond of 23 Feb 1771 in penal sum of 1400 pounds with condition of payment of 700 pounds...& one other bond of 18 May 1772 for 4111 11/12 pounds, condition for payment of 2055 15/9...Whereas one bond of 18 May 1783 Condition of payment of 258 pounds & Whereas for better securing of payment do sell & deliver to JOHN EWING CALHOUN & JOHN LEWIS GERVIS, Esq., Trustees to & for WILLIAM ANCRUM & GEORGE ANCRUM, Executors of LW&T GEORGE LORD who was surviving co partner of ANDREW LORD & GEORGE LORD & McCARTAN CAMPBELL for himself & as surviving co partner of McCARTAN CAMPBELL & son...the following negroes slaves to wit: TOM & MOSES, fellows; FRANK, MARCH, & PETER, Boys; LUCY & PAT, wenches. S/ JOHN PURVES. Wit: THOMAS LEE LEVINGSTON, who swore by oath 6 May 1791 before WILLIAM ANDERSON, J.P. Rcd. (no date).

Pp. 204-214. 5 May 1791: Colonel JOHN PURVES to JOHN EWING CALHOUN & JOHN LEWIS GERVAIS, Esq., Trustee, for 5 shillings, & for better securing of payment of some bonds of pp. 199-203, sold

DEED BOOK 10:   1791-1794   EDGEFIELD COUNTY S.C.

2216 acres being of 8 tracts to & for WILLIAM ANCRUM & GEORGE ANCRUM, Executors of LW&T of GEORGE LORD, dec'd., who was the surviving copartner of ANDREW & GEORGE LORD also McCARTEN CAMPBELL for himself & as Survivor of MARTIN CAMPBELL & son. (1) 100 acres granted to THOMAS WILLIAMS, (first six on Turkey Creek;) (2) 150 acres granted to JOHN PERVES in 1770 (which adj. above tract); (3) 150 acres to BARKLEY JONES 17--; & adj. above grants to THOMAS WILLIAMS; (4) 100 acres to JOHN PURVIS joining the following tract of; (5) 500 acres to WM. COURSEY 178-; (6) 500 acres to WILLIAM COURSEY 1772 adj. last tract; (7) 216 acres being part of a grant to WILLIAM BROOKS 178- on Bedingfield Creek of Savannah River; (8) 500 acres on Bedingfield Creek originally granted JOHN DEAS, Esq. afterwards the property of Lord CHARLES GREENVILLE MONTAGUE & conveyed to said JOHN PURVES by the Commissioners of forfeited Estate. S/ JOHN PURVIS. Wit: THOMAS LEVINGSTON, THOMAS LEE, who swore by oath 6 May 1791 before WILLIAM ANDERSON, J.E.C. Rcd. (no date).

Pp. 214-219. 25 Mar 1791: EPHRAIM SIZEMORE to ROLLEY ROBUCK, both of Edgefield Co. SC for 15 pounds, sold 100 acres granted 7 Apr 1770 said SIZEMORE on Horse Creek of Savannah River in Craven Co. SC. S/ EPHRIAM (E) SIZEMORE. Wit: JOAB WOOTEN, PHEBE RANDOL, GEORGE (X) RANDOL, who swore by oath 12 Apr 1791 before RUSSELL WILSON, J.P. Rcd. (no date).

Pp. 219-225. 11 Apr 1791: HENRY WARE, Senr. of Wilks Co. GA & HENRY WARE, Junr., of Edgefield Co. SC, Planter, to DANIEL BARKSDALE, Planter of Edgefield Co. SC for 100 pounds, 100 acres being part of a tract originally granted 5 Apr 1765 to JOHN SCOTT & being where said BARKSDALE is now living on South side of Stephens Creek of Edgefield Co. SC. S/ HENRY WARE, Senr., HENRY WARE, Junr. Wit: HENRY WARE, Junr., WILLIAM LONGMIRE, ROBERT WARE, who swore by oath 11 Apr 1791 before AQUILA MILES, J.P. Rcd. (no date).

Pp. 225-229. 4 Dec 1787: CHARLES GOODWIN of SC to WILLIAM GUERRY of Edgefield Co. SC for 30 pounds, sold 1/4 acre known as Lot No. 2 in the Village of Campbelton. S/ CHAS. GOODWIN. Wit: BENJAMIN COOK, PETER CARNES, Esq., who swore by oath 11 Apr 1791 before AQUILA MILES, J.P. Rcd. (no date).

Pp. 229-235. 15 Oct 1783: JOHN DUGLESS, Yeom. of Collenton Co. SC of Cane Break branch of Little Saluda to WRIGHT NICHOLSON of Edgefield Co. SC for 57 pounds, sold 350 acres being part of 500 acres originally granted 20 Jan 1773 comprehending the plantation formerly called JOHN DUGLESS & adj. BARTLETT BLEDSOE being on Cane Break branch of Little Saluda River. S/ JOHN (‡) DUGLESS. Wit: WILLIAM (X) NICHOLSON, RACHEL (X) DUGLESS, BARTLETT BLEDSOE, who swore by oath 20 Aug 1784 before SOLOMON POPE, J.P. Rcd. (no date).

Pp. 235-238. 29 Nov 1790: JOHN HENDRICKS to JOHN & WILLIAM BARRS, both of Ninety Six Dist. SC for 45 pounds, sold 200 acres granted 3 Jul 1786 to JOSHUA DEEN on Glade Lick branch of the Great Saluda River, but now by its lawful owner the said JOHN HENDRICKS. S/ JOHN (X) HENDRICKS. Wit: FRANCIS (X) GILLERY, BARNETT (B) BARNES, who swore by oath 29 Nov 1790 before JAMES SPANN, J.P. Rcd. (no date).

Pp. 239-243. 9 Jul 1790: ABRAHAM RICHARDSON & WINEAFRED, his wife to JOSHUA THORN,Planter, both of Edgefield Co. SC for 50 pounds, sold 275 acres being part of 350 acres originally granted 6 Feb 1773 to FREDERICK GLAZIER & was conveyed to WM. BANKS 177- & afterwards part thereof by said BANKS to GEORGE ROGERS it being on the NE corner of said tract containing 75 acres, the remainder part of said tract was left to CHARLES BANKS by named WM. BANKS as his only heir; said tract being on Stephens Creek on a small creek Such water. S/ ABRAHAM RICHARDSON, WINEFRED (X) RICHARDSON. Wit: WILLIAM WILLIAMS, LEONARD NOBLES, WILLIAM COVINGTON, who swore by oath 14 Apr 1791 before (blank). Rcd. (no date).

Pp. 243-248. 2 Nov 1784: JOHN CRAWFORD of Ninety Six Dist SC to DRURY PACE of same place for 100 pounds, sold 500 acres granted 9 Sep 1774 to said CRAWFORD being on Catfish Creek of Savannah River. S/ JOHN CRAWFORD. Wit: CHARLES ASHLEY, HUGH MIDDLETON, J.P., THOMAS SNELSON, who swore by oath 14 Feb 1789 before HUGH MIDDLETON, J.P. Rcd. (no date).

Pp. 248-255. 17 Sep 1784: PHILEMON WATERS, Esq. of Ninety Six Dist. SC to JOHN DUGLESS of same place for 71 pounds, sold 200 acres being part of 400 acres originally granted 2 Jan 1754 to JACOB KELLY on Buffelow Creek in the fork between Saludy & Broad River adj. when surveyed, S by JOHN RAGNESS, Junr., other sides vacant & conveyed by L&R 11 Sep 1776. The 200 acres is to be taken off the upper part of the 400 acres (within deed has a blank for name of PHILEMON WATER's wife). S/ P. WATERS. Wit: GEORGE MASON, WILLIAM NICHOLSON, HENRY KING, who swore by oath 30 Sep 1784 before SOLOMON POPE, J.P. Rcd. (no date).

Pp. 255-260. 17 Apr 1789: NATHANIEL BULLOCK & MARY, his wife of Wilks Co. GA to JOHN BULLOCK of Ninety Six Dist. for 250 pounds, sold 250 acres (excepting & reserving a possession of 20 feet square for a Buring place (including the place where ROBT. DICKEY's wife's mother was buried), being part of 350 acres granted 13 May 1768 to ROBERT DICKEY on waters of Saluda River adj. MARKERNESS GOODE, HECTOR DICKEY & other sides vacant. S/ NATHANIEL BULLOCK, MARY BULLOCK. Wit: DAN BULLOCK, RICHARD BULLOCK, JAMES COLEMAN, who swore by oath 10 Mar 1790 before WILLIAM ANDERSON, J.P. Rcd. (no date).

Pp. 261-268. 3 Apr 1786: Bond: FIELDS PARDUE, Planter of Edgefield Co. SC to LAWSON & PRICE assigns of WILLIAM CUNNINGHAM, Merchant of Charleston SC obligation of Total 1425 pounds with Interest, condition being payment of bonds be made 4 Apr 1789 & for better securing of payment sold 330 acres being two several plantations being part of lands late the property of the Checkesaw Indians in Ninety Six Dist. now Edgefield Co. on east side of Savannah River known by numbers of 15 & 16. No. 15 has 174 acres & No. 16 has 156 acres bounded on the SW of Savannah River. S/ FIELDS PARDUE, JULIUS SMITH, Atto. for LAWSON & PRICE. Wit: MELINES C. LEAVENSWORTH, JAM THOMSON, who swore by oath 19 May 1786 before PETER FRENEAU, J.P. Rcd. (no date).

Pp. 268-274. 9 Mar 1769: MOSES YARBOROUGH & ANN, his wife of Beach Hill in the province to MACKERNESS GOODE of Ninety Six for 5 pounds, sold 250 acres surveyed by JOHN CALDWELL, D.S. 5 Feb 1768 & granted 15 Jul 1768 unto MOSES YARBOROUGH in Berkley Co. SC on Little River adj. NE by RICHARD ROBERTSON, SW by WILLIAM McLAUGHLIN; S by SAMUEL CALDWELL & SE by WILLIAM BAILEY. S/ MOSES YARBOROUGH, ANN (X) YARBOROUGH. Wit: GEORGE BURNS, WILLIAM MARTIN, SAMUEL RAMSEY, who swore by oath 26 Aug 1769 before JOHN SAVAGE, J.P. of Colleton Co. SC.

DEED BOOK 10: 1791-1794 EDGEFIELD COUNTY S.C.

Pp. 274-279. 10 Apr 1789: ABSOLUM TILLEY to ROLLEY ROBUCK, both of Edgefield Co. SC for 60 pounds, sold 351 acres being part of 451 acres certified 7 Aug 1786 & granted 1 Jan 1787 adj. THOMAS RODE's land, new survaid land & vacant land. S/ ABSOLOM TILLEY. Wit: ISAAC HOPKINS, ZELPHA KIRKLAND, ISAAC KIRKLAND, who swore by oath 25 Dec 1790 before HUGH MIDDLETON, J.P. Rcd. (no date).

Pp. 279-285. 23 Apr 1790: THOMAS KEELING SMITH & ELENOR his wife, of Ninety Six Dist. SC to ROBERT McCOMBS for 90 pounds, sold 137 acres being part of 450 acres originally granted ROGER McKINNEY Senr, dec'd, & then land fell to ROGER McKINNEY, Junr, dec'd, & said ROGER McKINNEY Junr did transfer said 450 acres to TIMOTHEY McKINNEY who conveyed to THOMAS KEELING SMITH 300 acres of the 450 acres. Said land being on Ninety Six Creek adj. SW by Governour BEE's land; NW by HECTOR DICKY; NE by BEATY; SE & NE by PENDERGRASS; & E by ROGER McKINNEY. S/ KEELING SMITH, ELENOR SMITH. Wit: JOSEPH BENTON, D. CUNNINGHAM, DAVIS MOORE, who swore by oath 23 Apr 1790 before WILLIAM MOORE J.P. of Abbeville Co. Rcd. (no date).

Pp. 285-289. MICHAEL BUCKHALTER to PENIX HOWLET, both of Edgefield Co. SC for 50 pounds, sold 100 acres originally granted 24 Jan 1761 to CHATHARINE HOFFMANNER in Granville Co. on both sides of Hornes Creek of Stevens Creek adj. NE by FREDERICK DUBBER & vacant lands. Said land conveyed by CATHERINE HOFFMANNER to JOHN CONRAD GALLMAN by L&R. S/ MICHAEL (MB) BUCKHALTER. Wit: DRURY MURPHEY, JOHN BUCKHALTER, ROBERT LANG, who swore by oath 11 Sep 1789 before AQUILA MILES, J.P. Rcd. (no date).

Pp. 289-294. 1 Apr 1791: RICHARD JOHNSON, Junr. & MARY his wife, to REUBEN ROBERTS, both of Edgefield Co. SC for 25 pounds, sold 160 acres surveyed 12 Jan 1787 & granted 7 Apr 1788, being on Turkey Creek. S/ RICHD. JOHNSON, MARY JOHNSON. Wit: JERRY HATCHER, JOHN JOHNSON, JAMES (E) BARRINGTON, who swore by oath 12 Apr 1791 before RUSSELL WILSON, J.P. Rcd. (no date).

Pp. 294-300. 27 Feb 1775: JOHN ADAMS & SALLY his wife to JAMES ADAMS, both of Ninety Six Dist SC for 250 pounds, sold 100 acres, being part of 200 acres originally granted 5 Oct 1763 to LEWIS POWELL on a branch of Cuffee Town Creek of Stevens Creek. Lewis Powell & SARAH his wife, conveyed to DANIEL SULLIVAN by L&R 26 & 27 May 1767 & said SULLIVAN & ANN, his wife conveyed to JOHN ADAMS by L&R 30 & 31 Dec 1773. S/ JOHN ADAMS, SALLY (X) ADAMS. Wit: SAMUEL STALNAKER, ROBERT BRYAN, who swore by oath 28 Feb 1775 before BENJAMIN TUTT, J.P. Rcd. (no date).

Pp. 301-306. 4 Jun 1790: ZACHARIAH MARTIN, Planter to ANN HILL, both of Ninety Six Dist. SC for 2 pounds, sold 50 acres being part of a tract granted 5 Sep 1787 to PHILOMON WATERS & conveyed 23 & 24 Aug 1788 to THOMAS SNODIN who conveyed to ZACHARIAH MARTIN. S/ ZACHARIAH MARTIN, ELIZTH. (X) MARTIN, his wife. Wit: DANIEL LANGSDON, SION MITCHELL, WILLIAM PRESCOTT, who swore by oath in Lexington Co. SC 23 Oct 1790 before THOMAS FAIRCHILD, J.P. Rcd. (no date).

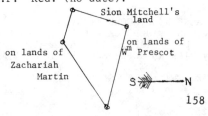

Sion Mitchell's land

on lands of Zachariah Martin

on lands of Wm Prescot

S — N

I have ameasured from ZACHARIAH MARTIN to ANN HILL 38 acres (sic). WM. WRIGHT, D.S.

158

Pp. 307-310. 15 Jan 1788: CHARLES GOODWIN, Esq. of SC to EDWARD CHURCH of Edgefield Co. SC for 20 pounds, sold 1/4 acre, Town Lot No. 6 in Campbellton. S/ CHAS GOODWIN. Wit: R.G. HARPER, JOHN HAMMOND.
14 Feb 1791: EDWARD CHURCH to CHARLES GOODWIN for 40 pounds, sold the within mentioned lot. S/ EDWD. CHURCH. Wit: LEROY HAMMOND.
14 Feb 1791: LEROY HAMMOND, Justice of SC gave oath that he did see the memorandum or reconveyance on the back the deed before ERO WHITFIELD, J.P. Rcd. (no date).

Pp. 310-313. 17 Sep 1790: MORRIS CALLYHAM to WILLIAM PRICHARD for 10 pounds, sold 150 acres being part 250 acres granted 5 Sep 1785 to JOHN RUTLEDGE, Esq. & conveyed 9 May 1788 by JOHN PURVES to MORRIS CALLYHAM, being on Crooked run of Turkey Creek of Savannah River. S/ MORRIS (M) CALLYHAM. Wit: JAMES COURSEY, CALL COLLINS, who swore by oath 18 Sep 1790 before JOHN PURVIS, J.P. Rcd. (no date).

Pp. 313-315. 24 Jul 1790: SUSANNAH COODY, Relict of LEWIS COODY, dec'd. of Edgefield Co. SC to FLOODE MITCHEL of same place for 30 pounds, sold 77 2/3 acres being her right of dowry of 233 1/3 acres being on Walnut Branch to be laid out agreeable to the award of the arbutrators LEWIS TILMAN & GEORGE MARTIN which award can be found on record in Clerk's office of Cambridge Court. Said 77 2/3 acres being under lease at this time to Mr MORRIS PARDUE for a certain term & said FLOODE MITCHELL shall be entitled to the benefit of said leased land from the beginning of the year 1791. S/ SUSANNAH (X) COODY. Wit: WILLIAM WASH, ADAM PARDUE, LEWIS TILMAN, who swore by oath 12 Apr 1791 before JOSEPH HIGHTOWER, J.P. Rcd. (no date).

Pp. 315-317. 24 Dec 1790: WILLIAM YARBOROUGH Planter, of Fairfield SC to JOHN BURRUS, Planter of Edgefield Co. SC (in his actual possession now), for 50 pounds, sold 200 acres originally granted 15 May 1772 & by the decease of MOSES YARBOROUGH descended to above WILLIAM YARBOROUGH, son & heir of said MOSES YARBOROUGH. S/ WILLIAM YARBOROUGH. Wit: WM. COURSEY, ALLEN (X) COURSEY, HENRY KEY, who swore by oath 12 Mar 1791 before WILLIAM ANDERSON, J.P. Rcd. (no date).

Pp. 318-322. 14 Jul 1788: JESSE ROUNDTREE to JOHN GLOVER, both of Ninety Six Dist SC for 500 pounds, sold 730 acres granted 19 Oct 1784 said ROUNDTREE being on both sides of Little Horse creek of Savannah River. S/ JESSE ROUNDTREE. Wit: JACOB SMITH, HENRY WARE, JOHN HATCHER, who swore by oath 15 Jul 1788 before BENJ. TUTT, J.P. Rcd. (no date).

Pp. 322-323. 12 Jul 1788: Bill of Sale: JESSE ROUNDTREE to JOHN GLOVER, both of Edgefield Co. SC for 800 pounds, sold the following negroes: wench TILLIS about 30 yrs. old; wench ISABEL about 25 yrs.; wench DOLL, about 35 yrs.; wench CLOAEY about 25; fellow, BEN about 30 yrs.; fellow JESSEY about 20 yrs.; fellow, ISAAC about 17 yrs.; boy, JACOB about - yrs.; girl, SUE about ?9 yrs.; girl, CREASE; girl, LUSE; & boy, ARRE. S/ JESSE ROUNTREE. Wit: JOHN HATCHER, BETSEY (also ELIZABETH) MEALOR, who swore by oath 26 Apr 1791 before JOSEPH HIGHTOWER, J.P. Rcd. (no date).

Pp. 323-325. 21 Dec 1790: JOHN LOGAN, Esq., of Collington Co. SC, Executor to his father's JOHN LOGAN, Senr., Estate, to JOHN

DEED BOOK 10: 1791-1794 EDGEFIELD COUNTY S.C.

THURMOND of Edgefield Co. SC for 105 pounds, sold 300 acres being part of 2 tracts; (1) 100 acres granted SAMUEL HARRIS; (2) 200 acres granted JOHN LOGAN on Gunnels Creek of Stephen Creek adj. LEVY HARRIS, SAMUEL HARRIS & CHAMPNESS TERRY. S/ JNO. LOGAN. Wit: THOS. SWINDEN, PHILLIP THURMOND, who swore by oath 11 Apr 1791 before AQUILA MILES, J.P. Rcd. (no date).

P. 325. 24 Feb 1791: Bill of Sale: ANDREW HARKNESS of Town of Campbeltown, to JAMES McQUEEN, one house & Lott in said Town now occupied by HAMMOND & WHITFIELD. Me having received the Value thereof if not paid on or before my return in the space of two months & pay Mr McQUEEN his account against me. He is to make whatever use he pleases of said house & Lot & be in full possession of same. S/ ANDW. HAKNESS. Wit: HENRY GREER, who swore by oath 13 Apr 1791 before HUGH MIDDLETON, J.P. Rcd. (no date).

P. 326. 12 Apr 1791: Bill of Sale: THOMAS H. HOWLE to JAMES McQUEEN for 25 pounds already paid, sell 1 negroe boy. S/ THOS. H. HOWLE. Wit: PETER CHASTAIN, who swore by oath 27 May 1791 before HUGH MIDDLETON, J.P. Rcd. (no date).

Pp. 326-327. 12 Jan 1791: Bill of Sale: JOEL CHANDLER to ISAAC FOREMAN, both of Ninety Six Dist. for 135 pounds, sold 5 negroes Viz: one wench SILVA; 1 girl, MARYANN; one girl named CATE; one boy POMPEY & 1 boy named HARNEY. S/ JOEL CHANDLER. Wit: ARTHUR ROBERTS, JOHN SIMKINS, who swore by oath 9 May 1791 before ARTHUR SIMKINS, J.E.C. Rcd. (no date).

Pp. 327-331. 2 Jan 1791: CHARLES RHODES & ISABELLA, his wife to WILLIAM COVINGTON, both of Edgefield Co. SC for 20 pounds, sold 188 acres granted 1 Jan 1787 said RHODES adj. SE by JOHN PURVES, Esq.; SW by JAMES MARTIN & Colo LEROY HAMMOND, Esq.; NW vacant; & NE by DANIEL GILL & SIMON MARTIN, being on waters of Savannah River. S/ CHARLES RHODES, ISABELLA (X) RHODES. Wit: ABRAHAM PEARCE, SIMON MARTIN, WILLIAM WILLIAMS, who swore by oath 9 May 1791 before JOSEPH HIGHTOWER, J.P. Rcd. (no date).

Pp. 331-335. 9 Feb 1791: WILLIAM RHODES & FRANCES, his wife to WILLIAM COVINGTON, both of Edgefield Co. SC for 20 pounds, sold 112 acres granted 5 Feb 1787 said RHODES adj. NE by REUBIN FRAZER, DANIEL GILL & CHARLES RHODES; SW & NW by LEROY HAMMOND, Esq., being on waters of Savannah River. S/ WM. RHODES, FRANCES (X) RHODES. Wit: ADAM PARDUE, WILLIAM WILLIAMS, who swore by oath 9 May 1791 before JOSEPH HIGHTOWER, J.P. Rcd. (no date).

Pp. 335-341. 5 Nov 1791: THOMAS WEST of Berkley Co. SC to WILLIAM BORROUM of Edgefield Co. SC for 130 pounds, sold 225 acres being part of 450 acres originally granted 13 Oct 1772 to THOMAS SHILES & conveyed 14 Apr 1773 being on South side of Saluda River on Little Saluda River & Indian Creek. Said tract of 450 acres was equally devided between said THOMAS WEST & NATHAN MELTON. S/ THOMAS (X) WEST. Wit: WILLIAM DOZER, HENRY KING, who swore by oath 22 Jan 1791 before RUSSELL WILSON, J.P. Rcd. (no date).

Pp. 341-342. 19 Feb 1791: To ARTHUR SIMKINS, Esq., appointed Judge of Court of Edgefield - Given under the seal of the state by Governour CHARLES PINCKNEY. S/ CHARLES PINCKNEY. Rcd. (no date).

DEED BOOK 10: 1791-1794 EDGEFIELD COUNTY S.C.

Pp. 342-343. 19 Feb 1791: To JOHN PURVES, Esq. - Appointed to a Judge of County Court of Edgefield. Given under the seal of the state by Governor CHARLES PINCKNEY Commander in Chief in & over the said state at Columbia. S/ CHARLES PINCKNEY. Secretary's office. Certified by PETER FRENEAU, Secretary.

Pp. 343-344. 19 Feb 1791: To WILLIAM ANDERSON, Esq. - Appointed to be a Judge of County Court of Edgefield. Given under the Seal of this State by CHARLES PINCKNEY our Governor over said state at Columbia. S/ CHARLES PINCKNEY. Secretary's Office. Certified by PETER FRENEAU, Secretary.

Pp. 344-345. 9 May 1793: Deed of Gift: MOSES LUCAS for love & affection of my nephew, JAMES FORGESON, give my goods & chattels to wit: 153 acres where I now live another tract of 90 acres adj. the above land. To wit: 1 negroe man named ROBERT; a negroe woman named MILLY; 13 cattle; 1 horse; 1 mare; my notes & accounts due me. S/ MOSES (X) LUCAS. Wit: JOHN ANDERSON, JOHN STRINGER, who swore by oath 23 May 1793 before RD. TUTT, C.E.C. Rcd. 20 Jun 1793.

Pp. 345-346. 31 Jan 1794: Power of Attorney: JOSEPH BRADBERRY of Columbia Co. GA ordain my friend, GEORGE B. MOORE of Edgefield Co. SC - My attorney to recover, bring Suit or at his pleasure to omit written judgement obtained by JULIUS SCRUGS against ENOCK GRIGSBY in the County of Henry, VA for 200 pounds, also 200 pounds damage. S/ JOSEPH (X) BRADBERRY. Wit: WILLIAM SPENCER, CLAYBURN ROZAR, who swore by oath 4 Feb 1794 before RICHARD TUTT, J.P. Rcd. 4 Feb 1794.

Pp. 346-347. 31 Aug 1793: Bill of Sale: JULIUS DEEN to ENOCH GRIGSBY, both of Edgefield Co. SC, certain property to wit: 1 negroe man named TOM about 25 yrs.; 1 bay Gilden; 1 sorrel horse; 1 bay mare; 14 head of cattle; 2 feather beds & furniture; 2 iron pot; 1/2 dozen pewter plates, 1 dish, 2 basons which said property is pledged & mortgaged to said ENOCH GRIGSBY which will come due 25 Dec next...S/ JULIUS DEEN. Wit: R. GRIGSBY, SAMUEL MAYS, who swore by oath 10 Sep 1793 before RICHARD TUTT, J.P. Rcd. 10 Sep 1793.

P p. 347-348. 9 Dec 1793: Bill of Sale: AMBROUS RIPLEY to WILLIAM HARDEN for 50 pounds, sold one negro slave named CAIN. S/ AMBROUS RIPLEY. Wit: WILLIAM DUCKER, NATHAN WHITE. (the "t" was not crossed, gch).

Pp. 348-350. 11 Apr 1793: BARBAREY TUTT, Widow & Relict of BENJAMIN TUTT, Senr., dec'd., late of Edgefield Co. SC, Esq., to RICHARD TUTT, Senr., Planter of same place for 300 pounds... Whereas BENJAMIN TUTT in his lifetime & during his intermarrige with said BARBARA, was seized in Demesne of fee of several tracts of land totaling 5500 acres in Edgefield Co. SC & now in possession of THOMAS BACON, Esq.:
(1) 2871 acres in Edgefield Co. SC on Cuffee Town Creek of Stephens Creek of Savannah River adj. NE heirs of ANDREW WILLIAMSON; S by HUGH MIDDLETON & JOHN WALLAN; W by BENJAMIN TUTT;
(2) 2638 acres on Hard Labor creek of Stephens Creek adj. N by ABNER PERRIN; E by Majr. TUTT; W by Mrs Yeldin;
And every Compensation in lew of her dower except 4 tracts included in aforesaid 5500 acres:

161

DEED BOOK 10: 1791-1794 EDGEFIELD COUNTY S.C.

(1) 100 acres granted to a certain WILLIAMS & titles given to
JAMES TUTT;
(2) 250 acres granted ISAAC MITCHELL, titles given to SAMUEL
STALNAKER, from him to JAMES TUTT;
(3) 100 acres granted to SWELLING, titles to SAML. STALNAKER, from
him to JAMES TUTT;
(4) 547 acres granted JOHN CRAB, titles given to WILLIAM DAWSON.
S/ BARBARA (X) TUTT. Wit: RICHARD TUTT, Junr., GABRIEL TUTT, who
swore by oath 28 Jun 1794 before AQUILA MILES, J.P. Rcd. 28 Jun
1794.

Pp. 350-351. 7 Mar 1794: Mortgage: ENOCH GRIGSBY to SAMPSON POPE,
both of Ninety Six Dist. SC for 134 pounds, one negroe man named
ABRAHAM & his wife named ALLEY & their six children. S/ ENOCH
GRIGSBY. Wit: ASAEL ROBERTS, RUSSELL WILSON, Senr., who swore by
oath 11 Mar 1794 before NATHAL. ABNEY, J.P. Rcd. 12 Mar 1794.

Pp. 351-352. 31 Jan 1787: Bill of Sale: HENRY GREER & JUDITH, his
wife of Edgefield Co. SC to JOHN PURSEL for 60 pounds, sold a
certain negroe named JOE. S/ HENRY GREER, JUDITH (X) GREER. Wit:
ELIJAH LYON, THOMAS SWENDIN, JOHN G. COOKE, who swore by oath 8
July 1794 before JOSEPH HIGHTOWER, J.P. Rcd. 12 Jul 1794.
[Note: gch: THOS. CLARK. Can not determine if he signed deed or
was a witness. His name does not appear in the oath.]

Page 352-354. 2 Apr 1793: Deed of Gift: JOHN MOORE, hereunto
moving & for natural love & affection to my sons, GREEN MOORE, &
JAMES McMILLAN, all of Edgefield Co. SC, give 9 negroes to wit:
HANDY; MINGO; SAM; TUBB; PENNY; JACOB; BOB; PHEBE; & JENNY; 7
feather beds & furniture; 1 waggon; 6 horses; 28 cattle; 25
sheep; 45 hogs; 1 walnut desk and plantation tools together with
other household & kitchen furniture. S/ JOHN MOORE. Wit: WILLIAM
(X) DILLARD, JOHN (X) MORGAN, MARTIN MORGAN, who swore by oath 12
Apr 1793 before JULIUS NICHOLS, Junr., J.P. Rcd. 2 Sep 1793.

Pp. 354-356. 2 Apr 1793: Deed of Gift: JOHN MOORE of Edgefield
Co. SC here unto moving & for natural love & affection for my
son, GREEN MOORE & JAMES McMILLIAN, give 292 acres originally
granted to JOHN & ROBERT CUNNINGHAM & conveyed from them to said
JOHN MOORE being on Ninety Six Creek adj. SE by COLBARD ANDERSON;
SW by SAMUEL RAMSEY & all other sides vacent when surveyed. S/
JOHN MOORE. Wit: MARTIN MORGAN, WILLIAM (X) DILLARD, JOHN MORGAN.
Abbeville Co. SC: MARTIN MORGAN swore by oath 12 Apr 1793 before
JULIUS NICHOLS, Junr., J.P. Rcd. 2 Sep 1793.

Pp. 356-357. 8 Jun 1793: Deed of Gift: JOHN WOOTAN of Edgefield
Co. SC for love & affection I bear my daughter, PRISCILLA MOSELY,
give unto the heirs of her body all the female part with their
female increase of that stock of cattle now ranging at her
plantation. And to my daughter PRISCILLA MOSLEY & her husband
THOMAS MOSELEY, all the male cattle for their good love & trouble
with said cattle. As the heirs become of age or marry they are to
receive their share. JOAB WOOTAN to be Executor over said cattle
to see they are not defrauded of their rights given under my
hand. S/ JOHN WOOTAN. Wit: AGNES (‡) RICHARDSON, DARRICK
HOLSONBACK, JONATHAN (‡) RICHARDSON, who swore by oath 11 June
1793 before RICHARD TUTT, J.P. Rcd. 11 Jun 1793.

Pp. 357-358. 5 Sep 1793: Bill of Sale: THOMAS LAMAR of Horse

162

Creek of Edgefield Co. SC to SAMUEL MAYS, Sheriff of said county, for 100 pounds, three negroe boys to wit: CAROLINE a boy (sic), 15 yrs. of age; HANNAH, a wench 30 yrs. old & her child 6 months old. S/ THOS. LAMAR. Wit: WILEY POPE, SOLOMON POPE, who swore by oath 1 Jan 1794 before HENRY KING, J.P. Rcd. 4 Jan 1794.

Pp. 358-359. This deed marked through & appears in full in Deed Book 10, p. 362, gch.

P. 359. 22 Mar 1794: Affidavit: Personally appeared CHARITY & MARTHA FOREMAN before RICHARD TUTT, J.P. & said they heard THOMAS McLENDEN (say) that he would have nothing to say to the settling his wife's portion of her father's estate with ISAAC FOREMAN, Guardian to said McCLENDON's wife whose name was NANCY FOREMAN, a daughter to JACOB FOREMAN, dec'd. Deliver a negro girl to said NANCY McCLENDON in full her part of her father's Estate. S/ CHARITY (X) FOREMAN, MARTHA (X) FOREMAN.

Pp. 359-361. 22 Jan 1788: Bond: JAMES WILSON bound to ALEXANDER HALL for the sum of 500 pounds, & for better securing of payment sell the following tracts of land, 300 acres being part of two tracts; (1) 200 acres granted said WILSON &; (2) 100 acres granted to JANE WILSON the said JAMES WILSON's daughter, being on Cuffey Town creek adj. Widow MILLER; HENRY LIGHTMAN; ANDREW MIMS & JAS. HARRISON. Also 42 acres now in the office & should said 42 acres come out of the office in said JAMES WILSON's name. Should payment be made in full this deed is null & void. S/ JAMES (X) WILSON. Wit: JAMES HARRISON, SAMUEL (X) CARTER, who swore by oath 24 May 1794 before J. HARRISON, J.P. Rcd. 2 Jun 1794.

P. 361. 10 Apr 1794: Bill of Sale: WILLIAM DICK to THOS. PARROT a negro slave woman named AGNESS. S/ WILLIAM DICK. Wit: JANE (X) DICK, SARAH (X) ACOMS, WILLIAM TOBLER, who swore by oath 14 Apr 1794 before AQUILA MILES, J.P. Rcd. 15 Apr 1794.

P. 362. 15 Oct 1791: JAMES BUTLER of Edgefield Co. SC to Methodist Meeting House of Methodist Episcopal Church of America, 2 acres now where the meeting house is erected on Chaves's creek. S/ JAMES BUTLER. Wit: JOHN (+) LOWE, WILLIAM JETER, Junr., who swore by oath 11 Mar 1794 before JOSEPH HIGHTOWER, J.P. Rcd. 12 Mar 1794.

Pp. 363-364. 19 Dec 1793: Bill of Sale: WM. LANIER Planter, formerly of Green Co. GA to KEVAN TAYLOR & MURREN of Campbellton, Edgefield Co. SC for 47 pounds, sold a negro man named MINGO, now in possession of FIELDS PARDUE with the condition that said WILLIAM LANIER pay in four months, the sum of 47 pounds this deed become null & void. S/ WILLIAM LANIER. Wit: FIELDS PARDUE, WILLIAM COVINGTON, who swore by oath 19 May 1794 before JOSEPH HIGHTOWER, J.P. Rcd. 2 Jun 1794.

Pp. 1-5. 15 Feb 1794: ALEXANDER HANNAH to ROBERT LAMAR, both of
Edgefield Co. SC for 130 pounds, sold 280 acres granted 7 Feb
1791 adj. CRANEMUS ZINN; MEYERS & ADAM HILES. S/ ALEXANDER (ᴎ)
HANNAH. Wit: JAMES (X) MALONE, PHILIP LAMAR, who swore by oath 6
Jun 1794 before JOSEPH HIGHTOWER, J.P. Rcd. 10 Jun 1794.

Pp. 5-11. 12 Nov 1772: JAMES HARRIS of Granville Co. SC to JOHN
LUCAS (LUKIS) of same place for 550 pounds, sold 200 acres being
between Savannah & Saludy River on waters of the Savannah adj. W
by LAWRENCE RAMBO, other sides vacant. S/ JAMES (H) HARRIS,
ELIZABETH HARRIS, his wife. Wit: EDWARD (X) MORRIS, JOHN HERNDON,
who swore by oath 17 Nov 1772 before PATRICK CUNNINGHAM, Justice
for Colleton Co. Rcd. 10 Jun 1794.

Pp. 11-14. 23 Jan 1793: Power of Attorney: THOMAS SUMERLIN of the
Creek Nation, Yeoman, here unto moving...appoint power of
attorney to my friend JOHN WELDON of Fairfield County, Yeoman, to
sell two tracts of land. S/ THOMAS (X) SUMERLIN. Executed before
ALEXANDER McGILLWRAY of Creek Nation.
27 May 1794: before JOSEPH HIGHTOWER, J.P. appeared BENJAMIN
DERANT who duly swore that the said DERANT now lives on the
Allabama River when at home near the intersection of Talapoocy &
Coosey Rivers in the Creek Indian Nation that about one year ago
he heard THOMAS SUMMERALL otherwise called THOMAS SUMMERLIN said
he lived heretofore on Horns Creek in Ninety Six Dist. & that he
had employed JOHN WELDON of Fairfield Co. in Camden Dist. SC to
sell lands belonging to said SUMMERALL which lay on Horns in
Ninety Six Dist. He further states that he married a sister of
ALEXANDER McGELVERY who appears as a Subscribing witness to the
deed & he is acquainted with the handwriting of said ALEXANDER
McGILVERY, Federal Brigadier General of the Creek Nation & the
signature is that of said McGILVERY & he further sayeth that the
said ALEXANDER McGILVERY is dead. S/ BENJ. DERANT.
10 Jun 1794: before JOSEPH HIGHTOWER, J.P. appeared JOHN WELDON
of Fairfield Co. SC & made oath concerning the power of attorney
given him...Rcd. 10 Jun 1794.

Pp. 14-21. 22 May 1794: JOHN WELDON, Yeoman of Fairfield Co. SC,
Camden Dist. SC, attorney of THOMAS SUMMERLIN, Hunter, of the
Allabama River in the Creek Nation in State of Georgia, to JOHN
RAINFORD, Planter of Edgefield Co. SC for 40 pounds, is & shall
be discharged by & with one gilding worth 35 pounds & one rifle
worth 5 pounds, sold 100 acres liable to the right of dower of AN
SUMMERALL, Widow of JACOB SUMMERALL, dec'd., being on Horns Creek
& originally granted 3 Nov 1770 unto JACOB SUMMERALL, Senr.,
dec'd., & sold by said JACOB SUMMERALL, Senr. to his son, THOMAS
SUMMERALL. S/ JOHN WELDON. Wit: RICHARD WITHINGTON, JOHN HALL,
who swore by oath 28 May 1794 before JOSEPH HIGHTOWER. Rcd. 10 Jun
1794.

Pp. 21-24. 23 May 1792: JULIUS NICHOLS, Junr. of Cambridge SC to
GARLAND GOODE of Edgefield Co. SC for 31 pounds, 140 acres adj.
lands of said GOODE. S/ JULIUS NICHOLS. Wit: JOSEPH BICKLEY,
WILLIAM HAGOOD, GABRIEL SMITHERS, who swore by oath 3 Jun 1793
before JOHN MOORE, J.P.

Pp. 24-28. 3 Jun 1794: SAMUEL GOODE to GARLAND GOODE, both of
Edgefield Co. SC for 5 pounds, sold 33 acres adj. GARLAND GOODE's
land. S/ SAMUEL GOODE. Wit: THOMAS EDWARDS, JOHN GOODE, PAUL

DEED BOOK 11: 1794-1795 EDGEFIELD COUNTY S.C.

HOLLAWAY, who swore by oath 5 Jun 1794 before JOHN MOORE, J.P. Rcd. 10 Jun 1794.

Pp. 28-30. 13 Aug 1793: MACKERNESS GOODE to GARLAND GOODE, both of Edgefield Co. SC for love & affection, gives 363 acres on Ninety Six Creek on South side of Saluda River. S/ MACKERNESS (MC) GOODE. Wit: JOHN HAMILTON, LEWIS MATHEWS, PAUL HOLLOWAY, who swore by oath 5 Jun 1794 before JOHN MOORE, J.P. Rcd. 10 Jun 1794.

Pp. 30-32. Cambridge - 13 Aug 1792: Bill of Sale: JOSEPH SANDERS, Junr., WILLIAM SANDERS, ELIZABETH SANDERS & GABRIEL SMITHERS of Abbeville Co. SC to BENJAMIN GLOVER for 55 pounds, sold a negro woman slave named PATTY. S/ JOSEPH SANDERS, WILLIAM SANDERS, ELIZABETH (I) SANDERS, GABRIEL SMITHERS. Wit: WILLIAM NIBBS, PATRICK MECKIE, J. SMITHERS.
Memo - 13 Nov 1793: I certify that I bought the within named slave woman (PATTY) from BENJAMIN GLOVER upon condition said BENJ. GLOVER. Do warrant & defend the title in the premeses against all persons except from WILLIAM SANDERS - ADAM SANDERS. S/ GARLAND GOODE. Wit: JAMES LESLIE, JOHN BURNS, who swore by oath 5 Jun 1794 before JOHN MOORE, J.P. Rcd. 10 Jun 1794.

Pp. 32-38. 8 Nov 1793: THOMAS HAGINS to WILLIAM ROBINSON, both of Edgefield Co. SC for 20 pounds, sold 50 acres granted 3 Apr 1786 said HAGINS on branches of Cedar Creek adj. N by JOHN CHANEY; W & S by DRURY MIMS & E by said HAGIN. S/ THOS. HAGIN. Wit: JOHN ROBERTSON, WILLIAM HAGIN, who swore by oath 16 Jun 1794 before RICHARD TUTT, J.P. Rcd. 16 Jun 1794.

Pp. 38-43. 18 Oct 1793: HENRY GEDDES & ELIZABETH his wife to WILLIAM BUTLER, Esq. for 40 pounds, sold 320 acres In the name of CHARLES ATKINS on Beaver Dam Creek of Little Saluda River known in the general plat of Confiscated Estates No. 7 & sold by the Commissioners to said GEDDIS adj. lands No. 6 of CHARLES ATKINS & land formerly the property of CHARLES ATKINS & also CORNELIOUS ROWE & EDWARD COWES. S/ HENRY GEDDIS, ELIZABETH (X) GEDDIS. Wit: DAVIS MOORE, JOHN HERRON, JOHN GEDDIS, BRITON MIMS, who swore by oath 27 Jun 1794 before RICHARD TUTT, J.P. Rcd. 27 Jun 1794.

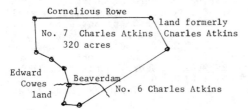

A true copy taken from the original in Com. F. Estate's office.

Surveyed 8 Jul 1783 by HARWOOD JONES, D.S.

Pp. 44-50. 20 Feb 1794: ZACHARIAH MARTIN & JANE, his wife to ROBERT O. WILLIAMS, both of Edgefield Co. SC for 100 pounds, sold 100 acres being part of 400 acres originally granted 5 May 1773 to JOHN DAY & sold 9 Oct 1783 to BRYANT GREEN who sold by Lease 11 Jan 1789 to DUDLEY CARTER who sold by L&R 6 & 7 Sep 1792 unto said MARTIN being on Chavous Creek adj. WILLIAM WILLIAMS, LEROY HAMMOND, JOHN LOWE, THOMAS BURNET, JOHN CLACKLER. S/ ZACHARIAH MARTIN, JANE (+) MARTIN. Wit: DAVID (X) MORGAN, THOMAS WILLIAMS, ANTHONY BUTLER, who swore by oath 24 Feb 1794 before JOSEPH HIGHTOWER, J.P. Rcd. 2 Jul 1794.

DEED BOOK 11: 1794-1795 EDGEFIELD COUNTY S.C.

Pp. 50-55. 30 May 1794: WILLIAM MURFEY of GA to JAMES BUTLER of Edgefield Co. SC for 100 pounds, sold 81 acres being part of 200 acres originally granted WILLIAM ANDERSON who sold to WILLIAM MURFEY on Chavous Creek adj. JAMES BUTLER, JOHN MORRIS; near the Ridge road & WILLIAM MURPHEY. S/ WM. MURFEY. Wit: ROBERT LANG, JAMES COBB, Junr., SETH HOWARD, who swore by oath 28 Jun 1794 before JOSEPH HIGHTOWER, J.P. Rcd. 7 Jul 1794.

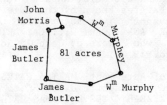

Plat: p. 55. Survey 31 May 1794, ROBERT LANG, D.S.

Pp. 56-60. 10 Nov 1777: MORRIS CALLINGHAM & Mary, his wife to SETH HOWARD, both of Granville Co. SC for 300 pounds, sold 150 acres originally granted to JOHN MITCHELL & sold to said CALLINGHAM on Buckhalters Creek near Stephens Creek of Savannah river. S/ MORRIS (M) CALLINGHAM, MARY (+) CALLINGHAM. Wit: DAVID HOLLIMAN, JOHN HAMMOND, DUDLEY CARTER, who swore by oath 19 Apr 1782 before WILL JONES, J.P. Rcd. 7 Jul 1794.

Pp. 61-66. 10 Jan 1777 - also 10 Nov 1777: MORRIS CALLINGHAM Planter, & MARY his wife to SETH HOWARD Planter, both of Ninety Six Dist. for 200 pounds, (also 360 pounds, the full consideration), 100 acres originally granted 23 Jan 1773 on Stephens Creek adj. MORRIS CALLINGHAM, THOMAS CARTER, FRANCIS SINQUEFIELD. S/ MORRIS (M) CALLINGHAM, MARY (+) CALLINGHAM. Wit: DAVID HOLLIMON, JOHN HAMMOND, DUDLEY CARTER, who swore by oath 19 Apr 1782 before WILLIAM JONES, J.P. Rcd. 7 Jul 1794.

Pp. 66-69. 3 Feb 1794: Mortgage: KATHARINE THWEATT & EDWARD THWEATT of Edgefield Co. SC to THOMAS WADSWORTH & WILLIAM TURPIN, Merchants, Obligation dated 3 Feb 1794 in sum of 102 pounds, condition of payment of 56 pounds & for better securing of payment sold one negro fellow named JIMMY about 45 yrs; a wench named SARAH, country born about 24 yrs. old; a wench SUKY, country born about 22 yrs; a fellow PETER, a girl JENNY about 3; a boy BILLY about 6 mo. S/ K. THWEATT, EDWARD THWEATT. Wit: DANIEL SYMMES.
Newberry Co. SC, 12 May 1794: DANIEL SYMMES swore by oath before ROBERT GILLMAN, J.P. Rcd. 7 Jul 1794.

Pp. 69-72. 1 Feb 1794: Mortgage: THOMAS WILLIAMS of Edgefield Co. SC to THOMAS WADSWORTH & WILLIAM TURPIN, Merchants of Newberry Co. SC, obligation dated 1 Jan 1794 penal sum 94 pounds condition of payment of 46 pounds, sold a negro girl named JENNY, about 10, a boy Cambridge, a girl LEAH, 13 yrs. S/ THOS. WILLIAMS. Wit: DANIEL SYMMES swore by oath 5 Apr 1794 in Newberry Co. SC before ROBERT GILLAM, J.P. Rcd. 7 Jul 1794.

Pp. 72-74. 15 Jan 1793: JAMES MARTIN & MILLY his wife to WILLIAM MATHEWS, Store keeper, both of Edgefield Co. SC for 80 pounds sold 230 acres originally granted JAMES MARTIN on Foxes Creek of

167

DEED BOOK 11: 1794-1795 EDGEFIELD COUNTY S.C.

Savannah River adj. MORGAN WARING, Colo. CHARLES HAMMOND. S/ JAMES MARTIN, MILLEY (+) MARTIN. Wit: SIMON MARTIN, LEROY HAMMOND, who swore by oath 6 May 1793 before JOSEPH HIGHTOWER, J.P. Rcd. 13 Jul 1794.

Pp. 74-79. 13 Nov 1788: THOMAS LAMAR & ANN his wife of Horse Creek to JAMES LAMAR of Horse Creek for 10 pounds, sold 167 acres being part of grant to THOMAS LAMAR & General ANDREW PICKENS by Commissioners for Confiscated Estates known by the name of the Chickesaw, on Horse Creek of Savannah River adj. THOMAS LAMAR & NATHANIEL BACON. S/ THOS. LAMAR, ANN LAMAR. Wit: CATHARINE (C) LAMAR, MELONES C. LEAVENWORTH, who swore by oath 15 Nov 1788 before WILLIAM ANDERSON, J.P. Rcd. 19 Jul 1794.

Pp. 79-81. 19 Apr 1794: Article of Agreement: MARTHA CATES, wife of THOMAS CATES, late deceased of Edgefield Co. SC to JOSEPH CATES, JOHN CATES, HULDA CATES, KEZEAH CATES & THOMAS CATES, for consideration of moveable property of THOMAS CATES dec'd., & dowry rights to tract of land whereon said THOMAS CATES dec'd. & further agree that MARTHA CATES will pay all debts of dec'd. for penal sum of 100 pounds. S/ MARTHA (+) CATES, JOSEPH (+) CATES, JOHN(+)CATES, KESIAH(+)CATES, THOMAS (+) CATES, HULDA (+) CATES. Wit: ROBERT CATES, ELENOR SILLIVEN, JAMES OGILVIE, who swore by oath 3 May 1794 before RUSSELL WILSON, J.P. Rcd. 23 Jul 1794.

P. 81. 13 Mar 1794: Bill of Sale: SAMUEL MAYS, Esq., Sheriff of Edgefield Co. SC to MARY PURVES for 50 pounds, sold a negro girl CLOE being mortgaged by the Colo. JOHN PURVES to JOHN LEWIS GEARVIS which said girl was sold under said mortgage to said MARY PURVIS. Wit: EUGENE BRENAN, who swore by oath 25 Jul 1794 before RICHARD TUTT, J.P. Rcd. 25 Jul 1794.

P. 82. (no date): Bill of Sale; SAMUEL MAYS, Esq., Sheriff of Edgefield Co. SC to CHARLES PURVES, Junr., for 50 pounds, sold a negro BILLY being mortgaged by late Colo. JOHN PURVES to JOHN LEWIS GERVAIS which negro was sold by mortgage to CHARLES PURVES. S/ S. MAYS, S.E.C. Wit: EUGENE BRANAN, who swore by oath 25 Jul 1794 before RICHARD TUTT, J.P. Rcd. 25 Jul 1794.

Pp. 82-86. 4 Sep 1782: ADAM PARDUE to THOMAS ADAMS of Ninety Six Dist. SC for 150 pounds, sold 100 acres being part of 200 acres granted 14 Aug 1772 to CHARLES STROTHER & bought by said PARDUE 12 & 13 Jul 1773 on Nobles Creek adj. land said ADAMS now lives on, & SHAW. S/ ADAM PARDUE, PHEBE (X) PARDUE. Wit: EDWARD MITCHEL, BENIJAH RAMBOW, LITTLEBERRY ADAMS, who swore by oath 28 Dec 1782 before AQUILA MILES, J.P. Rcd. 28 Jul 1794.

Pp. 86-93. 12 Jul 1773: CHARLES STROTHERS of Charles Town neck, SC to ADAM PARDUE of Bute Co. NC for 130 pounds, sold 200 acres on Nobles Creek Granville Co. SC adj. SPENCER & VANN. S/ CHARLES STROTHER. Wit: ROBERT MITCHELL, WILLIAM MOORE, who swore by oath 19 Nov 1776 before JAMES MOORE, J.P. Rcd. 23 Jul 1794.

Pp. 93-96. 13 Jun 1788: JAMES WEST Planter, to THOMAS ADAMS, both of Edgefield Co. SC for 7 pounds, sold 28 1/2 acres originally granted 7 Aug 1786 to JAMES WEST on Horns Creek of Savannah river adj. THOMAS ADAMS, BENJAMIN HARREY & widow FURNED. S/ JAMES (+·) WEST. Wit: ELIZABETH HARRY, ROBERT STARK, Junr., who swore by oath 12 Jan 1790 before AQUILA MILES, J.P. Rcd. 28 Jul 1794.

Pp. 96-104. 15 Nov 1793: Mortgage: ABRAHAM RICHARDSON to JOSEPH HIGHTOWER, Esq., both of Edgefield Co. SC By his bond dated 15 Nov instant in penal sum of 1000 pounds for payment of 500 pounds & for better securing of payment sell 890 acres, part of tract granted to ABSALEM NAPPER & the remainder granted to ABRAHAM RICHARDSON on Big Horse Creek being land where RICHARDSON's saw mill stands. Also the following negroe slaves BEN, WILL, LONDON, SAWNEY, BOB, CEZAR & PATT - Bond due 25 Dec 1789 & become null & void at payment. S/ ABRAHAM RICHARDSON, JOSEPH HIGHTOWER. Wit: DAVID (+) GENTRY, BENJAMIN HIGHTOWER, who swore by oath 16 Jan 1794 before RICHARD TUTT, J.P. Rcd. 16 Jan 1794.

Pp. 104-109. 19 Mar 1794: CHRISTIAN LIMBACKER & JANE ANNE, his wife to SHURLEY WHATLEY, both of Edgefield Co. SC for 50 pounds, sold 55 acres being part of that granted 4 Aug 1772 to ABRAHAM HOLSENBACK & sold 29 Jul 1775 to MATHEW DEVORE, Junr. who sold 6 Oct 1787 to said LIMBACKER on Dry Creek adj. the Five Notch road, a survey by MOSES KIRKLAND. S/ CHRISTIAN LIMBACKER, JANE ANNE (+) LIMBACKER. Wit: EDMUND PURSELL, WILLIS WHATLEY, who swore by oath 23 May 1794 before JOSEPH HIGHTOWER, J.P. Rcd. 2 Aug 1794.

Pp. 109-111. 6 Jun 1794: SAMUEL MAYS, Sheriff of Edgefield Co. to JOHN CATLET of Augusta GA: Whereas DRURY ADAMS obtained a Judgement at Edgefield Court against JOHN GARRET for 32 pounds & a writ of Fiere Facias dated 8 Apr 1793 attested by RICHARD TUTT was issued. Whereas SAMUEL MAYS, Sheriff, did sieze 3 Aug 1793, 351 acres on Stevens Creek where JOSEPH BARKSDALE formerly lived & sold said land at Public auction to highest bidder JOHN CATLET for 26 pounds. S/ S. MAYS, S.E.C. Wit: JONATHAN MOORE, BRITON MIMS, who swore by oath 6 Aug 1794 before RICHARD TUTT. Rcd. 6 Aug 1794.

Pp. 111-114. 8 Jan 1794: JOSHUA THORNE to CHARNAL H. THORNE, both of Edgefield Co. SC for 35 pounds, 97 acres on Sweet Water Creek originally granted FREDERICK GLAZER & sold to WILLIAM BANKS & by his heir, CHARLES BANKS sold to ABRAHAM RICHARDSON who sold to said THORNE. S/ JOSHUA THORNE. Wit: BENJAMIN HIGHTOWER, JOHN G. COOKE, who swore by oath 8 Feb 1794 before JOSEPH HIGHTOWER, J.P. Rcd. 7 Aug 1794.

P. 115. 3 Mar 1794: Bond: JAMES BAKER to GEORGE DELAUGHTER for $60.00, delivered a negro boy, JOHN. Now if said BAKER pays $60 to said DELAUGHTER by 25 Dec next said bond be null & void...S/ JAMES BAKER. Wit: JOHN HITT, JAMES RHODES, who swore by oath 23 Jul 1794 before HUGH MIDDLETON, J.P. Rcd. 3 Aug 1794.

Pp. 115-116. 29 Aug 1793: Bill of Sale: JOHN HITT of Edgefield Co. SC to GEORGE DELAUGHTER for 25 pounds, sold a negro girl, PAT. S/ JOHN HITT. Wit: JAMES DELAUGHTER, JOHN ANDERSON, who swore by oath 2 Jan 1794 before HUGH MIDDLETON, J.P. Rcd. 8 Aug 1794.

Pp. 116-120. 20 Mar 1794: JOHN HOLSONBACK to JAMES MOSLEY, both of Edgefield Co. SC for 40 pounds, sold 40 acres being part of 547 acres granted 2 Oct 1786 to JOHN HERNDON on Kine Fork of Horse creek adj. JAMES MOSELEY, THOMAS MOSELY, said HOLSONBACK. S/ JOHN HOLSONBAKE. Wit: JOAB WOOTAN, JONATHAN (I) RICHARDSON, who swore by oath 7 Aug 1794 before RICHARD TUTT, J.P. Rcd. 16 Aug 1794.

Pp. 121-124. 27 Jan 1793: JOSEPH DAY & MARY, his wife to JOHN COOK, both of Edgefield Co. SC for 100 pounds, sold 100 acres being part of 300 acres originally granted 5 Dec 1769 to PETER DAY, Senr., dec'd., & was willed to said JOSEPH DAY on Sweet water branch of Stephenes Creek. S/ JOSEPH (D) DAY, MARY (+) DAY. Wit: WILLIAM POND, RICHARD (+) JONES, who swore by oath 2 Mar 1793 before JOSEPH HIGHTOWER, J.P. Rcd. 21 Aug 1794.

P. 124. 1 Jun 1794: Deed of Gift: WILLIAM MURPHEY to MARY DINKINS, formerly called my wife, assign my wright of 50 acres & all line stock, except my horse, & household furniture. S/ WM. MURPHEY. Wit: JAMES BOOTH, BURET (X) JOHNSTON, MARY (M) GOM BRITON, SON- (her mark) BOOTH, SETH HOWARD, who swore by oath 25 Aug 1794 before RICHARD TUTT, J.P. Rcd. 21 Aug 1794.

Pp. 124-126. 7 Apr 1794: DRURY GLOVER to JACOB MILLER, both of Edgefield Co. SC for 50 pounds, sold 200 acres originally granted 1765 to HENRY RUPARD on Cuffey Town Creek at mouth of Beaver Dam Creek binding on two sides of said creek. S/ DRURY GLOVER. Wit: JOHN SLATER, WILLIAM ARNETT, JOHN GLOVER, who swore by oath 30 Aug 1794 before J. HARRISON, J.P. Rcd. 1 Sep 1794.

Pp. 126-131. 29 Jan 1794 - (also 13 Jan 1794): JOHN HOPKINS, heir at law to JOHN HOPKINS, dec'd., to SIMON BROOKS of Edgefield Co. SC for 50 pounds, sold 100 acres in Craven Co. when surveyed, but now Edgefield Co. originally granted 10 Jun 1775 to JOHN HOPKINS. On branch of Little Saluda called Simmons Lick Creek but now persimon lick creek adj. JAMES BROOKS, GEORGE ABNEY. S/ JOHN HOPKINS. Wit: WILLIAM HOPKINS, THOMAS HOPKINS. Richland Co. SC: WILLIAM HOPKINS swore by oath 30 Jan 1794 before JOHN HERONS, J.P. Rcd. 5 Sep 1794.

Pp. 131-136. 5 Sep 1794: BARTLEY MARTIN, Esq., Late Sheriff of Edgefield Co. SC to MARY SULLIVANT of Edgefield Co. SC for 40 pounds, sold 200 acres on Horns Creek adj. SAMUEL GARDNER, JOHN SWILLIVANT, AARON HERRING, JONATHAN LIMBACKER, JOHN PURSELL...Whereas THOMAS BRITMAN, absent Debtor of Edgefield Co. SC was seized of 200 acres & wheres JOHN HOWELL, the plaintiff in Edgefield Court Jul term, 1790 obtained a Judgment for 50 pounds to be levied against THOMAS BRITMAN & said MARTIN then sheriff did sell said land 20 Oct 1790 for 47 pounds to hightest bidder, MARY SULLIVANT. S/ BARTLEY MARTIN. Wit: JOSEPH TUCKER, who swore by oath 5 Sep 1794 before AQUILA MILES, J.P. Rcd. 6 Sep 1794. 11 Aug 1795:

Jonathan Limbacker

John Persell land agreed on by him & David Nelson

200 acres

Aron Herron

Samuel Gardner

John Sullivant

Resurvey made of land where Mrs. MARY SWILLIVANT now lives originally granted DAVID NELSON being part of 400 acres adj. SAMUEL GARDNER, JOHN SWILLIVANT, AARON HERRON, JONATHAN LIMBACKER, JOHN PERSEL. By ROBERT LANG, D.S.

Pp. 136-141. 17 Nov 1788: WILLIAM ENGLISH, Baker & SARAH his wife to LEWIS CLARK, both of Edgefield Co. SC for 63 pounds, sold 100 acres originally granted (bounty) 13 Apr 1769 to JOSEPH RISHTON who sold to WILLIAM ENGLISH 31 Dec 1776 being on Red Bank creek adj. Mrs JONES, AMOS RICHARDSON. S/ WILLIAM (X) ENGLISH, SALLY (X) ENGLISH. Wit: THOMAS SMEDLY, JOSEPH (D) THOMAS, HENRY KING, who swore by oath 6 Sep 1794 before RICHARD TUTT, J.P. Rcd. 6 Sep 1794.

Pp. 141-144. 13 Apr 1794: SAMUEL SAXON, Sheriff of Edgefield Co. SC to THOMAS BURNETT, last & hightest bidder for 54 pounds, sold 100 acres Whereas creditors of Lately in Court at Cambridge obtained a Judgement against LEROY HAMMOND, dec'd., & writ of Fieri Facias issued 13 Apr 1794. S/ S. SAXON, Sheriff of Ninety Six District. Wit: WILLIAM MATTHEWS, BARKLEY MARTIN. Rcd. 20 Sep 1794.

Pp. 144-146. 24 Aug 1791: FIELDING RENNOLDS & ELIZABETH, his wife to WILLIAM WASH, both of Edgefield Co. SC for 60 pounds, sold 100 acres being part of 750 acres granted LAWRENCE RAMBO, dec'd., who by LW&T gave to his son BENIJAH RAMBO who sold 100 acres 5 Apr 1787 to said RENNOLDS & his wife ELIZABETH. Said land on Dry creek of Horns Creek adj. BENJAMIN ADAMS, JOHN HOGG, WILLIAM JEATER, WILLIAM DOBY, JAMES HARGROVE, & FIELDING RUNNELS. S/ FIELDING REONNOLDS, ELIZABETH RUNNELS. Wit: LEANNA JONES, THOMAS JONES, who swore by oath 2 Sep 1791 before JOSEPH HIGHTOWER, J.P. Rcd. 27 Sep 1794.

Pp. 147-148. 20 May 1794: THOMAS LAMAR of Bellmount to PHILIP LAMAR, both of Edgefield Co. SC for 1000 pounds, sold 500 acres originally granted 1761 to THOMAS LAMAR, Sen., dec'd., on Savannah River adj. THOMAS SMITH...said tract free & clear of all former gifts, sales or conveyance from either me or my father. S/ THOS. LAMAR, B--- M. Wit: ZACHA. LAMAR, Senr., JOHN BUTLER, who swore by oath 2 Oct 1794 before JOHN CLARK, J.P. Rcd. 4 Sep 1794.

Pp. 148-151. 5 Jul 1794: CASPER NAIL, Junr., Planter to JOHN SAVAGE, Planter both of Edgefield Co. SC for 62 pounds, sold 125 acres, being part of original granted to BENJAMIN HARRIS late of GA & sold 21 Aug 1787 to said NAIL & recorded in Book D pp. 48-51, 27 Mar 1790, in New Windsor Township near Beech Island adj. WILLIAM EAVANS, originally granted JOHN RICHARDSON, CASPER NAIL, Junr., CASPER NAIL, Senr. S/ CASPER NAIL, Junr. Wit: WILLIAM EAVANS, WILLIAM SKINHOLSER, who swore by oath 5 Jul 1794 before JOHN CLARKE, J.P. Rcd. 10 Oct 1794.

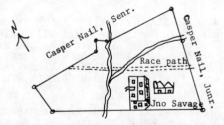

Plat: p. 150. 125 acres being 1/2 of land granted BENJAMIN HARRIS & sold to CASPER NAIL, Junr. Surveyed copied from original 14 Jul. WM. EVANS, D.S.

Pp. 151-152. 5 Jun 1794: Bill of Sale: ABRAHAM JONES to ANDREW PICKENS: Received in Augusta from ANDREW PICKENS, Esq. by the hand of JOSEPH HIGHTOWER A Judgement obtained by Maj. FIELDS PARDUE against the Adms. of WILLIAM BUGG, dec'd., in amount of 58 pounds with interest being full consideration for a negroe girl

DEED BOOK 11: 1794-1795 EDGEFIELD COUNTY S.C.

named FANNY now in possession of Maj. JONES (?JAMES) PEARRIE
which said girl FANNY do warrant to ANDREW PICKENS against all
lawful claims.. S/ ABRAM JONES, guardian for Heirs. Wit: JOSEPH
HIGHTOWER, who swore by oath 9 Oct 1794 before RICHARD TUTT, J.P.
Rcd. 10 Oct 1794.

Pp. 152-154. 3 Oct 1794: Bill of Sale: THOMAS ELLIS, Junr., to
MOODY BURT for 469 pounds, sold nine negroes to wit: BOB, SAMPSON,
JENNEY, VINEY, ANACAY, ELLICK, NEWORKEE, ISAAC, EDEY. Also waggon
& gear, 7 horses, 10 cows, stock of hogs, corn fodder & Tobacco.
Also plantation utensils, household & kitchen furniture. S/ T.
ELLIS, Junr. Wit: SHADRACK STOKES, EVAN STOKES, who swore by oath
9 Oct 1794 before JAMES HARRISON, J.P. Rcd. 10 Oct 1794.

Pp. 154-155. 3 Oct 1794: Bill of Sale: WILLIAM BLACKLEY of
Edgefield Co. SC to MOODY BURT for 460 pounds, sold 13 negroes to wit:
BEN, BIDDY, IRIS, PHILLIS, BETTY, JIMMEY, BOB, SCOTT, ORSON, TOM,
CYRUS, ANTHONY, & DOUGLASS. Also 5 horses, 14 head of cattle, 8
sheep, hogs, corn fodder & Tobacco. Also plantation utensil &
household & kitchen furniture. S/ WM. BLACKLEY. Wit: SHADRACK
STOKES, EVAN STOKES, who swore by oath 9 Oct 1794 before JAMES
HARRISON, J.P. Rcd. 10 Oct 1794.

Pp. 155-157. 3 Oct 1794: Bill of Sale: WILLIAM BLACKLEY of
Edgefield Co. SC to MOODY BURT for 54 pounds, a negro lad named
BEN which I left in Nottoway Co. VA 1791 in hands of THOMAS
JORDAN. S/ WM. BLACKLEY. Wit: SHADRACK STOKES, EVAN STOKES, who
swore by oath 9 Oct 1794 before JAMES HARRISON, J.P. Rcd. 10 Oct
1794.

Pp. 157-161. 4 Jul 1794: BRIANT GREEN to ENOS HOWARD, both of
Edgefield Co. SC for 50 pounds, sold 150 acres being part of 663
granted by JOHN CARTER to BRIANT GREEN 3 Jul 1794; adj. BRIANT
GREEN, JACOB FUDGE. S/ BRIANT (B) GREEN, PHEBE GREEN. Wit: REUBEN
HARLSON, EDWARD GREEN, who swore by oath 9 Jul 1794 before JOSEPH
HIGHTOWER, J.P. Rcd. 10 Oct 1794.

Pp. 161-162. 23 May 1794: ANN VALENTINE, a free negroe to JAMES
CARSON, both of Edgefield Co. SC, puts herself two full years &
her son ANDREW to the full age of 21 yrs. in service of said
JAMES CARSON...S/ ANN (X) VALENTINE, JAS. CARSON. Wit: NATHANIEL
ABNEY, Esq., J.P., who swore by oath 10 Oct 1794 before RICHARD
TUTT, J.P. Rcd. 10 Oct 1794.

Pp. 162-168. 29 Dec 1788: WILLIAM DEAN to WILLIAM ABNEY, both of
Edgefield Co. SC for 50 pounds, sold 360 acres originally granted
2 Oct 1786 WILLIAM DEAN on Persimmon Creek of Little Saluda River
adj. WILLIAM DEEN, GEORGE DEEN, ELISHA ABNEY, DENNITT ABNEY. S/
WILLIAM (D) DEEN. Wit: SARAH ABNEY, ELIZABETH MARY ANN ABNEY,
JOHN LOWE, who swore by oath 8 Oct 1794 before RUSSELL WILSON,
J.P. Rcd. 10 Oct 1794.

Pp. 168-173. 9 Sep 1794: MATTHEW WILLS to RICHARD COLEMAN, both
of Edgefield Co. SC for 50 pounds, sold 174 acres: (1) 74 acres
on Saluda River being part of 569 acres granted said WILLS 5 Dec
1785; (2) 100 acres near above land on Berrys creek of Saluda
River being part of 1000 acres originally granted WILLS 4 Sep
1786 adj. JOHN BERRY, JOHN ABNEY & MATTHEW WILLS. S/ MATTHEW
WILLS. Wit: ESAU BROOKS, MARY CARSON, JOHN HAVERD, who swore by
oath 13 Sep 1794 before NATHANIEL ABNEY, J.P. Rcd. 10 Oct 1794.

Pp. 173-174. 5 May 1794: For a priveledge "Bond": WILLIAM SPRAGINS to MATTHEW WILLS, both of Edgefield Co. SC give priveledge to make a Dam across my spring branch...S/ WM. SPRAGINS. Wit: SAMUEL SPRAGINS, JOHN ABNEY, JAMES CARSON, who swore by oath 9 Oct 1794 before NATHANIEL ABNEY, J.P. Rcd. 10 Oct 1794.

Pp. 174-180. 6 Sep 1794: WILLIAM SPRAGINS to MATTHEW WILLS, both of Edgefield Co. SC for 52 pounds, sold 162 acres being land of 3 tracts on South side of Saluda River; (1) 150 acres being part of 375 acres originally granted 5 Jun 1786 to said SPRAGINS adj. said WILLS; SPRAGINS, & JOHN GORMAN: (2) 10 acres being part of 250 acres originally granted PETER HUBER & sold by JOHN HUBER his son & heir to THOMAS CURTIS who sold to said SPRAGINS adj. the Rocky ford on Mills Creek below said WILLS mill; WM. MOORE; said WILLS; (3) 2 acres being part of above said 250 acre tract. S/ WILLIAM SPRAGINS. Wit: ESAU BROOKS, SARAH (X) WILLS, JACOB BROOKS, who swore by oath 7 Sep 1794 before NATHANIEL ABNEY, J.P. Rcd. 10 Oct 1794.

Pp. 180-185. 8 Feb 1792: WILLIAM SPRAGINS to MATTHEW WILLS, both of Edgefield Co. SC for (blank), 40 acres being part of 250 acres originally granted 24 Apr 1752 unto PETER HUBER & sold by his son & heir at law JOHN HUBER to THOMAS CURTIS who sold by L&R the last day of Aug & 1 Sep 1789 to said SPRAGINS. Said land on South side of Saluda River. S/ WILLIAM SPRAGINS. Wit: WILLIAM (W) CARTER, SARAH (X) CARSON, JAMES CARSON, who swore by oath 9 Oct 1794 before NATHANIEL ABNEY, J.P. Rcd. 10 Oct 1794.

Pp. 185-189. 28 Nov 1787: JACOB FUDGE, Junr to JACOB FUDGE, Senr., both of Edgefield Co. SC for 100 pounds, sold 640 acres originally granted 5 Jun 1786 said JACOB FUDGE, Junr. on both sides of Little Horse Creek of Savannah River. S/ JACOB FUDGE, Junr. Wit: CORNELIUS CARGILL, WILLIAM WATSON, Senr., who swore by oath 25 Aug 1792 before JOSEPH HIGHTOWER, J.P. Rcd. 11 Oct 1794.

Pp. 189-191. 8 Oct 1794: Deed of Gift: THOMAS REED to JAMES RUTHERFORD, both of Edgefield Co. SC for Love & affection for his son in law gives 100 acres, being part of 300 acres originally granted ANN DEEN & sold by her son GEORGE DEEN being her oldest son & heir at law to SAMUEL MAYS who sold to said REED. Said tract is where said JAMES RUTHERFORD now lives on Southside of Persimmon Lick Creek the generality of it lays waters of Big Creek of Little Saluda River adj. lands originally surveyed for GAVIN POU; JOHN BROOKS; JAMES BROOKS & said REED. S/ THOMAS REED. Wit: HENRY KING, FRANCIS WHITE, AVENILLAH (A) KING, who swore by oath 8 Oct 1794 before HENRY KING, J.P. Rcd. 11 Oct 1794.

Pp. 191-195. 24 May 1785: BENJAMIN TUTT to ANDREW CROWSER, both of Ninety Six Dist. SC for 50 pounds, sold 58 acres being on Cuffee Town Creek adj. PETER MAIL & said CROWSER. S/ BENJ. TUTT. Wit: RICHARD WORSHAM, JAMES TUTT, who swore by oath 11 Oct 1794 before RICHARD TUTT, Esq., J.P. Rcd. 11 Oct 1794.

Pp. 195-197. 25 Mar 1791: JAMES GAUDY, adm. (sic) of LW&T of ROBERT GOUEDY, Merchant late of Ninety Six Dist. SC, dec'd., to WILLIAM SHAW of Cambridge, attorney at Law, for 21 pounds, sold the remaining tract, whereon the said ROBERT GOUDY lived until his death - at a public Sale. S/ JAMES GOUEDY. Wit: STEPHEN

NORTHCUTT, JOHN McCONNEL - Abbeville Co. SC, Court 14 Sep 1793, swore by oath before JOHN BOWIE, C.C. Rcd. 13 Oct 1794.

Pp. 197-201. 2 Apr 1794: WILLIAM HART, Esq. Treasurer of SC residing in Charleston by Virture of an act passed by Legislature 19 Feb 1791, to WILLIAM SHAW, Esq. for 405 pounds, lease 1202 acres composed of several tracts; (1) 400 & 200 acres formerly belonging to BENJAMIN DARBIOUS; (2) 150 acres formerly Colonel JAMES MASON's; (3) 250 acres formerly HENRY PATRICK's partly in the fork & partly on both sides of road leading to Augusta & the road to Old Saluda Town & Ninety Six Creek & Hendleys Creek, late the property of ISAAC CROWTHERS, known by reference of Plat No. 240 filed in Office of Commissioners for "leaning the paper medium."
Release - 3 Apr 1794: Whereas 16 May 1786 ISAAC CROWTHERS borrowed 200 pounds by act passed 12 Oct 1785 from JOHN HUGER, THOMAS JONES, & JOHN POSTELL, Commissioners of the Loan Office & Mortgaged said land. Said CROWTHERS failed to make payment of interest due 1st Mar in present year & said land was advertized for sale agreeable to Direction of the Act...S/ WILLIAM HART. Wit: WM. SKRINE, JOHN HAMILTON, who swore by oath 29 Sep 1794 before JULIUS NICHOLS, J.P. Rcd. 13 Oct 1794.

Pp. 201-203. 3 Dec 1785: JOHN WEITZELL & ELINOR, his wife of the town of Ninety Six of Edgefield Co. SC to WILLIAM SHAW of Charleston for 108 pounds, sold 1 1/2 acres & other buildings in town of Ninety Six adj. lands formerly belonging to ROBERT GOUDY, dec'd., DAVID CUNNINGHAM's Lot no. 1 & hereby bargined premeses formerly belonging to said ROBERT GOUDY & sold by him to ROBERT WARING who mortgaged the same to WILLIAM MOORE, DAVIS MOORE & JULIUS NICHOLS who fore closed & sold 3 Jan 1780 to said WEITZELL. S/ JOHN WEITZEL, EALINER WEITZEL. Wit: ROBERT STARK, TIMOTHY McKINNEY. Acknowledged in open court 13 Apr 1786. Rcd. 13 Oct 1794.

Pp. 204-211. 9 Jun 1776: JACOB SUMMERALL Planter, & NANCY, his wife of Granville Co. SC to JESSE SUMMERALL, Planter of same place for 100 pounds, sold 400 acres originally granted 25 Apr 1765 to HENRY SUMMERALL, Senr., dec'd., father of said JACOB SUMMERALL, on Savannah River, Granville Co. adj. JOHN GRANT. S/ JACOB SUMMERALL, ANN (A) SUMMERALL. Wit: G.W. CLEMM, SANDERS (X) COLSON.
Orangeburg Dist. SC: Received date above written of JESSE SUMMERALL & SARAH his wife 700 pounds, being the full consideration. S/ JACOB SUMMERALL.
17 Feb 1785 Charleston Dist. SC: GEO. ROBERSON was called upon to prove the handwriting of GEO. WM. CLEMM as a witness to above L&R & said hand mark of SANDERS COLSON before J. LIGHTWOOD, J.P. Rcd. 13 Oct, 1794.

Pp. 211-218. 29 May 1784: JESSE SUMMERALL & SARAH his wife, late of Orangeburg Dist. SC to JOHN HAMPTON, Planter for 200 pounds, sold 400 acres, it being land granted 25 Apr 1765 HENRY SUMMERALL, Senr., dec'd., Father of JACOB SUMMERALL on Savannah river in Orangeburg Dist. adj. JOHN GRANT. Said tract was sold to said JESSE SUMMERALL 9 Jun 1776 by his brother JACOB SUMMERALL. S/ JESSE (X) SUMMERALL, SARAH (X) SUMMERALL. Wit: ALLEN ROBISON, JAMES MONTGOMERY, JOHN WILLIAMS.
Orangeburg Dist: JESSE SUMMERAL received the full consideration

of 200 pounds.
Charleston Dist. SC 13 Feb 1785: ALLEN ROBESON gave oath to above
before J. LIGHTWOOD, J.P. Rcd. 13 Oct 1794.

Pp. 219-221. 21 Feb 1794: Article of Agreement: JOHN HAMPTON of
Orangeburg Dist. SC to WILLIAM PRICE, Merchant of Charleston SC
in consideration of being exonerated of a debt originally Due
BANKS & FORSYTH by PETER PICKENS of VA & him the said JOHN
HAMPTON as surity & by them assigned to LAWSON & PRICE for 1215
pounds does agree to make titles within 3 months to 4000 acres in
Ninety Six Dist on Horse Creek being land granted said HAMPTON.
Also said HAMPTON does promise to relinquish title to 400 acres
at Stoney Point in Granville Co. on Savannah River which was
granted to HENRY SUMMERALL & is now mortgaged to the public by
said HAMPTON for 250 pounds paper medium. S/ WILLIAM PRICE, JOHN
HAMPTON. Wit: JULIUS SMITH, FRANCIS BREMAR, who swore by oath 24
Feb 1794 before JOHN SANDFORT DART, J.P. Rcd. 13 Oct 1794.

Pp. 221-223. 8 May 18th year of Republic: By Citizen EDANUS
BURKE, a Judge of Superior Court of SC to SPENCER MORGAN, SAMUEL
KENNER & JOHN ADAM SUMMER of Lexington Co. SC, Commissioned by
this instrument to examine MARGARET, the wife of JOHN HAMPTON, if
she be willing to renounce claim of dower of a 4000 acre tract in
Orangeburg Dist. SC on Savannah river sold by said HAMPTON to
WILLIAM PRICE of Charleston. Also one 400 acre tract in Ninety
Six Dist on Horse Creek...30 May the year written, MARGARET
HAMPTON renounced her dower of said land. S/ JOHN ADAM SUMER,
SPENCER MORGAN, SAMUEL KENNER. Rcd. 13 Oct 1794.

PP. 224-227. 5 May 1794: SAMUEL SAXON, Sheriff of Ninety Six
Dist. to WILLIAM PRICE of Charleston SC...Whereas FRANCIS BREMAR
lately in Court of Common Pleas in Orangeburg SC obtained a
Judgement against JOHN HAMPTON for 1800 pounds & a writ dated 10
Apr 1794 & said Sheriff did seize 4000 acres on Horse Creek in
Edgefield Co. SC originally granted JOHN HAMPTON 3 Apr 1786 & was
disposed 5 May 1794 at Public Auction to said WILLIAM PRICE for
102 pounds. S/ SAMUEL SAXON, Sherf. Ninety Six Dist. Wit: JAMES
SAXON, FRIDAY ARTHUR.
Orangeburg Dist. SC: FRIDAY ARTHUR swore by oath 30 May 1794
before JOHN ADAM SUMMER,J.P. Rcd. 13 Oct 1794.
Plat: pg. 226. 4000 acres
measured & laid out unto
JOHN HAMPTON 2 Nov 1785
by P. WATERS, D.S. A true
copy from Surveyors
Generals office
Charleston 19 Feb 1794.
S/ EPHRAIM MITCHELL, S.
GENL.

Pp. 227-229. 5 May 1794: SAMUEL SAXON, Sheriff of Ninety Six
Dist. to WILLIAM PRICE of Charleston SC...Whereas LAWSON PRICE &
Co. in Nov term 1793 Court of Common Pleas obtained an order for
the Sale of real Estate belonging to WILLIAM MOORE, dec'd.
(mortgaged to said LAWSON PRICE & Co.) for the credit of 12
months & in obedience to the order said SAXON did inter into 130
acre tract in Abbeville Co. SC adj. the Town of Cambridge known
in general Plat of Confiscated Estates by #2 surveyed by HARWOOD
JONES 9 Jul 1763 & said SAXON on 5 May 1794 to satisfy the
mortgage of said WILLIAM MOORE dec'd. to said LAWSON PRICE & Co.

DEED BOOK 11: 1794-1795 EDGEFIELD COUNTY S.C.

Assignees of WILLIAM CUNNINGHAM dated 4 May 1786 for 2225 pounds - sold 130 acres at Public Auction for 141 pounds...WILLIAM PRICE being the last & highest bidder. S/ S. SAXON, Sheriff of Ninety Six Dist. Wit: THOMAS LIVINGSTON, Major JOHN TROTTER, who swore by oath 8 Sep 1794 before JULIUS NICHOLS, J.P. Rcd. 13 Oct 1794.

Pp. 229-232. 5 May 1794: SAMUEL SAXON, Sheriff of Ninety Six Dist. to WILLIAM PRICE of Charleston SC...Whereas LAWSON PRICE & Co. at Nov term 1793 Court of Common Pleas obtained an order for the Sale of all the real Estate of WILLIAM MOORE, dec'd. (Mortgaged to said LAWSON PRICE & Co.) on credit of 12 mo...Said SAXON sold 5 May 1794, 44 acres adj. WILLIAM WHITE, OSWELL EVE, Estate of JAMES PARSONS, dec'd., to satisfy the mortgage of WILLIAM MOORE, dec'd., to said LAWSON PRICE & Co. assignee to WILLIAM CUNNINGHAM dated 4 May 1786 for 2225 pounds...said land disposed at Public Auction for 22 pounds...S/ S. SAXON, Sheriff of Ninety Six Dist. Wit: THOMAS LIVINGSTON, Major JOHN TROTTER, who swore by oath 8 Sep 1794 before JULIUS NICHOLS, J.P. Rec. 13 Oct 1794.

Pp. 232-234. 5 May 1794: SAMUEL SAXON, Sheriff of Ninety Six Dist. SC to WILLIAM PRICE of Charleston SC...Whereas LAWSON PRICE & Co. in Nov term 1793, Court of Common Pleas, obtained an order to sell the real Estate of WILLIAM MOORE, dec'd., on a credit of 12 months for the benefit of said LAWSON PRICE & Co...said SAXON at a Public auction 5 May 1794 sold two lots in Town of Cambridge where the said WILLIAM MOORE resided in his lifetime. Lots known as No. 61 & 62 with a two story dwelling house, kitchen & stove...sold for satisfaction of a mortgage of WILLIAM MOORE, dec'd., to said LAWSON PRICE & Co. assignees of WILLIAM CUNNINGHAM, dated 4 May 1786 for 2225 pounds & sold for 165 pounds to WILLIAM PRICE. S/ S. SAXON, Sheriff of Ninety Six Dist. Wit: THOMAS LIVINGSTON, Major JOHN TROTTER, who swore by oath 8 Sep 1794 before JULIUS NICHOLS, J.P. Rcd. 13 Oct 1794.

Pp. 234-236. 7 Jun 1794: SAMUEL MAYS, Sheriff of Edgefield Co. SC to GEORGE KER of Edgefield Co. SC...Whereas GEORGE KER in the County of Edgefield obtained a judgement against the Administrators of DANIEL MATHEWS for 10 pounds & 8 Jul 1793 said MAYS in obedience to the writ sold to said GEORGE KER 5 Oct...160 acres on Stephens Creek adj. JOHN COVINGTON for 3 pounds he being the last & highest bidder. S/ S. MAYS, Sheriff of Edgefield Co. Wit: JONATHAN MOORE, BRITON MIMS, who swore by oath 6 Aug 1794 before RICHARD TUTT, J.P. Rcd. 6 Aug 1794.

Pp. 237-242. 12 Feb 1794: JAMES EASON & MARY, his wife to ROBERT POU, both of Edgefield Co. SC for 17 pounds, sold 28 acres being part of 300 acres originally granted 2 May 1770 unto ARTHUR FORT & was conveyed to his son OWEN FORT by his LW&T who sold to WILLIAM HUMPHREYS who sold to MOSES PHELPS who sold to above JAMES EASON...28 acres is on Dry creek of Little Saluda River beginning at Mine Creek & adjs. said POU, Dry Creek, CHARLES PARTIN & Mine Creek. S/ JAMES (X) EASON, MARY (X) EASON. Wit: SOLOMON EIKNER, SAMUEL HUMPHREYS, who swore by oath 29 Mar 1794 before RUSSELL WILSON, J.P. Rcd. 13 Oct 1794.

Pp. 242-247. 24 Mar 1794: CHARLES PARTEN & ANN, his wife to ROBERT POU, both of Edgefield Co. SC for 40 pounds, sold 144 acres being part of 200 acres originally granted 11 Feb 1773 unto

DEED BOOK 11: 1794-1794 EDGEFIELD COUNTY S.C.

CHARLES PARTEN in Colleton Co. when surveyed but now Edgefield
Co. being on Dry Creek of Mine Creek of Little Saluda River adj.
originally THOMAS ROOK, GAVEN POU but now belonging to ROBERT POU
& ARTHUR FORT. S/ CHARLES (CP) PARTIN, ANN (X) PARTIN. Wit:
SOLOMON EIKNER, SAMUEL HUMPHREY, who swore by oath 29 Mar 1794
before RUSSELL WILSON, J.P. Rcd. 13 Oct 1794.

Pp. 247-252. 2 Jan 1788: ANTHONY ARGO, Yeoman to WILLIAM CORLEY,
Hatter, both of Ninety Six Dist. SC for 100 pounds, sold 325
acres granted 3 Jul 1786 to said ARGO being on the fork of Little
Saluda River & Big Creek adj. JOHN WHEELER, & ARON ETHRIDGE when
surveyed. S/ ANTHONY (X) ARGO, MARY (X) ARGO, his wife. Wit:
HEZEKIAH GENTRY, JOSEPH (X) WHITTLE, JESSE SANFORD, who swore by
oath 9 Aug 1794 before HENRY KING, J.P. Rcd. 13 Oct 1794.

Pp. 252-258. 9 Aug 1793: WILLIAM CORLEY, Hatter to JOHN WAIT,
Yeoman, both of Edgefield Co. SC for 32 pounds, sold 225 acres
being part of 325 acres granted 3 Jul 1786 ANTHONY ARGO & sold 2
& 3 Jan 1788 to said WILLIAM CORLEY & was transferred to one
GENTRY by Contract tho not being satisfied whilst there was a
third conveyance to said WAIT by contract from the said GENTRY in
Consequience of which it is that the present conveyance is from
WILLIAM CORLEY to said WAIT. Said land adj. JOHN WHEELER & ARON
ETHREDGE being on the fork of Little Saluda River & Big Creek. S/
WM. CORLEY. Wit: JOHN DAVIS, HENRY KING, LOT (X) ETHREDGE, who
swore by oath 9 Aug 1794 before HENRY KING, J.P. Rcd. 13 Oct
1794.

Pp. 258-262. 2 Jul 1794: JOHN CARTER to BRIANT GREEN, both of
Edgefield Co. SC for 100 pounds, sold 663 acres being part of a
larger grant to JOHN CARTER surveyed 10 Aug 1793 by CHARLES
BANKS, D.S. being on Jornegans waters of Horse Creek adj. JACOB
FUDGE & BENJAMIN FRANKLIN. S/ JOHN CARTER, ELIZABETH CARTER, his
wife. Wit: JOHN WISE, ENOS HOWARD, who swore by oath 9 Jul 1794
before JOSEPH HIGHTOWER, J.P. Rcd. 13 Oct 1794.

Pp. 262-266. 3 Oct 1794: BRIANT GREEN to RALPH CARTER, both of
Edgefield Co. SC for 20 pounds, sold 40 acres being part of a
survey granted to JOHN DAY & sold by DAY to BRYANT GREEN, being
on North side of Chavous Creek adj. WILLIAM PURSLEY, said GREEN &
JOHN BARNES. S/ BRIANT (B) GREEN. Wit: RICHARD WITHINGTON,
BENJAMIN HIGHTOWER, who swore by oath 4 oct 1794 before JOSEPH
HIGHTOWER, J.P. Rcd. 13 Oct 1794.

Pp. 266-268. 13 Jun 1794: CHARLES OLD to GEORGE B. MOORE & Co,
both of Edgefield Co. SC, for sum of 22 pounds, mortgage one
negro fellow named FRANK, age 22 yrs...Whereas the above sum with
Interest should be paid by 1st of Nov next...S/ CHARLES OLDS.
Wit: WILLIAM F. TAYLOR, who swore by oath 13 Oct 1794 before
RICHARD TUTT, J.P. Rcd. 13 Oct 1794.

Pp. 268-271. 28 Aug 1793: JOHN HARDY to GEORGE SEGAR, both of
Edgefield Co. SC for 50 pounds, sold 300 acres, being part of
tract granted JOHN HARDY being on Joices branch & Gibson branch.
S/ JOHN HARDY. Wit: RICHARD HARDY, ANN HARDY, DAVID SIGLER, who
swore by oath 11 Nov 1793 before JOSEPH HIGHTOWER, J.P. Rcd. 13
Oct 1794.

Pp. 271-278. 24 Feb 1772: NICHOLAS DILLARD, Planter to GEORGE

TILLMAN, Planter both of Granville Co. SC for 400 pounds, sold 125 acres being part of 250 originally granted 25 Oct 1764 unto DANIEL ROGERS on Crooked branch of Stephens Creek adj. JENKINS HARRIS & NOBLES. Said land was sold by DANIEL ROGERS to JENKINS HARRIS who sold to above DILLARD. S/ NICHOLOS DILLARD, DELILIAH (X) DILLARD, his wife. Wit: CHRISMAS RAY, THOMAS (T) MORRIS, LEWIS TILLMAN, who swore by oath 25 Feb 1772 before LEROY HAMMOND, Esq., J.P. Rcd. 13 Oct 1794.

Pp. 278-280. 15 May 1794: RICHARD POND, Cooper to WILLIAM MORGAN, Planter, both of Edgefield Co. SC for 12 pounds, sold 49 acres being part of a 274 acres granted 5 Nov 1792 to RICHARD POND on Foxes Creek of Savannah River. S/ RICHARD POND. Wit: DEMSEY TINER, CHRISTOPHER SHAW, who swore by oath 4 Oct 1794 before JOSEPH HIGHTOWER, J.P. Rcd. 13 Oct 1794.

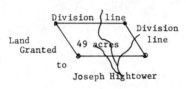

Land Granted to Joseph Hightower — Division line, Division line, 49 acres

Plat: p. 280.
49 acres being part of 274 acres on the Chalk hill fork of Foxes Creek surveyed 5 Jul 1794. CHARLES BANKS, D.S.

Pp. 281-282. 9 Oct 1794: WILLIAM COVINGTON & PHEBE, his wife to JOHN COOK, both of Edgefield Co. SC for 28 pounds, sold 28 acres being part of a tract granted 1772 unto WM. UFERY (sic) near Stephens Creek adj. land granted PETER DAY 1770, Sweet Water Creek, JOHN COVINGTON, WILLIAM COVINGTON. S/ WM. COVINGTON, PHEBE COVINGTON. Wit: CHARLES CARTER, DAVID SANDIDGE, who swore by oath 14 Oct 1794 before AQUILA MILES, J.P. Rcd. 14 Oct 1794.

Pp. 282-284. 9 Oct 1794: WILLIAM COVINGTON & PHEBE, his wife to JOHN COOK, both of Edgefield Co. SC for 5 pounds, sold 13 acres being part of 500 acres originally granted 1772 unto JOHN HAMMOND near the mouth of Stephens Creek adj. said COVINGTON, the road leading from Martintown to Campbelton & PETER DAY. S/ WM. COVINGTON, PHEBE COVINGTON. Wit: CHARLES CARTER, DAVID SANDIDGE, who swore by oath 14 Oct 1794 before AQUILA MILES, J.P. Rcd. 14 Oct 1794.

Pp. 284-289. 13 Nov 1789: JOHN GOODE, Planter of SC to WILLIAM ROBERTSON, Planter of Granville Co. for 50 pounds, sold 200 acres originally granted 7 May 1774 on South side of Stephens Creek. S/ JOHN (X) GOODE. Wit: CHARLES NIX, THOMAS (X) STILL. Winton Co. SC: CHARLES NIX swore by oath 26 Jan 1791 before THOMAS O'BANNON, J.P. Rcd. 13 Oct 1794.

P. 289. 13 Oct 1794: Bill of Sale: DAVID GAINS to REBECKAH HOGAINS, widow, both of Edgefield Co. SC for 100 pounds, sold a stud horse gray roan named Fearnought, 30 head of Cattle, 9 head of sheep, 25 head of hogs, 3 men saddles, 1 womans saddle, 2 feather beds & furniture, 1 large trunk, a parcel of pewter, 1 waggon & hind gears, sundry carpenters tools & other working tools...S/ DAVID GAINS. Wit: WILLIAM SIMKINS, JOHN DAVIS, who swore by oath 12 Oct 1794 before HENRY KING, J.P. Rcd. 13 Oct 1794.

Pp. 290-291. 13 Aug 1794: WILIAM EVANS, Deputy Surveyor to DANIEL

NAIL, Planter both of Edgefield Co. SC for 70 pounds, sold 100 acres being part of 640 acres granted 15 Oct 1784 to JOHN RICHARDSON, & sold to said EVANS 1 Jul 1793 being near Beach Island adj. BENAJMIN HARRIS, CASPER NAIL, JOHN CLARKE, Esq., & RICHARDSON. S/ WM. EVANS. Wit: CASPER NAIL, Junr., WILLIAM SHINHOLSER, who swore by oath Aug 1794 before JOHN CLARKE, Esq., J.P. Rcd. 14 Oct 1794.

Pp. 291-293. 9 Oct 1794: JOHN COOK & ANNE, his wife to WILLIAM COVINGTON, both of Edgefield Co. SC for 5 pounds, sold 5 acres being part of 200 acres on both sides of Sweet Water Creek near the mouth of Stephens Creek; adj. said COVINGTON, land granted in 1772 to JOHN HAMMOND, land granted PETER DAY in 17 (blank) & land granted WM. UFREY 1772. S/ JOHN COOK, ANNE COOK. Wit: CHARLES CARTER, DAVID SANDIDGE, who swore by oath 14 Oct 1794 before AQUILA MILES, J.P. Rcd. 14 Oct 1794.

Pp. 293-294. 18 Jul 1793: Deed of Gift: MARGARET MORRIS, Spinster, to daughter, RACHEL MORRIS, both of Edgefield Co. SC for love & affection, all my goods & chattles in my possession (that is to say), 1 roan & colt, 2 cow & calf, 2 sows, 1 feather bed & furniture, 1 pewter dish, 2 pewter basons, 6 pewter plates, 1 Iron pot, & the cloths of REBECKAH MORRIS, dec'd., & my cloths at my decease. S/ MARGARET (X) MORRIS. Wit: JOHN SLATER, JAMES BUTLER, Junr., WILLIAM WATSON, Senr., who swore by oath 3 May 1794 before JOSEPH HIGHTOWER, J.P. Rcd. 14 Oct 1794.

Pp. 294-298. 10 Mar 1794: SETH HOWARD of Edgefield Co. SC to CHARLES GOODWIN, Esq. Atty. at Law for 28 pounds, sold 40 acres being on both sides of Chavers Creek adj. said GOODWIN & HOWARD. S/ SETH HOWARD. Wit: ROBERT SAMUEL, who swore by oath 10 Sep 1794 before JOSEPH HIGHTOWER, J.P. Rcd. 15 Oct 1794.

Pp. 298-299. 1 Jul 1793: JOHN RICHARDSON of Charleston Dist. SC to WILLIAM EVANS of Edgefield Co. SC for 300 pounds, sold 640 acres originally granted 15 Oct 1784 unto JOHN RICHARDSON, adj. CASPER NAIL, Senr. & BENJAMIN HARRIS, DAVID ZUBLY, JOHN STURZENEGGER, Esqr. & JOHN CLARK. S/ JOHN RICHARDSON. Wit: THOMAS MURPHY, MICHAEL ALLEN.
Charleston Dist. SC: MICHAEL ALLEN swore by oath 7 Jun 1794 before MATTHEW DRESWELL, J.P. Rcd. 15 Oct 1794.

Pp. 300-305. 13 Oct 1794: JOHN WAITE to THOMAS ADAMS, both of Edgefield Co. SC for 45 pounds, sold 200 acres originally surveyed 20 Jun 1768 by JOHN DOOLY, D.S. On Red Bank Creek of Saluda River. S/ JOHN (X) WAITE. Wit: CHARLES GOODWIN, WILLIAM NIBBS, who swore by oath 15 Oct 1794 before JOHN CLARKE, J.P. Rcd. 15 Oct 1794.

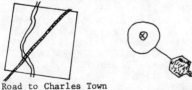
Red Bank a branch of Saluda River

Road to Charles Town

Plat: p. 304. Persuant to a warrant 13 Feb 1768 laid out to JOHN WAITE 200 acres in Colleton Co. all sides Vacant. Certified 20 Jun 1768 JOHN DOLY, D.S. JAMES BERWICK, S. Genl.

Pp. 305-306. 6 Nov 1793: Bill of Sale: WILLIAM JETER, Senr., to JOSEPH JETER for 4 pounds, sold a negro girl named EDEAS. Said negro is not to be moved until the death of myself & my wife. S/ WILLIAM JETER. Wit: HALL (+) JETER, WILLIAM JETER, Junr., who swore by oath 16 Oct 1794 befrore RICHARD TUTT, J.P. Rcd. 16 Oct 1794.

Pp. 306-307. (no date): Bill of Sale: PHILIP & WILLIAM JOHNSON to WILLIAM JETER, Senr. for 50 pounds, sold a negro woman named ROSE & two children one named TABB & one younger. S/ PHILIP JOHNSON, WILLIAM (X) JOHNSON. Wit: THOMAS CHILDERS, WILLIAM JETER, Junr., who swore by oath 16 Oct 1794 before RICHARD TUTT, J.P. Rcd. 16 Oct 1794.

Pp. 307-310. 29 Jan 1790: MACARTAN CAMPBELL, Esq. of Charleston SC to WEST COOK of Edgefield Co. SC for 20 pounds, sold 1/4 acre Lot known as Lot No. 7 in Campbellton Village. S/ MACARTAN CAMPBELL. Wit: JAMES STEWART, JOHN COOK, who swore by oath 10 Apr 1790 before LEROY HAMMOND, J.P. Rcd. 17 Oct 1794.

Pp. 310-313. 29 Jan 1790: MACARTAN CAMAPBELL, Esq. of Charleston SC to WEST COOK of Edgefield Co. SC for 20 pounds, sold 1/4 acre known as Lot #52 in Campbellton Village. S/ MACARTAN CAMPBELL. Wit: JAMES STEWART, JOHN COOK, who swore by oath 10 Apr 1790 before LEROY HAMMOND, J. P. Rcd. 17 Oct 1794.

Pp. 313-314. 10 Nov 1793: Deed of Gift: HENRY KEY to my children, one son JOHN KEY, also my three daughters, MARY KEY, LUCY KEY, & ELIZABETH KEY, all of Edgefield Co. SC for Love & affection, six negroe slaves: a woman named SARAH, Boy FRANK, girl JANNY, girl CATY, Boy FRIDAY & girl GRACE all now in my possession. To be divided amongst them when my daughter, ELIZABETH KEY becomes of age. S/ HENRY KEY. Wit: JOHN BURRESS, WILLIAM KEY, who swore by oath 15 Mar 1794 before JOHN CLARKE, J.P. Rcd. 20 Oct 1794.

Pp. 314-315. 21 Mar 1791: Bill of Sale: JOSEPH BARKSDALE to DUNCAN CAMPBELL for 32 pounds, sold a negro boy about 8 yrs. old named HARRY. S/ JOSEPH BARKSDALE. Wit: ROBERT GARDNER, ELLIS PALMER, who swore by oath 20 Oct 1794 before RICHARD TUTT, J.P. Rcd. 20 Oct 1794.

Pp. 315-317. 19 Aug 1794: NANCY BLAND, widow, to JAMES BLAND, both of Edgefield Co. SC for 5 pounds, sold 100 acres being part of 2 tracts; (1) bought of WILLIAM LITTLE &; (2) bought of GEORGE MASON by L&R being on Mine Creek on North side of road from Cambridge to Charleston adj. WORMLY BLAND, BARRATT TRAVIS, MUMFORT PEREMON, JOSEPH NIM & PATEN BLAND... it being the plantation where I now live. S/ NANCY (A) BLAND. Wit: JEREMIAH MOBLEY, WORMLY BLAND, who swore by oath 18 Oct 1794 before RUSSELL WILSON, J.P. Rcd. 20 Oct 1794.

Pp. 317-319. 5 Jun 1790: JOHN HOLLOWAY, Senr. to JOHN HOLLOWAY, Junr., both of Edgefield Co. SC for 25 pounds, sold 141 acres where he now lives being part of a tract purchased of CHRISTIAN RUMPH on both sides of Half-Way swamp of Saluda River. S/ JOHN (I) HOLLOWAY. Wit: PHILEMON BOZMAN, PAUL HOLLOWAY, CALEB HOLLOWAY, who swore by oath 17 Oct 1794 before JOHN MOORE, J.P. Rcd. 20 Oct 1794.

Pp. 319-322. 5 Jun 1792: JOHN POOL to JOHN HOLLOWAY, Junr., both of Edgefield Co. SC for 20 pounds, sold 13 acres. S/ JOHN

POOL. Wit: PHILLEMAN BOZMAN, PAUL HOLLOWAY, CALEB HOLLOWAY, who swore by oath 17 Oct 1794 before JOHN MOORE, J.P. Rcd. 20 Oct 1794.

Pp. 322-335. 5 May 1794: SAMUEL SAXON, Sheriff of Ninety Six Dist. to THOMAS BACON, Esq. of Edgefield Co. SC...Whereas BARBARA TUTT, widow of BENJAMIN TUTT, Esq., dec'd., in Court of Common Pleas obtained a judgement against THOMAS BACON for 314 pounds, writ dated 16 Nov 1793 directed the said Sheriff to seize 3462 acres in Edgefield Co. lately known to be the property of BENJAMIN TUTT, Esq., dec'd., but now the property of THOMAS BACON, Esq. where he now lives...On 5 May 1794 for satisfaction of Judgment disposed at a Public Auction for 157 pounds to said THOMAS BACON being the last & highest bidder. SAML. SAXON, Sheff. Ninety Six Dist. Wit: JAMES CRISWELL, THOMAS BUTLER, who swore by oath 24 Oct 1794 before RICHARD TUTT, J.P. Rcd. 24 Oct 1794.

Pp. 325-327. 31 May 1794: LEROY HAMMOND to ROBERT COCKRAN, Farmer, both of Edgefield Co. SC for 10 pounds, sold 34 acres on Savannah River being part of 631 acres granted 4 Apr 1785 to said HAMMOND. S/ LEROY HAMMOND. Wit: WILLIAM F. TAYLOR, WILLIAM COVINGTON, who swore by oath 31 May 1794 before JOSEPH HIGHTOWER, J. P. Rcd. 29 Oct 1794. Plat: p. 326.

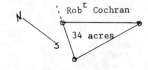

Pp. 327-330. 27 Feb 1790: MACARTAN CAMPBELL, Esq. of Charleston SC to JAMES McQUEEN of Edgefield Co. SC for 25 pounds, sold 1/4 acre Lot in Campbellton Village being a small strip of land between the Warehouse & street. S/ MACARTAN CAMPBELL. Wit: JAMES STUART, JOHN COOK, who swore by oath 18 Oct 1794 before JOSEPH HIGHTOWER, J.P. Rcd. 19 Nov. 1794.

Pp. 330-333. 8 Oct 1794: JAMES McQUEEN, Planter to WILLIAM FORBES TAYLOR, both of Edgefield Co. SC for 250 pounds, sold 1/4 acre Lot in Campbellton Village adj. Campbells Warehouse & a lot conveyed by me say SHADRACH ROZAR to BARTLEY MARTIN & street. S/ JAMES McQUEEN. Wit: JESSE CLARK, LEROY HAMMOND, who swore by oath 30 Oct 1794 before JOSEPH HIGHTOWER, J.P. Rcd. 19 Nov 1794.

Pp. 334-337. 5 Jun 1789: THOMAS PULLEY to JOHN McMANUS, both of Edgefield Co. SC for 30 pounds, sold 100 acres adj. JOHN BILLOPS & THOMAS REACE, SAMUEL ESKRIDGE & ARTHUR SIMKINS. S/ THOS. PULLEY. Wit: BARTLET BLEDSOE, NANCY NICHOLSON, MARY NICHOLSON, MARY LEWIS, swore by oath 20 Aug 1794, formerly MA NICHOLSON, before HENRY KING, J.P. Rcd. 3 Nov 1794.

Pp. 337- . 1 Sep 1794 (received): Receipt: DANIEL BROONER, to MICHAEL BROONER, 170 pounds for four negro slaves, CHLOE, BETT, FANNEY, & DICK. S/ DANIEL (DB) BROONER. Wit: JOHN N. FRY, SAMUEL BERRY HILL, who swore by oath 1 Sep 1794 before JOHN CLARKE, J.P.

Pp. 338-342. 8 Aug 1794: JONATHAN RICHARDSON to JOAB WOOTAN, both of Edgefield Co. SC for 100 pounds, sold 50 acres being part of 547 acres originally granted 2 Oct 1786 to JOHN HERNDON on Kines Fork of Big Horse Creek of Savannah River adj. Wild Cat branches, said RICHARDSON & WOOTAN. S/ JONATHAN (I) RICHARDSON. Wit: DANIEL

RITCHY, DARRICK HOLSONBAKE, who swore by oath 3 Dec 1794 before RICHARD TUTT, J.P. Rcd. 3 Dec 1794.

Pp. 342-347. 21 Aug 1794: CHARLES BANKS to JOAB WOOTAN, both of Edgefield Co. SC for 50 pounds, sold 116 acres being part of 361 acres granted 3 Dec 1792 to CHARLES BANKS on the drafts of Kines Fork of Horse Creek of Savannah River adj. JONATHAN RICHARDSON. S/ CHARLES BANKS. Wit: JAMES MOSLEY, DERRICK HOLSONBAKE, who swore by oath 3 Dec 1794 before RICHARD TUTT, J.P. Rcd. 3 Dec 1794.

Pp. 347-348. (no date): Bill of Sale: RICHARD JOHNSON, Adm. of JAMES BAKER, dec'd., to JAMES MALLETT, Attorney for RACHEL MALLETT, one of the Legatees, under & by the Will of WILLIAM BAKER, dec'd., for 170 pounds, which sum was due from WILLIAM BAKER Estate & to be discharged & paid by BENJAMIN POSTELL, Executor of said Estate it being part of the sum I was obliged to refund to Estate of WILLIAM BAKER on account of Debts & which negroes I sold by pursuant to an order from Mr LINING, Ordinary of Charleston District. S/ RICHD. JOHNSON, Administrator. Wit: PETER CARNS, JOHN JOHNSON, who swore by oath 6 Dec 1794 before RICHARD TUTT, J.P. Rcd. 6 Dec 1794.

Pp. 348-349. 28 Nov 1794: Receipt: RACHEL & JAMES MALLETT...Received from RICHARD JOHNSON, Adm. of JAMES BAKER Estate three negros, DRUMMER, BEC & JACK at 60 pounds each, fellow & BECK 52 pounds in cash at the different times hereafter mentioned, the cash in 1792, the negroes in 1793, DRUMMER & BECK, the 7 Aug, JACK the 9 Sep on account of what was due us by BENJAMIN POSTELL, Executor of WILLIAM BAKER. S/ RACHAL (X) MALLETT, JAMES MALLETT. Wit: JOHN JOHNSON, who swore by oath 6 Dec 1794 before RICHARD TUTT. Rcd. 6 Dec 1794.

Pp. 349-350. 8 Feb 1793: MARY WADE, Widow to JAMES MALLET, Planter, both of Edgefield Co. SC, my third of a tract granted to JOHN WADE, adj. MELLOR, LUCKOSES, NOBLE. S/ MARY (X) WADE. Wit: GIDN. PARDUE, RICHARD JOHNSON, Junr., who swore by oath 6 Dec 1794 before RICHARD TUTT, J.P. Rcd. 6 Dec 1794.

Pp. 350-354. 12 Aug 1779: MORRIS GUINN, Planter of Ninety Six Dist. SC to FRANCES SINQUEFIELD of same place for 1200 pounds, sold 250 acres being part of 2 tracts; (1) 200 acres on Saluda River originally granted 6 Aug 1765 said GUINN & (2) 50 acres originally granted 10 Apr 1771 WILLIAM ANDERSON & sold to said MORRIS GUINN being on Saluda River adj. WILLIAM LOW & said GUINN. S/ MORRIS (M) GUINN, RUTH (R) GUINN, his wife. Wit: NATHANIEL (F) FOOSHE, FRANCES BROOKS, THOMAS ANDERSON, who swore by oath 17 Aug 1779 before WILLIAM ANDERSON, J.P. Rcd. 8 Dec 1794.

Pp. 354-358. 3 Oct 1774: PETER CHASTAIN to EDMUND HOLLEMAN of Edgefield Co. SC for 100 pounds, sold 150 acres surveyed 30 Aug 1771 & granted to JOSEPH THOMAS being on both sides Loyds Creek. Said THOMAS conveyed to PETER CHASTAIN. S/ PETER CHASTAIN. Wit: WILLIAM COURSEY, PHILLIP CAPEHART, WILLIAM HOWLE, Junr., who swore by oath 5 Dec 1794 before AQUILA MILES, J.P. Rcd. 8 Dec 1794.

P.358. 14 Nov 1787: Bond: NATHON JOHNSON to JOHN KELLEY, promise to pay 60 pounds...The Condition is to pay 30 pounds against the

25 Nov 1789 to make title to 100 acres of upper end of the plantation now the said KELLEY lives on, then the above obligation be void...S/ NATHAN JOHNSON. Wit: WILLIAM HUGGINS, STEPHEN (X) HUTCHINSON, who swore by oath 8 Dec 1794 before RICHARD TUTT, J.P. Rcd. 8 Dec 1794.

Pp. 359-361. 15 Jan 1794: PETER & DAVID ANDERSON of Edgefield Co. SC to JOHN HILL of Newberry Co. SC for 25 pounds, sold 100 acres on Saluda River being part of 150 acres surveyed 1 Oct 1771 & granted 3 Apr 1772 to THOMAS ANDERSON dec'd., & the said 100 acres was conveyed to PETER & DAVID ANDERSON by LW&T of said ANDERSON. S/ PETER (X) ANDERSON, DAVID (R) ANDERSON. Wit: BENJAMIN TAYLOR, RUBIN TAYLOR, JOHN ABNEY, who swore by oath 12 Apr 1794 before NATHANIEL ABNEY, J.P. Rcd. 8 Dec 1794.

Pp. 361-363. 13 Sep 1793: SAMUEL GARNER & LYDDA, his wife to THOMAS ROBERTSON, all of Edgefield Co. SC for 55 pounds, 125 acres originally granted ELISHA ROBERTSON on waters of Savannah River adj. OAKLERS, SCOTS, & said ROBERTSON. S/ SAMUEL (X) GARNER, LIDDAY (X) GARNER. Wit: ADAMS PARDUE, THOMAS MORRIS, CHARLES (Λ) FINDLEY, who swore by oath 9 Dec 1794 before RICHARD TUTT, J.P. Rcd. 9 Dec 1794.

Pp. 363-365. 1 Dec 1794: AARON TOMLINSON of Pendleton Co. SC, Washington Dist. to MATHEW COCHERHAM of Edgefield Co., Ninety Six Dist. for 50 pounds, sold 125 acres originally granted 4 Jul 1791 unto LEWIS COLLANS who conveyed 1 Oct 1794 unto said TOMLINSON on branch of Turkey Creek of Stephens Creek of Savannah river adj. JOHN PURVES, Esq., JAMES COURSEY, ARGO GARNER, & ABSOLAM WILLIAMS. S/ AARON TOMLINSON.

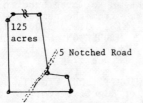

125 acres

5 Notched Road

Wit: WILLIAM BROOKS, ROBERT COURSEY, ROBERT (X) BROOKS, who swore by oath 16 Dec 1794 before AQUILLA MILES, J.P. Rcd. 16 Dec 1794.
Plat: p. 365.
WM. COURSEY, D. S.

Pp. 365-367. 23 Feb 1793: CONSTANT OGLESBY, Planter, & ANNE his wife to ISAAC BRUNSON, Senr., all of Edgefield Co. SC for 30 pounds, sold 65 acres being part of 946 acres granted 7 Aug 1786 to WM. COURSEY, part thereof transferred by said COURSEY to said OGLESBY by Deed of Gift dated 28 Nov 1789 on North side of Beaverdam of Turkey Creek of Savannah River adj. GOODE.
S/ CONSTANT OGLESBY, ANN (+) OGLSBY. Wit: ISAAC BRUNSON, JESSE MORRIS, who swore by oath before AQUILA MILES, J.P. Rcd. 16 Dec 1794.

Plat: p. 367.

Creek
Beaverdam
Goodes land
Goodes land

Land held by Isaac Brunson

Pp. 368-373. 24 Jan 1794: ABRAHAM HERNDON to JAMES PICKETT, both of Edgefield Co. SC for 250 pounds, sold; (1) 100 acres on the Main Road that leads from Augusta to the Pine Wood house known by the name of the Old Wells granted to FIELDING REYNOLDS 3 Apr 1786 & conveyed to JOHN HERNDON who conveyed to said ABRAHAM HERNDON & also; (2) 147 acres on the Main Road that leads from Augusta to the Pine Wood house granted to JOHN RYAN 1 Jan 1787 & was conveyed to said ABRAHAM HERNDON. S/ ABRAHAM HERNDON. Wit: DANIEL RITCHY, JOSHUA HAMMOND, who swore by oath 16 Dec 1794 before JOSEPH HIGHTOWER, J.P. Rcd. 16 Dec 1794.

Pp. 373-380. 27 Nov 1794: HUGH MIDDLETON & EDWARD PRINCE of SC, Planters, & ROBERT MIDDLETON of Augusta GA, Esq., to JOHN HALL, Esq. of the City of Philadelphia, Pennsylvania for 10 shillings, sold 227,000 acres granted HUGH MIDDLETON & EDWARD PRINCE in grants or patents of 1000 acres each dated 6 Oct 1794 being between twenty-three & twenty-six miles creek of Savannah River in Pendleton Co. SC of Washington Dist. The Plats are distinguished by the letter A & are numbered from one to twelve inclusive. Also, 22,000 acres granted HUGH & ROBERT MIDDLETON in grants of Equal quantity being between Little River & Hencoop creek of Savannah River in Pendleton Co. SC & the Plats are distinguished by the Letter B & numbered from one to twenty-two inclusive. Also, 15,000 acres granted HUGH & ROBERT MIDDLETON between Twenty-three & Twenty-six mile creek in Pendleton Co. SC & the Plats are distinguished by the Letter C & are numbered from one to fifteen inclusive. Also, 84,000 acres granted to ROBERT MIDDLETON in grants of the like quantity & dates of those first before described in Edgefield Co. SC & the Plats distinguished with the letter E & numbered one to Eighty four; Also, 94,000 acres granted as above described to ROBERT MIDDLETON in Washington District on waters of Keowee River, Saluda River, Twelve Mile River & Twenty-Six Mile Creek & the Plats are numbered from Two hundred & eighteen to Three hundred & twenty three inclusive. Deductions there from the numbers: 295, 296, 303, 304, 305, 311, 312, 313, 318, 319, 320, 321. S/ HUGH MIDDLETON, EDWARD PRINCE, ROBERT MIDDLETON. Wit: SAMUEL JACK, WILLIAM H. JACK, SAMUEL BARNETT, who swore by oath 18 Dec 1794 before JOSEPH HIGHTOWER, J.P. Rcd. 18 Dec 1794.

Pp. 380-387. 28 Oct 1794: FREEMAN WIGHTT, JOHN WIGHTT, JOHN FLINT & ANN his wife & SARAH WIGHTT of Edgefield Co. SC to STEPHEN TILLMAN, for 100 pounds, sold 25 acres on Horns Creek being part of two tracts; (1) 250 acres originally granted 21 Jul 1769 to JAMES THOMAS; (2) originally granted to LANCELOTT WARNER 26 Jul 1774 & conveyed to JAMES THOMAS by L&R 27 & 28 May 1775 & he conveyed the 2 tracts to JONATHAN WIGHTT, dec'd., & said 25 acres was invested in the above names by LW&T of JONATHAN WIGHTT. Said land adj. JAMES BRIAN, EDWARD MITCHELL, STEPHEN TILLMAN, WIGHTTS & FLINTS.

& FLINTS. S/ FREEMAN WIGHTT, JOHN WIGHTT, JOHN FLINT, ANN FLINT, SARAH WIGHTT. Wit: FREDERICK FREEMAN, Junr., SAMUEL MARSH, who swore by oath 29 Dec 1794 before RICHARD TUTT, J. P. Rcd. 29 Dec 1794.

White's land

Freeman

25 acres

Edward Mitchell part of Tillman's

Peter Carnes

Plat: p. 386.

Plat surveyed 11 Oct 1794. ROBERT LANG, D. S.

DEED BOOK 11: 1794-1795 EDGEFIELD COUNTY S.C.

Pp. 387-389. 24 Nov 1794: FREEMAN WIGHTT to JOHN WIGHTT, both of Edgefield Co. SC for 21 pounds, sold 1 negroe boy named ADAM formerly the property of JONATHAN WIGHTT, dec'd., Condition that said FREEMAN WIGHTT pay JOHN WIGHTT the sum of 21 pounds before 1 Jan 1796...S/ FREEMAN WIGHTT. Wit: JOHN FLINT, STEPHEN TILLMAN, who swore by oath 29 Dec 1794 before RICHARD TUTT, J.P. Rcd. 29 Dec 1794.

Pp. 390-394. 25 Dec 1794: JAMES PICKETT to BENJAMIN REYNOLDS, both of Edgefield Co. SC for 250 pounds, sold 100 acres on the Main road from Augusta to the Pine Wood house known by the name of the Old Wells granted to FIELDING REYNOLDS 3 Apr 1786 who conveyed to JOHN HERNDON & who conveyed to ABRAHAM HERNDON who conveyed to said PICKETT..Also, 147 acres granted 5 Jan 1787 JOHN RYAN on the main road from Augusta to the Pine Wood house. Said RYAN conveyed 147 acres to ABRAHAM HERNDON who conveyed to said PICKETT. S/ JAMES PICKETT. Wit: JAMES PICKETT, DANIEL RITCHY, who swore by oath 29 Dec 1794 before RICHARD TUTT, J.P. Rcd. 29 Dec 1794.

Pp. 394-400. 13 May 1771: JENKINS HARRIS, Planter to NICHOLAS DILLARD, Planter, both of SC for 150 pounds, sold 125 acres being part of 250 acres originally granted 25 Oct 1764 to DANIEL ROGERS in Granville Co. SC on North side of Crooked branch on Stevens Creek adj. NOBLES, DANIEL ROGERS, JENKINS HARRIS. S/ JENKINS (IH) HARRIS. Wit: JAMES NAPER, LEONARD NOBLES, who swore by oath 14 May 1771 before LEROY HAMMOND, J.P. Rcd. 29 Dec 1794.

Pp. 400-401. 29 Dec 1794: Bill of Sale: NATHANIEL SHEARLY to DANIEL PARKER, both of Edgefield Co. SC for 7 pounds, sold 4 cows, 1 heffer, 1 calf, 12 head of hogs, 2 beds & furniture, 2 pots, 6 plates, 3 basons & a dish, 1 spinning wheel, 1 bed stid, 1 chest, 1 powdering tub, 2 axes, 2 weeding hoes, 2 pates. S/ NATHANIEL (X) SHEARLY. Wit: PETER HARPER, who swore by oath 29 Dec 1794 before RICHARD TUTT, J.P. Rcd. 29 Dec 1794.

Pp. 401-404. 24 Mar 1794: WILLIAM COURSEY & MARY, his wife to ROBERT BROOKS, Blacksmith, both of Edgefield for 50 pounds, sold 206 acres being part of 1000 acres originally granted EDWARD VANN in Columbia by Gov. Moultrie 6 May 1793 & was conveyed by VANN to WM. COURSEY 10 Jun 1793 on North side Beaverdam creek of Savannah River. S/ W. COURSEY, MARY (X) COURSEY. Wit: ARGE GARNER, JAMES COURSEY, who swore by oath 2 Jan 1795 before RICHARD TUTT, J.P. Rcd. 2 Jan 1795.

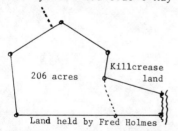

206 acres

Killcrease land

Land held by Fred Holmes

Plat: p. 403.

Pp. 404-405. 1 Nov 1794: Deed of Gift: TIRE FIKE, Planter to daughter, MARY FIKE, both of Edgefield Co. SC for love & affection, all my goods & chattels viz: 100 acres where I now live, 2 horses, 15 head of cattle, 20 hedd of hogs, 4 feather beds, bedsteads & their furniture. S/ TIRE (X) FIKE. Wit: WILLIAM HILL, SIMON FIKES, who swore by oath 2 Jan 1795 before RICHARD TUTT, J.P. Rcd. 2 Dec (sic) 1795.

Pp. 405-406. 1 Jan 1795: DANIEL BAUGH to JOHN FRAZIER, Senr., for 50 pounds, sold one negroe wench, PATIENCE. S/ DANIEL BAUGH. Wit: JOHN FRAZIER, LEVI JESTER, who swore by oath 3 Jan 1795 before RICHARD TUTT, J.P. Rcd. 3 Jan 1795.

P. 406. (no date): SAMUEL MESSER, Blacksmith, of Edgefield Co. SC to JACOB ODUM, Planter for 106 pounds, sold 1 negroe man named SAM. S/ SAML. MESSER. Wit: EZEKIEL PERRY, ELIJAH WATSON, who swore by oath 13 Dec 1794 before RUSSELL WILSON, J.P. Rcd. 3 Jan 1795.

Pp. 407-410. 2 Jul 1794: THOMAS ROGERS to HENRY BUCKHALTER, both of Edgefield Co. SC for 100 pounds, sold 153 acres on Beaverdam Creek adj. MICHAEL BUCKHALTER & ABSOLAM NAPPER. S/ THOMAS ROGERS. Wit: JOHN E. COOKE, JOHN (IB) BUCKHALTER, SOLOMAN (X) FUDGE, who swore by oath 2 Jan 1795 before JOSEPH HIGHTOWER, J.P. Rcd. 5 Jan 1795.

Pp. 410-411. 17 Nov 1794 at Augusta GA: Bill of Sale: RICHARD JOHNSON to BROWN & Co. of Augusta Ga for 60 pounds, sold one negroe man named BEN. S/ RICHD. JOHNSON. Wit: WILLIAM WYSE, who swore by oath in Edgefield Co. 10 Jun 1795 before JOHN CLARKE, J.P. Rcd. 23 Jul 1795.

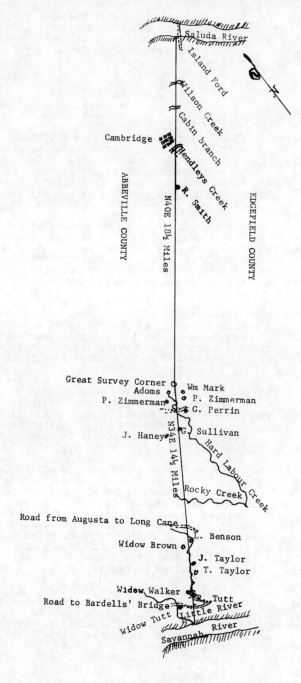

DEED BOOK 12: 1794-1796 EDGEFIELD COUNTY S.C.

In obedience to a Resolution of the Hon. House of Senate & the Hon. House of Representatives of SC dated 8 Dec 1792 we have surveyed the line between the Counties of Abbiville & Edgefield at the lower corner of the Great Saluda River to the Savannah River at the conference of Little River.

Surveyed 25 May 1793
PAT CALHOUN
W. ANDERSON
Recorded 11 Mar 1794   Commissioners

Pp. 2-3. 6 Feb 1792: WILLIAM MELTON to JAMES WHITEHEAD, both of Edgefield Co. SC for 10 pounds, sold 100 acres being part of 346 acres granted 1 Mar 1790 unto said MELTON being on Rocky Creek of South Edisto River adj. BENJAMIN JORREGEN; BIBBY BUSH. S/ WILLIAM (X) MELTON, HANNAH (H) MELTON, his wife. Wit: ELEANOR SHARP, JOHN (J) HESTER, EDWARD COUCH, who swore by oath 3 May 1792 before HENRY KING, J.P. Rcd. 1 Jan 1795.

Pp. 3-5. 8 Dec. 1788: JULAS DEEN, Yeoman & MARY his wife of Edgefield Co. SC to THOMAS SPIERMAN of Newberry Co. SC for 60 pounds, sold 240 acres granted 3 Jul 1786 said DEEN on Pessimmon Lick Creek of Big Creek of Saluda River adj. DANNETT ABNEY. S/ JULES DEEN, MARY (X) DEEN. Wit: SAMUEL MAYS, WILLIAM POWERS, who swore by oath 24 Dec 1795 before NATHANIEL ABNEY, J.P. Rcd. 5 Jan 1795.

Pp. 5-6. 12 Sep 1794: Deed of Gift: MARY BRUNSON, widow of Edgefield Co. SC hereunto moving, to MARY BRUNSON, wife of JOSHUS BRUNSON, for 10 pounds, sold the following negroes, Slaves (To Wit) CHLOE & CELA. S/ MARY BRUNSON. Wit: MARGET (X) BUCKHALTER, HENRY BUCKHALTER, who swore by oath 2 Jan 1795 before JOSEPH HIGHTOWER, J.P. Rcd. 5 Jan 1795.

Pp. 6-8. 11 Oct 1789: SAMUEL (sic) MARSH to JOHN MOSELEY, both of Edgefield Co. SC for 72 pounds, sold 100 acres originally granted 8 Jul 1774 to WILLIAM ENGLISH who sold to said MARSH 13 J an 1778 on Little Saluda River. S/ SARAH (X) MARSH, SHILES MARSH. Wit: SAMUEL MARSH, Junr., JOHN WATSON of Little Saluda who swore by oath before RUSSELL WILSON, J.P. Rcd. 5 Jan 1795.

Pp. 8-11. 18 May 1793: JAMES BROOKS of Edgefield Co. SC to RICHARD BUFFINGTON, late of Georgia for 50 pounds, sold 200 acres being part of 2 tracts; (1) 100 acres part of 300 acres originally granted 8 Jul 1774 to said BROOKS; (2) 190 acres part of 1190 acres originally granted 5 Jun 1786 to JOHN ABNEY who sold 190 acres to said BROOKS being on Persimmon Lick Creek of Little Saluda River being on a road leading from WM. ANDERSON's Ferry towards Charleston; adj. PETER BUFFINGTON & JOHN ROE. S/ JAMES (J) BROOKS. Wit: GEORGE (A) ABNEY, PETER BUFFINGTON, who swore by oath 3 Jun 1794 before NATHANIEL ABNEY, J.P. Rcd. 5 Jan 1795.

Pp. 11-13. 3 Sep 1793: WILLIAM ENGLISH to WILLIAM DOZER & HUDSON BENNETT, all of Edgefield Co. SC for 10 Shillings, sold 1 acre being part of 100 acres sold to WM. ENGLISH by ROBERT DAVIS, now dec'd. out of 200 acres originally granted 15 May 1772 to said ROBERT DAVIS adj. MOSES KIRKLAND on Little Saluda River. S/ WM. (X) ENGLISH. Wit: SAMUEL ESKREDGE, JOHN CORLEY, ENOCH GRIGSBY, who swore by oath 17 Sep 1793 before RUSSELL WILSON, J.P. Rcd. 5 Jan 1795.

DEED BOOK 12: 1794-1796 EDGEFIELD COUNTY S.C.

Pp. 13-14. 3 Jan 1795: Mortgage: JAMES MILLS to JOHN ABNEY, both of Edgefield Co. SC for 10 pounds, sold one horse about 12 yrs. old, 3 cows, 2 yearlings, 1 sow & pigs, 50 bushels of corn & all my household furniture upon the condition that JAMES MILLS pays the sum of 10 pounds 1 Jan 1796 & this instrument will be null & void. S/ JAMES MILLS. Wit: JOEL ABNEY, JAMES (X) LOVE, who swore by oath 3 Jan 1775 (sic) before NATHANIEL ABNEY, J.P. Rcd. 5 Jan 1795.

Pp. 14-16. 1 Jan 1789: JAMES KETCHERSIDES to JOHN MOSELEY, both of Ninety Six Dist. SC for 30 pounds, sold 100 acres originally granted 5 Jun 1786 said KETCHERSIDE being on Big Creek on the Road leading from Augusta to Saludy Old Town adj. WILLIAM ENGLISH. S/ JAMES KETCHERSIDE, SARAH (X) KETCHERSIDE, his wife. Wit: JOHN WATSON, JOSEPH MOSELEY, who swore by oath 22 Apr 1791 before JAMES SPANN, J.P. Rcd. 5 Jan 1795.

P. 17. 11 Apr 1794: Bill of Sale: ENOCH GRIGSBY to SAMUEL MAYS for 100 pounds, sold three negroes to wit: SILVY a wench about 20 yrs. old, Black Complection strong big made wench; WILLIS a boy about 18 yrs. old, yellow complection large mouth & thick lips - spare made; LIDIA, a girl about 5 yrs. old, a yellow complection - spare made, hansome girl. S/ ENOCH GRIGSBY. Wit: GEORGE MAYS, WILLIAM BUTLER, who swore by oath 6 Jan 1795 before W. ANDERSON, J.C.E. Rcd. 6 Jan 1795.

Pp. 17-18. Bond To Make Titles: PHILIP MEYER & CATHARINE, his wife of Charleston S.C. are bound unto JOHN GORMAN, Planter of Ninety Six Dist. SC for 100 pounds, which payment will be made 27 Sep 1791...The Condition of the obligation is such that PHILIP MEYER & CATHERINE MEYERS before the 1 Jan next should make legal titles in fee simple with the renunciation of Inheritance of the said CATHARINE MEYER of 150 acres originally granted 6 Dec 1768 to NICHOLAS FITTING being on a small branch of Saludy River near Old Town on both sides of the Road leading to Charleston...S/ PHILIP MEYER, CATHARINE MEYER. Wit: ROBERT THORNLY, EDWARD THOMAS, who swore by oath 7 Jun 1794 in Charleston Dist. SC. Rcd. 6 Jan 1795.

Pp. 18-20. 5 Jul 1794: WILLIAM DONAHO to THOMAS ADAMS, both of Edgefield Co. SC for 40 pounds, sold 150 acres being part of 700 acres originally granted 5 Aug 1793 unto ELVENTON SQUIRES, who conveyed to said DONOHO. Said tract being on Rocky Creek & Beech Creek head branches of the Edisto River adjs. said DONOHO & land where THOMAS ADAMS lives on at this present date, 1794. S/ WILLIAM DONAHO. Wit: THOMAS (X) FARES, JAMES ADAMS, who swore by oath 31 Oct 1794 before HENRY KING, J.P. Rcd. 6 Jan 1795.

Pp. 20-23. 8 Jun 1791: JOHN DOUGLAS, Planter to LEWIS DOUGLAS, both of Edgefield Co. SC for 30 pounds, sold 50 acres & 100 acres, being part of 2 tracts; (1) 100 acres of a 150 acre tract originally granted 3 Apr 1772 unto said JOHN DOUGLAS on waters of Little River; (2) 50 acres being part of 100 acres originally granted AARON WEAVER, now deceased & was conveyed by said WEAVER 3 Jan 1776 to JOHN DOUGLAS. S/ JOHN (ɫ) DOUGLAS. Wit: ASAEL ROBERTS, JANE (X) WEAVER, HENRY KING, who swore by oath 10 Jun 1791 before JAMES SPANN, J.P. Rcd. 6 Jan 1794.

Pp. 23-26. 31 Jan 1789: MICHAEL DELOACH of Red Bank of Little

DEED BOOK 12: 1794-1796 EDGEFIELD COUNTY S.C.

Saluda River to MOSES BROWN, both of Ninety Six Dist.
SC for 30 pounds, sold 50 acres - LEASE - taken from 400 acres on waters of Red Bank Creek of Little Saluda River adj. & beginning at Pen Creek; JACOB BROWN, to the ford of the branch between said MICHAEL DELOACH & his brother SAMUEL DELOACH & RUSSELL. Said tract originally granted 31 Aug 1774... S/ THOMAS DELOACHE, Senr., MICHAEL DELOACH, Sr. Wit: JACOB BROWN, JAMES ALLEN, XPHER BROOKS, Senr. - RELEASE - Same description of grant except adjs. SAMUEL ETHERIDGE, JACOB SMITH, JOSEPH HOGAN, Mr. RUSSELL; SAUNDERS WALKER & JAMES DAVIS. Rcd. from the within named JOHN DOUGLAS 30 pounds, being the full consideration in presences of JACOB BROWN. S/ MOSES BROWN. JACOB BROWN swore by oath 22 May 1792 he saw MICHAEL sign the within Release & that he saw MICHAEL & THOMAS DELOACHE sign the receipt hereon Indorsed & likewise saw JAMES ALLEN & CHRISTOPHER BROOKS sign their names before HENRY KING, J.P. Rcd. 6 Jan 1795.

Pp. 26-28. 15 Mar 1794: MICHAEL BUCKHALTER of GA to JAMES QUARLES of Edgefield Co. SC, 300 acres being part of 500 acres originally granted 6 Sep 1772 unto JOHN BUCKHALTER, Senr. & fell to MICHAEL BUCKHALTER by heirship being on Stephens Creek adj. said JAMES QUARLES. S/ MICHAEL (M) BUCKHALTER. Wit: WILLIAM WATSON, Senr., RICHARD QUARLES, Junr., who swore by oath 29 Mar 1794 before HUGH MIDDLETON, J.P. Rcd. 12 Jan 1795.

Pp. 28-30. 13 Oct 1790: ELIJAH PADGET, Planter to MOSES HOLSTEIN, Planter for 50 pounds, sold 100 acres being part of 200 acres granted to said PADGET on Cloud Creek of Little Saludy River. S/ ELIJAH PADGETT. Wit: JOSHUA GUNTER, WILLIAM HOLSTEIN, Senr., WILLIAM HOLSTEIN, Junr., who swore by oath 16 Oct 1790 before RUSSELL WILSON, J.P. Rcd. 16 Jan 1795.

Pp. 30-31. 13 Oct 1790: ELIJAH PADGET to WILLIAM HOLSTEIN, both of Ninety Six Dist. for 50 pounds, sold 100 acres being part of 200 acres originally granted 1773 unto said PADGETT being on Cloud Creek of Little Saluda River. S/ ELIJAH PADGET. Wit: JOSHUA GUNTER, WILLIAM HOLSTEEN, MOSES HOLSTEIN, who swore by oath 16 Oct 1790 before RUSSELL WILSON, J.P. Rcd. 16 Jan 1795.

P. 32. 10 May 1794: Bill of Sale: ENOCH GRIGSBY to RYDON GRIGSBY, both of Edgefield Co. SC for 150 pounds, sold four negroes namely JACK, ZILPH, PATT & TOM. S/ ENOCH GRIGSBY. Wit: RUSSELL WILSON, Senr., LODWICK HILL, who swore by oath 13 Jan 1795 before RUSSELL WILSON, J.P. Rcd. 16 Jan 1795.

Pp. 32-33. Bill of Sale: ENOCH GRIGSBY to LODWICK HILL for 50 pounds, sold one negroe woman named JUDE & her four children, HANNAH, PETER, SARAH & LUCY. S/ ENOCH GRIGSBY. Wit: RUSSELL WILSON, Senr., RHDON GRIGSBY, who swore by oath 13 Jan 1795 before RUSSELL WILSON, J.P. Rcd. 16 Jan 1795.

Pp. 33-35. 22 Mar 1793: WILLIS FEDERICK, Planter to WILLIAM HOLSTEEN, both of Ninety Six Dist. SC for 25 pounds, sold 220 acres including part where said HOLSTEEN now lives originally granted JOHN FEDRICK by WILLIAM MOULTRIE, Esq. Governor. Now this indenture witnesses that said WILLIS FEDRICK is the lawful owner. S/ WILLIS FEDRICK, JINNEA (X) FEDRICK, his wife. Wit: SAMPSON WILLIAMS, LEWIS FREDRICK, MOSES HOLSTEEN, who swore by oath 16 Nov 1793 before RUSSELL WILSON, J.P. Rcd. 16 Jan 1795.

190

P. 35. 17 July 1794: Deed of Gift: BENJAMIN LOVELESS to my son, JOHN LOVELESS, both of Edgefield Co. SC for Love & affection, gives all my goods & chattels in my present dwelling also all my stock and my plantation of 400 acres. S/ BENJAMIN (B) LOVELESS. Wit: SAMSON WILLIAMS, EDWARD COUCH, who swore by oath 16 Jan 1795 before VAN SWEARENGEN, J.P. Rcd. 16 Jan 1795.

Pp. 36. 5 Jan 1795: Bill of Sale: JAMES BAKER to WILLIAM FUQUA for Valuable consideration, one negro boy named DENNIS, age 12 yrs; one negro girl named JENNY, 8 years old; one negro boy named WILL, age 10 years. Said negroes were bequeath by LW&T of MARY FUQUA to said JAMES BAKER. S/ JAS. BAKER. Wit: SAMPSON BUTLER, RICHARD GANTT, who swore by oath 17 Jan 1795 before RICHARD TUTT, J.P. Rcd. 17 Jan 1795.

Pp. 36-37. 5 Jan 1795: Bill of Sale: JAMES BAKER to JOSEPH FUQUA for valuable consideration, sold one negro man named MATT; one negro boy named ISAC; one negro boy REUBIN. S/ JAS. BAKER. Wit: SAMPSON BUTLER, RICHARD GANTT, who swore by oath 17 Jan 1795 before RICHARD TUTT, J.P. Rcd. 17 Jan 1795.

P. 37. 5 Jan 1795: Bill of Sale: JAMES BAKER to STEPHEN TERRY of VA for valuable consideration sold one negro woman named HANNAH & her two children. S/ JAS. BAKER. Wit: RICHARD GANTT, SAMPSON BUTLER, who swore by oath 17 Jam 1795 before RICHARD TUTT, J.P. Rcd. 17 Jan 1795.

Pp. 37-38. 5 Jan 1795: Bond: JOSEPH FUQUA & WILLIAM FUQUA, both of Edgefield Co. SC, are bound to JAMES BAKER for 500 pounds...Whereas JOSEPH FUQUA & WILLIAM FUQUA, Brothers of SARAH wife of STEPHEN TERRY of VA have received a bill of sale on behalf of STEPHEN TERRY the following negroes to wit: one negro woman named HANNAH & her two children and whereas said JAMES BAKER is apprehensive and fearful that STEPHEN TERRY or some other person may endeavor to Revoke the Will of MARY FUQUA of SC for the purpose of obtaining a distributive share of her estate by virtue of a claim set up by STEPHEN TERRY. The condition of obligation is if JAMES BAKER is sued by STEPHEN TERRY, husband of SARAH who is a sister of MARY FUQUA, deceased, is to stay in full force & otherwise to have no effect. S/ JOSEPH FUQUA, WILLIAM FUQUA. Wit: SAMPSON BUTLER, RICHARD GANTT, who swore by oath 17 Jan 1795 before RICHARD TUTT, J.P. Rcd. 17 Jan 1795.

Pp. 38-40. 5 Nov 1790: JOHN MOSLEY of Winton Co. SC to DAVID MATHEWS of Edgefield Co. SC for 40 pounds, sold 191 acres originally granted 7 Aug 1786 unto JOHN MOSELEY being on Horns Creek adj. Widow HERNDON, JAMES HARGROVES, JOHN HOGG, JOHN RAINSFORD & WILLIAM MOSELEY. S/ JOHN (X) MOSELEY. Wit: WILLIAM (M) MOSELEY, STEPHEN TILMAN, who swore by oath 24 Jan 1795 before RICHARD TUTT, J.P. Rcd. 24 Jan 1795.

P. 41. 18 Oct 1794: Bill of Sale: GABREL TUTT of Abbeville Co. SC to BENJAMIN TUTT of Edgefield Co. SC for (blank), sold Five negroes (viz) CHARLES, SAM, CHARITY & child. MOD & PATT. S/ GABL. TUTT. Wit: JOHN CHASTAIN, CLEMT. CARGILL, who swore by oath 21 Nov 1794 before HENRY KING, J.P. Rcd. 22 Jan 1795.

P. 41. 1 Jul 1794: Bill of Sale: JAMES CHRISSUP to NANCY NEWSOM, both of Edgefield Co. SC for 15 pounds, sold one mare, two colts,

DEED BOOK 12: 1794-1796 EDGEFIELD COUNTY S.C.

one feather bed, furniture, one woman saddle, 2 pots, 1 dutchoven, & a lot of pewter, a lot of Earthenware, one heifer. S/ JAMES (X) CHRISSUP. Wit: EDWARD BLAND, WILLIAM BLAND, who swore by oath 26 Jan 1795 before HENRY KING, J.P. Rcd. 27 Jan 1795.

Pp. 41-44. 25 Jan 1785: JAMES WILSON, Planter to ROBERT McCAN, School master, both of SC, for 110 pounds, sold 100 acres originally granted 25 May 1774 in Coleton Co. being on Rocky Creek of Turkey Creek of Stevens Creek. S/ JAMES (C) WILSON. Wit: MORRIS (M) CALLIHAM, RICHARD WORSHAM, who swore by oath 27 Jan 1785 before RICHARD TUTT, J.P. Rcd. 6 Feb 1795.

Pp. 44-45. 1 Jul 1794: THOMAS BROUGHTON & MARY, his wife, to JOSEPH ACTON, both of Edgefield Co. SC for 50 pounds, sold 279 acres on Bird Creek of Stevens Creek of Savannah River, being part of a tract granted SAMUEL HOWARD, deceased, & convaid to said BROUGHTON by will of said HOWARD. S/ THOS. BROUGHTON, MARY BROUGHTON. Wit: JACOB HIBBLER, GEORGE (X) HAMILTON, WILLIAM (X) CARSON, who swore by oath 29 Nov 1794 before JAMES HARRISON, J.P. Rcd. 6 Feb 1795.

Pp. 45-47. 3 Feb 1795: ROBERT MOSELEY & PENELOPE his wife to EDWARD MOSELEY, all of Edgefield Co. SC for 50 pounds, sold 100 acres on Rockey Creek & Cedar Creek of Horns Creek adj. BUTLER WILLIAMS, ROBERT & EDWARD MOSELEY, JOHN MARTIN, JOHN RAINSFORD. S/ ROBERT (R) MOSELEY, PENELOPE (X) MOSELEY. Wit: LEWIS TILMAN, MARY (X) STALIONS, JOHN MOSELEY, who swore by oath 7 Feb 1795 before RICHARD TUTT, J.P. Rcd. 7 Feb 1795.

Pp. 47-48. 4 Feb 1795: ROBERT MOSELEY & PENELOPE his wife to JOHN MOSELEY, all of Edgefield Co. SC for 20 pounds, sold 70 acres on Cedar Creek adj. EDWARD MOSELEY, BUTLER WILLIAMS, RICHARD CHRISTMAS, LEWIS TILMAN, JOHN MOSELEY. S/ ROBERT (R) MOSELEY, PENELOPE (X) MOSELEY. Wit: LEWIS TILMAN, MARY (X) STALIONS, EDWARD MOSELEY, who swore by oath 7 Feb 1795 before RICHARD TUTT, J.P. Rcd. 7 Feb 1795.

P. 49. Bill of Sale: MARSHALL MARTIN to MATT MARTIN, both of Edgefield Co. SC for 200 pounds, sold one negroe man named JACOB, one negroe wench & child named WINEY & SAM, 4 horses, 8 head of Cattle, stock of hogs, 2 feather beds, my crop of corn & tobacco. S/ MARSHALL MARTIN. Wit: SAMUEL (X) LYONS, JOHN (+) DELANY, JAMES (X) MURRAH, who swore by oath 23 Jan 1795 before AQUILLA MILES, J.P. Rcd. 7 Feb 1795.

Pp. 49-52. GEORGE DEEN of Edgefield Co. SC to SAMUEL BEAKS, late of Edgefield Co. SC, but formerly of Newberry Co. SC for 92 pounds, sold 100 acres being part of 300 acres originally granted 8 Jul 1774 to ANN DEAN, mother of said GEORGE DEAN, the heir at law, on Perryman Creek of Little Saluda adj. DENIT ABNEY, JOHN BROOKS, GAVEN POU, ISAAC DECOSTS. S/ GEORGE DEEN. Wit: THOMAS REED, DANNITT ABNEY, SAMUEL (X) ABNEY, who swore by oath 22 Jan 1795 before NATHAL. ABNEY, J.P. Rcd. 7 Feb 1795.

Pp. 52-53. JOSHUA HAMMOND to JOHN COOK, both of Edgefield Co. SC for 5 pounds, sold 100 acres on Sweet Water Creek adj. JOHN HARDY, PETER DAY. S/ JOSHUA HAMMOND. Wit: JOSEPH HIGHTOWER, WEST COOK, who swore by oath 10 Apr 1790 before LEROY HAMMOND, J.P. Rcd. 11 Feb 1795.

192

DEED BOOK 12: 1794-1796 EDGEFIELD COUNTY S.C.

Pp. 54-55. 2 Oct 1790: PETER DAY to JOHN COOK, both of Edgefield
Co. SC for 5 pounds, sold 5 acres on Sweet Water Creek adj. PETER
DAY, JOSHUA HAMMON. S/ PETER (X) DAY. Wit: JOSEPH CUNNINGHAM,
RICHARD (X) JONES, who swore by oath 9 Mar 1791 before WILLIAM
ANDERSON, J.P. Rcd. 11 Feb 1795.

Pp. 55-56. 26 Nov 1794: Bill of Sale: JOHN COOK to JAMES HARDY
for 50 pounds, sold a negro girl named MARY. S/ JOHN COOK. Wit:
JOHN HARDY, DUDLEY CARTER, who swore by oath 9 Feb 1795 before
JOSEPH HIGHTOWER, J.P. Rcd. 11 Feb 1795.

P. 56. 11 Nov 1794: Bill of Sale: THOMAS CLARK, of GA, Adm. of
Estate of JOHN CLARK, Junr. dec'd., & JAMES CLARK of Edgefield
Co. SC, & JESSE CLARK of GA all legatees to EDMOND PURSELL of
Edgefield Co. SC, for 60 pounds sold one negro man named JOE. S/
THOS. CLARK, JAMES CLARK, JESSE CLARK. Wit: GEORGE FARRAR,
WILLIAM MILLER, WILLIAM PURSELL, who swore by oath 12 Nov 1794
before AQUILA MILES, J.P. Rcd. 13 Feb 1795.

Pp. 56-57. 1 Jan 1795: Mortgage: ANDREW BURNEY to EDMUND PURSSELL
for 20 pounds, sold one negro fellow named ?QUODO? S/ ANDW.
BURNEY. Wit: RICHARD (X) PARDUE, who swore by oath 13 Jan 1795
before AQUILLA MILES, J.P. Rcd. 13 Feb 1795.

Pp. 57-58. 26 Dec 1793: JOSEPH TOLBERT & SARAH his wife to
GARROTT FREEMAN, both of Edgefield Co. SC for 60 pounds, sold 150
acres originally granted 4 Dec 1771 unto EZEKIEL HANLIN, Senr.,
on Savannah River adj. JOHN McCOY. S/ JOSEPH TOLBERT, SARAH (T)
TOLBERT. Wit: HENRY KEY, EZEKIEL HUDNALL, JESSE COPELAND, who
swore by oath 25 Jun 1794 before JAMES HARRISON, J.P. Rcd. 13 Feb
1795.

P. 58. Deed of Gift: LUCY LOWERY of Edgefield Co. SC, having 22
pounds left me by my Father JOHN GARROT in the hands of HENRY
WARE, Senr. of Wilks Co. GA & HENRY (sic) of Edgefield Co. SC
they being left Executors to the will of my Father, JOHN GARROT &
having no brothers or sisters left in this part of the world but
one that is MARTHA WARE & for the love & affection I have for her
& her husband HENRY WARE, Senr. of Wilks Co. GA - I give the 22
pounds left by my father...S/ LUCY (X) LOWERY. Wit: THOMAS
MURRAH, MOSES (X) ROBERTSON, who swore by oath 10 Feb 1795 before
AQUILA MILES, J.P. Rcd. 13 Feb 1795.

Pp. 58-59. 2 Feb 1795: Bill of Sale: WEST COOK of Campbellton SC
to KEVAN & TAYLOR of same place for 60 pounds, sold the Undivided
one half of a Boat or Platt known by the name of the South
Carolina Planter. S/ WEST COOK. Wit: CHARLES COVINGTON, ROBERT
LIVINGSTON, who swore by oath 12 Feb 1795 before JOHN RYAN, J.P.
Rcd. 16 Feb 1795.

P. 59. 8 Nov 1794: Bill of Sale: JOHN VARDELL, Planter of
Edgefield Co. SC to JOHN McKENNEY for 36 pounds, sold one negro
boy named PRINCE. S/ JOHN VARDELL. Wit: SAMUEL MESSER, ROBERT
WILLIS, JACOB ODOM, who swore by oath 10 Nov 1794 before JOSEPH
HIGHTOWER, J.P. Rcd. 21 Feb 1795.

Pp. 59-61. 27 May 1794: HUGH YOUNG, Atty. of HUGH ROSE, Merchant
of Charleston SC to JOHN BRIDGERS of Edgefield Co. SC for 20
pounds, sold 285 acres being part of 1500 acres originally

granted 17 Dec 1772 unto HUGH ROSE on Little Stephens Creek of Savannah River. S/ HUGH YOUNG. Wit: SILVS. WALKER, JAMES JONES.

Laurens Co. SC: SILVS. WALKER swore by oath 11 Feb 1795 before JNO. DAVIS, J. P.

Plat: p. 61. Edgefield Co. SC: Certified a true Plat of 285 acres taken out of 1500 acres granted HUGH ROSE 17 Dec 1772. WM. COURSEY, Mathematicion.

Robert Starks land

Jacob ?Motts? Esq. land

Jacob Fudge

285 acres   Mazysks land

Jacob Fudge

John Courseys land from the original grant

Josiah Stephens

Pp. 61-63. 27 May 1794: HUGH YOUNG of Charleston Sc to ELISHA STEPHENS of Edgefield Co. SC for 20 pounds, sold 238 acres being part of 1500 acres originally granted 17 Dec 1772 unto HUGH ROSE & by Removal or decease of said ROSE, said 1500 acres descended unto HUGH YOUNG; on little Stephens Creek of Savannah River adj. JOHN FUDGE, JOSIAH STEPHENS, ------- JOHN BRIDGERS, JOHN COURSEY, LEWIS's line, JOHN STILL, RICHARD BUCKELEW, ALEXANDER BEAN. S/ HUGH YOUNG. Wit: SILVS. WALKER, JAMES JONES. Plat: p. 62.

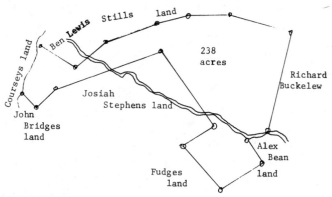

Stills land

Ben Lewis

Courseys land

238 acres

Richard Buckelew

Josiah Stephens land

John Bridges land

Alex Bean land

Fudges land

Certified Plat of 238 acres taken from 1500 acres granted 17 Dec 1772. 3 Mar 1793 by WM. COURSEY, Dep. Surv. Laurens Co. SC: SILVS. WALKER swore by oath 11 Feb 1795 before JNO. DAVIS, J.P. Rcd. 20 Feb 1795.

Pp. 63-64. 27 May 1794: HUGH YOUNG, Atty of HUGH ROSE of Charleston SC, Merchant, to OGDON COCKEROFF of Edgefield Co. SC for 28 pounds, sold 220 acres being part of 1500 acres originally granted 17 Dec 1772 on Little Stephens Creek of Savannah River Edgefield Co. SC. S/ HUGH YOUNG. Wit: SILVS. WALKER, JAMES JONES. Plat: p. 64. True Plat for OGDON COCKEROFF taken from original Plat of 1500 acres originally granted 17 Dec 1772 to HUGH ROSE by

DEED BOOK 12: 1794-1796 EDGEFIELD COUNTY S.C.

WM. COURSEY, Math.

Laurens Co. SC:
SILVS. WALKER
swore by oath 11
Feb 1795 before
JNO. DAVIS, J.P.
Rcd. 20 Feb 1795.

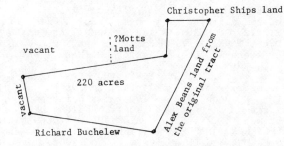

Pp. 64-65. 27 May 1794: HUGH YOUNG, Atty. of HUGH ROSE of
Charleston SC,. Merchant, to ALEXANDER BEAN of Edgefield Co.
SC for 20 pounds, sold 110 acres being part of 1500 acres originally
granted 17 Dec 1772 unto HUGH ROSE on Little Stephen Creek of
Savannah River. Wit: SILVS. WALKER, JAMES JONES.

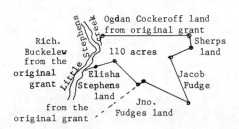

Plat: p. 65. 110 acres
Platted for ALEX. BEANS
taken from 1500 acres
granted unto HUGH ROSE
17 Dec 1772. WM.
COURSEY, Mathermatn.
Laurens Co. SC:
SILVS. WALKER swore by
oath 11 Feb 1795 before
JNO. DAVIS, J.P. Rcd.
20 Feb 1795.

Pp. 66-67. 24 Dec 1794: JAMES DAVIS of SC to SPENCER BOULWARE &
ROBERT RUTHERFORD BOULWARE of Edgefield Co. SC for 80 pounds,
sold a parcel of land on Saluda River which 100 acres originally
granted said DAVIS 30 Aug 1784, 150 acres dated 3 Apr 1788; adj.
JAMES BROOKS, JOHN WATSON. S/ JAMES DAVIS, LESBETH (X) DAVIS.
Wit: JOHN MOSELEY, WILLIAM BOULWARE, who swore by oath 27 Dec
1794 before NATHL. ABNEY, J.P. Rcd. 21 Feb 1795.

Pp. 67-68. 5 Dec 1794: DANNETT ABNEY to JOSEPH GRIFFIN, both of
Edgefield Co. SC for 5 shillings, sold 25 acres being part of 200
acres originally granted 19 Mar 1773 to said DANNETT ABNEY in
Colleton, but now Edgefield on Little Saluda River adj. JOSEPH
GRIFFIN's land originally granted to JULUS DEEN, BAILEY CHANEY.
S/ DENNETT ABNEY. Wit: SIMON BROOKS, GEORGE (A) ABNEY, WILLIAM
CROW, who swore by oath 14 Feb 1795 before NATHAL. ABNEY, J.P.
Rcd. 21 Feb 1795.

Pp. 69-70. 1 Oct 1794: LEWIS COLLINS of Pendleton Co. SC to AARON
TOMLINSON for 20 pounds, sold 125 acres originally granted 4 Jul
1791 at Columbia SC on a Stony Branch of Turkey Creek of Savannah
River adj. Col. JOHN PURVIS, JAMES COURSEY, DAVID BURKS, ABSOLOM
WILLIAMS. S/ LEWIS COLLINS. Wit: JOHN WILSON, WALKER (X) BRIANT,
who swore by oath 24 Jan 1795 before JOHN WILSON, J.P. of
Pendleton Co. SC. Rcd. 26 Feb 1795.

Pp. 70-71. 26 Jan 1795: JOSHUA DEEN, Planter & TABATHA his wife,

JOSEPH GRIFFITH, all of Edgefield Co. SC for 7 pounds, sold 60 acres surveyed for him 4 Jul 1792 on Little Saluda River adj. WILLIAM POWERS, BARNETS BARNS land, JAMES GOOD's. S/ JOSHUA (I) DEEN, TABETHA (X) DEEN. Wit: AARON CLARK, SIMON BROOKS, who swore by oath 20 Feb 1795 before NATHAL. ABNEY, J.P. Rcd. 21 Feb 1795.

Pp. 71-72. 22 Jan 1795: THOMAS SPEARMAN & MARGARET, his wife of Newberry Co. SC Planter, to JOSEPH GRIFFIN of Edgefield Co. SC for 40 pounds, sold 100 acres being part of 240 acres originally granted 3 Jul 1786 unto JULIUS DEEN on Glade lick of Little Saluda River adj. said JULIUS DEEN's & DANAT ABNEY. S/ THOS. SPEARMAN, MARGET (+) SPEARMAN. Wit: WILLIAM POWERS, EDMUND SPEARMAN, WILLIAM CROW, who swore by oath 14 Feb 1795 before NATHL ABNEY, J.P. Rcd. 21 Feb 1795.

Pp. 72-73. 22 Jan 1795: JAMES BROOKS, Planter & UNITY his wife, to JOSEPH GRIFFITH, all of Edgefield Co. SC for 5 pounds, sold 15 1/2 acres being part of 300 acres originally granted 8 Jul 1774 to JAMES BROOK on Persimon lick Creek of Saluda River adj. JAMES BROOK. S/ JAMES (J) BROOKS, UNITY (X) BROOKS. Wit: WILLIAM POWERS, JOHN (+) BROOKS, WILLIAM CROW, who swore by oath 14 Feb 1795 before NATHAL. ABNEY, J.P. Rcd. 21 Feb 1795.

Pp. 73-74. 29 Nov 1794: Deed of Gift: WILLIAM HOWLE, for divers causes & me here unto moving, to LACON RYAN, my great grandson, son of BENJAMIN RYAN & FRANCES his wife of Edgefield Co. SC, for Valuable Consideration, sold one negro girl called NAN but should LACON RYAN die before he comes of lawful age with out lawful issue, I give to his brother or sister or brothers or sisters as the case may be with respect to his mothers having children while she is in state of marriage & if said FRANCES RYAN has no other children to arrive at age without issue then I give the negroe & her issue to be equally divided among the children of PETER CHASTAIN...S/ WILLIAM HOWLE. Wit: MATT MARTIN, ORAN ELLISON, EDMUND HOLLEMAN, who swore by oath 7 Mar 1795 before JOHN RYAN, J.P. Rcd. 7 Mar 1795.

Pp. 74-75. 27 Feb 1795: Affidavit: JOSEPH STEPHENSON appeared before AQUILA MILES & sworn by oath that he lent to DAVID BURKS a set of Leases of 125 acres adj. WILLIAMS on South side Main Turkey Creek 12 Jul 1792 conveyed by LEWIS COLLINS & his wife to said STEPHENSON & that WILLIAM COURSEY, JAMES COURSEY & JOHN CAMFIELD are witnesses & that above titles were never returned by said BURK or any other person. S/ JOSEPH STEPHENSON. Rcd. 7 Feb 1795.

Pp. 75-76. 25 Sep 1794: ABSOLAM WILLIAMS, Planter to COLL COLLINS, Planter both of Edgefield Co. SC for 50 pounds, sold 100 acres originally granted 12 Dec 1768 to CHARLES WILLIAMS & at his decease descended to said ABSOLAM WILLIAMS his son & heir. Said tract is on Turkey Creek a branch of Stephens Creek a branch of Savannah River. S/ ABSOLAM WILLIAMS. Wit: WILLIAM BLACKLEY, MOODY BURT, who swore by oath 7 Mar 1795 before RICHARD TUTT, J.P. Rcd. 7 Mar 1795.

Pp. 76-77. 5 Jan 1793: JOHN CALLIHAM, son & heir of DAVID CALLIHAM, deceased, of Washington Co. GA to THOMAS BRISMORE of Edgefield Co. SC for 50 pounds, 150 acres being part of 300 acres (see plat surveyed 6 Feb 1792 by JOHN BOYD, D.S.) & granted to DAVID CALLIHAM, deceased; adj. said BRISMORE, DAVID CALLIHAM,

ELISHA ROBERTSON. S/ JOHN CALLIHAM, DAVID CALLIHAM, MARY CALLIHAM. Wit: THOMAS (X) JACKSON, JAMES THOMAS, who swore by oath 6 Jun 1793 before HUGH MIDDLETON, JP. Plat: p. 76.

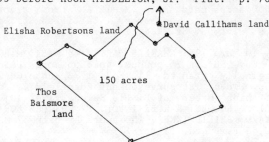

Elisha Robertsons land

David Callihams land

150 acres

Thos Baismore land

Pp. 77-78. 2 Nov 1792: JOSEPH THOMAS & JOYCE his wife of Burk Co. GA to THOMAS BAISMORE of Edgefield Co. SC for 25 pounds, sold 150 acres originally granted 21 Apr 1774: adj. ELISHA ROBERTSON, DAVID CALLIHAM, EBENEZER STERNS. S/ JOSEPH THOMAS, JOYCE THOMAS. Wit: ABSALOM GRIFFIN, DAVID THOMAS, JAMES THOMAS, who swore by oath 6 Jun 1793 before HUGH MIDDLETON J.P. Rcd. 11 Mar 1795.

Pp. 78-80. 21 Oct 1794: JOHN LOWE to MOSES WALTON, both of Edgefield Co. SC for 25 pounds, sold 40 acres being part of 100 acres originally granted Dec 1771 unto WILLIAM LOWE & now being conveyed by JOHN LOWE, son & heir at law to WILLIAM LOWE, deceased; adj. MOSES WALTONS, SAMUEL ABNEY. S/ JOHN LOWE. Wit: GILSON YARBOROUGH, SAMUEL (X) ABNEY, WILLIAM SPRAGGIN, who swore by oath 14 Jan 1795 before NATHL. ABNEY, J.P. Rcd. 11 Mar 1795.

Pp. 80-81. 13 Dec 1794: Bill of Sale: THOMAS YOUNG of Edgefield Co. SC to JOHN CRABTREE for 20 pounds, sold one negro boy named ENOCH about 16 yrs. old. S/ THOMAS YOUNG. Wit: DAVIS WILLIAMS, JOHN HARKINS, THOMAS SMITH, who swore by oath 13 Dec 1794 before JAMES HARRISON. Rcd. 11 Mar 1795.

P. 81. 21 Oct 1794: Bond: WILLIAM COVINGTON WRIGHT, Sen. Planter to JOSEPH COVINGTON CUNNINGHAM, Blacksmith, both of Edgefield Co. SC, Bound for 25 pounds, payment to be made of 12 pounds by 4 Sep next & for better securing of payment to be held one grey mare, one bay mare, bay horse, 4 feather beds with furniture, 4 head of cattle, some sheep, 4 hogs, & all other property said WRIGHT now possesses. S/ WILLIAM WRIGHT. Wit: SAMUEL (X) GARNER, WILLIAM STANHOPE WRIGHT, who swore by oath 10 Mar 1795 before AQUILA MILES. Rcd. 11 Mar 1795.

Pp. 81-83. 26 Jan 1793: WILLIAM DAWSON & MARY, his wife to ABNER McMILLAN, both of Edgefield Co. SC for 100 pounds, sold 350 acres being part of 547 acres originally granted JOHN CROW on Cuffeetown Creek of Savannah River adj. MAJOR BENJAMIN TUTT, THOMAS BACON, Esq.

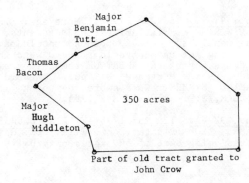

Major Benjamin Tutt

Thomas Bacon

Major Hugh Middleton

350 acres

Part of old tract granted to John Crow

DEED BOOK 12: 1794-1796 EDGEFIELD COUNTY S.C.

HUGH MIDDLETON. S/ WILL. DAWSON, MARY DAWSON. Wit: THOMAS BACON, JOHN TERRY, ICHABAL COX, THOMAS BROUGHTON, who swore by oath 9 Mar 1793 before JAMES HARRISON. Request of WILLIAM DAWSON have laid off 350 acres unto ABNER McMILLAN from tract granted JOHN CROW 6 Mar 1776 for 547 acres...Certified 26 Jan 1793, SHADR. STOKES, D.S. Plat: p. 82. Rcd. 11 Mar 1795.

Pp. 83-86. 10 Mar 1794: CHARLES PARTIN to WILLIAM HOLMES, both of Edgefield Co. SC for 25 pounds, sold 56 acres being part of 200 acres originally granted 11 Feb 1773 unto CHARLES PARTIN in Coleton Co. when 1st surveyed but Edgefield Co. on Dry Creek a branch of Mine Creek of Little Saluda river adj. ARTHUR FORT, said WILLIAM HOLMES & ROBERT POU. S/ CHARLES (CP) PARTIN. Wit: JOHN DRINKARD, PHILIP IKNER, who swore by oath 17 May 1794 before HENRY KING, J.P. Rcd. 11 Mar 1795.

Pp. 86-88. 25 Nov 1794: BRYANT GREEN to FRANCIS COLEMAN, both of Edgefield Co. SC for 70 pounds, sold 100 acres being part of original tract granted 5 May 1773 to JOHN DAY who conveyed to BRIANT GREEN who conveyed to DAVID BOSWELL who conveyed back to said GREEN. N. side of Chavouries Creek adj. Chavouries Creek at the mouth of Spring Branch, JOHN PURSLEY, MATTHEW DEVORES, JOHN LOWE, ROBERT O'WILLIAMS, WILLIAM WILLIAMS, RALPH CARTER. S/ BRYANT (B) GREEN, PHEBE GREEN. Wit: HEZEKIAH COLEMAN, WILLIAM GRIFFIN, JOHN HALL, who swore by oath 17 Jan 1795 before JOSEPH HIGHTOWER, J.P. Rcd. 12 Mar 1795.

Pp. 89-90. 2 Mar 1795: DAVID BURNS, Senr. of Laurence Co. SC to GARLAND GOOD for 40 pounds, sold 250 acres on head of Ninety Six Creek adj. MARCONESS GOODE, JANE BROWNLEE, ROBERT DUKE. S/ DAVID (D) BURNS. Wit: THOMAS WADSWORTH, JAMES YOUNG, who swore by oath 9 Mar 1795 before THOS. WADSWORTH, J.S.C. Rcd. 12 Mar 1795.

P. 90. 11 Mar 1795: Bill of Sale: WILLIAM EVANS, Planter to JOHN LYON, both of Edgefield Co. SC for 35 pounds, sold one negro boy named JAMES. S/ WILLIAM EVANS. Wit: JAMES LYON, JOHN KILLEREASE, who swore by oath 11 Mar 1795 before JAMES HARRISON, J.P. Rcd. 12 Mar 1795.

Pp. 90-91. 30 Oct 1793: DRURY PACE & MARY, his wife to ABIAH MORGAN, both of Edgefield Co. SC for 40 pounds, sold 244 acres being part of tract originally granted JOHN CRAWFORD adj. JOEL CRAWFORD, said PACE, WILLIAM RENNOLDS. S/ DRURY PACE, MARY (n) PACE. Wit: WILLIAM PACE, ONIAS MORGAN, RODAH (X her) MORGAN, who swore by oath 7 Mar 1795 before HUGH MIDDLETON, J.P. Rcd. 12 Mar 1795.

Pp. 91-93. 6 Jan 1795: Mortgage: THOMAS WILLIAMS to THOMAS WADSWORTH & WILLIAM TURPIN, Merchants, by bond dated 1 Jan 1794 in penal sum of 460 pounds, should pay 1 Feb 1794 & for better securing of payment sold a negro wench named MERIAH about 30 yrs old, a boy named CAMBRIDGE about 10 yrs. old & should payment be made, said Mortgage be null & void. S/ THOS. WILLIAMS. Wit: DANIEL SYMMES, who swore by oath 11 Mar 1795 before ROBERT GILLAM, J.P. Rcd. 12 Mar 1795.

Pp. 93-94. 12 Mar 1795: WILLIAM COURSEY of Edgefield Co. SC to JAMES LYON Planter, of Wilks Co. Ga for 150 pounds, sold 150 acres being part of 500 acres originally granted 21 May 1772 said

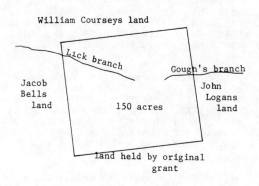

William Courseys land

Lick branch

Gough's branch

Jacob
Bells
land

150 acres

John
Logans
land

land held by original
grant

WILLIAM COURSEY on branch of Beaverdam & turkey Creek of Savannah River crossing GOUGH's branches adj. JOHN LOGAN, Esq., ABRAM MARTIN, JACOB BELL, & WILLIAM COURSEY. S/ WM. COURSEY. Wit: ROBERT COURSEY, WILLIAM KILLCREASE, who swore by oath 12 Mar 1795 before JOHN BLOCKER, J.P. Rcd. 12 Mar 1795. Plat: p. 94.

Pp. 94-96. 19 Jan 1792: WILLIAMS REONOLDS & PEGGY his wife, to ONIAS MORGAN, both of Edgefield Co. SC for 100 pounds, sold 100 acres, part of a tract granted to JOHN HARRIS of Stephens Creek on Catfish waters of Savannah River adj. WILLIAM & KIT COX, DARTON's (DALTON) old survey, DAVID CALLEYHAM & JOHN HERRINGTON. S/ WILLIAM REONALDS, PEGGY (+) REONALDS. Wit: DRURY PACE, NANCY MORGAN, MARY PACE, ABIAH MORGAN, who swore by oath 7 Mar 1795 before HUGH MIDDLETON, J.P. Rcd. 12 Mar 1795.

Pp. 96-97. 9 Nov 1793: Deed of Gift: ELINOR SILLIVAN to OWEN HEATON for 10 shillings, sold 81 acres being part of a tract granted said ELENOR SILLIVAN on north side of Cow Creek. If said OWEN HEATON should decease before reaching age 21 or without lawful heirs of his body then this becomes void...S/ ELENOR SILLIVAN. Wit: MEAL (MEALKEY) DEEN, SARAH (+) YOUNG, SAMUEL DEEN, who swore by oath 4 Oct 1790 before RUSSELL WILSON. Rcd. 12 Mar 1795.

Pp. 97-99. 6 Aug 1793: Sheriff Sale: SAMUEL SAXON, Sheriff of Ninety Six District to WILLIAM SHAW, Esq., Atty. at Law ... Whereas JOHN GORDON, lately in Orangeburg Court of Common Pleas obtained a judgement against Admins. of JOHN CALDWELL, dec'd. for 1000 pounds & Writ was issued 18 Apr 1792 & Sheriff did seize 150 acres in Edgefield Co. SC originally granted Feb 1768 said JOHN CALDWELL adj. JAMES ATKINS...Said Sheriff did sell to WILLIAM SHAW, Esq. for 35 pounds being the last & highest bidder. S/ S. SAXON, Sheriff of Ninety Six Dist. Wit: HENRY WILSON, JOHN TROTTER, who swore by oath 13 Mar 1795 before R. TUTT, J.P. Rcd. 13 Mar 1795.

Pp. 99-100. 14 Feb 1794: Bill of Sale: ABRAHAM RYLEY, Planter of Edgefield Co. SC to SOLOMON POPE for 5 pounds, sold 5 head of Cattle. S/ ABRAHAM RYLEY. Wit: HENRY KING, SUSANNAH (X) POPE, the Younger, who swore by oath 17 Feb 1795 before HENRY KING, J.P. Rcd. 13 Mar 1795.

Pp. 100-102. 23 Dec 1793: CASPER NAIL, Senr., Planter to MARY MEYER, both of Edgefield Co. SC, Adm'trix of Estate of JOHN MEYER, dec'd., for 5 shillings, in Trust & for the only proper use & benefit of the Heirs of said JOHN MEYER, dec'd., sold 150 acres originally granted 5 Jun 1786 to said CASPER NAIL, Senr.,

199

being near Beach Island (excepting a small parcel which runs into JOSEPH HIX's land bounded by said CASPER NAIL, BENJAMIN HARRIS & JOSEPH HIX. S/ CASPER NAIL. Wit: WILLIAM SHINHOLSER, WILLIAM STEWART, who swore by oath 8 Dec 1793 before JOHN CLARKE, J.P. Rcd. 13 Mar 1795.

Pp. 102-105. 5 Jan 1795: GEORGE DEEN, Carpenter to THOMAS DAVIS, Planter, both of Edgefield Co. SC for 10 shillings, sold 145 acres originally granted 29 Jun 1793 to ABSOLOM DEEN, Soldier & he being deceased, fell to GEORGE DEEN, his heir; being on Red Bank Creek of Saluda River adj. THOS. DOZER, RICHARD DOZER, JOHN ABNEY, & LOYAR PERSONS. S/ GEORGE DEEN. Wit: LUD WILLIAMS, ELISHA NIGHT, ARTHUR H. DAVIS, who swore by oath 9 Jan 1795 before RUSSELL WILSON. Rcd. 13 Mar 1795.

P. 105. 23 Feb 1795: Bill of Sale: JAMES JOHNSON, Planter of Lincoln Co. NC to JOHN POPE, for 18 pounds sold one bay horse. S/ JAMES JOHNSON. Wit: CHARITY POPE, SUSANNA POPE, who swore by oath 24 Feb 1795 before HENRY KING, J.P. Rcd. 13 Mar 1795.

Pp. 105-107. 25 Jun 1794: Article of Agreement: ROBERT SAMUEL & CHARLES GOODWIN, Esq., Atty. at Law agree to exchange 2 tracts of land on Chavers Creek; ROBERT SAMUEL to CHARLES GOODWIN, for 5 shillings, 5 acres on S side Chavers Creek & CHARLES GOODWIN to ROBERT SAMUEL for 5 shillings, 7 acres on N side of Jenakin or Judges Branch being south most fork of Chavers Creek. S/ ROBERT SAMUEL CHAS. GOODWIN. Wit: SETH HOWARD, who swore by oath 28 Jun 1794 before JOSEPH HIGHTOWER, J.P. Rcd. 14 Mar 1795.

Pp. 107-108. 28 Oct 1794: Deed of Gift: THOMAS JOHNSON to ROBERT & JOSEPH HUTSON for love & affection my two grandchildren to be equally divided betwixt them - 5 head of cattle, 10 head of hoggs, 1 spinning wheel, 1/2 doz. chairs, 1 set of tea ware, 2 large bowls, 1 bed, 2 bed steads, 1 cupboard, 1 chest, 1 frying pan, 1 pr. of fine irons, 1 blanket, 1 matrass, 1 table, 1 churn & 2 prs. of cards, 6 plates, 3 dishes, 1 silver watch. S/ THOMAS JOHNSON. Wit: WILLIAM BURNS, WILLIAM MOORE, who swore by oath 14 Feb 1795 before W. ROBINSON, J.P. Rcd. 14 Mar 1795.

Pp. 108-109. 5 Dec 1795: Mortgage: JOHN COVINGTON & WILLIAM FUGUA of Edgefield Co. SC to ELIAS & HENRY SMERDON, Merchants, of Augusta GA by bond for 157 pounds, payable by 16 Nov 1795 & for better securing of payment sell 2 negroe boys named PETER & ABRAHAM about 14 years each, on condition that 78 pounds be payed by 16 Nov 1795 & then agreement be null & void. S/ JOHN COVINGTON, WILLIAM FUQUA. Wit: JOHN GIBSON, CHARLES CARTER, who swore by oath 13 Mar 1795 before RICHARD TUTT, J.P. Rcd. 13 Mar 1795.

Pp. 109-110. 15 Mar 1795: Deed of Gift: JOHN COOK to WEST COOK, my son, both of Edgefield Co. SC for love & affection; after my death one negroe man named DANIEL. S/ JOHN COOK. Wit: JAMES BAKER, WILLIAM FUGUA, JOSEPH CUNNINGHAM, who swore by oath 16 Mar 1795 before JOHN BLOCKER, J.P. Rcd. 16 Mar 1795.

P. 110. 15 Mar 1795: Deed of Gift: JOHN COOK to ANN COOK, my loving wife, for love & good will, give two negroes named CHARLES & ANAKA during her life then to return to my daughter, POLLY COOK. Also give to my daughter POLLY COOK 136 acres, & 5 negroes

DEED BOOK 12: 1794-1796 EDGEFIELD COUNTY S.C.

(to wit:) HARKLESS, SELA, HARRY, TOM & SAM, also my household
furniture, stock of horses, cows & hogs. If said POLLY COOK dies
without heirs said property returns to me & my heirs. Also my
desire is that my wife, ANN COOK keep possession of my land etc.
during her life & of above mentioned negroes, HARKLESS, SELA,
HARRY, TOM & SAM I give to my daughter POLLY until she comes of
age or marries. S/ JOHN COOK. Wit: JAMES BAKER, WILLIAM FUQUA,
JOSEPH CUNNINGHAM, who swore by oath 16 Mar 1795 before JOHN
BLOCKER, J.P. Rcd. 15 Mar 1795.

P. 111. 23 Apr 1794: Bill of Sale: JAMES CLARKE of Edgefield Co.
SC to Capt. THOMAS KEY for 25 pounds, sold one negro girl age 11,
named NELLY. S/ JAMES CLARK. Wit: JOSEPH BARKSDALE, RICHARD
GANTT, who swore by oath 14 Mar 1795. Rcd. 16 Mar 1795.

Pp. 111-112. 26 Dec 1794: WILLIAM HOWLE, Senr. to WILLIAM
STANHOPE WRIGHT, both of Edgefield Co. SC for 25 pounds, sold 100
acres being part of 135 acres on Loyd & Stephens Creek adj. Mrs.
BRAZEAL; formerly NATHAN EVAN, & MICAJAH PHILLIPS. S/ WILLIAM (X)
HOWLE, Senr. Wit: MILLY (O) HOWLE, JOHN (K) BALEY, WILLIAM HOWLE,
Junr., who swore by oath 6 Mar 1795 before AQUILA MILES, J.P.
Rcd. 16 Mar 1795.

Pp. 112-115. 16 Mar 1795: THOMAS BACON, Esq. Planter, to WILLIAM
HALL, Planter both of Edgefield Co. SC for 100 pounds, sold 150
acres originally granted 7 Feb 1764 unto JOHN WILLIAMS on Cuffee
Town Creek a branch of Stephens Creek of Savannah River adj.
heirs of HUMPHREY BARROTT. S/ THOS. BACON. Wit: DAVIS MOORE,
HARTWELL JONES, EUGENE BRENAN, who swore by oath 23 Mar 1795
before RD. TUTT, J.P. Rcd. 23 Mar 1795.

Pp. 115-118. 16 Mar 1795: THOMAS BACON, Esq. Planter, to WILLIAM
HALL, Planter both of Edgefield Co. SC for 15 pounds, sold 40
acres granted to JOHN WILLIAMS on Cuffee Town Creek of Savannah
River adj. THOMAS BACON, WILSON, STOKES. S/ THOS. BACON. Wit:
DAVIS MOORE, HARTWELL JONES, EUGENE BRENAN, who swore by oath 23
Mar 1795 before RICHARD TUTT, J.P. Rcd. 23 Mar 1795.

P. 118. Bill of Sale: DANIEL GUNNELS to MARGARET CARTER: ROSANNAH
CARTER delivered to MARGARET CARTER for 3 pounds due my mother
one cow & calf delivered in 1790. Also 1 Iron pot to discharge
above debt certified by me in 1790 DANIEL GUNNELS which goods I
recieved in behalf of my child MARGET I say recieved by me. S/
ROSANAH (+) CARTER. Wit: MOSES CARTER, EDWARD COUCH, who swore by
oath before VAN SWEARENGEN, J.P. Rcd. 24 Mar 1795.

Pp. 118-120. 20 Dec 1794: ROBERT BROOKS & ANNE his wife,
Planters, to DANIEL BRUNSON, both of Edgefield
Co. SC for 30 pounds, sold
174 acres, part of 206
acres conveyed 24 Mar 1794
from WILLIAM COURSEY to
said BROOKS which was part
of 1000 acres granted 6
May 1793 at Columbia unto
EDWARD VANN, who conveyed
10 Jun 1793 to WILLIAM
COURSEY on branch of
Beaverdam Creek of Turkey

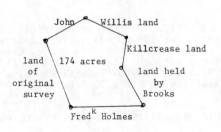

201

Creek of Savannah River. S/ ROBT. (+) BROOKS, ANNE (+) BROOKS. Wit: WILLIAM COURSEY, JOHN (‡) WITT, who swore by oath 27 Mar 1795 before RICHARD TUTT, J.P. Plat: p. 120.

Pp. 120-122. 28 Mar 1795: Rev. JOHN MONK to JOHN SLOAN, 1150 acres on South Edisto River being all that two tracts; (1) 150 acres originally granted 8 Jul 1774 to JAMES HARRISON in Ninety Six Dist. on Edisto Creek so called at that time & was conveyed by said HARRISON 24 Mar 1787 to DAVIS RICHARDSON who conveyed 19 Nov 1790 unto said Rev. JOHN MONK; (2) 1000 acres originally granted 2 Sep 1793 to said REV. JOHN MONK. Said land includes the Iron Works lately built by Rev. JOHN MONK & said SLOAN & known as Edisto Iron Works. Also the Grist & saw mills & all the Iron ore banks. Said 1150 acres lying within 3 miles of navagable water & within 25 miles of Augusta & Campbell Town & Savannah River. S/ JOHN MONK. Wit: ISAAC KIRKLAND, JAMES (+) BANISTER, MOSES ARMSTRONG, who swore by oath 30 Mar 1795 before VANN SWEARENGEN, J.P. Rcd. 30 Mar 1795.

Pp. 122-123. 7 Nov 1793: WILLIAM USERY of Spartenburg Co. SC to WEST HARRIS of Edgefield Co. SC for 50 pounds, sold 276 acres originally granted 4 Feb 1793 on Sleepy Creek of Stephens Creek of Savannah River. S/ WILLIAM (V) USERY. Wit: RICHARD (R) MORRIS, WILLIAM MORRIS, JOHN MORRIS, who swore by oath 23 Nov 1793 before HENRY KING, J.P. Rcd. 30 Mar 1795.

Pp. 123-126. 2 Feb 1795: JONATHAN LIMBACKER & REBECCA his wife to MATHEW DEVORE, both of Edgefield Co. SC for 100 pounds, sold 100 acres on Chavers Creek being part of 300 acres originally granted to MICHAEL BUCKHALTER & conveyed unto GEORGE LIMBACKER, Sr. & then invested in GEORGE LIMBACKER, Jr. by LW&T of GEO. LIMBACKER, Sr. & from GEORGE LIMBACKER, Jr. conveyed 27 Dec 1784 to JONATHAN LIMBACKER. S/ JONATHAN (L) LIMBACKER, REBECCA (X) LIMBACKER. Wit: WILLIAM WATSON, Senr., JOHN ROBERTS, Jr., ABSOLAM (A) ROBERTS, who swore by oath 31 Mar 1795 before RICHD. TUTT, J.P. Rcd. 20 Apr 1795.

Pp. 126-128. 26 Dec 1787: JOHN PURSELL to AARON HERRIN, both of Edgefield Co. SC for 70 pounds, sold 70 acres being part of a tract originally granted JOHN MORRIS & conveyed by said MORRIS to JOHN PURSELL on Stephens Creek adj. DAVID MELONE old line, TUTT's old line. S/ JOHN (↔) PURSELL, BARBARA (+) PURSELL. Wit: ELIJAH LYON, ABSALOM (A) ROBERT. Rcd. 2 Apr 1795.

Pp. 128-129. 17 Mar 1795: Bill of Sale: WILLIAM EVANS of Edgefield Co. SC to JOHN LYON for 40 pounds, sold one negro girl named MERIER. S/ WILLIAM EVANS, JOHN LYON. Wit: JENSEY HIBBLER, THOMAS BACON, Jr., who swore by oath 23 Mar 1795 before THOS. BACON, J.E.C. Rcd. 4 Apr 1795.

Pp. 129-130. 15 Feb 1794: JOHN CARTER, Planter of Fairfield Co. SC to BENJAMIN LINDSEY, Blacksmith for 200 pounds, sold 200 acres originally granted 16 May 1773 unto JOHN MORRIS on Nobles Creek of Horns Creek of Savannah River; adj. BN. RYAN. S/ JOHN CARTER, JANE (+) CARTER, his wife. Wit: THOS. MALONE, JAMES PARKS, who swore by oath 25 Mar 1794 before JOHN PRATT, J.P. Rcd. 4 Apr 1795.

P. 131. 22 Dec 1794: BENJAMIN CROOKSHANKS, formerly of SC, now

DEED BOOK 12: 1794-1796 EDGEFIELD COUNTY S.C.

of GA to JOSEPH FARGUSON, Sr. Planter, of Warren Co. GA for 25
pounds, sold 100 acres in Edgefield Co. SC on Savannah River adj.
HUGH MIDDLETON, Esq., STEPHEN SMITH, being part of 400 acres
originally granted 18 Mar 1754 unto JOHN CROOKSHANKS OF SC
dec'd., being the father of above mentioned BENJAMIN CROOKSHANKS.
Said land afterwards conveyed or bequeath to his three sons(viz)
JOHN, DAVID & BENJAMIN CROOKSHANKS jointly as heirs by Deed Will

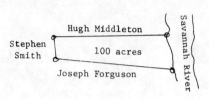

10 Mar 1765. S/
BENJAMIN (B.C.)
CROOKSHANKS. Wit:
JOHN GRAY, ELKANAH
LOFTIN, who swore by
oath 4 Apr 1795
before JOSEPH
HIGHTOWER, J.P. Rcd.
6 Apr 1795. Plat: p.
131.

10 May 1794 by ROBERT LANG, D.S.

Pp. 132-134. 25 Oct 1794: WILLIAM COURSEY & MARY his wife, Deputy
Surveyor & Spinstress, to JOHN FRANKS, Planter, all of Edgefield
Co. SC for 84 pounds, sold 460 acres being part of 1000 acres
originally granted EDWARD VANN 6 May 1793 & conveyed to said
WILLIAM COURSEY 10 Jun 1793 on Goughs branch of Turkey Creek of
Savannah River adj. the Ridge path, WHIT, ROBERT BROOKS, COURSEY,
FREDERICK HOLMES. S/ WM. COURSEY, MARY (+) COURSEY. Wit: ALLEN
COURSEY, ELIJAH (X) BOND, who swore by oath 10 Apr 1795 before
RD. TUTT, J.P. Rcd. 10 Apr 1795. Plat: p. 134.

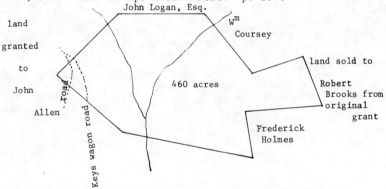

Pp. 134-135. 11 Jan 1794: Bond: JOHN SLOAN of Spartenburg Co. SC
to JOSEPH REED of Edgefield Co. SC, his certain attorney,
Indorsed to THOMAS BROUGHTON, In penal sum of 1000 pounds;
condition of obligation that JOHN SLOAN should persue the search
after a vain of Led oar supposed to be on a tract of land
conveyed from said JOSEPH REED unto the bound JOHN SLOAN & when
found said SLOAN will deliver on the oar banks one half of all
the lead or silver or par the value thereof to said JOSEPH REED
then said above obligation be null & void. I, Indorse the within
Bond to THOMAS BROUGHTON 9 Oct 1794. S/ JOSEPH REED. Wit: WILLIAM
WILLIAMS, JOHN SMITH, who swore by oath 13 Apr 1795 before
RICHARD TUTT, J.P. Rcd. 13 Apr 1795.

Pp. 135-136. 6 Apr 1795: Mortgage: REUBIN FRAZOR, Planter of
Edgefield Co. SC to JAMES FLETCHER: give Bond for 100 pounds to

203

DEED BOOK 12: 1794-1796 EDGEFIELD COUNTY S.C.

JAMES FLETCHER to be paid 9 months from now & for better securing of payment give & grant certain property (to wit) one negro woman named TINER, 11 head of cattle, 2 horses, a bay mare, 6 head of sheep, the rest bought at the sale of JOHN CUNNINGHAM's Sale, 3 fether beds & furniture 1/2 doz. plates, 2 dishes, 3 pewter basons, tble, 4 chears, 1 case of bottles, one chest, 1 weavers lume - If obligation met...becomes null & void. S/ REUBIN FRAZER. Wit: LUCY MIDDLETON, MATHEW TURPIN, who swore by oath 8 Apr 1795 before HUGH MIDDLETON, J.P. Rcd. 14 Apr 1795.

Pp. 136-137. 9 Mar 1795: HENRY WARE, Esq. & MARTHA his wife of Wilks Co. GA to JAMES MONDAY of Edgefield Co. SC for 50 pounds, sold 800 acres originally granted 16 Apr 1773 to said HENRY WARE; on waters of Stephens Creek, Martin & Rockey Creeks waters of Savannah River adj. MURPHEY, GIBARs. S/ HENRY WARE, MARTHA (+) WARE. Wit: JAMES WARE, BENJAMIN MAY, who swore by oath 14 Apr 1795 before JOHN RYAN, J.P. Rcd. 17 Apr 1795.

Pp. 137-139. 21 Oct 1794: SAMUEL MAYS, Sheriff of Edgefield Co. SC to EPHRAM BROWN...Whereas ANDREW PICKENS & Co. lately in Edgefield Co. Court obtained a judgement against THOMAS LAMAR for 290 pounds & a Writ was issued 8 Jul 1793 which directed the goods & chattels & real estate of THOMAS LAMAR be levied & SAMUEL MAYS, Sheriff, did sieze 200 acres on horse creek adj. MELINE C. LEVENWORTH, THOMAS LAMAR, NATHANIEL BACON the 6 Sep 1794 sold for 30 pounds to highest & last bidder, EPHRAM BROWN. S/ S. MAYS, Sheriff, Edgefield County. Wit: JEREMIAH HATCHER, THOMAS BUTLER, who swore by oath 24 Oct 1794 before RICHARD TUTT, J.P. Rcd. 20 Apr 1795.

Pp. 139-141. WILLIAM TENNANT, Sheriff of Ninety Six Dist. to JOHN FOX, Merchant, of Augusta, GA...Whereas THOMAS LAMAR of Edgefield Co. SC was siezed of 600 acres on Horse Creek adj. BENJAMIN BEVIN, GEORGE KING: Said land originally granted 8 Jul 1774 unto JOSEPH JOHNSON & by him conveyed 3 Jun 1788 to THOMAS LAMAR for 100 pounds & Whereas THOMAS LAMAR became indebted unto KEVAN TAYLOR & MURRIN, Merchants, who obtained a judgement for 168 pounds, did Commence action in Court of Common Pleas at Cambridge 22 Nov 1793 & said Sheriff, WILLIAM TENNANT did sieze & sell at public auction to highest & last bidder, JOHN FOX for 9 pounds... S/ WM. TENNENT, Sheriff of Ninety Six Dist. Wit: JOHN TROTTER, SAMUEL SAXON, who swore by oath 22 Apr 1795 before JOHN TROTTER, J.P. Rcd. 30 Apr 1795.

Pp. 141-144. 6 Mar 1795: WILLIAM TENNANT, Sheriff of Ninety Six Dist. to JOHN FOX, Merchant of Augusta GA...Whereas THOMAS LAMAR of Edgefield Co. SC was seized of 640 acres on Horse Creek adj. on lands surveyed for one BRANNON, lands formerly held by BEVEN, ARCHD. OFFATT, being land originally granted 5 Dec 1785 to THOMAS LAMAR...Whereas THOMAS LAMAR became indebted to KEVAN TAYLOR & MURAIN, Merchants & they obtained a judgement for 168 pounds 22 Nov 1793 & Sheriff, WILLIAM TENNANT did sieze & sell for 12 pounds to the last & highest bidder, JOHN FOX. S/ WM. TENNANT, Sheriff of Ninety Six Dist. Wit: JOHN TROTTER, SAMUEL SAXON, Esq., who swore by oath 22 Apr 1795 before JOHN TROTTER, J.P. Rcd. 30 Apr 1795.

Pp. 144-147. 24 Apr 1795: NATHAN JOHNSON, Jr. late of Edgefield Co. SC & JAMES GOUEDY, Planter of Edgefield Co. SC to DIONYSIAS

OLIVER, Planter, of Edgefield Co. SC for 80 pounds, sold 160 acres being part of 200 acres originally granted 24 Dec 1772 unto JOHN MASON on Beaver Dam Creek a branch of Stephens Creek of Savannah River. S/ NATHAN JOHNSON, Jr., JAMES GOUEDY. Wit: JAMES McCRACKAN, EUGENE BRENAN, who swore by oath 2 May 1795 before RICHARD TUTT, J.P. Rcd. 2 May 1795.

Pp. 147-149. 20 Apr 1795: Newberry Co. SC: WILLIAM GOGGINS & PHEBY, his wife, of Newberry Co. SC to JOHN SLOAN of Spartinburgh Co. SC for 50 pounds, sold 100 acres being part of 200 acres originally granted 31 Aug 1774 unto THOMAS WHITEHEAD & was conveyed to DANIEL GOGGINS 23 Dec 1779. Said DANIEL GOGGINS, dec'd. & it fell to WILLIAM GOGGIN, being his Eldest son & heir; Said land on North side of Edisto with 1 1/2 acres on the South side at a shoal trap or suitable place for a mill or fish. S/ WILLIAM GOGGANS, PHEBE (+) GOGGANS. Wit: DANIEL GOGGINS, CHARLES SCOTT.
Edgefield Co. SC: BENJAMIN CLARK swore by oath 1 May 1795 before VAN SWEARENGEN, J.P. Rcd. 2 May 1795.

Pp. 149-151. 27 May 1794: HUGH YOUNG, Esq. to JOHN COURSEY, both of Edgefield Co. SC for 25 pounds, sold 179 acres being part of 1500 acres originally granted 17 Dec 1772 unto HUGH ROSE & at his deceased, descended to HUGH YOUNG. On Little Stephens Creek of Savannah River adj. BENJAMIN MAZYCK; near Saluda & Savannah Road; JAMES WILLIAMS, WHEYLEY, ELISHA STEPHENS, BRIDGES & said YOUNG. S/ HUGH YOUNG. Wit: JAMES JONES, SYLVANUS WALKER, who swore by oath 22 Apr 1795 before W. ROBINSON, J.P. Rcd. 2 May 1795. Plat: p. 150.

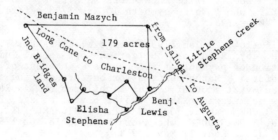

WM. COURSEY, D.S.

Pp. 151-154. 29 Apr 1795: DANIEL GUNNELS & ELIZABETH, his wife to DANIEL PARKER, both of Edgefield Co. SC for 60 pounds, sold 150 acres originally granted 31 Aug 1774 unto JOHN VERNON & a memorial entered 25 Feb 1775 in Auditor General's Office, & on a branch of Log Creek of Savannah River adj. bounty land, when surveyed. S/ DANIEL (X) GUNNELS, ELIZABETH (+) GUNNELS. Wit: SANDERS GUNNELS, JOSEPH GRIFFIN, who swore by oath 7 May 1795 before RICHARD TUTT, J.P. Rcd. 7 May 1795.

Pp. 154-155. 27 May 1795: Bill of Sale: DANIEL GUNNELS to DANIEL PARKER, both of Edgefield Co. SC for 30 pounds, sold (viz) one horse, 1 Mair, 1 cow, 1 calf, 1 heifer, 1 feather bed & furniture, 1 chest, 1 trunk, 1/2 doz. Chairs, 1/2 doz. plates, 4 pewter plates, 5 basons, 1 dish, 1 case of knives & forks, 1/2 doz. spoons, 1 coffee pot, 5 other pots, 1 spinning wheel, 1 frying pan, 1 washing tub, 2 pails, 3 hives of bees, 1 grind stone, 1 narrow ax, 3 weeding hoes, 1 bridle, 1 plow & gairs, 7 head of geese, 40 head of hogs, 2 sows, 12 pigs. S/ DANIEL (X) GUNNELS. Wit: JOSEPH GRIFFIN, SAMUEL MARSH, SANDERS (+) GUNNELS, who swore by oath 7 May 1795 before RICHARD TUTT, J.P. Rcd. 7 May 1795.

Pp. 155-158. 7 Dec 1794: CHARLES FENDLEY & HANNAH, his wife to JOHN HOULSONBACK, both of Edgefield Co. SC: 100 acres being part of 113 acres originally granted 5 Oct 1786 CHARLES ASHLEY; on a branch of Middle Creek adj. JACOB CLACKER, JOHN HOULSONBACK, MELSON, THOMAS BURKHAM, ABSOLOM RHANES. S/ CHARLES (C) FENLEY, HANNER (X) FENLEY. Wit: RICHARD SEARLES, JAMES PICKETT, who swore by oath 7 May 1795 before HENRY KEY, J.P. Rcd. (not on page).

P. 159. 16 Nov 1792: Bond: THOMAS DOOLY & GEORGE DOOLY of Wilks Co. GA to EZEKIEL WIMBLEY of Edgefield Co. SC for 500 pounds; The condition of above obligation & for better securing of payment sell a plantation - on a road leading to Long Cane Settlement including PATRIDGE's old fields - if above obligation paid... becomes null & void. S/ THOMAS DOOLY, GEORGE DOOLY. Wit: ALEXANDER McMILLON, ROBERT ROSS, LEWIS WIMBERLEY, who swore by oath 15 May 1793 before HENRY KING, J.P. Rcd. 2 May 1795.

Pp. 159-162. 15 Nov 1792: THOMAS DOOLY of Wilks Co. GA to EZEKIEL WIMBLEY of Edgefield Co. SC for 35 pounds, sold 100 acres on the waggon Road leading to Long Cane Settlement including PATRIDGE's old field adj. CRAWFORD, DOOLY, SIMON BECK. S/ THOMAS DOOLY, GEORGE DOOLY. Wit: ALEXANDER McMILLAN, ROBERT ROSS, LEWIS WIMBLEY, who swore by oath 15 May 1793 before HENRY KING, J.P. Rcd. 2 May 1795.

Pp. 162-164. 23 Jan 1795: Mortgage: RICHARD TUTT, Jr. to BERKLEY MARTIN: by Bond or obligation for penal Sum 200 pounds with condition of payment of 100 pounds & interest of 7 % per annum on or before 8 March next, & for better securing of payment sold 3 negroes viz: MOLLEY & her 2 children BETT & RACHEL. MOLLY is a yellow complexion about 25 or 6 yrs. of age, BETT about 5 yrs. old, RACHEL about 3 yrs old. S/ RICHARD TUTT, JR. Wit: EDMOND HOLLEN, THOMAS ODEN, who swore by oath 18 Apr 1795 before AQUILLA MILES, J.P. Rcd. 11 May 1795.

Pp. 164-166. 15 Aug 1794: JOSEPH DAWSON & ELIZABETH his wife, Planter & Spinstress, to OBEDIAH CLEMENT, Planter, all of Edgefield Co. SC for 100 pounds, sold 203 acres on Turkey Creek a prong of Stephens Creek of Savannah River, being two tracts of land adj. each other as seen in plat; (A) 100 acres originally granted ANDREW JONES & transferred to said DAWSON the 18th Apr 1793; (B) 103 acres being part of 150 acres originally granted said

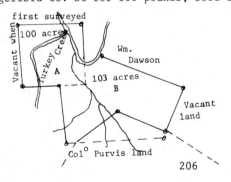

DEED BOOK 12: 1794-1796 EDGEFIELD COUNTY S.C.

DAWSON 1 Jan 1787; take off 47 acres part of said grant in Plat C, included by the dotted lines fell in an old grant held by Colo. PURVIS being measured & plotted out by WM. COURSEY, D.S. 23 Nov 1791. S/ JOSEPH DAWSON, ELIZABETH (+) DAWSON. Wit: DORIS WILLIAMS, WILLIAM TERRY, who swore by oath 11 May 1795 before R. TUTT, C.E.C. Plat: p. 165.

Pp. 166-169. 15 May 1794: SAMUEL SAXON, Esq. Sheriff of Ninety Six Dist. to WILLIAM MATTHEWS, Storekeeper, being last & highest bidder...Whereas SAMUEL SAXON, Sheriff did seize, advertise & sell at Campbellton, toward satisfactions of a public auction, 200 acres originally granted JOSHUA SNOWDON, bounded by Savannah River, DANIEL PEPPER, WILLIAM McMULLAN & a memorial was entered in the Aud. General's office & recorded in Secretary's office... Whereas creditors entered a judgement at Court of Common Pleas at Cambridge against the Estate of LEROY HAMMOND, Esq. dec'd., with the Adm. of said estate MARY ANN HAMMOND, LEROY HAMMOND, CHARLES GOODWIN & GEORGE WHITEFIELD; (1) Debt of 14,380 pounds to JOHN BLAKE, HENRY POOLE, WILLIAM DAWSON, JOHN YARSTON & WILLIAM HORNBY... suit witnessed by Hon. JOHN RUTLEDGE, Esq. 18 Apr 1792; (2) Debt of 286 pounds to JOHN & HENRY SCHOOLBREAD, witnessed by Hon. JOHN RUTLEDGE, Esq. 28 Apr 1793. S/ S. SAXON, Sheriff Ninety Six Dist. Wit: JOHN TROTTER, DAVID SANDIDGE, who swore by oath 27 Apr 1795 before JNO. TROTTER, J.P. Rcd. 18 May 1795.

Pp. 169-170. 23 Dec 1793: Articles of Agreement: JOSEPH BRADBERRY of Columbia Co. GA sold to RICHARD JOHNSON a Judgement upon ENOCH GRIGSBY which was obtained in VA in favor of JULIOUS SCRUGS against said GRIGSBY. RICHARD JOHNSON is to give 125 pounds in TOM P. CARNES Bond & in horse flesh for said Judgement in full against GRIGSBY & said RICHARD is to be all expenses that may accure on said suit now in Cambridge against GRIGSBY & the said BRADBERRY & RICHD. JOHNSON is to meat at PETER CARNS, Esq. on 1 Jan 1794 in order to finally receive the payment of JOHNSON in full for Judgement. S/ JOSEPH (X) BRADBERRY, RICHD. JOHNSON. Wit: JOHN JOHNSON & EPHRAM FERRELL swore by oath 5 May 1795 before JOHN RYAN, J.P. Rcd. 18 May 1795.

Pp. 170-171. 5 Aug 1793: RICHARD CORLEY of Edgefield Co. SC to JOHN THOMAS, Jr. of Green Co. GA for 125 pounds, sold one negro woman, LIZZE (or ELIZABETH), about 30 yrs. old of yellow complexion & her 4 children: 1 negro girl, DOLLY, about 12 yrs. old; 1 negro girl, NANCY, about 9 yrs. old; 1 negro boy, TONEY, about 7 yrs. old; 1 negro boy, MANUEL about 6 months old. S/ RICHARD CORLEY. Wit: GARLAND GOODE, & SAMPSON POPE swore by oath 1 Apr 1795 before W. ROBINSON, J.P. Rcd. 7 May 1795.

Pp. 171-174. 2 Dec 1794: HENRY WARE of Stephen Creek, Planter, to WILLIAM WRIGHT, both of Edgefield Co. SC for 140 pounds, sold 200 acres being part of 150 acres originally granted 7 Jan 1772 JOHN DAVIS & 100 acres granted 21 Apr 1774 to NATHAN REED, & conveyed over from ISOM DAVIS by being heir at law unto HENRY WARE 24 Jan 1784; on NE side of Loyd's Creek adj. JONES RIVERS, MICHAEL BLOCKER, STEPHEN GARROTT. S/ HENRY WARE. Wit: EDMOND HOLLEMAN, LUCY (her mark) HOLLIDAY, JOHN (X) KING, who swore by oath 29 May 1795 before HUGH MIDDLETON, J.P. Rcd. 29 May 1795.

Pp. 174-178. 21 Dec 1794: WILLIAM WRIGHT, Planter of Abbeville Co. SC to JAMES LOMAX, for 28 pounds, sold 200 acres being part of 150 acres originally granted 7 Jan 1772 to JOHN DAVIS & 100 acres granted 21 Apr 1774 to NATHAN REED & conveyed from ISOM DAVIS by virtue of his being heir at law to HENRY WARE 24 Jan 1784 who conveyed 2 Dec 1794 to WILLIAM WRIGHT, on Loyds Creek adj. JONES RIVERS, MYCHAL BLOCKER, STEPHEN GARROTT. S/ WILLIAM WRIGHT. Wit: ABSOLOM FARRINGTON, ARCHABALD (X) FRASHOR, WILLIAM LOMAX, who swore by oath 3 Apr 1795 before W. ROBINSON, J.P. Rcd. 29 May 1795.

Pp. 178-181. 22 May 1795: WILLIAM MAYSON, as attorney for WM. HART in Charleston, to HENRY HERRON of Edgefield Co. SC for 50 pounds, sold 200 acres being part of 2 tracts granted to the Revd. SAMUEL HART & in a general Plat surveyed by WILLIAM DANIEL 18 Jun 1794 said to contain 1007 as a lot off said Plat on Pen Creek of Little Saluda River. S/ WM. HART by his agent, WM. MAYSON. Wit: BARRET (X) TRAVERS, WILLIAM HERRIN, who swore by oath 24 May 1795 before JAS. MAYSON. Rcd. 2 Jun 1795.

Pp. 181-184. 11 Jan 1794: JOSEPH REED of Edgefield Co. SC to JOHN SLOAN of Spartinburg Co. SC for 50 pounds, sold 329 acres originally granted 4 Mar 1790 & 1793 on head of Beaverdam Creek of Turkey Creek & Stephens Creek of Savannah River adj. WALKER, HOLMES, MARSH, JOSEPH READ, & ISAAC KIRKLAND. S/ JOSEPH REED. Wit: WILLIAM WILLIAMS, BENJAMIN ARRINGTON, JOHN SMITH, who swore by oath 7 Jun 1795 before RICHARD TUTT, J.P. Rcd. 6 June 1795.

Pp. 184-187. 11 Jan 1794: JOSEPH REED of Edgefield Co. SC to JOHN SLOAN of Spartenburg Co. SC for 50 pounds, sold 100 acres originally surveyed & granted 10 Nov 1761 unto ISREAL ROBINSON & by LW&T 10 Feb 1773 of ISREAL ROBINSON devised to DAVID ROBINSON & by said ROBINSON conveyed 31 Dec 1791 unto JOSEPH REED; on Beaverdam Creek otherwise Rocky Creek, a branch of Turkey Creek of Stephens Creek & Savannah River. S/ JOSEPH REED. Wit: WILLIAM WILLIAMS, BENJAMIN ARRINGTON, JOHN SMITH, who swore by oath 6 Jun 1795 before R. TUTT, J.P. Rcd. 6 Jun 1795.

Pp. 187-190. 31 Dec 1791: DAVID ROBINSON & ELINOR, his wife of GA to JOSEPH REED of Edgefield Co. SC for 50 pounds, sold 100 acres originally granted 10 Nov 1761 unto ISREAL ROBINSON & by LW&T of 10 Feb 1773 conveyed to said DAVID ROBINSON; on Beaverdam branch otherwide Rocky Creek, a branch of Turkey Creek of Stephens Creek & Savannah River. S/ DAVID ROBINSON, ELINOR ROBINSON. Wit: HENRY JOHNSON, JOSEPH WHITE, NATHAN WHITE, who swore by oath 13 Jan 1792 before ARTHURS SIMKINS, J.E.C. Rcd. 6 Jun 1795.

Pp. 190-194. 11 Jan 1794: NATHANIEL FORD of Fairfield Co. SC to JOHN OLLIPHANT, Planter of Edgefield Co. SC for 15 pounds, sold 300 acres being part of 384 acres originally granted 7 Jan 1793 unto NATHANIEL FORD, on branches of Beaverdam Creek of Turkey Creek of Stephens Creek of Savannah River adj. CHARLES PINKNEY, LEROY JESTER, NATHAN JOHNSON. S/ NATHANIEL FORD. Wit: DANIEL BAUGH, WILLIAM WILLIAMS, JOHN FRAZIER, who swore by oath 26 Jun 1795 before RICHARD TUTT, J.P. Rcd. 26 Jun 1795.

Pp. 194-195. 10 Feb 1795: JAMES WEST to JOHN OLIPHANT, both of Edgefield Co. SC for 100 pounds, sold 7 acres originally surveyed 19 May 1783 for JAMES WEST & granted 1 Oct 1787, on branch of Cedar Creek adj. THOMAS HAGENS, OLIPHANTS, WILLIAM HAGEN. S/ JAMES (⊢⊣) WEST. Wit: WILLIAM HAGENS, WILLIAM ROBERTSON, who swore by oath 26 Jun 1795 before RICHARD TUTT, J.P. Rcd. 26 Jun 1795.

DEED BOOK 12: 1794-1796 EDGEFIELD COUNTY S.C.

Pp. 195-198. 29 Nov 1794: THOMAS SWEARENGEN, Edgefield Co. SC to JOHN SLOAN of Spartenbugh Co. SC, Tygor River, for 30 pounds, sold 150 acres, the lower part of 298 acres originally granted 1 Aug 1793 THOS. SWEARENGEN, Shaws Creek of Edisto River adj. JOHN SWEARENGEN. S/ THOS. SWEARENGEN. Wit: JESSE LOTT, VAN SWEARENGEN, Jr., who swore by oath 6 Jun 1795 before RICHARD TUTT, J.P. Rcd. 6 Jun 1795.

Pp. 199-200. 21 May 1795: Deed of Gift: JAMES BARKER, Sr., Planter of Rocky Creek to my son, JAMES BARKER, Jr., a minor, for love & affection, gives 50 acres being land where said JAMES BARKER, Sr. now lives, being on Rocky Creek. S/ JAMES BARKER. Wit: JEREMIAH (X) YOUNGBLOOD, JAMES SCOTT, MARY YOUNGBLOOD (her mark), who swore by oath 6 Jun 1795 before RICHARD TUTT, J.P. Rcd. 6 Jun 1795.

Pp. 200-201. 21 May 1795: Deed of Gift: JAMES BARKER, Sr. of Rocky Creek, Edgefield Co. SC to my beloved son, JAMES BARKER, Jr., for Love & affection, give all my chattles & substances; mare & colt; horse, 2 heifers & calves; 2 sows & pigs, crop in ground; 2 feather beds & furniture; 1 Loom, chest; gun, 2 pots, oven, pewter & other shelf ware, 2 plows, 1 hoe, 1 axe, 1 mattock. S/ JAMES BAKER. Wit: JEREMIAH YOUNGBLOOD, JAMES SCOTT, MARY (X) YOUNGBLOOD, who swore by oath 6 Jun 1795 before RICHRD. TUTT, J.P. Rcd. 6 Jun 1795.

Pp. 202-203. 24 Jan 1795: PHILIP LAMAR to JAMES JONES, both of Edgefield Co. SC for (blank) 188 acres, being part of tract originally granted PHILIP LAMAR on waters of Savannah River; adj. JACOB GUYTON. S/ PHILIP LAMAR. Wit: JACOB GUYTON, SION (X) WEST, who swore by oath 9 May 1795 before JOHN CLARK, J.P. Rcd. 6 Jun 1795.

Pp. 203-204. 5 Aug 1793: Agreement: PETER CARNS, Esq., DAVID GLOVER, & THOMAS DOOLY: THOMAS DOOLY & PETER CARNS agree for himself & ABRAHAM RICHARDSON...Whereas said RICHARDSON as owner of a judgement given to MARY RODGERS has now under Executor several tracts of land among others 1000 acres on Chaverus Creek & has sold to DAVID GLOVER 522 acres & also 200 acres of same tract & to PETER CARNES, Esq. & Whereas said DOOLY has received $50.00. Now it is agreed between said GLOVER & above parties that the whole tract shall be sold at Sheriff's Sale & said GLOVER shall be the purchaser & land shall not sell for under 150 pounds & said GLOVER is to pay CARNES & RICHARDSON in proportion & said sell satisfy said Judgement & said GLOVER retain 572 acres... S/ PETER CARNS, THOMAS DOOLY, DAVID GLOVER. Wit: JOHN RYAN, who swore by oath 6 Jun 1795 before RICHARD TUTT, J.P. Rcd. 6 Jun 1795.

P. 204. 11 May 1795: Bill of Sale: SAMUEL DENNIS of Edgefield Co. SC to JAMES HOGE, sold sundry articles to wit: 1 mare & colt, 2 cows & calves, 4 hoggs, 2 pots, dutch oven, 2 fether beds & furniture, & all corn, cotton & potatoes. S/ SAMUEL DENIS. Wit: THOMAS SWEARENGEN, who swore by oath 6 Jun 1795 before VAN SWEARENGEN, J.P. Rcd. 6 Jun 1795.

Pp. 204-206. 28 Apr 1795: BENJAMIN CLARK to JOHN SLOAN of Spartenburgh Co. SC for 200 pounds, sold 191 acres surveyed 12 Jan 1786 for & granted 5 Nov 1787 to GEORGE RODEN, on west side

of south fork of Edisto River on both sides of gumpingut adj. WM.
HOG GOGENS, & DAVID RICHARDSON: also 191 acres, part of tract of
419 acres bounded by the other tract excepting that part, 54 1/2
acres, which a certain SWIFT took from said CLARK by an older
grant adj. EZEKIEL WALKER, DANIEL GOGENS, DAVID RICHARDSON. S/
BENJAMIN CLARK. Wit: WILLIAM CLARK, WILLIAM (+) SMITH, READICK
(X) GRANEY, who swore by oath 5 Jun 1795 before VAN SWEARENGEN,
J.P. Rcd. 6 Jun 1795.

Pp. 206-208. 7 Nov 1794: NATHAN JOHNSON of VA & Logan Co. KY, to
JOHN OLIPHANT of Edgefield Co. SC for 30 pounds, sold 279 acres
being part of 379 acres originally surveyed 25 Apr 1787 & granted
1 Mar 1790 for said NATHAN JOHNSON, on little Beaver Dam Creek a
branch of the big beaver Dam Creek of Turkey Creek of Stephens
Creek of Savannah River beginning at Warhoo bell Station adj.
JOHN KELLY, JOHN OLIPHANT, a dividing line now by WILLIAM
COURSEY, CHARLES JONES, ELIMS. S/ NATHAN JOHNSON. Wit: JOHN
KELLY, THOMAS HAGENS, WILLIAM ROBERTSON, who swore by oath 26 Jun
1795 before RICHARD TUTT, J.P. Rcd. 26 Jun 1795.

Pp. 208-210. 25 Jul 1792: Mrs ANN ZUBLY, Executrix of DAVID ZUBLY
of New Windsor, dec'd., of Edgefield Co. SC to NICHOLAS SHAFFER,
Planter of Edgefield Co. SC for 25 pounds, sold 1000 acres
originally granted 2 Oct 1786 on hollow creek & Winton Co. in
Orangeburg Dist. SC. S/ ANN ZUBLY, Executrix. Wit: WILLIAM
SHINHOLSER, WILLIAM EVANS, who swore by oath 18 Apr 1792 before
JOHN CLARKE, J.P. Rcd. 10 Jun 1795.

Pp. 210-212. Bond: ROBERT SAMUEL to GEORGE KERR, Merchant of
Edgefield Co. SC...Whereas by Bond dated 27 May 1795 in penal sum
of 215 pounds, with condition for payment of 107 pounds &
interest payable to GEORGE KERR before 1 Jan 1796 & for better
securing of payment, sold 2 negro slaves viz: CHARLES about 23
yrs. old & DANGERFIELD, about 20 yrs. old...to be null & void if
payment made...S/ ROBERT SAMUEL. Wit: HENRY CROPLE, GEORGE
HOGARTH, who swore by oath 2 Jul 1795 before RICHARD TUTT, J.P.
Rcd. 2 Jul 1795.

Pp. 212-213. 17 Sep 1794: JAMES MATHEWS & DINAH, his wife to
SARAH BRAZIEL, all of Edgefield Co. SC for (blank), sold 100
acres being part of a grant 25 Dec 1768 to WILLIAM BRAZIEL on
Loyd's Creek of Savannah River. S/ JAMES MATHEWS, DINAH (+)
MATHEWS. Wit: PHILIP CAPEHART, ELIZABETH (X) BRAZIEL, HENRY
CAPEHART, who swore by oath 7 May 1795 before HUGH MIDDLETON,
J.P. Rcd. 4 Jul 1795.

Pp. 213-215. 24 Jun 1794: WILLIAM BRUNER of Orange Co. SC to
WILLIAM TODD of Edgefield Co. SC for 10 pounds, sold 100 acres
originally granted 25 May 1774 unto CATHARINE FLICK on Turkey
Creek of Savannah River & by way of Marriage conveyed to said
WILLIAM BRUNER. Said land adj. MARY PACEHURETT. Wit: ARCHABALD
McNIEL, HENRY DULHEUER, of Orangeburg Dist. SC, who swore by oath
28 Jun 1794 before LEWIS LESTARYETTE, J.P. Rcd. 4 Jul 1795.

Pp. 215-217. 5 Jun 1795: WILLIAM COURSEY & MARY, his wife to
WILLIAM TERRY, all of Edgefield Co. SC for 100 pounds, sold 365
acres, being part of 946 acres granted 7 Aug 1786 unto WILLIAM
COURSEY; on Beaverdam Creek of Turkey Creek of Stephens Creek of
Savannah River. S/ W. COURSEY, MARY (+) COURSEY. Wit: JOHN

ELAMS, JURDIAN (also JURDASH) BROOKS, who swore by oath 6 July 1795 before JOHN BLOCKER, J.P. Rcd. 6 Jul 1795. Plat: p. 217.

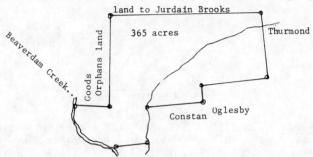

land to Jurdain Brooks

Beaverdam Creek

Goods Orphans land

365 acres

Thurmond

Constan Oglesby

Pp. 217-219. 4 Apr 1793: MOSES CLARK, Planter & RUTH, his wife to CHRISTOPHER WARD, all of Edgefield Co. SC for 20 pounds, sold 100 acres being part of 640 acres granted 4 Apr 1793 unto MOSES CLARK; on head branch of Little Stephens Creek of Savannah River crossing Mill Creek...S/ MOSES CLARK, RUTH (+) CLARK. Wit: JOHN COCKER, DANIEL (+) WARD, JOSEPH LEWIS, who swore by oath 6 Jul 1795 before R. TUTT, J.P. Rcd. 6 Jul 1795.

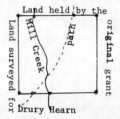

Land held by the

Land surveyed for

Mill Creek

path

original grant

Drury Hearn

Pp. 219-220. 10 Mar 1795: GRISIA ROWAN & EDWARD COUCH her attorney to WILLIAM TERRY, all of Edgefield Co. SC for 20 pounds, sold 194 acres being part of 250 acres, originally granted unto JAMES ROWAN, dec'd. & descended unto GRISIA ROWAN, one of said

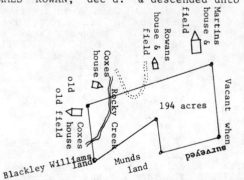

Rowans house & field

Martins house & field

Coxes house

old field

Rocky Creek

Coxes house

old field

194 acres

Vacant when surveyed

Blackley Williams land

Munds land

dec'd. daughters; on Rocky Creek of Turkey Creek of Savannah River adj. ACCEBUD COX, MARTIN, RICHD. MUNDS, THOS. WILLIAMS. S/ GRIZIA (+) ROWAN, EDWARD COUCH. Wit: JOSEPH MINTER, WILL THOMAS, WILLIAM EVANS, OBEDIAH CLEMENTS, JOHN TERRY, who swore by oath 6 Jul 1795 before JOHN BLOCKER, J.P. Rcd. 6 Jul 1795.

Plat: p. 220.

Pp. 220-222. 4 Aug 1794: NERY TAYLOR & ANNE TAYLOR, Planter & Spinstress, to JESSE COX, Planter, all of Edgefield Co. SC for 50 pounds, sold 100 acres, being part of 425 granted unto WARD TAYLOR 1 Aug 1791? & by his decease, descended to NERY & ANNE TAYLOR, son & widow of WARD TAYLOR; on branch of Turkey Creek of Savannah River adj. ARBEN MOORE, JOSEPH & WM. DAWSON. S/ NERY (+) TAYLOR, NANCY (+) TAYLOR. Wit: ROBERT COURSEY, JESSE MORRISS, who swore by oath 29 Apr 1795 before JOHN BLOCKER, J.P. Rcd. 6 Jul

DEED BOOK 12: 1794-1796 EDGEFIELD COUNTY S.C.

1795. Plat: p. 222.

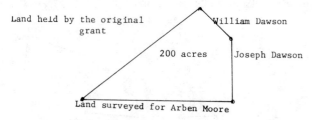

Land held by the original grant

William Dawson

200 acres

Joseph Dawson

Land surveyed for Arben Moore

Pp. 222-224. 5 Jun 1795: WILLIAM COURSEY & MARY, his wife, D.S. & Seamstress, to JORDAN BROOKS, all of Edgefield Co. SC for 40 pounds, sold 200 acres being part of 946 acres granted 7 Aug 1786 unto WILLIAM COURSEY on branch of Beaver Dam Creek of TurkeyCreek of Stephens Creek of Savannah River crossing the Augusta Road, adj. NATHAN TALLEY & WM. GOODE. S/ W. COURSEY, MARY (+) COURSEY. Wit: ROBERT COURSEY, CHARLES COURSEY, SCARBURGH BROADWATER, who swore by oath 6 Jul 1795 before JOSEPH BLOCKER, J.P. Rcd. 6 Jul 1795. Plat: p. 223.

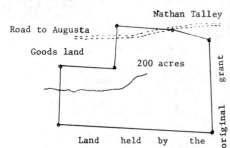

Nathan Talley

Road to Augusta

Goods land

200 acres

original grant

Land held by the

Pp. 224-225. 11 Mar 1795: WILLIAM COURSEY & MARY his wife, D.S. & Seamstress, to SCARBOROUGH BROADWATER, Shoemaker, all of Edgefield Co. SC, for 15 pounds, sold 100 acres, being part of 946 acres granted 7 Aug 1786 unto WILLIAM COURSEY on branch of

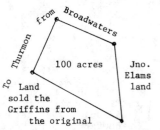

from Broadwaters

Thurmon

100 acres

Jno. Elams land

To Land sold the Griffins from the original

Beverdam a branch of Turkey Creek of Stephens Creek of Savannah River. S/ W. COURSEY, MARY (+) COURSEY. Wit: ROBERT COURSEY, CHARLES COURSEY, JURDAIN BROOKS, who swore by oath 6 Jul 1795 before JOHN BLOCKER, J.P. Rcd. 6 Jul 1795.

Plat: p. 225.

Pp. 225-227. 21 Oct 1794: SAMUEL MAYS, Sheriff, to CONRAD GALMAN...Whereas JOHN SMITH of Fairfield Co. SC obtained a judgement against KEMP TOLIFERE STRAWTHER & HENRY HUNTER for 81 pounds & a writ was issued 12 Apr 1792 attested by DAVID EVINS & The Sheriff in obedience to writ seized 600 acres in Edgefield Co. on Log Creek adj. ARTHUR SIMKINS, Esq., JOHN YOUNGBLOOD, LEWIS YOUNGBLOOD, & SAMUEL LANDRUM & advertized said lands 1 Mar 1794 & toward satisfaction, sold at public auction to last & highest bidder, CONRAD GALMAN. S/ S. MAYS, Sheff., Edgefield Co. Wit: THOMAS BUTLER, J. HATCHER, who swore by oath 6 Jul 1795 before R. TUTT, J.P. Rcd. 6 Jul 1795.

212

Pp. 227-229. 3 Feb 1795: JOHN LOGAN of the "Round O" to WILLIAM KEY of Ninety Six for 77 pounds, sold 500 acres originally granted RICHARD WARING adj. formerly the Estate of JOHN LOGAN, WILLIAM HOLMES, ANDERSON, YOUNG, & land run by LANG. S/ JNO. LOGAN. Wit: RICHARD WALTON, JOHN KILLCREASE, who swore by oath 7 May 1795 before HENRY KING, J.P. Rcd. 6 Jul 1795.

Pp. 229-231. 29 May 1795: JOHN HOLSONBAKE, Sadler, to CHARLES BANKS, Deputy Surveyor, both of Edgefield Co. SC for 100 pounds, sold 1000 acres originally granted 5 Apr 1793 said HOLSONBAKE on Good Spring branch of Big Horse Creek of Savannah River adj. Major JOHN HAMPTON, GEORGE GREGORY & CHARLES BANKS. S/ JOHN HOLSONBAKE. Wit: ELIZABETH (X) SEARLS, ROBERT JENNINGS, who swore by oath 29 May 1795 before HENRY KEY, J.P. Rcd. 2 Jul 1795.

Pp. 231-233. 10 May 1790: GEORGE BUCKELEW to CHRISTOPHER WARD, both of Edgefield Co. SC for 20 pounds, sold 50 acres on main branch of Little Stephens Creek adj. OGDEN COCKEROFT, WILLIAM GREEN. S/ GEORGE BUCKELEW, MARY (+) BUCKELEW. Wit: WILLIAM COCKEROFT, WILLIAM (I) GREEN, OGDEN COCKEROFT, who swore by oath 6 Jul 1795 before RICHARD TUTT, J.P. Rcd. 6 Jul 1795.

Pp. 233-235. 7 May 1794: WILLIAM BURDETT to DAVID PITTS for 5 pounds, sold 50 acres originally granted 5 Feb 1787 on branch of Red bank Creek of Little Saluda River adj. AMBROSE GAINS. S/ WILLIAM (⊢⊷⊣) BURDITT, PATIENCE (+) BURDITT. Wit: AVENILLAH (A) KING, ELIZABETH (X) SMEDLEY, HENRY KING, who swore by oath 27 Jun 1795 before WM. DANIEL, J.P. Rcd. 6 Jul 1795.

Pp. 235-236. 31 Nov 1793: ELISHA PALMER & MILDRED his wife, to JOHN HUFFMAN, both of Edgefield Co. SC for 50 pounds, sold 100 acres being part of a grant to THOMAS KEY adj. Mrs. LOGAN, GEORGE BUSSEY, Junr., said PALMER, & Mrs. BRAZIEL. S/ ALISHA (X) PALMER, MILDRED (X) PALMER. Wit: DEMCY BUSSEY, DEMCY (X) HUGHS, GEORGE BUSSEY, Junr.

In open Court 6 Jul 1795 ELISHA PALMER acknowledges deed before R. TUTT, J.E.C.

Plat: p. 235.

George Bussey
Mrs. Logan
100 acres
Mrs. Braziel
Elisha Palmer

Pp. 236-238. 8 Jan 1795: WILLIAM EVANS & KIZIAH, his wife of Edgefield Co. SC to JOHN LOWE of Lexington Co. SC for 40 pounds, sold 373 acres being part of a grant 7 Nov (sic) 1791 unto WILLIAM EAVANS on waters of Rockey Creek of Stevens Creek of Savannah R. S/ WILLIAM EVANS, KEZIA EVANS. Wit: JOSEPH WALLACE, GILLIAM EVANS, BATTE EVANS, who

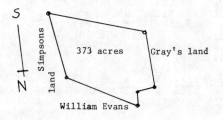

S
Simpsons land
N
373 acres
Gray's land
William Evans

213

swore by oath before THOMAS BACON, J.E.C. Plat: p. 237. Plat of 373 acres from a Survey made 9 Sep & granted 10 Oct 1791 This survey made 2 Jan 1795 by SHADK STOKES, D.S.

Pp. 238-240. 15 Mar 1795: JOHN COOK to JOHN HARDY, both of Edgefield Co. SC for 100 pounds, sold 105 acres on Sweet Water Creek adj. JOSEPH DAY, PETER DAY, dec'd. S/ JOHN COOK. Wit: JAMES BAKER, CHARLES OLD, RICHARD HARDY, who swore by oath 9 May 1795 before JOSEPH HIGHTOWER, J.P. Rcd. 6 Jul 1795.

Pp. 240-244. 2 Mar 1795: WILLIAM HOLSTON, Planter to HEZEKIAH HALLMAN, Planter, both of Edgefield Co. SC for 5 pounds, sold 100 acres being part of a tract granted 6 Nov 1786 unto JOHN FREDRICK who conveyed same to WILLIS FREDRICK who conveyed to said HOLSTON. S/ WILLIAM
HOLSTUN. Wit: WILLIAM
WRIGHT, REBECCAH HALMAN
(ALMAN), MOSES HOLSTUN,
who swore by oath 7 Mar
1795 before RUSSELL
WILSON, J.P. Rcd. 6 Jul
1795 Also saw SARAH
HOLESOM, (HOLSTUN), wife
of said WILLIAM HOLESON
(HOLSTUN) sign. Plat: p.
242.

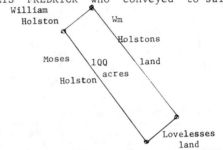

Pp. 244-247. 28 Jan 1795: THOMAS SELLERS, Planter to HOWELL SELLERS, Planter, both of Edgefield Co. SC for 10 pounds, sold 123 acres, being part of 2 tracts; (1) 114 acres being the lower side of 193 acres originally granted 3 Apr 1786 on waters of Log Creek of Turkey Creek adj. THOMAS McGINNES, WESCOATS, JOHN YOUNGBLOOD; (2) 9 acres being part of land originally granted THOMAS McGINNES on Log Creek. S/ THOMAS SELLERS. Wit: JAMES BROWN, CONRAD GALLMAN, who swore by oath 6 Jul 1795 before RICHARD TUTT, J.P. Rcd. 6 Jul 1795.

Pp. 248-250. 14 Dec 1793: ROBERT STARK, the Younger, & MARY his wife & ALEXANDER BOLLING STARK of Lexington Co. Orangeburg Dist. to JAMES McGOWAN, Planter of Edgefield Co. SC for 40 pounds, sold 100 acres being part of 1570 acres known by the name of the level or STARK's old store & distinguished by division of said 1570 acres by Letters & figures No. 13; below the old Ridge on south side Cloud creek adj. Division No. 12 & No. 1, lately sold to WM. BELL, HARTLY tract now or
lately EDWARD PRINCE & by
him sold to EDWARD
JOHNSON. S/ R. STARK,
ALEXR. BOLLG. STARK. Wit:
JOHN BYNUM, JOHN HIDLE,
WILLIAM BELL, who swore
by oath 21 May 1795
before RUSSELL WILSON,
J.P. Rcd. 7 Jul 1795.
Plat: p. 250.

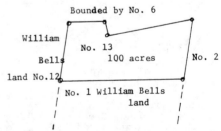

Pp. 251-254. 14 Dec 1793: ROBERT STARK, Jr., the Younger & MARY his wife & ALEXANDER BOLLING STARK of Orangeburg Dist, Esq. to WILLIAM BELL of Edgefield Co. SC, Innholder, for 250 pounds, sold

406 acres being part of 1570 acres commonly known by the name of
the Level or STARK's old Store on headwaters of Cloud Creek &
waters of Edisto marked in the plan & division of said 1570 acres
as No. 1 & No. 12 adj. No 2, No. 13, No. 8, No. 11 & No. 11;
heirs of Capt. MICHAEL WATSON, WILLIAM LAMAR...Lastly said ROBERT
STARK, the younger & ALEXANDER BOLLING STARK appoint ROLAND
WILLIAMS & SIMON BECK of Edgefield Co. SC, Planters, their
attornies jointly. S/ R. STARK, ALEXR. BOLLG. STARK. Wit: JOHN
BYNUM. JOHN HIDLE. Rcd. 7 Jul 1795.

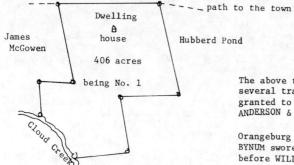

path to the town

Dwelling & house

James McGowen

Hubberd Pond

406 acres

being No. 1

Cloud Creek

The above tract is part of those
several tracts of land originally
granted to JAMES RAVENEL, JOHN
ANDERSON & JOHN ADAM WINGART.

Orangeburg District SC: JOHN
BYNUM swore by oath 18 May 1795
before WILLIAM FITZPATRICK J.P.

Pp. 254. 14 Aug 1794: WILLIAM HENRY HOWARD hath highhard two
negroes of Capt. THOS. KEY (viz) GEORGE about 18 yrs. old &
HANNAR, a girl about 15 yrs. old, a horse, a feather bead &
furniture which property I oblige myself to pay 5 shillings per
year during the said KEY's pleasure. S/ W.H. HOWARD. Wit: MARTHA
KEY, JAMES LIVINGSTON, who swore by oath 24 Mar 1795 before
AQUILLA MILES, J.P. Rcd. in this Book N, 7 Jul 1795.

Pp. 255-258. 27 Mar 1794: THOMAS HALSEL to JAMES PERRY, both of
Edgefield Co. SC for 120 pounds, sold a total of 250 acres; (1)
100 acres originally granted 7 Oct 1762 to MOSES POWELL near
Cloud Creek a branch of Little Saluda River adj. WM. WATSON, &
ANDREW SHIPES; (2) 150 acres originally granted 24 Jan 1770 to
WILLIAM DOOLY near Cloud Creek, a branch of Little Saluda River
adj. HENRY HARTLEY, MOSES POWELL. S/ THOMAS HALSEL. Wit: LEWIS
WIMBERLEY, RICHMOND WATSON, JOHN WIMBERLEY, who swore by oath 6
Jul 1795 before JOHN BLOCKER, J.P. Rcd. 7 Jul 1795.

Pp. 258-261. 15 Jul 1793: EZEKIEL McCLENDON & TERRY, his wife to
BENJAMIN DARBY, all of Edgefield Co. SC for 100 pounds, sold 180
acres being part of 200 acres originally granted 11 Aug 1774 to
DENNIS NOWLAND on branches of Shaws Creek of Edisto. S/ EZEKIEL
McCLENDON, TERRY (+) McCLENDON. Wit: THOMAS (+) HUNT, THOS.
SWEARENGEN, who swore by oath 3 Aug 1793 before RICHARD TUTT,
J.P. Rcd. 12 Jul 1795.

Pp. 261-264. 15 Jul 1793: EZEKIEL McCLENDON & TERRY, his
wife, to BENJAMIN DARBY, all of Edgefield Co. SC for 200 pounds,
sold 470 acres granted 5 Jun 1786 said EZEKIEL McCLENDON. S/
EZEKIEL McCLENDON, TERRY (X her) McCLENDON. Wit: THOMAS (X)
HUNT, THOMAS SWEARINGEN, who swore by oath 3 Jun (sic) 1793
before RICHARD TUTT, J. P. Rcd. Jul 1795.

Pp. 264-266. 21 Dec 1793: WILLIAM EVANS, Deputy Surveyor to JOHN CLARK, Esq., Planter, both of Edgefield Co. SC for 15 pounds, sold 33½ acres being part of 270 acres which was part of 640 acres originally granted JOHN RICHARDSON who conveyed 8 Sep 1790 to said EVANS. Said land on branch of Savannah River adj. JOHN CLARK & JOHN RICHARDSON. S/ WM. EVANS. Wit: WILLIAM STEWART, WILLIAM SHINHOLSER, who swore by oath 12 Oct 1795 before RICHARD TUTT, J.P. Memo: WILLIAM SHINHOLSER renounces all right title, Interest in said 32 1/2 acres. Wit: WILLIAM STEWART. S/ WM. SHINHOLSER. Plat: p. 266. 32 1/2 acres divided from 640 acres granted to JOHN RICHARDSON & sold to JOHN CLARK Esq by WM. EVANS, D.S. Certified 21 Dec 1793 by WM. EVANS, D.S.

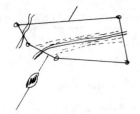

Pp. 266-267. 12 Jun 1795: Bill of Sale: ABIGAIL JONES to ISAAC FOREMAN for 35 pounds, sold a stock of Cattle - 35 head...S/ ABIGAIL JONES. Wit: ABIGAIL DYAL, BENJAMIN DARBY, who swore by oath 12 Jul 1795 before RICHARD TUTT, J.P. Rcd. 12 Jul 1795.

Pp. 267-269. 7 Jul 1795: SAMUEL MAYS, late Sheriff of Edgefield Co. SC to SAMUEL SCOTT...Whereas WILLIAM GARROTT, lately of Edgefield Co. obtained a judgement against WILLIAM DAWSON lately in Co. Court of Edgefield for 8 pounds & a writ was issued by RICHARD TUTT, Clerk of Court 10 Apr 1793. SAMUEL MAYS, Sheriff of Edgefield Co. seized 174 acres in Edgefield Co. adj. HUGH MIDDLETON, JOSEPH TUCKER & JOHN CROW & duly advertizing same 2 Nov 1793 & sold at public auction to last & highest bidder, SAMUEL SCOTT for 8 pounds. S/ S. MAYS, Late Sherf. Edgefield Co. Wit: ERO? H. PERRIN, SAMPSON BUTLER, who swore by oath 13 Jul 1795 before RICHARD TUTT, J.P. Rcd. 13 Jul 1795.

Pp. 269-272. 7 Oct 1794: DAVIS MOORE to MOSES HARRIS, both of Edgefield Co. SC for 60 pounds, sold 150 acres originally surveyed 11 Sep 1767 for JOSEPH NOBLE & granted 23 Feb 1768 near the head of a branch of Horns Creek of Stephens Creek. Said land was conveyed 17 Dec 1786 (sic) by JOSEPH NOBLE & RACHEL, his wife to JOHN MOCK & said JOHN MOCK & MARY, his wife by deed 15 Apr 1783 under their bonds to JOHN CHANEY & by said CHANEY to TOLIVER DAVIS, Senr. 9 Apr 1789 & by said DAVIS to DAVIS MOORE 19 Dec 1792. S/ DAVIS MOORE. Wit: BRITON MIMS, JONATHAN MOORE, SAMPSON BUTLER, who swore by oath 13 Jul 1795 before RICHARD TUTT, J.P. Rcd. 13 Jul 1795.

Pp. 272-274. 1 Feb 1795: WILLIAM SHINHOLSER Planter, & ANN his wife to WILLIAM EVANS, D.S., both of Edgefield Co. SC for 100 pounds, sold 240 acres near Beech Island adj. BENJAMIN HARRIS, JOHN RICHARDSON. S/ WM. SHINHOLSER, ANNE SHINHOLSER. Wit: ALEX. (X) HANNAH, PHILIP LAMAR, who swore by oath 26 Jul 1795 before JOSEPH HIGHTOWER, J.P. Rcd. 13 Jul 1795.

Pp. 274-275. 4 Jul 1795: Deed of Gift: JONATHAN RICHARDSON for love & affection for my daughter JORIAH RICHARDSON give Cattle (cows describing Marks). S/ JONATHAN (Ŧ) RICHARDSON. Wit: JOAB WOOTAN, DANIEL RITCHEY, who swore by oath 15 Jul 1795 before VAN SWEARENGEN, J.P. Rcd. 15 Jul 1795.

DEED BOOK 12: 1794-1796 EDGEFIELD COUNTY S.C.

Pp. 275-276. 27 Mar 1795: Bill of Sale: JOHN WHITE of Wilks Co.
GA to MARY ANN HAMMOND for 25 pounds, sold one negroe fellow
named BEN & his wife BENER. S/ JOHN WHITE. Wit: WILLIAM MATTHEWS,
ANDREW WILLIAMSON, who swore by oath 27 Mar 1795 before JOSEPH
HIGHTOWER, J.P. Rcd. 20 Jul 1795.

Pp. 276-277. 4 Jun 1793: WILLIAM FORT, Adm. of HENRY BOLTON,
dec'd., of Washington Co. GA to EDWARD HOLMES of Edgefield Co. SC
for 25 pounds, sold 25 acres being part of a larger tract
originally granted 1765 to DRURY FORT & conveyed by said FORT to
HENRY BOLTON ; said tract is on Mine Creek of Little Saluda adj.
Estate of FREDERICK SISON, dec'd., said HOLMES, & PHILIP EKNER.
S/ WILLIAM FORT. Wit: ARNOLD BERRY, NATHANIEL BOLTON, who swore
by oath 24 Jun 1793 before HENRY KING, J.P. Rcd. 24 Jul 1795.

Pp. 277-279. 9 Mar 1785: DRURY FORT, Planter of Colleton Co. to
EDWARD HOLMES, Planter of same place, for 20 pounds, sold 100
acres originally granted 21 May 1769 unto DRURY FORT on a branch
of Mine Creek of Litel Saludeay in Collenton Co. S/ DRURY FORT.
Wit: CHARLES (X) PARTIN, WILLIAM HOLMES, who swore by oath 11 Apr
1785 before SOLOMON POPE, J.P. Rcd. 24 Jul 1795.

Pp. 279-281. 28 Jan 1795: Deposition: SUSANNAH MELTON to JOHN
HESTER. Appeared & Swore before VAN SWEARENGEN, J.P. SUSANAH
MELTON, the older, made oath that 27 Feb 1792 that WILLIAM
MELTON, her son with HANAH, his wife came forth & made her Rights
to a 146 acre tract of land & afterwards she lived on & is now
living on said land being the remainder of the grant over & above
what the said WILLIAM MELTON sold to JAMES WHITEHEAD & JOHN
HESTER which grant was of 346 acres granted 1 Mar 1790. She, the
Desponant declares further that she has reason to believe that
the rights have since been stolen out of her house in her absence
by some El desposed person by finding JAMES WHITEHEAD's Lease in
her yeard which was folded together with her one lease & also
said SUSANAH has misplaced them so that she can't find them to
record in the Clerk's office - And further EDWARD COUCH appeared
with JAMES WHITEHEAD & JOHN HESTER & swore they were all present
& subscribed their names as witnesses & that said COUCH that he
wrote the Lease & Release according to the laws above mentioned &
subscribed his name to Probate when proven before HENRY KING,
Esq. S/ EDWARD COUCH, JAMES WHITEHEAD, JOHN (+) HESTER. Rcd. 25
Jul 1795.

Pp. 281-283. 18 Apr 1793: Orangeburg Dist. SC: JOHN MESSER of
Edgefield Co. SC to WILLIAM MESSER of Orangeburgh Dist. for 20
pounds, sold 40 acres being part of 305 acres granted 7 Jun 1788
on Chinquepen branch of North Edisto adj. CANNON's line. S/ JOHN
(X) MESSER. Wit: JOHN P. BOND, REDMOND JOHNSON, WILLIAM NORRIS,
of Orangeburgh Dist. swore by oath before JOHN THOMAS FAIRCHILD,
J.P. Rcd. 29 Jul 1795.

Pp. 284-286. 29 Jan 1794: Orangeburgh Dist. SC: WILLIAM MESSER of
Orangeburgh Dist., Lexington Co. SC to JOHN STONE for 25 pounds,
sold 40 acres being part of 305 acres granted 7 Jun 1788 to JOHN
MESSER, who sold 17 Apr 1793 to said WILLIAM MESSER, on a branch
of Chinquepen, the head branch of North Edisto. S/ WILLIAM
MESSER. Wit: JOHN DYE, MARY (also MARGARET) JAMES, Orangeburgh
Dist., who swore by oath 10 May 1794 before JAMES WELLS, J.P.
Rcd. 29 Jul 1795.

DEED BOOK 12:   1794-1796 EDGEFIELD COUNTY S.C.

Pp. 287-288. 9 Apr 1794: WHEATON PINES of Orangeburg Dist.,
Lexington Co. SC to JOHN STONE, of same place for 50 pounds, sold
130 acres being part of 200 acres granted 3 Apr 1786 to WHEATON
PINES. S/ WHEATON (M) PINES, CATHARINE (X) PINES, his wife. Wit:
JOHN DYE, GEORGE GODFREY, MARGARET JAMES, Orangeburgh Dist. SC,
who swore by oath 10 May 1794 before JAMES WELLS, J.P. Rcd. 29
Jul 1795.

Pp. 288-292. 16 Mar 1795: WILLIAM MARSH & ANNE, his wife to
JOSEPH GRIFFIN, all of Edgefield Co. SC for 50 pounds, sold 205
acres being part of 410 acres originally granted 1786 unto SAMUEL
MARSH & conveyed 16 Jan 1787 to said WILLIAM MARSH...Land on
Beaverdam waters adj. JAMES FRAZIER, WILLIAM FRAZIER. S/ WILLIAM
MARSH, ANNE (+) MARSH, JOSEPH GRIFFIN. Wit: SAMUEL MARSH,
ELISABETH MARSH, ROBERT MARSH, who swore by oath 5 Aug 1795
before RICHARD TUTT, J.P. Rcd. 5 Aug 1795.

Pp. 292-295. 16 Jan 1787: SAMUEL MARSH to WILLIAM MARSH for 50
pounds, sold 205 acres being part of 410 acres granted 1786 said
MARSH on Beaverdam waters adj. JAMES FRAZIER & WILLIAM FRAZIER.
S/ SAML. MARSH. Wit: ELISABETH MARSH, ROBERT MARSH, SAMUEL MARSH,
who swore by oath 5 Aug 1795 before RICHARD TUTT, J.P. Rcd. 5 Aug
1795.

Pp. 295-296. 16 Apr 1795: Deed of Gift: EDWARD COUCH of Edgefield
Co. SC to MOORE JOHNSON & CHARITY, his wife for love & affection,
gives a negro boy named TOM about 11 yrs old & an inventory...S/
EDWARD COUCH. Wit: JOHN JOHNSON, ROBERT WILLIS, who swore by oath
15 Aug 1795 before RICHARD TUTT, J.P. Rcd. 15 Aug 1795.

Pp. 297-301. 2 Mar 1795: Lease & Mortgage: JOHN FUDGE to EPHRAM
FERRELL, both of Edgefield Co. SC for 10 shillings, sold 300
acres being part of a tract granted JACOB FUDGE, dec'd., & willed
to JOHN FUDGE on Little horse creek. S/ JOHN FUDGE. Wit: FIELDING
REONOLDS, JOHN GLOVER.
3 Mar 1795: Whereas JOHN FUDGE by his bond of 28 Feb 1795 became
bound to EPHRAIM FERRELL in penal sum of 39 pounds, under
condition of payment of 19 pounds...This Indenture witnesseth for
better securing of payment 300 acres being on horse pen & Little
Horse creek being part of a tract granted unto JACOB FUDGE,
dec'd. & willed to said JOHN FUDGE.
4 Mar 1795: JOHN GLOVER swore by oath before JOSEPH HIGHTOWER,
J.P. Rcd. 29 Aug 1795.

Pp. 301-303. Mortgage: ROBERT WARE - by 3 bonds; (1) bond 29 Apr
1795, bond in penal sum 938 pounds ... with condition for payment
of 469 pounds to GEORGE KER payable 1 Jan 1796 for 156 pounds...;
(2) bond payable 1 Jan 1797 for 156 pounds...; (3) bond payable 1
Jan 1798 for 156 pounds...; & for better securing of payment of
bonds ROBERT WARE sells thirteen slaves. Viz: BOB about 30 yrs.
old; MILLEY about 30 yrs. old; BETTY about 7 yrs. old; CHARLES
about 5 yrs. old; STEPHEN about 3 yrs. old; TOM about 2 yrs. old;
HARRIOT 4 weeks old; AGGE about 32 yrs. old; ALIJAH about 6 yrs.
old; JOE about 4 yrs. old; HANNAH about 6 wks. old; RACHEL about
18 yrs. old; DELPH about 3 yrs. old...& their future increase...
If payment made of bonds this be null & void... S/ ROBERT WARE at
Campbelton. Wit: GEORGE HOGARTH, A.B. MURRAY, JOSIAS H.
McPHERSON. Rcd. 1 Sep 1795.
GEORGE HOGARTH swore by oath 1 Sep 1795 before RICHARD TUTT, J.P.
Rcd. 1 Sep 1795.

218

Pp. 303-307. 21 May 1795: BENJAMIN REYNOLDS of Edgefield Co. SC to ABRAHAM HERNDON for 200 pounds, sold 247 acres, being of two tracts; (1) 100 acres granted 3 Apr 1786 unto FIELDS REYNOLDS on the Main road from Augusta to the Ridge known by the Name of old wells also; (2) 147 acres granted 1 Jan 1787 unto JOHN RYAN on the Main Road that leads from the pine wood house to Augusta known by the name of the old well. S/ BENJA. REYNOLDS. Wit: JONATHAN (ł) RICHARDSON, DANIEL RITCHEY, who swore by oath 22 May 1795 before JOSEPH HIGHTOWER, J.P. Rcd. 4 Sep 1795.

Pp. 307-308. 10 Jun 1795: Receipt: JOHN RYAN, Esq. to SAMUEL WALKER for 50 pounds, being full payment for a negroe boy named JOSEPH 14 or 15 yrs. old... S/ JOHN RYAN. Wit: JOSEPH T. BELL, JOHN ADDISON, who swore by oath 5 Sep 1795 before RICHARD TUTT, J.P. Rcd. 5 Sep 1795.

P. 308. 9 Sep 1795: Bill of Sale: TRUMAN WIGHTT to JOHN WIGHTT & JOHN FLINT, for valuable consideration, sold two negroes (To Wit:) negro wench named PEGG about 30 yrs. old & negro wench named MARY about 14 yrs. old. S/ TRUMAN WIGHTT. Wit: JAMES (↦) WEST, ESOTT PERRIN, who swore by oath 10 Sep 1795 before RICHARD TUTT, J.P. Rcd. 10 Sep 1795.

Pp. 308-309. 18 Mar 1795: Agreement: JAMES PIKE & his wife to ELIJAH MARTIN, six cows & calves for which he promises to pay JOHN FEESTER 2 guineas & interest when he is of age & to SALLY FEESTER 1 guinea & interest; to POLLY FEESTER 1 guinea & interest; to ELIZABETH FEESTER 1 guinea & interest; when of age I promise to pay ?ELLY. Received as witness MARY (+) PIKE. S/ ELIJAH MARTIN. Rcd. 14 Sep 1795.
JAMES PIKE & I do sel & bargin to ELIJAH MARTIN a Bay horse cald Prins for which sade MARTIN promises to pay JOHN FEESTER my step son a horse Cider when he is of age I promise to pay value received this horse of PIKE this 18 Mar 1794. MARY (X) PIKE. S/ ELIJAH MARTIN.
27 Apr 1795 sworn by oath of MARY PIKE to contract between JAMES PIKE & ELIJAH MARTIN made 18 Mar last before RUSSELL WILSON, J.P. Rcd. 14 Sep 1795.

Pp. 309-310. 20 Feb 1795: Agreement & Indenture: PATIENCE HICKS, late of Edgefield Co. SC to RICHARD BUSH; Puts herself voluntarily apprentice to RICHARD BUSH, Senr., Sitizen of Edisto, Planter Edgefield Co. SC for 7 years. S/ PATIENCE (X her) HICKS, RICHARD BUSH. Wit: JOHN BUSH, PRESCOTT BUSH, who swore by oath 11' Mar 1795 before VAN SWEARENGEN, J.P. Rcd. 21 Sep 1795.

Pp. 311-312. 20 Oct 1794: JOHN HILL & JANE, his wife of Edgefield Co. SC to JOHN BERRY for 30 pounds, sold 122 acres granted 25 Jan 1792 being on Mountain Creek of Turkey Creek & Savannah River. S/ JOHN HILL, JANE (+) HILL. Wit: WILEY (X) BERRY, who swore by oath 12 Sep 1795 before RICHARD TUTT, J.P. Rcd. 12 Sep 1795.

Pp. 313-316. 26 Mar 1795: CALL COLLINS, Planter & BETSY his wife to CHRISTOPHER GLANTON, all of Edgefield Co. SC for 50 pounds, sold 100 acres granted 12 Dec 1768 unto CHARLES WILLIAMS & by his decease, descended to son & heir ABSOLOM WILLIAMS; on Turkey Creek a branch of Stephens Creek of Savannah River. S/ CAUL COLLINS, BETSY (+) COLLINS. Wit: JOHN McFARTRICK, THOMAS PENNINGTON, who swore by oath 17 Sep 1795 before HENRY KEY, J.P. Rcd. 21 Sep 1795.

DEED BOOK 12: 1794-1796 EDGEFIELD COUNTY S.C.

Pp. 316-318. 25 Apr 1795: STEPHEN SMITH & SARAH his wife to JEREMIAH JONES, both of Edgefield Co. SC for 15 pounds, sold 100 acres being part of 461 acres granted 1791. S/ STEPHEN (X) SMITH, SARAH (X) SMITH. Wit: JEREMIAH JONES, HUGH MIDDLETON, EDWARD PRINCE, who swore by oath 25 Apr 1795 before HUGH MIDDLETON, J.P.

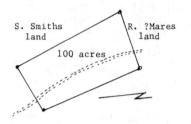

S. Smiths
land

100 acres

R. ?Mares
land

Plat: 100 acres part of 461 acres granted 6 Jan 1787 (sic) STEPHEN SMITH. Surveyed 19 Nov 1794 by JNO. BOYD, D.S. Rcd. 24 Sep 1795.

Pp. 318-322. 27 Sep 1795: DAVID GLOVER of Edgefield to ELIZABETH CARNES, Executrix of PETER CARNES, Esq., dec'd., for 500 pounds, sold 848 acres being two tracts; (1) 810 acres granted DANIEL MITCHELL on Mills Creek adj. JOHN HENRY MEALING, ABSOLOM ROBERT, JOHN ANDERSON, RICHARD QUARLES, DAVID GLOVER... except 50 acres (which is in description of land in lines belonging to THOMAS KEY); (2) 38 acres being part of afsd. tract of land granted 14 Aug 1772 DANIEL MITCHELL & divided by elder survey now belonging to said GLOVER adj. THOMAS BURNETT, RICHARD QUARLES, said GLOVER. DANIEL MITCHELL's grant of 14 Aug 1772 for 1000 acres, but on resurvey found to be 1529 acres. S/ DAVID GLOVER. Wit: ROBERT LANG, JOHN RYAN, Esq., who swore by oath 1 Oct 1795 before RICHARD TUTT, J.P. Rcd. 1 Oct 1795.

Pp. 322-325. 15 Sep 1795: BENJAMIN MAY to JOAB WOOTAN, both of Edgefield Co. SC for 100 pounds, sold 100 acres originally granted 5 Dec 1785 DRURY NAPPER on Chaveres Creek of Savannah River. S/ BENJAMIN MAY. Wit: DANIEL RITCHEY, JONATHAN (‡) RICHARDSON. Rcd. 3 Oct 1795.

Pp. 325-328. 14 Sep 1795: PHILL MAY, Senior to JOAB WOOTAN for 200 pounds, sold 99 acres being part of 300 granted 12 Jul 1772 unto RICHARD KIRKLAND, being on Chavers Creek, a branch of Savannah River adj. GEORGE GARBETT's Spring being the dividing line between said GARBETT & PHILL MAY, JOHN RYAN, JACOB FUDGE & SOLOMON LUCAS. S/ PHILL MAY, Senr. Wit: DANIEL RITCHEY, JONATHAN (‡) RICHARDSON, who swore by oath 3 Oct 1795 saw PHILL MAY, Junior (sic) sign above before VAN SWEARENGEN, J.P. Rcd. 3 Oct 1795.

Pp. 328-330. 17 Oct 1795: HENRY KEY, Esq. to GEORGE TURNER, Hatter, both of Edgefield Co. SC for 20 pounds, sold 100 acres being part of 250 acres granted 16 Sep 1774 said HENRY KEY; on Stephens Creek of Savannah River. S/ HENRY KEY. Wit: CHARLES (c) FENDLY, JOHN SEARLS, who swore by oath 4 Nov 1795 before RICHARD TUTT, J.P. Rcd. 4 Oct 1795. Plat: p. 330.

(Please see plat on following page.)

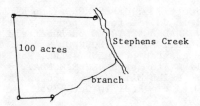

Wm COURSEY DS

Pp. 330-331. 8 May 1795: Mortgage: DAVID JOHNSTON, Planter Edgefield Co. SC to JAMES COX of Newberry Co. SC, bind for 120 pounds & to secure payment set over my titles to two negroes: HALL a negro fellow 16 or 17 yrs. old & MILL a black wench 18 or 19 years old with her toes gone off her left foot...payment of 60 pounds be made 1 Dec 1795 & this be void. S/ DAVID JOHNSTON. Wit: MORRIS GWYN, ISAAC NORRELL, JOSEPH TOWLES, who swore by oath 1 Oct 1795 before S. MAYS, J.P. Rcd. 5 Oct 1795.

Pp. 331-333. 10 Apr 1795: MATTHEW COCKERAM, Planter to ROBERT BROOKS, Blacksmith, for 5 pounds, sold 127 acres being part of 460 acres originally granted 4 Jul 1791 to LEWIS COLLINS. The said 127 acres was conveyed unto ARON TOMLINSON 1 Oct 1794 who conveyed 1 Oct

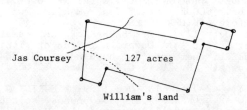

1795 to said COCKERAM, on branch of Turkey Creek of Savannah River adj. THOS. & CHS. WILLIAMS, LEWIS COLLINS, PURVIS. S/ MATTHEW (X) COCKERAM. Wit: JONES HOLMES, JAMES COURSEY, who swore by oath 5 Oct 1795 before RICHARD TUTT, J. P. Rcd. 5 Oct 1795. Plat: p. 333.

Pp. 333-335. 1 Oct 1795: Deed of Gift: JOHN LEWIS of Edgefield Co. SC to son, JAMES LEWIS, for good will & affection, negro man named JAMES alias TIM about 20 yrs. old, swarthy complexion, 5 ft. 7 or 8 inches. Also 4 sows & pigs...
To son, SAMUEL LEWIS, one negro woman named DINAH about 35 yrs. of age. Also 1 feather bed & furniture & 3 cows...
To daughter, ELIZABETH LEWIS, one negro girl named JUDE about 9 yrs. old. Also 1 feather bed & furniture & 1 heifer. S/ JOHN LEWIS. Wit: BENJAMIN HIGHTOWER, who swore by oath 1 Oct 1795 before JOSEPH HIGHTOWER, J.P. Rcd. 5 Oct 1795.

P. 335. 2 Mar 1795: Receipt: JOHN McDANIEL of Edgefield Co. SC acknowledges receipt from MARGARET LANE, late MARGARET McDUGEL all my wife's portion of land, stock & furniture which is thought to be her part of her father, PATRICK McDUGEL's Estate & JOHN McDANIEL gives Quit Claim to MARGARET LANE forever. S/ JOHN McDANIEL, ELENDER McDANIEL. Wit: ELIZABETH (X) McDUGEL, WILLIAM NICHOLS, who swore by oath 27 Aug 1795 before NATHAL. ABNEY, J.P. Rcd. 10 Oct 1795.

DEED BOOK 12:   1794-1796 EDGEFIELD COUNTY S.C.

Pp. 335-337. 9 Oct 1795: JAMES MONDAY to RICHARD BARROTT, Senr., both of Edgefield Co. SC for 50 pounds, sold 132 acres surveyed 30 Sep 1794 by SHADRACK STOKES on Bumefield Creek of Sav. River adj. REUBEN MONDAY, GEORGE HOGWOOD & JAMES HOGWOOD. Said tract was originally granted to HENRY WARE, Esq. of GA 31 Aug 1774 & was conveyed 1794 to said JAMES MONDAY. S/ JAMES MONDAY. Wit: PHILL MAY, Senr., PHILL MAY, Junr., who swore by oath 10 Oct 1795 before JOHN RYAN, J.P. Rcd. 10 Oct 1795.

Pp. 337-339. Mortgage: JOHN CURETON of Edgefield Co. SC to THOMAS WADSWORTH & WILLIAM TURPIN, Merchants of Newberry SC...Whereas JOHN CURETON gave his bond 11 May 1795 in penal sum of 116 pounds with condition of payment of 58 pounds on or before 19 Oct next. For better securing of payment sells a negro fellow named ARTHER about 34 yrs. old; a negro girl named MIMA about 12 yrs. old; & a negro fellow named GEORGE about 21 yrs. old...S/ JOHN CURETON. Wit: DANIEL SYMMES, who swore by oath 5 Sep 1795 before ROBERT GILLAM, J.P. Rcd. 12 Oct 1795.

Pp. 339-342. 9 Jul 1792: JOHN PURSEL & BARBARY, his wife to JESSE MEACHUM, both of Ninety Six Dist. for 100 pounds, sold 55 acres originally granted 26 Jul 1774 on branches of Horns Creek adj. SAMUEL WHORTON, MOCK, & PHILIP GOODE... S/ JOHN (J) PURSEL. Wit: MACK. GOODE, Col. JOHN MARTIN, who swore by oath 10 Oct 1795 before AQUILLA MILES.
12 Oct 1795: Mrs BARBARY PURSEL came into Court & acknowledged her right of Dower & thirds of within land conveyed from JOHN PURSEL, her dec'd. husband, to JESSE MECCHUM. Extract from the Minutes: R. TUTT, C.E.C. Rcd. 12 Oct 1795.

Pp. 342-345. 13 Dec 1789: FREDRICK GLOVER & SARAH his wife, to THOMAS EDWARDS for 35 pounds, sold 60 acres being part of 500 acres originally granted 15 Mar 1771 unto WILLIAM BEAN, who conveyed 60 acres 11 & 12 Jul 1771 unto said GLOVER. Said 60 acres surveyed by WILLIAM ANDERSON, D.S.; adj. SW ELISHA BROOKS, SE WILLIAM BEAL & FREDERICK GLOVER, NE said BEAN's land. S/ FREDK. GLOVER, SARAH (+) GLOVER. Wit: TOLAVER BOSTICK, WILLIAM JONES, JAMES WILSON, who swore by oath 30 Dec 1789 before JOHN MOORE, J.P. Rcd. 12 Oct 1795.

Pp. 345-348. 31 Dec 1789: ISHAM GREEN & MARY his wife to THOMAS EDWARDS, both of Edgefield Co. SC for 113 pounds, sold 139 acres; was divided from 150 acres being part of 450 acres surveyed 11 Oct 1763 by JOHN LIVINGSTON, D.S. to ELISHA FOWLER who transfer legally to ELISHA BROOK who with his wife FRANCES conveyed 4 & 5 Sep 1772 - 150 acres unto ROBERT MITCHELL, who conveyed 17 & 18 Apr 1775 to PETER GREEN, who conveyed 30 & 31 Aug 1785 unto said ISHAM GREEN. Said land adj. NW on ISHAM GREEN & the Charleston Road & JOEL LIPSCOMB; SW by JOEL LIPSCOMB, NW by JACOB SMITH & FREDERICK GLOVER; NE JAMES MOORE & WILLIAM MOORE, dec'd. & Ninety Six Creek. S/ ISHAM GREEN, MARY (+) GREEN. Wit: MARK SMITH, JOEL LIPSCOMB, who swore by oath 23 Apr 1795 before W. ROBINSON, J.P. Rcd. 12 Oct 1795.

Pp. 348-350. 29 May 1795: JOHN SULLIVAN & SARAH his wife, Planter & Spinster, to NATHAN TALLEY, Blacksmith, both of Edgefield for 32 pounds, sold 240 acres being part of 375 acres granted said SULLIVAN 5 Jun 1786 whereas 135 acres of said 375 acres fell into Old Survey formerly granted JOSIAH LOCKWOOD, being on branch of

222

Beaverdam Creek a branch of Turkey Creek, of Big Stephens   Creek of   Savannah   River
adj.   PURVES,   JOHN
THURMOND,   CHARLES
BROADWATER,JOSHUA(sic)
LOCKWOOD,   COCKERAM,
FREDK.   TILLMAN   &
JOHN PURVES, Esq. S/
JNO.   (X)   SULLIVAN,
SARAH   (X)   SULLIVAN.
Wit: PRESLY   (X)
SWILLIVAN,   ARON
HERRON,   JOHN   LYON,
who swore by oath 12
Oct 1795 before JOHN
BLOCKER,   J.P.   Rcd.
12 Oct 1795.

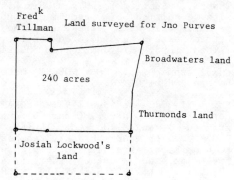

Fred^k Tillman   Land surveyed for Jno Purves

unknown   240 acres

Broadwaters land

Thurmonds land

Josiah Lockwood's land

P. 351 - missing.

Pp.   352-357. 1793: OBEDIAH HENDERSON to ALEXANDER BURNET for 70 pounds, sold 200 acres in neighborhood of Cuffee Town Creek originally granted MICHAEL PLIFER & 100 granted to MARTIN PLIFER all granted 23 Aug 1765. S/ OBEDIAH HENDERSON, JUDAH (+) HENDERSON, his wife. Wit: WILLIAM THORNTON, JEREMIAH BURNETT, who swore by oath 6 Dec 1794 before JAMES HARRISON, J.P. Rcd. 12 Oct 1795.

Pp.   357-359. 13 Feb 1795: JOHN MOBLEY, Senr. to JOHN COCKEROFT, both of Edgefield Co. SC for 5 pounds, sold 200 acres being part of 600 acres granted 7 Oct 1793 said MOBLEY, on Mine Creek of Little Saluda River adj. REUBIN KIRKLAND, OGDEN COCKEROFT. S/ JOHN (+) MOBLEY, ELIZABETH (+) MOBLEY, his wife. Wit: JEREMIAH MOBLEY, JESSE CLARK, OGDEN COCKEROFT, who swore by oath 12 Oct 1795 before RICHARD TUTT, J.P. Rcd. 12 Oct 1795.

Pp.   359-362. 27 Feb 1795: GARLAND GOODE, Planter to ROBERT THOMAS, Esq., both of Edgefield Co. SC for 288 pounds, sold 320 acres as seen by plat attached to lease laid out by WM. ANDERSON, Esq., being land bequeath to said GOODE by LW&T of his father, MACKERNES GOOD, Dec 1794; on Ninety Six Creek adj. LUALLEN GOOD, SAMMUEL GOOD. S/ GARLAND GOODE. Wit: SAMUEL OSBORN, SAMPSON POPE, L.M. GOODE, proved in open court 12 Oct 1795 before R. TUTT, C.E.C. Rcd. 12 Oct 1795.
12 Oct 1795: Mrs ELIZABETH GOODE, Widow of the within GARLAND GOODE came into Court & ack. her right of Dower & Third to the within mentioned land which was ordered recorded. R. TUTT, C.E.C.

Pp. 362-365. 8 Jan 1792: ABRAM RIELY, Planter to JOSIAH LANGLEY, Planter, both of Edgefield Co. SC for 60 pounds, sold 100 acres being part of tract originally granted 24 Dec 1772 to THOMAS BARTON, who conveyed to BENJAMIN LEWIS who conveyed to WILLIAM BRYAN who conveyed 6 & 7th Nov 1789 to said ABRAM RIELY on branch of Stephens Creek of Turkey Creek. S/ ABRAHAM RILEY, ANN (X) RILEY. Wit: JOHN BRATCHER, ALEXANDER BURNETT, who swore by oath 17 Aug 1792 before HENRY KING, J.P. Rcd. 12 Oct 1795.
(ANN RILEY signed the Lease & witnessed receipt of money, did not sign the Release nor was she ack. in the oath, gch)

Pp. 365-371. 5 Oct 1795: Mortgage: JAMES HOLLINSWORTH to WILLIAM TENNENT, Sheriff of Ninety Six Dist. for penal sum of 18 pounds with condition of payment of 9 pounds & for better securing of payment sold 215 acres, late the property of MOSES KIRKLAND on Little Stephens & Mine Creek on the main Road from Augusta to the Island ford. S/ JAMES (X) HOLLINSWORTH. Wit: ROBERT McCOMBS, ROGERS HARKINS.
Charleston Dist. SC: ROBERT McCOMBS swore by oath 9 Oct 1795 before JOHN TROTTER, J.P. Rcd. 13 Oct 1795.

Pp. 371-374. 18 Sep 1794: ABSOLAM SHIRLEY to EPHRAIM FRANKLIN, both of Edgefield Co. SC for 40 pounds, sold 250 acres originally granted 7 Aug 1786 to WILLIAM DOBY & was assigned by WILLIAM DOOBY to ABSOLAM SHIRLEY, on head of Coutches branch of South Edisto River including the plantation the said ABSOLAM SHIRLEY lives at the present date. S/ ABSOLOM (X) SHIRLEY, CLOEY (X) SHIRLEY. Wit: THOMAS FRANKLIN, RICHARD KNOWLES, BENJAMIN SUTTON, who swore by oath 6 Oct 1795 before VAN SWEARENGEN, J.P. Rcd. 13 Oct 1795.

Pp. 374-375. 29 Jul 1795: Deed of Gift: RODY MORGAN, widow of ONIAS MORGAN, to my daughter FANNEY MORGAN, dau. of the dec'd., ONIAS MORGAN, both of Edgefield Co. SC for love & affection, 100 acres, all my part as a widow, on waters of Savannah river & I delivered unto ABIAH MORGAN as guardian for the above named FANNY, a true & legal deed. S/ RODY (X) MORGAN. Wit: JOHN (X) RODEN, TRAVERS HILL, who swore by oath 8 Oct 1795 before HENRY KEY, J.P. Rcd. 13 Oct 1795.

Pp. 375-377. 25 Aug 1795: PHILIP LAMAR & LEMUEL YOUNG to ROBERT LAMAR, both of Edgefield Co. SC for 15 pounds, 150 acres being part of a tract originally granted PHILIP LAMAR & WILLIAM EVANS, dec'd., & the 1/2 of said tract of land now by heirship falling to LEMUEL YOUNG; adj. ALEX HANNAH & now in possession of said ROBERT LAMAR, being on Town Creek of Savannah River. S/ PHILIP LAMAR, LEMUEL (X) YOUNG. Wit: JOSEPH HIGHTOWER, BENJAMIN HIGHTOWER, who swore by oath 25 Aug 1795 before JOSEPH HIGHTOWER, J.P. Rcd. 13 Oct 1795.

P. 377. 18 Apr 1795: Receipt: Received in full of JAMES VESSELS, JESSY ROUNDTREE & DAVID BARNET satisfaction for the Judgement obtained against them in Edgefield Co. SC. S/ JOHN HIGHTOWER. EPHRODITUS HIGHTOWER, made oath he saw his father, JOHN HIGHTOWER sign the above receipt before W. ANDERSON, J.C.E. Rcd. 14 Oct 1795.

Pp. 378-380. 5 Oct 1795: Sheriff's Title: WILLIAM TENNENT, Sheriff of Ninety Six Dist. to CHARLES GOODWIN of Cambridge for 72 pounds, sold 650 acres on both sides Cedar Creek formerly called Walnut creek adj. HENRY PARKMAN, WILLIAM TILLERY & THOMAS DAVIS & GRANGE SHAW PARKMAN & REUBIN FRAZIER. Whereas ZEPHENIAH CLEMENTS, JAMES COODIE & EDWARD VAN, Senr. were indebted by joint bond to MARY ANN HAMMOND, Executrix, & LEROY HAMMOND, GEORGE WHITEFIELD & CHARLES GOODWIN, Executors of LW&T of LEROY HAMMOND, Esq. dec'd., for 150 pounds with Interest & did obtain a writ at Court of Common Pleas in Cambridge 12 Nov 1794...Said WILLIAM TENNENT, Sheriff of Ninety Six Dist. did seize & sell from ZEPHANIAH CLEMENTS (see above prop.) & sold at public auction for payment of said debt...to last & highest bidder... S/ WM.

TENNENT, Sheriff of Ninety Six Dist.
WILLIAM TENNENT, Esq. Sheriff of Ninety Six came into Court &
ack. his deed to CHARLES GOODWIN, Esq. for 500 (sic) acres &
ordered recorded. R. TUTT, Clk. Rcd. 14 Oct 1795.

Pp. 380-383. 3 Aug 1795: Sheriff's Title: WILLIAM TENNENT,
Sheriff to CHARLES GOODWIN of Cambridge, both of Ninety Six Dist,
sold 100 acres on Pretty Run joining lands of Colonel HAMMOND...
Whereas JOHN DOOLY was seized of land (see land) being indebted
to MARY RODGERS for 198 pounds & for recovery of such obtained a
writ from Court of Common Pleas at Cambridge 29 Apr 1793 for 190
pounds & cost of suit & said property was seized by WILLIAM
TENNANT, Sheriff of Ninety Six Dist. & sold at public auction to
CHARLES GOODWIN... S/ WM. TENNANT, Sheriff of Ninety Six Dist.
Oct. Term 1795: WILLIAM TENNANT, Esq. Sher. of Ninety Six Dist.
came into Court & ack. his deed to CHARLES GOODWIN & ordered
Recorded. RD. TUTT, Clk. Rcd. 14 Oct 1795.

Pp. 383-384. 14 Oct 1795: Bill of Sale: CHARLES JONES COLCOCK to
JOHN MARTIN & CATHARINE MARTIN, sold 3 negroe slaves to wit:
FLORA, SAM, & NANNY for the purpose mentioned...to wit to and for
the use benefits and behalf of BENJAMIN MARTIN & MILLY TUTT
MARTIN, son & daughter of EDMOND MARTIN & in case of death of
said children, underage or before marriage then benefits to the
survivor. S/ CHAS. J. COLCOCK.
In presence of RD. TUTT, J.P.
Oct. Term: CHARLES JONES COLCOCK came into Court & ack. within
Bill of Sale & was ordered recorded. R. TUTT, C.E.C. Rcd. 14 Oct
1795.

Pp. 384-389. Jun 1785: PHILLIP MAY, Senr. of Chavers Creek,
Ninety Six Dist. to SOLOMON LUCAS, both of Ninety Six Dist. for
200 pounds, sold 111 1/4 acres being part of 300 acres originally
granted 20 Jul 1772 to RICHARD KIRKLAND & was conveyed to PHILLIP
MAY, Senr. 14 Apr 1783 on South side Chavers Creek adj. &

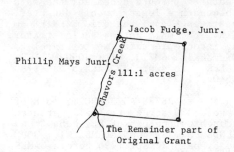

inclosing 1 acre of land
purchased from PHILLIP
MAY, Junr. for a Mill
seat, PHILLIP MAY, Junr.,
JACOB FUDGE, Junr., &
the remainder part of
the original grant. S/
PHILL MAY. Wit: GEORGE
GARBET, JONATHAN RICHARD-
SON, who swore by oath 24
Nov 1788 before ARTHUR
SIMKINS, J. P. Rcd. 14
Oct 1795.
Plat: p. 388. Surveyed
by ROBERT LANG, D.S. 10
May 1785.

P. 389. 22 Sep 1795: Bill of Sale: JOHN RYAN, Esq. of Edgefield
Co. SC to JOHN GLOVER for 140 pounds, sold 2 negro fellows named
GUY & JIM. S/ JOHN RYAN. Wit: JOSEPH HIGHTOWER, who swore by oath
14 Oct 1795 before JOHN CLARKE, J.P. Rcd. 14 Oct 1795.

Pp. 390-392. 13 Oct 1795: ISAAC FOREMAN to JOHN GRAY, Senior,
both of Edgefield for 50 pounds, sold 100 acres granted 5 Jun

DEED BOOK 12: 1794-1796 EDGEFIELD COUNTY S.C.

1786 unto LOTT WARREN & conveyed to said ISAAC FOREMAN; being on
Horns Creek... S/ ISAAC FOREMAN. Wit: J. HALL, THOMAS SWEARENGEN,
ISAAC KIRKLAND, who swore by oath 14 Oct 1795 before JOHN
BLOCKER, J.P. Rcd. 14 Oct 1795.

Pp. 392-396. 6 Jul 1795: THOMAS COTTEN & ANNA his wife, to DANIEL
PARKER, both of Edgefield Co. SC for 30 pounds, sold 150 acres
originally granted 25 Feb 1775 JOHN VERNON who sold 14 Nov 1787
to said COTTON, on branch of Log Creek of Savannah River. S/
THOS. COTTON. Wit: HARTWELL JONES, EUGENE BRENAN, who swore by
oath 7 Jul 1795 before JOHN RYAN, J.P. Rcd. 14 Oct 1795.
Oct. Term 1795: Mrs ANN COTTEN relinq. dower right before R.
TUTT, C.E.C.

Pp. 396-397. 13 Feb 1795: Bill of Sale: THOMAS HUNT of Washington
Co. GA, Planter, to KEVAN & TAYLOR of Village of Campbelton SC,
Merchants for 25 pounds, sold a negroe woman, KATE, about 42 yrs.
old. S/ THOS. HUNT. Wit: ROBERT LIVINGSTON, GEORGE LESLIE, who
swore by oath 15 Oct 1795 before R. TUTT, J.P. Rcd. (no date).

Pp. 397-401. 9 Sep 1795: SHURLEY WHATLEY & PHEBY, his wife to
WILLIS WHATLEY, both of Edgefield Co. SC for 50 pounds, sold 55
acres being part of original grant 4 Aug 1772 to ABRAHAM
HOLSONBACK & sold 28 Jul 1775 to MATHEW DEVORE, Jr., & by said
DEVORE, Jr., sold 6 Oct 1787 to CHRISTIAN LEMBACKER who sold 20
Mar 1794 to said SHIRLEY WHATLEY; on Dry Creek of Stephens Creek
adj. the five knotched road, ABRAHAM HOLSONBAKE, BENJAMIN TUTT &
land surveyed by MOSES KIRKLAND. S/ SHURLEY WHATELY, PHEBY (+)
WHATLEY. Wit: ROBERT MELTON, DAVID SHAW, who swore by oath 15 Oct
1795 before JOSEPH HIGHTOWER, J.P. Rcd. 15 Oct 1795.

Pp. 401-402. 21 Nov 1794: EZEKIEL SMITH of Hancock Co. GA to my
brother, T. KELAND SMITH of Edgefield Co. SC appoints my lawful
attorney to act in my behalf...Where as JOHN CARRAWAY, dec'd.,
father to ELIZABETH, the wife of AARON SMITH & parents to us,
EZEKIEL & T. KELING SMITH, both of parents deceased; the said
JOHN CARRAWAY did by LW&T bequeath a legacy to his daughter,
ELIZABETH & her legal representatives & as I the said EZEKIEL am
the oldest son of said ELIZABETH & the only acting administrator
of my said father & it being inconvenient for me to travel to
N.C. to receive said legacy. S/ EZEKIEL SMITH. Wit: JOHN WALLER,
JOHN N. WALLER, THOMAS B. WALLER, who swore by oath 5 Jan 1795
before JOHN MOORE, J.P. Rcd. 15 Oct 1795.

Pp. 402-405. 16 Feb 1794: JOHN ADAMS to JEREMIAH BURNETT, both of
Edgefield Co. SC for 50 pounds, sold 330 acres originally granted
15 Jun 1786 said ADAMS on branch Cuffeetown of Stephens Creek
adj. MIZE, JAMES ANDERSON, HENDERSON. S/ JOHN ADAMS. Wit: JOHN
SPRATT, SAMUEL MAYS, who swore by oath 23 Apr 1795 before JAMES
HARRISON, J.P. Rcd. 16 Oct 1795.

Pp. 406-410. 3 Jun 1794: EDWARD PENMAN, Merchant of Charleston SC
to JAMES HAREGROVE, Planter of Edgefield Co. SC for 50 pounds,
sold 100 acres being part of 500 acres originally granted 28 Aug
1772 JAMES SIMPSON & sold to JOHN BOWMAN & RICHARD WELDS & by
them sold to said EDWARD PENMAN; on Dry Creek a branch of
Savannah River adj. land sold by EDWARD PENMAN to PATRICK
CUNNINGHAM, WILLIAM MOSELEY, EDWARD PENMAN, JOSEPH & SAMUEL
DOOLITTLE. S/ ED. PENMAN. Wit: JAMES GARDNER, CHARLES J. COLCOCK,

226

who swore by oath 5 Oct 1795 before JAMES HARRISON, J.P.

Plat: p. 410. Plat
of 100 acrés part
of 500 acres
Certified 11 Mar
1795 by W.
ANDERSON, D.S.
Rcd. 16 Oct. 1795.

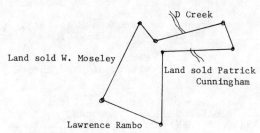

D Creek

Land sold W. Moseley

Land sold Patrick Cunningham

Lawrence Rambo

Pp. 410-411. 19 Sep 1791: Deed of Gift: STEPHEN SMITH, Planter of Edgefield Co. SC to son, ISAAC SMITH of same place for love & affection gives 361 acres where I now live on; one negroe fellow named GEORGE; one negrow wench JUDE & her two children; five head of horses; thirty head of horned cattle; & all my hogs marked with a Crop & a hole in each year (sic); all my household furniture. S/ STEPHEN (+) SMITH. Wit: ZEPHENIAH HARVEY, DRURY GLOVER, Abbeville Co. SC, who swore by oath 7 Nov 1792 before JULIUS NICHOLS, Jr. J.P. Rcd. 16 Oct 1795.

Pp. 411-414. 17 Oct 1795: BARKLEY MARTIN to GEORGE LESLIE & ARCHABALD CAMPBELL or otherwise called GEORGE LESLIE & CO. of the Village of Campbelltown, we of Edgefield Co. SC for 100 pounds, sold 3 Lots of land containing one & a quarter in the village of Campbellton known in the plan of the village by the Number 27, 28, & 29. S/ BARKLEY MARTIN. Wit: WILLIAM WASH, JONATHAN MOORE, who swore by oath 17 Oct 1795 before JOSEPH HIGHTOWER, J.P. Rcd. 17 Oct 1795.

Pp. 414-417. 27 Dec 1778: GEORGE MASON to JOSEPH NUNN, Planter, both of Ninety Six district SC for 2100 pounds, sold 150 acres being the North half of 300 acres originally granted 5 Sep 1769 Colleton County on Dry Creek of Saluda River adj. CHARLES PARTON & GAVIN POU. S/ GEORGE MASON. Wit: JOHN DAVIS, SAMUEL GRIGSBY, BURDITT ESKRIDGE, who swore by oath 28 Dec 1778 before RUSSELL WILSON, J.P. Rcd. 17 Oct 1795.

Pp. 417-419. 12 Oct 1795: SAMUEL MAYS, Late Sheriff of Edgefield Co. SC to BARKLEY MARTIN for 3 pounds: Whereas JOSEPH DICK obtained a Judgement in Edgefield Court against McCARTAN CAMPBELL & THOMAS GOLPHIN for 12 pounds & a Writ of Fieri Facias was issued 7 Feb 1792 by RICHARD TUTT, Clerk of Court... Said MAYS did sieze of JOSEPH DICK a certain lot #29 of 1/2 acre in the town of Campbellton adj. McCARTAN CAMPBELL & advertized same 3 Mar 1792 for sale at public auction to the last & highest bidder... S/ S. MAYS. Wit: DRURY MIMS, HARTWELL JONES, who swore by oath 17 Oct 1795 before JOSEPH HIGHTOWER, J.P. Rcd. 17 Oct 1795.

Pp. 419-420. 12 Oct 1795: SAMUEL MAYS, Sheriff of Edgefield Co. SC to BARKLEY MARTIN... Ibid, 17 Feb 1792... 1/2 acre Lot #28. S/ S. MAYS, Shff. Edgefield Co. Wit: DRURY MIMS, HARTWELL JONES, who swore by oath before JOSEPH HIGHTOWER, J.P. Rcd. 17 Oct 1795.

Pp. 421-423 25 Apr 1795: THOMAS WITHERTON to DAVID GLOVER, both
of Edgefield Co. SC for 30 pounds, sold 55 acres originally
granted 1 May 1786 unto RICHARD WITHERTON on a branch of
Chavoures Creek of Stephens Creek adj. JONATHAN LIMBACKER, JOHN
DOOLY. S/ THOMAS (T) WEIGHERINGTON. Wit: MATHEW (M) DEVORE,
JOHN DEVORE, ISAAC HOPKINS, who swore by oath 19 Oct 1795 before
RICHARD TUTT, J.P. Rcd. 19 Oct 1795.
[Note: gch. In content of deed in one place is written THOMAS
?COTTON? WITHERTON.]

P. 424. 12 Jun 1795: Bill of Sale: ISAAC FOREMAN of Edgefield Co.
SC to ABIGAL JONES for 35 pounds, sold one negro boy named POMPY.
S/ ISAAC FOREMAN. Wit: ABIGAIL DYAL, BENJAMIN DARBY, who swore by
oath 12 Oct 1795 before VAN SWEARINGEN, J.P. Rcd. 19 Oct 1795.

Pp. 424-425. 17 Oct 1795: Bill of Sale: MARGARET GOMILLIAN to
ABIGAL JONES for 15 pounds, sold 3 cows & calves; 2 heifers
marked CG; 2 beds & furniture; dutch oven & 1 small pot; horse
colt of brown coulour...S/ MARGARET (+) GOMILIAN. Wit: WILLIAM
NICHOLS, ADAM PARDUE, who swore by oath 19 Oct 1795 before VAN
SWEARINGEN, J.P. Rcd. 19 Oct 1795.

Pp. 425-426. 29 Oct 1795: Deed of Gift: FANNY BURT, widow, to
niece, LUCY WILLIAMSON EVANS, both of Edgefield Co. SC for love &
affection, at the time of my decease one negro woman called
GRACE; one negroe boy named JACOB; & one negro girl called
HANNAH; one bed & furniture; 1 horse & Riding chair with all my
stock household & kitchen furniture. S/ FANNY (+) BURT. Wit:
HINCHEY MITCHELL, GEORGE H. PERRIN, who swore by oath 30 Oct 1795
before R. TUTT, J.P. Rcd. 30 Oct 1795.

Pp. 426-430. 25 Nov 1778: MICHAEL ABNEY to CHRISTOPHER GORMAN,
both of Ninety Six Dist. SC for 500 pounds, sold 100 acres being
part of 200 acres originally granted 13 Oct 1772 said ABNEY on
south side of Saluda River adj. East on part of original grant
now in possession of JOHN GORMAN. S/ MICHAEL ABNEY. Wit: JOHN (Ɏ)
GORMAN, HANNAH GORMAN, ROBERT LANG, who swore by oath 5 Nov 1795
before RICHARD TUTT, J.P. Rcd. 5 Nov 1795.

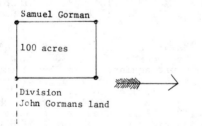

13 Oct 1792: I have
ameasured & laid out 100
acres, part of 200 acres
originally granted M.
ABNEY on south side
Saluda...   Certified
ROBERT LANG.

Pp. 431-434. 3 Aug 1794: JOHN PURSLEY & ELIZABETH his wife to
ZACHARIAH MARTIN, all of Edgefield Co. SC for 100 pounds, sold
114 acres on north side Dry Creek adj. WILLIS WHATLEY, ROBERT
MELTON, JACOB HAVERLIN, MOSES PURSLEY. S/ JOHN (X) PURSLEY,
ELIZABETH (X) PURSLEY. Wit: WILLIAM (M) PURSLEY, JAMES (X)
SUTLEY, WILLIAM WATSON, Senr., who swore by oath 11 Apr 1795
before JOSEPH HIGHTOWER, J.P. Rcd. 5 Nov 1795.

(Please see following page for plat)

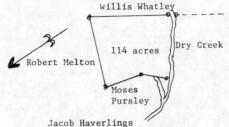

Plat: p. 434. 30 Jul
1794 Plat represents
114 acres conveyed
from JOHN PURSLEY to
ZACHARIAH MARTIN
surveyed & laid off
by ROBERT LANG, D.S.

Pp. 434-436. 4 Jul 1795: EDMOND HOLLEMAN, Arithmatior, to HUGH
MOSS, Planter, both of Edgefield Co. SC for 20 pounds, sold 85
acres granted in Columbia 5 Sep 1791 said HOLLEMAN on Gunnels

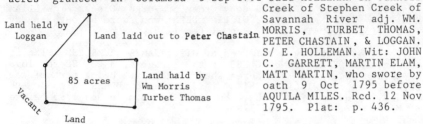

Creek of Stephen Creek of
Savannah River adj. WM.
MORRIS, TURBET THOMAS,
PETER CHASTAIN, & LOGGAN.
S/ E. HOLLEMAN. Wit: JOHN
C. GARRETT, MARTIN ELAM,
MATT MARTIN, who swore by
oath 9 Oct 1795 before
AQUILA MILES. Rcd. 12 Nov
1795. Plat: p. 436.

Pp. 436-439. 5 Oct 1795: WILLIAM TENNANT, Sheriff of Ninety Six
District SC to ANDREW GLOVER for 10 pounds, sold 94
acres...Whereas THOMAS LAMAR, Planter, was seized in his
demence... a certain tract of land of 94 acres adj. Horse Creek,
GLOVER, land near Chalk Hill, as per plat, late property of the
Chickersaw Indians known by the No. 29. Whereas THOMAS LAMAR &
RICHARD JOHNSON by their joint & several Bonds became indebted to
WILLIAM PARKER & EDWARD BLAKE, Commissioners of the Treasury for
34 pounds & interest. And where as the Commissioners for recovery
of said debt did commence action in the Court of Common Pleas at
Cambridge against LAMAR & JOHNSON 23 Apr 1795... And where as a
Judgement was issued 16 Nov 1794 against said LAMAR & JOHNSON &
the said Sheriff in obedience to the writ of Fiere Facias did
seize said property & give legal notice of a public sale to the
highest & last bidder...ANDREW GLOVER. S/ WM. TENNENT, Sheriff of
Ninety Six Dist. Wit: THOMAS BUTLER, WILLIAM HARKINS, who swore
by oath 20 Nov 1795 before R. TUTT, J.P. Rcd. 20 Nov 1795.

Pp. 439-442. 25 Sep 1795: PETER FRENEAU of Charleston SC to
CRADOCK BURNELL of Edgefield Co. SC for 25 Spanish milled
dollars, sold 25 acres being part of a survey made 13 May 1737
for JOHN ELLERS & granted 4 Jul 1785 to said PETER FRENEAU in the
township of New Windsor. The survey at the time made adj. HANS
ZURCHER, LEONARD BRUDER, CONRAD ANDEROWER, ULRICK EGGERS. S/
PETER FRENEAU, CRADK. BURNELL. Wit: PETER J. SEAVER, ISAAC MOTTE
DART, who swore by oath 26 Sep 1795 before CHARLES LINNING, J.P.
in Charleston, SC. Rcd. 25 Nov 1795.

Pp. 442-443. 8 Sep 1795: Bill of Sale: JOHN BURT of Edgefield Co.
SC to HANNAH BLAIR & POLLY BLAIR for Goodwill & consideration of
5 shillings, sold 2 cows & calvs; 12 head of hogs; 1 feather bed;

1 side saddle; 2 dishes; 2 basons; 6 plates; 1 cotton wheel & 1 linning wheel. S/ JOHN BURT, Senr. Wit: JOHN BURT, Jr., WILLIAM BURT, JOHN WHITE, who swore by oath 27 Nov 1795 before AQUILA MILES, J.P. Rcd. 30 Nov 1795.

Pp. 443-444. 3 Sep 1795: Bill of Sale: JOHN BURT to JESSE HILL for good will & consideration of 5 shillings, sold two mares & working tools. S/ JOHN BURT, Sr. Wit: JOHN BURT, Jr., WILLIAM BURT, JOHN WHITE, who swore by oath 26 Nov 1795 before AQUILA MILES, J.P. Rcd. 30 Nov 1795.
[Comment: gch. deed Titled Bill of Sale but called Deed of Gift in oath.]

Pp. 444-445. 13 Oct 1793: WILLIAM ROBINSON to JAMES McCRELESS, both of Edgefield Co. SC for 25 pounds, sold 110 acres originally granted 3 Oct 1785 on Sleepy Creek of Turkey Creek. S/ WILLIAM ROBINSON. Wit: NANCY DEEN, WILLIAM DEEN, who swore by oath 26 Nov 1795 before S. MAYS, J.P. Rcd. 1 Dec 1795.

Pp. 445-446. 18 Nov 1795: Deed of Gift: JAMES McCRELESS, Planter to son, GEORGE LEWIS McCRELESS, both of Edgefield Co. SC for love & affection, gave 70 acres where I now live being part of 110 acres granted WILLIAM ROBINSON. S/ JAMES McCRELESS. Wit: JOSEPH ESSERY, JOHN (Ϯ) BUCKELEW, who swore by oath 26 Nov 1795 before S. MAYS, J.P. Rcd. 1 Dec 1795.

Pp. 446-449. 1 Jun 1795: ALEXANDER WILSON & MARTHA his wife, of Edgefield Co. SC to HENRY GESKIN, Merchant of Charleston SC for (blank) sold 197 acres originally granted 4 Dec 1787 to CHRISTOPHER BROOKS on Deloach branch of Little Saluda River. Said land conveyed by CHRISTOPHER BROOKS to said WILSON. S/ ALEXDR. WILSON, MARTHA WILSON. Wit: WILLIAM WEEKS, DAVID RICHARDSON, who swore by oath 25 Nov 1795 before WM. ROBINSON, J.P. Rcd. 2 Dec 1795.

Pp. 449-450. 3 Nov 1795: Bill of Sale: SAMUEL LANDRUM to JOHN LANDRUM, both of Edgefield Co. SC for 30 pounds, sold one negro boy about 11 yrs. old named ABRAM. S/ SAMUEL LANDRUM. Wit: PHEBE LANDRUM, HOWEL SELLERS, who swore by oath 4 Nov 1795 before JOHN BLOCKER, J.P. Rcd. 5 Dec 1795.

Pp. 450-451. 3 Nov 1795: Bill of Sale: SAMUEL LANDRUM of Edgefield Co. SC to PHEBE LANDRUM for 25 pounds, sold one negro girl about 6 yrs. old named JENNY. S/ SAMUEL LANDRUM. Wit: JOHN LANDRUM, HOWELL SELLERS, who swore by oath 4 Nov 1795 before JOHN BLOCKER, J.P. Rcd. 5 Dec 1795.

Pp. 451-452. 9 Jul 1795: Bill of Sale: JAMES COBB, Sr. of Edgefield Co. SC to JAMES COBB, Jr. for 500 pounds, sold 7 negroes (to wit) JANEY, CREASY, NED, SALLY, JESSE, AGGY & MIMA. S/ JAMES COBB, Sr. Wit: MARY SNEAD, RICHARD JOHNSON, who swore by oath 1 Nov 1795 before JOHN RYAN, J.P. Rcd. 5 Dec 1795.

Pp. 452-454. 5 May 1795: ABDEL STOT & MARY his wife, to JOHN LANDRUM, both of Edgefield Co. SC for 40 pounds, sold 988 acres originally granted 7 Jan 1793 on big Horse Creek of Savannah River adj. JOHN HERNDON, Esq., & VAN SWEARENGEN's. S/ ABDEL (+) STOT. Wit: JAMES BROWN, HOWEL SELLERS, who swore by oath 4 Nov 1795 before JOHN BLOCKER, J.P. Rcd. 5 Dec 1795.

Pp. 454-460.   4 May 1795: Bond: EPHRIAM RAMSAY of Cambridge to
THOMAS RADCLIFFE of Charleston, Executor of LW&T of ANDREW
WILLIAMSON, dec'd., for 21 pounds with interest, sold 100 acres
originally granted 23 Aug 1765 unto PHILIP PETER KNOB in Colleton
Co. on Cuffeetown Creek adj. PETER KNOB. S/ E. RAMSEY. Wit: R.A.
RAPLEY, ABRAHAM DOZIER, who swore by oath 1 Dec 1795 before JOHN
TROTTER, J.P.   Rcd. 5 Dec 1795.

Pp. 460-465. 4 May 1795: Land by Way of Mortgage: EPHRIAM RAMSEY
of Cambridge to THOMAS RADCLIFF of Charleston, Executor of LW&T
of ANDREW WILLIAMSON, dec'd., by his bond & obligation 4 May for
sum of 25 pounds...and payment of 12 pounds... 100 acres in
Granville Co. on Stephenson Creek. Wit: R.A. RAPLY, ABRAHAM
DOZIER, who swore by oath 1 Dec 1795 before JNO. TROTTER, J.P.
Rcd. 5 Dec 1795.

Pp. 466-469.   10 Dec 1795: DRURY MIMS to RICE CLEVELAND, Planter,
both of Edgefield Co. SC for (blank) sold 50 acres being part of
200 ares originally granted 1772 unto NICHOLAS DILLARD adj.
THOMAS HAGENS & was conveyed by NICHOLAS DILLARD to PHILIP
DILLARD & by PHILLIP DILLARD to DRURY MIMS 19 Dec 1789. S/ DRURY
MIMS. Wit: R. TUTT, GEORGE H. PERRIN, who swore by oath 11 Dec
1795 before R. TUTT, J.P.   Rcd. 11 Dec 1795.

Pp. 469-470.   25 Jan 1793: WILLIAM DAWSON & MARY, his wife to
THOMAS BACON, Esq., both of Edgefield Co. SC for 50 pounds, sold
70 acres being part of 547 acres originally granted to JOHN CROW
on Cuffee Town Creek
of Savannah River adj.
BENJ. TUTT, Maj. HUGH
MIDDLETON.   S/ WILL.
DAWSON. Wit: SHADRACK
STOKES,   JAMES
McMILLAN, who swore by
oath 8 Feb 1793 before
JAMES HARRISON, J.P.
Rcd. 22 Dec 1795.

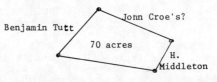

Pp. 470-471.   17 Dec 1795: Deed of Gift: WILLIAM BRASWELL unto
my children (viz) My sons, JACOB, WILLIAM, RICHARD, JOHN & ALLEN
BRASWELL, each one horse, 1 cow & calf for love & affection.
To   dau. NANCY, one cow, calf, feather bed & furniture;
To dau. ELIZABETH, Ibid;
To dau. SALLY, Ibid;
Also to son ALLEN - 15 head of hogs, pewter, pot, working tools.
S/ WILLIAM (X) BRASWELL. Wit: BRITTIAN BRASWELL, JAMES BRASWELL,
who swore by oath 22 Dec 1795 before WM. DANIEL, J.P. Rcd. 23 Dec
1795.

Pp. 471-472.   6 Aug 1795: Deed of Gift: JAMES BURGESS, Shop
Joiner, appoint as my lawful attorney JACOB NORRILL, Planter, all
of Edgefield Co. SC for recovery of said debts & legacies due me.
S/ JAMES BURGESS. Wit: GREEN MOORE, WILLIAM MOORE., who swore by
oath 19 Dec 1795 before WILLIAM ROBINSON, J.P. Rcd. 23 Dec 1795.

Pp. 472-475. 28 Dec 1795: MOSES HARRIS to VINCENT PETER
WILLIAMSON, both of Edgefield Co. SC for 100 pounds, sold 100
acres being part of 300 or 350 (sic) acres granted Mar 1768 unto
JAMES ROBINSON who transferred to his son THOMAS ROBINSON by Deed

of Gift & he sold by L&R 30 & 31 Jan 1778 to JENKINS HARRIS & he by his LW&T of said JENKINS HARRIS, dec'd., 100 acres of the original grant descended unto MOSES HARRIS. Said land on Beaverdam Creek of Stephens Creek of Savannah River, adj. MEZEAK, WILLIAM SIMKINS. S/ MOSES HARRIS. Wit: JOHN ROBERTSON, GEORGE H. PERRIN, who swore by oath 29 Dec 1795 before RICHARD TUTT. Rcd. 29 Dec 1795.

Pp. 475-479. 28 Dec 1795: WILLIAM SIMKINS to VINCENT PETER WILLIAMSON, both of Edgefield Co. SC for 100 pounds, sold 4 acres being part of 325 acres granted 2 May 1785 unto WILLIAM SIMKINS on Beaverdam Creek a branch of Horns Creek (sic) (in release said Stephens Creek, gch) of Savannah River as seen by original plat & plat of 4 acres by WILLIAM COURSEY, D.S. S/ WILLIAM SIMKINS. Wit: FREEMAN WIGHTT, MOSES HARRIS, who swore by oath 29 Dec 1795 before RICHARD TUTT, J.P.

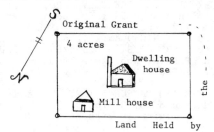

16 Mar 1795: I have ameasured unto VINCENT PETER WILLIAMSON 4 acres of land in Edgefield Co. SC near the Court house where WILLIAMSON now dwelleth adj. all sides by original grant of 325 acres granted 2 May 1785. S/ WM. COURSEY, D.S. Rcd. 29 Dec 1795.

Pp. 479-482. 13 Nov 1795: HUGH MIDDLETON of Edgefield Co. SC to PATSAY MIDDLETON (daughter in witnesses oath), for natural love & 10 shillings, 350 acres being of 2 tracts; (1) 200 acres granted RICHARD MEDERS (also MEADS) on Savannah River adj. Savannah River & runs down said river until it takes 2/3 of the uncleared grounds to the old mill where it joins 170 acres granted HUGH MIDDLETON.. thence along lines joining another tract of 353 acres granted said MIDDLETON; (2) part of above mentioned 353 acres at the mouth of Ready Branch up that fork of Deep step until it intersects the head of the schoolhouse branch.. thence down the line until it joins above 170 acres. S/ HUGH MIDDLETON. Wit: RICHARD QUARLES, HUGH MIDDLETON, Jr., Charleston Co. SC, who swore by oath 5 Dec 1795 before JOHN TROTTER, J.P. Rcd. 29 Dec 1795.

Pp. 482-483. 1 Dec 1795: Deed of Gift: HUGH MIDDLETON of Edgefield Co. SC hereunto moving, to daughter PATSY MIDDLETON, for love & affection give 4 negroes named JUNO, SARAH, PRINCE & TOM. S/ HUGH MIDDLETON. Wit: RICHARD QUARLES, HUGH MIDDLETON, Jr., who swore by oath 5 Dec 1795 before JOHN TROTTER, J.P. Rcd. 29 Dec 1795.

Pp. 483-485. 2 Dec 1795: PATSAY MIDDLETON of Edgefield Co. SC to HUGH MIDDLETON & CHARLES J. COLCOCK, for 5 shillings, sold 350 acres being part of 200 acres granted to RICHARD MEADERS on Savannah River running down said river until it takes 2/3s of enclosed low goods... to old mill where it joins 170 acres granted HUGH MIDDLETON... to tract of 353 acres granted said HUGH MIDDLETON... also part of the above 353 acres at mouth of Ready Branch... up that fork of deepstep until it intersects head of

DEED BOOK 12: 1794-1796 EDGEFIELD COUNTY S.C.

the Schoolhouse branch... to 170 acres before mentioned. S/ PATSY MIDDLETON. Wit: RICHARD QUARLES, HUGH MIDDLETON, Jr., Charleston Co. SC, who swore 5 Dec 1795 before JOHN TROTTER, J.P. Rcd. 29 Dec 1795.

Pp. 485-490. 3 Dec 1795: Settlement by Way of Marriage: WILLIAM TENNENT of Cambridge & PATSAY MIDDLETON of Edgefield Co. SC to HUGH MIDDLETON & CHARLES J. COLCOCK of Edgefield Co. SC (Trustees nominated & appointed by them said WILLIAM TENNANT & CHARLES J. COLCOCK for the purpose after mentioned), for 10 shillings... Whereas a marriage is shortly intended between WILLIAM TENNENT & PATSAY MIDDLETON... trustees for 350 acres & 4 negroes named JUNO, SARAH, PRINCE, & TOM. S/ WILLIAM TENNENT, PATSAY MIDDLETON. Wit: RICHARD QUARLES, HUGH MIDDLETON, Jr., who swore by oath 5 Dec 1795 before JOHN TROTTER, J.P. Rcd. 29 Dec 1795.

Pp. 490-493. 21 May 1794: WILLIAM RICE CLARK, Planter to EBENITES STEVENS, Planter, both of Edgefield Co. SC for 7 pounds, sold 100 acres being part of 330 acres granted 7 May 1787 unto said CLARK on Rocky Creek a branch of Turkey Creek of Savanna River said 330 acres & all 330 acres being claimed taken by former or older grant; adj. JOHN BELL, JAMES THOMAS. S/ WILLIAM RICE CLARK. Wit: JAMES GOLMAN, SAMUEL (∿) WILLIAMS, who swore by oath 27 Sep 1794 before HENRY KING, J.P. Rcd. 2 Jan 1796.

Pp. 493-496. 7 Dec 1795: JOHN JULIUS PRINGLE, Esq. & SUSANNAH his wife of Charleston SC to ARTHUR WATSON of Edgefield Co. SC for 54 pounds, sold 500 acres originally granted 26 Jul 1774 to ROBERT PRINGLE, Esq., dec'd., on Fauls Creek of Cloud Creek adj. ARTHUR WATSON, JAMES DANIEL, ROBERT STARK, EDWARD COUCH & MICHAEL WATSON. S/ JOHN J. PRINGLE, SUSANNA PRINGLE. Wit: HARY GRANT, WILLIAM LEE, JOHN EDSON, who swore by oath 14 Dec 1795 before RUSSELL WILSON, J.P. Rcd. 4 Jan 1796.

Pp. 496-497. 12 Nov 1795: JOHN KILLCREASE to RUSSELL PUCKETT, both of Edgefield Co. SC for 20 pounds, sold 50 acres originally granted JOHN LOGAN of the "Round O" on Blue branch of Turkey Creek adj. said LOGAN. S/ JOHN KILLCREASE. Wit: SAMUEL SELLARS, JESSE PUCKETT, who swore by oath 4 Jan 1796 before RD. TUTT, J.P. Rcd. 4 Jan 1796.

Pp. 497-500. 18 Oct 1795: DANIEL PARKER & ELIZABETH, his wife to EDWARD MITCHELL, all of Edgefield Co. SC for 30 pounds, sold 120 acres being part of 150 acres originally granted 25 Feb 1775 unto JOHN VERNON & which other part of 30 acres was sold by DANIEL GUNNELS unto SARAH GUNNELS. Said land on branch of Log Creek of Turkey Creek of Savannah River & adj. said SARAH GUNNEL & Bounty land when surveyed. S/ DANIEL PARKER. Wit: STARLING MITCHELL, HINCHY MITCHELL, who swore by oath 4 Jan 1796 before RICHARD TUTT, J.P. Rcd. 4 Jan 1796.
Mrs ELIZABETH PARKER relinq. dower before RICHARD TUTT, J.P.

Pp. 500-502. 29 Apr 1795: THOMAS FARRAR, Esq. formerly Sheriff of Ninety Six district to MATHEWS WELLS of Edgefield Co. SC for 12 pounds, sold 350 acres...Whereas: HENRY WELSH lately in Court of Common Pleas at Cambridge entered a judgement against JAMES OLIPHANT & a writ of Fiere Facias attested by Hon. JOHN RUTLEDGE, Esq. Chief Justice, was issued & in obedience to Judgement THOMAS FARRAR, Sheriff of Ninety Six did sieze, advertize & sell to last & highest bidder, MATTHEW WELLS 350 acres on south side of Saluda

233

DEED BOOK 12:   1794-1796 EDGEFIELD COUNTY S.C.

adj. RICHARD TEET, WILLIAM STEWART, MOSES KIRKLAND & WILLIAM
LEGG. S/ THOMAS FARRAR, Late Sheff. Ninety Six Dist. Wit: ALLEN
GLOVER, JAMES McCRACKAN, who swore by oath 1 Dec 1795 before JNO.
TROTTER, J.P. Rcd. 4 Jan 1796.

Pp. 502-504. 14 Apr. 1795: ELISHA PALMER (also PALMAR & PALMORE),
of Edgefield Co. SC to AGNESS CUNNINGHAM, Adm'trix of JOHN
CUNNINGHAM, dec'd., of SC for 10 pounds, sold 10 acres on
Stephens Creek of Savannah River being part of a tract formerly
belonging to ABRAHAM RUMP. S/ ELISHA (X) PALMORE. Wit: WILLIAM
BIBB, WILLIAM HOWLE, who swore by oath 17 Apr 1795 before AQUILA
MILES, J.P. Rcd. 4 Jan 1795.

Pp. 504-505. 23 Jan 1795: THOMAS DOZER to REUBIN LISENBY, both of
Edgefield Co. SC for 30 pounds, sold 600 acres being part of 2
tracts originally granted said DOZER; (1) tract of 1000 acres
granted 1 Sep 1788 &; (2) tract granted 7 Jan 1793 on Big Creek
of Little Saluda River adj. THOMAS SCOTT, JOHN GREEN, said THOMAS
DOZER, JOSHUA DEEN & ALEXR. BOLING STARK. S/ THOMAS DOZER, CATEY
(X) DOZER. Wit: PRESLEY BLAND, JOEL BROWN, HENRY KING, who swore
by oath 30 May 1795 before WILLIAM DANIEL, J.P. Rcd. 4 Jan 1796.
Memordm: 23 Jan 1795 Peasble & Quiet on Possession & Seizia was
given to RUBIN LISENBY of the within lands by me. S/ THOMAS
DOZER, CATEY (X) DOZER.

Pp. 505-506. 7 Feb 1794: THOMAS DOZER to JOHN GREEN, all of
Edgefield Co. SC for 25 pounds, sold 200 acres being part of 350
acres originally granted 7 Jan 1793 to said DOZER & being that
part that joins JOHN GREEN's land, THOMAS SCOTT, LEWIS CLARK &
greens branch. S/ THOMAS DOZER. Wit: WILLIAM (X) GREEN, WILLIAM
STROTHERS, JESSE GAINS, who swore by oath 12 Feb 1794 before
HENRY KING, J.P. Rcd. 4 Jan 1796.

Pp. 507-508. 13 Apr 1794: SAMUEL SAXON, Sheriff of Ninety Six
district to LEROY HAMMOND of Edgefield Co. SC for 51 pounds, sold
6 acres in Cambleton, Edgefield Co. SC on Savannah River.
Whereas: sundry creditors lately in the Cambridge Court of Common
Pleas entered a judgement against LEROY HAMMOND, dec'd., & a writ
of fiere Facias was issued 18 Apr 1792 attested by Hon. JOHN
RUTLEDGE, Esq. Chief Justice... directed SAMUEL SAXON, Sher. of
Ninety Six to seize, advertize & sell goods, chattels,
hereditaments & real estate of LEROY HAMMOND, dec'd. S/ S. SAXON,
Sheff. Ninety Six Dist. Wit: GEO. WHITFIELD?, JOHN TROTTER, who
swore by oath 4 Jan 1796 before JULIUS NICHOLS, J.P. Rcd. 4 Jan
1796.

Pp. 508-511. 29 Dec 1795: LEROY HAMMOND of New Richmond,
Edgefield Co. SC to JOHN HAMMOND, Merchant of Mount Airy,
Edgefield Co. SC for 100 pounds, sold 6 acres in Cambleton,
Edgefield Co. SC adj. Savannah River & Union Street. S/ LEROY
HAMMOND. Wit: EPHRAIM RAMSEY, ABRAHAM DOZER, who swore by oath 14
(sic) Jan 1796 before JOHN TROTTER, J.P. Rcd. 4 Jan 1796.
[Note: gch: The word "Mistake" written on next two blank
unnumbered pages then deed continues.]

Pp. 511-514. 4 Dec 1775: RICHARD DEEN to ELISHA ROBINSON, both of
Ninety Six Dist. SC for 50 pounds, sold 50 acres originally
granted 9 Sep 1774 said DEEN on Savannah River. S/ RICHD. (R)
DEEN. Wit: STEPHEN ANDERSON, JOHN MURPHEY, JAMES BAYLAY, who

swore by oath 6 Dec 1775 before WILLIAM ANDERSON, J.P. Rcd. 5 Jan 1796.

Pp. 514-515. 19 Jan 1796: Bill of Sale: JOHN SEARLS to DANIEL RITCHEY, both of Edgefield Co. SC for 45 pounds, sold one negro boy named ANTHONY about nine years old, black complected. S/ JOHN SEARLS. Wit: ABSOLEM NAPPER, ABRAM HERNDON, who swore by oath 29 Jan 1796 before VAN SWEARINGEN, J.P. Rcd. 29 Jan 1796.

Pp. 515-518. 24 Jun 1791: ROBERT LANG to DANIEL MACKEY, both of Edgefield Co. SC for 50 pounds, sold 458 acres on the head of Turkey Creek & on the waggon road from Augusta to the Ridge & road from Edgefield courthouse to Columbia adj. JOHN RYAN, CHARLES WILLIAMS & JOHN CRAWFORD. S/ ROBERT LANG. Wit: MACKERNESS GOODE, EDMUND WHATLEY, ROGER WILLIAMS, who swore by oath 1 Jul 1791 before AQUILA MILES, J.P. Rcd. 14 Jan 1796.

P. 518. 13 May 1795: Bill of Sale: JOHN PHILLIPS to WALTER ABNEY for 30 pounds, sold one negro girl named RACHEL. The condition of the above Bill of Sale is - if said JOHN PHILLIPS replaces said 30 pounds by 1 January next, the above obligation is void... S/ JOHN PHILLIPS. Wit: ELIZABETH (X) McCREA, ROBERT McCREA, who swore by oath 12 Jan 1796 before WILLIAM ROBINSON, J.P. Rcd. 19 Jan 1796.

Pp. 519-521. 6 Apr 1795: WILLIAM TENNANT, Sheriff of Ninety Six District to JOHN FOX, Merchant of Augusta, GA for 615 pounds, sold 717 acres...Whereas: THOMAS LAMAR by his Bond became indebted to DAVID McCREEDEE for 300 pounds with lawful interest & for the recovery of said debt a judgment was obtained in the Court of Common Pleas in Cambridge & a writ of fiere facias was issued 27 Mar 1791 attested by Hon. JOHN RUTLEDGE, Esq. Chief Justice... directing the Sheriff to sieze, advertise & sell to the last & highest bidder the goods, chattels, & real estate of THOMAS LAMAR...Said 717 acres being on Savannah River & is adj. by mouth of Horse Creek, NATHANIEL BACON, Capt. NATHL. BACON, land known in the general plat of the Chickasaw Lands (as surveyed by BENNETT CRAFTON) by the Number 8, Number 24, & General ANDREW PICKENS. S/ WM. TENNANT, Sheff. Ninety Six Dist. Wit: JOHN TROTTER, ROGER HAWKINS, who swore by oath 16 Dec 1795 before JOHN TROTTER, J.P. Rcd. 25 Jan 1796.

Pp. 521-523. 1 Aug 1795: THOMAS BACON & MARTHY, his wife, to JACOB SHIBBLEY (also SHIBLEY), all of Edgefield Co. SC for 120 pounds, sold 250 acres originally granted unto ISAAC MITCHELL on Cuffytown Creek of Savannah River adj. JOHN STUART & BRYANT at the time of survey. S/ THOS. BACON, MARTHA BACON. Wit: JACOB HIBBLER, JOSEPH WALLACE, SAMUEL HALL, who swore by oath Aug 1795 before JAS. HARRISON, J.P. Rcd. 25 Jan 1796.

26 Jan 1796: MARTHA BACON, wife of THOMAS BACON relinq. her dower before ARTHUR SIMKINS, J.C.E.

Plat: p. 522.

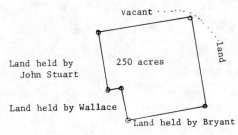

vacant

Land held by John Stuart

250 acres

...land

Land held by Wallace

Land held by Bryant

DEED BOOK 12:   1794-1796 EDGEFIELD COUNTY S.C.

Pp. 523-524. 24 Jan 1796: JAMES FRAZIER to MOSES CARTER, both of
Edgefield Co. SC for 50 pounds, sold 50 acres on the Augusta &
Edgefield Road of Beaverdam Creek adj. DANIEL GUNNELS, WILLIAM
CRANE & WILLIAM MARSH. S/ JAMES FRAZIER. Wit: SANDERS (X)
GUNNELS, JOHN (X) OLLIPHANT, GEORGE H. PERRIN, who swore by oath
26 Jan 1796 before RICHARD TUTT, J.P. Rcd. 26 Jan 1796.

P. 524. 26 Jan 1796: MOSES CARTER to ARON (also AARON) CARTER,
Jr., both of Edgefield Co. SC for 50 pounds, sold 50 acres on the
Augusta & Edgefield Road of Beaverdam Creek adj. DANIEL GUNNELS,
WILLIAM CRANE & WILLIAM MARSH. S/ MOSES (W) CARTER. Wit: JOHN
ROBERTSON, GEORGE H. PERRIN, who swore by oath 26 Jan 1796 before
RICHARD TUTT, J.P. Rcd. 26 Jan 1796.

Pp. 525. 1 Aug 1795: Bond: DANIEL ROGERS, Sr. to MARY JOHNSON,
dau. of DAVID JOHNSON, all of Edgefield Co. SC for 100 pounds, to
be received by said DAVID JOHNSON which sum is now given in
marriage with 1/3 part of all my real & personal estate as her
dividend after my decease...Condition is the DAVID JOHNSON be
trustee for said MARY JOHNSON... & said DANIEL ROGERS, Sr. doth
covenant & again to & with MARY JOHNSON to Join in the Holy Estate
of Matrymony & secrets of Wedlock... S/ DANIEL (X) ROGGERS. Wit:
JOSEPH TOWLS, CHARITY JOHNSON, SAMUEL JOHNSON, who swore by oath
23 Jan 1796 before NATHL. ABNEY, J.P. Rcd. 29 Jan 1796.

Pp. 526-257. Jan 1796: FIRE FIKE & MARY FIKE to GASPER GALLMAN,
all of Edgefield Co. SC for valuable considertion, sold 85 acres
being of 2 tracts; (1) 50 acres &; (2) 35 acres adj. each other &
GALLMAN, DANIEL PARKER, JOHN GRAY & SAMUEL WALKER. S/ MARY (X)
FIKE, FIRE (his X) FIKE. Wit: JAMES BROWN, HOWELL SELLERS, CONRAD
GALLMAN, who swore by oath 25 Jan 1796 before ARTHUR SIMKINS,
J.C.E.
25 Jan 1796: SARAH (X) FIKE, wife of FIRE FIKE, relinq. her dower
before ARTHUR SIMKINS, J.C.E. Rcd. 30 Jan 1796.

Pp. 527-528. 10 Jun 1793: EDWARD VANN, Sr. & MARY, his wife,
Planter & Spinster to WILLIAM COURSEY, all of Edgefield Co. SC
for 500 pounds, sold 1000 acres surveyed for EDWARD VANN 17 Dec
1792 by WM. COURSEY, D.S., Certified 20 Apr 1793 by PETER BREMAR
pro Surv. General & granted 6 May 1793 in Columbia SC being in
Edgefield Co. SC on both sides of Beaverdam Creek of Turkey Creek
of Savannah River adj. JOHN LOGAN, JOHN ALLEN, WM. COURSEY, JNO.
THURMOND, WM. MINTER, OBEDIAH KILLCREASE, FREDERICK HOLMES & WM.
KEYS. S/ EDWARD VAN, Senr., MARY (M) VANN. Wit: HENRY WARE, Jr.,
ALLEN COURSEY, who swore by oath 27 Jun 1793 before AQUILA MILES,
J.P. Rcd. 30 Jan 1796.

Pp. 528-530. 2 Jan 1796: JEREMIAH HATCHER, Sheriff of Edgefield
Co. SC to RICHARD TUTT, Esq. for 4 pounds, sold 258
acres...Whereas: DAVIS MOORE & PETER CHASTAIN lately in Edgefield
County Court obtained a Judgment against WILLIAM COURSEY for 4
pounds... & a Writ of Fiere Facias was issued 10 Oct 1794
attested by RICHARD TUTT, Clerk of said Court & the Sheriff was
directed to sieze, advertize & sell, on 3 Apr 1795, goods
chattels & lands of said WM. COURSEY to the last & highest bidder
being RICHARD TUTT. Said 258 acres being on Mountain Creek of
Turkey Creek of Savannah River. S/ J. HATCHER, S.E.C. Wit: SAMPSON
BUTLER, GEORGE H. PERRIN, who swore by oath 2 Jan 1796 before
JOHN RYAN, J.P. Rcd. 2 Feb 1796.

236

Pp. 530-534. 4 Nov 1793: ADAM BROONER (also BRUNER) , Planter, to
WILLIAM BRYANT, both of Edgefield Co. SC for 25 pounds, sold 100
acres being part of 273 acres originally granted 7 May 1787 unto
said ADAM BRUNER & has such marks on plat Certified 16 Oct 1793
by DAVID BURKS, D.S. S/ ADAM (A) BROONER. Wit: JOHN STUART,
ABRAHAM (A) RILEY, who swore by oath 20 Nov 1795 before JOHN
BLOCKER, J.P. Rcd. 2 Feb 1796.

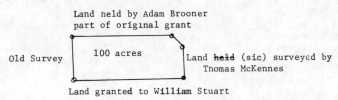

Land held by Adam Brooner
part of original grant

Old Survey   100 acres   Land held (sic) surveyed by
                               Thomas McKennes

Land granted to William Stuart

Plat: p. 532. Certified 16
Oct 1793, DAVID BURK, D.S.

Pp. 534-537. 21 Dec 1795: DANIEL MACKLEY (also McKIE), Planter,
to JAMES BARRINGTON, both of Edgefield Co. SC for 50 pounds, sold
458 acres on head of Turkey Creek & the waggon road from Augusta
to the Ridge & on the Road from Edgefield Courthouse to Columbia
adj. JOHN RYAN, heirs of CHARLES WILLIAMS & JOHN CRAWFORD. S/
DNL. McKIE. Wit: SAWNEY McKIE, JAMES LIVINGSTON, JONATHAN NEAL
(also NAIL), who swore by oath 23 Dec 1795 before WM. DANIEL,
J.P. Rcd. 5 Feb 1796.

Pp. 537-538. 23 Dec 1795: The Judges of County Court of Edgefield
to THOMAS BACON & CHARLES GOODWIN, Esq's., or either one of them
greetings: You are directed to examine according to law & to
receive the acknowledgement & Renounciation of Inheritance Dower
& all other her Estate & interest of ANN otherwise NANCY DAY,
wife of DANIEL DAY in 400 acres called (sic) New Richmond, being
on Savannah River with all sides vacant at time of survey to
LEROY HAMMOND of New Richmond. S/ RICHARD TUTT, J. C.E.C.
The Execution of this Commission returned here with CHAS.
GOODWIN. Rcd. 5 Feb 1796.

Pp. 538-539. 24 Dec 1795: THOMAS BACON, Esq. Judge of Edgefield
County Court. To Whom it May Concern: NANCY DAY, wife of DANIEL
DAY of said County late DRAKE relinq. her rights to inheritance
to LEROY HAMMOND to the form & effect of a certain Deed of Lease
& Release dated 16 & 17 Jan 1792 between DANIEL DAY & said LEROY
HAMMOND. S/ NANCY (+) DAY. Rcd. 5 Feb 1796.

Pp. 539-541. 13 Jan 1796: EPHRAIM BROWN of Augusta GA, House
Carpenter, to JOHN ROLSTON of New York City, Merchant, for
$500.00 due & owing said JOHN ROLSTON & for the better securing
of payment sells 100 acres being purchased by said BROWN at a
Sheriff's Sale as the property of THOMAS LAMAR & is the place
where HALY JOHNSTON has Tended or cultivated for some years last
past. Said 100 ares on lower side of Horse Creek adj. heirs of
McCARTAN CAMPBELL, heirs of JAMES LAMAR & lands now or late
THOMAS LAMAR. S/ EPM. BROWN. Wit: JAMES COOPER, JOHN STUART, who
swore by oath 8 Feb 1796 before RICHARD TUTT, J.P. Rcd. 8 Feb
1796.

Pp. 541-542. 12 Jan 1796: RICHARD TUTT, Jr. to PAUL WILLIAMS, both of Edgefield Co. SC for 100 pounds, sold 100 acres on Hardlabor Creek of Stevens Creek of Savannah River adj. ABNER PERRIN, GEORGE SULLIVANT, WILLIAM PERRIN & SAMUEL PERRIN. S/ RD. TUTT. Wit: MARTHA PERRIN, GEORGE H. PERRIN, who swore by oath 6 Feb 1796 before JOHN BLOCKER, J.P. Rcd. 8 Feb 1796.

Pp. 542-545. 21 Dec 1794: VALENTINE BRAZEL to JOSEPH McKINNEY, both of Edgefield Co. SC for 30 pounds, sold 100 acres originally granted 4 Apr 1791 at Columbia SC being on the south side of the Saluda River below the ancient boundary line on the Edisto River at the Sisters Pond adj. MANOAH HUBERT, BENJAMIN McKINNEY, & JAMES HERRING. S/ VALENTINE (V) BRAZEL. Wit: BENJAMIN McKINNEY, WILLIAM PARDUE, JOHN McKINNEY, who swore by oath 6 Feb 1795 before VAN SWEARINGEN, J.P. Rcd. 8 Feb 1796.

Pp. 545-546. 8 Feb 1796: Bill of Sale: RICHARD BURTON to EUGENE BRENAN, both of Edgefield Co. SC for 55 pounds... One negro slave named ELSY, 4 feather beds & furniture, 3 bedsteads, 1 mare, 1 two yr. old filley, 1 gelding, 15 head of cattel, 20 head of hoggs, 12 chairs, 3 trunks & also all household & kitchen furniture. S/ RICHD. BURTON. Wit: FRANCIS BURT, PHILIP BURT, who swore by oath 8 Feb 1796 before RICHARD TUTT, C.E.C. [Note: gch: Written on side of deed was: "Satisfaction Entered 16 August 1802". S/ EUGENE BRENAN, also the deed had X marked through it.]

P. 546. 5 Nov 1795: Receipt: ANDREW & WILLIAM BURNEY: Received from MACKERNESS GOODE 10 pounds in full for a mill seate of 6 1/4 acres on hon's (?horn?) Creek near the mouth being a part of a tract originally granted to JOHN TOBLER. S/ A. BURNEY, WM. BURNEY. Wit: ZACHEUS PURSSELL, who swore by oath 11 Feb 1796 before AQUILA MILES, J.P. Rcd. 11 Feb 1796.

Pp. 547-548. 6 Feb 1796: JAMES BARRONTINE & MARY his wife, Planter & Spintress to JONATHAN NEAL, Sr., Planter, all of Edgefield Co. SC for 30 pounds, sold 200 acres being part of 687 acres originally granted to ROBERT LANG 7 May 1787 whereof 229 acres of said tract fell in an old grant to one SWIFT the remaining 458 acres transferred by said LANG unto DANIEL MACKEY & by DANIEL MACKEY unto said JAMES BARRENTINE being on Turkey Creek of Big Stevens Creek of Savannah River & near the Court House Road, adj. JOHN RYAN & part of original grant as can be seen by plat surveyed by WM. COURSEY, D.S. S/ JAMES (I) BARRENTINE, MARY BARRENTINE. Wit: WILLIAM COURSEY, WILLIAM (X) BARRENTINE, REUBIN ROBERTS, who swore by oath 8 Feb 1796 before RICHARD TUTT, J.P. Rcd. 15 Feb 1796.

15 Feb 1796: MARY BARRENTINE, wife of JAMES BARRENTINE relinq. her dower before ARTHUR SIMKINS, J.C.E.

Land held by original grant

Swifts land

Court House Road

.John Ryan Esq.

Land held for . . . .

DEED BOOK 12: 1794-1796 EDGEFIELD COUNTY S.C.

Pp. 549-550. 23 Oct 1794: JOHN THOMAS & ELIZABETH, his wife to THOMAS HILL, all of Edgefield Co. SC for 15 pounds, sold 50 acres originally granted 12 Aug 1784 said THOMAS being on South side of Turkey Creek adj. NICHOLAS GLASSER, JOHN STIDHAM, JOHN COURSEY & GRIMKEY. S/ JOHN THOMAS, ELIZABETH (X) THOMAS. Wit: WILLIAM GLEN, JOHN (O) HILL, who swore by oath 16 Feb 1796 before RICHARD TUTT, J.P. Rcd. 16 Feb 1796.

Pp. 551-552. 23 Oct 1794: JOHN THOMAS & ELIZABETH his wife, to THOMAS HILL, all of Edgefield Co. SC for 40 pounds, sold 144 acres originally granted 13 Aug 1765 unto NICHOLAS GLASSER being on the south side of Turkey creek. S/ JOHN THOMAS, ELIZABETH (X) THOMAS. Wit: WILLIAM GLEN, JOHN (O) HILL, who swore by oath 16 Feb 1796 before RICHARD TUTT, J.P. Rcd. 16 Feb 1796.

Pp. 552-556. 14 Jul 1783: NICHOLAS GLASSER & BARBARY his wife, to JOHN THOMAS, all of Ninety Six District SC for 144 pounds, sold 144 acres originally granted as 200 acres 13 Aug 1765 unto NICHOLAS GLASSER but on a resurvey found to be dificit of 56 acres so that the tract contained only 144 acres, being in Granville County on Turkey Creek. S/ NICHOLAS GLASSER, BARBARY (O) GLASER. Wit: JOHN (X) ARLEDGE, ESTHER STEWART, THOMAS McGINNIS, who swore by oath 11 Dec 1783 before JOHN PURVIS, J.P. Rcd. 16 Feb 1796.

Pp. 557-559. 2 Mar 1795: WILLIAM TENNANT, Sheriff of Ninety Six Dist. SC to TOLIVER BOSTICK, Planter of Edgefield Co. SC for 146 pounds...Whereas: JAMES MOORE In his lifetime was seized of a certain tract of land adj. THOMAS EDWARDS, REAVES MARTIN, MATHEW RAMSEY & CHARLES HEARD as can be seen in a plat surveyed by J. ROBERT MAYSON 29 Mar 1794 & Whereas: ANNY BOSTICK, late widow of JAMES MOORE, dec'd., was entitled to her Dower in the Estate of JAMES MOORE, dec'd., & Whereas: the sum of 137 pounds... was assigned as her Dower by Commissioners legally appointed for that purpose 28 Mar 1794. And Whereas a Writ of Fiere Facias was issued by Court of Common Pleas at Cambridge to recover said sum 137 pounds...also 9 pounds... for damages to said ANNY BOSTICK... & said WILLIAM TENNANT, Sher. did seize, advertize & sell tract of land to last & highest bidder TOLIVER BOSTIC. S/ WM. TENNANT, Sheriff of Ninety Six Dist. Wit: REUBIN CHILES, WILLIAM MOORE, who swore by oath 17 Aug 1795 before JOHN TROTTER, J.P. Rcd. 17 Feb 1796.

Pp. 559-563. 14 Dec 1794: WILLIAM HUMPHREYS & NANCY his wife, of Ninety Six Dist. SC to DAVID GAINS of same place for 50 pounds, sold 200 acres being of several tracts of land; (1) 100 acres being part of 300 acres originally granted 2 May 1770 unto ARTHUR FORT & was willed by said FORT to OWEN FORT who conveyed 150 acres of the 300 acres to said WILLIAM HUMPHREYS & said 100 acres is part of the 150 acres...; (2) 30 acres originally granted 19 Aug 1784 unto HENRY BOLTON; (3) 70 acres being part of 312 acres originally granted 4 Dec 1786 unto said HUMPHREYS lying on Mine creek of Little Sauldy adj. ROBT. POU, SAMUEL HUMPHREY, new road, & BOLTON. S/ WILLIAM HUMPHREYS, ANN HUMPHREYS. Wit: SAMUEL HUMPHREYS, WILLIAM (X) NICHOLSON, WILLIAM GAINS, who swore by oath 27 Feb 1795 before WM. DANIEL, J.P. Rcd. 22 Feb 1796.

Pp. 563-564. Nov 1795: LAZARUS GURLEY of Warren Co. GA to JOHN FRAZIER, Jr. gives as surity 300 acres on Beaverdam Creek adj.

239

BARTON HARRISes old place near the head of said creek & THOS. COTTON. Said LAZARUS GURLEY shall pay two notes of hand due; (1) 1 Mar in 1796 for 17 pounds... one half cash & the other half trade &; (2) due 25 Dec 1797 one half cash & the other trade. When notes are paid this deed is null & void. S/ LAZARUS GURLEY. Wit: EZEKIEL McCLENDON, VAN SWEARENGEN, who swore by oath 24 Feb 1796 before RICHARD TUTT, J.P. Rcd. 24 Feb 1796.

Pp. 564-566. 25 Feb 1796: JAMES MONDAY of Edgefield Co. SC to ENOCH BRAZIEL of Abbeville Co. SC for 25 pounds, sold 120 acres on Bennifields Creek of Savannah River adj. Cambelton Road, JAMES HAGWOOD (also HAGOOD) & said MONDAY. S/ JAMES MONDAY. Wit: JAMES HAGOOD, JOHN G. COOKE, GEORGE HAGOOD, who swore by oath 5 Mar 1796 before RICHARD TUTT, J.P. Rcd. 5 Mar 1796.

Pp. 566-567. 7 Mar 1796: RICE CLEVELAND to DIONYSIUS OLIVER, Jr. all of Edgefield Co. SC for 3 pounds, sold 3 acres near Edge-field Courthouse adj. RICHARD TUTT, DIONYSIUS OLIVER & CLEVELAND. S/ RICE (X) CLEVELAND. Wit: SUSANNAH (X) WILLIS, GEORGE HENRY PERRIN, who swore by oath 10 Mar 1796 before RICHARD TUTT, J. P. Rcd. 10 Mar 1796.

Pp. 567-568. 7 Mar 1796: THOMAS MANN to THOMAS WARREN, both of Edgefield Co. SC for $500.00, sold 300 acres being a part of 2 tracts; (1) 150 acres being part of 250 acres originally granted 1 Mar 1775 to JOHN WATS MANN, lying on Round Crees pond of Cloud Creek adj. WM. JOHNSON & JOHN WATS MAN's. All of said tract except the 100 acres "to be taken off joining where the Widow JOHNSON now lives it to extend to the District post", &; (2) 150 acres originally granted 13 Aug 1774 unto JOHN WATS MAN being on Cloud Creek adj. JOHN WATS MAN. Said THOMAS MAN being Eldest Son & heir of JOHN WATS MAN. S/ THOMAS (+) MANN. Wit: WILLIAM NORRIS, STEPHEN NORRIS, who swore by oath in Orangeburg Dist SC Mar 1796 before JOHN P. BOND, J.P. Rcd. 10 Mar 1795.

Pp. 568-571. 13 Nov 1795: EZEKIEL WIMBERLEY & MARY, his wife of Edgefield Co. SC to JOHN SPANN of Wayne Co. NC for 150 pounds, sold 100 acres on the waggon Road leading Cain Settlement including PARTRIDGE's old field adj. DOOLY, CRAWFORD & SIMON BEEK. S/ EZEKIEL WIMBERLY, MARY WIMBERLY. Wit: WILLIAM BUSH, NOAH SMITH, BIDDY BUSH, who swore by oath 11 Mar 1796 before JOHN BLOCKER, J.P. Rcd. 11 Mar 1796.

P. 571. 17 Oct 1795: Bill of Sale: SAMUEL LANDRUM to MARTHA DRAKE, both of Edgefield Co. SC for 24 pounds, sold one negro girl about fore years old named AMY. S/ SAMUEL LANDRUM. Wit: JOHN LANDRUM, REUBIN LANDRUM, who swore by oath 5 Mar 1796 before JOHN BLOCKER, J.P. Rcd. 11 Mar 1796.

Pp. 571-573. 26 Feb 1796: EDWARD COUCH, Late of Edgefield Co. SC to WILLIS ANDERSON of Edgefield Co. SC for 40 pounds, sold 90 acres being part of 113 acres granted 15 Jan 1792 unto said EDWARD COUCH on both sides of the Charlestown waggon road on Horse Creek of South Edisto River adj. BENJAMIN LOVELESS, JACOB ODOM, WILLIS ANDERSON, JACOB REED, Esq. & land formerly belonging to MARTIN GARNER. S/ EDWARD COUCH. Wit: ISAAC KIRKLAND, JAMES BRUTON, ROBERT HATCHER, who swore by oath 11 Mar 1796 before JOHN BLOCKER, J.P. Rcd. 11 Mar 1796.

Pp. 573-574. 5 Mar 1796: WILLIS ANDERSON & PATIENCE his wife, to JAMES BRUTON, all of Edgefield Co. SC for 40 pounds, sold 90 acres being part of 113 acres granted 15 Jan 1792 to EDWARD COUCH being on both sides of the Charlestown waggon road on Horse Creek of South Edisto River adj. BENJAMIN LOVELESS, JACOB ODOM, WILLIS ANDERSON, JACOB REED, Esq. & land formerly belonging to MARTIN GARNER. Said land was conveyed 26 Feb 1796 to said ANDERSON. S/ WILLIS ANDERSON, PATIENCE (X) ANDERSON. Wit: ROBERT WILLIS, MARTHA ODOM, JAMES PERRY, who swore by oath 11 Mar 1796 before JOHN BLOCKER, J.P. Rcd. 11 Mar 1796.

Pp. 574-577. 11 May 1792: WILLIAM BROWN, late from Ireland to THOMAS BROWN of Newberry Co. SC for 20 pounds, sold 200 acres being part of 2 tracts of land originally granted to JOHN ABNEY & conveyed to said WILLIAM BROWN on Persimmon lick Creek of Little Saluda River adj. JOHN WATSON, MOSELEY, said WILLIAM BROWN, JOHN ABNEY, WILLIAM ABNEY & WILLIAM DEEN. S/ WILLIAM BROWN. Wit: WILLIAM SPRAGGINS, JOHN ABNEY, who swore by oath 12 May 1792 before NATHAL. ABNEY, J.P. Rcd. 11 Mar 1796.

Pp. 577-578. 4 Jan 1796: THOMAS BACON & MARTHA, his wife to GARRETT LONGMIRE, all of Edgefield Co. SC for 100 pounds, sold 150 acres originally granted 18 Jan 1765 to ROBERT BRYAN lying on Hawtree Creek now called Cuffee Town creek of Stephens Creek. S/ THOMAS BACON, MARTHA BACON. Wit: RICHARD TUTT, Jr., WILLIAM HALL, who swore by oath 11 Mar 1796 before JAS. HARRISON, J.P. Rcd. 11 Mar 1796.

Pp. 578-579. 16 Nov 1795: Renounnuation of Dower: JAMES HARRISON & JOHN BLOCKER or any two of you are authorized by law to receive ack. of relinq. of dower by MARTHA BACON, wife of THOMAS BACON of 2 tracts of land...; (1) 150 acres &; (2) 40 acres, to be the property of WILLIAM HALL if she concents... S/ RICHARD TUTT, C.E.C.
5 Feb 1796: MARTHA BACON, wife of THOMAS BACON did relinq. her dower to a conveyance made 16 & 17 Mar 1795 by THOMAS BACON, Esq. to WILLIAM HALL of two tracts of land...: (1) 150 acres &; (2) 40 acres in Edgefield Co. SC. S/ MARTHA BACON. Wit: JAS. HARRISON, J.P. & JOHN BLOCKER, J.P., who swore by oath 5 Feb 1796. Rcd. 11 Mar 1796.

Pp. 579-580. 18 Feb 1796: Power of Atty: Abbeville Co. SC THOMAS SPRAGGIN of Pitsylvannia Co. VA to TOLAVER BOSTICK of Abbeville Co. SC - all my share of the late JAMES NORRELL, dec'd., of Edgefield Co. SC as son-in-law to said NORRELL. S/ THOMAS (+) SPRAGGIN. Wit: JOSEPH BECKLEY, JACOB NORRELL, who swore by oath 11 Mar 1796 before CHAS. J. COLCOCK, J.P. Rcd. 11 Mar 1796.

P. 581. 17 Oct 1795: HENRY KEY, Jr. to WILLIS JOHNSON, both of Edgefield Co. SC for 18 pounds, sold 40 acres being part of a tract originally granted 5 Jan 1773 to said KEY on Stephens Creek. S/ HENRY KEY. Wit: JOHN SEARLS, GEORGE (X) TURNER, who swore by oath 11 Mar 1796 before HUGH MIDDLETON, J.P. Rcd. 11 Mar 1796.

Pp. 582-583. 22 Sep 1795: SIMON TOTEVINE of Edgefield Co. SC to PHILIP LAMAR, for 50 pounds, sold 816 acres originally surveyed 9 Mar 1786 for THOMAS LAMAR afterwards elapsed & was granted 1 Jan 1787 to AYERS GORLEY & conveyed to REUBIN PYLE who conveyed to

said TOTEVINE. Said land on Savannah River near Horse Creek. S/
SIMON TOTEVINE. Wit: WILLIAM NICHOLS, BENJAMIN EXUM, who swore by
oath 10 Mar 1796 before JOSEPH HIGHTOWER, J.P. Rcd. 11 Mar 1796.

Pp. 584-585. 11 Jan 1796: JESSE HARVIN to DENNIS McCARTY, both of
Edgefield Co. SC for 20 pounds, sold 50 acres originally granted,
(old grant) JOSEPH WARREN on Mours Creek adj. DENNIS McCARTY. S/
JESSY (X) HARVIN, MARY (+) HARVIN. Wit: THOMAS (X) WARREN,
WILLIAM (X) McCARTY, who swore by oath 29 Jan 1796 before RUSSELL
WILSON, J.P. Rcd. 11 Mar 1796.

Pp. 585-590. 1 Feb 1796: Mortgage: Capt. WILLIAM ANDERSON to
SIMON THEUS & JOHN G. GIUGNARD, Com. of the Treasurer, for penal
sum of 90 pounds with condition of payment of 45 pounds... and
for better securing of payment, sell 398 acres being of two
tracts; (1) 174 acres known as # 17 &; (2) 224 acres known as #
18 being in Edgefield Co. SC (opposite the town of Augusta GA) at
a place known by the name of Chicasaw Indian Lands adj. # 19 & 20
now in possession of SAMUEL WILLISON, & # 15 & 16 in possession
of FIELDS PARDUE. S/ W. ANDERSON. Wit: CHARLES TENNENT, CHAS. J.
COLCOK, who swore by oath 12 Mar 1796 before R. TUTT, J.P. Rcd.
12 Mar 1796.
[Note: gch: The deed was X through & written in margin was:]
Satisfaction, 5 Jul 1798: Sir: Capt. ANDERSON Has paid me his
bond due to the Publick for land purchased by him & for which he
gave a mortgage...S/ CHARLES J. COLCOCK.

Pp. 590-591. 16 Jan 1796: GREEN JACKSON to DAVID GWIN, both of
Edgefield Co. SC for
40 pounds, sold 100
acres on Saluda
River originally
granted 12 Oct 1770
to JOHN COBB who
conveyed to SAMUEL
RAMSEY, who conveyed
to WILLIAM
MERRIWEATHER, who
conveyed to JOHN
JACKSON, Father to
said GREEN JACKSON,

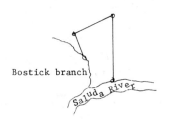

Bostick branch

who left to same by LW&T. Said land adj. JANE DICKIE & Bosticks
branch. S/ GREEN JACKSON. Wit: ELISHA HUNT, MATHEW SULLIVAN, who
swore by oath 10 Mar 1796 before WILLIAM ANDERSON, J.P. Rcd. 12
Mar 1796.
SC: Pursuant to a warrant 2 Jan 1770... for JOHN COBB 100 acres
on Saludy River adj. NW by JANE DICKIE, W. vacant, SE Bostick
branch & E by Saludy River. Surveyed 20 Jun 1770. W: ANDERSON,
D.S.

Pp. 591-593. 20 Feb 1794: THOMAS DOZIER to THOMAS SCOTT, both of
Edgefield Co. SC for 25 pounds, sold 350 acres being part of 2
tracts; (1) 1000 acres granted 1 Sep 1788 to said DOZER on Big
Creek &; (2) 315 acres granted 7 Jan 1793 said DOZER. Said land
adj. PARSON, Greens branch, THOMAS SCOTT & BRATCHER. S/ THOMAS
DOZIER. Wit: JAMES DOZER, WILLIAM SMEDLEY, JOHN (X) PERRYMAN, who
swore by oath 19 Mar 1796 before HENRY KING, J.P. Rcd. 12 Mar
1796.

Pp. 593-597. 12 Oct 1792: THOMAS DOZER, Yeoman, to THOMAS SCOTT, both of Edgefield Co. SC for 75 pounds, sold 150 acres originally granted 13 Sep 1774 unto AMOS RICHARDSON on Red Bank Creek of Little Saludy River & was conveyed 9 & 10 Apr 1787 by said RICHARDSON to said DOZER. S/ THOMAS DOZER. Wit: DAVID LILLY, JAMES SCOTT, WILLIAM BRISON, who swore by oath 22 May 1793 before HENRY KING, J.P. Rcd. 12 Mar 1796.

Pp. 597-598. 26 Feb 1796: Bill of Sale: JAMES ALLISON of Edgefield Co. SC to JAMES FANNING of Spartanburg Co. SC for 429 pounds... sold one negro man named MACK @ 80 pounds, negro man named JACK @ 60 pounds, negro woman named BELLOW @ 30 pounds, negro woman named LYLL & 4 children @ 170 pounds, negro boy named TOM @ 40 pounds, 3 head of horses @ 25 pounds, 2 feather beds & furniture @ 10 pounds, 2 cows & calves @ 4 pounds, 20 head of hogs @ 7 pounds, 2 pots @ 2 pounds, a quanity of Pewter @ 1 pound... S/ JAS. ALLISON. Wit: JOSEPH CULBREATH, WILLIAM (M) DEEN, who swore by oath 12 Mar 1796 before JOHN BLOCKER, J.P. Rcd. 12 Mar 1796.

Pp. 598-600. 1 Feb 1796: Sheriff Title: WILLIAM TENNANT, Sher. of Ninety Six Dist. to WILLIAM ANDERSON, Esq., of same place, for 45 pounds, sold 398 acres. Whereas: a Writ of fiere facias was issued from the Court of Common Pleas at a suit of WILLIAM HART & BENJAMIN WEARING, Treasurers of the State against ELIZA ANN PURVIS, Extrix. of Estate of JOHN PURVIS & directed said sheriff to seize, advertize & sell said land to the 1st & highest bidder; said 398 acres is of 2 tracts; (1) 174 acres known as #17 &; (2) 224 acres known as #18 being in Edgefield Co. SC (opposite the town of Augusta GA) at a place known by the name of Chicasaw Indian Lands adj. #19 & 20 now in possession of SAMUEL WILLISON & #15 & 16 in possession of FIELDS PARDUE. S/ WM. TENNENT, Sheff. Ninety Six Dist. Wit: CHARLES TENNENT, CHARLES JONES COLCOCK, who swore by oath 12 Mar 1796 before ARTHUR SIMKINS, J.P. Rcd. 12 Mar 1796.

The below plat of 2 tracts of 398 acres represent land sold by the Com. of Confiscated Estates to JOHN PURVIS, Esq. & was mortgaged to the Com. of Treas. by said PURVIS to secure purchase money & was again sold in consequence of a Judgement obtained 23 Apr 1795 in Court of Common Pleas by the Treas. against Ex'trix. of JOHN PURVIS...

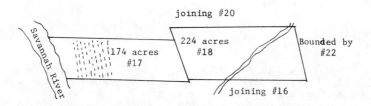

Pp. 600-606. 25 Jan 1796: Mortgage: JOHN MOORE to BENJAMIN GLOVER & ARCHIBALD CAMPBELL, otherwise called BENJAMIN GLOVER & Company, for penal sum of 81 pounds... with condition of payment of 40 pounds... & for better securing of payment, sold 150 acres

originally granted 17 Feb 1767 unto ROBERT CUNNINGHAM who conveyed 23 Jul 1772 to said MOORE being the place where said MOORE formerly lived. Land is on branch of Ninety Six Creek & adj. CULBERD ANDERSON, JOHN CUNNINGHAM, & SAMUEL RAMSEY. S/ JOHN MOORE. Wit: JOHN MOORE, Jr., WILLIAM McMILLAN, who swore by oath 10 Mar 1796 before J. NICHOLS, J.P. Rcd. 12 Mar 1796.

Pp. 606-610. 22 Jul 1772: ROBERT CUNNINGHAM & MARGARET his wife, of Craven Co. SC to JOHN MOORE, Planter of Colleton Co. SC for 100 pounds, sold 150 acres in Colleton Co. SC originally granted 17 Feb 1767 said CUNNINGHAM on branch of Ninety Six Creek adj. COLBERT ANDERSON, JOHN CUNNINGHAM, & SAMUEL RAMSEY. S/ ROBT. CUNNINGHAM, MARGARET (W) CUNNINGHAM. Wit: MOSES YARBOROUGH, DAVID CUNNINGHAM, WILLIAM MOORE, who swore by oath 2 Jul 1773 before CHAMP TERRY. Rcd. 12 Mar 1796.

Pp. 610-612. 19 Feb 1795: JOHN HILL, Sr., to JOHN HILL, Jr., both of Edgefield Co. SC for 10 pounds, sold 196 acres originally granted 4 Mar 1785 to said HILL, Sr. on Mountain Creek of Turkey Creek. S/ JOHN HILL. Wit: W. HAMILTON, JOHN HARRIS, JOHN (+) HUNTER, who swore by oath 12 Mar 1796 before RICHARD TUTT, J.P. Rcd. 12 Mar 1796.

Pp. 612-615. 23 Jul 1794: HENRY HAZEL, to EDWARD CULBREATH for 50 pounds, sold 185 acres originally granted 3 Apr 1786 to BENJAMIN SMITH on Tarripin Creek of Saluda River adj. SAMUEL SAVAGE, JOHN SMITH, TOWLES, & NATHANIEL FOESHEA. Said land was conveyed by SMITH to WILLIAM ANDERSON, who conveyed to HENRY HAZEL for 132 acres (sic). S/ HENRY (X) HAZEL, ELIZABETH (X) HAZEL, (his wife in oath). Wit: JOHN ABNEY, JOHN CLARK, JOSEPH CULBREATH, who swore by oath 29 Aug 1794 before WILLIAM ANDERSON, J.P. Rcd. 12 Mar 1796.

Pp. 615-617. 1 Feb 1796: BENJAMIN DARBY to EUGENE BRINAN (also BRENAN), for 40 pounds, sold 45 acres on a branch of Horns Creek. S/ BENJAMIN DARBY. Wit:
WILLIAM WASH, TRUMAN
WIGHTT, who swore by
oath 14 Mar 1796 before
JOHN BLOCKER, J.P. Rcd.
14 Mar 1796.
12 Mar 1796: OLIF (X)
DARBY, wife of BENJAMIN
DARBY, relinq. dower
before ARTHUR SIMKINS,
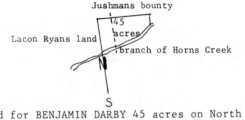
J.P. Plat: p. 616. Surveyed for BENJAMIN DARBY 45 acres on North side of branch of Horns Creek sold by LACON RYAN. Certified 27 Oct 1784. S/ JNO. PERRY.

Pp. 617-621. 3 Sep 1789: OLIVER PRIDE to FEDDERICK WILLIAMS, both of Edgefield Co. SC for 11 pounds, sold 180 acres (in Lease & 108 acres in Release, gch.), being part of a tract of 208 acres originally granted 5 Mar 1787 & was conveyed by JOSEPH WRIGHT to said PRIDE 15 Apr 1789. Land on Cloud Creek of Little Saludah River adj. formerly the property of THOMAS SNOWDEN. S/ OLIVER PRIDE, MARY (X) PRIDE, (wife in oath). Wit: JOHN MITCHELL, FRANCIS BENTON, SION MITCHELL, who swore by oath 9 Jan 1790 before RUSSELL WILSON, J.P. Rcd. 14 Mar 1796.

DEED BOOK 12: 1794-1796 EDGEFIELD COUNTY S.C.

Pp. 621-622. 13 Mar 1796: FRANCIS WALKER to ANN BLALOCK, LEWIS CLARK & JAMES CLARK, heirs of LEWIS CLARK, dec'd., all of Edgefield Co. SC for valuable consideration, part of 170 acres on waters of the South Edisto River adj. POSEY, BUCKNER BLALOCK, formerly the property of LEWIS CLARK, dec'd., DEES, WILLIAM SMITH & the old Beach Island Road. S/ FRANCIS WALKER. Wit: ROBERT THOS. JACK, RICHARD BUSH, who swore by oath 14 Mar 1796 before VAN SWEARENGEN, J.P. Rcd. 14 Mar 1796.

Pp. 622-624. 2 Apr 1795: WILLIAM HUMPHREYS to SAMUEL HUMPHREYS, both of Edgefield SC for 50 pounds, sold 150 acres being part of 2 tracts; (1) 130 acres granted 6 Mar 1786 to HENRY BOLTON &; (2) 300 acres granted 2 May 1770 to ARTHUR FORT who conveyed 150 acres to OWEN FORT, who conveyed to WM. HUMPHREY. Land adj. TRAVERS, PARTIN, WM. HUMPHREY, POU, & GAIN. S/ WILLIAM HUMPHREYS. Wit: RICHD. LEWIS, HENRY KING, WORMLEY BLAND, who swore by oath 10 Aug 1795 before WM. DANIEL, J.P. Rcd. 14 Mar 1796.

Pp. 624-625. 14 Mar 1796: Relinquishment: MICHEL VESSELLS, wife of JAMES VESSELLS, relinquished her dower in 400 acres on Foxes Creek which CHRISTOPHER SHAW purshased at a Sheriff's sale as the property of her husband JAMES VESSELL before WILLIAM ANDERSON Judge of Edgefield Court. S/ MICHEL (X) VASSELLS. Rcd. 14 Mar 1796.

Pp. 625-626. 2 May 1762: JOHN STEWART, Sr., Planter of Turkey Creek to JOHN STEWART, Jr., of same place: obligate myself for 400 pounds with payment of 200 pounds. Condition is such that 200 pounds paid in full by 1 Dec 1763 this be null & void. For better securing of payment sell all my stock, swine with household stuff & furniture, plantation tools, my books with all other goods & chattels, lands... S/ JOHN STEWART. Wit: ROBT. WALLACE, THOMAS WALLACE, THOMAS McGINNIS, who made oath 3 Sep 1762 before ANDREW BROWN, one of his Majesties Justices for Berkley County. Rcd. 4 Mar 1796.

Pp. 626-627. 18 Apr 1793: Deed of Gift: GIDEON PARDUE to my three sisters - PATSY PARDUE, LEUELLAH HOLLY PARDUE & ELIZA PARDUE, for love & affections, one Bay mare & colt & one Bay Mare & their increase which I have lent unto my father FIELDS PARDUE for six years & at expiration of six years or sooner, if agreeable to said F. PARDUE, to be equally among my sisters. S/ GIDN. PARDUE. Wit: JAMES HARGROVE, JOHN PERRY, who swore by oath 27 Apr 1793 before JOSEPH HIGHTOWER, J.P. Rcd. 14 Mar 1796.

Pp. 627-628. 22 Feb 1796: WILLIAM MAYSON of Salluda SC as Attorney of WILLIAM HART, Ship carpenter in Charleston, SC to BARROT TRAVIS, Tavernkeeper of Mine Creek, for 50 pounds, sold 400 acres being part of a tract originally granted 21 Jul 1775 unto the Reverent SAMUEL HART. Rev. SAMUEL HART, father of said WILLIAM, died without a will & the land fell to him being the Eldest son. S/ WM. HART by his Attorney WM. MAYSON. Wit: GILSON YARBOROUGH, PRESLY BLAND, who swore by oath 14 Mar 1796 before JOHN BLOCKER, J.P. Rcd. 14 Mar 1796.

Pp. 628-631. 7 Nov 1795: ROBERT O. WILLIAM & KEZIA, his wife to THOMAS BURNETT, all of Edgefield Co. SC for 32 pounds, sold 50 acres originally granted 5 May 1773 to JOHN DAY on Chavours Creek adj. WILLIAM's old survey, THOMAS BURNETT, WILLIAM WILLIAMS, JOHN

CLACKLER & ROBERT O. WILLIAMS. S/ ROBERT O. WILLIAMS, KEZIA WILLIAMS. Wit: THOMAS WILLIAMS, DAVID BOSWELL, who swore by oath 14 Mar 1796 before JOHN BLOCKER, J.P. Rcd. 14 Mar 1796.

Pp. 631-632. 7 Mar 1796: Bill of Sale: BENJAMIN BRUTON & JAMES BRUTON of Edgefield Co. SC to WILLIS ANDERSON for 65 pounds, sold a negro boy named SAMPSON. S/ BENJA. BRUTON, JAMES BRUTON. Wit: WILLIAM FELLMATE, ROWLAN WILLIAMS, who swore by oath 14 Mar 1796 before VAN SWEARENGEN, J.P. Rcd. 14 Mar 1796.

P . 632-633. 29 Feb 1796: WILLIAM NICHOLS, Jr. of Edgefield Co. SC to JOHN FOX of Augusta GA for 500 pounds, sold 600 acres being part of 3 tracts; (1) 200 acres on Chaverses Creek originally granted 20 Oct 1772 to DANIEL SHOMACK & conveyed by him 14 & 15 Oct 1773 to JOHN HERNDEN which adj. JOHN HERNDEN & JAMES NAPPER; (2) 150 acres on Chaverses Creek originally granted 4 Jul 1769 to JOHN HERNDEN which adj. JAMES HARRIS & one NAPPER, &; (3) 250 acres on Chavours Creek being part of 300 acres originally granted 26 Sep 1772 to SWAN RAMBO. S/ WILLM. NICHOLS. Wit: JAMES EXUM, BENJAMIN MOBLEY, who swore by oath 14 Mar 1796 before JOSEPH HIGHTOWER, J.P. Rcd. 15 Mar 1796.

Pp. 634-635. 14 Feb 1795: GEORGE KER, Mercht., to RICHARD ROBINSON, both of Edgefield Co. SC for 25 pounds, sold 200 acres (formerly belonging to DANIEL MATTHEWS & sold by Sher. of Edgefield Co.) being near Stevens Creek adj. WM. COVINGTON, Widow PURVES, CARMICHAL & others. S/ GEORGE KER. Wit: ROBERT LANG, SAMUEL CRAFTON, who swore by oath 15 Mar 1796 before RICHARD TUTT, J.P. Rcd. 15 Mar 1796.

Pp. 635-639. 15 Feb 1788: ELKANAH SAWYER & MARIAM, his wife of Edgefield Co. SC to FREDERICK WILLIAMS for 60 pounds, sold 150 acres on West Creek of Santee River originally granted 20 Jan 1773 to GEORGE ROBINSON & adj. WILLIAM WEST. S/ ELKANAH SAWYER, MARIAM (X) SAWYER. Wit: JAMES BELVIN, FREDERICK WILLIAMS, Jr., JOHN MITCHELL, who swore by oath 2 Aug 1788 before RUSSELL WILSON, J.P. Rcd. 15 Mar 1796.

Pp. 639-642. 21 Dec 1790: JAMES MARTIN, Esq. of Ninety Six Dist. SC to SAMUEL CRAFTON for 50 pounds, sold 45 acres on Savannah River originally granted 5 Nov 1787 to said JAMES MARTIN & adj. DANIEL GILL, heirs of DANIEL MITCHELL & JAMES GLOVER. S/ JAMES MARTIN. Wit: JOHN BELL, DANIEL MAZYCK, who swore by oath 11 Feb 1791 before HUGH MIDDLETON, J.P. Rcd. 15 Mar 1796.

Pp. 643-646. 3 Mar 1789: GEORGE DELAUGHTER, Planter to SAMUEL CRAFTON, Planter, both of Edgefield Co. SC for 25 pounds, sold 135 acres originally granted 15 Oct 1784 & signed by the Governor 18 Sep 1787 being near the Savannah River & adj. DANIEL GILL, & said DELAUGHTER. S/ GEORGE (+) DELAUGHTER. Wit: ALEXANDER McMILLAN, JAMES McDANIEL, who swore by oath 3 Mar 1794 before HUGH MIDDLETON, J.P. Rcd. 15 Mar 1796.

Pp. 646-649. 19 Jan 1791: WILLIAM RHODES, Planter to SAMUEL CRAFTON, Planter, both of Edgefield Co. SC for 20 pounds, sold 149 acres on west side of Stephens Creek of Savannah River originally granted 5 Feb 1787 to said RHODES & adj. DANIEL GILL & CHARLES RHODES. S/ WILLM. RHODES. Wit: WILL DAWSON, JAMES COURSEY, who swore by oath 20 Apr 1794 before RICHARD TUTT, J.P. Rcd. 15 Mar 1796.

DEED BOOK 12:   1794-1796 EDGEFIELD COUNTY S.C.

Pp. 649-653.   13 Sep 1794: HENRY WARE, JOHN CATLETT GARRETT &
ELIZABETH GARRET, his wife, Planters to MATHEW CAPS, Planter, all
of Edgefield Co. SC for 20 pounds, sold 160 acres on a branch of
Stephens Creek originally granted 2 Oct 1786 to NICHOLAS WARE. S/
HENRY WARE,   JOHN CATLETT GARRETT, ELIZABETH GARRETT. Wit: PETER
(X) PRINCE,   FREDERICK (X) CAPS, who swore by oath 10 Oct 1794
before HUGH MIDDLETON, J.P. Rcd. 15 Mar 1796.

Pp. 654-655.   14 Mar 1796: JOHN RANDOL of Winton Co. SC to JOHN
GRAY,   Sr. of Edgefield Co. SC for 3 pounds, sold 199 acres
originally granted 5 Nov 1792, being on the Road to Charleston at
the beaver pond of Horse Creek adj. ABRAHAM HOLSUMBACK. S/ JOHN
RANDOL. Wit: STEPHEN NORRIS, EUGENE BRENAN, who swore by oath 14
Mar 1796 before JOSEPH HIGHTOWER, J.P.
14 Mar 1796: MARY (X) RANDOL, wife of JOHN, relinq. dower before
ARTHUR SIMKINS, J.E.C. Rcd. 15 Mar 1796.

Pp. 655-656. 10 Mar 1796: Agreement: Georgia: JAMES ARMSTRONG to
JOHN GARRETT for $1834.00, sold 315 acres on North side of
Savannah River being Confiscated by SC & bought by RICHARD
JOHNSON & now property of said ARMSTRONG. S/ J. ARMSTRONG, JOHN
GARRETT. Wit: SAMUEL CRAFTON, STEPHEN GARRETT, who swore by oath
15 Mar 1796 before JOSEPH HIGHTOWER. Rcd. 15 Mar 1796.

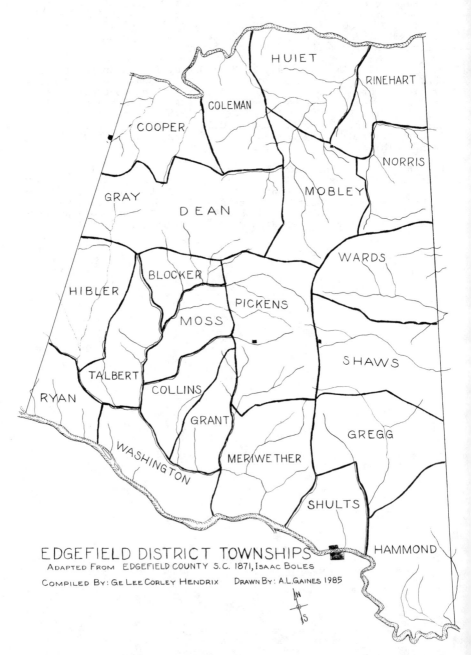

EDGEFIELD DISTRICT TOWNSHIPS
Adapted From EDGEFIELD COUNTY S.C. 1871, Isaac Boles
Compiled By: Ge Lee Corley Hendrix   Drawn By: A.L. Gaines 1985

APPENDIX

The Statutes at Large of South Carolina
by Thomas Cooper, M.D.-L.L.D.
Volume Third 1716-1752

Act No. 532   A. D. 1731

An Act for Remission of Arrears of Quit-Rents, and for Registering of Patents, Grants, or Memorials of Patents and Grants, and Memorials of Title-Deeds, for the better ascertaining and regulating the payment of his Majesty's Quit-Rents for the future, and for the supplying the defect of those Patents and Grants where any lands have been meeted out and ascertained to the patentees or grantees, and of the Titles of persons claiming under the same Patents and Grants, and for the confirming and establishing the Titles and possessions of the several inhabitants of this Province to their respective lands, tenements and hereditaments within the same; and for keeping the office of Publick Register of this Province from being united to other office or offices, appointed or to be appointed by his Majesty, for Registering, Enrolling or Recording of Grants or Deeds; and for suspending the Act for calling in and sinking the paper bills; and for appropriating the monies arisen and to arise, by virtue of an Act entituled an Act for granting to his Majesty a duty and imposition on negroes, liquors and other goods and merchandizes, for the use of the publick of this Province, to the services of this Province; and for repealing of an Act to ascertain the prices of lands, the form of conveyances and the manner of recovering of rents for lands, and the prices of the several commodities the same may be paid in, passed the sixteenth of March, one thousand six hundred ninety-five; and for repealing part of an Act of the General Assembly entituled a declaratory Act concerning several Acts of the General Assembly of this Province that are repealed, and also concerning the adjournments of the Commons House of Assembly, passed the eighteenth of September, one thousand seven hundred and thirteen.

WHEREAS, by an Act of Parliament, passed in Great Britain, in the second year of the reign of his present Majesty King George the second, entituled an Act for establishing an agreement with seven of the Lords Proprietors of Carolina, for the surrender of their title and interest in that Province, by virtue of which said Act, the several parts and shares of seven of the late Proprietors therein named (except as therein is excepted,) are now become vested in his Majesty, his heirs and sucessors, together also with seven eight parts of all and every the arrears of quit-rents, and other rents, sum and sums of money, debts, dues, accounts, reckonings, claims and demands whatsoever, due to the said last mentioned proprietors, to the first day of June, one thousand seven hundred and twenty-nine; and whereas his Majesty, as a mark of his royal bounty and indulgence to his people in South Carolina, under the Government of his Excellency, Robt. Johnson, Esq., did empower his Excellency the said Robt. Johnson, to give his assent to a law for remitting the arrears of quit-rents, provided the Assembly do by the same law repeal one Act formerly consented to by the late Lords Proprietors, entituled an Act to ascertain the prices of land, the forms of conveyances, and the manner of recovering the rents of lands, and the prices of the several commodities the same shall be paid in, and do thereby provide that all possessors of land in his Majesty's Province of South Carolina, do forthwith register their respective grants by which they claim such land, in the office of his Majesty's auditor general or his deputy, and that every person possessing land in the said Province by virtue of any grant from the late Lords Proprietors, for the future pay unto his Majesty, his heirs and successors, the annual quit-rent reserved upon such grants respectively, in proclamation money; We, therefore, your Majesty's most dutiful and loyal subjects, desiring ever more to be mindful of all your Majesty's royal favours, and more especially of this your Majesty's royal bounty and fatherly indulgence, in remitting to us the seven eight parts of all arrears of quit-rents, do hereby declare our ready acceptance of your Majesty's remission of the said arrears, and to the end therefore that your Majesty's quit-rents may be better ascertained, and the future payment thereof better regulated, we humbly pray your most sacred Majesty, that it may be enacted.

I.   And be it enacted by his Excellency Robert Johnson, Esq. Governour, by and with the advice and consent of the Council and Assembly of this your Majesty's Province, and by the authority of the same, That all and every person or persons whatsoever, being and residing within the Province of South Carolina, who do hold or claim any messuages, lands, tenements or hereditaments within the said Province, by virtue of any patents or grants from and immediately under the Lords Proprietors, or any of them, or from or under any of their Governours, deputies, commissioners or trustees, do and shall within eighteen months after the passing of this Act, register all and every such their patents or grants, respectively, or memorials thereof, at the election of the patentee or grantee, in the office of his Majesty's auditor general or his deputy, or such other proper person or register as his Majesty hath, or shall be graciously pleased to appoint for and within this Province, to do and perform the same, by leaving a true copy of such patent or grant or memorial thereof with the said auditor general or his deputy, or other proper officer or register to be appointed by his Majesty for this Province, and residing within the same, the said officer having first examined and compared such memorial with that part of the original as is hereby required to be registered; and all and every such patentees or grantees shall at the same time declare and discover before the said auditor of his deputy, the several and particular quantities of land such patentee or grantee holds in his own right, by virtue of such patent or grant, as far as he hath knowledge thereof, and the county, parish and place where situate, and the particular buttings and boundings of the same, and the rents now reserved thereon; provided always nevertheless, that nothing herein before contained, shall extend or be construed to oblige any person to register any grants or deeds of the lots within the town plots of townships already laid out, in regard to the quit-rents thereon reserved, if any are so inconsiderable that they are not worth the trouble of receiving or collecting the same.

II. And be it further enacted by the authority aforesaid, That all and every person and persons whatsoever being and residing within the said Province of South Carolina, who do now hold, possess or claim any messuages, lands, tenements or hereditaments whatsoever by virtue of any mesne conveyances under such original patentees or grantees shall within eighteen months next after the passing this Act, exhibit and deliver unto his Majesty's auditor general or deputy, or other proper officer or register appointed or to be appointed by his Majesty for that purpose, for and within this Province, a short memorial in writing, to be signed by the party exhibiting the same, containing the purport, substance and effect of the last mesne conveyance, deed or will under whom the party immediately claims, (except town lots, as before excepted,) that is to say, every memorial of any such deed, conveyance or will, shall contain the year and day of the month when such deed bears date, and the names and additions of all the parties of such deed or conveyance, and if by will, the devisor, testator or testatrix of such will, and shall express or mention such messuages, lands, tenements or hereditaments contained in such deed, conveyance or will, and the place where situate, that is to say the county, parish, township, precinct or extraparochial places within the said Province where such messuages, lands and tenements or hereditaments, are situate or do lie, in such manner as the same are expressed in such deed, conveyance or will, or probate of the same, and the said auditor, his deputy or register aforesaid, at the time of entering such memorial, shall endorse a certificate, on every such deed, conveyance or will or probate of the same, and therein mention the day and time on which such memorial was registered, and shall sign the same certificate, and shall note therein the book and number of page of such a book, and shall duly file every such memorial in order of time, as the same shall be brought to the said office, and number, register and enter the said memorials in the same order that they shall respectively come to his hands; and the auditor or his deputy shall not register any lands whatsoever, without some patent, grant or title deed produced, except as is hereafter mentioned, all which entries or registers of all and every such grants and memorials as aforesaid, shall and are hereby declared to be sufficient evidence in the law, and valid to charge the parties, their heirs

and assigns with the rents respectively therein mentioned and reserved, saving and excepting nevertheless, all such grants or patents heretofore granted by the late Lords Proprietors, whereon one penny per acre was heretofore reserved and afterwards reduced by an order of the late Lords Proprietors, dated the thirteenth day of May, one thousand six hundred ninety-one, to the rent or sum of twenty pounds a barony, which amounts to three shillings and four pence per hundred acres.

III. And to the end that none of the said grants or the quit-rents thereon reserved may be concealed or his Majesty defrauded of his quit-rents, Be it further enacted by the authority aforesaid, That all guardians, executors, trustees and attornies, being possessors of such original patents or grants, immediately from or under the said late proprietors, or from and immediately under their governours and deputies, commissioners or trustees, shall likewise register the same grants and last mesne conveyance or memorials thereof, as aforesaid, and also all mortgages of lands and tenements in this Province having any such original grants or last mesne conveyance in their hands, or the mortgagor, shall likewise register the same, or a memorial thereof, in manner aforesaid: Provided, nothing herein contained shall extend to the registring of leasehold estates only, nor to such grants or deeds as have at any time once before been registered by the said auditor, his deputy or register, and certificate thereon endorsed or given as aforesaid. And the said Auditor or his deputy shall be allowed for registring every grant or memorial, and for giving certificate thereof, seven pence half-penny proclamation money, or the value thereof in the currency of this Province, for every copy-sheet, that is to say, for every ninety words, and no more.

IV. And to the end that all persons may know where to resort for registring their said grants and memorials of deeds, It is hereby further enacted and declared, That the Auditor, his deputy or register, or other person appointed or to be appointed by his Majesty to register such grants or deeds, or memorials of such grants or deeds, shall reside in Charlestown, and give due attendance in his office every day, from the hours of nine to twelve in the forenoon and from two to five in the afternoon, Sundays and holidays excepted.

V. And be it further enacted by the authority aforesaid, That the seven-eight parts of all and every the annual quit-rents reserved and hereafter to grow due on all and every such grants and deeds, shall be deemed and accounted to be and paid unto his Majesty, his heirs and successors, for ever, in proclamation money, yearly and every year, on every five and twentieth day of March, to commence from the five and twentieth of March last past, or within three months then next after at farthest; and that for and notwithstanding any other days or times given or expressed in any such patent, grant or deed, for payment thereof, the first payment to begin and be made on the five and twentieth day of March now next ensuing.

VI. And be it further enacted by the authority aforesaid, That where any original grant made by the said late Lords Proprietors, or their deputies, commissioners or trustees, hath been casually lost or destroyed by fire or other accident, and no record or register of the same can be found, nor the quit-rents thereon reserved, sufficiently ascertained by any deed under which the party in possession doth claim the same, that all and every such person shall pay unto his Majesty, his heirs and successors, for ever, the quit-rent of twelve pence per hundred acres, in proclamation money, (being the usual quit-rent for all lands granted for thirty-five years past and upwards,) yearly, and every year, on every twenty-fifth day of March, or within three months then next after at farthest.

VII. And be it further enacted by the authority aforesaid, That all land whatsoever lying and being within the said Province of South Carolina, now in the tenure or occupation of any person or persons whatsoever living and residing within the same, that shall not be registered in the office of the said Auditor General or his deputy, within eighteen months after the said office shall be erected and established in Charlestown, as aforesaid, and publick notice given thereof by the said auditor or his deputy, by posting the same at each parish church throughout the said Province, (and where there is no parish church, at some other noted place of such parish) the same shall be reputed, deemed and taken as vacant lands, and it shall be lawful for any person to take up the same; saving the right, nevertheless, of all minors and orphans, who shall have three years after they come of the age of one and twenty years, to register their said deeds and grants, (paying the arrears of quit-rents that shall be then due); saving the rights of feme coverts and persons beyond the seas, which persons now residing beyond the seas or out of this Province, may register the same within five years from the passing of this Act, unless they shall sooner return into this Province: Provided always, nevertheless, that if any person or persons who are possessed of any lands or tenements in this Province have, by fire or other accident, lost their original grant or deed or will, under which they immediately claim, and do and shall make oath of the same before the auditor or his deputy, who is hereby impowered to administer such oath, that then and in such case, if a record of such grant, deed or will, can be found in the Secretary's or publick Register's office of this Province, the party claiming under any such lost grant, deed or will, shall produce an attested copy of such grant, deed or will, or probat of the same, from the said Secretary or Register, unto his Majesty's Auditor or his deputy, who shall register the same in manner as before directed for original grants, deeds or wills, and shall indorse a special certificate of the same on the attested copy of such grant, deed or will, or probat of the same; and the record of such grant, deed or will, in the Secretary's and publick Register's office, together with the actual possession of the party claiming under the same, shall be deemed good evidence of a title at law, until better evidence of a title appears.

Provided also, nevertheless, that where any person or persons, by fire or other accident, have lost their original grant or title-deed under which they claim, or where such grants or deeds are much torn, obliterated or defaced by casualties, and no record can be found thereof in the Secretary's or Register's office, nor of the will under which he claims, and the party making oath that he claimeth under a grant, deed or will, which hath been bona fide lost, or where the same appears to be casually obliterated, torn or defaced, and shall prove by other evidence that he or those under whom he claimes have been in the actual and peaceable possession of the lands he now claimeth, for the full space and term of seven years and upwards, that it shall and may be lawful for such person to purchase a new grant from his Majesty for the same, paying the same quit-rents, at twelve pence per hundred acres, proclamation money, so that such new grant shall not be construed to extend to bar him that better title had before the taking out such new grant, nor to strengthen his title against any other person that layeth claim to the same lands, but that such other person, then living and residing within this Province, may at any time within seven years next after the issuing thereof, pursue his title at law, notwithstanding any such new grant; and such new grant shall not be given in evidence to bar him that better right had at or immediately before the obtaining such new grant; saving the right also of infants, feme coverts, and persons beyond the seas or out of this Province, as aforesaid.

VIII. And be it further enacted by the authority aforesaid, That all and every the quit-rents whatsoever, which from and after the passing of this Act shall grow due to his Majesty, his heirs or successors, for any messuages, lands, tenements or hereditaments whatsoever, in the said Province of South Carolina, by virtue of any patents, grants or deeds heretofore made by the late Lords Proprietors of Carolina, or any of them, their governors, deputies or trustees, or other commissioners appointed for selling of lands in this Province, or by virtue of any mesne conveyances from and under such patents, grants or indentures, or by virtue of any patents, grants or indentures already made or to be made by his Majesty, his heirs or successors, or by any officer or officers appointed by his Majesty, his heirs or successors, for that purpose, of any messuages, lands, tenements or hereditaments whatsoever, within the said Province of South Carolina, the same shall be paid to his Majesty, his heirs and successors, or to his Majesty's receiver-general of his quit-rents, or his deputy, yearly and every year, on every five and twentieth day of March, or within three months then next after, at farthest, in manner following; that is to say, if the person or persons so in arrear shall live or reside in Granville County, he and they shall be at liberty to pay in his and their quit-rents to a deputy receiver, to be appointed, to reside at Port Royal, in Granville county, for that purpose; and if the person so in arrear shall live or reside in Craven county, he and they shall be at liberty to pay in his and their quit-rent at some certain place to be for that purpose appointed by his Majesty's receiver-general, or his deputy, at Winyaw, in Craven county, and not elsewhere, unless any persons, so living and residing in Granville county, or Craven county, shall find it more for his or their conveniency to pay it at the office of his Majesty's receiver-general, or his deputy, at Charlestown; and all persons living or residing in Berkley county or Colleton county shall pay in their quit-rents to his Majesty's receiver general, or his deputy, at the office of such his Majesty's receiver-general, or his deputy, in Charlestown.

IX. And for the more speedy and effectual recovery and getting in his Majesty's said quit-rents for the future, Be it further enacted by the authority aforesaid, That if any of the quit-rents whatsoever, that shall become due to his Majesty, his heirs or successors, from and after the passing of this Act, out of any messuages, lands, tenements or hereditaments, whatsoever, within this Province, (town lots excepted) shall happen to be behind and unpaid by the space of three months next over or after the said twenty-fifth day of March, that then it shall and may be lawful to and for his Majesty, his heirs and successors, by his and their officers, ministers and bailiffs, appointed or to be appointed, and duly sworn for that purpose, into all or any messuages, lands or tenements respectively whatsoever, to enter and make reasonable distress upon the goods and chattels of the owners, in whatsoever part of the Province the same can be found, nearest to Charlestown, and the goods and chattels so distrained (except nevertheless, as herein after is excepted) shall drive and carry away, and them detain, or impound, in some place within the parish, where such distress is taken; and if the tenant or owner of the goods or chattels so distrained, shall not within five days exclusive, next after the taking of such distress, and notice thereof in writing, with the cause of such taking, left at the owner's house, upon the lands where such distress is made, and in case there is no house, at the parish church where such lands lye, or for want of such parish church in some noted place of such parish, redeem the same, that then and in such case, after such distress and notice as aforesaid, and expiration of the said five days exclusive of the days of taking, the constable of the parish where such distress shall be taken, who is hereby required also to be aiding and assisting therein, shall well and truly appraise the goods and chattels so distrained, according to the best of his understanding, and after such appraisement, the person distraining the same shall and may lawfully sell the goods and chattels so distrained, at out-cry, for the best price that can be got for the same, towards satisfaction of the quit-rent, for which the said goods and chattels shall be so distrained, and of the charges of such distress, appraisement and sale; leaving the overplus, if any, in the hands of the said constable, for the owner's use.

X. And be it further enacted by the authority aforesaid, That there shall be allowed and paid by the person so in arrear, to his Majesty's bailiff, who shall be appointed to make such distress or distresses, the sum of one shilling in the pound, proclamation money, or the value thereof in the present currency, for every pound or twenty shillings proclamation money so in arrear, where the same is not paid before such distress be taken, and three pence per mile, proclamation money, to be computed from the house of the receiver of the district where such distress is made, and three pence proclamation money, or the value thereof in the currency of this Province, per head, for the pasturage of each horse or cattle distrained or sold, for every twenty-four hours, till redeemed, so that such distress be not unreasonable; and to the constable assisting the officer, each day, half a crown proclamation money, or the value thereof in the current bills of this Province.

XI. And be it further enacted by the authority aforesaid, That upon any pound-breach or rescues of any goods and chattels distrained for any quit-rent, it shall and may be lawful for his Majesty, his heirs and successors, by his and their officers and ministers appointed or to be appointed by his Majesty to receive or collect the said quit-rents, to bring a special action on the case, for the wrong thereby sustained, and recover treble damages against the offender or offenders in any such rescues or pound-breach, any or either of them, or against the owners of the goods, in case the same be afterwards come to his use and possession.

XII. And be it further enacted by the authority aforesaid, That in case any person or persons whatsoever, possessed of any messuages, lands or tenements in this Province, after having registered their patents, grants or deeds, or memorials thereof, or memorials of the last will or probate thereof, in the office of his Majesty's auditor or deputy, as aforesaid, shall sell or dispose of such messuages, lands or tenements, or any part thereof, he shall cause a new memorial to be made of the indenture or deed by which the said messuages, lands or tenements are so disposed of, (town lots excepted,) to be exhibited and filed with his Majesty's auditor or his deputy; and if devised away by will, then the devisee, executors or administrators, shall exhibit a memorial of such will, that is to say, the testator and devisee's names, the date of the will, and the clause of such will whereby the same is devised away; and then and from thenceforth, upon payment of all arrears then due, the persons only to whom such messuages, lands or tenements are conveyed over or devised, shall stand chargeable only with the payment of the quit-rents from thenceforth to grow due out of such messuages, lands or tenements; and in case only part thereof be conveyed away or devised, then upon exhibiting a memorial in manner as aforesaid, and paying all arrears of quit-rents then due, the said auditor or his deputy is hereby required to apportion the rent accordingly, and to charge the same on such new purchaser or devisee, paying the usual fees, as aforesaid.

XIII. And be it further enacted by the authority aforesaid, That in case any person or persons who have any right or title to any lands or hereditaments in this Province, for which any quit-rents or other rents are due and payable to his Majesty, his heirs or successors, shall suffer the said lands and hereditaments to lye fresh and the rents due and payable for the same to be at any time hereafter in arrear and remain unpaid for the space of five years, and no distress can be found on such lands and hereditaments, or any other lands, tenements or hereditaments of the owner and proprietor of such lands within this Province, that then, in such case, on inquisition thereof duely taken and office found, the said lands for which the rent is so in arrear shall again become vested in his Majesty, his heirs and successors; and then and from thenceforth it shall and may be lawful for his Majesty, his heirs and successors, by his and their bailiffs, ministers and officers, into such lands to enter, and to grant the same in fee or for any other estate, to any other person or persons whatsoever; saving the rights of infants, who shall have three years after they come of age, and of feme coverts, who shall have three years after the removal of such coverture.

XIV. And be it further enacted by the authority aforesaid, That no rice,corn, or other grain, whilst in the sheaf or ear, either in the field or barn, shall be liable to any distress for quit-rents or other rents whatsoever, till threshed out, nor negroes or any other slaves, nor wagons, carts or carriages, loaden or unloaden, going in the King's highroad or private path, to and from a landing, nor oxen or horses drawing the same, nor the loading so carried or drawn, nor any goods in boats, periagoes, or other vessels on the water, nor oxen, nor horses of the plow, on any plantation where other horses or cattle are shewn and delivered, nor mills, or other plantation tools or utensils, or canoes, boats or periagoes, belonging to the owner or any other person, when other sufficient distress is shewn or produced, nor shall any distress be severed and drove or carried to more than one place, to put the parties to charge.

XV. And be it further enacted by the authority aforesaid, That in case any distresses and sales as aforesaid shall be made by colour of this Act or otherwise of any quit-rents pretended to be due and in arrears, where in truth no such quit-rents are due or in arrears, or if any distress or distresses shall be taken and sold contrary to the true intent and meaning of this Act, that then the owner of such goods so distrained and sold as aforesaid, his executors or administrators, shall and may, by action of trespass, or upon the case, to be brought against the person or persons by whose warrant or command such distress was made, any or either of them, his or their executors or administrators, recover double the value of the goods or chattels so distrained and sold, together with full costs of suit.

XVI. And be it further enacted by the authority aforesaid, That where any distress or distresses shall happen to be made for any quit-rents which hereafter shall become due to his Majesty, his heirs and successors, and the person or persons so distrained upon, shall at any time within five days, exclusive of the day of taking such distress, produce a certificate or certificates from the Receiver General or Collector of his Majesty's quit-rents or his deputy; to the person making such distress, that the quit-rent or quit-rents so in arrears, is or are paid and satisfied, or that he hath taken sufficient suretys for satisfying the same, that then such distress shall immediately cease on satisfying the charges of such distress.

XVII. And be it further enacted by the authority aforesaid, That the receiver general or collector of his Majesty's quit-rents or his deputy, shall immediately give a receipt to the party paying in his quit-rent, and shall cause every receipt to be immediately entered at large, into a book to be kept for that purpose, with his name subscribed thereto, which entry or an attested copy thereof, shall be a sufficient discharge in law as well as the original receipt.

XVIII. And whereas, for the preventing frauds in conveyances, double mortgages and other collisions in making over and conveying lands and other estates, an officer is by a law of this Province appointed for recording deeds, conveyances and mortgages, in like manner as is appointed by certain Acts of Parliament in Great Britain, for the appointing registers in the county of Middlesex and other parts of that kingdom; and it having been found by experience that the said office has had the good effects expected by the same, and has been of great use and service to this Province, as it has been distinct and separate from any other office, Be it therefore enacted by the authority aforesaid, That the recorder or register of deeds or conveyances of land and mortgages, shall be and continue separated and distinct from any other office or officer whatsoever, for registering of deeds; and the said register of this Province, and the register of this Province for the time being, who whilst register of this Province or deputy register, shall take upon him to execute the office of secretary or deputy secretary, or of his Majesty's auditor general or his deputy, or his Majesty's register or his deputy, or of receiver general or his deputy, or as any other officer whatsoever, established or to be established for registering, enrolling or recording of grants or deeds, shall forfeit the sum of five hundred pounds proclamation money, to him or them that will inform and sue for the same by action of debt, bill, plaint or information, in any court of record in this Province, together with the loss of his office of register of this Province, and wherein no essoyn, protection, injunction or wager of law shall be allowed or admitted of.

XIX. And whereas, divers questions and doubts have been heretofore had and moved concerning the titles of the several inhabitants of this Province to their respective estates, viz. that the late Lords Proprietors being joint tenants by the two charters granted to them by his late Majesty King Charles the second, could not alien any part of the said Province, without the joynt consent of the whole of such Proprietors; and all such patents and grants so made, were for that reason said to be invalid and void in law, and that the Governours and their deputys who were empowered and commissioned from time to time from the late Lords Proprietors, to grant and sell lands in this Province, could not execute such an authority without the joynt power and consent of all the said Proprietors, whereby all grants made of any lands under such a defective power were likewise said to be void, and that all or most of such powers were defective, for the reasons aforesaid, at other times that many of the Lords Proprietors were not named, or had not been rightly named in the said patents or grants, and at other times that significant and necessary words were wanting in the patents, grants and indentures, so made by the said proprietors themselves and their Governours, deputys and commissioners, to convey such estates were thereby intended to be conveyed, so that nothing passed thereby to the grantees, nor to the purchasers claiming under such patents, grants, indentures or deeds, to the great disturbance and disquietude of all the inhabitants who were more or less concerned as original purchasers, or claiming estates by mesne conveyances, from and under such original purchasers; wherefore for the supplying all the defects aforesaid, and for the quiet and ease of his Majesty's subjects, it being no wise the intent and meaning of the said Lords Proprietors or any of them, to take advantage of such defects, by a certain Act entituled an Act to ascertain the prices of land, the forms of conveyances, and the manner of recovery of rents for lands, and the prices of the several commodities the same may be paid in, passed the sixteenth day of March, one thousand six hundred and ninety-five, it was enacted by his Excellency William Earl of Craven, Palatine, and the rest of the late true and absolute Lords and Proprietors of the said Province of South Carolina, by and with the advice and consent of the rest of the members of the General Assembly, among other things, that all grants and deeds indented for the sale and conveyance of lands lying within the said Province of South Carolina, which at any time thentofore were made by the said Palatine or his deputy, and any three more of the said Lords Proprietors or their deputys, commissioned or impowered to sell and grant lands, were and are thereby declared to be and forever thenafter should be taken and held to be good, strong, substantial, stable, firm and lawful, according to the true intent and meaning thereof, any misnomer, omission of the said names of the said Lord Proprietors, any want of any significant and necessary words in law for conveying of lands, any omission, commission or mistake whatsoever in the said grants, done, omitted or committed by any or all of the trustees commissioned by the said Lords Proprietors for the selling of lands, notwithstanding. And for the better security and quiet of all persons who should thereafter become purchasers, it was further enacted by the same Act, that all grants and sales of lands, all

publick instruments a writing, all private contracts and agreements, with any person or persons, all acts and orders of Assembly, all rules and instructions of Government, and all other papers relating thereto, which should be made and signed and sealed by the Palatine and three more of the said Lords Proprietors, or by any five of the Lords Proprietors, and all acts and matters one by virtue thereof, should be taken and held to be as good and substantial in law, as if the same had been agreed and consented to and signed and sealed by all the Lords Proprietors themselves; as in and by the said last recited Act, relation being thereunto had, doth more fully and at large appear; Be it therefore further enacted by the authority aforesaid, That all and every person and persons who are now possessed of or do hold any messuages, lands, tenements or hereditaments whatsoever in the said Province of South Crolina, by and under any original patents, grants, deeds, indentures or poll, either made by the said Lords Proprietors or by their Palatine or his deputy, and any three more of the Lords Proprietors or their deputies, or by any of their late Governours of the said Province, and any three or more of the said Lords Proprietors, or the said Lords Proprietors's deputys, or by any other person or persons whatsoever, commissioned by their Palatine and any three or more of the said Lords Proprietors, or by any five of the said Lords Proprietors, their deputys or commissioners, as of fee simple or fee simple conditional, or for life or for terms of years, and all other person and persons whatsoever, who are now possessed of or do hold any such estate or estates, by virtue of any mesne conveyances, derived from and under all or any such original patents, grants, deeds, indented or poll, shall and may from hence forth quietly and peaceably have, hold, use, occupy, possess and enjoy, all and every such messuages, plantations, lands, tenements and hereditaments whatsoever to them, their heirs, executors, administrators and assigns respectively, according to the several tenures in such original patents, grants, deeds indented or deeds poll and mesne conveyances, or last wills derived from and under them respectively mentioned and expressed, and that against his said Majesty, his heirs and successors for ever, and against all and every the said Lords Proprietors and their heirs, and all and every person and persons whatsoever, save and except as hereinafter is saved and excepted, and that for and notwithstanding any misnomer or omission of the names of any of the said Lords Proprietors or their deputys, any want of significant and necessary words in law, for conveying of such lands, any omission, commission or mistake whatsoever, in the said grants done, omitted or committed by all or any of the said Lords Proprietors, their deputys or trustees commissioned by the said Lords Proprietors, for selling of lands in this Province, according to the true intent and meaning of this Act; and also for and notwithstanding any proper seal or seals not being used or affixed by the said Proprietors, their Governours, deputys, commissioners or trustees, to all or any such patents, grants, indentures, deeds or commissions;

254

and also for and notwithstanding the lands granted or conveyed, or intended to be granted and conveyed by such patents, grants, deeds indented or poll, have not been sufficiently described or ascertained in such patents, grants, deeds indented or poll, so that nevertheless any such lands, or some part thereof, have been surveyed or meeted out, or ascertained by survey to such patentees, grantees or purchasers, or to their heirs or assigns, or to the heirs or assigns of the persons named as patentees or grantees or assigns, in such patents or grants, or deeds or assignment, or to their or any of their attorneys or agents in their behalf, by a survey of a sworn surveyor or surveyors, as part of such patent lands, or certified or returned into the office of the surveyor general by a sworn surveyor or surveyors thereto appointed; or so that the same lands, or some part thereof, have been described or ascertained by subsequent grants thereof, to such original patentees, grantees or to persons named as such, their heirs or assigns, or to underpurchasers by mesne conveyances from such original patentees, grantees or assignees, or persons named as such, their heirs or assigns, or to persons claiming under them as such, or to their attornies or agents, in their or any of their behalf, before the passing of this Act; or so that any lands which at any time within two years after a surveyor general shall be appointed by his Majesty, and after his the said surveyor general's arrival in this Province, be meeted out and ascertained to any patentee or patentees, their heirs or assigns, or persons claiming under them as such by virtue of any patents, grants, indentures or deeds heretofore made by the said Proprietors before the said Act of Parliament passed in Great Britain, for vesting the same in his Majesty; and also for and notwithstanding any want of livery and seisin, enrollment, attornment or any other defect whatsoever, in the execution of all or any such patents, grants, deeds, indented or poll, so made by the said Lords Proprietors or any of them, their Governours, deputies or commissioners, or in the not timely execution, or for the non-execution of the same, by reason of the first or former patentee or patentees dying before such lands were meeted out to him or them, in part of such patents, or otherwise howsoever, so that nevertheless the heir or heirs of the persons who were named as patentees or grantees, or purchasers in such patents, grants or deeds of assignment, or the heirs or assigns of such first or former patentee or patentees, or any person or persons whatsoever, claiming as such, under all or any of them, their agents or attorneys, did cause any part of such vacant and unoccupied lands to be meeted out or ascertained to them or any of them, their heirs or assigns, or persons named as such in such deeds of assignment, conveyances or last wills, or to their attornies or agents in their behalf, by survey or surveys of a sworn surveyor or surveyors, or certified or returned into the surveyor general's office, for and in part of such patent lands before conveyed or intended to be conveyed by such original patents, grants, indentures or deeds; or so that such lands be meeted out to such patentee

or patentees, at any time within two years after a surveyor shall be appointed and arrive in this Province as aforesaid; and also for and notwithstanding any other defect, omission or commission in form or substance, law or fact, in all or any such original patents, grants, indentures or deeds, or assignments of the same, or in the execution thereof, or of any of them, so that such lands or some part of them, have been meeted out or ascertained to such patentees, grantees or assigns, or to persons named as such in any such patents, grants or deeds or assignment, or to their attorneys or agents in their behalf, or returned into the surveyor general's office as aforesaid, at any time before the passing of this Act; and all and every such patents, grants, indentures and deeds, and all other patents, grants, indentures and deeds from the said Proprietors, their Governours, deputies, commissioners or trustees, where any lands have been so meeted or ascertained or returned as aforesaid, and the assignments thereof, are hereby ratified and confirmed, for and notwithstanding all or any such defects in the patents, grants or deeds aforesaid, or any of them, or the assignments thereof, or other defects whatsoever, in not timely executing, undue or non-execution thereof as aforesaid, or so that such lands be meeted out to such patentee or patentees, at any time within two years after the arrival of a surveyor to be appointed by his Majesty as aforesaid: Saving to every person and persons whatsoever, bodies politick and corporate, their executors, administrators and assigns, other than to the King's Majesty, his heirs and successors, and other than to the said Lords Proprietors, and their heirs, and other than to such person and persons who do or may stand seized or possessed in trust, for his said Majesty, his heirs and successors, or for the said Lords Proprietors, all such right, title, interest and demand whatsoever, which they or any of them now have and may claim of, in or to the said lands, messuages, tenements and hereditaments whatsoever, so granted as aforesaid, or any part thereof, as fully and effectually to all intents and purposes, as if this Act had not been made, this Act or any thing therein contained to the contrary notwithstanding: Provided also, that nothing in this Act contained shall extend or be construed to alter or abridge the right honourable John Lord Carteret, his heirs, executors, administrators or assigns, or the said Lords Proprietors or their heirs, of any estate, right, title or interest whatsoever, which have or hath been saved and reserved unto the said John Lord Carteret, or to the late Lords Proprietors, or any of them, in and by the said Act, entituled an Act for establishing an agreement with seven of the Lords Proprietors of Carolina, for the surrender of their title and interest in that Province to his Majesty; nor to revive or enlarge any estate or right or interest whatsoever in the said Lords Proprietors, or any of them, their or any of their heirs, of, in and to the Provinces and territories aforesaid, or any part thereof, which they or any of them have granted and conveyed as aforesaid, to any person or persons whatsoever, or which they have surrendered to his Majesty by virtue of the last herein before recited Act.

XX. And whereas, divers new comers and others, being desirous to take up lands in this Province, in order to settle, cultivate and improve the same, but have no patents or grants from the late Lords Proprietors, their Governours, deputys or commissioners, nor any deeds of purchase, derived under any such patents or grants, although many have paid their purchase money to the late Lords Proprietors's receiver general, and in pursuance thereof have meeted out and ascertained the same by legal warrants and surveys, yet could obtain no grants, by reason of the land office being shut up for several years past; we therefore pray your most sacred Majesty that it may be enacted, And be it enacted by the authority aforesaid, That such persons may be enabled to take out grants from his Majesty before others who have made no such purchase, nor obtained and made such legal warrants and surveys; and that the persons who have made such purchases, and obtained legal warrants, and made surveys in pursuance thereof, may hold the same by grants from his Majesty, at the quit-rents respectively and usually reserved on lands, when such purchases were made, preferable to all others: Provided such persons do produce purchase receipts, or copy thereof from the receiver's books, for the purchase money of such land, to his Excellency the Governor, and shall make oath before him that the land he claims, was surveyed and ascertained to him or his ancestor, or some person under whom he claims, by virtue of a warrant and such purchase receipt; and that no other land whatsoever is held by him or any other person whatsoever, by virtue of the said warrant and purchase receipt, to the best of his knowledge: Provided also, that the person possessing such lands, by virtue of such purchase receipt and survey, agreeable thereto, do prove that he, his ancestor, or the person under whom he claims, have constantly paid the usual taxes for such land, either by receipt, or from the tax books of the publick receiver of this Province: And to prevent all disputes that may arise, who are lawful surveyors, it is hereby enacted and declared, that the surveyor general and his deputies, who have been appointed by the late Lords Proprietors, or by virtue of any power or authority derived from them, were, shall be and are hereby declared to be lawful surveyors, and so shall be and continue until such time as others are or shall be appointed by his Majesty, and for and until such time as the surveyor or surveyors, so appointed or to be appointed, by his Majesty, shall take on him or them the execution of their said office.

XXI. And be it further enacted by the authority aforesaid, That no surveyor or surveyors, auditor or his deputy, secretary or his deputy, or other officer whatsoever, shall take any premium, fee, present, gratuity or reward, directly or indirectly, other than the legal fees, by himself or by any other in his behalf, either for the preferring or postponing of any grant whatsoever, or for the renewing thereof, under the penalty of forfeiting ten times the value of the premium, fee, present, gratuity or reward

so taken, to be recovered by action of debt, bill, plaint or information, in any court of record in this Province, wherein no essoign, protection, injunction or wager of law shall be allowed or admitted of; the one half of which shall be to his Majesty for the support of this Government, the other half to him or them that will sue for the same; and for the better preventing and detecting thereof, it is hereby declared that the person giving such premium, fee, present, gratuity or reward, may give the same in evidence upon the trial.

XXII. And be it further enacted by the authority aforesaid, That one Act entituled an Act to ascertain the prices of Lands, the forms of Conveyances, the manner of recovering Rents for Lands, and the prices of the several commodities the same may be paid in, passed the sixteenth day of March, one thousand six hundred ninety-five, from and immediately after the passing of this Act, be and is hereby repealed.

XXIII. And be it further enacted by the authority aforesaid, That the seven-eight parts of all and every arrears of quit-rents reserved and payable to the late Lords Proprietors, or to his Majesty, out of any messuages, lands, tenements or hereditaments whatsoever, within this Province, from any person or persons being within or without the same, and also all other rents and arrears of rent whatsoever, due unto his Majesty until the 25th of March last, be and are hereby declared to be absolutely remitted and for ever discharged.

XXIV. And be it further enacted by the authority aforesaid, That the execution of one Act entituled an Act for calling in and sinking the Paper Bills, passed the fifteenth day of February, in the year of our Lord one thousand seven hundred and twenty-three, be and is hereby suspended for the space of seven years, to commence from the passing of this Act.

XXV. And be it further enacted by the authority aforesaid, That all the monies which hath arisen or due upon the duties of the imports, to the five and twentieth day of March, one thousand seven hundred and thirty-one, shall be appropriated and applied toward payment of the publick debts to the said twenty-fifth day of March, one thousand seven hundred and thirty-one, in such order and manner as in and by an Act of the General Assembly hereafter to be made or passed, shall be directed and appointed; and that the sum of five thousand pounds per annum, in the present currency, which shall hereafter arise upon the duties of the imports of this Province, be appropriated and applied for the space of seven years, to commence from the said five and twentieth day of March, one thousand seven hundred and thirty-one, to the charge of surveying and laying out townships, and to the purchasing of tools, provisions and other necessaries, for any poor Protestants that shall be desirous to settle in the said Province, according to his Majesty's twentieth instruction to his Excellency the Governour; and that the residue of the duties which hereafter shall arise upon the imports of this Province, be appropriated and applied for the space of seven years, to commence from the passing of this Act, towards payment of the residue of the publick debts now due, and in such manner and order as in and by any Act of the General Assembly hereafter to be made or passed shall be directed and appointed as aforesaid; the said Act entituled for calling in and sinking the paper bills, or any other Act, to the contrary thereof in any wise notwithstanding.

XXVI. And whereas, by an Act entituled a Declaratory Act concerning the several Acts of Assembly of this Province that are repealed, and also concerning the adjournments of the said Commons House of Assembly, it is enacted in the first clause of the said Act that no Act of Assembly of this Province that now standeth or hereafter shall stand repealed by any other Act or clause or paragraph of any Act of this Province, shall be revived by the repealing of such repealing Act, but that the same shall stand repealed and so continue to be always repealed, excepting the same shall by express words of some other Act or Acts of the Assembly of this Province, be revived and enacted to be again of force, any law or custom to the contrary thereof in any wise notwithstanding, and the said clause hath been found inconvenient: Be it therefore enacted by the authority aforesaid, that the said first clause of the said Act be and is hereby repealed.

XXVII. And be it further enacted by the authority aforesaid, That if any officer or officers whatsoever, who are required to put this Act or any part thereof in execution, shall happen to be sued for any breach or pretended breach thereof, he and they shall be at liberty to plead the general issue, and to give this Act or any other special matter in evidence for his justification.

XXVIII. And to the end that no person may hereafter suffer any inconveniency by producing their grants or title deeds before the said auditor, or by registering such grants or memorials of such grants and title deeds, by exposing the defects of such grants of title deeds, It is hereby enacted and declared, That no grant, deed of feoffment, deed of bargain and sale, deeds of gift, or other conveyance of any lands or tenements whatsoever, heretofore made, shall be impeached or set aside in any courts or law or equity for want of attornment or of livery and seisin or enrollment thereof, or for that such conveyance hath been made by way of assignment or endorsement on such deeds or grants without other ceremony, nor for any other defect in the form or in the manner of the execution of such deeds or grants, or of the endorsements or assignments thereof, either by the first grantor or in any of the mesne conveyances derived therefrom, so that the right were or would have been in the person conveying, if such defects had not happened in the form of such grants, deeds or conveyances, or in the manner of the execution of the same as aforesaid; provided always nevertheless, that nothing in the last mentioned clause shall extend, or be construed to extend, to suits now actually depending for any lands or tenements in any courts of law or equity, but that the same be and

remain in such plight and condition as they would have been if this Act had never passed.

XXIX. And whereas, no office or offices have hitherto been established whereby any fine might be passed for barring any feme covert of her right and inheritance, or of her dower or thirds, in any lands or tenements, but such feme coverts have only joined with their husbands in such conveyances, and by the practice of late years being privately examined before the chief justice of the Province have acknowledged that they did freely and voluntarily join with their husbands in such conveyances, without any compulsion, dread or fear of their said husbands, which being certified by the chief justice, the same hath been entered of record in the office of pleas, yet no law hath hitherto passed for establishing and confirming such practice, so that such titles may be still deemed defective, Be it therefore enacted by the authority aforesaid, that all deeds and conveyances heretofore made, where the wife hath joined with her husband in the conveying of any lands and tenements which were the estate or inheritance of the wife, or for the barring of her dower and thirds, shall be deemed good and effectual in the law to all intents and purposes to bar such feme covert and her heirs of such estate as therein in expressed, so that the right were in such feme covert at the time of making such conveyance, and for the barring of her dower and thirds, where any such estate might accrue to her after the decease of her husband, unless it shall hereafter appear that such feme covert was under some restraint or force at the time of doing thereof; and that all feme coverts, who have heretofore joined with their husbands in the conveying of their estates, or for the barring of their dower and thirds of any lands and tenements, and have been privately examined before the Governour or chief justice, or any justice of the court of pleas, or before any commissioners thereto authorized by the Governour or chief justice, and have acknowledged that they did freely join with their said husbands in conveying such their estates and releasing their right thereto, and the same hath been certified by the said chief justice or justices, and recorded in the office of pleas in this Province, that all and every such feme coverts and their heirs, shall and are hereby declared to be effectually barred of their right of, in and to such lands and tenements, from the time of acknowledging the same; and the persons claiming under such conveyances, shall and may hold such lands and tenements against all persons whatsoever, for such terms and estates as were mentioned in such conveyance, where the rights were in such feme coverts at the time of executing such conveyances, or her acknowledging or passing away the same in manner as aforesaid, and for the barring of her dower and thirds where any right of dower or thirds might accrue to her after the decease of her husband; and that the usual method and practice now observed for the barring of any feme covert of her estate or inheritance, or of her dower and thirds, by joining freely and voluntarily with her husband in any conveyance for the purposes aforesaid, and acknowledging the same before the chief justice for the time being, or before any persons by him thereunto authorized, and certified by the said chief justice and recorded in the office of pleas, shall be deemed as effectual and valid in the law to all intents and purposes whatsoever, as any fine passed in due form of law in his Majesty's court of pleas at Westminter for conveying of lands in Great Britain.

XXX. And be it further enacted by the authority aforesaid, That the records of all grants in the office of the said auditor general or his deputy, and the records of all grants and deeds duely proved before a justice of the peace, according to the usual method, and recorded or to be recorded in the register's office of this Province, and also the attested copies thereof, shall be deemed to be as good evidence in the law and of the same force and effect as the original would have been if produced, in all courts of law and equity.

XXXI. And be it further enacted by the authority aforesaid, That if upon any survey hereafter to be made of any person's lands it shall appear that there are more acres of land contained within the bounds of his plot, or the marked trees or stakes specified in the said plot, than is expressed in the grant or deed by which any person holds the same, that then the person claiming such overplus as being contained or supposed to be contained within the bounds of his plot or marked trees, shall be preferred to the new grant thereof before any other person whatsoever, at the same quit-rent reserved on his original grant or deed, provided no person hath purchased the same before the passing of this Act and if it appears that any person hath a less number of acres than by his grant or deed is expressed, that then and in such case he shall pay no more quit-rent than what he shall appear to be possessed of on such new survey, any thing herein before contained to the contrary thereof in any wise notwithstanding; and when there is a less quantity of acres of lands in any person's grant or deed than his grant or deed expresses, such person shall be entitled to a new grant of vacant land to make up the deficiency, at the same quit-rent that is reserved on such grant or deed.

WM. DONNING, Speaker.
Charlestown, Council Chamber, **the Twentieth of August, 1731.**
Assented to: ROBT. JOHNSON

APPENDIX B

The Statutes at Large of South Carolina by Thomas Cooper, M.D. - L.L.D.
Volume Third 1716-1752

Act No. 545   A. D. 1733

AN ACT To Ascertain The Fees Of The Surveyor General For the Time Being And His Deputies; And To Prevent Any Irregularities Being Committed In The Office Of The Said Surveyor General, Or By Any Of His Deputies.

WHEREAS, in and by an Act of the General Assembly of this Province, ratified the twenty-first day of September, in the year of our Lord one thousand seven hundred and twenty-one, entituled an Act for ascertaining Publick Officers' Fees, it is among other things enacted, that the Surveyor General shall have for running out any quantity of land, the sum of one penny proclamation money per acre, to be paid in the current bills of this Province, at three hundred per cent advance: And whereas, the several fees appointed and allowed to the Surveyor of this Province, by the said Act, were so appointed to him in full of all claims or demands relating hereto, as well by himself and his deputies, or any other acting by or under his appointment or authority; notwithstanding which, the practice of James St. John, Esq. Surveyor General, and his deputies in that office, has lately been to take the sum of four pence per acre, current money of this Province, for running out every tract of land, and also the deputy surveyors two pence per acre, or three pounds per diem, current money of this Province, and some more, as they could exact from the parties that employed them, for running the same tract of land, whereby the force, elect and true intent and meaning of the said Act, hath been eluded, which is a great grievance and imposition on his Majesty's subjects; for the prevention whereof for the future, and also for the prevention of any other irregularities being committed in the said Surveyor General's office, may it pleass your most sacred Majesty that it may be enacted,

I. And be it enacted by his Excellency Robert Johnson, Esq., Governour, and with the advice and consent of his Majesty's honourable Council, and the Assembly of this Province, and by the authority of the same, that the Surveyor General for the time being, shall not directly or indirectly have, receive, take or demand any sum of money, fee or reward for any business, matter or thing done by him or his deputies, relating to his price, other than such and so much fees as are in the table of fees hereunto annexed, particularly set down, limited and appointed, upon pain that the Surveyor General for the time being, shall forfeit twelve pence current money, for every penny current money that he shall take and receive over and above what is mentioned in the said table of fees, for any business, matter or thing done by him or his deputies, relating to the said office, one moiety of the said forfeiture to his Majesty for the support of the Government, to be paid to the publick treasurer for the time being, and the other moiety to the party grieved, or to him or them that will sue for the same, with full costs of suit; all which forfeitures, that shall be under twenty pounds current money, shall be recovered upon information, on the oath of one or more witness or witnesses, before any one or more of his Majesty's Justice or Justices of the Peace, who are hereby authorized and required to issue out his or their warrant or warrants to bring before him or them such offender or offenders; and in case he or they shall refuse to pay such penalty or forfeiture as aforesaid, to grant his or their warrant or warrants to levy the same, with the charges of such warrant or warrants, by distress and sale of the offender's goods; and in case no distress

258

can be found, to commit the offender or offenders to the common goal of this Province in Charlestown, there to remain until he or they shall pay the same; and all forfeitures that shall be above twenty pounds current money, shall be recovered, with full costs of suit, by action of debt, bill, plaint or information, in any of the courts of record within this Province, wherein no wager of law, essoign, privilege or protection shall be allowed.

II. And be it further enacted by the authority aforesaid, That the Surveyor General for the time being, shall not directly or indirectly receive any sum or sums of money for any other articles or charges that he may contrive or invent, for any business, matter or thing, which he or his deputies, or any other person or persons acting by or under him or them, may do and perform in his said office, save what are mentioned in the table of fees hereunto annexed, upon pain of the forfeiture of twelve pence current money, for every penny current money that he shall so receive for any article or charge not mentioned in the table of fees hereunto annexed, to be recovered by the same persons, and in the same manner as is herein before mentioned, wherein no wager of law, essoign, priviledge or protection, shall be allowed, nor any more than one imparlance.

III. And whereas, for sixty years past, it has been usual to pay the deputy surveyor who surveys the land one moiety for his trouble and pains in surveying, Be it therefore further enacted by the authority aforesaid, That the said Surveyor General shall pay and satisfy his said deputies for their trouble and expences out of the aforesaid fee of four pence, that is to say, the sum of two pence current money per acre, for running out lands in this Province; and the deputies of the said Surveyor General shall and may, and they are hereby authorized and impowered from time to time, to receive to their respective uses, out of the said four pence per acre, the said sum of two pence current money per acre, for any lands they shall run out for any person or persons whatsoever, and no more; and a receipt for the said sum of two pence per acre, given under the hand of any of the said deputies, shall be a good discharge in law for the person or persons to whom the same shall be given, against the said Surveyor General, his heirs, executors and administrators, and shall and may be given in evidence on the general issue, in any action or suit in any court in this Province; any law, custom or usage to the contrary thereof in any wise notwithstanding.

IV. And be it enacted by the authority aforesaid, That **any person having a warrant from** his Excellency **the Governour**, or the Commander-in-chief for the time being, **to run out land**, shall carry the same to the office of the Surveyor General for the time being, who is hereby required immediately to give such person an attested copy thereof, with a general precept thereon endorsed, on such person's paying the said Surveyor General the sum of ten shillings current money, which copy shall be in all respects of equal force with the original; **and upon** any **person's delivering** such attested copy and precept thereon **to any deputy surveyor**, the said deputy shall immediately number and indorse such warrant, with the time when he received the same, and shall be obliged, upon notice, **to survey the same, within any part of this Province**, to the person first applying and giving such notice, and **indorse the quantity so surveyed, returning** the copy so indorsed to the owner, and **a plat unto the owner of the warrant and precept, on his or their paying** to the deputy surveyor his **lawful fees** for the same, on pain of the forfeiture of fifty pounds current money to the party grieved, to be recovered with full costs of suit, in any of the courts of record in this Province, by action of debt, bill, plaint or information, wherein no wager of law, essoign, privilege or protection, shall be allowed, nor any more than one imparlance; and that the plat or plats so received, shall by the party owner of the **said warrant, be returned in to the Surveyor General's office within thirty days** after he shall receive it from the deputy surveyor, on penalty of the land being deemed and actually becoming vacant; and that **the Surveyor General shall certify and deliver the plat or plats within twenty days after their being so received into his office (provided the fees are duly paid or satisfied)** on the penalty of forfeiting the sum of two hundred pounds current money, to be recovered as aforementioned.

V. And be it further enacted by the authority aforesaid, That **the said Surveyor General or his deputies shall set down the course and distance of the lines in all plats,** and also in case of driving any stakes the same shall be mentioned, and the course and distance from any and what tree, **that they may be so recorded**; and that the said Surveyor General shall not return any plat but what shall be mae in such manner, upon pain of the forfeiture for every such offence, the sum of fifty pounds current money, to him or them that will sue for the same, to be recovered with full costs of suit, by action of debt, bill, plaint or information, in any of the courts of record in this Province, wherein no wager of law, essoign, priviledge or protection shall be allowed, or any more than imparlance.

VI. And be it further enacted by the authority aforesaid, That **the said Surveyor General**, within one month after the ratification of this Act, and every Surveyor General hereafter to be appointed for this Province, before he or they take upon him or them the execution of his or their office, **shall record in the Secretary's office of this Province, his commission** for the said office, together with his instructions, on pain of the forfeiture of five hundred pounds current money, one half to his Majesty, and the other half to him or them that will sue for the same, to be recovered, with full costs of suit, in any court of record in this Province, by action of debt, bill, plaint or information, wherein no wager of law, essoign, priviledge or protection shall be allowed, or any more than one imparlance.

VII. And be it further enacted by the

authority aforesaid, That the said Surveyor General, within one month after the ratification of this Act, and the Surveyor General for the time being, before he enter upon the execution of his said office, shall take the following oath, viz: I, A.B., do swear, that I will, according to the best of my skill and knowledge, faithfully execute my office of Surveyor General, according to the directions of an Act entituled An Act to ascertain the Fees of the Surveyor General for the time being, and his deputies, and to prevent any irregularities, being committed in the office of the Surveyor General, or by any of his deputies; and that I will not postpone executing any warrant, or give any undue preference unto any person or persons, for favour or affection, or on any account whatsoever: So help me God. And all the deputy surveyors, appointed or to be appointed by the said Surveyor General, shall take the same oath, mututis mutandis, which oath shall be taken before the Governour or Commander-in-chief for the time being, or before one or more of his Majesty's justices of the peace, to be commissioned by the Governour or Commander-in-chief for the time being, or before one or more of his Majesty's justices of the peace, to be commissioned by the Governour or Commander-in-chief for the time being, for that purpose, upon pain that every person so neglecting or refusing to take such oath, shall forfeit the sum of five hundred pounds current money, one moiety of the said forfeitures to his Majesty for the support of the Government, and the other half to him or them that will sue for the same, to be recovered with full costs of suit, in any court of record in this Province, by action of debt, bill, plaint or information, wherein no wager of law, essoign, priviledge or protection shall be allowed, nor any more than one imparlance.

VIII. And be it further enacted by the authority aforesaid, That the Surveyor General or his deputy shall certify every respective plat on the days the respective surveys were finished, and that the Surveyor General's return shall bear the same date with the certificate of the surveyor that runs out the land.

IX. And be it further enacted by the authority aforesaid, That any of the deputy surveyors within this Province, are hereby impowered to execute any copy of a warrant and precept thereon certified, from his Excellency the Governour, by the Surveyor General for the time being, in any part of this Province.

X. And be it further enacted by the authority aforesaid, That all and every the deputy surveyors, within one month, after the taking of the said oath of office, shall record in the Secretary's office of this Province, the instructions which they have received from the Surveyor General, which instructions shall not at any time be altered by the said Surveyor General, without the approbation and consent of his Excellency the Governour for the time being, and his Majesty's honourable Council, upon pain that every deputy surveyor, for every offence, shall forfeit the sum of one hundred pounds current money, to him or them that will sue for the same, to be recovered with full costs of suit, in any court of record in this Province, by action of debt, bill, plaint or information, wherein no wager of law, priviledge or protection shall be allowed, or any more than one imparlance.

XI. And be it further enacted by the authority aforesaid, That if any of the deputy surveyors shall directly or indirectly receive or take any sum or sums of money for running out any land in this Province, or for any other business in the execution of their office, more than is hereby limited and appointed, shall forfeit the sum of twelve pence current money for every penny current money that he shall so receive and take, to be recovered by such persons and in such manner as the first forfeiture mentioned in this Act.

The Table of the Surveyor General's Fees, mentioned in the above Act.

To running any quanity of land, per acre, four pence current money, for him and his deputy.

For a plat, record of that plat, and certificate and copy of that plat delivered to the party, two pounds ten shillings current money.

To an attested copy of a plat, taken out of the Surveyor General's books, thirty shillings current money.

For running out of lines between party and party at their request, and not otherwise, three pounds per diem.

For a copy of a warrant, and a precept indorsed thereon, ten shillings current money.

To the Deputy for every day he shall ride to the place of survey and back, if above twenty miles, fifty shillings current money.

PAUL JENYS, Speaker
In the Council Chamber, Charlestown, South Carolina **April 13th, 1733.**
Assented To: ROBT. JOHNSON

APPENDIX C

The Public Laws of South Carolina
to 1790
by John Faucheraud Grimke, A.B.-L.L.D.

Act No. 1320   A. D. 1784

AN ACT for establishing the Mode and Conditions of surveying and granting the vacant Lands within this State.[1]

Whereas the granting of the vacant lands of this State will be greatly conducive to its strength and prosperity, by increasing the agriculture and population thereof: Be it enacted, **That** all **the lands** lying and being **to the north-west of the** ancient **boundary line** heretofore established **between the Cherokee nation** of Indians **and this State**, running from Savannah river north 50 degrees east to Reedy river, and then due north until it intersects the North Carolina boundary; **shall be** granted and **sold for** the sum of[2]

10 pounds sterling for every 100 acres, in the manner and form, and under the several regulations and restrictions hereinafter mentioned.

II. Any person or **persons who have** located **lands** within the ancient limits of this State, on or **before the 1st day of January, 1775,** on warrants of survey legally obtained, and were prevented from procuring grants of the same, by the abolition of the British government, or other good and sufficient causes, which **shall appear** upon oath, to be made **before the commissioner of locations of the district where such lands were located, within 6 months after the passing of this act, shall, and they are hereby entitled to grants for the said lands:** And that any persons who have settled vacant lands within the ancient limits of this State, and have been prevented by the aforesaid reasons from surveying and obtaining grants for the same, shall be, and they are hereby entitled, for the term of six months, to the preference of the said settled lands; and that all lands coming within the above description, and **also all other vacant lands within the limits of this State shall be granted and sold for the sum of 10 dollars per 100 acres.**

III. A **commissioner of locations** shall be appointed in each circuit court district, who shall take and receive the original entry of all vacant lands, lying and being within the ancient boundaries of such district (except **for the district of 96, where 2 commissioners** shall be appointed, one **to reside on the north side of Saluda river, and the other to reside on the south side of the same river,** and which said[3] river shall be the division line between the said 2 commissioners) for which **a warrant of survey shall be demanded,** and shall thereupon issue such warrant of survey, **directed** to some **deputy surveyor,** authorising and **requiring him, within a** calendar months from the date of such **warrant, to lay off and locate the lands** directed to be surveyed; which said warrant, **when executed,** together with a **true and correct platt** of the survey, shall be received by the said commissioner, who shall make a fair record of the same, and **within 3 months after such return, shall transmit the original platt to the office of the surveyor-general of the State** for the time being, where the same shall be delivered.

IV. Each and every of the said commissioners of locations shall be appointed in the same manner as the surveyor-general is by law to be appointed, and shall enter into bond for the faithful discharge of his duty together with 2 good and sufficient securities, in the full and just sum of 10,000 pounds sterling, payble to the treasurers of this State for the time being, in trust, and to and for the use of this State; and shall also at the same time before some magistrate take and subscribe the following oath of office:
I, A.B. do solemnly swear, or affirm, that I will well and faithfully execute the office of Commissioner of Locations for the district of (-----) without giving a preference to any through favour, fear, or reward, according to the best of my skill and ability. So help me God.

V. The surveyor-general of this State, on the return of the entry and platt of survey to his office from the office of commissioner of locations, shall make out a platt of the lands surveyed as aforesaid, and record and transmit the same certified to the office of the Secretary of the State, **who shall cause a grant to be prepared for the same, and the great seal affixed** thereto; and shall **within 3 months** thereafter cause a fair record of all such grants to be made and kept in his said office with alphabetical indexes; and **on every 3d Friday in the** months of[4] January, April, July, and October, **the said Secretary of the State,** on the said days respectively, **shall lay before his excellency the Governor** for the time being, all such **grants** by him prepared as aforesaid, who is hereby empowered and **directed to sign the same,** and thereupon deliver them to the Secretary of the State, **to be delivered to the respective grantees,** or to their order: Provided, That in all cases previous to the signing of the said grants, where there shall appear to be any fraud or collusion in the progress of the said entry, warrant and survey, the Governor and commander in chief for the time being, and any[5] 5 members of the privy council, shall have full power and authority to cause all parties to appear before them, and without delay, in a summary manner, decide in such, as to justice and equity shall appertain.

VI. The said surveyor-general shall enter into bond for the faithful discharge of his duty, with 2 good and sufficient securities, in the same sum, payable in the same manner, and shall also take and subscribe the same oath, or affirmation, before the secretary of this State in the presence of his excellency the governor, as is herein-before prescribed to be entered into and taken by the several commissioners of locations to be appointed as aforesaid; which bond and oath, or affirmation, shall be thenceforth recorded in the secretary's office.

VII. **The surveyor-general shall have full power** and authority **to appoint** such and so many **deputy-surveyors in each** of the said **districts,** as he may judge sufficient, not exceeding[6] 6 for each district, for executing all such warrants of survey as shall be to them directed by the respective commissioners of locations, for whose conduct in office the said surveyor-general shall be responsible both to the State and to the party grieved, any thing herein contained to the contrary notwithstanding.

VIII. The said deputy surveyors of the respective districts shall take the same oath, or affirmation of office on their appointment, and in the same manner as is herein-before prescribed to be taken by the commissioners of locations, before they shall be qualified to locate any warrant of survey, under the penalty of being for ever disabled to act in the said office; and shall also within 3 calendar months from the date and delivery of all warrants of survey to them directed, well and faithfully locate and survey the same, and return a fair and correct platt thereof to the office of commissioners of locations from whence the same had issued: And the said deputy-surveyors are hereby required, authorised, and empowered to administer the following oath to the chain-carriers, to wit,

I, A.B. do solemnly swear, or affirm, that I will well and truly execute the employment of chain-carrier, without favour or affection.

IX. Repealed by A.A. 24th March, 1785.

X. and XI. Repealed by A.A. 12th October, 1785.

XII. On all creeks or rivers, navigable for shipping or boats, whereon any vacant lands shall lie, the deputy-surveyors shall, and they are hereby directed, to lay off the same by measuring 4 chain back from such river or creek, for every one, fronting on and bounded by the same; and all surveys not made and regulated by this rule, and any grants which may be obtained thereupon, are hereby declared to be null and void to all intents and purposes.

XIII. All treasury indents of money due and payable by this State to individuals, shall, and they are hereby declared to be a lawful tender at the treasury as so much money in payment of all monies accruing and to become due to this State, for lands hereby directed to be granted and sold, any thing herein contained to the contrary notwithstanding.

XIV. The following fees, and no other[7], shall be demanded or taken by the secretary of the State, surveyor-general, commissioners of locations, and deputy-surveyors, who shall make out a table of the same, and keep posted up in some conspicuous part of their said offices; and each and every of the said respective officers who shall demand or receive any greater or other fees than are allowed by this act, each and every such person shall be liable to an indictment for extortion, and on conviction thereof shall pay a fine of 100 pounds sterling, one half to be paid to the prosecutor, and the other to the treasurers for the time being, for the use of this State.

Secretary of State's fees

For making out the grant, recording the same and fixing the great seal thereto.
  0 10 0

Surveyor-General's fees

For every search	0	1	2
Copy platt		4	8
Recording and sending the same to the Secretary's office	0	7	6

Commissioner of Locations

For receiving applications, making entries, and granting warrants of survey, under hand and seal of office   0 4 8
For receiving returns of, and recording platts and transmitting the same to the surveyor-general's office   0 7 0

Deputy Surveyor's fees

For surveying every acre, a half-penny sterling

Deputy Surveyor's fees (cont.)
Platting and returning the same   0 11 8
For running of old lines for any person, or between parties, 14s. sterling per day.

XV. Repealed by A.A. 12th October, 1785.

XVI. The said surveyor-general hereby to be appointed, shall not, during the time he is in office, on any pretence whatever, hold any other place or office of emolument, under the United States in Congress assembled, or under the legislature of this State.

XVII. And whereas many persons have caused surveys of land lying beyond the Indian boundary to be made, which practice is not only founded in deception, but contrary to the regulations heretofore established for taking up vacant lands --- Be it therefore enacted, That all grants and surveys passed or more for lands lying beyond the Indian boundary herein-before mentioned, before the passing of this act, shall, and are hereby declared to be null and void.

XVIII. The commissioners of locations, in the several districts, shall keep their respective offices at or near the center of the district wherein he is commissioner, and shall give regular attendance every day (Sundays excepted.) And no entry shall be made, or warrant given, to survey any lands until 2 months after the passing of this act, in which time the surveyor-general shall appoint and qualify the several deputy-surveyors respectively herein-before mentioned to be appointed.

Provided, That nothing in this act contained shall extend to entitle any person or persons to lay warrants of survey, or receive grants of land appropriated by the resolution of the legislature as a provision for the officers and soldiers of the continental line of this State, except such persons as are entitled thereto under the said resolution.

JOHN LLOYD, President of the Senate
21th March, 1784.
HUGH RUTLEDGE, Speaker of the House of Representatives

[1]See A.A. 24th March, and 12th October, 1785; 22d March, 1786, and 2 acts of 28th March, 1787.
[2]Altered to 10 dollars by A.A. 24th March, 1785.
[3]See this division more accurately ascertained by A.A. 24th March, 1785.
[4]Altered to the 1st Monday in every month by A.A. 24th March, 1785.
[5]Altered to 3 commissioners appointed for the circuit court districts by A. A. 24th March, 1785.
[6]Limitation taken off by A.A. 24th Mar 1785.
[7]See A.A. 24th March, 1785.

APPENDIX D

The Statutes of South Carolina
by David J. McCord
Volume Seventh

Act No. 1281   A.D. 1785

AN ACT for Establishing County Courts, and for regulating the proceedings therein.

WHEREAS, experience hath proved the utility of courts of inferior jurisdiction, for the more expeditious determination of suits and controversies, and the recovery of debts.

I. Be it therefore enacted, by the Honorable the Senate and House of Representatives, now met and sitting in General Assembly, and it is hereby enacted by the authority of the same, That **in every county of this State, a court shall be held once in every three months,** by the justices appointed in the manner hereinafter mentioned to preside in and hold the same at the several places assigned by law for holding the same, and on the several days hereinafter limited for each county, respectively, and at no other time or place; which courts shall be called county courts, **and shall be held and administered by seven justices of the peace, all of whom,** in the first instance, **shall be elected by a joint nomination of the Senate and House of Representatives,** who shall be qualified in the manner this Act directs; and if any vacancies shall happen by the death, resignation or removal out of the county, of any of the said justices, the remaining justices, or a majority of them, shall have full power to nominate and appoint other fit and proper persons to fill up such vacancies, who shall be qualified in like manner, until the next meeting of the Legislature thereafter, when such nomination and appointment shall be annulled or confirmed, and shall be commissioned by the Governor and Commander-in-chief for the time being, during good behavior; any three or more of whom shall have full power and jurisdiction to hold the said county courts, and to hear and determine all causes and other matters and controversies properly appertaining and referred by law to their jurisdiction; and every person so appointed shall, previously to his entering upon and executing the said office, before the Governor or Commander-in-chief for the time being, or some one judge of the court of Common Pleas, take and subscribe the oath of allegiance and fidelity to this State, and shall also take the following oath, to wit:

The oath of a justice of peace, authorized to sit in a county court:

I, AB, do solemnly swear, (or affirm, as the case may be,) that I will well and truly discharge the trust reposed in me, by administering justice according to law, in the county court of C, wherein I am appointed sit, according to the best of my knowledge, judgment and ability, without malice or partiality; and that I will not take any fee, gift or gratuity, except such as may be appointed by law, for any thing to be done by me in virtue of my said office; and that I will, without being influenced by fear, favor or affection, do equal justice and right to all manner of people, both high and low, rich and poor, without any equivocation or mental reservation. So help me God.

And if any person shall presume to execute the said office, without being first qualified as aforesaid, such person shall forfeit and pay, for every such offence, the sum of two hundred pounds sterling, one moiety thereof to the public treasury, towards the support of government, the other moiety to the informer, to be recovered, with costs by action of debt, in any court of record in this State having jurisdiction thereof.

II. **And be it further enacted by the authority aforesaid, That the said county courts shall be constantly held, every three months throughout the year,** upon the days hereinafter specified for each county respectively, that is to say: for the counties of Abbeville, Winyaw, Granville, York and Richland, on the first Monday in January, April, July and October; **for the counties of Edgefield,** Hilton, Williamsburgh and Clarendon, **on the second Monday in January, April, July and October;** for the counties of Newberry, Lincoln, Marlborough, Berkley and Kingston, on the first Monday in March, June, September and December; for the counties of Laurens, Bartholomew, Shrewsbery and Chesterfield, on the second Monday in March, June, September and December; for the counties of Spartanburgh, Washington, Lexington and Claremont, on the third Monday in March, June, September and December; for the counties of Chester, Lancaster, Winton, Darlington and Charleston, on the third Tuesday in January, April, July and October; for the counties of Clarendon, Union, Liberty, Lewisburgh and Marion, on the fourth Monday in March, June, September and December; for the counties of Orange, Colleton and Fairfield, on the fourth Monday in January, April, July and October: provided nevertheless, that if the business of the said courts, respectively, cannot be determined on the court day, the justices may sit from day to day, not exceeding six days in the whole, and such causes and controversies, then depending before them, as cannot be heard and determined within that time, shall be adjourned over to the next county court.

...

XXII. And be it further enacted by the authority aforesaid, That the clerks of the several county courts within this State, shall be appointed by a majority of the justices of the said county courts, respectively, and shall hold their offices during good behaviour, and moreover, shall enter into bond, with three good and sufficient surities, in the sum of one thousand pounds lawful money, for the well and faithful discharge of their duty, which bond shall be made payable to the treasurers of the State for the time being, and shall be recorded in the county court where such clerk shall be appointed to act, and shall be deposited in the treasury; and in case any clerk of any county court shall be guilty of such malpractice in the execution of his; trust as shall render his continuance in office injurious to the community, the justices of the said county courts, respectively, are hereby authorized to remove such clerk for such malpractice; and such clerk, with his; surities, shall be liable to all damages sustained by any person or persons, in consequence of any malpractices committed by such clerk;

263

provided, that no person shall be eligible to the said office, unless he shall have resided in the State one year immediately preceding his election to the said office.

XXIII. And be it further enacted by the authority aforesaid, That the clerks of the several county courts shall provide and keep, at their own expense, all necessary record books for the proceedings of the county courts, and shall make a fair record of such proceedings, together with all such other papers appointed by law to be by them recorded; and the justices presiding in the several county courts shall annually appoint two fit persons of their number to inspect the clerk's office of their county, and to report to the next court the condition in which they find the papers and records.

...

XXVII. And for the better regulation of the office of sheriff in the several counties of this State, Be it enacted by the authority aforesaid, That the justices presiding in the several counties, shall, on the court of every county which shall be first held, elect a sheriff for the county, and the clerk shall enter and record such election...

...

XLV. And whereas, it is necessary to settle the mode of proving and recording deeds and other conveyances in the several counties of this State, for preventing frauds; Be it further enacted by the authority aforesaid, That no conveyance of lands, tenements or hereditaments, within this State, shall pass, alter or change from one person or persons to another, any estate of inheritance in fee simple, or any estate for life or lives, nor shall any greater or higher estate be made or take effect in any person or persons, or any use thereof, to be made by bargain or sale, lease and release, or other instrument, unless the same be made in writing, signed, sealed, and recorded in the clerk's office of the county where the land mentioned to be passed or granted shall lie, in manner following, that is to say: - if the person or persons who shall make and seal such instrument of writing, shall be resident within the State at the time of making, signing and sealing the same, then the recording thereof shall be within six months from the signing, sealing and delivery, and if the person or persons so making, signing and sealing, shall be resident in any other of the United States at the time aforesaid, then the recording shall be within twelve months, and if without the limits of the United States, then the recording shall be within two years; and if any deeds or any other conveyances shall not be recorded within the respective times before mentioned, such deeds or other conveyances shall be legal and valid only as to the parties themselves and their heirs, but shall be void and incapable of barring the right of persons claiming as creditors, or under subsequent purchases, recorded in the manner hereinbefore prescribed; and no such deed or conveyance whatsoever of real estate, shall be admitted to record

in any county court, unless the same be acknowledged in such court by the grantor or grantors thereof, in person, or otherwise by proof of the signing, sealing and delivery thereof, to be made in open court, by the oath of two credible witnesses at the least.

And that when any such deeds or conveyances shall be acknowledged or proved in court as aforesaid, to their being recorded, the memorandum of livery and seizen thereupon made in deeds of feoffment shall in like manner be acknowledged or proved, and shall be recorded with the deed, and such memorandum proved and acknowledged as aforesaid, shall be taken and deemed a sufficient livery and seizen of the land or other real estate conveyed.

XLVI. And be it further enacted by the authority aforesaid, That all deeds or other conveyances hereafter made in writing, under the hand and seal of husband and wife, and by them personally acknowledged in the county court, (the wife being first examined separately and apart from her husband, by some justice of the court, and giving her free consent to the same,) shall be, and are hereby declared to be, good and effectual in law to pass and convey all the estate, title and interest of such wife and her heirs; and where any feme covert shall relinquish her right of dower in any real estate, and acknowledge the same in court, or before a commissioner or commissioners, and such acknowledgment shall be recorded, the same shall be effectual in law, to convey and pass away the right of such feme covert, although she has not executed or acknowledged any deed of conveyance for that purpose.

And where any feme covert cannot conveniently travel to the county court to acknowledge her deed for passing away her estate, it shall be lawful for the clerk of the county court to issue a commission to two or more commissioners, being justices of the peace in the county where such feme covert resides, for receiving the acknowledgment of any deed of conveyance of such feme covert for passing away her estate real; and such deed, so acknowledged before them, after they shall have examined her privily and apart from her husband, touching her consent without compulsion or threats, and thereof certify the justices before whom such commission shall be returnable, shall be recorded, together with the commission and return, and shall be as effectual as if the same had been personally acknowledged in court by such feme covert.

XLVII. And to the end that persons who are inclined to lend money upon the security of lands or negroes, or to become purchasers thereof, may more easily discover whether the lands or slaves offered to be sold or mortgaged, be free from incumbrances, Be it further enacted by the authority aforesaid, That a memorial of sales and conveyances, mortgages, marriage settlements, deeds of trust, whereby any lands or slaves, the property of any persons residing in this State, charged, incumbered or passed from one person to another, shall be registered in the secretary's office, in books to be kept for that purpose; which memorial shall contain the date of the deed or conveyance, the names, surnames and additions of the parties thereto, the consideration mentioned therein, the lands conveyed, settled or mortgaged, and where the same lies, and the number, names and ages of the slaves, if any be sold, settled or mortgaged; and the clerks of all and every of the county courts within this State are hereby required, twice in every year, in the months of January and June, to transmit memorials of all such deeds, settlements, mortgages, or other conveyances, as shall have been proved and recorded in their respective courts the preceding half year, to the secretary's office, to be there registered as aforesaid...

...

JOHN LLOYD, President of the Senate
In the Senate House 24th March 1785
JOHN FAUCHEREAUD GRIMKE, Speaker of the House of Representatives.

APPENDIX E

The Public Laws of South Carolina
to 1790
by John Faucheraud Grimke, A.B.-L.L.D.

Act No. 1377   A. D. 1785

AN ACT for laying off the several Counties therein mentioned, and appointing Commissioners to erect the public Buildings.

Be it enacted, That from and immediately after the passing of this act, the following counties shall be established, with the several names, descriptions and boundaries, hereinafter set forth and expressed: That is to say, six counties for the district now called 96; - One county situate, lying and being on Savannah river, and adjoining the old Indian boundary, and known in the map of 96 district by the name of Abbeville; - One other county adjoining the above, and also bounded on Savannah river, known by the name of Edgfield; - One other county, beginning at the Island Ford on Saluda river, thence along the Old Road to Odel's Ford on Enoree river, thence down Enoree to Anderson's Ford, thence along the road to Hill's Ford on Tyger river, thence down the same to the mouth, thence down Broad river to a point thereon 8 miles below the district line, thence to the mouth of Bear creek, thence up Saluda to the beginning, and known by the name of Newbury; - One other county beginning at the Island Ford, thence up Saluda river to the Indian boundary, thence along the said boundary to Enoree river, thence to Odel's Ford, and thence along the Old Road to the beginning, and shall be named Laurens county; - One other county bounded by Laurens county on the north, the Indian line on the westward, North-Carolina boundary and Broad river to Tate's ferry, thence along the road to John Ford's plantation on Enoree river including the same, and shall be called by the name of Spartanburgh; - One other county of the other part of the said district, and shall be called Union county...

...

JOHN LLOYD, President of the Senate

12th March, 1785.
JOHN FAUGHEREAUD GRIMKE, Speaker of the House of Representatives.

APPENDIX F

The Statutes at Large of South Carolina
by Thomas Cooper, M.D. - L.L.D.
Volume Fifth 1786-1814

Act No. 1373   A. D. 1787

AN ACT to restrain particular persons therein described, from obtaining Grants of Land; To make null and void certain Grants of Surplus Lands; to prevent Located Lands from being passed into Grants until the purchase money shall be paid; to compel persons who have obtained Grants to pay for the same within six months; and for other purposes therein mentioned.

WHEREAS, the surveyor general and his deputies, the commissioners of locations, and the secretary of the State and his deputy, have great advantages over their fellow citizens, from having it in their power to take up elapsed grants, and such other lands as may be vacant within this State: and such advantages being injurious to the repose and well-being of the republic.

I. Be it therefore enacted, by the honorable the Senate and House of Representatives, now met and sitting in General Assembly, and by the authority of the same, That from and immediately after the passing of this Act, it shall not be lawful for the surveyor general, secretary of the State, commissioners of locations, the clerks in the surveyor general's and secretary's offices, to take up any elapsed grant, or run out, either directly or indirectly, in his or their own name or names, or in the name or names of any other person or persons, for his or their use or uses, any lands now vacant within this State, without being subject and liable to the penalty of five thousand pounds, to be recovered in any court of record in this State; the one-half to the use of this State, and the other half to the use of the informer or person suing for the same; and he or they shall also be discharged from his or their respective offices, and forever rendered incapable of holding any office of trust or emolument in this State.

II. And whereas, surveys have been made, and grants obtained, of surplus lands situate lying and being within known and established lines, to the great injury of many good citizens, as it is not just and right that the said grants should be held and deemed good and valid; Be it therefore enacted by the authority aforesaid, that all grants which have been obtained by any person or persons, for lands situate, lying, and being within the lines, buttings, and boundings of former plats and grants, which are commonly known by the name of surplus lands, (except where the grant of such surplus land hath been made to the proprietor of such granted land,) be, and they are hereby declared to be, made null and void to all intents and purposes whatsoever, and as if the same had never been granted.

265

III. And whereas, the revenue of this State is greatly injured by the non-payment of the purchase money for lands granted; Be it further enacted by the authority aforesaid, that no grants already obtained shall be delivered by the secretary to the owner thereof, until the purchase money be paid into the public treasury; and that all grants hereafter to be obtained shall be deemed forfeited to the State, if the purchase money be not paid within six months after the passing of the said grants.

IV. And be it further enacted by the authority aforesaid, That it shall and may be lawful for all and every person and persons forever hereafter to collect and carry off oysters and oyster shells below highwater mark, from all lands for which warrants of survey have been taken out, and which have not been passed and confirmed by grants under the signature of his Excellency the Governor, since the opening of the land office by the Act passed the twenty-first day of March, one thousand seven hundred and eighty-four.

V. And be it further enacted by the authority aforesaid, That the secretary shall furnish the commissioners of the treasury with a list of forfeited grants, with a particular description of the same, within one month after the same shall become forfeited as aforesaid.

VI. And be it further enacted by the authority aforesaid, That the present proprietors of wharves and low-water lots in Charleston, shall have the exclusive privilege for six months after the passing of this Act, of obtaining grants for the land covered by water in front of their present wharves and low water lots, as far as the western edge of the channel of Cooper river, and the northern edge of the channel of Ashley river.

VII. And be it further enacted by the authority aforesaid, That every grant of land which has been obtained since the twenty-first day of March, one thousand seven hundred and eight-four, or which may hereafter be obtained, for Sullivan's island, Middle Bay island, commonly called the Light-house island, or any other lands whatever which have been or are now appropriated for any particular public purposes, shall be deemed and held null and void.

VIII. And be it further enacted by the authority aforesaid, That an actual, peaceable, and quiet possession of lands five years previous to the fourth day of July, one thousand seven hundred and seventy-six, shall be deemed a good and sufficient title, and any grant obtained since that time, or which may be obtained, for the said land, is hereby declared null and void; and the possessors of the said lands are are hereby declared subject to the payment of all taxes which have been or may be imposed by any law since the fourth day of July, one thousand seven hundred and seventy-six.

In the Senate House, **the twenty-eighth day of March, in the year of our Lord one thousand seven hundred and eighty-seven,** and in the eleventh year of the Independence of the United States of America.

JOHN LLOYD, President of the Senate.
JOHN J. PRINGLE, Speaker of the House of Representatives.

APPENDIX G

The Public Laws of South Carolina
to 1790
by John Faucheraud Grimke, A.B.-L.L.D.

Act No. 1576   A. D. 1789

An Act to enlarge the Time for the recording of Mortgages, and other Conveyances.

WHEREAS, by a clause of an act of this State, entitled, "An act for establishing county courts, and for regulating the proceedings therein," passed on the 17th day of March, 1785, it was enacted "That no conveyance of lands, tenements or hereditaments, within this State, shall pass, alter or change from 1 person or persons to another, any estate of inheritance, in fee simple, or any estate for life or lives, nor shall any greater or higher estate be made or take effect in any person or persons, or any use thereof, to be made by bargain or sale, lease, and release or other instrument, unless the same be made in writing, signed, sealed and recorded in the clerk's office of the county, where the land mentioned to be passed or granted, shall lie in manner following: That is to say, if the person or persons who shall make and seal such instrument of writing, shall be resident within this State at the time of making, signing, and sealing the same, then the recording thereof shall be within 6 months from the signing, sealing, and delivery, and if the person or persons so making, signing and sealing, shall be resident in any other of the United States at the time aforesaid, then the recording shall be within 12 months, and if without the limits of the United States, then the recording shall be within 2 years, and if any deed or any other conveyances shall not be recorded within the respective times before mentioned, such deeds or other conveyances shall be legal and valid only as to the parties themselves and their heirs, but shall be void and incapable of barring the right of persons claiming as creditors, or under subsequent purchases, recorded in the manner hereinbefore prescribed."
And Whereas, by reason that so material an alteration in the law of this State with respect to mortgages and other conveyances of lands being concealed in the body of an act, which from its title expressly related only to the "establishment of county courts, and the regulation of the proceedings therein;" it has so happened that very few or no mortgagees or purchasers have discovered the same, but have permitted the aforesaid time to elapse without recording their said mortgages, or other conveyances, whereby numbers of such mortgages and purchasers, contrary to the just intent and meaning of the said act, may be utterly deprived of all benefit from their said mortgages and other conveyances: Be it therefore enacted, That all such mortgages and other conveyances, as by the said act are required, to be recorded in manner therein mentioned, shall be held and

266

deemed valid and sufficient in law, any thing in the said act contained to the contrary therof, in any wise notwithstanding.

Provided, That the same be recorded in the clerk's office of the county, the Secretary's office, or register of mesne conveyances of any district, where county courts are not established, where such lands lie, within 12 months from the passing of this act.

D. DESAUSSURE, President of the Senate
13th March, 1789.
J. REID, Speaker of the House of Representatives.

APPENDIX H

The Statutes at Large of South Carolina
by Thomas Cooper, M. D. - L. L. D.
Volume Fifth 1786-1814

Act No. 1448   A. D. 1789

AN ACT for the removal of the Public Records out of Charleston, and for other purposes therein mentioned.

WHEREAS, by an Act passed on the twenty-second day of March, one thousand seven hundred and eighty-six, the town of Columbia was fixed on for the future seat of government and deposite of public records; and whereas, it is essential to the general interests of the State that the same be carried into effect, and that the public records should be removed thereto;

I. Be it therefore enacted by the honorable the Senate and House of Representatives, now met and sitting in General Assembly, and by the authority of the same, That on the first day of December, one thousand seven hundred and eighty-nine, all the public records, except such as relate to the property within the districts of Charleston, Georgetown, and Beaufort, shall be removed to Columbia. Provided, the commissioners shall certify to the Governor or Commander-in-chief for the time being, that the public buildings mentioned in the said Act are erected as therein directed. And his Excellency the Governor is hereby authorized and empowered to nominate and appoint three commissioners to separate and set apart the records hereby required to be retained.

II. And be it further enacted by the authority aforesaid, That all such State papers, necessary at the meeting of the Legislature, as shall be directed by the Governor and Council to be removed, and such records as shall be separated or copied at the time of the removal of the seat of Government to Columbia, shall be removed thereto as is directed in the first clause of this Act; and that nothing contained in this Act shall be construed to extend to remove any of the old records from Charleston, which relate to the districts of Charleston, Georgetown, and Beaufort.

III. And be it further enacted by the authority aforesaid, That his Excellency the Governor or the Commander-in-chief for the time being, to authorized and empowered to draw on the Treasury for

paying the expenses to be incurred in consequence of the removal of the said records.

In the Senate House, the seventh day of March, in the year of our Lord one thousand seven hundred and eighty-nine, and in the thirteenth year of the Independence of the United States of America.

D. DESAUSSURE, President of the Senate
JACOB READ, Speaker of the House of Representatives

APPENDIX I

The Statutes at Large of South Carolina
by Thomas Cooper, M. D. - L. L. D.
Volume Fifth 1786-1814

Act No. 1489   A. D. 1791

AN ACT for the abolition of the Rights of Primogeniture, and for giving an equitable distribution of the Real Estates of Intestates; and for other purposes therein mentioned.

WHEREAS, the Convention of this State, by the fifth section of the tenth article of the Constitution, passed the third day of June, in the year of our Lord one thousand seven hundred and ninety, did direct that the Legislature should, as soon as might be convenient, pass laws for the abolition of the rights of primogeniture, and for giving an equitable distribution of the real estates of intestates;

I. Be it therefore enacted, by the honorable the Senate and House of Representatives, now met and sitting in General Assembly, and by the authority of the same, That the right of primogeniture be, and the same is hereby, abolished; and that when any person possessed of, interested in, or entitled unto a real estate in his or her own right in fee simple, shall die without disposing thereof by will, the same shall be distributed in the following manner:

1st. If the intestate shall leave a widow and one or more children, the widow shall take one-third of the said estate, and the remainder shall be divided between the children, if more than one, but if only one, the remainder of the estate shall be vested in that one absolutely forever.

2d. The lineal descendants of the intestate shall represent their respective parents, and be entitled to receive and divide equally among them the shares to which their parents would respectively have been entitled, had they survived the ancestor.

3d. If the intestate shall not leave a child, or other lineal descendant, but shall leave a widow and a father or mother, the widow shall be entitled to one moiety of the estate, and the father, or if he be dead, the mother, shall be entitled to the other moiety.

4th. If the intestate shall not leave a lineal descendant, father or mother, but shall leave a widow and brothers and sisters, or brother or sister, of the whole blood, the widow shall be entitled to one moiety of the estate, and the brothers and sisters, or brother or sister, to the other moiety, as tenants in common. The children of a deceased brother or sister shall have among them respectively the share which their respective ancestors would have been entitled to had they survived the intestate.

5th. If the intestate shall leave no lineal descendant, father, mother, brother or sister of the whole blood, but shall leave a widow, and a brother or sister of the half blood, and a child or children of a brother or sister of the whole blood, the widow shall take one moiety of the estate, and the other moiety shall be equally divided between the brothers and sisters of the half blood, and the children of the brothers and sisters of the whole blood. The children of every deceased brother or sister of the whole blood taking among them a share equal to the share of a brother or sister of the half blood. But if there be no brother or sister of the half blood then a moiety of the estate shall descend to the child or children of the deceased brother or sister; and if there be no child of a deceased brother or sister of the whole blood, then the said moiety shall descend to the brothers and sisters of the half blood.

6th. If the intestate shall leave no lineal descendant, father, mother, brother or sister of the whole blood, or their children, or brother or sister of the half blood, then the widow shall take one moiety, and the lineal ancestor or ancestors, if any there be, the other moiety.

7th. If the intestate shall leave no lineal descendants, father, mother, brother or sister of the whole blood, or their children, or brother or sister of the half blood, or lineal ancestor, then the widow shall take two-thirds of the estate, and the remainder shall descend to the next of kin.

8th. If the intestate shall leave no widow, the provision made for her shall go as the rest of his estate is directed to be distributed in the respective clauses in which the widow is provided for.

9th. In reckoning the degrees of kindred, the computation shall begin with the intestate, and be continued up to the common ancestor, and thence down to the person claiming kindred, inclusively, each step inclusively being reckoned as one degree.

10th. On the death of any married woman, the husband shall be entitled to the same share of her real estate as is herin given to the widow out of the estate of the husband, and the remainder of her real estate shall be distributed among her descendants and relations in the same manner as is heretofore directed in case of the intestacy of a married man.

11th. If the intestate shall leave no husband, the provision herein made for him shall go as the rest of her estate is directed to be distributed in the preceding clauses.

II. And be it further enacted That in all cases of intestacy the personal estate of the intestate shall be distributed in the same manner as real estates are disposed of by this Act.

III. And be it further enacted by the authority aforesaid, That nothing herein contained shall be construed to give to any child or issue (or his or her legal representatives) of the intestate, a share of his or her ancestors estate where such child or issue shall have been advanced by the intestate in his lifetime, by portions or portion equal to the share which shall be allotted to the other children. But in case any child, or the issue of any child, who shall have been so advanced, shall not have received a portion equal to the other children shall be due to the other children, (the value of which portion being estimated at the death of the ancestor, but so as that neither the improvements of the real estate by such child or children, nor the increase of the personal property, shall be taken into the computation,) then so much of the estate of the intestate shall be distributed to such child or issue as shall make the estate of all the children to be equal.

IV. And be it further enacted by the authority aforesaid, That no lands or personal estate which shall be acquired by any person after the making of his or her will shall pass thereby, (unless the said will be republished,) but every such person shall be considered as having died intestate, as to the said lands and personal estate, and the same shall be distributable according to the directions of this Act.

V. And be it further enacted by the authority aforesaid, That where any person shall be at the time of his or her death seized or possessed of any estate in joint tenancy, the same shall be adjudged to be severed by the death of the joint tenant, and shall be distributable as if the same was a tenancy in common.

VI. And be it further enacted by the authority aforesaid, That in all cases where provision is made by this Act for the widow of a person dying intestate, the same shall, if accepted, be considered as in lieu of, and in bar of, dower.

VII. And be it further enacted by the authority aforesaid, That from and after the first day of May next, it shall and may be lawful to and for any person who may be entitled to a distributive share of any estate, real or personal, and shall have arrived to the age of twenty-one years, or be married, to apply by petition to the court of equity or common pleas (at the option of the party,) for a writ of partition to be Petition for distribution of property directed to certain commissioners, authorizing & requiring them to divide the same estate; and the court shall therefore issue a writ of partition in the same manner as is directed for the admeasurement of dower, by an Act entitled "An act for the more easy and expeditious obtaining the admeasurement of dower to widows, of the lands of which their deceased husbands were seized in fee at any time during their marriage;" and the commissioners so to be appointed, being first duly sworn fairly and impartially to discharge their duty, shall proceed to execute the said writ, and return the same to the court; and when the said estate cannot, in the opinion of the commissioners, be fairly and equally divided between the parties interested therein, without manifest injury to them, or some or one of them, then they shall make a special return of the whole property and the value thereof, truly appraised, and certify their opinion to the court whether it will be most for the benefit of all parties to deliver over to one or more of the parties interested therein the property which cannot be fairly divided, upon the payment of a sum of money to be assessed by the said commissioners, or to sell the same at public auction; and the court shall proceed to consider and determine the same, and if it shall appear to the court that it will be for the benefit of all parties interested in the said estate that the same should be vested in one person or more persons entitled to a portion of the same, on the payment of a sum of money, they shall determine accordingly; and the said person or persons, on the payment of the consideration money, shall be vested with the estate so adjudged to them, as fully and absolutely as the ancestor was vested. But if it shall appear to the court that it would be more for the interest of the parties that the same should be sold, then they shall direct a sale to be made, on such a credit and on such terms as to them shall seem right; and the property so sold shall stand pledged for the payment of the purchase money.

VIII. And be it further enacted by the authority aforesaid, That the judges of the respective courts shall be, and they are hereby, authorized from time to time to make such rules and orders as may be necessary for the purpose of carrying the foregoing clause into effect.

IX. And be it further enacted by the authority aforesaid, That this Act shall commence its operation on the first day of May next, but not sooner.

In the Senate House, **the nineteenth day of February, in the year of our Lord one thousand seven hundred and ninety-one,** and in the fifteenth year of the Independence of the United States of America.

DAVID RAMSAY, President of the Senate.

JACOB READ, Speaker of the House of Representatives.

APPENDIX J

Listing of Names and Years of
Justices and other Judges, Sheriffs, and Surveyors
who are cited in
Abstracts of Edgefield County Deed Books 1 through 12

Justices and other Judges

ABNEY, Nathaniel 1792-96
ALEXANDER, J. 1790, Camden Dist.
ANDERSON, Robert 1789, Pendleton Co.
ANDERSON, William 1773, 1775-76, 1779-80, 1786 - 91, 1793-96
BACON, Thomas 1791, 1792
BELL, John 1791 Camden
BENTHAN, J. 1792, Charlestown
BLOCKER, John 1795, 1796
BOND, John P. 1796 Orangeburg Dist.
BOWIE, John 1793 Abbeville
BROWN, Andrew 1762 Berkley
BROWNLEE, John 1790
CALDWELL, John 1771 Craven
CALVERT, John 1791, Richland Co.
CLARK, John 1792-95
COLCOCK, Chas. J. 1796 Abbeville
CUNNINGHAM, Patrick 1772, Colleton Co.
CUNNINGHAM, Robert 1771, Berkley Co.
DANIEL, Wm. 1795
DART, John Sandford 1791, 1794, Charleston
DAVIS, John 1795, Laurens
DICK, John 1772, Granville

DRESWELL, Matthew 1794, Charleston Co.
FAIRCHILD, John 1776, Orangeburg
FAIRCHILD, John Thomas 1788, Lexington; 1790, 1791; 1791-93 Orangeburg
FITZPATRICK, William 1795, Orangeburg
FRANCIS, James 1759, Berkley
FRENEAU, Peter 1786, 1789, 1792, Charleston
GILLAM, Robert 1793-95, Newberry Co.
GOODWIN, Charles 1795
GRAYBILL, Henry 1791, Green Co., GA
GREEN, Daniel 1787, 1790, Winton Co.
HAMILTON, John 1790-91, Prov. of New Brunswick, Kings Co.
HAMMOND, John 1789
HAMMOND, Leroy 1771-74, 1777, 1785, 1787-90
HAMPTON, John 1793, Lexington
HARRISON, James 1793-96
HEATLY, William. 1792, Orangeburg
HERNDON, John 1784-85
HERONS, John 1794, Richland Co.
HIGHTOWER, Joseph 1791-96
HOUSEL, Wm. 1785
HUNTER, Dalziel 1791-92,

HUNTER, Dalziel (cont.) Richmond Co. GA
HUNTER, Edward 1791, Green Co. GA
HORRY, Peter 1787 Charlestown
JONES, William 1782
JULIEN, Pet 1792, Newberry Co., SC
KEY, Henry 1795
KING, Henry 1792-95
KIRKLAND, Moses 1771, 1774
LESTARYETTE, Lewis 1794 Orangeburg
LIGHTWOOD, J 1785 Charlestown
LINDSEY, John 1790, Newberry Co.
LINNING, Charles 1795, Charleston
MASON, James 1771-2, 1795
MAYSON, James 1794, Newberry Co.
MAZYCK, D. L. 1789-90
MIDDLETON, Hugh 1774?, 1788-96
MILES, Aq. 1782, 1788-96
MOORE, James 1776
MOORE, John 1788-95
MOORE, William 1784, 1786, 1788-90, Abbeville, Edgefield & Ninety Six
MORRISON, John 1788, Burke Co. GA
MURRAY, John 1783
NICHOLS, Julius (& Jr.) 1791-96, Abbeville

NOTE

The writer has not made any effort to interpert the spelling of personal and proper names in the text. Therefore, the reader is advised to search all variant spellings of any surname.

A plus sign has been placed by the page number in the index when the same name appears in more than one deed on a page, i. e. **CORLEY, William 177+**

A number of sub-indices are in the main entry index. They are:

Miscellaneous trivia

Occupations

Places

Plats

Slaves

and

Waterways

Other listings found in **APPENDIX J** are:

Justices & other Judges

Sheriffs

and

Surveyors

INDEX

By: WILMA COPELAND KIRKLAND

BROOKS 201
  Aaron 63
  Anne 201, 202
  Christopher 230
  Christopher, Jr. 69
  Christopher, Sr.
  69, 89, 101, 190
  Elisha 1+, 23, 222+
  Esau 172, 173
  Frances 1, 182, 222
  Honour 101
  Jacob 173
  James 63, 170, 173, 188,
  195, 196
  John 37, 116, 173, 192,
  196
  Jordan 212+
  Jourdan 85
  Jurdash 211
  Jurdian 211
  Nancy 23
  Richard 1
  Robert 183, 185, 201,
  202, 203, 221
  Simon 170, 195, 196
  Susannah 44+
  Unity 196
  William 8, 44+, 48, 59,
  141, 156, 183
BROONER, Adam 237
  Daniel 181
  Michael 181
BROUGHTON, John 34
  Mary 192
  Thomas 192, 198, 203
BROWN & Co. 186
  Andrew 136, 245
  Bartlett 153
  Ephraim 204, 237
  Frances 90
  Jacob 190
  James 19, 107+, 110+,
  214, 230, 236
  Joel 234
  Joseph 3
  Moses 122, 190
  Pudy Pitts 60
  Ruthy 136
  Thomas 104+, 132, 241
  Widow 187
  William 7, 19, 22, 37,
  42, 112+, 117, 153, 241
BROWNLE, Jane 89+, 92, 198
BROWNLEE, John 92, 118
BRUDER, Leonard 229
BRUNER, Adam 237
  Daniel 75
  William 210
BRUNSON, Daniel 201
  Isaac 183
  Isaac, Jr. 45
  Isaac, Sr. 49, 183
  Joseph 49
  Joshus 188
  Mary 188
BRUTON, Benjamin 246
  James 240, 241, 246
BRYAN, Robert 158, 241
  Thomas 121
  William 223
BRYANT 235
  Lewis 71
  Robert 29, 30
  Sarah 29
  William 237
BRYDE, John 125
BUCK, Edward 23, 26
  Sara 26
BUCKELEW, Efphama 111
  Garret 60
  George 26, 139, 213
  James 25, 26
  John 230
  Mary 81, 111, 213

BUCKELEW, Moses 139
  Rachel 26
  Richard 26, 194, 195+
BUCKHALTER (BURKHALTER,
  BURCKHALTER) 135
  Agness 105
  Christian 5, 11, 20, 36,
  105, 147
  David 40, 91
  Henry 105, 186, 188
  John 26+, 40, 47, 91,
  158, 186
  John, Sr. 190
  Marget 188
  Michael 7, 11, 27, 35,
  40, 91, 105, 131, 158,
  186, 190, 202
  William 26, 27
BUCKHAM, Thomas 12+, 206
BUCKLEW, Frederick 60
BUCKLUE, Garret 111
  George 81, 111
  James 111
  Richard 81, 111
BUFFINGTON 95
  Ezekiel 25, 52
  Mary 46
  Oburn 25, 50, 52, 138,
  139
  Peter 188
  Richard 188
  Thomas 152
BUGG, Edward, Jr. 63
  William 129, 171
BULLOCK, Dan 157
  Daniel 15, 32, 37, 112,
  137
  Hannah 15, 86
  John 78, 137, 157
  Mary 157
  Nathaniel 157
  Richard 157
BUNTER, Joshua 22
BURDEN, Mathew 22
BURDETT, William 213
BURDITT, Patience 112, 213
  William 112, 151, 213
BURGES (BURGESS) 76
  Elizabeth 126
  James 231
  Samuel 53, 76, 91+, 92,
  120, 126
  William 58+, 134+
BURK (BURKE, BURKES)
  Adamus 3
  David 17, 18, 35, 38,
  45, 48, 53, 57, 65, 76,
  86, 94+, 95, 108, 195,
  196, 237
  Edanus 175
  Jane 45, 76
  Jean 38
  John 37
BURKMYERS, Catharine 150
BURNE 85
BURNELL, Chadock 154, 229
BURNET (BURNETT)
  Alexander 223+
  Daniel 59, 137
  Ellexander 39
  Hezekiah 109
  Jeremiah 223, 226
  Pleasant 13, 109
  Thomas 144, 166, 171,
  220, 245
BURNEY, Andrew 193, 238
  William 238
BURNS 128
  David 89+
  George 1, 157
  John 166
  Sarah 71
  William 200
BURRESS, John 180

BURROWS, William 4
BURRUS, John 159
BURT (BURTS)
  Fanny 90, 228
  Francis 90, 130+, 238
  Harwood 35, 48
  John 229, 230
  John, Jr. 230+
  John, Sr. 230+
  Matthew 98, 134
  Moody 35, 46, 48, 96,
  172+, 196
  Moody, Jr. 46, 84
  Moody, Sr. 90
  Phillip 31, 238
  Robert 35, 46, 48, 95,
  98, 135
  William 230+
BURTON, James 17
  Joseph 104
  Richard 49, 138+, 238
  Robert 18, 20, 135
  Sarah 135
BUSH, Biddy 6, 7, 188, 240
  Isaac 6, 7
  John 219
  Prescot 219
  Richard 219, 245
  Richard, Jr. 127
  Richard, Sr. 219
  William 6, 7, 240
BUSSEY, Charles 89, 131
  Chearls 101
  Demay 66, 125, 132, 212
  George, Jr. 132, 213
  George, Sr. 125, 132
  Joshua 132
  Libba 132
  Richard 142
  Zadock 132
BUTLER, Anthony 23, 36,
  166
  Bethethland 4
  James 10, 24, 36, 163,
  167
  James, Jr. 179
  John 93, 171
  Sampson 127, 191+, 216+,
  236
  Sarah 10
  Thomas 21+, 32, 37, 81,
  136, 139, 181, 204, 212,
  229
  William 4, 9, 26, 66,
  81, 115, 139, 143, 166,
  189
BYNUM, John 103, 214, 215

C

CAILS, Sarah 5
CAIN, William 117
CALDWELL, Elizabeth Ann 37
  Henry 27
  John 1, 26, 90, 114,
  140, 157, 199
  Robert 133
  Samuel 157
  William 37, 120, 121+,
  137
  William Thomas 90
CALAHAM (CALEHAM, CALLAHAM
  CALLEHAM, CALLEHAN, CALLE-
  HAN, CALLIHAM, CALLINGHAM,
  CALLYHAM) 40
  David 40, 135, 196,
  197+, 199
  Elizabeth 9+
  John 135, 143, 196, 197
  Lucy 135
  Mary 6, 46+, 110, 167,
  197

280

282

283

289

Plats: (cont.)
  BELL, Joseph Tucker 151
  BRITMAN, Thomas 170
  BROOKS, Elisha 1
  BROOKS, James 63
  BROOKS, Robert 201
  BROONER, Adam 237
  BUCKHALTER, Michael 105
  BURKS, David 45
  BUSSEY, George 132
  CALLAHAM, Morris 6
  CALLIHAM, John 197
  CAMPBELL, Marcantan 113, 129
  CLARK, Moses 211
  COCKERAM, Matthew 221
  CORLEY, William 109
  COURSEY, William 85, 141, 185, 198, 203, 211, 212 (2)
  CROOKSHANKS, Benjamin 203
  DARBY, Benjamin 244
  DAWSON, Joseph 206
  DAWSON, William 197, 231
  EDGEFIELD- ABBEVILLE County line 187
  EVANS, William 213, 216
  GRIFFIN, Absolom 141
  HAMMOND, Joshua 19
  HAMMOND, Leroy 181
  HAMPTON, John 175
  HARRIS, John 99
  HOLLEMAN, Edmond 229
  HOLMES, John 128
  HOLSTON, William 214
  JACKSON, Green 242
  JAMES, James 114
  JOEL, Richard 125
  JOHNSON, Philip 33
  JOHNSON, Richard 96
  JONES, Andrew 122
  KENNEDY, David 107
  KEY, Henry 144, 220
  LAMAR, Phillip 96
  LAMAR, Thomas, Sr. 21, 25
  LEHRE, Thomas 135
  LONGMIRE, William 49
  MARTIN, Zachariah 158
  MAY, Phillip 225
  McDANIEL, John 102
  MILLER, George 94
  MIMS, Drury 17, 18
  MURPHY, Thomas 16
  MURPHY, William 24, 167
  NAIL, Casper, Jr. 171
  NAIL, Casper, Sr. 6
  OGLESBY, Constant 183
  PALMER, Elisha 213
  PENMAN, Edward 79, 227
  PERRIN, Abner 90, 128
  POND, Richard 178
  PURSLEY, John 229
  PURVIS, John 142, 243
  RAMBO, Swan 142
  ROSE, Hugh 194 (2), 195 (2), 205
  ROWAN, James 211
  SIMKINS, William 232
  SMITH, Jacob 131
  SMITH, Stephen 220
  STARK, Robert 214, 215
  SULLIVAN, John 223
  SWEARENGEN, Capt. Vann, Jr. 65
  TAYLOR, Ward 31, 211
  THOMAS, Joseph 145 (2)
  TOMLINSON, Aaron 183
  TUTT, James 35
  VESSELS, James 72
  WAITE, John 179
  WALLACE, Robert 30
  WEST, James 42

Plats: (cont.)
  WIGHTT, Jonathan 184
  YOUNGBLOOD, Peter 70
  ZUBLY, Ann 91
  ZUBLY, David 8
PLIFER, Martin 223
  Michael 223
POAGE, John Lewis 47
POLLOCK, Matt 97
POND, Richard 37, 38, 178
  William 170
Ponds: See Waterways
PONMAN, Edward 3
  Jas. 3
POOL (POOLE)
  John 23, 75, 180, 181
  Henry 207
POPE, Charity 200
  Jacob 13
  John 74, 200
  Sampson 162, 207, 223
  Solomon 11, 50, 73, 112, 139, 156, 157, 163, 199, 217
  Susanna 200
  Susannah the younger 199
  Wiley 163
PORTER 16
POSEY 245
POSTELL, Benjamin 69, 70, 182+
  John 174
POU 136, 245
  Ann 134+
  Gaven (Gavin) 11, 37, 116, 134+, 173, 177, 192, 227
  John 134+
  Margaret 134+
  Robert 134+, 176+, 177, 198, 239
  William 134+
POUND (POUNDS) Mary 151
  John 34, 52+, 151
POWEL (POWELL), Henery 148
  Lewis 23, 105, 158
  Mary 131
  Moses 10, 104, 105+, 131, 215
  Sarah 158
POWERS, William 188, 196+
PRATT, John 202
PRESCOTT, William 158
PREWIT, Dudly 74
PRICE 90, 157
  & LAWSON Co. 175, 176+
  William 175+, 176+
PRICHARD, James 35, 83
  William 9, 10, 83, 159
PRIDE, Mary 244
  Oliver 244
PRINCE, Edward 16, 61, 62, 138, 150, 184, 220, 214
  Joseph 16
  Lucy 150
  Peter 247
PRINGLE, John Julius 233
  Robert 148, 233
  Susannah 233
PRIOR, John 51
PRYOR (PRYER), John 51, 52, 76, 118+
PUCKET (PUCKETT)
  Ephraim 24, 77, 78
  Jesse 48, 233
  Russell 233
PUCKITT, Elizabeth 78
  Thomas 78
PUET, Dudley 74
PUGH, Gavin 11, 22
PULLEY, Thomas 49, 119, 181
PULLIM, J. 82+
PURDUE, Gideon 129

PURSEL (PURSELL)
  Barbara 202
  Barbary 82, 222
  Edmond (Edmund) 110, 143, 169, 193+
  James 151
  John 75, 82, 94+, 103, 162, 170, 202, 222
  Mary 94
  William 82, 193
  Zacheus 94, 238
PURSLEY (PURSLY)
  Elizabeth 228
  John 153, 198, 228, 229
  Moses 228
  William 8, 177, 228
PUSLY, William 8
PURVIS (PURVES) 221, 223
  Charles, Jr. 168
  Col. 206, 207
  Eliza Ann 243
  John 2, 3, 4+, 5+, 6+, 8, 9+, 10+, 21, 23, 29+, 31, 33, 35+, 37+, 38, 40, 43, 45+, 46+, 48+, 49+, 53, 47, 59+, 61+, 65, 66+, 67+, 71+, 83, 113, 142, 144, 152, 153+, 154, 155+, 156, 159, 160, 161, 183, 223, 239, 243
  Col. John 98, 142, 168+, 195
  Mary 168
  Widow 246
PYLE, Reubin 120, 241
PYTNHYLN, Isaac 147

Q

QUARLES, James 190
  Richard 144, 220, 232+, 233+
  Richard, Jr. 190
QUARLS, William 101+

R

RABAN, William 134+
RABORN, William 12, 22
RABOURN, Joseph 39
  William 134
RABUN, John 11
RADCLIFFE, Thomas 231+
RAGLAND, George 20
RAGNESS, John, Sr. 157
RAILEY 66
RAILY, Elizabeth 60
RAINES, Giles Y. 137
RAINFORD, John 165
RAINSFORD, John 18, 20, 32+, 33, 104, 151, 191, 192
RAIRDEN, Timothy 35, 38
RAMBEY, Peter 79, 90
RAMBO, Joseph 19, 33, 34, 41+, 125
  Lawrence 15, 19, 26, 27, 28, 41, 79+, 97, 138, 147, 165, 171, 227
  Mary 15, 41+, 138
  Rachel 15
  Rubin 43
  Susanna 125
  Swain 116
  Swan 142+, 246
RAMBOW, Benjah 15, 97, 168, 171
RAMSEY, Charles 6, 126
  Ephraim 138+, 139, 150,

SKINHOLSER, William 171
SKINNER, Jesse 28
SKIRVING, William 133
SKRINE, Wm. 174
SLATER, John 170, 179
  Levi 101+
Slaves:
  Abey 84
  Abraham 84, 162, 200
  Abram 42, 126, 230
  Adam 25, 130, 185
  Ag 47
  Agge 218
  Aggy 230
  Aggey 143
  Agness 163
  Aleck 70
  Alesey 149
  Alley 162
  Alijah 218
  Amy 240
  Anacay 172
  Anaka 200
  Andrew 84
  Anner 47
  Annica 126
  Anthony 172, 235
  April 70
  Arre 159
  Arther 222
  Bason 87
  Bec 182
  Beck 13
  Bellaney 32
  Bellow 243
  Ben 13, 22, 58, 70, 84,
    110, 117, 118, 159, 169,
    172+, 186, 217
  Bener 217
  Benter 84
  Bett 32, 74, 181, 206
  Betty 13, 25, 70, 141,
    149, 154, 172, 218
  Biddy 4, 172
  Big Amy 70
  Big Betty 87
  Big Fortune 70
  Big Lewis 70
  Big Mary 70
  Big Sam 70
  Billy 10, 70, 73, 167,
    168
  Binah 55
  BLACK, James 52
  Bob 9, 49, 87, 114, 118,
    153, 169, 172+, 218
  Bobb 137, 162
  Bram 10, 70
  Bristo 118
  Briston 70
  Burton 107
  Cain 161
  Calliener 66
  Cambridge 167, 198
  Caroline 163
  Cat 42
  Cate 30, 47, 160
  Cato 4, 84
  Caty 180
  Cela 188
  Cesar 55, 70
  Ceaser 104
  Cezar 169
  Charity 22, 49, 130, 191
  Charles 42, 49, 102,
    126, 191, 200, 210+, 218
  Charlotte 10
  Chaney 66
  Chloe 10, 181, 188
  Clacy 42
  Clark 127
  Clary 87, 154
  Cleark 117
  Cloaey 159

Slaves: (cont.)
  Cloe 168
  Cork Primus 25
  Creasy 230
  Crese 78, 159
  Cresey 33
  Cutor 42
  Cyrus 84, 172
  Daniel 73, 125, 200
  Dangerfield 210
  Daphney 120
  Darkees 80
  Darkiss 79
  David 117
  Davy 78
  Deffeney 4
  Delph 218
  Dennis 191
  Dick 33, 42, 45, 60,
    103, 137, 140, 181
  Dinah 13, 32, 92, 221
  Doll 126, 159
  Dolly 24, 207
  Dominy 79
  Dorcus 9, 115, 130
  Douglass 172
  Drummer 13, 182
  Dublin 115
  Eamy 115
  Easter 28
  Easther 115
  Eleas 179
  Eley 60, 172
  Ellick 172
  Elsey 138
  Elsy 238
  Enoch 197
  Esther 117
  Fancy 55
  Fanny 87, 171, 181
  Feb 118
  Fed 22
  Feribie 118
  Flora 225
  Florah 115
  Frank 10, 87, 140, 155,
    177, 180
  Fred 73
  Friday 180
  George 75, 78, 87, 93,
    215, 222, 227
  Goodgame 84
  Grace 68, 70, 90, 180
  Greenberry Boling 127
  Guy 225
  Guye 127
  Hagar 84
  Hager 66, 69, 73+
  Hall 221
  Hampton 69
  Handy 162
  Hanna 218
  Hannah 3, 10, 21, 25,
    33, 36, 45, 60, 70, 87,
    127, 163, 190, 191+, 228
  Hannar 117, 215
  Harkless 201
  Harney 160
  Harriott 218
  Harry 13, 66, 73, 80,
    87, 180, 201
  Henry 42
  Hercules 25
  Isaac 13, 21, 30, 159,
    172
  Isac 191
  Isabel 159
  Isabelle 70
  Iris 172
  Jack 13, 32, 47, 49, 58,
    65, 70, 92, 94, 182,
    190, 243
  Jacob 42, 90, 159, 162,
    192, 228

Slaves: (cont.)
  James 21, 24, 66, 112,
    198, 221
  Jane 42, 145
  Janey 230
  Jenny 180
  January 138
  Jeff 20
  Jeffre 53
  Jem 81
  Jenney 172
  Jenny 24, 70, 105, 115,
    162, 167+, 191, 230
  Jesse 230
  Jessey 159
  Jim 87, 225
  Jimmy 87, 89, 167, 172
  Joan 126
  Jodah 120
  Joe 51, 87, 92, 117,
    127, 162, 193, 218
  John 42, 169
  John Caluner 69
  Johnny 50
  Joseph 219
  Juba 74
  Judah 154
  Jude 58, 190, 221, 227
  Judy 33
  June 84
  Juno 232, 233
  Kate 226
  Lance 70
  Leah 120, 167
  Lesar 103
  Lett 97, 154
  Lettice 80
  Lettie 55
  Lidia 189
  Little Amy 70
  Little Betty 87
  Little Fortune 70
  Little Lewis 70
  Little Mary 70
  Little Rachel 70
  Little Sam 70
  Lizze (Elizabeth) 207
  London 92, 169
  Luck 117, 127
  Lucy 10, 13, 42, 55, 87,
    155, 190
  Luce 159
  Lydda 126
  Lyll 243
  Mack 94, 243
  Mansfield 70
  Manuel 207
  March 155
  Marinda 22
  Mary 84, 193, 219
  Mary Ann 70
  Maryann 160
  Mat 68, 181
  Meriah 198
  Merier 202
  Mill 221
  Milley 120, 218
  Milly 161
  Mima 66, 222, 230
  Mingo 162, 163
  Mingoe 25, 70
  Mod 191
  Moll 13, 137
  Molley 206
  Moly 30
  Moses 4, 130, 155
  Nan 4, 117, 196
  Nancy 10, 13, 30, 33,
    66, 85, 207
  Nanney 141
  Nanny 225
  Ned 120, 121, 126, 130,
    230
  Nell 10, 87

293

Slaves: (cont.)
Nelly 201
Neworkee 172
Nim 154
Nimrod 97
Orson 172
Pat 87, 155, 169
Patience 22
Patt 49, 70, 169, 190, 191
Patty 166
Pegg 9, 10, 69, 70, 219
Penny 162
Peter 55, 66, 70, 110, 115, 118, 126, 155, 167, 190, 200
Phebe 4, 162
Phib 22
Philles 141
Phillis 10, 21, 52, 70, 94, 172
Poll 55
Polydore 10
Pomp 117
Pompey 138, 160
Pompy 228
Ponpy 4
Prime 115
Prince 10, 29, 33, 55, 138, 145, 193, 232, 233
Pumpkin 84
Qua 30
Quach 73
Quodo 193
Queen 80
Rachel 13, 60, 70, 85, 126, 130, 206, 218, 235
Reubin 191
Robert 161
Rose 117, 127, 180
Sal 107
Sall 126
Sally 13, 117, 230
Sam 9, 49, 58, 59, 73, 139, 162, 186, 191, 192, 201, 225
Sambo 69
Samp 3, 36
Sampson 87, 136, 172, 246
Sandy 9, 84
Sarah 47, 87, 167, 180, 190, 232, 233
Saviay 130
Sawney 169
Scippo 25
Scott 172
Seal 118
Sela 78, 201
Sharlott 130
Silas 117
Siller 70
Silva 55, 70, 160
Silvia 30, 42, 110, 119
Sillvey 55, 117
Silvy 79, 189
Simity 32
Simmeria 66
Simon 33
Sinah 70, 79
Slyva 10
Sylvy 87
Solsbury 70
Squash 47
Squire 4
Stephen 29, 55, 84, 154, 218
Stepney 55
Sterling 66
Suck 75
Sue 25, 70, 117, 159
Suie 117
Suky 167
Sulviain 2

Slaves: (cont.)
Sweep Stackes 75
Tabb 180
Talley 70
Tamar 130
Tamer 66
Tellery 25
Tenah 92
Tillis 159
Tim 55, 221
Tiner 204
Toby 10
Toe Cak 22
Tom 21, 22, 24, 42, 47, 70, 72, 84, 115, 161, 172, 190, 201, 218+, 232, 233, 243
Toney 80, 207
Tubs 162
Venus 27
Vice 83
Viney 172
Wenney 55, 75
Will 2, 73+, 84, 87, 117, 118, 119, 126, 169, 191
William 66
Willis 189
Wina 2
Winey 192
Zadock 84
Zilph 190
SLEE, William 67
SLOAN, John 202, 203, 205, 208+, 209+
SMEDLY (SMEDLEY), Elizabeth 213
James 49
John 22, 89
Thomas 12, 150, 171
William 242
SMERDON, Elias 200
Henry 32+, 61, 200
SMITH, Aaron 226
Abraham 106
Benjamin 37, 38, 118, 244
Elenor 136, 158
Elizabeth 226
Ezekiel 226
Harris 117
Isaac 227
Jacob 4+, 10, 15, 17, 112, 131+, 151, 159, 190, 222
James 132, 155
John 118, 133, 150, 203, 208+, 212, 244
JohnJacob Messer 35, 62
Julius 157, 175
Keating 47
Mark 222
Martha 110
Mary 53, 78
Noah 240
R. 187
Richard 116
Robert 154, 155
Rev. Robert 2
Roger 3, 102
Sarah 220
Stephen 203, 220, 227
Thomas 126, 171, 197
Thomas Keeling 136, 158
T. K. 136
T. Keland 226
Tom Keeling 47
William 148, 210, 245
SMITHERS, A. 220
Christopher 86
Gabriel 69, 85, 165, 166
J. 166
John 69, 81
SNEAD, Mary 230

SNEARLS, John 235
SNEED, John 151
SNELGROVE, Edward 133
SNELSON, Thomas 140, 141, 157
SNODIN, Thomas 158
SNOWDEN, Thomas 244
SNOWDON, Joshua 207
SPANN, Francis 60
James 9, 60+, 74, 81, 112, 150, 151, 152+, 156, 189+
John 66, 81, 152+, 240
John, Sr. 9, 60
Sarah 152+
William 99
SPEAR, Abraham 1, 142
Robert 98
SPEERS, Elizabeth 20
Roland 15
Robert 20, 38, 56+
SPENCER 42, 60, 168
John 43, 151, 152
John Thomas 24
Mary 24, 43
Ray 151
William 19+, 24, 59, 61, 161
SPEARMAN, Edmund 196
Margaret 196
Thomas 196
SPIERMAN, Thomas 188
SPRAGINS (SPRAGGINS, SPRAGENS), Samuel 117, 173
Thomas 13, 15, 119, 121, 241
Wm. 43, 74, 117, 143, 173+, 197, 241
SPRAT, John 127, 226
SPRINGER, John 53, 78
SPULLOCK, James 11
SQUIRES, Elventon 189
STALIONS, Mary 192+
STALNAKER, Adam 143
Samuel 2, 6, 39, 40, 66, 107, 158, 162
STANLEY, Susannah 60+
STANTENBOUGH, Sarah 146
STAUTENBOUGH, William 147
STARK, Alexander Bolling 102, 214+, 215, 234
Bolen 57, 108
Mary 214+
Rebecca 57, 109
Robert 8, 12, 21, 26, 28+, 38, 45, 61, 62, 77, 102, 103, 148, 174, 194, 233
Robert, Jr. 8, 19, 86, 101, 168
Robert, Sr. 8, 39
Robert, the younger 102, 214+, 215
STARE, John 5
STARNES, Levy 80
STARR, John 6
STEDAM, Jane 59+
STEDHAM, Zachariah 93
STEDMAN, Samuel 79
STEPHEL, James 61
STEPHENS, Ebenatus 7, 19
Elisha 111, 194, 195, 205
Joseph 7, 19
Josiah 194
Mary 3
STEPHENSON, Joseph 196
STERK 85
STERNS, Ebenezer 197
STEVENS, Ebenites 233
Elisha 71, 117
Isiah 71
Josiah 71
Sylvanus 18

294

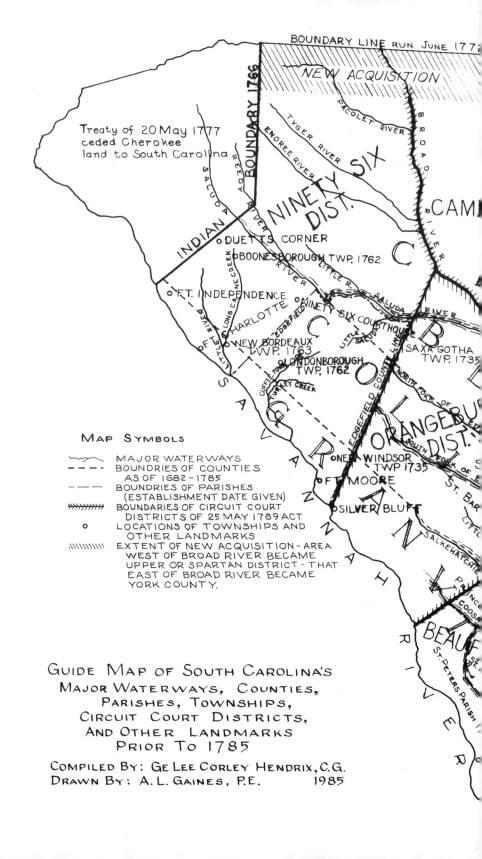

BOUNDARY LINE RUN JUNE 177?

NEW ACQUISITION

Treaty of 20 May 1777
ceded Cherokee
land to South Carolina

NINETY SIX DIST.

CAM

PACOLET RIVER

TYGER RIVER

ENOREE RIVER

BROAD RIVER

BOUNDARY 1766

INDIAN

SALUDA R

REEDY RIVER

LONG CANE CREEK

o DUETTS CORNER

o BOONESBOROUGH TWP. 1762

o FT. INDEPENDENCE

CHARLOTTE

o EDGEFIELD

NINETY SIX COURTHOUSE

LITTLE R.

SALUDA RIVER

C

B

E

L

COOSAW

LITTLE RIVER

LITTLE SALUDA

o NEW BORDEAUX
TWP. 1763

o LONDONBOROUGH
TWP. 1762

CUFFEE TOWN

TURKEY CREEK

SAXE GOTHA
TWP. 1735

EDGEFIELD COUNTY LINE

NORTH FORK OF

S
A
V
A
N
N
A
H

R
I
V
E
R

ORANGEBURG DIST.

SOUTH FORK OF S

ST. BAR

o NEW WINDSOR
TWP 1735

o FT. MOORE

o SILVER BLUFF

SALKEHATCHIE

MAP SYMBOLS

⌇⌇⌇ MAJOR WATERWAYS
- - - BOUNDRIES OF COUNTIES
        AS OF 1682-1785
— — BOUNDRIES OF PARISHES
        (ESTABLISHMENT DATE GIVEN)
»»»»»» BOUNDARIES OF CIRCUIT COURT
        DISTRICTS OF 25 MAY 1769 ACT
 o   LOCATIONS OF TOWNSHIPS AND
        OTHER LANDMARKS
\\\\\\\ EXTENT OF NEW ACQUISITION - AREA
        WEST OF BROAD RIVER BECAME
        UPPER OR SPARTAN DISTRICT - THAT
        EAST OF BROAD RIVER BECAME
        YORK COUNTY.

NC
COOSA

BEAUF

ST. PETERS PARISH 1

St.

GUIDE MAP OF SOUTH CAROLINA'S
MAJOR WATERWAYS, COUNTIES,
PARISHES, TOWNSHIPS,
CIRCUIT COURT DISTRICTS,
AND OTHER LANDMARKS
PRIOR TO 1785

COMPILED BY: GE LEE CORLEY HENDRIX, C.G.
DRAWN BY: A.L. GAINES, P.E.   1985